THE ULTIMATE FAN'S GUIDE
PRO SPORTS TRAVEL

AAA PUBLISHING
1000 AAA Drive, Heathrow, Florida
32746

AAA PUBLISHING

President & CEO: Robert Darbelnet
Executive Vice President, Publishing & Administration:
  Rick Rinner
Managing Director, Travel Information:
  Bob Hopkins

Director, Product Development: Bill Wood
Director, Sales & Marketing: John Coerper
Director, Purchasing & Corporate Services:
  Becky Barrett
Director, Business Development: Gary Sisco
Director, Tourism Information Development (TID):
  Michael Petrone
Director, Travel Information: Jeff Zimmerman
Director, Publishing Operations: Susan Sears
Director, GIS/Cartography: Jan Coyne
Director, Publishing/GIS Systems & Development:
  Ramin Kalhor

Product Manager: Cynthia Psarakis
Managing Editor, Product Development:
  Margaret Cavanaugh

AAA Travel Store & e-store Manager:
  Sharon Edwards

Print Buyer: Laura Cox
TID Regional Managers: Todd Cronson,
  Larry Hamilton, Michel Mousseau, Stacey Mower,
  Patrick Schardin, Bob Sheron
TID Field Operations Manager: Laurie DiMinico
Manager, Product Support: Linda Indolfi
Manager, Electronic Media Design: Mike McCrary
Manager, Pre-Press & Quality Services: Tim Johnson
Manager, Auto Travel: Josette Constantino

*AAA Publishing wishes to acknowledge the following
for their assistance:*
  ESPN, Major League Baseball, National Basketball
  Association, National Football League, National
  Hockey League, Courtney Canova, Fay Dallas
  and Tim Reilly, and special thanks to Bob
  Modrzejewski

Published by AAA Publishing, 1000 AAA Drive,
Heathrow, Florida 32746

ISBN 1-56251-521-7

Cataloging-in-Publication Data is on file with
the Library of Congress.

First Edition 10 9 8 7 6 5 4 3 2 1
Printed in Canada

Book Production: St. Remy Media Inc.

President: Pierre Léveillé
Vice President, Finance and Operations:
  Natalie Watanabe
Managing Editor: Carolyn Jackson
Managing Art Director: Diane Denoncourt
Production Manager: Michelle Turbide
Systems Director: Edward Renaud
Director, Business Development:
  Christopher Jackson

Art Director: Anne-Marie Lemay
Editor: Neale McDevitt
Writers: Lance Blomgren, Rob Lutes
Research Editor: Heather Mills
Researchers: Tal Ashkenazi, Jessica Braun,
  Peter Fedun
Designer: Roxanne Tremblay
Cartographers: Dimension DPR Inc.
Illustrators: Vincent Gagnon, Jacques Perrault
Photo Researcher: Linda Bryant
Production Editor: Brian Parsons
Production Coordinator: Dominique Gagné
Pre-Press Technician: Jean Angrignon Sirois
Scanner Operator: Martin Francoeur

*The following people also assisted in the
preparation of this book:*
  Danny-Pierre Auger, Lorraine Doré,
  Joey Fraser, Pascale Hueber, Jim Hynes,
  Justyna Pietralik

Foreword

Okay, I'll admit it — I love my job. Believe me, I've had my fair share of lousy ones, so I don't take for granted for one second that I have every sports fan's dream job: talking about sports on television. About the only real DOWNSIDE to what I do is that I'm anchored to a desk five days a week. One of the best things about sports is going to the games ... going to the ballparks and arenas ... finding out all the great little out-of-the-way places in the stadiums and the cities that make every venue special. If there were a way to combine travel with what I do, it would be the best job on this planet.

And this book from AAA Publishing is exactly what you'd need for that job. A road map to the best and most unique places in and around the major stadiums and arenas. For example, where else are you going to find out just how many Cardinals besides Wally Moon have won Rookie of the Year awards, as well as discover the best hotels near Soldier Field?

Sports are America's passion, and this book takes you right through the heart and soul of America. If you've ever wanted to go coast-to-coast and just watch baseball all summer, or find out exactly where to stay and where to eat for a one-day trip to see your favorite team play, this is your book. I mean, who else is going to tell you about The Varsity in Atlanta and the world's largest retractable stainless steel roof at Mellon Arena? Travel and sports: To borrow a line from Field of Dreams, *"Is this heaven?"*

Enjoy.

Trey Wingo

Table of Contents

Baseball

Basketball

Football

Hockey

How To Use This Book

THIS BOOK IS DESIGNED to give sports fans all the essential information regarding their favorite teams and sporting venues. Each of the major pro sports has its own chapter, complete with sections on history, records and Halls of Fame. The majority of the book is dedicated to current teams, providing franchise history and records, individual awards and honors, and interesting bits of trivia. You will also find invaluable facts about each venue, including box-office and gate hours, pertinent phone numbers, prohibited items and insider seating tips. Directions to each venue are also provided, along with information on parking and access for people who are disabled.

THE OPENERS

Conferences and Divisions
List of each sport's teams, conferences and divisions.

Picture Collage
Trivia questions for each photo in the opening collage appear on pages 286–287.

THE GAME AND THE STARS

The Stars
The records page lists each sport's all-time greats and lets you compare them to today's stars.

Key Moments
Timeline covers the major events that helped shape each game.

The Game
Each sport's heroes and lore are celebrated in a detailed two-page essay.

Leagues and Divisions
Historical overview of the formation of each league and its evolution to the present day.

Hall of Fame
Each of the four major Halls of Fame is outlined. Important visitor information includes directions, admission prices, operating hours and details on the collections and displays.

Best-Loved Venues
This sidebar pays tribute to some of sport's most hallowed venues, past and present.

TAILGATING

Tailgating
Four pages on tailgating include everything from a historical overview and practical tips to tailgating etiquette and can't-miss recipes. Although tailgating is primarily associated with football, this section applies to tailgaters following all sports.

Tailgating Checklist
This helps tailgaters cut down on preparation time by providing an extensive list of items to pack on game day.

THE TEAMS AND VENUES

Quote
Provides colorful quotes from players, coaches and members of the media.

Venue Information
Includes address and phone number, web address, box office hours, media coverage, and training facility.

Game Day Tips
Pointers on each venue's concessions, gate hours and prohibited items, as well as seating tips.

Team Spread
A two-page write-up on each team includes information on the franchise and its venue.

Seating Chart
Detailed chart gives readers a good idea of each section's proximity to the action. Wheelchair- and scooter-accessible seating is also included. (Note: ATM locations are listed, but the machines may be moved.)

Postseason, Records and Awards
Lists the postseason appearances by each team, as well as team records and individual awards.

Locator Map
Shows exact location of venue and gives directions for drivers, as well as information on public transportation and parking.

Timeline
Traces the history of each team.

Lodging and Restaurants
Nearby AAA-RATED® and unrated establishments.

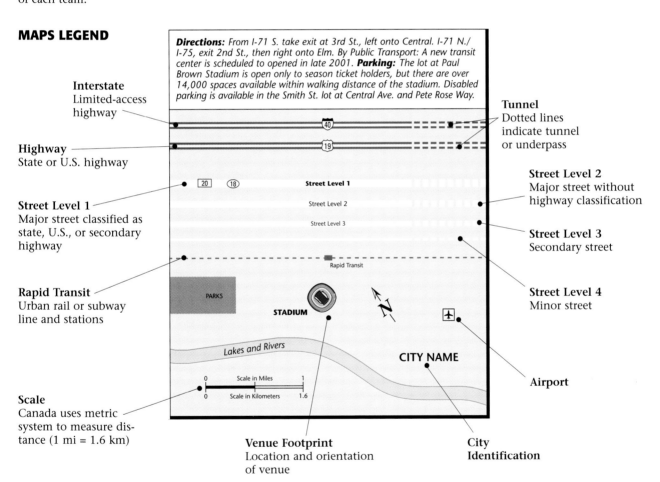

MAPS LEGEND

Directions: From I-71 S. take exit at 3rd St., left onto Central. I-71 N./I-75, exit 2nd St., then right onto Elm. **By Public Transport:** A new transit center is scheduled to opened in late 2001. **Parking:** The lot at Paul Brown Stadium is open only to season ticket holders, but there are over 14,000 spaces available within walking distance of the stadium. Disabled parking is available in the Smith St. lot at Central Ave. and Pete Rose Way.

Interstate
Limited-access highway

Highway
State or U.S. highway

Street Level 1
Major street classified as state, U.S., or secondary highway

Rapid Transit
Urban rail or subway line and stations

Scale
Canada uses metric system to measure distance (1 mi = 1.6 km)

Tunnel
Dotted lines indicate tunnel or underpass

Street Level 2
Major street without highway classification

Street Level 3
Secondary street

Street Level 4
Minor street

Airport

Venue Footprint
Location and orientation of venue

City Identification

TICKET BROKERS AND SCALPERS

On the surface, ticket brokers seem like they provide a great service. With a single phone call, fans can reserve seats and avoid long lineups at the box office. Brokers also give fans access to games or events that are usually sold out. They can also provide people with premium seating that is not always readily available for a single game. Of course, brokers charge a service fee, which can vary greatly depending on the demand. In some states, ticket resellers must obtain a license. Many fans have learned the hard way that a number of unlicensed brokers inflate prices to astonishing levels, including a recent case in which World Series tickets were being sold for $1,500. The best policy is to check with each team to see if they are affiliated with licensed brokers. This information is often given on the team website. Unlike licensed brokers, scalpers are breaking the law. When you buy tickets from a scalper you always run the risk of getting ripped off.

BASE

1

2

3

4
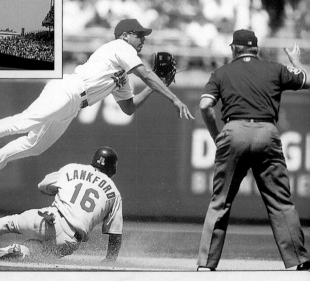

BALL

American League East
Baltimore Orioles
Boston Red Sox
New York Yankees
Tampa Bay Devil Rays
Toronto Blue Jays

American League Central
Chicago White Sox
Cleveland Indians
Detroit Tigers
Kansas City Royals
Minnesota Twins

American League West
Anaheim Angels
Oakland Athletics
Seattle Mariners
Texas Rangers

National League East
Atlanta Braves
Florida Marlins
Montreal Expos
New York Mets
Philadelphia Phillies

National League Central
Chicago Cubs
Cincinnati Reds
Houston Astros
Milwaukee Brewers
Pittsburgh Pirates
St. Louis Cardinals

National League West
Arizona Diamondbacks
Colorado Rockies
Los Angeles Dodgers
San Diego Padres
San Francisco Giants

THE GAME

BASEBALL IS A MIX, BOTH SUBTLE AND SUBLIME, of diverse elements. It is one part math, in which statistical milestones such as 20 wins, a .300 batting average and 100 RBIs are the measure of a great season. The game magically imbues numbers with lives of their own. Just as every fan knows that the distance between home plate and the pitcher's mound is 60 feet 6 inches, they will also tell you that 56 means only one thing: Joe DiMaggio's remarkable consecutive-game hitting streak; and that .406 belongs to Ted Williams' 1941 season. Cal Ripken Jr. will forever be remembered for playing in 2,632 consecutive games, "Hammerin' Hank" Aaron for clubbing 755 career homers and Mark McGwire for belting 70 home runs in the glorious 1998 season.

But baseball is also one part myth, in which the magical mix of fact and fancy combine to create heroes in double knit. There are tales that Denton True Young earned his nickname Cy, short for Cyclone, by destroying a wooden fence with warmup pitches. Fanciful reports tell of Honus Wagner throwing out a runner even though a small dog had bolted from the stands and clamped onto the ball. Mickey Mantle rose from Oklahoma farm boy

and miner to feared slugger, whose prodigious homers — some estimated at 650 feet — gave birth to the term "tape-measure home run." The most famous bit of lore is Babe Ruth's famed "called shot," in which Ruth, irritated by heckling coming from the opposing dugout, pointed to a spot in the outfield bleachers and, on the very next pitch, blasted a home run right to that exact place.

GREAT PLAYERS AND GREAT MEN

Baseball is populated with larger-than-life personalities, both great and questionable. Some of the most celebrated players were anything but good role models off the field. Ty Cobb, one of the charter members of the Baseball Hall of Fame, was a notorious racist and a bully who sharpened the spikes on his cleats to frighten opposing infielders when he came sliding in on close plays. In 1883 Cap Anson, another Hall of Famer, refused to play an exhibition game because the opposing team had a black catcher.

But these examples are counterbalanced by the men who managed to combine both talent and integrity. People such as Ruth, who, despite being courted by presidents and movie stars, never forgot his humble beginnings and always took the time to talk to his young fans. Players such as Ted Williams, Bob Feller and Joe DiMaggio set an example for the nation by putting their careers on hold and signing up to fight in World War II. Warren Spahn, the winningest left-hander in National League history, was awarded the Purple Heart for wounds he received in a battle on the Rhine.

In 1947 Jackie Robinson became the major league's first black player when he jogged onto the field for the Brooklyn Dodgers. Accepting the season-long maelstrom of insults hurled at him by fans, members of the media, opposing players and even some of his own teammates, Robinson continually turned the other cheek and let his talent speak for him. His daring exploits on the base paths electrified fans and propelled the Dodgers to a World Series showdown with the Yankees. He was named National League Rookie of the Year.

Robinson did not make his stand alone. Dodgers President Branch Rickey signed Robinson and stood by him, even when the rookie started the season going 0-20 at the plate. When a team threatened to strike rather than compete on the same field as a black player, baseball Commissioner Ford Frick threatened sweeping suspensions, adding, "This is the United States of America, and one citizen has as much right to play as any other."

Pedro Martinez won three Cy Young Awards — in 1997, '99 and 2000.

THE RISE AND FALL OF OUR HEROES

Baseball is also part Greek tragedy, with many of its greatest stars taking epic falls from Olympus. "Shoeless Joe" Jackson rose from rural illiteracy to become a bona fide superstar in the early 1900s. However, Jackson was banned from the game forever for his part in the infamous Black Sox scandal, in which he and seven Chicago White Sox teammates accepted money from gamblers to throw the 1919 World Series. Just four years after setting the all-time single-season RBI record of 191 in 1930, slugger Hack Wilson had drunk and brawled his way out of the majors and, not long after that, all the way to an early grave.

Many people consider Babe Ruth, who ended his career with 714 home runs, to be the greatest hitter ever to swing a bat.

Not all of baseball's early demises are self-inflicted. Lou Gehrig overcame broken bones, illness and near-crippling back problems to play in an incredible 2,130 consecutive games for the Yankees in the 1920s and 1930s, establishing himself as one of the most feared hitters of all time. In the end, however, it took a fatal illness — amyotrophic lateral sclerosis, now commonly referred to as Lou Gehrig's Disease — to end his streak and force him from the game he loved. Two years after his streak ended, the "Iron Horse" was dead at the age of 37.

The game lost one of its great ambassadors on New Year's Eve in 1972, when Roberto Clemente, the Pirates' All-Star right fielder, was killed in an airplane crash as he carried relief supplies to Nicaraguan earthquake victims.

HAVING FUN

More than anything else, however, baseball is about having fun. How else can one explain how the game's marquee player — and one of its most physically imposing men — was nicknamed Babe?

Giving people nicknames is a pastime in childhood, but its practice has long been embraced by the adults playing and watching baseball. "Stan the Man," "Leo the Lip," "the Yankee Clipper," "Mr. Cub," "the Say Hey Kid," "the Georgia Peach," "Mr. October" and "the Sultan of Swat" are often as easily recognized as each player's given name.

But lesser known monikers such as "Buttermilk Tommy" Dowd, Buck "Leaky" Fausett, Johnny "Ugly" Dickshot, Jack "Death to Flying Things" Chapman, and brothers Paul "Big Poison" and Lloyd "Little Poison" Waner all have their spot in baseball's irreverent history book.

Venues of the Past

Ebbets Field, Brooklyn, New York: *This was the cramped but comfortable home of the Brooklyn Dodgers from 1913 to 1957. Kids watched games for free by peeking through a gap under the gate in right center. Theirs were among the best spots to watch as line drives took crazy caroms off the in-play scoreboard, handcuffing generations of frustrated outfielders. Long-suffering Brooklyn fans were renowned for their boisterous backing of even the most laughable Dodgers teams, but their frustration peaked from 1947 to 1956, when the Yankees won four of five World Series against the hard-luck Dodgers. The first televised game was played in Ebbets Field on Aug. 26, 1939, against the Cincinnati Reds. It was also the setting for Jackie Robinson's landmark game on April 15, 1947, when he became the first black major-leaguer.*

Polo Grounds, New York: *Perhaps the most unusual ballpark ever, the Polo Grounds was home to the New York Giants, the early New York Yankees and later the New York Mets. The bathtub-shaped park was a cavernous 480 to 500 feet to straight-away center, but only 279 and 258 feet to the left- and right-field foul poles. Because the outfield was sunken, players in the dugout could see only the upper torsos of the outfielders. This was where Willie Mays made his electrifying over-the-shoulder catch in the 1954 World Series.*

Forbes Field, Pittsburgh: *The Pittsburgh Pirates played their home games at Forbes Field from 1909 to 1970. The Negro League's Homestead Grays also played here from 1939 to 1949. Although the park was designed with a center field that was nicknamed "Death Valley" because it measured more than 450 feet from home plate, its short left-field fence made it easy pickings for noted Pirates slugger Ralph Kiner.*

Comiskey Park, Chicago: *The White Sox played here from 1910 through the 1990 season. In 1960 team owner Bill Veeck equipped the stadium with baseball's first exploding scoreboard — complete with pinwheels and fireworks. In times when the Chicago infield was suspect, the grounds crew let the grass grow long to slow ground balls. They also tinkered with the height of the mound in the opposing bullpen to throw off the timing of rival pitchers.*

PLAYING THE GAME

Perhaps Commissioner Frick said it best when, at the end of his terse 1947 message to rebellious players looking to chase Jackie Robinson from their ranks, he asserted that it was every person's right to "play" baseball. More than anything else, baseball is about playing a game.

Unlike the trench warfare and violence inherent in football and hockey and the high-flying freneticism of basketball, baseball is a quiet and reflective game played at a leisurely pace. There are no clocks to beat, no rude buzzers heralding the end of a game in mid-play. It is one of the first sports that we try as children and one, if we are so inclined, that we can play well into later life. It is, after all, a pastime — our National Pastime.

Childlike exuberance simmers at the core of the game of baseball, and there is joy to be had both in watching and playing. Even when a game is at its busiest and most exciting, be it the crack of a monstrous home run, a daring base runner breaking for second or the deft turning of a double play, the majority of players on the field — even the multimillionaire stars of today — are mere spectators, little boys in men's bodies waiting for their turn to play.

KEY MOMENTS

While experts can't seem to agree on who actually invented the game of baseball, most believe that it was born as a variation of a British children's game called rounders. The following is a list of key moments in baseball's history.

• 1845 First Organized Team
Bank teller Alexander Cartwright founds the New York Knickerbockers, the country's first organized baseball team. Some experts maintain that Cartwright establishes some of baseball's fundamentals, including nine innings, the same year.

• 1871 First Pro League
The National Association becomes baseball's first pro league. Players are often drunk and disorderly, games are frequently fixed and a number of teams fold before the end of the first season. As can be expected, the fledgling league lasts only five years.

• 1876 NL Founded
The National League of Professional Base Ball Clubs is salvaged from the wreckage of the first pro league. Although the league's early years are somewhat tumultuous, it manages to hang on, and with the arrival of the American Association in the early 1880s Major League Baseball is formed.

• 1894 Most Runs Scored
"Sliding Billy" Hamilton sets all-time record by scoring 192 runs for the Philadelphia Phillies. The speedy center fielder also hits .404 for the season.

• 1903 First Official World Series
While there had been postseason championships since 1884, the first official World Series is in 1903 between the Boston Pilgrims and the Pittsburgh Pirates. The underdog Pilgrims take the series, five games to three.

• 1919 Black Sox Scandal
Eight members of the Chicago White Sox are given lifetime suspensions for throwing the 1919 World Series.

• 1920 Babe Sets the Tone
Babe Ruth changes the game forever by belting 54 homers. Prior to the arrival of "the Bambino" on the baseball scene, the single-season record had been 27.

• 1924 Century's Best Batting Average
Rogers "the Rajah" Hornsby sets the modern major-league record for highest batting average in a single season with .424. His .358 lifetime mark is still tops in the NL.

• 1927 Yankees' Lineup Murders the Rest
Led by Ruth (60 homers) and Lou Gehrig (175 RBIs), the Yanks' unstoppable starting lineup demolishes the rest of the American League for 110 wins and is dubbed "Murderers' Row." The team goes on to sweep the Pittsburgh Pirates in the World Series.

• 1936–37 24 Straight
Pitching for the New York Giants, Carl Hubble wins 24 consecutive games over two seasons, a major-league record.

• 1941 DiMaggio Goes 56 Straight
"Joltin' Joe" DiMaggio hits safely in 56 games. DiMaggio edges Boston's Ted Williams for MVP honors even though Williams hits .406 — the last player to do so.

• 1947 Robinson Arrives
Jackie Robinson breaks baseball's color barrier by playing with the Brooklyn Dodgers. Along the way he leads the league in stolen bases and wins Rookie of the Year honors. Two years later he will be crowned NL MVP.

• 1960 Mazeroski Paces Bucs
Pirates second baseman Bill Mazeroski delivers a clutch, bottom-of-the-ninth, game-seven home run that propels the Bucs to the World Series title.

• 1968 Pitchers Rule
Detroit's Denny McLain wins 31 games, the highest total since 1931. His NL counterpart, Bob Gibson of the Cardinals, finishes the year with an ERA of 1.12.

• 1969 Miracle Mets Win Fall Classic
Perennial doormats of the 1960s, the New York Mets upset the heavily favored Orioles in the World Series.

• 1973 Ryan Fans 383
Fireballer Nolan Ryan sets a modern major-league record by striking out 383 batters in a season. By the end of Ryan's illustrious career, a record 5,714 batters will go down in flames.

• 1977 Reggie Delivers
Reggie Jackson earns the nickname "Mr. October" by belting five homers in the Yankees' six-game World Series win over the Los Angeles Dodgers. He saves his best for last, smacking three long balls in his final three at-bats.

• 1992 Blue Jays Win World Series
The Toronto Blue Jays' six-game World Series win marks the first time that the title resides outside the United States. The Jays repeat in 1993.

• 1998 McGwire Versus Sosa
St. Louis Cardinals strong man Mark McGwire beats Chicago Cubs slugger Sammy Sosa in one of the most exciting home run derbies ever. Both men best Roger Maris' 1961 single-season mark of 61, with Sosa ending at 66 and McGwire hammering 70 long balls.

• 2000 Yanks Win Again
The Yankees begin the new millennium where they left off the old one: with a World Series win. Led by series MVP Derek Jeter, the Bronx Bombers beat the Mets.

In 1998 Mark McGwire of the St. Louis Cardinals shattered Roger Maris' long-standing home-run record by smashing 70 homers in a single season.

National Baseball Hall of Fame

BASEBALL'S SHRINE

If baseball's greatest players can be likened to Greek gods — both heroic and flawed at the same time — then the National Baseball Hall of Fame and Museum is their Mount Olympus. To be elected into the Hall of Fame is, for many inductees, a thrill even greater than winning a World Series. More so than any other sporting hall of fame, baseball's shrine infuses visitors with a palpable sense of awe and wonder for the men who are enshrined here.

This is especially true in the Hall of Fame Gallery, the Museum's main attraction. Here more than 200 of the game's greatest players, managers, pioneers and executives are honored. Each day hundreds of visitors file past the rows of bronze plaques, pausing to read the simple inscriptions and pay quiet homage to the men who once made hearts soar with a simple swing of the bat.

And while many of the names inscribed here are well known to all — Mays, Berra, Mantle, Koufax, for example — others are less so. Lesser-known luminaries such as Luke "Old Aches and Pains" Appling, Ray "Cracker" Schalk and Mordecai "Three Fingers" Brown are also immortalized here.

In 1971 the Hall of Fame began admitting players and coaches from the Negro League, many of whom were lauded by their white counterparts in the major league. Oscar Charleston, James "Cool Papa" Bell, Josh Gibson and Satchel Paige are just some of the great players who excelled at baseball despite the barriers they faced on a daily basis. When asked who was the greatest player of all time, Babe Ruth answered John Henry "Pop" Lloyd, a brilliant black shortstop who at age 44 hit .564 and led his league in homers.

A young fan admires a display at the Baseball Hall of Fame.

Vital Stats

Address: 25 Main St., Cooperstown, N.Y.
Phone: (607) 547-7200
Web: baseballhalloffame.org
Hours: Daily 9–9 May–Sept.; Sun.–Thurs. 9–5, Fri.–Sat. 5–9 April, Oct.–Dec.; daily 9–5 rest of year. Closed Jan. 1, Thanksgiving, Dec. 25.
Admission: Adult $9.50; senior citizen $8; child 7–12 $4; child under age of 7 free.
Directions: From Albany, take I-90 northwest to exit 29 at Canajoharie. From there, take Hwy. 5S to Fort Plain, then Hwy. 80 south to Cooperstown. From Syracuse, take I-90 to exit 30 at Herkimer, then follow Hwy. 28 south. From Binghamton, take Hwy. 88 east to Oneonta, then Hwy. 28 north.

HISTORY OF THE HALL

Although the official Hall of Fame didn't open until June 29, 1939, the first inductees were announced back in 1936. These charter members of the Hall, the so-called "Five Immortals," were Babe Ruth, Ty Cobb, Cy Young, Christy Mathewson and Honus Wagner, all voted in by a committee of baseball executives. Since that time, election into the Hall requires that a candidate's name appears on 75 percent of the ballots of the selection committee, which includes members of the Baseball Writers Association of America. This is no easy feat — no one, not even Ruth, DiMaggio or Cobb, has ever been voted in unanimously.

The Hall of Fame has changed drastically from when it first opened. Originally its modest collection centered on the famous "Doubleday ball," the rag-stuffed ball that one of the game's supposed creators, Abner Doubleday, used in an early match. Today the Hall boasts some 30,000 items in its extensive collection. Every facet of the game is represented, from antique and modern equipment to ballpark artifacts and players' personal belongings, along with hundreds of collectibles and valuable pieces of artwork. Where else can someone admire Ty Cobb's sliding pads, baseball sheet music, Babe Ruth's monogrammed bowling ball and Norman Rockwell originals all under the same roof? Visitors can also listen to famous radio calls of the past before sneaking peeks at television reruns of past World Series and clips from baseball films starring everyone from Gregory Peck to Madonna. And, yes, the "Doubleday ball" is still on display.

The Hall traces baseball's history back to its earliest roots, with reproductions of ancient Egyptian hieroglyphics depicting young athletes hitting stones with a staff. The evolution of the game from its early pre-20th century days to the present is best illustrated in the numerous displays of ever-changing equipment.

Early bats have no nub at the end and look hand-carved and awkward, whereas the graceful taper of today's sleek models belies the power that they are capable of generating in the right hands. By the same token, the first mitts look almost like cycling gloves, dwarfed in comparison to the monstrous models worn by modern players patrolling the field. Visitors can only marvel at "Shoeless Joe" Jackson's impossibly small glove, the place where it was said that "triples went to die."

But perhaps nowhere is the discrepancy between old and new best illustrated than in the Hall's displays of uniforms. The oldest versions are baggy woolen flannels, quaint reminders of a time when comfort and modesty were placed at a premium. Today's form-fitting, often brightly colored models speak of the brashness of the modern era.

HEROES OF THE GAME

Sometimes a single item sums up one of these heroes better even than film clips. Babe Ruth's gigantic spring-training bat, topping the scales at four pounds, eight ounces, speaks eloquently about the giant who wielded it with such success and panache.

A smaller bat sits nearby, one used by Hank Aaron to tie Ruth's mark of 714 career home runs. Despite the constant death threats and racial slurs, Aaron went on to surpass Ruth and set the career standard at 755 home runs, earning himself a rightful place among the immortals.

THE STARS

NO SPORT IS AS ENAMORED with numbers as baseball. In every ballpark you will find legions of fans poring over their scorecards, keeping detailed records of each at-bat. Milestones are marked in big, round numbers: 3,000 hits will guarantee a batter baseball immortality, as will 3,000 strikeouts for a pitcher. Here is a list of some of the game's most impressive records. Active players appear with an asterisk beside their name. For all the career records, we've included the nearest active player so you can gauge how today's stars rank with the greats of eras past.

BASEBALL RECORD BOOK
Hitting Records
Batting Avg. (career):
1. Ty Cobb .366
2. Rogers Hornsby .358
3. Joe Jackson .356
16. Tony Gwynn* .338 (tie)

Hits (career):
1. Pete Rose 4,256
2. Ty Cobb 4,189
3. Hank Aaron 3,771
17. Tony Gwynn* 3,108
32. Rickey Henderson* 2,914

Runs (career):
1. Hank Aaron 755
2. Babe Ruth 714
3. Willie Mays 660

The Chicago Cubs' Sammy Sosa belted 66 homers in 1998.

7. Mark McGwire* 554

Runs (career):
1. Ty Cobb 2,246
2. Rickey Henderson* 2,178
3. Hank Aaron 2,174
   Babe Ruth 2,174

RBIs (career):
1. Hank Aaron 2,297
2. Babe Ruth 2,213
3. Lou Gehrig 1,995
21. Harold Baines * 1,622

Stolen Bases (career):
1. Rickey Henderson* 1,370
2. Lou Brock 938
3. Billy Hamilton 912

Walks (career):
1. Babe Ruth 2,056
2. Rickey Henderson* 2,060
3. Ted Williams 2,019

Batting Avg. (season):
1. Hugh Duffy .440 (1894)
2. Tip O'Neill .435 (1887)
3. Ross Barnes .429 (1876)

Hits (season):
1. George Sisler 257 (1920)
2. Lefty O'Doul 254 (1929)
   Bill Terry 254 (1930)

HRs (season):
1. Mark McGwire* 70 (1998)
2. Sammy Sosa* 66 (1998)
3. Mark McGwire* 65 (1999)

Runs (season):
1. Billy Hamilton 192 (1894)
2. Tom Brown 177 (1891)
   Babe Ruth 177 (1921)

RBIs (season):
1. Hack Wilson 191 (1930)
2. Lou Gehrig 184 (1931)
3. Hank Greenberg 183 (1937)

Stolen Bases (season):
1. Hugh Nichol 138 (1887)
2. Rickey Henderson* 130 (1982)
3. Arlie Latham 129 (1887)

Walks (season):
1. Babe Ruth 170 (1923)
2. Mark McGwire* 162 (1998)
   Ted Williams 162 (1947)
   Ted Williams 162 (1949)

Pitching Records
Appearances (career):
1. Jesse Orosco* 1,095
2. Dennis Eckersley 1,071
3. Hoyt Wilhelm 1,070

Lowest ERA (career):
1. Ed Walsh 1.82
2. Addie Joss 1.89
3. Mordecai Brown 2.06
53. John Franco* 2.68
    Pedro Martinez* 2.68

Saves (career):
1. Lee Smith 478
2. John Franco* 420
3. Dennis Eckersley 390

Shutouts (career):
1. Walter Johnson 110
2. Pete Alexander 90
3. Christy Mathewson 79
28. Roger Clemens* 45

Strikeouts (career):
1. Nolan Ryan 5,714
2. Steve Carlton 4,136
3. Bert Blyleven 3,701
8. Roger Clemens* 3,504

Wins (career):
1. Cy Young 511
2. Walter Johnson 417
3. Pete Alexander 373
   Christy Mathewson 373
34. Roger Clemens* 260

Appearances (season):
1. Mike Marshall 106 (1974)
2. Kent Tekulve 94 (1979)
3. Mike Marshall 92 (1973)

Lowest ERA (season):
1. Tim Keefe 0.86 (1880)
2. Dutch Leonard 0.96 (1914)
3. Mordecai Brown 1.04 (1906)

Saves (season):
1. Bobby Thigpen 57 (1990)
2. Trevor Hoffman* 53 (1998)
   Randy Meyers* 53 (1993)

Shutouts (season):
1. George Bradley 16 (1876)
   Pete Alexander 16 (1916)
3. Jack Coombs 13 (1910)
   Bob Gibson 13 (1968)

Strikeouts (season):
1. Matt Kilroy 513 (1886)
2. Toad Ramsey 499 (1886)
3. Hugh Daily 483 (1884)

Wins (season):
1. Charley Radbourn 59 (1884)
2. John Clarkson 53 (1885)
3. Guy Hecker 52 (1884)

Leagues and Divisions

EARLY HISTORY

The National Association (NA), America's first professional baseball league, was formed in 1871. The fledgling circuit was saddled with problems from the start. Lopsided games made visiting teams feel they had no chance of winning and often they just didn't show up for games. These were the frontier days of baseball and many of the players gambled, drank too much and weren't above throwing the occasional game. Franchises came and went, often folding in mid-season. As a result of the constant turmoil, the NA lasted a mere five seasons before it ran aground at the end of 1875.

BIRTH OF THE NATIONAL LEAGUE

Undaunted by the failure of the NA, William A. Hulbert, owner of the NA's Chicago White Stockings, helped found the National League of Professional Base Ball Clubs in 1876. Hulbert stabilized things by ruling with an iron fist. When the Philadelphia Athletics and New York Mutuals refused to play their final games of the season, Hulbert tossed both franchises out of the league. He also handed down lifetime bans to four players from the Louisville team for their part in game-fixing in 1877.

As a result of Hulbert's unflinching leadership, the NL garnered support from fans who had grown weary of baseball's shady dealings. This, in turn, enabled the NL to stave off challenges from the upstart leagues, such as the Union Association. However, just after the turn of the 20th century, an agreement was reached between NL officials and those from another contender, the American League (AL), in which the best team from each would square off in a championship. In 1903 the AL's Boston Pilgrims upset the Pittsburgh Pirates of the NL in the first World Series match pitting AL against NL.

EXPANSION AND REALIGNMENT

The first major change to baseball's structure came in 1969, when expansion necessitated that both leagues be split into two divisions, East and West. Thus was born the League Championship Series, in which the top team in each division played off for the league pennant and the right to compete for the World Series.

In 1994 Major League Baseball realigned once again, adding a Central Division to each league and an extra layer to the playoffs. Today the top teams in the East, West, and Central Divisions are joined by a wild-card entry — the team with the best record that didn't win a division title — in the postseason.

A new twist was added in 1997. For the first time, teams from the AL and NL met in regular-season competition. Designed to create new rivalries and take advantage of built-in ones such as Mets versus Yankees and White Sox versus Cubs, interleague play has its share of detractors. Purists claim it tampers with the schedule, makes for fewer games between divisional rivals and waters down the AL/NL confrontation in the World Series.

DESIGNATED HITTERS

The major difference between the AL and NL is the designated hitter. Since 1973 AL pitchers have been replaced in the batting order by another hitter. The

Johnny Bench, one of the main cogs of Cincinnati's "Big Red Machine" of the mid-1970s, which won two World Series.

AL implemented the designated hitter rule in an effort to boost lagging offensives. In 1968, for example, 20 percent of all major-league games ended in a shutout. Hitting was so anemic that in 1968 Carl Yaztremski was the only AL player to hit over .300, winning the batting crown with a .301 average. The effect of the DH was immediate. In 1972, the year before the switch, AL hitters combined for a measly .238 average. The following season, the league average jumped to .259.

Traditionalists say the DH rule eliminates much of the managerial strategy, such as deciding when a pitcher should be removed for a pinch hitter. They also maintain that while the original experiment came at a time when baseball needed an offensive jump-start, the pendulum has swung the other way, with too many games ending in blowouts. Boosters argue that the DH rule has prolonged the careers of players who, though still capable at the plate, are unable to play in the field. They also say that the majority of fans would rather see a designated hitter belt a 400-foot home run than watch a pitcher strike out feebly on three straight pitches.

WHO RULES?

Since the first World Series confrontation in 1903, the AL has won 57 fall classic titles to just 39 for the NL. The AL's winning percentage in World Series play is .594, compared to .406 for the NL.

However, of the 71 All-Star Games, the NL has taken 40, 10 more than the AL (the 1961 midsummer classic ended in a 1-1 tie when a heavy deluge at the end of the ninth inning forced the game to be cancelled). The NL's All-Star winning percentage is a stellar .563 to the AL's .422. Of the 167 combined World Series and All-Star games, the AL holds a slight edge with 87 wins to the NL's 79.

ANAHEIM ANGELS

GENE AUTRY ATTENDED THE AMERICAN LEAGUE expansion meeting in St. Louis in 1960 with the goal of securing broadcast rights for his Golden West Broadcasting firm. He left that meeting as the owner and chairman of the expansion Los Angeles Angels. With Bill Rigney as its manager, the team amazed everyone with a winning record in its second year. The real trappings of winning would have to wait for nearly two decades, however, until original Angel infielder Jim Fregosi took the managerial reins and led the team to its first ever AL West title in 1979. The squad's hero that year was big DH Don Baylor, who led the league with 120 runs and 139 RBIs. In 1982 the team lured free agent Reggie Jackson from the Yankees. The move paid immediate dividends, with the free-swinging Jackson leading the league with 39 homers. That, combined with Rod Carew's 14th consecutive .300+ season, drove the Angels to top spot in the AL West. The team would win its third division title in 1986. Unfortunately they lost both the '82 and '86 ALCS series to the eventual world champion. With Autry's death in 1998, The Walt Disney Company assumed full ownership of the team. Today's Angels fans look to young stars like Darin Erstad and Troy Glaus to lead the way to the most heavenly destination — a World Series crown.

Vital Stats

Stadium Address:
2000 Gene Autry Way,
Anaheim, Calif.
Phone: (714) 940-2000
Web: angelsmlb.com
Box Office:
(714) 940-2054,
Mon.–Sat. 9–5:30,
during home games
Media Coverage:
Radio: KLAC (570 AM),
TV: KCAL 9 (Channel 9),
Fox Sports Net
Spring Training:
Tempe Diablo Stadium,
Tempe, Ariz.

> *"Hitting is an art, but not an exact science."*
>
> — *Rod Carew, a 1979–85 Angel and one of the greatest hitters in baseball's modern era*

POSTSEASON
• AL West Titles 3
(1979, '82, '86)

RETIRED NUMBERS
• Jim Fregosi (11)
• Gene Autry (26)
• Rod Carew (29)
• Nolan Ryan (30)
• Jimmie Reese (50)

TEAM RECORDS
Hitting Records
• Don Baylor (1972–82)

The Inside Pitch

• During their first season, the Angels played their home games at Wrigley Field in Los Angeles. The team moved to the Dodgers' Chivas Ravine the following year and stayed there until Anaheim Stadium opened in 1966.
• Hall-of-Fame pitcher Nolan Ryan threw four of his seven no-hitters while with the Angels.

RBIs (game): 8 (tie)
(Aug. 25, 1979)
RBIs (season): 139 (1979)
• **Rod Carew (1979–85)**
Batting Avg. (career): .314
• **Brian Downing (1979–90)**
At-Bats (career): 5,854
Extra Base Hits (career): 526
Hits (career): 1,588
HRs (career): 222
RBIs (career): 846
2B (career): 282
• **Jim Edmonds (1993–99)**
2B (season): 42 (1998)
• **Darin Erstad
(1996–present)**
Batting Avg. (season):
.355 (2000)
Hits (season): 240 (2000)
Runs (season): 121 (2000)
Total Bases (season):
366 (2000)
• **Troy Glaus (1998–present)**
Extra Base Hits (season):
85 (2000)
HRs (season): 47 (2000)
• **Reggie Jackson (1982–86)**
HRs (game): 3 (tie)
(Sept. 18, 1986)

Pitching Records
• **Bert Blyleven (1989–92)**
Winning Pct. (season): .773
(1989)
• **Dean Chance (1961–66)**
Shutouts (season): 11 (1964)
• **Chuck Finley (1986–99)**
Innings Pitched
(career): 2,675
Starts (career): 379
Wins (career): 165

• **Bob Lee (1964–66)**
ERA (season): 1.33 (1964)
ERA (career): 1.99
• **Nolan Ryan (1972–79)**
Complete Games
(season): 26 (1973, '74)
Complete Games
(career): 156
Innings Pitched (season):
332.2 (1974)
No-Hitters (career): 4
Shutouts (career): 40
Strikeouts (game): 19
(Aug. 12, 1974)
Strikeouts (season): 383
(1973)
Wins (season): 22 (tie) (1974)

LEAGUE HONORS
AL MVP
• Don Baylor
(1979)

AL Rookie of the Year
• Tim Salmon
(1993)

AL Cy Young
• Dean Chance
(1964)

AL Silver Slugger
• Rick Burleson
(1981)
• Bobby Grich
(1981)
• Doug
DeCinces
(1982)

• Reggie Jackson (1982)
• Lance Parrish (1990)
• Tim Salmon (1995)

AL Gold Glove
• Mark Langston 5
• Bob Boone 4
• Bobby Knoop 3
• Jim Edmonds 2
• Gary Pettis........................2
• J.T. Snow...........................2
• Devon White......................2
• Ken Berry 1
• Jim Fregosi 1
• Rick Miller 1
• Vic Power 1
• Jim Spencer......................1

The Angels look to Darin Erstad, among the AL's top hitters, to lead them to glory.

Timeline

1960	1961	1964	1971	1979	1982	1984	1986	1991	1998	2000
Cowboy legend Gene Autry is awarded Angels franchise	Angels win first AL game, 7-2 over Baltimore	Pitcher Dean Chance becomes Angels' first 20-game winner and wins AL Cy Young	Angels acquire pitcher Nolan Ryan in trade with Mets	Angels win first AL West title, posting 88-74 record	Led by Reggie Jackson's league-leading 39 home runs, Angels capture second division title	Mike Witt pitches perfect game against Texas	Angels lose dramatic seven-game ALCS to Boston	Pitcher Mark Langston wins first of five consecutive Gold Glove Awards	Anaheim Stadium renovated and renamed Edison International Field	Angels slugger Darin Erstad finishes second in AL batting race

16

EDISON INTERNATIONAL FIELD OF ANAHEIM: THE BIG A

EDISON INTERNATIONAL FIELD has seen many changes over the years. Opened as Anaheim Stadium in 1966, the building was renovated in 1979 to provide more seating for the NFL's Los Angeles Rams. Capacity went from 43,250 to 64,600, a boon at the time since the Angels were enjoying great success and drawing record crowds. Adapted again in 1998 to a baseball-only park, Edison Field now features state-of-the-art facilities. However, the stadium also hearkens back to its early days — it's still a power hitters' park and the centerpiece of the original stadium, a 230-foot-high letter "A" with a golden halo around it, stands proudly in the parking lot.

CONCESSIONS

Edison Field offers a wide variety of food, from gourmet Chinese to sausages, pizza, barbecue, hot dogs, nachos and burgers. A smoke house, named after late team owner Gene Autry, is a particular favorite with hungry fans.

Stadium Facts

Opened: April 9, 1966
Cost: $24 million
Capacity: 45,050
Type: Outdoor
Surface: Grass
Home Sweet Home:
• To make it easier for batters to pick up the ball once it leaves the pitcher's hand, a green canvas covering was placed over some center-field sections of the ballpark. This is a boon to Angels batters, who play half their games at Edison International Field.

GAME DAY TIPS

• **Gate hours:** Gates open 90 minutes prior to games.
• **Tailgating:** Some tailgating takes place about two hours before games in the designated right-field parking lot.
• **Weather:** Expect warm, sunny weather. Make sure to pack sunscreen and a hat. Anaheim games rarely get rained out.
• **Prohibited items:** Cans, bottles, thermoses, ice chests and glass containers are all prohibited. Alcohol and large quantities of food cannot be brought into the stadium. Smoking, while forbidden in most areas, is allowed in certain spots such as the ramps and the Plaza Courtyard area.
• **Ticket tips:** Same-day tickets are generally available. Expect big crowds (and far fewer available tickets) on Opening Day and the Fourth of July as well as games against the Yankees, Red Sox and LA Dodgers.
• **Lost and found:** (714) 940-2115.

Seating Plan

Field MVP	$35
Terrace MVP	$24
Field Box	$22
Terrace Box	$20
Lower View MVP	$15
Lower View Box	$12
View	$10
Terrace/Club Pavilion	$8
Left Field Family Pavilion	$7
Premium Seating-Diamond Club	$55
Premium Seating-Club MVP	$35
Premium Seating-Club Lodge	$22
Premium Seating-Suites	N/A

ATM Sections 110, 126, 418
♿ Sections 213–247, 221–233, 350–352

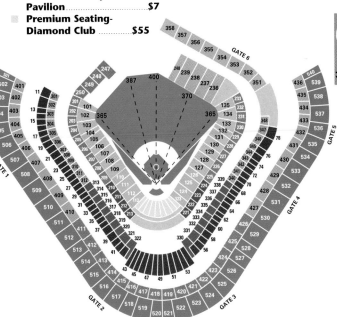

HOME PLATE GATE

Directions: From CA-57 north, exit at Katella Ave. Go left on E. Katella Ave. to the park. From the I-5 north, exit at Chapman Ave. Turn left onto W. Chapman Ave. and right onto The City Dr., which becomes State College Blvd. By Public Transport: The No. 50 bus will take you to Edison Field. For schedules call 714-636-RIDE. The Amtrak station is near the park. **Parking:** An on-site lot holds 15,000 cars and is wheelchair accessible. More lots are on The City Dr., W. Katella Ave. and W. City Blvd.

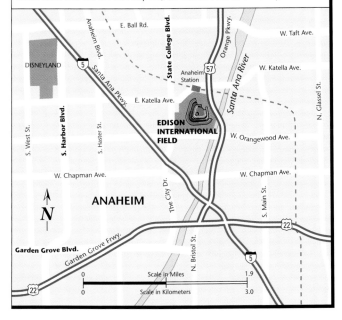

Nearby Hotels

▼▼▼ **Anaheim Towneplace Suites by Marriott** (*Motel*), 1730 S. State College Blvd. (Anaheim), (714) 939-9700, $69-$99
▼▼▼ **Comfort Inn & Suites** (*Motel*), 300 E. Katella Blvd. (Anaheim), (714) 772-8713, $89-$119
▼▼▼ **Hilton Suites Anaheim/Orange** (*Suite Hotel*), 400 N. State College Blvd. (Orange), (714) 938-1111, $105-$210
▼▼▼ **Peacock Suite Resort** (*Suite Motel*), 1745 S. Anaheim Blvd. (Anaheim), (714) 535-8255, $94-$130
▼▼▼ **Residence Inn by Marriott** (*Apartment*), 1700 S. Clementine St. (Anaheim), (714) 533-3555, $199-$329

Nearby Restaurants

▼▼ **The Catch** (*Steak & Seafood*), 1929 S. State College Blvd. (Anaheim), (714) 634-1829, $13-$25
▼▼▼ **Citrus City Grille** (*American*), 122 N. Glassell St. (Orange), (714) 639-9600, $12-$24
ESPN Zone (*American*), 1545 Disneyland Dr. (Anaheim), (714) 300-ESPN, $8-$22
▼▼▼ **Mr. Stox Restaurant** (*American*), 1105 E. Katella Ave. (Anaheim), (714) 634-2994, $16-$28
▼▼▼ **Rafaello Ristorante** (*Northern Italian*), 1998 N. Tustin Ave. (Orange), (714) 283-8230, $11-$19

ARIZONA DIAMONDBACKS

SINCE HIS EARLIEST DAYS AS GENERAL MANAGER of the NBA's Suns, the name Jerry Colangelo has been synonymous with professional sports in Phoenix. His reputation was enhanced in 1995, when his bid to bring a major-league baseball franchise to the city was successful. Colangelo hired former Yankees skipper Buck Showalter to manage the team and the Diamondbacks played a respectable inaugural season in 1998, finishing with 65 wins, one of the best performances by any first-year expansion franchise. But Colangelo has always set winning as a high priority, so he gave GM Joe Garagiola Jr. the go-ahead to sign some free agents who would make the team a contender in 1999. Garagiola did his job well, signing, among others, Arizona native and reigning strikeout king Randy Johnson, speedy infielder Tony Womack, and outfielders Steve Finley and Luis Gonzalez. The acquisitions, combined with the power hitting of original third baseman Matt Williams, instantly turned the Diamondbacks into a force to be reckoned with. The following season was pure magic for the team, as it completed the single greatest reversal of fortune in baseball history, going 100-62 to win the NL West. The unprecedented two-year rise from expansion team to division winner set the entire state of Arizona on fire with baseball fever and attendance reached more than 3.6 million in 1999. The team enjoyed a second consecutive winning season in 2000, but finished third in the division. With Johnson and crew back again, the D'backs are poised for another run at the postseason in the near future.

Vital Stats

Stadium Address:
401 E. Jefferson St.,
Phoenix, Ariz.
Phone: (602) 462-6000
Web:
diamondbacks.mlb.com,
bankoneballpark.com
Box Office:
(602) 514-8400,
Mon.–Sat. 9–5,
game days until
seventh inning
Media Coverage:
Radio: KTAR (620 AM)
TV: KTVK-TV (Channel 3),
Fox Sports Net
Spring Training:
Tucson Electric Park,
Tucson, Ariz.

POSTSEASON
• NL West Titles 1
(1999)

TEAM RECORDS
Hitting Records
• **Jay Bell (1998–present)**
Hits (career): 459
HRs (season): 38 (1999)
HRs (career): 76

The Inside Pitch

• Arizona ace Randy Johnson currently stands second to Roger Clemens in strikeouts among active players. His 364 strikeouts in 1999 is the fourth-best single-season total in major-league history.

• During its division-winning 1999 season, the team was an astounding 52-21 after the All-Star break, an amazing .712 winning percentage.

• The General Manager of the Diamondbacks is Joe Garagiola Jr., son of the legendary player/commentator Joe Garagiola. The senior Garagiola works as a TV analyst on the Diamondbacks' weekend games.

Runs (season): 132 (1999)
Total Bases (career): 812
Walks (season): 82 (1999)
2B (career): 91
• **Luis Gonzalez
(1999–present)**
Batting Avg. (season):
.336 (1999)
Batting Avg. (career): .323
Hits (season): 206 (1999)
Total Bases (season):
337 (1999)
2B (season): 45 (1999)
• **Matt Williams
(1998–present)**
At-Bats (season): 627 (1999)
Grand Slams (career): 5
RBIs (season): 142 (1999)
RBIs (career): 260
• **Tony Womack
(1999–present)**
Steals (season): 72 (1999)
Steals (career): 117
3B (season): 14 (2000)
3B (career): 24

Pitching Records
• **Brian Anderson
(1998–present)**
Innings Pitched
(career): 551.1
Pickoffs (season): 12 (1998)
• **Andy Benes (1998–99)**
HRs By Pitcher (career): 2
• **Randy Johnson
(1999–present)**
Complete Games (season):
12 (1999)
Complete Games

(career): 20
ERA (season): 2.48 (1999)
ERA (career): 2.56
Shutouts (season): 3 (2000)
Starts (season): 35
Strikeouts (season):
364 (1999)
Strikeouts (career): 711
Wins (season): 19
Wins (career): 36
Winning Pct. (season):
.731 (2000)
Winning Pct. (career): .692
• **Gregg Olson (1998–99)**
Games (season):
64 (tie) (1998)
Games (career): 125
Saves (season): 30 (1998)
Wins in Relief (season):
9 (1999)
• **Greg Swindell
(1999–present)**
Games (season):
64 (tie) (2000)

Managing Records
• **Buck Showalter
(1998–2000)**

"I can't remember being more excited about seeing this team on the field."

— D'backs GM Joe Garagiola Jr.,
on the 2001 squad

Wins (season): 100 (1999)
Wins (career): 250
Winning Pct. (season):
.617 (1999)

LEAGUE HONORS
NL Cy Young
• **Randy Johnson**
(1999, 2000)

NL Gold Glove
• **Steve Finley** 2

NL All-Star Selections
• **Devon White (1998)**
• **Luis Gonzales (1999)**
• **Randy Johnson (1999)**
• **Matt Williams (1999)**

In his second Cy Young season, Randy Johnson had 347 Ks.

Timeline

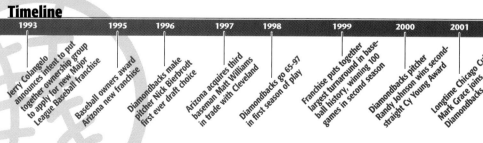

1993	1995	1996	1997	1998	1999	2000	2001
Jerry Colangelo announces intent to put together ownership group to apply for new Major League Baseball franchise	Baseball owners award Arizona new franchise	Diamondbacks make pitcher Nick Bierbrodt first ever draft choice	Arizona acquires third baseman Matt Williams in trade with Cleveland	Diamondbacks go 65-97 in first season of play	Franchise puts together largest turnaround in baseball history, winning 100 games in second season	Diamondbacks pitcher Randy Johnson wins second-straight Cy Young Award	Longtime Chicago Cub Mark Grace joins Diamondbacks

BANK ONE BALLPARK: FUN AT POOLSIDE

OPENED IN 1998 as home to the new Arizona franchise, Bank One Ballpark joins a host of new baseball facilities that have put the emphasis on fan comforts and field quality. From its trademark pool beyond the wall in right center to its full air conditioning and unobstructed sight lines, Bank One Ballpark is an excellent facility for watching the grand old game. The retractable roof insulates fans from Arizona's infamous heat and unpleasant monsoons. Although most games at Bank One are played with the roof closed, the field is natural grass.

CONCESSIONS

Bank One Ballpark has hamburgers, pizza and Mexican food as well as a farmer's market selling fresh produce.

GAME DAY TIPS

• **Gate hours:** Gates open two hours prior to games.

Stadium Facts

Opened: *March 31, 1998*
Cost: *$354 million*
Capacity: *49,033*
Type: *Enclosed (with retractable roof)*
Surface: *Blend of turf grasses*
Home Sweet Home:
• *The BOB (as the ballpark is known to fans) is the second-highest in MLB. The 1,100-foot elevation makes this a hitter's park.*

• **Weather:** The ballpark has an 8,000-ton cooling system and the roof is kept shut on sunny days. These efforts keep the temperature from getting too high. You may even want to bring along a sweatshirt because a seat in front of a cooling vent can prove chilly. When the roof is open during day games, the third base side gets the shade while the first base side gets the sun.
• **Prohibited items:** Blow horns, noisemakers, laser pointers, fishing nets, beach balls, glass bottles, cans and thermoses are all forbidden. Smoking is allowed only in designated areas.
• **Ticket tips:** More than 80 percent of the seats in this ballpark are inside the foul poles and all the seats are angled toward home plate to ensure a clear sight line. Three-hundred-and-fifty $1 tickets are always reserved for same-day sales, and more expensive seats are generally available as well.
• **Lost and found:** (602) 462-6173.

Seating Plan

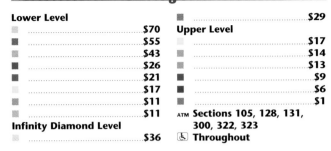

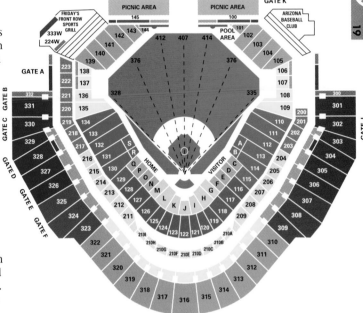

Lower Level

▪	$70
▪	$55
▪	$43
▪	$26
▪	$21
▪	$17
▪	$11
▪	$11

Infinity Diamond Level

▪	$36

▪	$29

Upper Level

▪	$17
▪	$14
▪	$13
▪	$9
▪	$6
▪	$1

ATM Sections 105, 128, 131, 300, 322, 323
♿ **Throughout**

Directions: *Take the I-17 or the I-10 to the 7th St. exit. The park is on the corner of East Jefferson and 7th streets and is visible from the exit. By Bus: The No. 7 bus runs along 7th St. to the park. For schedule information, call (602) 253-5000.* **Parking:** *The ballpark's garage holds only 1,500 cars, but there are more than 30,000 spots available in downtown Phoenix lots within a 15-minute walk on 1st, 2nd, 3rd, 4th, 5th or 7th streets. Guests with disabilities can use one of 31 on-site reserved spots.*

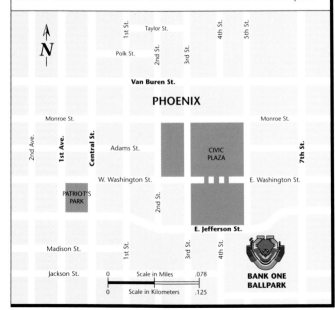

Nearby Hotels

▼▼▼ **Best Western Executive Park Hotel** *(Hotel)*, 1100 N. Central Ave. (Phoenix), (602) 252-2100, $61-$91
▼▼▼ **Embassy Suites Hotel Airport West** *(Suite Hotel)*, 2333 E. Thomas Rd. (Phoenix), (602) 957-1910, $69-$139
▼▼▼ **Hilton Suites-Phoenix** *(Suite Hotel)*, 10 E. Thomas Rd. in Phoenix Plaza (Phoenix), (602) 222-1111, $59-$239
▼▼▼ **Hyatt Regency Phoenix** *(Hotel)*, 122 N. 2nd St. (Phoenix), (602) 252-1234, $224-$249
▼▼▼ **La Quinta Inn Thomas Rd** *(Motel)*, 2725 N. Black Canyon Hwy. (Phoenix), (602) 258-6271, $49-$99

Nearby Restaurants

▼▼▼ **Eddie Matney's** *(French)*, 2398 E. Camelback Rd. in Northern Trust Bank Tower (Phoenix), (602) 957-3214, $17-$25
▼▼ **Omaha Steakhouse** *(Southwest American)*, 2630 E. Camelback Rd. in Embassy Suites-Biltmore (Phoenix), (602) 955-3992, $11-$34
▼▼ **Rennicks** *(American)*, 2435 S. 47th St. (Phoenix), (480) 894-1600, $10-$19
▼▼ **Rose's** *(American)*, 1100 N. Central Ave. in Best Western Executive Park Hotel (Phoenix), (602) 252-2100, $9-$18
▼ **Stockyards Restaurant** *(American)*, 5001 E. Washington Ave. (Phoenix), (602) 273-7378, $14-$32

ATLANTA BRAVES

Vital Stats

THE ATLANTA BRAVES IS THE OLDEST CONTINUOUSLY operating franchise in professional sports. Despite its incredible longevity, however, the team has been anything but stable. The Braves underwent several name changes and three moves before becoming the team we know today. Located in Boston from 1876 to 1951, the franchise was known as the Red Stockings, Beaneaters, Doves, Rustlers and Bees before choosing the name Braves in 1912. The Braves won just one World Series in Boston, but the franchise did have some illustrious roster members, including Olympic decathlon champion Jim Thorpe in 1919 and Babe Ruth in 1935. With fan support sagging, the team relocated to Milwaukee in 1953 and, led by sluggers Hank Aaron and Eddie Mathews, captured the 1957 World Series. The team landed in Atlanta in 1966 and struggled, winning just two division titles in the next 25 years. But in the 1990s, behind a stellar starting rotation anchored by Tom Glavine and Greg Maddux, the team won an incredible eight division titles and a world championship, earning the nickname "Team of the '90s." And with another NL East win in 2000, the Braves show no signs of slowing down this decade.

Stadium Address:
755 Hank Aaron Dr., Atlanta, Ga.
Phone: *(404) 522-7630*
Web: *braves.mlb.com*
Box Office:
(404) 522-7630
Mon.–Fri. 8:30–6, Sat. 9–5, Sun. 1–5, game days until seventh inning
Media Coverage:
Radio: News/Talk 750 WSB (750 AM)
TV: TBS (Channel 17), Fox Sports Net, Turner South
Spring Training:
Disney's Wide World of Sports Complex, Kissimmee, Fla.

The Inside Pitch

• Atlanta Fulton County Stadium was the site of Hank Aaron's record-breaking 715th homer. The pitcher he hit it off, Al Downing, is now a Braves broadcaster.
• Hall-of-Famer Eddie Mathews played for the Braves in Boston, Milwaukee and Atlanta.

"Spahn and Sain and two days of rain."

— Sportswriter Gerry Hearn, on the Boston Braves 1948 pitching rotation, which included greats Warren Spahn and Johnny Sain, and not much else

Batting Avg.
(season): .438 (1894)
Hits (season): 236 (1894)
RBIs (season): 145 (1894)
Runs (season): 160 (1894)
2B (season): 51 (1894)
• Billy Hamilton (1896–1901)
Batting Avg. (career): .338
Steals (season): 93 (1896)
• Eddie Mathews (1952–66)
Walks (career): 1,444

Pitching Records
• John Clarkson (1888–92)
Innings Pitched (season): 620 (1889)
Wins (season): 49 (1889)

• **Greg Maddux (1993–present)**
ERA (season): 1.56 (1994)
Winning Pct. (season): .905 (1995)
Winning Pct. (career): .712
• Phil Niekro (1966–83, '87)
Games (career): 740
Strikeouts (career): 2,912
Walks (career): 1,458
• Warren Spahn (1942–52)
Complete Games (career): 374
Starts (career): 635
Shutouts (career): 63
Strikeouts (game): 18 (June 14, 1952)
Wins (career): 356
20-Game Seasons (career): 13

Managing Records
• Bobby Cox (1978–81, 1990–present)
Wins (career): 1,261
Games (career): 2,078
Wins (season): 106 (1998)
• Frank Selee (1890–1901)
Winning Pct. (career): .607

POSTSEASON
• World Series Titles............3
(1914, '57, '95)
• NL Pennants.....................9
(1914, '48, '57, '58, '91, '92, '95, '96, '99)

RETIRED NUMBERS
• Dale Murphy (3)
• Warren Spahn (21)
• Phil Niekro (35)
• Eddie Mathews (41)
• Hank Aaron (44)

TEAM RECORDS
Hitting Records
• Hank Aaron (1954–74)
At-Bats (career): 11,628
Games (career): 3,076
Grand Slams (career): 16
Hits (career): 3,600
HRs (season): 47 (tie) (1971)
HRs (career): 733
RBIs (career): 2,202
Runs (career): 2,107
2B (career): 600
• Hugh Duffy (1892–1900)

LEAGUE HONORS
NL Rookie of the Year
• Alvin Dark (1948)
• Samuel Jethroe (1950)
• Earl Williams (1971)
• Bob Horner (1978)
• David Justice (1990)
• Rafael Furcal (2000)

NL Cy Young
• Warren Spahn (1957)
• Tom Glavine (1991)
• Greg Maddux (1993, '94, '95)
• John Smoltz (1996)
• Tom Glavine (1998)

NL MVP
• Robert Elliott (1947)
• Hank Aaron (1957)
• Dale Murphy (1982, '83)
• Terry Pendleton (1991)
• Chipper Jones (1999)

NL Gold Gloves
• Greg Maddux 8
• Dale Murphy 5
• Phil Niekro 5
• Del Crandall 4
• Andruw Jones 3
• Marquis Grissom 2
• Felix Millan 2
• Clete Boyer 1
• Terry Pendleton 1
• Joe Torre 1

Greg Maddux, one of the game's best pitchers, garnered four Cy Young Awards in the 1990s.

Timeline

1876	1877	1890	1914	1942	1953	1957	1966	1982	1993	1995	2000
Braves join National League as Boston Red Stockings	Braves win franchise's first pennant	Frank Selee becomes manager, leads team to five pennants in 12 years	Braves win first World Series, four games to three over the Philadelphia Athletics	Warren Spahn is signed and appears in just four games	Braves move to Milwaukee	Hank Aaron hammers three home runs as Milwaukee defeats the Yankees in WS	Braves move to Atlanta	Dale Murphy wins NL MVP as Braves take NL West title	Greg Maddux wins second consecutive Cy Young in his first year with team	After fourth straight NL East title, Braves win World Series, Atlanta's first major pro sports championship	Braves win ninth NL East title in 10 years

TURNER FIELD: GOLD MEDAL PARK

THE ATLANTA BRAVES' TIMING couldn't have been better. Just as Fulton County Stadium was becoming obsolete, Atlanta was preparing to host the 1996 Summer Games. Along with the Olympics came a new, all-purpose stadium, later converted for only baseball use. The result, the retro-style Turner Field, was named for then team owner, multimillionaire Ted Turner. Dwarfing the Braves' former home, the new stadium, nicknamed "the Ted," is immaculately clean and comfortable, and should serve the Braves for many years to come.

CONCESSIONS

Among Turner Field's many food choices (including vegetarian options) is the "Taste of the Major Leagues." Found in the Entry Plaza, this stand offers food favorites from the visiting team's town.

Stadium Facts

Opened: April 4, 1997
Cost: $240 million (for Olympics stadium and conversion)
Capacity: 50,062
Type: Outdoor
Surface: Athletic turf and hybrid Bermuda grasses
Home Sweet Home:
• Turner Field is not a home-run park. The conditions seem to favor pitchers as home runs and scoring are generally lower than the league average.

GAME DAY TIPS

• **Gate hours:** Gates open three hours prior to games.
• **Weather:** Expect the weather to be hot, hot, hot, especially during day games. Come equipped with sun block, lots of water (plastic bottles only) and a sun hat.
• **Prohibited items:** Cans and glass bottles are forbidden. Foam rubber tomahawks (which are waved to start Braves' rallies) are sold at the stadium — wooden or metal tomahawks are forbidden. Smoking is allowed only in designated areas around the concourse.
• **Ticket tips:** Same-day tickets (178) go on sale at the stadium when the gates open. These land you in the

Skyline seating area, but cost only $1. Good seats may be harder to come by, especially if the Braves are in a division race or playing a big team —

Yankees, Mets or Red Sox. Standing-room tickets are available for sold-out games.
• **Lost and found:** (404) 614-1396.

Seating Plan

■ **Dugout Level**	$40		■ **Upper Levels**	$12
■ **Private Suites**	N/A		■ **Upper Pavilion Level**	$5
□ **Club Level**	$32		■ **Skyline**	$1
■ **Field & Terrace Levels**	$27		ATM **Sections 106, 128, 140,**	
■ **Field & Terrace**			**147, 230, 241, 411**	
Pavilions	$18		♿ **Throughout**	

Directions: I-75 or I-85 to the Fulton St./Stadium exit (246). From the east, take the I-20 west to the Capitol Ave. exit (24). From the west, take the I-20 east and exit at the Windsor St./Stadium exit (22). By Public Transport: Take the MARTA to the Five Point station. Shuttle buses go from there to the park beginning 90 minutes before the game. **Parking:** A lot with more than 8,500 spots is right next door. Handicapped parking is available in the south (Green) lot (east of I-75/85). Additional lots are on Fulton, Glenn and Richardson streets and Central Ave.

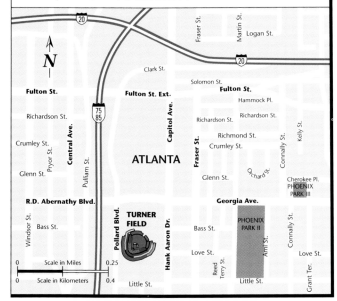

Nearby Hotels

▼▼▼ **Country Inn & Suites by Carlson** *(Motel)*, 1365 Hardin Ave. (East Point), (404) 767-9787, $79-$115
▼▼▼ **Drury Inn & Suites Atlanta Airport** *(Motel)*, 1270 Virginia Ave. (East Point), (404) 761-4900, $82-$102
▼▼▼ **La Quinta Inn Airport** *(Motel)*, 4874 Old National Hwy. (Atlanta), (404) 768-1241, $49-$69
▼▼ **Red Roof Inn-Atlanta Airport North** *(Motel)*, 1200 Virginia Ave. (East Point), (404) 209-1800, $70-$100
▼▼▼▼ **The Ritz-Carlton, Atlanta** *(Hotel)*, 181 Peachtree St. NE (Atlanta), (404) 659-0400, $139-$295

Nearby Restaurants

▼▼▼▼ **City Grill** *(Regional American)*, 50 Hurt Plaza, Ste. 200 (Atlanta), (404) 524-2489, $16-$36
▼▼ **Dailey's** *(American)*, 17 International Blvd. (Atlanta), (404) 681-3303, $20-$30
▼▼ **Lombardi's** *(Italian)*, 94 Upper Pryor St. #238 (Atlanta), (404) 522-6568, $10-$22
▼▼ **Malone's Grill & Bar-Airport** *(American)*, 1258 Virginia Ave. (East Point), (404) 762-5577, $11-$19
▼▼▼ **Mumbo Jumbo** *(International)*, 89 Park Pl. (Atlanta), (404) 523-0330, $16-$28

BALTIMORE ORIOLES

AFFECTIONATELY KNOWN AS THE O'S OR THE BIRDS, the Baltimore Orioles were formed in 1883, playing first in the American Association and then in the National League. Joining the American League in 1901, the team was moved to Manhattan two years later. Baltimore remained without a major-league team until 1954, when the St. Louis Browns moved there and changed their name to the Orioles. Led by future Hall-of-Famer Brooks Robinson — arguably the best third baseman in the history of the game — the O's gained stature throughout the 1950s and early '60s. In 1965 the team pulled off one of the greatest trades in franchise history, adding All-Star outfielder Frank Robinson to the Orioles' growing roster of powerhouse players. In 1966 the triumvirate of Frank Robinson, Brooks Robinson and young slugger Boog Powell fueled the Orioles to their first World Series victory. The team duplicated the feat four years later, thanks in large part to Brooks Robinson's defensive brilliance at third. The 1980s saw the next generation of Orioles greatness come to fruition. Led by stars such as Eddie Murray and Cal Ripken Jr., the franchise won its third World Series title in 1983. Ripken, in particular, remained the backbone of the team, eclipsing Lou Gehrig's consecutive-game record and setting the new standard at 2,632. The team now turns to its young stars to lead the team into the future.

Cal Ripken Jr. retired at the end of the 2001 season.

"I've been successful just trying to prepare myself one game at a time."

— Cal Ripken Jr., who prepared for 2,632 consecutive games

POSTSEASON
• World Series Titles 3
(1966, '70, '83)
• AL Pennants 6
(1966, '69, '70, '71, '79, '83)
• AL East Titles 2
(1996, '97)

RETIRED NUMBERS
• Earl Weaver (4)
• Brooks Robinson (5)

The Inside Pitch

• *The Orioles Hall of Fame is located at the north end of the warehouse of Oriole Park, at the base of the scoreboard. The plaques are similar to those found in Cooperstown.*
• *Look for the single red seat in the left field lower box. It was painted to honor the spot where Cal Ripken Jr.'s historic 278th homer touched down in 1993 — the most ever by a shortstop.*
• *Brass plaques on Eutaw Street commemorate all the homers belted over the right field wall.*

• Frank Robinson (20)
• Jim Palmer (22)
• Eddie Murray (33)

TEAM RECORDS
Hitting Records
• **Roberto Alomar (1996–98)**
Batting Avg. (career): .312
Runs (season): 132 (1996)
• **Brady Anderson (1988–present)**
HRs (season): 50 (1996)
Stolen Bases (career): 295
Total Bases (season): 369 (1996)
• **Cal Ripken Jr. (1981–2001)**
Hits (season): 211 (1983)
Hits (career): 3,070
Hits (game): 6 (June 13, 1999)
HRs (career): 417
RBIs (career): 1,627
Runs (career): 1,604
• **Brooks Robinson (1955–77)**
Games (season): 163 (1961, '64)
Games (career): 2,986
3B (career): 68
• **Ken Singleton (1975–84)**
Batting Avg. (season): .328 (1977)
Walks (season): 118 (1975)

Pitching Records
• **Dave McNally (1962–74)**

Vital Stats

Stadium Address:
333 W. Camden St., Baltimore, Md.
Phone: (410) 685-9800
Web: orioles.mlb.com, orioleparkat camdenyards.com
Box Office:
1-888-848-BIRD, Mon.–Sat. 9–5, Sun. 12–5
Media Coverage:
Radio: WBAL (1090 AM)
TV: WJZ (Channel 13), WNUB (Channel 54)
Spring Training:
Fort Lauderdale Stadium, Fort Lauderdale, Fla.

ERA (season): 1.95 (1968)
Winning Pct. (season): .808 (1971)
• **Mike Mussina (1991–2000)**
Strikeouts (season): 218 (1997)
Strikeouts (game): 15 (1997)
Winning Pct. (career): .645
• **Gregg Olson (1988–93)**
Saves (career): 160
• **Jim Palmer (1965–67, 1969–84)**
Games (career): 558
Strikeouts (career): 2,212
Shutouts (season): 10
Shutouts (career): 53
Wins (career): 268
• **Steve Stone (1979–81)**
Wins (season): 25 (1980)

Managing Records
• **Earl Weaver (1968–82, 1985–86)**
Wins (career): 1,480
AL Pennants: 4

LEAGUE HONORS
AL MVP
• Brooks Robinson (1964)
• Frank Robinson (1966)
• Boog Powell (1970)
• Cal Ripken Jr. (1983, '91)

AL Rookie of the Year
• Ron Hansen (1960)
• Curt Blefary (1965)
• Al Bumbry (1973)
• Eddie Murray (1977)
• Cal Ripken Jr. (1982)
• Gregg Olsen (1989)

AL Cy Young
• Mike Cueller (1968)
• Jim Palmer (1973, '75, '76)
• Mike Flanagan (1979)
• Steve Stone (1980)

AL Gold Glove
• Brooks Robinson 16
• Mark Belanger 8
• Paul Blair 8
• Bobby Grich 4
• Mike Mussina 4
• Jim Palmer 4
• Davey Johnson 3
• Eddie Murray 3
• Roberto Alomar 2
• Luis Aparicio 2
• Rafael Palmeiro 2
• Cal Ripken Jr. 2

Timeline

1872	1883	1903	1954	1962	1966	1968	1970	1975	1983	1992	1995	2000
Lord Baltimores baseball team founded Baltimore's first professional club	The Lord Baltimores adopt the name the Orioles	Team moves to Manhattan to become the Highlanders, and later the Yankees	St. Louis Browns move to Baltimore and become the Orioles	Boog Powell pops first homer over the center-field wall at Memorial Stadium – a 469-foot shot	O's win their first World Series Championship	Earl Weaver embarks on long career as Orioles manager	O's take their second World Series Championship	Former Oriole great Frank Robinson becomes the first black baseball manager	Jim Palmer becomes the only pitcher to win a World Series game in each of three decades	Oriole Park at Camden Yards opens	Cal Ripken Jr. plays his 2,131st consecutive game, breaking Lou Gehrig's record	Right-hander Jose Mercedes paces O's with 14-7 record

ORIOLE PARK: STADIUM REINVENTS THE PAST

Situated on the old Camden Yards railway site, this stadium is esteemed for its seamless blend of up-to-date technology and traditional design. Oriole Park was conceived as a "green cathedral," and provides spectators with an awe-inspiring view of the Baltimore skyline as well as an intimate game-viewing environment. Built just two blocks from Babe Ruth's birthplace and directly on the site of the Ruth family café, Oriole Park was designed with baseball's roots in mind. Steel trusses, an arched brick facade and a traditional asymmetrical field all tie this modern facility to the magnificent ballparks of yesteryear.

CONCESSIONS

All types of standard ballpark fare is available at the Yards, including Boog's BBQ (owned by legendary Oriole great Boog Powell), hamburgers, vegetarian, chicken, pizza, kosher and crab cakes.

Stadium Facts

Opened: *April 6, 1992*
Cost: *$110 million*
Capacity: *48,876*
Type: *Outdoor*
Surface: *Grass*
Home Sweet Home:
• *Oriole Park's luxurious, state-of-the-art team facilities are among the finest in the AL.*
• *Prevailing winds favor left-handed pull hitters.*
• *The asymmetrical field can result in strange caroms off the outfield wall — something Orioles fielders are adept at playing.*

GAME DAY TIPS

• **Gate hours:** Gates open 90 minutes prior to games on weekdays and two hours prior to games on weekends.
• **Weather:** Baltimore can be very muggy in the summer. Rain is fairly common in the fall.
• **Prohibited items:** Radios and stereos are prohibited at Oriole Park, as are glass bottles and cans. Smoking is prohibited in all areas except the concourses. Videotaping of games is also prohibited.
• **Ticket tips:** Tickets can be hard to come by since Baltimore has recently enjoyed one of the highest attendance rates in the major league. Reserve tickets early, if possible. All seats face north, offering a view of downtown Baltimore. The middle (Club) level seats are highly recommended, not only for the fabulous view they provide, but also for their easy access to the bars and lounges on this level.
• **Lost and found:** (410) 685-9800.

Seating Plan

■ Club Box	$35	
■ Field Box	$30	
■ Field Box	$27	
■ Left Field Club	$22	
■ Lower Box	$22	
■ Terrace Box	$23	
■ Terrace Box	$20	
■ Left Field Lower Box	$18	
■ Upper Box	$18	
■ Left Field Upper Box	$16	
■ Lower Reserve	$16	
■ Lower Reserve	$13	
■ Upper Reserve	$13	
■ Left Field Upper Reserve	$11	
■ Bleachers	$9	
■ Standing Room	$7	
ATM	Sections 17–19, 37–39, 90–92, 338, Upper Reserve 336–340	
♿	Throughout	

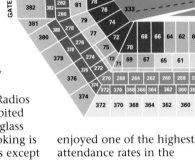

Directions: *From the north, take I-83 to the Fayette exit and follow Maryland or St. Paul St. south. From the west, take I-70 to I-695 and US 40. From the east, take US 40 or Eastern Ave. From the south, take I-395 (exit 53 from I-95) or Russell St. (exit 52 from I-95). By Train: The MARC train and light-rail trains both have stops at the park. By Bus: Buses are available. Call 1-410-539-5000.* **Parking:** *On-site lots hold 4,000 cars and have spots for the disabled. Other lots are within walking distance on W. Pratt, W. Camden, W. Conway, Light, S. Paca and S. Eutaw streets.*

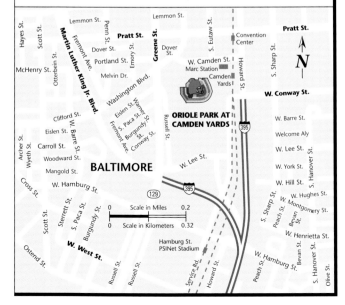

Nearby Hotels

▼▼▼ **Best Western Hotel & Conference Center** *(Motor Inn)*, 5625 O'Donnell St. (Baltimore), (410) 633-9500, $99-$119
▼▼ **Holiday Inn-Inner Harbor** *(Hotel)*, 301 W. Lombard St. (Baltimore), (410) 685-3500, $139-$1890
▼▼▼▼ **Hyatt Regency Baltimore** *(Hotel)*, 300 Light St. (Baltimore), (410) 528-1234, $215-$240
▼▼▼ **Sheraton Inner Harbor Hotel** *(Hotel)*, 300 S. Charles St. (Baltimore), (410) 962-8300, $119-$264
▼▼▼ **Tremont Plaza Hotel** *(Apartment)*, 222 St. Paul Pl. (Baltimore), (410) 727-2222, $109-$129

Nearby Restaurants

▼▼▼ **Della Notte Ristorante** *(Italian)*, 801 Eastern Ave. (Baltimore), (410) 837-5500, $11-$20
▼▼ **Germano's Trattoria** *(Italian)*, 300 S High St. (Baltimore), (410) 752-4515, $13-$25
▼▼ **Obrycki's Crab House and Seafood Restaurant** *(Seafood)*, 1727 E. Pratt St. (Baltimore), (410) 732-6399, $16-$28
▼▼▼ **Pisces** *(Seafood)*, 300 E. Light St. in the Hyatt Regency Baltimore (Baltimore), (410) 605-2835, $22-$32 (dinner only).
▼▼▼ **Windows** *(American)*, 202 E. Pratt St. in the Renaissance Harborplace Hotel (Baltimore), (410) 685-8439, $14-$30

BOSTON RED SOX

IN BOSTON, PEOPLE WILL tell you that all their baseball team's woes — no World Series title since 1918 — can be traced back to "the curse of the Bambino." It was December 1919 and the Red Sox's cash-strapped owner was forced to sell a talented outfielder named Babe Ruth, also known as "the Bambino," to the New York Yankees. In Ruth's first four years with Boston, the team won three World Series titles to go along with the crown the squad had taken in 1903 on Cy Young's powerful right arm. It isn't that the team has lacked great players since Ruth departed. Many a BoSox lineup card has included the names of baseball's greatest legends. Jimmie "Double X" Foxx rivaled Ruth as a home run hitter in the 1930s; Ted Williams, "the Splendid Splinter," forged a name for himself as one of the game's best hitters in the '40s and '50s. Williams was replaced in Fenway's left field in 1960 by another future Hall of Famer, Carl Yastrzemski, who along with teammates Carlton Fisk, Jim Rice, Louis Tiant and Dwight Evans took several good runs at baseball's top prize in the 1970s only to fall short. Fireballer Roger "Rocket" Clemens and hitting machine Wade Boggs led the team to the 1986 World Series, only to lose in a heartbreaking game seven. Current BoSox fans are hoping that stars such as Nomar Garciaparra and Pedro Martinez have the necessary magic to remove the dreaded curse once and for all.

Nomar Garciaparra is one of baseball's brightest stars.

POSTSEASON
• World Series Titles 5
(1903, '12, '15, '16, '18)

• AL Pennants 9
(1903, '12, '15, '16, '18, '46, '67, '75 '86)

RETIRED NUMBERS
• Bobby Doerr (1)
• Joe Cronin (4)
• Carl Yastrzemski (8)
• Ted Williams (9)
• Carlton Fisk (27)

TEAM RECORDS
Hitting Records
• Wade Boggs (1982–92)

The Inside Pitch

• *Ted Williams is considered one of the greatest hitters of all time. The last man to bat .400 in a season, he won six batting crowns despite missing five years to military service. In 1957 the 39-year-old Williams became the oldest man to lead the league in hitting (.388). He topped himself the following year, beating all AL batters, at age 40, by hitting .328. Fittingly, Williams homered in the very last at-bat of his Hall-of-Fame career.*

Hits (season): 240 (1985)
• **Jimmie Foxx (1936–42)**
HRs (season): 50 (1938)
RBIs (season): 175 (1938)
• **Nomar Garciaparra (1996–present)**
At-Bats (season): 684 (1997)
• **Tommy Harper (1972–74)**
Steals (season): 54 (1973)
• **Harry Hooper (1909–20)**
Steals (career): 300
3B (career): 130
• **Jim Rice (1974–89)**
Total Bases (season): 406 (1978)
• **Tris Speaker (1907–15)**
3B (season): 22 (1913)
• **Earl Webb (1930–32)**
2B (season): 67 (1931)
• **Ted Williams (1939–42, 1946–60)**
Batting Avg. (season): .406 (1941)
Batting Avg. (career): .344
HRs (career): 521
Runs (season): 150 (1949)
Slugging Pct. (career): .634
• **Carl Yastrzemski (1961–83)**
At-Bats (career): 11,988
Games (career): 3,308
Hits (career): 3,419
RBIs (career): 1,844
Runs (career): 1,816
Total Bases (career): 5,539
2B (career): 646

Pitching Records
• **Roger Clemens (1984–96)**
Innings (career): 2776.0
Shutouts (career): 38 (tie)

Strikeouts (career): 2,590
Wins (career): 192 (tie)
• **Tom Gordon (1996–99)**
Saves (season): 46 (1998)
• **Dutch Leonard (1913–18)**
ERA (season): 0.96 (1914)
• **Pedro Martinez (1998–present)**
Strikeouts (season): 313 (1999)
• **Bob Stanley (1977–89)**
Saves (career): 132
• **Smokey Joe Wood (1908–15)**
ERA (career): 1.99
Wins (season): 34 (1912)
• **Cy Young (1901–08)**
Complete Games (season): 41 (1902)
Complete Games (career): 275
Innings (season): 384.2 (1902)
Shutouts (career): 38 (tie)
Wins (career): 192 (tie)

LEAGUE HONORS
AL MVP Awards
• Jimmie Foxx (1938)
• Ted Williams (1946, '49)
• Jackie Jensen (1958)
• Carl Yastrzemski (1967)
• Fred Lynn (1975)
• Jim Rice (1978)
• Roger Clemens (1986)
• Mo Vaughn (1995)

"Fenway Park is a religious shrine. People go there to worship."

— *Bill Lee, former Red Sox pitcher*

Vital Stats

Stadium Address:
4 Yawkey Way,
Boston, Mass.
Phone: (617) 267-9440
Web: redsox.mlb.com
Box Office:
(617) 482-4SOX,
Mon.–Sat. 9–5, game days until one hour after game start
Media Coverage:
Radio: WEEI (850 AM)
TV: WFXT (Channel 25), NESN
Spring Training:
City of Palms Park,
Fort Myers, Fla.

AL Rookie of the Year
• Walter Dropo (1950)
• Don Schwall (1961)
• Carlton Fisk (1972)
• Fred Lynn (1975)
• Nomar Garciaparra (1997)

AL Cy Young
• Jim Lonborg (1967)
• Roger Clemens (1986, '87, '91)
• Pedro Martinez (1999, 2000)

Timeline

1901	1903	1904	1916	1919	1930	1938	1941	1953	1967	1974	1986	1991	1999	2000
Boston franchise plays in newly formed AL	Team wins first modern World Series	Cy Young pitches perfect game	Pitcher Babe Ruth wins 23 games; team wins second straight WS	Red Sox sell Babe Ruth to Yankees	Boston finishes last in AL for sixth straight year	Jimmie Foxx wins MVP with 50 HRs and 175 RBIs	Ted Williams hits .406	BoSox score 17 runs in one inning versus Tigers	Carl Yastrzemski wins triple crown; leads team to AL pennant	Louis Tiant notches second straight 20-win year	Roger Clemens fans 20 versus Mariners	Clemens wins third Cy Young Award	Nomar Garciaparra is AL batting champion	Pedro Martinez wins second straight Cy Young Award

FENWAY PARK: HOME OF "THE GREEN MONSTER"

OPENED IN 1912, Fenway Park is the oldest link to baseball's bygone era. While there is a movement afoot to build a new modernized version of the ballpark, Fenway's numerous supporters have been vocal in their support of the venerable old venue. They relish the park's cozy, if not somewhat cramped, confines and the diamond's wildly asymmetrical dimensions. Looming over the historic scene is Fenway's most notorious feature, "the Green Monster." Standing 315 feet from home plate, the famous left-field fence is a tempting target for sluggers looking to belt the long ball. However, at more than 37 feet in height, the Monster has turned many a certain dinger into a double off the wall.

CONCESSIONS

Fenway's food choices include sausage, burgers, seasoned fries, sandwiches and New England clam chowder. The famous "Fenway frank" comes regular or foot-long.

Stadium Facts

Opened: *April 20, 1912*
Cost: *$275,000*
Capacity: *33,871*
Type: *Outdoor*
Surface: *Bluegrass*
Home Sweet Home:
• *Dominated by the "Green Monster," Fenway's asymmetrical outfield fence can be a wild adventure for opposing outfielders unaccustomed to gauging its difficult caroms.*

GAME DAY TIPS

• **Gate hours:** Gates open 90 minutes prior to games.
• **Weather:** Typical northeast weather means cooler temperatures in early spring. Expect summer days to be hot and occasionally humid.
• **Prohibited items:** Beachballs, alcoholic beverages, bottles and cans are prohibited. No smoking is allowed in the seating area or the bathrooms.
• **Ticket tips:** Poles for banners affect the sight line from most of the grandstand seats at Fenway. Avoid the right-field corner; the bleachers, although a bit distant from the field, offer a less obstructed view of the game. Same-day standing-room and last-minute tickets are often available even for sold-out games. The team's big rival is the N.Y. Yankees and those series sell out fast. Look for discount nights in cooler spring months.
• **Lost and found:** (617) 267-9440.

Directions: *From I-93 north, take Storrow Dr. W. and then the Fenway exit. From I-90, exit at Cambridge tolls and proceed toward Cambridge. Turn right onto Storrow Dr. E. and take Fenway exit. From I-93 south, take Massachusetts Ave. exit.* **Parking:** *Fenway has no private lot and the downtown location means parking is limited. The public lots in the area are expensive, although the nearby Prudential Center offers a discount to people going to the game. People with disabilities can look for reserved spots on Landsdowne St. near Brookline Ave.*

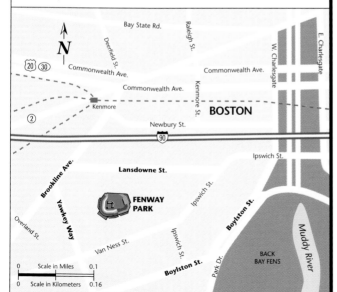

Seating Plan

- ☐ **Field Box Seats** $55
- ■ **Infield Roof Box** $55
- ☐ **Loge Seats** $55
- ■ **Right Field Box** $30
- ■ **Right Field Roof Box** $30
- ■ **Grandstand** $40
- ■ **Outfield Grandstand** $25
- ■ **Lower Bleacher** $20
- ■ **Upper Bleacher** $18
- **ATM Sections 19, 43**
- ♿ **Throughout**

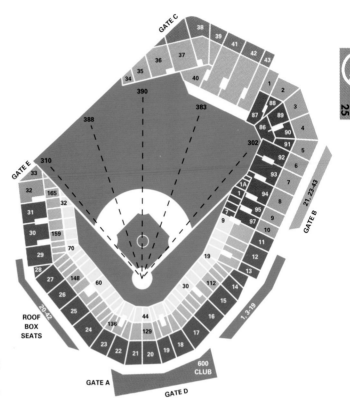

Nearby Hotels

▼▼▼▼ **The Eliot Suite Hotel** (*Historic Hotel*), 370 Commonwealth Ave. (Boston), (617) 267-1607, $275-$435
▼▼ **Hilton Boston Back Bay** (*Hotel*), 40 Dalton St. (Boston), (617) 236-1100, $249-$489
▼▼▼ **Howard Johnson Lodge Fenway** (*Motor Inn*), 1271 Boylston St. (Boston), (617) 267-8300, $105-$199
▼▼ **The Midtown Motel** (*Motel*), 220 Huntington Ave. (Boston), (617) 262-1000, $119-$279
▼▼▼ **Sheraton-Boston Hotel** (*Hotel*), 39 Dalton St. (Boston), (617) 236-2000, $349-$619

Nearby Restaurants

▼▼▼ **The Capital Grille** (*Steak & Seafood*), 359 Newbury St. (Boston), (617) 262-8900, $22-$35
▼▼▼ **Davio's** (*Northern Italian*), 269 Newbury St. (Boston), (617) 262-4810, $15-$29
▼▼ **The Elephant Walk** (*French*), 900 Beacon St. (Boston), (617) 247-1500, $12-$25
▼▼ **Hong Kong Café** (*Regional Chinese*), 575 Commonwealth Ave. in the Howard Johnson Hotel-Kenmore (Boston), (617) 434-8889, $8-$15
▼ **Marche Movenpick** (*Eclectic*), 800 Boylston St. in the Prudential Center (Boston), (617) 578-9700, $9-$15

CHICAGO CUBS

REVERED BY LOCALS FOR THEIR TEAM UNITY and strong work ethic, the Cubs have represented the spirit of Chicago for more than a century. Throughout the first decade of the 1900s, the Cubs endeared themselves to fans with their never-say-die attitude. The love affair peaked when the Cubbies enjoyed a pair of back-to-back World Series wins over Detroit in 1907–08. While the team has suffered through an incredible dry spell since then, Cubs' fans refuse to wallow in self pity. Instead they celebrate the great, charismatic players that have marked Cubs history: the "Big Three" powerhouse of Hack Wilson, Rogers "the Rajah" Hornsby and Kiki Cuyler who assaulted the record books in the late 1920s and early '30s; the dauntless Billy Williams, who played a whopping 1,117 consecutive games; and, of course, "Mr. Cub," Ernie Banks, who enchanted Chicago fans for 19 seasons. With his monstrous homers and charming personality, Banks always made the denizens of Wrigley Field feel like he was playing just for them. Today the Cubs are led by another smiling slugger, Sammy Sosa, whose easy-going attitude belies just how hard he is on opposing pitchers.

"Isn't it a beautiful day? . . . The Cubs of Chicago in beautiful, historic Wrigley Field. Let's go, let's go. It's Sunday in America."
— Ernie Banks, 1970

POSTSEASON
• World Series Titles............2
(1907, '08)
• NL Pennants...................10
(1906, '07, '08, '10, '18, '29, '32, '35, '38, '45)

RETIRED NUMBERS
• Ernie Banks (14)
• Billy Williams (26)

TEAM RECORDS
Hitting Records
• **Cap Anson (1876–97)**
Batting Avg. (career): .339
Hits (career): 3,081
RBIs (career): 1,879
Runs (career): 1,711

Singles (career): 2,330
2B (career): 530
• **Ernie Banks (1953–71)**
Games (career): 2,528
Grand Slams (career): 12
HRs (career): 512
• **Billy Herman (1931–41)**
At-Bats (season): 666 (1935)
2B (season): 57 (1935, '36)
• **Rogers Hornsby (1929–32)**
Batting Avg. (season): .380 (1929)
Hits (season): 229 (1929)
Runs (season): 156 (1929)
• **Ryne Sandberg (1982–94, 1996–97)**
Singles (career): 1,624
3B (season): 19 (1984)
• **Sammy Sosa (1992–present)**
HRs (season): 66 (1998)
• **Hack Wilson (1926–31)**
RBIs (season): 191 (1930)
Slugging Pct. (season): .723 (1930)
Slugging Pct. (career): .590
Total Bases (season): 423 (1930)

Pitching Records
• **Mordecai "Three-Finger" Brown (1904–12, '16)**
ERA (season): 1.04 (1906)
ERA (career): 1.80
Shutouts (career): 48
Winning Pct. (career): .686
Wins (season): 29 (1908)
• **Fergie Jenkins**

(1966–73, 1982–83)
Strikeouts (season): 274 (1970)
Strikeouts (career): 2,038
• **Charlie Root (1937–47)**
ERA (season): 1.64 (1943)
Games (career): 605
Wins (career): 201

Managing Records
• **Cap Anson (1879–97)**
Pre-1900 Wins (career): 1,282
• **Charlie Grimm (1932–38, 1944–49, '60)**
Post-1900 Wins (career): 946

LEAGUE HONORS
NL MVP
• **Rogers Hornsby** (1929)
• **Gabby Hartnett** (1935)
• **Phil Cavarretta** (1945)
• **Hank Sauer** (1952)
• **Ernie Banks** (1958, '59)
• **Ryne Sandberg** (1984)
• **Andre Dawson** (1987)
• **Sammy Sosa** (1998)

NL Rookie of the Year
• **Billy Williams** (1961)
• **Ken Hubbs** (1962)
• **Jerome Walton** (1989)
• **Kerry Wood** (1998)

NL Cy Young
• **Fergie Jenkins** (1971)
• **Bruce Sutter** (1979)
• **Rick Sutcliffe** (1984)
• **Greg Maddux** (1992)

NL Gold Glove
• **Ryne Sandberg** 9
• **Ron Santo** 5
• **Mark Grace** 4
• **Greg Maddux** 3
• **Andre Dawson** 2
• **Don Kessinger** 2
• **Glenn Beckert** 1
• **Jody Davis** 1
• **Bob Dernier** 1
• **Randy Hundley** 1

The Inside Pitch

• An old Cubs' tradition is the "Flying of the Flags" from the tall center-field flagpole after each game. A white flag with a blue "W" proclaims a Cubs victory to passersby, while a blue flag with a white "L" announces a loss.

• Since the Cubs' last World Series win in 1908, the team has made seven unsuccessful trips to the fall classic.

In 1998 Kerry Wood burst onto the scene by recording 233 strikeouts as a rookie.

Timeline

1876	1906	1907	1916	1930	1935	1945	1958	1960	1970	1978	1989	1995	1998

The first game in the history of Chicago's National League franchise takes place on April 25

Chicago rounds out the season 116-36, setting an all-time league record

The name "Cubs" is officially adopted by the team — which wins first World Series title

Team moves to Weeghman Park (now Wrigley Field)

Hack Wilson nails 56 HRs and drives in 191 RBIs — still a major-league record

Cubs win 21 straight games in September to take NL pennant

Cubs' 10th WS appearance ends in another loss

Ernie Banks wins his first MVP award

Don Cardwell throws no-hitter against St. Louis in first game with club

Billy Williams becomes first player to appear in 1,000 consecutive games

Largest Opening Day crowd ever at Wrigley Field – 45,777

Teammates Jerome Walton and Dwight Smith finish 1-2 in Rookie of the Year voting

Cubs win their 9,000th game

Sammy Sosa wins NL MVP after his 66-HR season

WRIGLEY FIELD:
87 SEASONS OF BASEBALL HISTORY

OPENED IN 1914, WRIGLEY FIELD IS THE second-oldest ball-park in Major League Baseball and one of America's most cherished sporting venues. The ballpark's ivy-strewn walls, original hand-turned scoreboard and classic field design all help to create an atmosphere that is steeped in baseball's rich history. At Wrigley, spectators are transported back to some of the game's greatest moments, including Babe Ruth's legendary "called-shot" during the 1932 World Series, in which he pointed to the bleacher section where he would deposit a home run with his very next swing; Ernie Banks' 500th career homer in 1970; and Pete Rose's 4,191st career hit in 1985, which tied him with Ty Cobb for the most ever. To see a game at Wrigley is to experience a part of baseball lore.

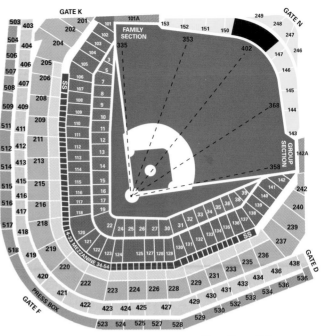

Stadium Facts

Opened: *April 23, 1914*
Cost: *$250,000*
Capacity: *39,056*
Type: *Outdoor*
Surface: *Grass*
Home Sweet Home:
• *Winds play a huge factor in games at Wrigley Field. Gusts off Lake Michigan favor pitchers, while wind blowing toward the lake turns fly balls into homers.*
• *If an opposing player hits a home run at Wrigley, the notorious "Bleacher Bums" show their disdain by throwing the baseball back onto the field.*

CONCESSIONS

A wide variety of food can be found at Wrigley Field, including pizza, hamburgers, sausages, baked goods, vegetarian food, ice cream and sandwiches. The hot dog and beer combo is the must-have for any die-hard Cubs fan.

GAME DAY TIPS

• **Gate hours:** Gates open two hours prior to games.
• **Weather:** Nicknamed the "Windy City" for its turbulent political history, Chicago remains infamous for its strong winds off Lake Michigan. Humidity can be oppressive in the summer and early autumn.
• **Prohibited items:** Cans and plastic and glass bottles are prohibited at Wrigley Field, as is any outside food. Videotaping games is also not allowed. Smoking is prohibited in the bleachers.
• **Ticket tips:** Tickets go fast at Wrigley, especially for games against the Mets, Cardinals and White Sox, with whom the Cubs have strong rivalries.
• **Lost and found:** (773) 404-4185.

Seating Plan

■ **Club Boxes**	**$30**
■ **Field Boxes**	**$28**
■ **Mezzanine**	
Suites	**call for prices**
▨ **Terrace Boxes**	**$23**
▨ **Terrace Reserved**	**$18**
■ **Upper Deck Boxes**	**$23**
■ **Upper Deck Reserved**	**$10**
□ **Bleachers**	**$20**
■ **Family Section**	**$23**
■ **Group Section**	
(seats 107)	**call for prices**

ATM **Sections 19–22, 137, 138, 247, 248, 420, 421**
♿ **Sections 113–115, 120–122, 128–130**

Directions: *Take I-94/90 to the Addison St. exit. Turn right (east) on Addison and travel three miles to the ballpark. By Subway (CTA): Take Howard/Dan Ryan red line to Addison St. stop. By Bus: Many buses are available to and from the stadium. Call the Chicago Transit Authority at (312) 836-7000 for more information.* **Parking:** *The Cubs operate a lot at 1126 Grace St. and there are other lots in the vicinity. For daytime games you can park on the street around Wrigley, but not during night games, when you will be towed. Wheelchair-accessible parking is available at lots on N. Sheffield Ave. and N. Broadway and N. Clark streets.*

Nearby Hotels

▼▼▼ **Best Western Hawthorne Terrace** *(Historic Motel)*, 3434 N. Broadway (Chicago), (773) 244-3434, $129-$179
▼▼▼ **City Suites Hotel** *(Historic Motel)*, 933 W. Belmont Ave. (Chicago), (312) 404-3400, $99-$179
▼▼ **Days Inn-Lincoln Park North** *(Historic Motel)*, 644 W. Diversey Pkwy. (Chicago), (773) 525-7010, $96-$136
▼▼▼ **Majestic Hotel** *(Historic Motel)*, 528 W. Brompton Pl. (Chicago), (773) 404-3499, $99-$179
▼▼▼ **The Willows** *(Historic Motel)*, 555 W. Surf St. (Chicago), (773) 528-8400, $119-$199

Nearby Restaurants

▼▼▼ **Bella Vista Restaurant** *(Italian)*, 1001 W. Belmont Ave. (Chicago), (773) 404-0111, $15-$25
▼▼▼ **Erwin-An American Café** *(American)*, 2925 N. Halsted St. (Chicago), (773) 528-7200, $15-$26 (dinner only)
▼▼ **PS Bangkok** *(Thai)*, 3345 N. Clark St. (Chicago), (773) 871-7777, $6-$11
▼▼ **Stefani's** *(Northern Italian)*, 1418 W. Fullerton Ave. (Chicago), (773) 348-0111, $11-$20
▼▼▼▼ **Yoshi's Café** *(Fusion)*, 3257 N. Halsted St. (Chicago), (773) 248-6160, $16-$21 (dinner only)

CHICAGO WHITE SOX

WITH A HISTORY THAT SPANS more than 100 years, the Chicago White Sox franchise has an all-time roster that reads like a baseball who's who. In all, some 23 players now immortalized in the Hall of Fame once donned the White Sox colors. One such player was "Big Ed" Walsh, the notorious spitballer whose gaudy 1908 numbers (40 wins, 269 strikeouts and a 1.42 ERA) rank as one of the best single-season pitching performances of all time. Walsh was the ace of a pitching staff that carried the light-hitting ChiSox, nicknamed "the Hitless Wonders," to a 1906 World Series upset of their crosstown rivals, the Chicago Cubs. The team won its second fall classic in 1917 with a line-up stocked with no less than three future Hall of Famers: Eddie "Cocky" Collins, Ray Schalk and Urban Charles "Red" Faber. In that World Series, pitching once again carried the day for the White Sox, with Faber winning three games. But perhaps the best player on that squad, and the most notorious ChiSoxer of all time, was "Shoeless Joe" Jackson, the immensely talented outfielder who, along with seven other members of the White Sox, was banned for life for throwing the 1919 World Series. The ensuing years have been both harsh (finishing 56.5 games out of first in 1932) and heady (17 straight winning seasons from 1951–67) for the team. Today's ChiSox fans pin their World Series hopes on two-time AL MVP Frank "Big Hurt" Thomas and wonder every time he belts another tape-measure home run if they are watching yet another White Sox player blazing a trail to the Hall of Fame.

Vital Stats

Stadium Address:
333 W. 35th St.,
Chicago, Ill.
Phone: (312) 674-1000
Web: whitesox.mlb.com
Box Office:
(312) 831-1SOX,
Mon.–Sat. 9–9, Sun. 9–4,
game days until bottom of
fifth inning; when team is
away Mon.–Fri. 10–6,
Sat.–Sun. 10–4
Media Coverage:
Radio: ESPN (1000 AM)
TV: WCIU-TV (Channel
26), WGN-TV (Channel 9),
Fox Sports Net
Spring Training:
Tucson Electric Park,
Tucson, Ariz.

"It would all depend on how well she was hitting."

— Early Wynn, ChiSox pitcher, on whether he would throw at his mother to move her off the plate

POSTSEASON
- World Series Titles...........2
(1906, '17)
- AL Pennants.....................4
(1906, '17, '19, '59)
- AL West Titles 2
(1983, '93)
- AL Central Titles..............1
(2000)

RETIRED NUMBERS
- Nellie Fox (2)

The Inside Pitch

- *The ChiSox were owned by Bill Veeck, a flamboyant showman who would do anything to sell tickets. As the owner of the St. Louis Browns, Veeck sent midget Eddie Gaedel up to bat against the Tigers in a 1951 game. Standing just 3 feet 7 inches tall, Gaedel presented such a miniscule strike zone that he drew a walk on four pitches.*

- Luke Appling (4)
- Minnie Minoso (9)
- Luis Aparicio (11)
- Ted Lyons (16)
- Billy Pierce (19)
- Carlton Fisk (72)

TEAM RECORDS
Hitting Records
- **Luke Appling (1930–50)**
At-Bats (career): 8,857
Batting Avg. (season):
.388 (1936)
Hits (career): 2,749
Runs (career): 1,319
- **Albert Belle (1997–98)**
HRs (season): 49 (1998)
RBIs (season): 152 (1998)
- **Eddie Collins (1915–26)**
Hits (season): 222 (1920)
Steals (career): 366
- **Nellie Fox (1950–63)**
At-Bats (season): 649 (1956)
3B (career): 104 (tie)
- **Joe Jackson (1915–20)**
Batting Avg. (career): .339
3B (season): 21 (1916)
- **Rudy Law (1982–85)**
Steals (season): 77 (1983)
- **John Mostil (1918, 1921–29)**
Runs (season): 135 (1925)
- **Frank Thomas (1990–present)**
HRs (career): 344
RBIs (career): 1,183

- **Robin Ventura (1989–98)**
Grand Slams (career): 10
Grand Slams (game): 2
(April 9, 1995)

Pitching Records
- **Jack Harshman (1954–57)**
Strikeouts (game): 16
(July 25, 1954)
- **Lamar Hoyt (1979–84)**
Consecutive Wins (season):
13 (1983)
- **Ted Lyons (1923–42, '46)**
Complete Games (career): 356
Wins (career): 260

Frank Thomas, one of baseball's most feared sluggers.

- **Billy Pierce (1949–61)**
Strikeouts (career): 1,796
- **Bobby Thigpen (1986–93)**
Saves (season): 57 (1990)
Saves (career): 201
- **Ed Walsh (1904–16)**
Complete Games (season):
42 (1908)
ERA (season): 1.27 (1910)
ERA (career): 1.81
Shutouts (season): 11 (1908)
Shutouts (career): 57
Strikeouts (season):
269 (1908)
Wins (season): 40 (1908)

LEAGUE HONORS
AL MVP
- Nellie Fox (1959)
- Dick Allen (1972)
- Frank Thomas (1993, '94)

AL Rookie of the Year
- Luis Aparicio (1956)
- Gary Peters (1963)
- Tommie Agee (1966)
- Ron Kittle (1983)
- Ozzie Guillen (1985)

AL Cy Young
- Early Wynn (1959)
- LaMarr Hoyt (1983)
- Jack McDowell (1993)

Timeline

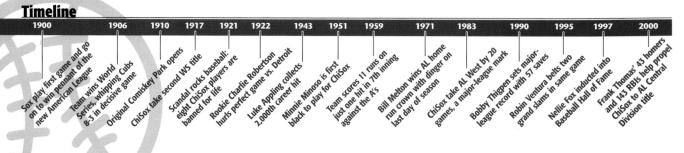

| 1900 | 1906 | 1910 | 1917 | 1921 | 1922 | 1943 | 1951 | 1959 | 1971 | 1983 | 1990 | 1995 | 1997 | 2000 |

Sox play first game and go on to win pennant of the new American League

Team wins World Series, whipping Cubs 8–3 in decisive game

Original Comiskey Park opens

ChiSox take second WS title

Scandal rocks baseball: eight ChiSox players are banned for life

Rookie Charlie Robertson hurls perfect game vs. Detroit

Luke Appling collects 2,000th career hit

Minnie Minoso is first black to play for ChiSox

Team scores 11 runs on just one hit in 7th inning against the A's

Bill Melton wins AL home run crown with dinger on last day of season

ChiSox take AL West by 20 games, a major-league mark

Bobby Thigpen sets major-league record with 57 saves

Robin Ventura belts two grand slams in same game

Nellie Fox inducted into Baseball Hall of Fame

Frank Thomas' 43 homers and 143 RBIs help propel ChiSox to AL Central Division title

COMISKEY PARK: THE TRADITION CONTINUES

THE NEW COMISKEY PARK opened in 1991 directly across the street from the old Comiskey Park, which had served as the club's home since 1910. In a tip of the hat to the old park, designers built a re-creation of its famous exploding scoreboard. The infield dirt from the original park, notorious for being watered down when teams with good base stealers came into town, was used to make the new field's base paths. On the minus side: The park is located in the city's South Side neighborhood — not the district you want to hang out in after the game.

CONCESSIONS

Concessions at Comiskey Park include the traditional hot dogs, hamburgers and pizza, as well as sandwiches (including steak, roast beef, corned beef and subs), brats, Tex/Mex and funnel cakes. Kids' specialties, such as peanut butter and jelly sandwiches, are also available.

Stadium Facts

Opened: April 18, 1991
Cost: $137 million
Capacity: 45,887
Type: Outdoor
Surface: Grass (bluegrass)
Home Sweet Home:
• Comiskey Park underwent major renovations during the winter of 2001. The outfield fences were moved in considerably, making the home team's already potent offense even more intimidating for opposing pitchers.

GAME DAY TIPS

• **Gate hours:** Gates open 90 minutes prior to games.
• **Tailgating:** Tailgating takes place two hours before a game in parking lots A–F.
• **Weather:** Known for its heat waves, Chicago is hot and humid in the summer. Fans can cool off in the shower room (left field) or rain room (right field). April, May and September typically have cooler evenings, so bring along a sweater for night games.
• **Prohibited items:** No alcoholic beverages, bottles, cans or hard coolers can be brought in. Banners and flags cannot have poles and may not be held up during play or placed on the field. Video cameras may be used to tape the game. There is no smoking in the seating area.
• **Ticket tips:** Although tickets are usually easy to get, watch out for sellout crowds when the crosstown rival Chicago Cubs are the opponents. Ticket prices are reduced by 50 percent for all Monday night home games.
• **Lost and found:** (312) 674-1000.

Seating Plan

■ Lower Deck Box $26
□ Club Level $26
▨ Lower Deck Reserved $20
■ Upper Deck Box $18
■ Bleachers $18
▨ Available for full-season
   tickets only $13

■ Upper Deck Reserved $12
ATM Sections 133, 533, outside
   Bullpen Sports Bar, Gate 4
♿ Sections in 100s, eight
   sections in 500s

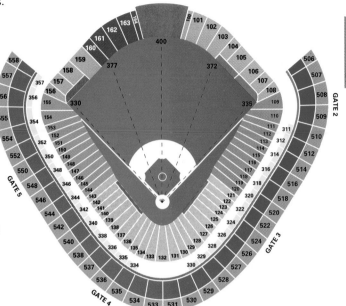

Directions: *From the Dan Ryan Expressway (I-94) going north or south, take the 35th St. exit (55A). By Subway/Elevated Train: Red line (Howard–Dan Ryan) to 35th St. stop. By Bus: Rte. 24 (Wentworth) or 35 (35th St.). Call Chicago Transit Authority at (312) 836-7000 for information.* **Parking:** *There are 7,000 spots in the stadium lot. Wheelchair-accessible parking and drop-off in Lot D; enter by 37th St. Non-residents cannot park on the street area around the ballpark, so public lots must be used. Illinois Institute of Technology has shuttle service from its lots.*

Nearby Hotels

▼▼ **Best Western Grant Park Hotel** (*Hotel*), 1100 S. Michigan Ave. (Chicago), (312) 922-2900, $139-$335
▼▼▼▼ **Hilton Chicago** (*Classic Hotel*), 720 S. Michigan Ave. (Chicago), (312) 922-4400, $129-$354
▼▼▼ **Hyatt Regency McCormick Place Chicago** (*Hotel*), 2233 S. Martin Luther King Dr. (Chicago), (312) 567-1234, $219-$244
▼▼ **Sleep Inn-Midway Airport** (*Motel*), 6650 S. Cicero Ave. (Bedford Park), (708) 594-0001, $99-$119
▼▼ **Wooded Isle Suites** (*Historic Apartment*), 5750 S. Stony Island Ave. (Chicago), (773) 288-5578, $119-$173

Nearby Restaurants

▼▼ **Emperor's Choice** (*Chinese*), 2238 S. Wentworth Ave. (Chicago), (312) 225-8800, $7-$20
▼▼▼▼ **Everest** (*French*), 440 S. LaSalle St. at One Financial Place (Chicago), (312) 663-8920, $28-$34 (dinner only)
▼▼ **Harry Caray's Restaurant** (*Steakhouse*), 33 W. Kinzie St. (Chicago), (312) 828-0966, $11-$33
▼▼ **Russian Tea Time** (*Russian*), 77 E. Adams St. (Chicago), (312) 360-0000, $15-$26
▼▼ **Tuscany** (*Italian*), 1014 W. Taylor (Chicago), (312) 829-1990, $9-$24

CINCINNATI REDS

A FERVENT BASEBALL TOWN, Cincinnati was one of the first cities to lavish widespread adoration on its team. Formed in 1866 as the Resolutes, the team soon gained the moniker "the Red Stockings" for its red socks and knickers-style pants. In the early years, the club cut a wide swath through baseball, going an incredible four years without a loss. In 1869, for the first time in baseball, the team signed its players to contracts, with shortstop George Wright topping the salaries at $2,000. Since then, each Reds generation has had its share of stars and big wins. With Edd Roush and Heinie Groh leading the way, the Reds won their first World Series in the ill-fated 1919 series against the Chicago White Sox — a series in which eight Sox players, including "Shoeless Joe" Jackson, were accused of throwing the games. The Reds' legacy peaked in the 1970s, when Pete Rose, Joe Morgan, Johnny Bench, George Foster, Ken Griffey and Tony Perez brought "the Big Red Machine" two more championship crowns. Over the last 25 years, the Reds have seen leaner days, but still reached the postseason in 1990 with "Nasty Boys" Randy Myers, Rob Dibble and Norm Charlton.

Vital Stats

Stadium Address:
100 Cinergy Field,
Cincinnati, Ohio
Phone: (513) 421-4510
Web: reds.mlb.com,
cinergy.com
Box Office:
(513) 381-REDS,
Mon.–Fri. 9–5
Media Coverage:
Radio: WLW (700 AM)
TV: Fox Sports Net
Spring Training:
Ed Smith Stadium,
Sarasota, Fla.

Ken Griffey Jr. has had seven 40+ HR seasons.

The Inside Pitch

- Fans seeking autographs on game days can hail their favorite Reds player from the Blue section seating near the dugouts until the end of batting practice.
- Check the left-field wall to view the uniforms of Reds' legends.
- In the early 1900s Cincinnati became the first team to use chalk foul lines when groundskeeper Will Weed got tired of local players tripping over the furrows that designated the game lines.

POSTSEASON
- **World Series Titles**...........5
(1919, '40, '75, '76, '90)
- **NL Pennants**.....................9
(1919, '39, '40, '61, '70, '72, '75, '76, '90)

RETIRED NUMBERS
- **Fred Hutchinson (1)**
- **Johnny Bench (5)**
- **Joe Morgan (8)**
- **Ted Kluszewski (18)**
- **Frank Robinson (20)**

TEAM RECORDS
Hitting Records
- **Johnny Bench (1967–83)**
Grand Slams (career): 11
HRs (career): 389
RBIs (career): 1,376
- **George Foster (1971–81)**
HRs (season): 52 (1977)
RBIs (season): 149 (1977)
Total Bases (season): 388 (1977)
- **Ted Kluszewski (1947–53)**
Slugging Pct. (season): .642 (1954)
- **Joe Morgan (1972–79)**
Steals (career): 406
- **Frank Robinson (1956–65)**
Runs (season): 134 (1962)
Slugging Pct. (career): .553
- **Pete Rose (1963–78, 1984–86)**
At-Bats (career): 10,934
At-Bats (season): 680 (1973)
Games (career): 2,722
Hits (season): 230 (1973)
Hits (career): 3,358
Hitting Streak: 44 games (1978)

Runs (career): 1,741
2B (career): 601
- **Edd Roush (1916–26, '31)**
Batting Avg. (career): .331
3B (career): 153

Pitching Records
- **Bob Ewing (1902–09)**
ERA (career): 2.37
- **John Franco (1984–89)**
Consecutive Saves (season): 23 (1988)
Saves (career): 148 Games
- **Noodles Hahn (1900–05)**
Complete Games (season): 41 (1901)
Complete Games (career): 207
- **Jim Maloney (1960–70)**
No-Hitters (career): 2
Strikeouts (game): 18 (June 14, 1965)
Strikeouts (career): 1,592
- **Eppa Rixey (1921–33)**
Innings Pitched (career): 2,890
Starts (career): 356
Wins (career): 179
- **Fred Toney (1915–18)**
ERA (season): 1.57 (1915)
- **Bucky Walters (1938–48)**
Shutouts (career): 32
Wins (season): 27 (1939)

LEAGUE HONORS
NL MVP
- Ernie Lombardi (1938)
- Bucky Walters (1939)
- Frank McCormick (1940)
- Frank Robinson (1961)
- Johnny Bench (1970, '72)
- Pete Rose (1973)

- Joe Morgan (1975, '76)
- George Foster (1977)
- Barry Larkin (1995)

NL Rookie of the Year
- Frank Robinson (1956)
- Pete Rose (1963)
- Tommy Helms (1966)
- Johnny Bench (1968)
- Pat Zachry (1976)
- Chris Sabo (1988)
- Scott Williamson (1999)

NL Gold Glove
- Johnny Bench 10
- Dave Concepcion 5
- Joe Morgan 5
- Cesar Geronimo 4
- Eric Davis 3
- Barry Larkin.....................3
- Roy McMillan 3
- Johnny Edwards 2
- Tommy Helms 2
- Pokey Reese......................2
- Pete Rose..........................2
- Bret Boone........................1
- Leo Cardenas 1
- Harvey Haddix 1
- Vada Pinson 1
- Frank Robinson 1

> *"I'm no different from anybody else with two arms, two legs and 4,200 hits."*
> — Pete Rose, baseball's all-time hits leader

Timeline

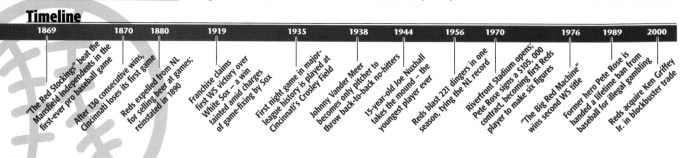

1869	1870	1880	1919	1935	1938	1944	1956	1970	1976	1989	2000

"The Red Stockings" beat the Mansfield Independents in the first-ever pro baseball game

After 130 consecutive wins, Cincinnati loses its first game

Reds expelled from NL for selling beer at games; reinstated in 1890

Franchise claims first WS victory over White Sox – a win tainted amid charges of game-fixing by Sox

First night game in major-league history is played at Cincinnati's Crosley Field

Johnny Vander Meer becomes only pitcher to throw back-to-back no-hitters

15-year-old Joe Nuxhall takes the mound – the youngest player ever

Reds blast 221 dingers in one season, tying the NL record

Riverfront Stadium opens; Pete Rose signs a $105,000 contract, becoming first Reds player to make six figures

"The Big Red Machine" wins second WS title

Former hero Pete Rose is handed a lifetime ban from baseball for illegal gambling

Reds acquire Ken Griffey Jr. in blockbuster trade

CINERGY FIELD: THE END OF AN ERA

OVER THE NEXT COUPLE OF YEARS, Cincinnati will see the end of Cinergy Field as construction of a new ballpark gets underway. Originally named Riverfront Stadium, Cinergy remains famous as the circular, modern facility that housed the legendary "Big Red Machine" lineup in the mid-1970s. Unfortunately, Cinergy has fallen on harder times since then — wear and tear to the stadium and field has cost millions in upgrades — and local feeling is that Cincinnati needs a newer facility to recapture the Reds' glory days. Although construction has only just begun, the plans for the new stadium call for larger, airier concourses, more field-level seating and more of an "old-time" baseball atmosphere.

CONCESSIONS

Cinergy Field offers pizza, hot dogs, Montgomery ribs, hamburgers, chicken, sausages, baked goods, vegetarian items, ice cream and sandwiches. The gold-star chili is the food of choice for discerning Reds fans.

Stadium Facts

Opened: June 30, 1970
Cost: $45 million
Capacity: 52,953
Type: Outdoor
Surface: Grass
Home Sweet Home:
• Baseball is an important part of the Cincinnati summer. Since 1919 fans have held the Findlay Market Parade just prior to the Reds home opener to celebrate the return of baseball season to the city.

GAME DAY TIPS
• **Gate hours:** Gates open two hours prior to games.
• **Weather:** Rain showers are common in the spring and autumn, while heat and humidity can be a factor in late summer.
• **Prohibited items:** Glass, cans and bottles are not allowed. Coolers must be able to fit under seats. Smoking is prohibited in the stands and concession and washroom areas.
• **Ticket tips:** The Reds have a keen state rivalry with the Cleveland Indians. Fans will line up early for tickets. For good comfortable seats, go for the cushioned seats in the yellow and lower red sections.
• **Lost and found:** (513) 421-4510.

Seating Plan

■ Blue Box A	$28
■ Blue Box B	$21
■ Green Box A	$21
■ Green Box B	$16
■ Yellow Box	$15
■ Red Box	$14
■ Red Reserved	$9
■ Top Six	$5

ATM **Sections 102, 202, Red Box**
♿ **Throughout**

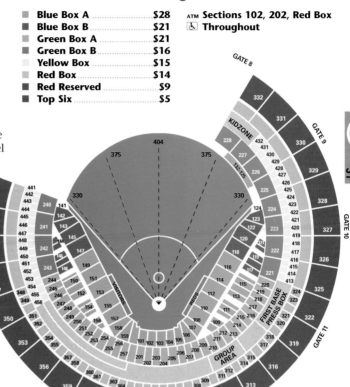

31

Directions: *From the south, take I-71/75 to the 5th St. exit and go to Central Ave., then to Pete Rose Way. From the north, take I-75 to the Freeman exit and go to Mehring Way, then to Pete Rose Way. From the west, take US 50 to the Freeman exit and go to Mehring Way, then to Pete Rose Way. From the east, take US 50 to the Eggleston Ave. exit, then go south to Pete Rose Way. **By Bus:** Many buses go to the park. Call the Cincinnati Transit Authority at (513) 621-4455 for information. **Parking:** There are 10 lots around Cinergy; all have spots with wheelchair access and free valet service for the disabled. There is more parking on 3rd, 4th, 6th and 7th streets.*

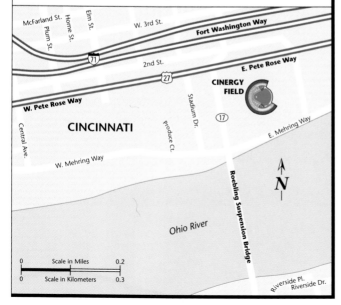

Nearby Hotels

▼▼▼ **Amos Shinkle Townhouse Bed & Breakfast** (*Historic Bed & Breakfast*), 215 Garrard St. (Covington, Ky.), (859) 431-2118, $79-$150
▼▼▼▼ **The Cincinnatian Hotel** (*Hotel*), 601 Vine St. (Cincinnati), (513) 381-3000, $225-$1500
▼▼▼ **Cincinnati's Weller Haus Bed & Breakfast** (*Historic Bed & Breakfast*), 319 Poplar St. (Bellevue, Ky.), (859) 431-6829, $89-$158
▼▼▼ **Hampton Inn Cincinnati Riverfront** (*Motel*), 200 Crescent Ave. (Covington, Ky.), (859) 581-7800, $84-$109
▼▼▼ **Holiday Inn-Riverfront** (*Motor Inn*), 600 W. 3rd St. (Covington, Ky.), (859) 291-4300, $79-$109

Nearby Restaurants

▼▼▼ **J's Fresh Seafood Restaurant** (*Seafood*), 2444 Madison Rd. (Cincinnati), (513) 871-2888, $14-$25
▼▼▼▼ **Maisonette** (*French*), 114 E. 6th St. (Cincinnati), (513) 721-2260, $22-$44
▼▼ **Montgomery Inn** (*American*), 9440 Montgomery Rd. (Cincinnati), (513) 791-3482, $12-$23
▼▼ **Montgomery Inn at the Boathouse** (*American*), 925 Eastern Ave. (Cincinnati), (513) 721-7427, $11-$24
▼▼▼ **Riverview Restaurant** (*Seafood*), 668 5th St. in the Clarion Hotel Riverview (Covington, Ky.), (859) 491-5300, $17-$25

CLEVELAND INDIANS

A MEMBER OF THE AL SINCE ITS INCEPTION IN 1901, the Cleveland Indians have seen it all. The franchise has endured tragedies. In 1911 future Hall-of-Famer Addie Joss died of spinal meningitis, just three years after tossing a perfect game. Nine years later, Indians shortstop Ray Chapman passed away after being beaned by Yankee Carl Mays. In 1993 pitchers Steve Olin and Tim Crews were killed in a boating accident. But the Indians have also been trailblazers. In 1947 the team signed the AL's first black player, center fielder Larry Doby. Doby was a catalyst for the team's 1948 World Series title, winning game four with a 400-foot homer. Frank Robinson became the major's first black manager when he signed on with the Tribe in 1974. Some of baseball's greatest players have played in Cleveland, including Cy Young, Tris Speaker, "Shoeless Joe" Jackson, Satchel Paige, Nap Lajoie, Lou Boudreau, Bob Feller and Bob Lemon. Of course, the Tribe has also had its share of colorful characters. Bronx native Rocky Colavito endeared himself to fans with his prodigious home runs, leading the AL with 42 in 1959. In 1980 "Super Joe" Charboneau burst onto the scene, winning Rookie of the Year honors and keeping his teammates in stitches by opening bottles with his eye socket and by dyeing his hair exotic colors. In recent years the Tribe has enjoyed an embarrassment of riches, winning five AL Central titles from 1995 to '99. Fans hope that such current stars as Omar Vizquel, Roberto Alomar, Jim Thome and newcomer Juan Gonzalez will help write a brilliant new chapter to the Indians' history.

Omar Vizquel, one of the finest infielders in baseball.

"Looks like it worked. I doubt that we'll get it back now. "

— *Paul Shuey, pitcher, after the removal of the clubhouse ping-pong table by management and the Indians went on to win 17 of their next 22 home games*

POSTSEASON
- **World Series Titles**...........2
(1920, '48)
- **AL Pennants**.....................5
(1920, '48, '54, '95, '97)
- **AL Central Titles**..............5
(1995, '96, '97, '98, '99)

RETIRED NUMBERS
- Earl Averill (3)
- Lou Boudreau (5)
- Larry Doby (14)
- Mel Harder (18)
- Bob Feller (19)
- Bob Lemon (21)

The Inside Pitch

- *From 1901–14, the club changed names frequently, being called the Bluebirds, the Bronchos and the Naps. Finally, in 1915 the team settled on the name Indians, in honor of Louis Francis Sockalexis, a Penobscot Indian and a star of the pre-1900 Cleveland teams.*

TEAM RECORDS
Hitting Records
- **Earl Averill (1929–39)**
RBIs (career): 1,084
Runs (season): 140 (1931)
Runs (career): 1,154
- **Albert Belle (1989–96)**
HRs (season): 50 (1995)
HRs (career): 242
- **George Burns (1920–21, 1924–28)**
2B (season): 64 (1926)
- **Larry Doby (1947–55, '58)**
20-HR Seasons: 7
- **Joe Jackson (1910–15)**
Batting Avg. (season): .408 (1911)
Batting Avg. (career): .375
Hits (season): 233
3B (season): 26 (1912)
- **Nap Lajoie (1902–14)**
At-Bats (career): 6,034
Hits (career): 2,046
- **Kenny Lofton (1992–96, 1998–present)**
Steals (season): 75 (1996)
Steals (career): 434
- **Manny Ramirez (1993–2000)**
RBIs (season): 165 (1999)
- **Tris Speaker (1916–26)**
Walks (career): 857
2B (career): 486
- **Jim Thome (1991–present)**
Walks (season): 127 (1999)
- **Terry Turner (1904–18)**
Games (career): 1,619

Pitching Records
- **Jim Bagby Sr. (1916–22)**
Wins (season): 31 (1920)
- **Bob Feller (1936–41, 1945–56)**
Complete Games (season): 36 (1946)
Complete Games (career): 279
Innings (season): 371 (1946)
Innings (career): 3,827.0
No-Hitters (career): 3
Shutouts (season): 10 (tie) (1946)
Starts (career): 484
Strikeouts (season): 348 (1946)
Strikeouts (career): 2,581
Wins (career): 266
- **Doug Jones (1986–91, '98)**
Saves (career): 129
- **Addie Joss (1902–10)**
ERA (season): 1.16 (1908)
ERA (career): 1.89
Shutouts (career): 45
- **Bob Lemon (1941–42, 1946–58)**
Shutouts (season): 10 (tie) (1948)
20-Win Seasons: 7
- **Jose Mesa (1992–98)**
Saves (season): 46 (1995)

- **Gaylord Perry (1972–75)**
Consecutive Wins (season): 15 (tie) (1974)
- **Louis Tiant (1965–69)**
Strikeouts (game): 19 (July 3, 1968)
- **George Uhle (1919–28, '36)**
Starts (season): 44 (1923)

LEAGUE HONORS
AL MVP
- Lou Boudreau (1948)
- Al Rosen (1953)

AL Rookie of the Year
- Herb Score (1955)
- Chris Chambliss (1971)
- Joe Charboneau (1980)
- Sandy Alomar Jr. (1990)

AL Cy Young
- Gaylord Perry (1972)

Vital Stats

Stadium Address:
2401 Ontario St., Cleveland, Ohio
Phone: *(216) 420-4200*
Web: *indians.mlb.com*
Box Office:
(216) 420-4200, Mon.–Fri. 9–5, Sat.–Sun. 9–4
Media Coverage:
Radio: WTAM (1100 AM) TV: WUAB (Channel 43), Fox Sports Net
Spring Training:
Chain of Lakes Park, Winter Haven, Fla.

Timeline

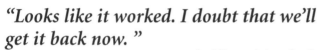

| 1869 | 1889 | 1901 | 1908 | 1920 | 1940 | 1947 | 1959 | 1972 | 1974 | 1981 | 1993 | 1995 | 2000 | 2001 |

Cleveland Forest City's baseball team finishes seventh in National Association

Team changes name to Spiders because it has many tall, skinny players

Cleveland joins new American League

Addie Joss hurls perfect game

Tribe's second baseman Bill Wambsganss makes unassisted triple play in WS to help team win first title

Bob Feller pitches Opening Day no-hitter in Chicago

Larry Doby becomes first black player in AL

Rocky Colavito hammers four HRs in one game

Gaylord Perry wins 24 games and AL Cy Young

Frank Robinson becomes first black manager in major-league history

Len Barker pitches perfect game

Pitchers Steve Olin and Tim Crews killed in boating accident

Tribe wins first of five straight AL Central crowns

Manny Ramirez leads all AL hitters with .697 slugging pct.

Eight-time Gold Glove shortstop Omar Vizquel signs two-year $15-million contract extension

JACOBS FIELD: FAN- AND PLAYER-FRIENDLY

NO ONE LIKES THE FRIENDLY confines of Jacobs Field as much as Cleveland players. Since moving into their new ballpark in 1994, the Indians have never finished lower than second in their division. Smaller and more intimate than cavernous Cleveland Stadium, the new ballpark is also centrally located, making it a hit with fans as well. Seats are angled toward home plate so that fans don't need to crane their necks to watch the action. The seating bowl has also been designed to offer more legroom and unobstructed sight lines.

CONCESSIONS

Jacobs Field has dozens of concession stands and outlets, giving fans a multitude of food choices. As well as standard ballpark fare, hungry fans will find Mexican, Polish and vegetarian food and desserts. Kidsland, located behind first base, has special concessions and play areas for children. Picnic areas can be found behind the outfield fence.

GAME DAY TIPS
• **Gate hours:** Gates open two hours prior to games.
• **Weather:** Cleveland summers are hot and relatively dry, with occasional showers.
• **Prohibited items:** Alcohol, cans, glass or plastic containers, thermos bottles and hard-sided coolers are not permitted. Banners and umbrellas are allowed, but laser pointers, poles and nets are not. Smoking is allowed only in designated areas.
• **Ticket tips:** Indians tickets are hard to come by and the park is often sold out. Given the chance, try to get a seat on the mezzanine.
• **Lost and found:** (216) 420-4932.

Stadium Facts

Opened: April 4, 1994
Cost: $169 million
Capacity: 43,368
Type: Open
Surface: Bluegrass
Home Sweet Home:
• *Jacobs Field has notoriously narrow foul territories. This makes it extremely difficult for fielders to track down foul pop-ups before running out of room. As a result, batters often get a second life.*

Seating Plan

- ▪ .... **Diamond Box**
- ▪ .... **Field Box**
- ▪ .... **Baseline Box**
- ▪ .... **Lower Box**
- ▪ .... **Infield Lower Box**
- ▪ .... **Lower Reserved**
- ▪ .... **Club Seating**
- ▪ .... **Mezzanine Seating**
- ▪ .... **View Box**
- ▪ .... **Infield Upper Box**
- ▪ .... **Upper Box**
- ▪ .... **Upper Reserved**
- ▪ .... **Reserved General Admission**
- ▪ .... **Field Bleachers**
- ▪ .... **Bleachers**

Call for information on ticket prices.
ATM Sections 116, 159, 519
♿ **Throughout**

Directions: Take I-77 north or I-90 west and exit at E. 9th St. Continue north on E. 9th St. or Ontario St. By Public Transportation: Buses and rapid transit trains go to and from the stadium. Call RTA at (216) 621-9500 for information. **Parking:** The ballpark parking garage is between Jacobs Field and Gund Arena. About 30,000 parking spaces are available on E. Prospect, Euclid and Summer Aves. and E. 9th and E. 14th Sts.

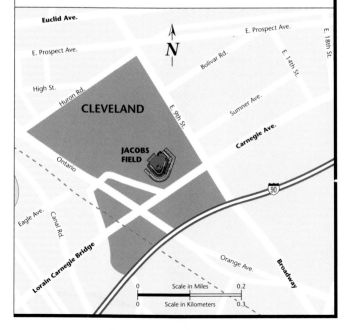

Nearby Hotels

▼▼▼ **Hampton Inn Cleveland-Downtown** *(Motel)*, 1460 E. 9th St. (Cleveland), (216) 241-6600, $99-$179
▼▼▼ **Radisson Hotel at Gateway-Cleveland** *(Hotel)*, 651 Huron Rd. (Cleveland), (216) 377-9000, $129-$149
▼▼▼▼ **The Ritz Carlton, Cleveland** *(Hotel)*, 1515 W. 3rd St. in Tower City Center (Cleveland), (216) 623-1300, $240-$264
▼▼▼ **Sheraton Cleveland City Centre** *(Hotel)*, 777 St. Clair Ave. (Cleveland), (216) 771-7600, $113-$129
▼▼▼ **Wyndham Hotel at Playhouse Square** *(Hotel)*, 1260 Euclid Ave. (Cleveland), (216) 615-7500, $109-$209

Nearby Restaurants

▼▼▼ **Blue Pointe Grille** *(Seafood)*, 700 W. St. Clair Ave. (Cleveland), (216) 875-7827, $15-$30
▼▼ **Café Sausalito** *(American)*, 1301 E. 9th St. in the Galleria at Erieview (Cleveland), (216) 696-2233, $10-$20
▼▼▼ **Johnny's Downtown** *(Northern Italian)*, 1406 W. 6th St. (Cleveland), (216) 623-0055, $18-$34
▼▼ **Li Wah** *(Chinese)*, 2999 Payne Ave. in Asia Plaza (Cleveland), (216) 696-6556, $8-$15
▼▼ **Hyde Park Chop House** *(Steak House)*, 123 Prospect Ave., (Cleveland), (216) 344-2444, $14-$36

COLORADO ROCKIES

NEVER HAS A BASEBALL TEAM been so influenced by its immediate surroundings as the Colorado Rockies. Studies prove that a ball will carry nine percent farther in mile-high Coors Field, the highest altitude of any major-league ballpark, than at sea-level Yankee Stadium. As such, the team has always been well stocked with sluggers who hammer homer after homer through the thin Denver air. In 1995, just two years after the team's first game, Dante Bichette won the NL home-run crown with 40 dingers. The following season, teammate Andres Galarraga topped the league with 47 round trippers only to have his title wrested from him in 1997 when another Rockies slugger, Larry Walker, belted 49 homers. That same year, the heavy-hitting Rockies, also called "the Blake Street Bombers," set a major-league team record with 239 home runs. While power will never be a problem in Colorado as long as the likes of Walker and Todd Helton are taking their cuts, management is fine-tuning the machinery to add speed and pitching to the mix. However, in case opposing pitchers feel too confident, all they have to do is look at the row of purple seats marking one mile above sea level to be reminded they are in hostile territory.

> "*I pitched there my second start of the year and for five starts after that I had brain damage.*"
>
> *— Expos pitcher Jim Bullinger, on the challenge of pitching at Coors Field*

POSTSEASON
• NL Wild Cards 1
(1995)

TEAM RECORDS
Hitting Records
• **Dante Bichette (1993–99)**
At-Bats (career): 4,050
Games (career): 1,018
Hits (season): 219
Hits (career): 1,278
RBIs (career): 826
Runs (career): 665
Total Bases (career): 2,187
2B (career): 270
• **Vinny Castilla (1993–99)**
HRs (career): 203
• **Andres Galarraga (1993–97)**

RBIs (season): 150 (1995)
• **Todd Helton (1997–present)**
Walks (season): 103
2B (season): 59 (2000)
• **Neifi Perez (1996–present)**
At-Bats (season): 690
3B (season): 11 (1999, 2000)
3B (career): 41
• **Larry Walker (1995–present)**
Batting Avg. (season): .379 (1999)
Batting Avg. (career): .334
HRs (season): 49 (1997)
Runs (season): 143 (1997)
Total Bases (season): 409 (1997)
Walks (career): 312
• **Eric Young (1993–97)**
Steals (season): 53 (1996)
Steals (career): 180

Pitching Records
• **Pedro Astacio (1997–present)**
Starts (career): 108
Complete Games (season): 7 (1999)
Complete Games (career): 10
Innings Pitched (season): 232.0 (1999)
Innings Pitched (career): 686.1
Strikeouts (season): 210 (1999)
Strikeouts (career): 624
Wins (season): 17 (1999)
Wins (career): 47

• **Curtis Leskanic (1993–99)**
Games (career): 356
• **Chuck McElroy (1998–99)**
Games: (season): 78 (tie) (1998)
• **Mike Meyers (2000–present)**
Games (season): 78 (tie) (2000)
• **Steve Reed (1993–97)**
ERA (career): 3.68
• **Kevin Ritz (1994–98)**
Wins (season): 17 (tie) (1996)
• **Bruce Ruffin (1993–97)**
Saves (career): 60
• **Dave Veres (1998–99)**
Saves (season): 31 (1999)

Managing Records
• **Don Baylor (1993–98)**
Wins (season): 83 (1996, '97)
Wins (career): 440

Vital Stats

Stadium Address:
2001 Blake St.,
Denver, Colo.
Phone: (303) ROCKIES
Web: rockies.mlb.com
Box Office:
(800) 388-ROCK
or (303) ROCKIES,
Mon.–Fri. 9–6, Sat. 9–4,
game days until after game
Media Coverage:
Radio: KOA (850 AM)
TV: KWGN (Channel 2),
Fox Sports Net
Spring Training:
Hi Corbett Field,
Tucson, Ariz.

LEAGUE HONORS
NL MVP
• Larry Walker (1997)

NL Gold Glove
• Larry Walker 3
• Neifi Perez 1

NL Silver Slugger
• Vinny Castilla 3
• Larry Walker 2
• Dante Bichette 1
• Ellis Burks 1
• Andres Galarraga.............1
• Todd Helton 1
• Eric Young 1

NL Batting Titles
• Larry Walker 2
• Andres Galarraga.............1
• Todd Helton 1

NL Manager of the Year
• Don Baylor (1995)

Rockies first baseman Todd Helton led the majors with 147 RBIs in 2000.

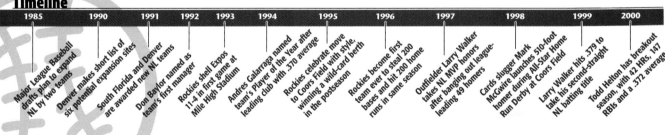

Timeline

1985 — Major League Baseball drafts plan to expand NL by two teams

1990 — Denver makes short list of six potential expansion sites

1991 — South Florida and Denver are awarded new NL teams

1992 — Don Baylor named as team's first manager

1993 — Rockies shell Expos 11-4 in first game at Mile High Stadium

1994 — Andres Galarraga named team's Player of the Year after leading club with .370 average

1995 — Rockies celebrate move to Coors Field with style, winning a wild-card berth in the postseason

1996 — Rockies become first team ever to steal 200 bases and hit 200 home runs in same season

1997 — Outfielder Larry Walker takes NL MVP honors after banging out league-leading 49 homers

1998 — Cards slugger Mark McGwire launches 510-foot homer during All-Star Home Run Derby at Coors Field

1999 — Larry Walker hits .379 to take his second-straight NL batting title

2000 — Todd Helton has breakout season, with 42 HRs, 147 RBIs and a .372 average

COORS FIELD: ROCKY MOUNTAIN HIGH

COORS FIELD WAS THE NL'S FIRST new stadium built solely for baseball since Dodger Stadium in 1962. The stadium evokes ballparks of the past with its striking red brick facade, exposed girders and old fashioned clock tower at the main gate greeting visitors. The asymmetrical field is another reminder of the quirky fields from baseball's golden years. The backdrop is even more appealing, with fans on the first base side of the stadium treated to views of the Rocky Mountains in the distance.

CONCESSIONS

The many food options at Coors Field include deli, Tex/Mex, gourmet pizza, barbecue and a wide selection of beer. Vegetarian choices include garden burgers, salads and wraps. The oysters and hot dogs are particularly good.

Stadium Facts

Opened: *April 26, 1995*
Cost: *$215 million*
Capacity: *50,445*
Type: *Outdoor*
Surface: *Grass*
Home Sweet Home:
• *No baseball team enjoys more fan support than the Rockies. Since Coors Field opened in 1993, Colorado has drawn more than 2.5 million more fans to its home games than any other team in baseball.*

GAME DAY TIPS

• **Gate hours:** Gates open two hours prior to games.
• **Weather:** Denver weather has a notorious range. Expect warm and sunny days in the summer, but go prepared for anything, maybe even snow, in the early days of spring.
• **Prohibited items:** The items prohibited at Coors Field include bottles, cans, fireworks, bull horns, confetti, beachballs and other inflatables, rollerblades, skateboards, large water guns, fish nets and laser pointers. Smoking is forbidden in the seating area, but is permitted in designated spots around the stadium.
• **Ticket tips:** Coors Field offers some of the best sight lines in the majors, no matter where you sit.

Seating Plan

- ▪ Club Level Infield **$37**
- ▫ Club Level Outfield **$35**
- ▪ Infield Box **$32**
- ■ Outfield Box **$22**
- ▪ Lower Reserved Infield .**$16**
- ▪ Lower Reserved Outfield **$13**
- ■ Right Field Box **$12**
- ▪ Upper Reserved Infield ..**$12**
- ■ Lower Reserved Corner .**$11**
- ▪ Right Field Mezzanine ...**$10**
- ▪ Pavilion **$9**
- ▪ Upper Reserved Outfield .**$9**
- ▪ Upper Reserved Corner ...**$7**
- ■ Lower Right Field Reserved **$6**
- ▪ Upper Right Field Reserved **$5**
- ▫ Rockpile .... **$4/$1**
- **ATM** Sections 114, 123, 147, 234, 330
- ♿ Throughout

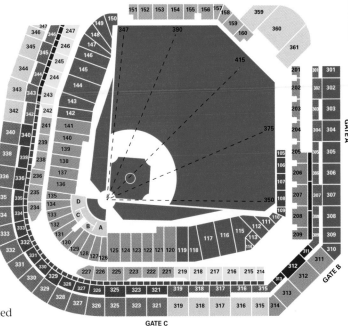

Even the inexpensive Rockpile seats, which are sold only on the day of the game, offer a decent view.
• **Lost and found:** (303) 312-2109.

Directions: *From I-25 south, take exit 213 (Park Ave., which becomes 22nd). From I-25 north, take exit 207A (Broadway/Lincoln). By Public Transport: The Regional Transportation District (RTD) offers shuttle buses from several metro areas. Regular buses and light rail are also options. Call (303) 299-6000 for information.* **Parking:** *Spots for 3,800 cars are available at the ballpark; 200 spots for the disabled are located in Lot A. Public lots are on Wazee, Blake, Market, Larimer, 17th and 18th streets.*

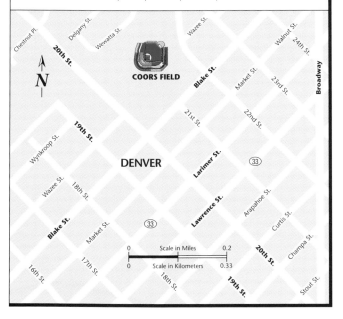

Nearby Hotels

▼▼▼▼ **Brown Palace Hotel** (*Classic Hotel*), 321 17th St. (Denver), (303) 297-3111, $234
▼▼ **Comfort Inn Downtown Denver** (*Hotel*), 401 17th St. (Denver), (303) 296-0400, $129
▼▼▼ **Denver Marriott Hotel City Center** (*Hotel*), 1701 California St. (Denver), (303) 297-1300, $189
▼▼▼ **Holiday Inn Denver Downtown** (*Hotel*), 1450 Glenarm Pl. (Denver), (303) 573-1450, $99-$139
▼▼▼▼ **Hotel Monaco** (*Hotel*), 1717 Champa St. (Denver), (303) 296-1717, $185-$240

Nearby Restaurants

▼▼▼ **McCormick's Fish House & Bar** (*Regional Seafood*), 1659 Wazee St. (Denver), (303) 825-1107, $8-$25
▼▼▼▼ **Palace Arms** (*Continental*), 321 17th St. in the Brown Palace Hotel (Denver), (303) 297-1311, $22-$38
▼▼▼ **Palm Restaurant** (*Steakhouse*), 1201 16th St. in the Westin Tabor Center Denver (Denver), (303) 825-2256, $14-$29
▼▼▼ **Rocky Mountain Diner** (*American*), 800 18th St. in the Ghost Building (Denver), (303) 293-8383, $9-$18
▼▼ **Rodizio Grill** (*Steakhouse*), 1801 Wynkoop St. (Denver), (303) 294-9277, $18

DETROIT TIGERS

As the second-most winning team in the American League, the Tigers have the dubious reputation of being a successful, yet second-best team. Often good, but only sometimes great, the Tigers' 100-year history is marred by numerous close calls and many disappointing losses. Founded in 1881, the Detroit franchise finally came into its own in the mid-1900s. Led by "the Georgia Peach," Ty Cobb — and his ruthless playing style — the Tigers fought their way to the top of the league in 1907, '08 and '09, but lacked the magic to put together a World Series title. In the following years, Cobb kept the Detroit hopes alive with his legendary slugging and controversial behavior. Known for sharpening his spikes and instigating fights, Cobb became as famous for his mean-spirited competitiveness as his brilliant bat work. The Tigers came back in the 1930s with the stellar lineup of Mickey Cochrane, Goose Goslin, Hank Greenberg and Charlie Gehringer; in 1935 the Tigers edged the Cubs to win the team's first World Series. Since then many greats have graced the Tigers uniform: "Prince Hal" Newhouser, Al Kaline, Denny McLain, Mickey Lolich, Alan Trammel, Mark Fidrych, Lou Whittaker and Jack Morris were all instrumental in the Tigers' World Series wins of '45, '68 and '84. In recent years the Tigers have been working to rebuild the Motown legacy. The power hitting of Tony Clark and Dean Palmer as well as the construction of Comerica Park have both acted to bolster Tigermania in Detroit.

"What a beautiful ballpark."

— Gregg Jefferies, on new stadium

Vital Stats

Stadium Address:
2100 Woodward Ave.,
Detroit, Mich.
Phone: (313) 962-4000
Web: tigers.mlb.com
Box Office:
(313) 962-4000,
Mon.–Sat. 10–6, Sun. 10–2
Media Coverage:
Radio: WJR (760 AM)
TV: WKBD (Channel 50),
Fox Sports Net
Spring Training:
Joker Marchant Stadium,
Lakeland, Fla.

POSTSEASON
• **World Series Titles**...........4
(1935, '45, '68, '84)
• **AL Pennants**.....................9
(1907, '08, '09, '34, '35, '40,
'45, '68, '84)

RETIRED NUMBERS
• **Charlie Gehringer (2)**
• **Hank Greenberg (5)**
• **Al Kaline (6)**
• **Hal Newhouser (16)**

TEAM RECORDS
Hitting Records
• **Ty Cobb (1905–26)**
At-Bats (career): 10,591
Batting Avg. (season): .420
(1911)

The Inside Pitch

• Tiger Stadium, Detroit's former site, hosted its first game on April 20, 1912, the same day as Fenway Park in Boston.
• Tiger great Ty Cobb was as smart as he was ornery. He began the practice of swinging several bats while on deck so one bat would feel light at the plate. He was also shrewd in business, investing in Coca Cola at $1.18 per share, a move that generated huge dividends later.

Bobby Higginson belted a team-high 30 homers in 2000.

Batting Avg. (career): .369
Hits (season): 248 (1911)
Hits (career): 3,900
RBIs (career): 1,804
Runs (season): 147 (1911)
Runs (career): 2,088
Total Bases (career): 5,466
• **Hank Greenberg (1930–46)**
Grand Slams (career): 10
HRs (season): 58 (1938)
RBIs (season): 183 (1937)
Slugging Avg. (season): .683 (1938)
Slugging Avg. (career): .616
Total Bases (season): 397 (1937)
2B (season): 63 (1934)
• **Al Kaline (1953–74)**

HRs (career): 399
Games (career): 2,834

Pitching Records
• **Hooks Dauss (1912–26)**
Wins (career): 221
• **"Wild Bill" Donovan (1903–12, '18)**
Winning Pct. (season): .862 (1907)
• **Mike Henneman (1987–95)**
Saves (career): 154
• **John Hiller (1965–70, 1972–80)**
Games (career): 545
Saves (season): 38 (1973)
• **Mickey Lolich (1963–75)**
Shutouts (career): 39
Starts (career): 459
Strikeouts (career): 2,679
Strikeouts (season): 308 (1971)
• **Denny McLain (1963–70)**
Wins (season): 31 (1968)
Shutouts (season): 9 (1969)
• **George Mullin (1902–13)**
Complete Games (career): 336
Complete Games (season): 42 (1904)
Innings Pitched (career): 3,394
• **Ed Summers (1908–12)**
ERA (season): 1.64 (1908)

Managing Records
• **Sparky Anderson (1979–95)**

Games (career): 2,579
Wins (career): 1,331
• **Mickey Cochrane (1934–38)**
Winning Pct. (career): .582

LEAGUE HONORS
AL MVP
• **Mickey Cochrane (1934)**
• **Hank Greenberg (1935, '40)**
• **Charlie Gehringer (1937)**
• **Hal Newhouser (1944, '45)**
• **Denny McLain (1968)**
• **Willie Hernandez (1984)**

AL Rookie of the Year
• **Harvey Kuenn (1951)**
• **Mark Fidrych (1976)**
• **Lou Whitaker (1978)**

AL Cy Young
• **Denny McLain (1968, '69)**
• **Willie Hernandez (1984)**

AL Gold Glove
• **Al Kaline**..........................10
• **Bill Freehan**......................5
• **Mickey Stanley**.................4
• **Alan Trammell**.................4
• **Lance Parrish**....................3
• **Lou Whitaker**....................3
• **Gary Pettis**.........................2
• **Frank Boling**.....................1
• **Ed Brinkman**.....................1
• **Frank Lary**.........................1
• **Aurelio Rodriguez**............1

Timeline

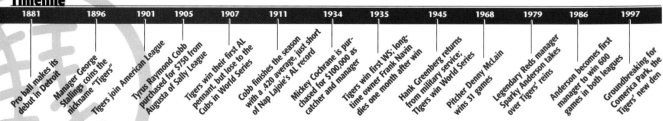

1881	1896	1901	1905	1907	1911	1934	1935	1945	1968	1979	1986	1997

Pro ball makes its debut in Detroit

Manager George Stallings coins the nickname "Tigers"

Tigers join American League

Tyrus Raymond Cobb purchased for $750 from Augusta of Sally League

Tigers win their first AL pennant, but lose to the Cubs in World Series

Cobb finishes the season with a .420 average, just short of Nap Lajoie's AL record

Mickey Cochrane is purchased for $100,000 as catcher and manager

Tigers win first WS; longtime owner Frank Navin dies one month after win

Hank Greenberg returns from military service; Tigers win World Series

Pitcher Denny McLain wins 31 games

Legendary Reds manager Sparky Anderson takes over Tigers' reins

Anderson becomes first manager to win 600 games in both leagues

Groundbreaking for Comerica Park, the Tigers' new den

36

COMERICA PARK: THE FUTURE IS NOW

CONCEIVED AS AN URBAN VILLAGE, Comerica Park contains shops, restaurants, bars and historic attractions, as well as a baseball field. Comerica also offers a ferris wheel, a merry-go-round and "liquid fireworks," which syncs music and lights to a large water fountain in center field for home runs. Although the ballpark has a smaller capacity than Tiger Stadium, fans will enjoy Comerica's improved comfort and sight lines, and the view of downtown Detroit over the right-field wall. This ballpark blends the traditional baseball experience with the entertainment demands of today's fan.

CONCESSIONS

There is a wide selection of restaurants, cafés and snack bars at Comerica. Popular eats include pizza, hot dogs, gyros, sausages, kielbasa, seafood, baked goods, elephant ears, vegetarian food, ice cream and sandwiches. The frozen daiquiris are especially popular among fans.

GAME DAY TIPS

• **Gate hours:** Gates open 90 minutes prior to games.
• **Weather:** Rain is a common factor at Comerica Park. Check the weather forecast before the game and consider taking along an umbrella.
• **Prohibited items:** Cans, bottles (glass or plastic), jugs, coolers and hard containers of any kind are prohibited. Noisemakers are also prohibited. Smoking is allowed only in specified areas.
• **Ticket tips:** The best deal at Comerica is the right-field bleachers. For less than $10 you have a great view and get pizza or a hot dog and a beverage. Show up early for games against the Cardinals, White Sox or Yankees. Seats go quickly!
• **Lost and found:** (313) 962-4000.

Stadium Facts

Opened: April 11, 2000
Cost: $300 million
Capacity: 40,000
Type: Outdoor
Surface: Grass
Home Sweet Home:

• The asymmetrical outfield wall features angles and corners that create special challenges for outfielders.
• Comerica has an expansive outfield, making it easier on pitchers to keep the ball in the park. Outfielders have to cover a lot of turf.

Seating Plan

LOWER LEVEL		UPPER LEVEL	
■ Tiger Den	$75	■ Club Seats	$35
■ Tiger Den	$60	■ Upper Box	$20
■ On-Deck Circle	$60	□ Upper Box Outfield	$20
■ The Terrace	$35	■ Mezzanine	$15
■ Infield Box	$30	■ Upper Reserved	$12
■ Outfield Box	$25	ATM Sections 120, 130, 213, 331
■ Outfield Box	$15	♿ Throughout
■ Pavilion	$14		
■ The Bleachers	$8		

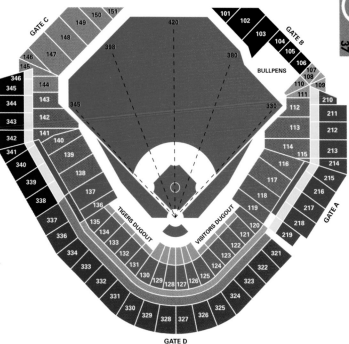

37

Directions: From the north, exit I-75 at Mack Ave. and turn right, then left onto Woodward Ave. From the south, exit I-75 at Grand River Ave.; follow service drive, then turn right onto Woodward Ave. From the east, take I-94 to I-75, exit at Mack Ave. and go right, then left onto Woodward Ave. From the west, take I-94 to I-75, exit at Grand River Ave. and follow service drive to Woodward Ave. and turn right. By Bus: Call 1-800-DDOT-BUS or (313) 962-5515. *Parking:* The stadium holds 4,500 cars and there are area lots on Adams and Gratiot avenues and Broadway, Brush and Madison streets; all are wheelchair accessible, as is Columbia St. entrance (Gate A).

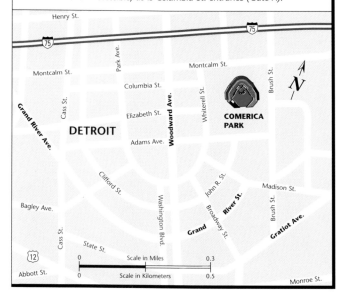

Nearby Hotels

▼▼▼▼ **The Atheneum Suite Hotel & Conference Center** *(Suite Hotel)*, 1000 Brush Ave. (Detroit), (313) 962-2323, $175-$700
▼▼ **Comfort Inn-Downtown Detroit** *(Motel)*, 1999 E. Jefferson Ave. (Detroit), (313) 567-8888, $79-$199
▼▼▼ **Courtyard by Marriott-Detroit Downtown** *(Motel)*, 333 E. Jefferson Ave. in the Millender Center (Detroit), (313) 222-7700, $139-$164
▼▼▼ **Crowne Plaza Pontchartrain** *(Hotel)*, 2 Washington Blvd., (313) 965-0200, $75-$139
▼▼ **Shorecrest Motor Inn** *(Motor Inn)*, 1316 E. Jefferson Ave. (Detroit), (313) 568-3000, $74-$104

Nearby Restaurants

▼ **America's Pizza Café** *(American)*, 2239 Woodward Ave. at the Fox Theater (Detroit), (313) 964-3122, $7-$13
▼▼ **Fishbones Rhythm Kitchen Café** *(Cajun)*, 400 Monroe St. in The Atheneum Suite Hotel & Conference Center (Detroit), (313) 965-4600, $5-$25
▼ **Lafayette Coney Island** *(American)*, 118 W. Lafayette St. (Detroit), (313) 964-8198, $2-$6
▼▼▼ **Opus One** *(American)*, 565 E. Larned St. (Detroit), (313) 961-7766, $20-$39
▼▼▼ **Whitney Restaurant** *(American)*, 4421 Woodward Ave. (Detroit), (313) 832-5700, $19-$35

FLORIDA MARLINS

THE EXPANSION FLORIDA MARLINS' first four seasons in the majors followed the same well-worn path that virtually every new franchise has taken — losing season followed losing season, with some improvement each year. But by 1996 the Miami-based club had climbed to within two games of a .500 record, thanks in large part to solid pitching by veteran starters Kevin Brown and Al Leiter, and the slugging of original Marlin Gary Sheffield. Some key additions were needed to bring the club into contention, however. Before the 1997 season General Manager Dave Dombrowski did his best to fill any holes in the lineup, acquiring batting specialists such as Moises Alou, Bobby Bonilla, Jim Eisenreich and Darren Daulton. Dombrowski also signed a hard-throwing Cuban rookie named Livan Hernandez. Although the Marlins had little chance to win the NL East with Atlanta winning 101 games, the team did have a shot at the wild-card spot. On Sept. 23, to the surprise of baseball pundits everywhere, Florida clinched a place in the postseason. The team went on to sweep the Giants in the divisional playoff, win a six-game duel with the powerhouse Braves in the NLCS and then outlast Cleveland in a dramatic extra-inning seventh game to capture the World Series. A veritable fire sale during the off-season denied the Marlins any realistic chance of repeating as champs, but a new crop of talent has recently brought the team back into contention. Is another miracle in the offing? Stay tuned.

POSTSEASON
- **World Series Titles** 1
(1997)

TEAM RECORDS
Hitting Records
- **Chuck Carr (1993–95)**
Steals (season): 58 (1993)
Steals (career): 115
- **Luis Castillo (1996–present)**
Batting Avg. (season): .334 (2000)
Hits (season): 180 (2000)

The Inside Pitch

- *Winning the World Series in just its fifth season, Florida beat the previous expansion record of eight, held by the New York Mets. The spikes worn by Marlins infielder Craig Cousel to score the winning run are on display in the Baseball Hall of Fame.*
- *In 1997 the Marlins became the first team to draw more than 500,000 fans in a single postseason.*

"I guess every little boy imagines this might happen at one time. It's a total fantasy for me."

— *Manager Jim Leyland, after the Marlins' World Series win in 1997*

- **Jeff Conine (1993–97)**
At-Bats (career): 2,531
Batting Avg. (career): .291
Consecutive Games: 307
Extra-Base Hits (career): 234
Games (season): 162 (1993)
Games (career): 718
Hits (career): 737
RBIs (career): 422
Total Bases (career): 1,181
2B (career): 122
- **Cliff Floyd (1997–present)**
2B (season): 45 (1998)
- **Mark Kotsay (1997–present)**
3B (season): 9 (1999)
3B (career): 22
- **Edgar Renteria (1996–98)**
At-Bats (season): 617 (1997)
Singles (season): 143 (1997)
- **Gary Sheffield (1993–98)**
Extra-Base Hits (season): 76 (1996)
HRs (season): 42 (1996)
HRs (career): 122
Runs (season): 118 (1996)
Runs (career): 365
Slugging Pct. (season): .625 (1996)
Slugging Pct. (career): .543
Total Bases (season): 324 (1996)
Walks (season): 142 (1996)

Walks (career): 424
- **Preston Wilson (1998–present)**
Pinch-Hit HRs (season): 3 (1999)
RBIs (season): 121 (2000)

Pitching Records
- **Kevin Brown (1996–97)**
Complete Games (career): 11
ERA (season): 1.89 (1996)
ERA (career): 2.30
Innings Pitched (season): 237.1 (1997)
Shutouts (season): 3 (1996)
Shutouts (career): 5
Wins (season): 17 (1996)
- **Ryan Dempster (1998–present)**
Strikeouts (season): 209 (2000)
- **Brian Harvey (1993–95)**
Saves (season): 45 (1993)
- **Charlie Hough (1993–94)**
Starts (season): 34 (1993)
- **Al Leiter (1996–97)**
Walks (season): 119 (1996)
- **Robb Nen (1993–97)**
Games (career): 269
Saves (career): 108
- **Pat Rapp (1993–97)**
Starts (career): 115
Strikeouts (career): 384
Wins (career): 37

Managing Records
- **John Boles (1996, 1999–present)**
Winning Pct. (career): .460

Vital Stats

Stadium Address:
2269 Dan Marino Blvd. (NW 199th St.), Miami, Fla.
Phone: *(305) 623-6100*
Web: *marlins.mlb.com, pro-player-stadium.com*
Box Office:
(305) 626-7426, Mon.–Fri. 8:30–6, Sat. 10–4, game days Sun. 10–4
Media Coverage:
Radio: WQAM (560 AM) TV: WAMI-TV (Channel 69), Fox Sports Net
Spring Training:
Space Coast Stadium, Melbourne, Fla.

- **Rene Lachemann (1993–96)**
Wins (career): 221
- **Jim Leyland (1997–98)**
Wins (season): 92 (1997)
Winning Pct. (season): .568 (1997)

LEAGUE HONORS
All-Star Game MVP
- Jeff Conine (1995)

World Series MVP
- Livan Hernandez (1997)

NL Gold Glove
- Charles Johnson 3

Antonio Alfonseca led all relief pitchers in 2000 with 45 saves.

Timeline

1991	1992	1993	1995	1996	1997	1998	1999	2000
South Florida chosen as site for expansion baseball franchise	Marlins select catcher Charles Johnson with first draft pick in amateur draft	Marlins win first-ever regular season game 6-3 over Dodgers	Florida first baseman Jeff Conine named MVP of All-Star game	Joe Robbie Stadium renamed Pro Player Stadium	Marlins win World Series	Florida drops to fifth in NL East, losing 108 games	Marlins announce plans for new baseball-only stadium	Florida finishes third in NL East, just three games below .500

PRO PLAYER STADIUM: MULTI-PURPOSE VENUE

IN 1987 JOE ROBBIE BUILT this stadium as a home for his Miami Dolphins football team. Joe Robbie Stadium was renovated to accommodate baseball by Marlin's owner Wayne Huizenga in 1994. It was renamed Pro Player Stadium, after the sports apparel brand of Fruit of the Loom, in 1996. The park is an original, with many odd wall angles in the outfield that frequently make for strange bounces. The tall wall in short left is referred to as the "Teal Monster." Plans for a new domed stadium had been considered, but have been shelved since the weather in south Florida has not proven as problematic as expected. Locations are being considered for a baseball-only facility in downtown Miami, however.

CONCESSIONS

Pro Player Stadium offers standard baseball fare including hamburgers, hot dogs, chicken, ice cream and cookies. The choice for vegetarians is limited to pretzels, nachos or desserts.

Stadium Facts

Opened: Aug. 16, 1987
Cost: $115 million
Capacity: 36,331
Type: Outdoor
Surface: Natural grass
Home Sweet Home:
• The stadium's outfield wall has a deep notch known as the "Bermuda Triangle." It is troublesome for outfielders and strange bounces often turn doubles off the wall into triples.

GAME DAY TIPS

• **Gate hours:** Gates open two hours prior to games. Fans can obtain autographs up to 45 minutes before a game.
• **Weather:** Rain delays are a relatively common occurrence at Pro Player Stadium. Because the stadium is outdoors, day games can get quite warm (in spite of partial air conditioning to the Club seats), so bring along some sunscreen or a protective hat.
• **Prohibited items:** Prohibited items, which may be checked at the stadium, include coolers, bottles, cans, jugs and thermoses as well as strollers, laser pointers, beachballs, oversized umbrellas and any food not purchased within the stadium. Smoking is permitted

only on the ramps of each stadium level.
• **Ticket tips:** Getting tickets to a Marlins game at the last minute is generally not a problem. The second deck outfield seats are covered with canvas during ball games, rendering the stadium more "baseball friendly."
• **Lost and found:** (305) 626-7275.

Seating Plan

■ **Founder's Club Box Seats** $55
■ **Infield Box Seats** $25
□ **Club Zone A** $32
■ **Club Zone B** $24
■ **Power Alley (Club Zone C)** $18
■ **Terrace Box Seats** $15
■ **Mezzanine Box Seats** $15
■ **Outfield Reserved** $10
■ **Mezzanine Reserved** $9
■ **Fish Tank** $4
ATM **Sections 149, 150, 456**
♿ **Sections 103, 107, 128, 146, 150, 153, 156**

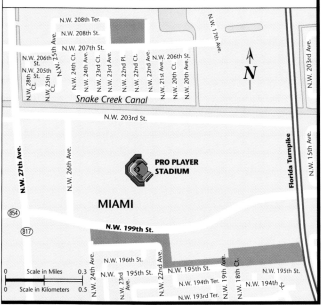

Directions: From I-95, take Ives Dairy Rd. and proceed west for 5 miles to stadium. From Florida Turnpike Interchange, take exit 2X (NW 199th St./Stadium exit). By Bus: The No. 27 bus will take you to the stadium. Call (305) 770-3131 for schedules and information. **Parking:** The stadium lot accommodates 14,970 cars. There are 262 spots reserved for people with disabilities and these are located in lots A, C, E and G.

Nearby Hotels

▼▼▼ **Don Shula's Hotel & Golf Club** (*Resort*), 15255 Bull Run Rd. (Miami Lakes), (305) 821-1150, $99-$129
▼▼▼ **El Palacio Resort Hotel & Suites** (*Motor Inn*), 16805 NW 12th Ave. (Miami), (305) 624-8401, $98-$170
▼▼▼ **Holiday Inn-Calder/Pro Player Stadium** (*Motor Inn*), 21485 NW 27th Ave. (Miami), (305) 621-5801, $82-$1000
▼▼▼ **TownePlace Suites by Marriott** (*Extended Stay Motel*), 10505 NW 36th St. (Miami), (305) 718-4144, $69-$139
▼▼▼▼ **Turnberry Isle Resort & Club** (*Resort*), 19999 W. Country Club Dr. (Aventura), (305) 932-6200, $275-$485

Nearby Restaurants

▼▼▼▼ **Chef Allen's** (*American*), 19088 NE 29th Ave. (Aventura), (305) 935-2900, $26-$38 (dinner only)
▼▼ **Mike Gordon Seafood Restaurant** (*Seafood*), 1201 NE 79th St. (Miami), (305) 751-4429, $12-$25
▼▼▼ **Shula's Steakhouse** (*Steakhouse*), 7601 NW 154th St. in Don Shula's Hotel & Golf Club (Miami Lakes), (305) 820-8102, $18-$33
▼▼ **Shula's Steak 2** (*Sports Bar*), 7601 NW 154th St. in Don Shula's Hotel & Golf Club (Miami Lakes), (305) 820-8047, $6-$20
▼▼ **Tuna's Waterfront Grille** (*Seafood*), 17201 Biscayne Blvd. (North Miami Beach), (305) 945-2567, $10-$25

HOUSTON ASTROS

IN 1962 HOUSTON WAS GRANTED an expansion franchise in the National League and fielded a team called the Colt .45s. Originally playing in mosquito-infested Colt Stadium, the team changed locales — and names — when the Astrodome opened its doors in 1965. Throughout the 1970s, the Astros built themselves into a team to be reckoned with. In these early years, it was the gutsy steals of Cesar Cedeno, the pitching excellence of Joe Niekro and fireballer J.R. Richard, and the batting prowess of Greg Gross and Lee May that kept Houston fans coming back to watch their team climb the ranks. Although Richard was felled by a career-ending stroke in June 1980, the Astros battled their way to a tie with the Dodgers at the top of the NL West. Niekro six-hit Los Angeles in the one-game playoff to give Houston its first divisional crown. In 1986 another pitcher would lead the Astros to its best season to date. Mike Scott, with his deceptive split-finger fastball, topped the league in strikeouts and ERA en route to 18 wins. However, a disappointing loss to the Mets in the NLCS prevented the team from advancing to the World Series. Since then, one name has become synonymous with the Astros' hopes for a World Series title: Jeff Bagwell. One of the strongest offensive players in the game, Bagwell owns the majority of Astros' records. Bagwell teamed up with star second baseman Craig Biggio to push the Astros to three straight NL Central Division titles to close out the 1990s.

> *"There is nothing that compares to the feeling of hitting a baseball."*
>
> — *Chuck Jackson, Astro 1987–88*

ERA (career): 2.42
• **Dave Smith (1980–90)**
Saves (career): 199
Games (career): 563
• **Billy Wagner (1995–present)**
Saves (season): 39 (1999)

Managing Records
• **Bill Virdon (1975–82)**
Most Wins (career): 544

LEAGUE HONORS
NL MVP
• Jeff Bagwell (1994)

NL Rookie of the Year
• Joe Morgan (1965)
• Greg Gross (1973)
• Jeff Bagwell (1991)

NL Cy Young
• Mike Scott (1986)

NL Gold Glove
• Cesar Cedeno 5
• Doug Rader 5
• Craig Biggio 4
• Jeff Bagwell 1
• Roger Metzger 1

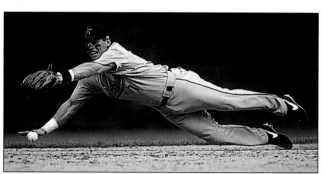

In 1999 Craig Biggio led all NL second basemen in putouts, assists, total chances and double-plays turned.

• **Craig Biggio (1988–present)**
At-Bats (career): 6766
Consecutive Games: 494
Hits (season): 210 (1998)
Hits (career): 1,969
Runs (career): 1,187
2B (season): 56 (1999)
2B (career): 402
• **Cesar Cedeno (1970–81)**
Steals (career): 487
• **Jose Cruz (1975–87)**
Games (career): 1870
Singles (career): 1384
3B (career): 80
• **Gerald Young (1987–92)**
Steals (season): 65 (1988)

Pitching Records
• **Larry Dierker (1964–76)**
Complete Games (season): 20 (1969)
Complete Games (career): 106
Starts (career): 320
Innings (season): 305.1 (1969)
Innings (career): 2,294.1
Shutouts (career): 25
• **Mike Hampton (1994–99)**
Wins (season): 22 (1999)
• **Joe Niekro (1975–85)**
Wins (career): 144
• **J.R. Richard (1971–82)**
Strikeouts (season): 313 (1979)
• **Dave A. Roberts (1972–75)**
Shutouts (season): 6 (1973)
• **Nolan Ryan (1980–88)**
ERA (season): 1.69 (1981)
Strikeouts (career): 1,866
• **Joe Sambito (1976–82, '84)**

POSTSEASON
• NL West Titles 2
(1980, '86)
• NL Central Titles 3
(1997, '98, '99)

The Inside Pitch

• *The new millennium brought a new look to Astros attire. Featuring pinstripes, a new color scheme and an updated logo, the Astros uniforms are the newest trend in a series of "retro-chic" baseball outfits.*

• *In 1997 Jeff Bagwell hit 43 home runs and swiped 31 bases to become the first Astro in history to join the exclusive 30-30 club. He did it again in 1999.*

RETIRED NUMBERS
• Jose Cruz (25)
• Jim Umbrict (32)
• Mike Scott (33)
• Nolan Ryan (34)
• Don Wilson (40)

TEAM RECORDS
Hitting Records
• **Jeff Bagwell (1991–present)**
Batting Avg. (seasons): .368 (1994)
Batting Avg. (career): .304
Games (season): 162 (1999)
HRs (season): 47 (2000)
HRs (career): 310
RBIs (season): 135 (1997)
RBIs (career): 1,093
Runs (season): 152 (2000)
Slugging Pct. (season): .750 (1994)
Total Bases (season): 363 (2000)
Total Bases (career): 2,955

Vital Stats

Stadium Address:
501 Crawford St., Houston, Texas
Phone: *(713) 259-8000*
Web: *astros.mlb.com*
Box Office:
(713) 259-8500, Mon.–Fri. 8–6, Sat.–Sun. 9–5, game days until 30 minutes after game
Media Coverage:
Radio: KTRH (740 AM) TV: KNWS-TV (Channel 51), Fox Sports Net
Spring Training:
Osceola County Stadium, Kissimmee, Fla.

Timeline

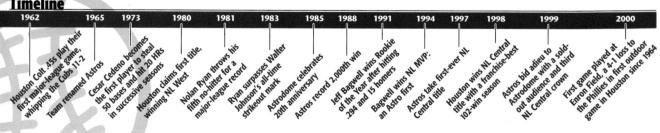

1962 Houston Colt .45s play their first major-league game, whipping the Cubs 11-2

1965 Team renamed Astros

1973 Cesar Cedeno becomes the first player to steal 50 bases and hit 20 HRs in successive seasons

1980 Houston claims first title, winning NL West

1981 Nolan Ryan throws his fifth no-hitter for a major-league record

1983 Ryan surpasses Walter Johnson's all-time strikeout mark

1985 Astrodome celebrates 20th anniversary

1988 Astros record 2,000th win

1991 Jeff Bagwell wins Rookie of the Year after hitting .294 and 15 homers

1994 Bagwell wins NL MVP; an Astro first

1997 Astros take first-ever NL Central title

1998 Houston wins NL Central title with a franchise-best 102-win season

1999 Astros bid adieu to Astrodome with a sold-out audience and third NL Central crown

2000 First game played at Enron Field, a 4-1 loss to the Phillies in first outdoor game in Houston since 1964

40

ENRON FIELD:
THE JEWEL OF THE HOUSTON SKYLINE

THE 1999 SEASON MARKED the last for the Astros at the Houston Astrodome. Heralded as an achievement in modern stadium design when it opened in 1965, the Astrodome was the first ballpark with an entire AstroTurf playing surface. With this reputation in mind, Houston enlisted famed stadium architects HOK Sport to create a new, hyper-modern facility that would live up to the innovative spirit of its predecessor. Featuring a retractable glass roof, a functioning locomotive, an interactive game room for children, a theater and a conference center, Enron provides a futuristic vision of "a day at the park." Furthermore, with wider seats, state-of-the-art climate control and great sight lines, Enron prides itself on being the spectator's stadium par excellence.

CONCESSIONS

Enron boasts one of the most eclectic assortments of foods of any ballpark. Cajun cooking, Mexican, Texas barbecue, pizza, bistro sandwiches and sausages all top the list of favorite fare.

Stadium Facts

Opened: *April 7, 2000*
Cost: *$248.1 million*
Capacity: *42,180*
Type: *Retractable roof*
Surface: *Grass*
Home Sweet Home:
• *The uneven wall heights, sloping outfield and center-field flag pole make Enron tricky for outfielders.*
• *Enron's deep center-field fence makes it tough to hit homers to straightaway center. The left-field fence, however, is very short.*

GAME DAY TIPS
• **Gate hours:** Gates open two hours prior to games.
• **Weather:** With the retractable roof, Enron Field enjoys minimal weather concerns.
• **Prohibited items:** Bottles and beverage containers are not allowed. All outside food or drink is also prohibited.
• **Ticket tips:** While Houston fans are famous for coming out in droves for home games, the Astros have an especially strong rivalry with fellow NL Central Division mates the Atlanta Braves. Plan ahead for tickets. The

Seating Plan

■ **Dugout Seats**	$29	■ **Mezzanine**	$12
■ **Field Boxes**	$25	■ **Terrace Deck**	$12
□ **Crawford Boxes**	$17	■ **Upper Deck**	$10
■ **Bullpen Boxes**	$15	□ **Outfield Deck**	$5
▨ **Club Seats**	$28	**ATM** **Sections 107, 112, 132, 315**
▨ **Club Seats**	$24	♿ **Throughout**

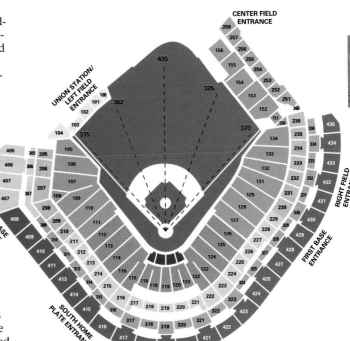

bullpen boxes provide one of the best viewpoints for the price. With fewer seats than many stadiums, Enron's upper deck also offers a decent view of the field for a good price.
• **Lost and found:** Contact the guest services desk or call (713) 259-8000.

Directions: From the west, take I-10 to Smith or McKee exit. From the south, take US 59 to Spur 527 exit to Travis and follow to downtown. From the north, take I-45 to Milam and follow to downtown. From the east, take I-10 to US 59 S, then exit at Hamilton and follow to downtown. By Bus: The Metro Ballpark and Ride Bus runs before and after all games. Call (713) 635-4000 for information. Parking: Spaces for 25,000 cars are available in private lots on Preston, Franklin, Prairie and Texas avenues. Wheelchair-accessible parking is widely available.

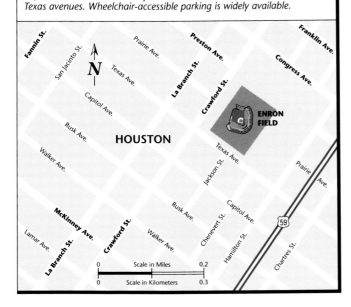

Nearby Hotels
▼▼▼ **Allen Park Inn (*Motor Inn*)**, 2121 Allen Pkwy. (Houston), (713) 521-9321, $98-$150
▼▼▼ **Doubletree Hotel at Allen Center (*Hotel*)**, 400 Dallas St. (Houston), (713) 759-0202, $250-$270
▼▼▼▼▼ **Four Seasons Hotel Houston (*Hotel*)**, 1300 Lamar St. (Houston), (713) 650-1300, $160-$365
▼▼▼ **Holiday Inn Select-Greenway Plaza (*Hotel*)**, 2712 Southwest Fwy. (Houston), (713) 523-8448, $59-$89
▼▼▼ **Hyatt Regency Houston (*Hotel*)**, 1200 E. Louisiana St. (Houston), (713) 654-1234, $195-$220

Nearby Restaurants
▼▼ **Cafe Noche (*Mexican*)**, 2409 Montrose Blvd. (Houston), (713) 529-2409, $8-$25
▼▼▼ **Clive's (*American*)**, 517 Louisiana St. (Houston), (713) 224-4438, $19-$32
▼▼▼▼ **DeVille (*Regional American*)**, 1300 Lamar St. in the Four Seasons Hotel Houston (Houston), (713) 650-1300, $18-$35
▼▼ **Kim Son (*Chinese*)**, 2001 Jefferson (Houston), (713) 222-2461, $7-$20
▼▼ **Ruggles Grill (*American*)**, 903 Westheimer Blvd. (Houston), (713) 524-3839, $10-$19

KANSAS CITY ROYALS

THE KANSAS CITY ROYALS ARE THE MODEL on which all expansion teams should be built. The team shocked the baseball world by finishing second in the AL West in 1971, just three years after its entry into the league. Over the next 20 seasons, the team finished first or second in its division 13 times. A strong farm system combined with timely trades built a strong, well-balanced dynasty that was equal parts offense, pitching and defense. One of the keys to the franchise's long-term excellence is that it built a core of talented young players and held on to them as they gained experience. By the time the Royals squared off against the St. Louis Cardinals in the 1985 World Series, established stars such as George Brett, Willie Wilson, Hal McRae, Frank White, Larry Gura and Dennis Leonard had all played at least nine seasons together. Their experience paid off: Down 3-1 in the series, the Royals didn't panic and went on to take the next three games and the World Series crown. Typically, it was KC's mix of veteran leadership and youthful talent that carried the day during the '85 fall classic. Playing in his 12th season, future Hall-of-Famer George Brett led all batters with 10 hits and a .370 average. But the series MVP went to the Royals second-year pitching phenom, Brett Saberhagen, who went 2-0 for the series with a pair of complete games and a showy 0.50 ERA. Today's Royals are hoping to build on its championship tradition, rebuilding the core of its lineup with young stars such as Jermaine Dye, fleet-footed Johnny Damon and team RBI king Mike Sweeney.

Vital Stats

Stadium Address:
1 Royal Way,
Kansas City, Mo.
Phone: (816) 921-8000
Web: royals.mlb.com
Box Office:
(816) 504-4040,
Mon.–Sat. 9–6, Sun. 10–4
Media Coverage:
Radio: KMBZ (980 AM)
TV: KMBC (Channel 9),
KCWE (Channel 29),
Fox Sports Net
Spring Training:
Baseball City Stadium,
Davenport, Fla.

"To this day I firmly believe that I am still the biggest Royals fan in the country."

— An emotional George Brett during his 1999 induction into the Hall of Fame

POSTSEASON
• **World Series Titles**...........1
(1985)
• **AL Pennants**.....................2
(1980, '85)
• **AL West Titles**.................6
(1976, '77, '78, '80, '84, '85)

RETIRED NUMBERS
• George Brett (5)
• Dick Howser (10)
• Frank White (20)

TEAM RECORDS
Hitting Records
• Steve Balboni (1984–88)
HRs (season): 36 (1985)
• George Brett (1973–93)
At-Bats (career): 10,349

The Inside Pitch

• *Trailing 4-3 in a 1983 game against the Yankees, the Royals appeared to take the lead on George Brett's two-run homer. But the homer was disallowed. Umpires deemed Brett had smeared pine tar too far up the barrel of his bat.*

Batting Avg. (season):
.390 (1980)
Games (career): 2,707
Hits (career): 3,154
HRs (career): 317
Runs (career): 1,583
RBIs (career): 1,595
2B (career): 665
3B (career): 137
Walks (career): 1,096
• **Johnny Damon**
(1995–present)
Runs (season): 136 (2000)
• **John Mayberry (1972–77)**
Walks (season): 122 (1973)
• **Hal McRae (1973–87)**
Games (season): 162 (1977)
2B (season): 54 (1977)
• **Jose Offerman (1996–98)**
Batting Avg. (career): .306
• **Mike Sweeney**
(1995–present)
RBIs (season): 144 (2000)
• **Willie Wilson (1976–90)**
At-Bats (season): 705 (1980)
Hits (season): 230 (1980)
3B (season): 21 (1985)
Steals (season): 83 (1979)
Steals (career): 612

Pitching Records
• Kevin Appier (1989–99)
Strikeouts (career): 1,451

• **Dennis Leonard**
(1974–86)
Complete Games (career): 103
Complete Games (season):
21 (1977)
Innings Pitched (season):
294 (1978)
Shutouts (career): 23
Starts (season): 40 (1978)
Strikeouts (season): 244 (1977)
• **Jeff Montgomery**
(1988–99)
Appearances (career): 686
Saves (career): 304
• **Roger Nelson**
(1969–72, '76)
ERA (season): 2.08 (1972)
Shutouts (season): 6 (1972)

Jermaine Dye led the Royals with 33 home runs in 2000.

• **Dan Quisenberry**
(1979–88)
Appearances (season):
84 (1985)
ERA (career): 2.55
Saves (season): 45 (tie) (1983)
• **Brett Saberhagen**
(1984–91)
Wins (season): 23 (1989)
• **Paul Splittorff (1970–84)**
Starts (career): 392
Wins (career): 166
Innings Pitched
(career): 2,555

LEAGUE HONORS
AL MVP
• George Brett (1980)

AL Rookie of the Year
• Lou Piniella (1969)
• Bob Hamelin (1994)
• Carlos Beltran (1999)

AL Cy Young
• Brett Saberhagen
(1985, '89)
• David Cone (1994)

AL Gold Glove
• Frank White 8
• Amos Otis 3
• Bob Boone 1
• George Brett 1
• Al Cowens 1
• Jermaine Dye 1
• Brett Saberhagen 1
• Willie Wilson 1

Timeline

1969 The expansion Royals finish 28 games out of first

1971 Team shocks league with second-place finish

1973 First year for George Brett, Frank White and Hal McRae trio goes on to drive in 3,493 runs for the franchise

1974 Steve Busby tosses second no-hitter as a Royal

1975 John Mayberry becomes first Royal to belt three HRs in a single game

1976 Kansas City reaches postseason for first time only to lose to Yankees in ALCS

1977 Team sets franchise record with 102 wins

1980 Royals beat Yankees to take first AL pennant

1985 Royals come back from 3-1 deficit in games to win first World Series

1987 Slugging roster, including Bo Jackson and Danny Tartabull, belts league-best 168 HRs

1989 Brett Saberhagen leads AL with 23 wins

1990 George Brett wins fourth AL batting title with .329 average

1999 George Brett inducted into Baseball Hall of Fame

2000 First baseman Mike Sweeney establishes club record with 144 RBIs

KAUFFMAN STADIUM: A PARK FOR THE PURISTS

IN 1973 THE KANSAS CITY BASEBALL TEAM MOVED into newly finished Royal Stadium. Over the next three decades, the stadium, renamed in 1993 in honor of the franchise's first owner, Ewing M. Kauffman, has seen a lot of great baseball, including seven AL playoff series and two World Series. Still considered one of the country's most picturesque ballparks, Kauffman Stadium is equipped with one of the largest video screens in the country and a massive water fountain. Purists take note: In 1995 the field's artificial surface was replaced by grass.

Seating Plan

■ Club Box	$19	■ Youth General	
■ Field Box	$17	Admission	$3.50
■ Plaza Reserved	$15	■ Dugout Suites	N/A
■ View Level Box	$12	■ Crown Seats	N/A
■ View Level Reserved	$11	ATM Sections 102, 300	
■ Price Chopper Games		♿ Sections 107–108, 139–145,	
(Mon., Thurs.)	$5.50	140–146, 317–318	
■ General Admission	$7		

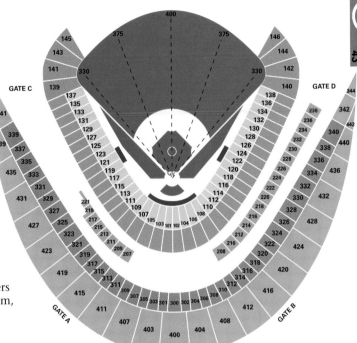

CONCESSIONS

Kauffman Stadium features standards such as hot dogs, burgers, nachos and peanuts, as well as a few special treats such as barbecue, pizza and grilled chicken sandwiches.

Stadium Facts

Opened: April 10, 1973
Cost: Approximately $30 million (part of $70 million sports complex)
Capacity: 40,793
Type: Outdoor
Surface: Grass
Home Sweet Home:
• Although visibility for hitters at Kauffman Stadium is among the best in baseball, few home runs are hit because of deep alleys and a fence that cuts away sharply from the 320-foot foul poles.

GAME DAY TIPS

• **Gate hours:** Gates open 90 minutes prior to games.
• **Weather:** Expect typical Midwest weather. Summers are generally hot and sunny.
• **Prohibited items:** Although banners are permitted, they may not have poles or sticks attached to them. Flash photography and video reproductions of the game are prohibited, as are laser pointers, bottles, cans and certain noisemakers. Coolers are permitted in the stadium, but they must be small enough to fit under the seats. Smoking is allowed only in designated areas.
• **Ticket tips:** Getting seats for games is generally easy. The general-admission tickets (about 5,000 seats) are sold

the day of the game. Avoid sitting near the foul poles on the upper deck — it can get quite dark.
• **Lost and found:** (816) 921–8000.

Directions: From east or west, take I-70 to exit 9 (Blue Ridge Cutoff/ Sports Complex). From north or south, take I-435 to exit 63C (Sports Complex). By Bus: A special bus called the Metro/Royals Express runs from several spots in town before the game and back after the game. Call (816) 221-0660 for route and schedule details. **Parking:** There is parking at the stadium for more than 19,000 cars. Lot M has 200 spots for people with disabilities and the ballpark is fully accessible from there.

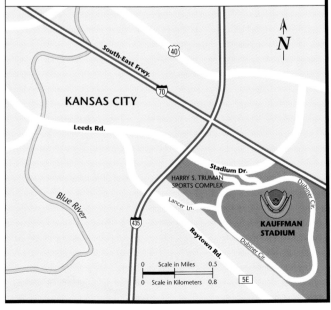

Nearby Hotels

▼▼▼ **Adams Mark-Kansas City** *(Hotel)*, 9103 E. 39th St. (Kansas City), (816) 737-0200, $99-$129
▼▼▼ **Drury Inn-Stadium** *(Motel)*, 3830 Blue Ridge Cutoff (Kansas City), (816) 923-3000, $69-$95
▼▼▼ **Holiday Inn-Sports Complex** *(Motor Inn)*, 4011 Blue Ridge Cutoff (Kansas City), (816) 353-5300, $72-$109
▼▼ **Red Roof Inn-Independence** *(Motel)*, 13712 E. 42nd Terr. (Independence), (816) 373-2800, $42-$60
▼▼ **Shoney's Inn-Independence** *(Motel)*, 4048 S. Lynn Court Dr. (Independence), (816) 254-0100, $49-$79

Nearby Restaurants

▼▼ **Michael Forbes Grill** *(American)*, 7539 Wornall Rd. (Kansas City), (816) 444-5445, $8-$15
▼▼▼ **Remington's** *(American)*, 9103 E. 39th St. in Adams Mark-Kansas City (Kansas City), (816) 737-4760, $15-$35
▼▼▼ **Stephenson's Apple Farm Restaurant** *(American)*, 16401 Hwy. 40E (Independence), (816) 373-5400, $9-$20
▼▼ **Stephenson's Red Mule Restaurant** *(American)*, 16506 Hwy. 40E (Independence), (816) 478-1810, $6-$13
▼▼▼ **V's Italiano Ristorante** *(Italian)*, 10819 Hwy. 40E (Independence), (816) 353-1241, $13-$18

LOS ANGELES DODGERS

ONE OF BASEBALL'S OLDEST FRANCHISES, the Los Angeles Dodgers began play in the National League in 1890 in Brooklyn, New York. The team name comes from "Trolley Dodgers," for the maze of trolley cars that crisscrossed Brooklyn at the time. In 1913 owner Charles Ebbets moved the team into a new stadium, Ebbets Field, but success was sporadic. Pennants in 1916 and '20 behind the hitting of star Casey Stengel were followed by a prolonged 20-year drought. It wasn't until the 1940s that the Dodgers took center stage of pro baseball. This was partly the result of the team's winning ways. Brooklyn captured seven pennants between '41 and '56, each year facing their arch rivals the New York Yankees in legendary World Series showdowns and winning just once, in 1955. But the Dodgers also came to prominence when, in 1947, the team started a young infielder named Jackie Robinson, breaking baseball's long-held color barrier. Enduring taunts and threats, Robinson batted .297 and rapidly won over Brooklyn fans. These same fans would be devastated 10 years later when Dodgers owner Peter O'Malley moved the team to Los Angeles, opening up the league's West Coast expansion. The Dodgers flourished in their new locale, winning the World Series in 1959, '63 and '65 behind the pitching of Sandy Koufax and Don Drysdale. Success has continued for the Dodgers with World Series titles in 1981 and '88 and two playoff appearances in the 1990s. Today a star-studded lineup anchored by veteran Eric Karros is hoping for yet another visit to the fall classic.

44

In 2000 Kevin Brown led the Dodgers with a 2.58 ERA.

POSTSEASON
- **World Series Titles**...........6
(1955, '59, '63, '65, '81, '88)
- **NL Pennants**...................21
(1890, '99, 1900, '16, '20, '41, '47, '49, '52, '53, '55, '56, '59, '63, '65, '66, '74, '77, '78, '81, '88)

RETIRED NUMBERS
- Pee Wee Reese (1)
- Tommy Lasorda (2)
- Duke Snider (4)
- Jim Gilliam (19)
- Don Sutton (20)
- Walter Alston (24)
- Sandy Koufax (32)
- Roy Campanella (39)
- Jackie Robinson (42)
- Don Drysdale (53)

TEAM RECORDS
Hitting Records
- **Tommy Davis (1959–66)**
RBIs (season): 153 (1962)
- **Babe Herman (1926–31, '45)**
Batting Avg. (season): .393 (1930)
Hits (season): 241 (1930)

The Inside Pitch

- *Incredibly, the Dodgers have been rained out only 17 times in the team's 39 seasons of home games at Dodger Stadium.*

- **"Wee Willie" Keeler (1893, 1899–1902)**
Batting Avg. (career): .360
- **Pee Wee Reese (1940–42, 1946–58)**
Runs (career): 1,338
- **Duke Snider (1947–62)**
HRs (season): 43 (tie) (1956)
HRs (career): 389
RBIs (career): 1,271
- **Maury Wills (1959–66, 1969–72)**
Steals (season): 104 (1962)
Steals (career): 490
- **Zack Wheat (1909–26)**
Hits (career): 2,804
2B (career): 464
3B (career): 171

Pitching Records
- **Sandy Koufax (1955–66)**
Shutouts (season): 11 (1963)
Strikeouts (season): 382 (1965)
- **Tom Lovett (1890–91, '93)**
Wins (season): 30 (1890)
- **Rube Marquard (1915–20)**
ERA (season): 1.58 (1916)
- **Jeff Pfeffer (1913–21)**
ERA (career): 2.31
- **Don Sutton (1966–80, '88)**
Shutouts (career): 52
Strikeouts (career): 2,696
Wins (career): 233

Managing Records
- **Chuck Dressen (1951–53)**
Wins (season): 105 (1953)
- **Walter Alston (1954–76)**

> *"The Dodgers hit short and run long."*
> — *Bill Roeder,* New York World-Telegram & Sun, *on 1947 team*

NL Pennants (career): 7
World Series Titles (career): 4
Wins (career): 2,040

LEAGUE HONORS
NL MVP
- Jake Daubert (1913)
- Dazzy Vance (1924)
- Dolph Camilli (1941)
- Jackie Robinson (1949)
- Roy Campanella (1951, '53, '55)
- Don Newcombe (1956)
- Maury Wills (1962)
- Sandy Koufax (1963)
- Steve Garvey (1974)
- Kirk Gibson (1988)

NL Rookie of the Year
- Jackie Robinson (1947)
- Don Newcombe (1949)
- Joe Black (1952)
- Jim Gilliam (1953)
- Frank Howard (1960)
- Jim Lefebvre (1965)
- Ted Sizemore (1969)
- Rick Sutcliffe (1979)
- Steve Howe (1980)
- Fernando Valenzuela (1981)
- Steve Sax (1982)

Vital Stats

Stadium Address:
1000 Elysian Park Ave.,
Los Angeles, Calif.
Phone: (323) 224-1500
Web: dodgers.mlb.com
Box Office:
(323) 224-1-HIT,
Mon.–Sun. 8:30–5:30
Media Coverage:
Radio: KXTA (1150 AM)
TV: KTLA (Channel 5),
Fox Sports Net 2
Spring Training:
Dodgertown,
Vero Beach, Fla.

- Eric Karros (1992)
- Mike Piazza (1993)
- Raul Mondesi (1994)
- Hideo Nomo (1995)
- Todd Hollandsworth (1996)

NL Cy Young
- Don Newcombe (1956)
- Don Drysdale (1962)
- Sandy Koufax (1963, '65, '66)
- Mike Marshall (1974)
- Fernando Valenzuela (1981)
- Orel Hershiser (1988)

Timeline

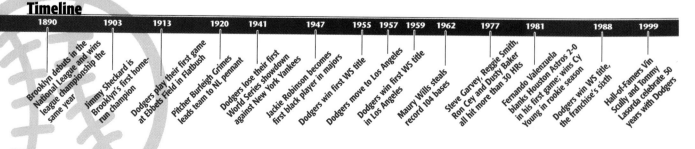

1890	1903	1913	1920	1941	1947	1955	1957	1959	1962	1977	1981	1988	1999
Brooklyn debuts in the National League and wins league championship the same year	Jimmy Sheckard is Brooklyn's first home-run champion	Dodgers play their first game at Ebbets Field in Flatbush	Pitcher Burleigh Grimes leads team to NL pennant	Dodgers lose their first World Series showdown against New York Yankees	Jackie Robinson becomes first black player in majors	Dodgers win first WS title	Dodgers move to Los Angeles	Dodgers win first WS title in Los Angeles	Maury Wills steals record 104 bases	Steve Garvey, Reggie Smith, Ron Cey and Dusty Baker all hit more than 30 HRs	Fernando Valenzuela blanks Houston Astros 2-0 in his first game; wins Cy Young in rookie season	Dodgers win WS title, the franchise's sixth	Hall-of-Famers Vin Scully and Tommy Lasorda celebrate 50 years with Dodgers

DODGER STADIUM: THE JEWEL AT CHAVEZ RAVINE

WHEN DODGERS OWNER WALTER O'MALLEY saw the empty 300-acre lot at Chavez Ravine, surrounded by freeways and within easy reach of downtown, he knew it was the right spot for a new stadium. Since it opened in 1962, the park has awed visitors with its incredible views: the LA skyline to the south; the tree-lined Elysian hills to the north and east; and the San Gabriel Mountains in the distance. Dodger Stadium is one of the finest historic stadiums in the majors and is the place where Kirk Gibson launched his dramatic ninth-inning homer to win game one of the 1988 World Series.

CONCESSIONS

Dodger Stadium has typical ballpark fare as well as several ice cream and baked goods stands. Vegetarian food is also available.

Stadium Facts

Opened: April 10, 1962
Cost: $23 million
Capacity: 56,000
Type: Outdoor
Surface: Grass
Home Sweet Home:
• Dodger Stadium is considered a classic pitcher's park. Expansive foul territories give fielders lots of room to chase foul balls. As well, the field's deep power alleys (385 feet in both right and left center) make it tough to hit the ball out.

GAME DAY TIPS

• **Gate hours:** Gates open 90 minutes prior to games. Parking lots open two hours before a game.
• **Weather:** Los Angeles is usually dry, with moderate temperatures in the summer and early fall; however, the city's smog level is worst at these times.
• **Prohibited items:** Banners, beachballs, noisemaking devices, cans, bottles (glass or plastic), jugs, coolers and hard containers of any kind are prohibited. Smoking is allowed in designated areas.
• **Ticket tips:** Among the toughest tickets to come by are for games against the much-hated Yankees. Fans in the know will tell you that

Seating Plan

■ **Top Deck** $6	■ **Dugout Club** $215
■ **Inner Reserved Level** ...$15	■ **Luxury**
■ **Outer Reserved Level** ...$10	**Suites** ......**Call for prices**
■ **Loge Box** $13	■ **Suites** ....**Call for prices**
■ **Field Box** $17	ᴀᴛᴍ **Top Deck, Reserved Level**
■ **Left/Right Field**	**Section 9, Field Level Gate**
Pavilion $6	**near Section 57, Section 109**
■ **Sold Out** ....N/A	⬧ **Throughout**

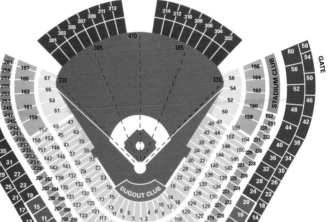

the best seats in the house are those in the left- and right-field pavilion. Batting practice begins 90 minutes before the game and many balls end up in the stands.
• **Lost and found:** (323) 224-1384, Mon. to Fri. 10–4.

Nearby Hotels

▼▼ **Best Western Dragon Gate Inn** (*Motor Inn*), 818 N. Hill St. (Los Angeles), (213) 617-3077, $79-$189
▼▼▼▼ **Hyatt Regency Los Angeles** (*Hotel*), 711 S. Hope St. (Los Angeles), (213) 683-1234, $210-$235
▼▼▼ **Los Angeles Downtown Marriott Hotel** (*Hotel*), 333 S. Figueroa St. (Los Angeles), (213) 617-1133, $190-$149
▼▼▼ **The Millennium Biltmore Los Angeles** (*Classic Hotel*), 506 S. Grand St. at 5th St. (Los Angeles), (213) 624-1011, $135-$155
▼▼▼ **Wyndham Checkers Hotel** (*Hotel*), 535 S. Grand Ave. (Los Angeles), (213) 624-0000, $99-$199

Nearby Restaurants

▼▼▼ **A Thousand Cranes Restaurant** (*Japanese*), 120 S. Los Angeles St. in the New Otani Hotel (Los Angeles), (213) 253-9255, $35-$90
▼▼▼ **Checkers Restaurant** (*Continental*), 535 S. Grand Ave. in the Wyndham Checkers Hotel (Los Angeles), (213) 891-0519, $16-32 (dinner only)
▼▼ **Engine Company No. 28** (*American*), 644 S. Figueroa St. (Los Angeles), (213) 624-6996, $10-$20
▼▼ **McCormick & Schmick's** (*Seafood*), 633 W. 5th St. in the First Interstate World Center Bldg., 4th floor (Los Angeles), (213) 629-1929, $9-$20
▼▼▼ **The Tower** (*Continental*), 1150 S. Olive St. in the Transamerica Center Bldg., 32nd floor (Los Angeles), (213) 746-1554, $35-$45

Directions: From I-5, take Stadium Way exit, then follow to Elysian Park Ave. and turn left. From I-110/Harbor Frwy., take Dodger Stadium exit and turn left on Stadium Way, then right on Elysian Park Ave. From US 101, take Alvarado exit and turn right on Sunset, then left on Elysian Park Ave. By Bus: Metro Buses 2, 3, 4, 302 and 304 stop at Sunset and Innes. Call Metropolitan Transit Authority at 1-800-COMMUTE for more information. *Parking:* Lots surrounding the stadium can accommodate 16,000 cars. Lot 10 is wheelchair accessible.

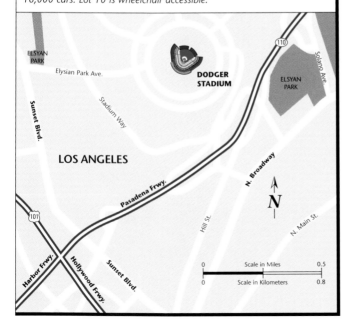

MILWAUKEE BREWERS

ALMOST FROM THE DAY THE MILWAUKEE BRAVES franchise left for Atlanta following the 1965 season, a group of prominent sports enthusiasts in the city, including current Baseball Commissioner Bud Selig, began to put together a plan for a new team. Local baseball fans were elated in 1970, when their efforts were rewarded and the Milwaukee Brewers Inc. became owners of the struggling Seattle Pilots franchise. The new Milwaukee baseball team began play that year in the same County Stadium that had witnessed so many great moments with the Braves, including the 1957 World Series. The "Brew Crew," as the team became known, would endure an expansion hangover that lasted several seasons. The doldrums were alleviated brilliantly, if only briefly, by the return to Milwaukee of superstar Hank Aaron, who chose to finish his career where it had begun. But through the early years, General Manager Frank "Trader" Lane was assembling a powerful team. Gorman Thomas arrived in 1973, followed by 18-year-old Robin Yount in '74, Cecil Cooper in '77, Paul Molitor in '78 and ace reliever Rollie Fingers in '81. Under manager Harvey Kuenn, "Harvey's Wall Bangers" — as the team was known — won the 1982 AL pennant and very nearly won the World Series, losing a seven-game contest to rival St. Louis. Success has been sporadic for the Brewers since that great year. The team has had several winning seasons, but the pennant has proven elusive. The 1998 realignment in baseball brought the Brewers to the National League. Now accustomed to their new opponents and with a brand new stadium, the "Brew Crew" hopes for a return to past glory.

Vital Stats

Stadium Address:
One Brewers Way,
Milwaukee, Wis.
Phone: (414) 902-4400
Web: brewers.mlb.com,
www.millerpark.org
Box Office:
(800) 933-7890, Mon.–Fri.
9–7, Sat. 9–5, Sun. 11–5
Media Coverage:
Radio: WTMJ (620 AM)
TV: WCGV (Channel 24),
Midwest Sports Channel
Spring Training:
Maryvale Baseball Park,
Phoenix, Ariz.

POSTSEASON
• AL Pennants.....................1
(1982)

RETIRED NUMBERS
• **Paul Molitor (4)**
• **Robin Yount (19)**
• **Rollie Fingers (34)**
• **Hank Aaron (44)**

TEAM RECORDS
Hitting Records
• **Jeff Cirillo (1994–99)**
Batting Avg. (career): .307
• **Cecil Cooper (1977–87)**
Hits (season): 219 (1980)
RBIs (season): 126 (1983)
• **Paul Molitor (1978–92)**
Batting Avg. (season):

.353 (1987)
Hitting Streak: 39 games
(1987)
Runs (season): 136 (1982)
Steals (career): 412
3B (season): 16 (1979)
• **Gorman Thomas
(1973–76, 1978–83, '86)**
HRs (season): 45 (1979)
• **Robin Yount (1974–93)**
Hits (career): 3,142
HRs (career): 251
RBIs (career): 1,406
Runs (career): 1,632
2B (season): 49 (1980)
2B (career): 613

Pitching Records
• **Mike Caldwell (1977–84)**
Complete Games (season):

23 (1978)
Complete Games
(career): 85
Shutouts (season):
6 (1978)
Wins (season): 22 (1978)
• **Cal Eldred (1991–99)**
ERA (season): 1.79 (1992)
Winning Pct. (season):
.846 (1992)
• **Teddy Higuera (1985–94)**
Strikeouts (season):
240 (1987)
Strikeouts (career): 1,081
• **Ken Sanders (1970–72)**
ERA (career): 2.22
• **Jim Slaton
(1971–77, 1979–83)**
Innings Pitched
(career): 2,025.1

> *"I never thought home runs were all that exciting."*
> — Hank Aaron, who hit the last of his record 755 homers as a Brewer

Shutouts (career): 19
Wins (career): 117
• **Bob Wickman (1996–99)**
Saves (season): 37 (1999)

Managing Records
• **George Bamberger
(1978–80, 1985–86)**
Wins (season): 95 (1979)
• **Phil Garner (1992–99)**
Wins (career): 563
• **Harvey Kuenn (1982–83)**
Winning Pct. career): .573

LEAGUE HONORS
AL MVP
• Rollie Fingers (1981)
• Robin Yount (1982, '89)

AL Rookie of the Year
• Pat Listach (1992)

AL Cy Young
• Rollie Fingers (1981)
• Pete Vuckovich (1982)

AL Gold Glove
• George Scott.......................5
• Cecil Cooper.......................2
• Sixto Lezcano....................1
• Robin Yount.......................1

The Inside Pitch

• The Brewers is one of the few baseball teams with a longstanding tradition of tailgating. Join the action about two hours before each game in the Miller Park parking lots or in the specially designated tailgating park. Call the ticket office for information.
• One of the game's great characters, former catcher Bob Uecker has brought his humor to Brewer's radio broadcasts since 1980.

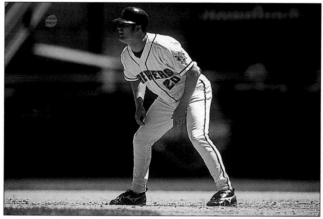

Jeromy Burnitz set a Brewers team record by drawing 99 bases on balls in the 2000 season.

Timeline

1969	**1970**	**1972**	**1974**	**1976**	**1978**	**1981**	**1982**	**1987**	**1989**	**1992**	**1998**	**2000**	**2001**

Expansion Seattle Pilots begin play in AL West

Milwaukee acquires Pilots franchise; team begins play as Brewers

Brewers switch to AL East

Robin Yount becomes regular shortstop at age 18

Hank Aaron plays final major-league season with Brewers; hits 10 homers

Brewers have first winning season, going 93-69

Brewers win second half of split season; lose to Yankees in division series

Brewers win AL pennant; lose dramatic seven-game World Series to Cardinals

Paul Molitor records 39-game hitting streak

Robin Yount becomes only player to win two MVP Awards at two different positions

Yount records 3,000th hit; Brewers finish second in AL East

Brewers play first season in National League

Jeromy Burnitz records third-straight 30 home-run season

Brewers move to Miller Park

MILLER PARK: A BALLPARK WITHIN A PARK

OPENED IN SPRING OF 2001, Miller Park is located in a large, 265-acre park on the Menominee River. Outside the ultra-modern baseball facilities, the park offers walking trails, environmental preservation areas and specifically designed picnic and tailgating areas (constructed in the former outfield of now dismantled Milwaukee County Stadium). Contrasting this rustic setting is the ballpark itself. With the only fan-shaped retractable roof in North America, Miller Park is part of a new generation of stadiums that offers the old-fashioned thrill of the game with modern amenities and high-tech viewing comforts.

CONCESSIONS
Apart from the standard ballpark fare of hot dogs and pizza, Miller Park offers a wide range of regional specialities. Some popular items are corned beef sandwiches, bison burgers, venison jerky and, of course, Wisconsin bratwurst.

GAME DAY TIPS
• **Gate hours:** Gates open 90 minutes prior to games.
• **Weather:** Due to the retractable roof, weather concerns at Miller Park are minimal. Still, consider bringing an umbrella on damp days since the roof will not be closed unless rain is very heavy.
• **Prohibited items:** Cans, bottles (glass or plastic), jugs, coolers and hard containers of any kind are prohibited at Miller Park. While cameras are permitted, tripods and monopods for photographic equipment are not. Video-taping the game is also not allowed. Smoking is permitted only in designated areas.
• **Ticket tips:** Seats in the loge bleachers are good value and have great views. Non-alcoholic beverage sections are good for families. For Cubs and Cardinals games, tickets sell very quickly.
• **Lost and found:** (414) 902-4400.

Stadium Facts

Opened: *April 6, 2001*
Cost: *$250 million*
Capacity: *43,000*
Type: *Retractable roof*
Surface: *Grass*
Home Sweet Home:
• *The "spilt-bowl" seating design brings fans closer to the action than older ballparks. This proximity has helped amplify the cheers of the Brewers faithful.*
• *Relatively deep power alleys help pitchers keep the ball in the park.*

Directions: *From the east or west, take I-94 to Miller Park Way off-ramp in the Stadium Interchange, then take Miller Park exit. From the south, take National Ave. to Miller Park Way, then take Miller Park exit. From the north, take Hwy. 41 to Miller Park exit. By Bus: Call Milwaukee County Transit System at (414) 344-6711 for schedules.* **Parking:** *Connected lots surround the stadium, providing 13,000 spots for cars. Wheelchair-accessible parking is available; disabled plate or permit is required and spots are allocated on first-come, first-served basis.*

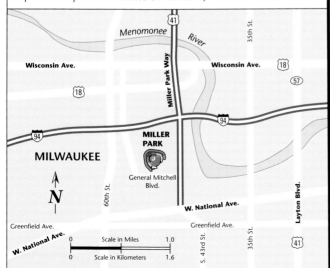

Seating Plan

▦ **Field Diamond Box**	$50	
■ **Field Infield Box**	$32	
▨ **Field Outfield Box**	$27	
▤ **Loge Diamond Box**	$27	
▩ **Loge Infield Box**	$23	
░ **Loge Outfield Box**	$20	
▧ **Club Infield Box**	$32	
░ **Club Outfield Box**	$24	
▦ **Terrace Infield Box**	$16	

■ **Terrace Outfield Box**	$14	
▨ **Terrace Reserved**	$10	
░ **Field Bleachers**	$10	
□ **Loge Bleachers**	$6	
▩ **Club Bleachers**	$6	
■ **Terrace Bleachers**	$5	

ATM **All levels left-field corner; Field, Terrace levels behind home plate**
♿ **Throughout**

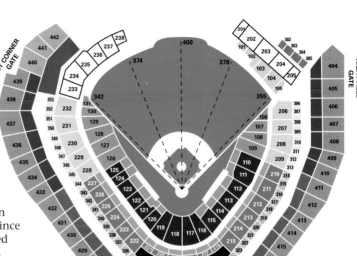

Nearby Hotels
▼▼▼ **Comfort Suites** *(Motel)*, 6362 S. 13th St. (Oak Creek), (414) 570-1111, $89-$229
▼▼▼ **Hilton Milwaukee City Center** *(Hotel)*, 509 W. Wisconsin Ave. (Milwaukee), (414) 271-7250, $89-$139
▼▼▼ **Hotel Metro-Milwaukee** *(Hotel)*, 411 E. Mason St. (Milwaukee), (414) 272-1937, $180-$190
▼▼▼ **Hyatt Regency Milwaukee** *(Hotel)*, 333 W. Kilbourn Ave. (Milwaukee), (414) 276-1234, $149-$174
▼▼▼▼ **The Pfister Hotel** *(Classic Hotel)*, 424 E. Wisconsin Ave. (Milwaukee), (414) 273-8222, $244-$314

Nearby Restaurants
▼▼▼ **Bartolotta's Lake Park Bistro** *(French)*, 3133 E. Newberry Blvd. (Milwaukee), (414) 962-6300, $8-$29
▼▼ **Benson's Steak House** *(Steakhouse)*, 509 W. Wisconsin Ave. in Hilton Milwaukee City Center (Milwaukee), (414) 271-7684, $18-$39
▼▼▼ **Eddie Martini's** *(Traditional American)*, 8612 W. Watertown Plank Rd. (Wauwatosa), (414) 771-6680, $15-$30
▼▼▼ **Ristorante Bartolotta** *(Northern Italian)*, 7616 W. State St. (Wauwatosa), (414) 771-7910, $13-$26
▼▼▼▼ **Sanford Restaurant** *(American)*, 1547 N. Jackson St. (Milwaukee), (414) 276-9608, $42-$69

MINNESOTA TWINS

THE MINNESOTA TWINS can be likened to the mythical phoenix. In 1961 the team rose from the ashes of the now-defunct Washington Senators — a club that finished above .500 only five times from 1934 to '60. But the change of scenery seemed to bolster the players. Pitcher Camilo Pascual rattled off seven straight winning seasons in Minnesota, including four in a row in which he had more than 200 strikeouts. Likewise, Harmon "Killer" Killebrew blossomed in the Twin Cities, winning six home-run crowns. But not all of Minnesota's early heroes were crossovers from the old club. In 1967 Rod Carew took AL Rookie of the Year honors. Carew went on to claim seven batting titles, peaking in 1977, when he led the league in hits, runs, triples and, of course, batting, with an incredible .388 average. Minnesota's ability to overcome adversity led to its first World Series crown in 1987. Despite having only the ninth-best record in baseball, the team defeated heavily favored Detroit to win the AL pennant. Led by Kirby Puckett, Don Gladden and Minnesota-born Kent Hrbek, the Twins took the World Series title in seven games over the Cards when Frank Viola shook off a game-four shelling to pitch eight strong innings in the decisive match. In 1991 the team made one of the biggest single-season turnarounds in baseball history when it ran away with the AL East after having finished in the cellar in 1990. The Twins completed their improbable story when Jack Morris shut out the Braves through 10 innings in game seven of the World Series, giving Minnesota another championship.

Matt Lawton is the Twins slugging star.

POSTSEASON
- World Series Titles...........2
(1987, '91)
- AL Pennants....................3
(1965, '87, '91)

RETIRED NUMBERS
- Harmon Killebrew (3)
- Tony Oliva (6)
- Kent Hrbek (14)
- Rod Carew (29)
- Kirby Puckett (34)

TEAM RECORDS
Hitting Records
- **Rod Carew (1967–78)**
Batting Avg. (season): .388 (1977)
Batting Avg. (career): .334
Hits (season): 239 (1977)
3B (career): 90

The Inside Pitch

- *Although none of the old Washington Senators records survived the franchise's move to Minnesota, one player is worth remembering. Playing for the Sens from 1907 to '27, Walter "Big Train" Johnson had 12 20-win seasons and recorded 3,509 strikeouts. His 110 career shutouts is a major-league record that may never be broken.*

- **Marty Cordova (1995–99)**
2B (season): 46 (1996)
- **Cristian Guzman (1999–present)**
3B (season): 20 (2000)
- **Harmon Killebrew (1961–74)**
Games (career): 1,939
HRs (season): 49 (1964, '69)
HRs (career): 475
RBIS (season): 140 (1969)
RBIS (career): 1,325
Walks (season): 145 (1969)
Walks (career): 1,321
- **Chuck Knoblauch (1991–97)**
Runs (season): 140 (1996)
Steals (season): 62 (1997)
Steals (career): 276
- **Ken Landreaux (1979–80)**
Hitting Streak: 31 games (1980)
- **Tony Oliva (1962–76)**
Extra-Base Hits (season): 84 (1964)
Total Bases (season): 374 (1964)
- **Kirby Puckett (1984–95)**
At-Bats (season): 691 (1985)
At-Bats (career): 7,244
Hits (career): 2,304
Runs (career): 1,071
Total Bases (career): 3,453
2B (career): 414

Pitching Records
- **Rick Aguilera (1989–99)**
Appearances: 490
Saves (career): 254

"I think this is great. The ball really shoots out of here. Now, if we can only learn to hit."
— Calvin Griffith, Twins owner, about the Metrodome in 1982

Saves (season): 42 (tie) (1991)
- **Allan Anderson (1986–91)**
ERA (season): 2.45 (1988)
- **Bert Blyleven (1970–76, 1985–88)**
Complete Games (season): 25 (1973)
Complete Games (career): 141
Shutouts (season): 9 (1973)
Shutouts (career): 29
Strikeouts (season): 258 (1973)
Strikeouts (career): 2,035
- **Dean Chance (1967–69)**
ERA (career): 2.67
- **Jim Kaat (1961–73)**
Starts (season): 42 (1965)
Starts (career): 422
Wins (season): 25 (1966)
Wins (career): 189
- **Mike Marshall (1978–80)**
Games (season): 90 (1979)
- **Jeff Reardon (1987–89)**
Saves (season): 42 (tie) (1988)
- **Frank Viola (1982–89)**
Win Pct. (season): .774 (1988)

LEAGUE HONORS
AL MVP
- Zoilo Versalles (1965)
- Harmon Killebrew (1969)
- Rod Carew (1977)

Vital Stats

Stadium Address:
400 S. 5th St.,
Minneapolis, Minn.
Phone: (612) 332-0386
Web: twins.mlb.com
Box Office:
(800) 338-9467,
Mon.–Fri. 9–5, game days
Sat. 9–4
Media Coverage:
Radio: WCCO (830 AM)
TV: KMSP-TV (Channel 9),
MSC
Spring Training:
Hammond Stadium,
Fort Myers, Fla.

AL Rookie of the Year
- Tony Oliva (1964)
- Rod Carew (1967)
- John Castino (1979)
- Chuck Knoblauch (1991)
- Marty Cordova (1995)

AL Cy Young
- Jim Perry (1970)
- Frank Viola (1988)

Timeline

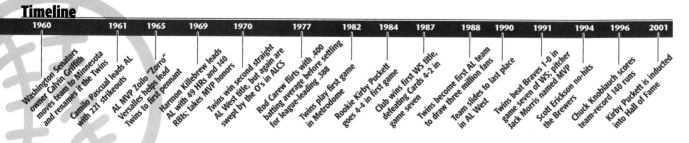

1960	1961	1965	1969	1970	1977	1982	1984	1987	1988	1990	1991	1994	1996	2001

Washington Senators owner Calvin Griffith moves team to Minnesota and renames it the Twins

Camilo Pascual leads AL with 221 strikeouts

AL MVP Zoilo "Zorro" Versalles helps lead Twins to first pennant

Harmon Killebrew leads AL with 49 HRs and 140 RBIs; takes MVP honors

Twins win second straight AL West title, but again are swept by the O's in ALCS

Rod Carew flirts with .400 batting average before settling for league-leading .388

Twins play first game in Metrodome

Rookie Kirby Puckett goes 4-4 in first game

Club wins first WS title, defeating Cards 4-2 in game seven

Twins become first AL team to draw three million fans

Team slides to last place in AL West

Twins beat Braves 1-0 in game seven of WS; pitcher Jack Morris named MVP

Scott Erickson no-hits the Brewers

Chuck Knoblauch scores team-record 140 runs

Kirby Puckett is inducted into Hall of Fame

48

HUBERT H. HUMPHREY METRODOME: FULL OF HOT AIR

THE METRODOME HAS THE DISTINCTION of being the only air-supported dome in the majors. The roof has deflated twice due to tears caused by heavy snow. In one 1984 game, Dave Kingman hammered a ball that hit the roof and disappeared into a drainage hole, never to be seen again. The stadium has hosted the 1985 Baseball All-Star Game, Super Bowl XXVI and the 1992 NCAA Final Four basketball tourney. However, Twins fans will always remember this as the ballpark where Minnesota clinched both its World Series crowns.

CONCESSIONS

The Metrodome has a variety of specialty sausages, ranging from bratwurst to Italian. There are also a number of choices for the health conscious and vegetarians, including salads, yogurt smoothies and sandwiches.

Stadium Facts

Opened: *April 3, 1982*
Cost: *$83 million*
Capacity: *48,678*
Type: *Enclosed*
Surface: *AstroTurf*
Home Sweet Home:
• The white dome of the ballpark makes it hard to see balls hit high in the air.
• Due to the curved wall behind home plate, wild pitches and passed balls bounce toward first base.

The "Walkaway Sundae" is a favorite with fans.

GAME DAY TIPS

• **Gate hours:** Gates open 90 minutes prior to games on Monday through Thursday and two hours prior to games on Friday through Sunday.
• **Prohibited items:** Items prohibited include cans, bottles, plastic containers, beverages, laser pointers, bats and brooms. Signs are permitted if they are not mounted on sticks or poles.
• **Ticket tips:** Getting last-minute tickets in a variety of seating areas at the Metrodome is no problem. Sight lines along the base paths are not great, however, so choose seats accordingly.
• **Lost and found:** (612) 375-7432.

Directions: *From the I-94 west, take the 5th St. exit. From the I-394 north, take the 4th St. exit. From the I-35W south, take the Washington Ave. exit. From the I-35W north, take the 3rd St. exit. By Bus: There are bus routes going to the Metrodome from around town. Call (612) 373-3333 for routes and schedules.* **Parking:** *Get to the ballpark early to take advantage of the eight-hour meters nearby. The Metrodome has no private lot, but there are public lots on S. 3rd, S. Park,, S. 5th, S. 11th and S. Washington streets. A lot reserved for people with disabilities can be found on Chicago Ave. between S. 3rd St. and S. 4th St.*

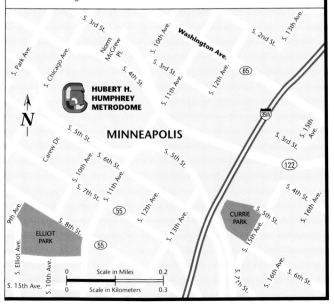

Seating Plan

- ■ Lower Club $25
- ■ Lower Diamond View ..$23
- ☐ Lower Reserved $15
- ■ Upper Club $10
- ■ Marquette Banks Family Section $10
- ■ Lower General Admission $10
- ■ Upper General Admission $5
- **ATM** Sections 106, 116, 123, 136
- ♿ Throughout

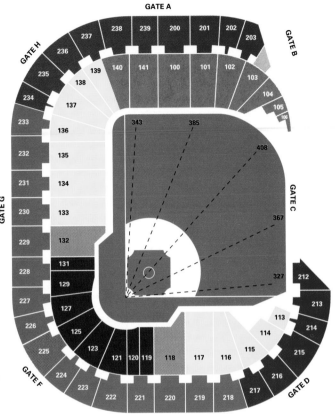

Nearby Hotels

▼▼▼ **Best Western Downtown** *(Motel)*, 405 S. 8th St. (Minneapolis), (612) 370-1400, $89-$104
▼▼▼ **Crowne Plaza Northstar Hotel** *(Hotel)*, 618 S. 2nd Ave. S. (Minneapolis), (612) 338-2288, $89-$149
▼▼▼ **Embassy Suites Minneapolis Downtown** *(Suite Hotel)*, 425 S. 7th St. (Minneapolis), (612) 333-3111, $170-$199
▼▼▼ **Holiday Inn Metrodome** *(Hotel)*, 1500 Washington Ave. S. (Minneapolis), (612) 333-4646, $115-$209
▼▼▼ **Hyatt Whitney** *(Hotel)*, 150 Portland Ave. (Minneapolis), (612) 375-1234, $155-$210

Nearby Restaurants

▼▼▼ **Basil's** *(American)*, 710 Marquette Ave. in the Marquette Hotel (Minneapolis), (612) 376-7404, $10-$30
▼▼▼ **Cafe Brenda** *(American)*, 300 1st Ave. N. (Minneapolis), (612) 342-9230, $7-$12
▼▼▼▼ **Goodfellow's** *(American)*, 40 S. 7th St. in the City Center Shopping Complex (Minneapolis), (612) 332-4800, $25-$35
▼▼▼ **Murray's Restaurant** *(American)*, 26 S. 6th St. (Minneapolis), (612) 339-0909, $11-$49
▼▼▼ **Palomino Euro-Bistro** *(American)*, 825 Hennepin Ave. on the Skyway level of Lasalle Plaza (Minneapolis), (612) 339-3800, $9-$27

MONTREAL EXPOS

KNOWN PRIMARILY AS A HOCKEY TOWN, Montreal has a long pro baseball history. A year before breaking the color barrier with the Brooklyn Dodgers in 1947, Jackie Robinson played in the minors for the Montreal Royals. Major League Baseball came to the city in 1969, with the Expos representing the first team located outside the U.S. Playing in tiny Jarry Park, the first-year team had its share of ups and down. The thrill of Bill Stoneman's no-hitter in April was tempered by a 20-game losing streak later that same season. Still, local fans were captivated by home team heroes such as Stoneman, Maury Wills, Mack Jones and Rusty Staub — lovingly referred to by the French populace as "le Grand Orange" (roughly translated: "the Big Redhead"). In 1977 the team left the comfy confines of Jarry Park and moved to the Olympic Stadium. That version of the Expos was buoyed by a talented cast that included Ellis Valentine, Andre Dawson, Gary Carter, and pitchers Steve Rodgers and Bill Gullickson. Through the years a host of future superstars were groomed in the team's farm system. Tim Raines, Andres Galarraga, Larry Walker, Marquis Grissom, and pitching aces Randy Johnson and Pedro Martinez are just some of the players who began their illustrious careers in Montreal. Today, under the guidance of new General Manager Jim Beattie, emerging stars such as Vladimir Guerrero and José Vidro hope to take the team where it has never been before: the World Series.

Vital Stats

Stadium Address:
4549 Pierre-de-Coubertin, Montreal, Que.
Phone: (514) 252-4679
Web: expos.mlb.com, rio.gouv.qc.ca
Box Office:
(800) GO-EXPOS,
Mon.–Fri. 9–5,
Sat. 10–4
Media Coverage:
Radio: CKAC (730 AM)
TV: RDS, TSN
Spring Training:
Roger Dean Stadium,
Jupiter, Fla.

"Montreal has always been a true baseball city."

— Jeffrey Loria, Expos owner

POSTSEASON
• NL East Titles 1
(1981)

RETIRED NUMBERS
• Gary Carter (8)
• Andre Dawson (10)
• Rusty Staub (10)

TEAM RECORDS
Hitting Records
• **Andre Dawson (1976–86)**
HRs (career): 225
RBIs (inning): 6
(Sept. 24, 1985)
• **Gary Carter (1974–84, '92)**
Grand Slams (career): 7
• **Warren Cromartie (1974, 1976–83)**
At-Bats (season): 659 (1979)
• **Mark Grudzielanek (1995–98)**
Singles (season): 157 (1996)
2B (season): 54 (1997)
• **Vladimir Guerrero (1996–present)**
Batting Avg. (season): .345 (2000)
Batting Avg. (career): .322
Consecutive Games Played (career): 276
(May 20, 1998–Aug. 29, 1999)

Extra-Base Hits (season): 84 (1999)
Hitting Streak: 31 games (1999)
HRs (season): 44 (2000)
RBIs (season): 131 (1999)
Slugging Pct. (season): .664 (2000)
Total Bases (season): 379 (2000)
• **Ron LeFlore (1980)**
Stolen Bases (season): 97 (1980)
• **Al Oliver (1982–83)**
Hits (season): 204 (1982)
• **Tim Raines (1979–90, 2001–present)**
Runs (season): 133 (1983)
Runs (career): 934
Steals (career): 634
3B (career): 81

The Inside Pitch

• Attached to the stadium is the 552-foot Montreal Tower, the world's tallest inclined structure. Visitors can ride the funicular to the observatory and get a great view of Montreal.
• Oct. 19, 1981, is known to Expos fans as "Blue Monday." A ninth-inning home run by L.A. Dodger Rick Monday ended the Expos first and only bid for a NL pennant.

• **Tim Wallach (1980–92)**
At-Bats (career): 6,529
Games (career): 1,767
Hits (career): 1,694
RBIs (career): 905
Total Bases (career): 2,728
2B (career): 360

Pitching Records
• **Tim Burke (1985–91)**
Games (career): 425
• **Ross Grimsley (1978–80)**
Wins (season): 20 (1978)
• **Bill Gullikson (1979–85)**
Strikeouts (game): 18 (Sept. 10, 1980)
• **Pedro Martinez (1994–97)**
ERA (season): 1.90 (1997)
Strikeouts (season): 305 (1997)
• **Jeff Reardon (1981–86)**
Saves (career): 152
• **Steve Rogers (1973–85)**
Complete Games (career): 129
Innings Pitched (career): 2,838.0
Innings Pitched (season): 301.2 (1977)
Shutouts (season): 5 (tie) (1979, '83)
Shutouts (career): 37
Strikeouts (career): 1,621
Wins (career): 158
• **Bill Stoneman**
Complete Games (season): 20 (1971)
No-hitters (career): 2
• **John Wetteland (1992–94)**
Saves (season): 43 (1993)

LEAGUE HONORS
NL Rookie of the Year
• Carl Morton (1970)
• Andre Dawson (1977)

NL Cy Young
• Pedro Martinez (1997)

NL Manager of the Year
• Felipe Alou (1994)

All-Star Game MVP
• Gary Carter (1981, '84)
• Tim Raines (1987)

NL Gold Glove
• Andre Dawson 6
• Gary Carter 3
• Tim Wallach 3
• Andres Galarraga 2
• Marquis Grissom 2
• Larry Walker 2
• Mike Jorgensen 1
• Ellis Valentine 1

Vladimir Guerrero is considered one of the game's best offensive players.

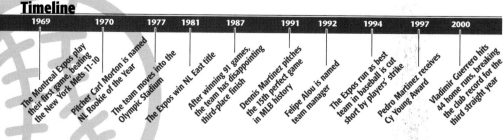

Timeline

1969 The Montreal Expos play their first game, beating the New York Mets 11-10

1970 Pitcher Carl Morton is named NL Rookie of the Year

1977 The team moves into the Olympic Stadium

1981 The Expos win NL East title

1987 After winning 91 games, the team has disappointing third-place finish

1991 Dennis Martinez pitches the 15th perfect game in MLB history

1992 Felipe Alou is named team manager

1994 The Expos run as best team in baseball is cut short by players' strike

1997 Pedro Martinez receives Cy Young Award

2000 Vladimir Guerrero hits 44 home runs, breaking the club record for the third straight year

OLYMPIC STADIUM: THE BIG O

OPENED IN 1976 AS ONE OF THE NEW FACILITIES for the 1976 Olympic Games, this unique structure with its leaning tower has seen its share of good times and bad times. Cost overrun and a problematic roof boosted the bill to taxpayers to more than $1 billion. This was the site where U.S. decathlete Bruce Jenner won his gold medal. Since then, "the Big O" (or "the Big Owe" as angry Montreal taxpayers have dubbed it) has hosted professional football games, trade shows and rock concerts. The Expos have been calling it home since 1977.

CONCESSIONS

A variety of foods is available, including pizza, hot dogs, sandwiches and hamburgers. Limited vegetarian choices are also on hand. Look for genuine Montreal smoked meat and beaver tails, a tasty dessert that contains no actual beaver parts.

Stadium Facts

Opened: July 17, 1976
Cost: More than $1 billion (whole complex)
Capacity: 46,620
Type: Enclosed
Surface: AstroTurf
Home Sweet Home:
• This symmetrical ballpark is usually kind to pitchers because unlike many fields, it doesn't have a short right- or left-field fence. However, in the fall the dome keeps out the cold weather and helps the ball carry a little more than it would outdoors.

GAME DAY TIPS

• **Gate hours:** Gates open 90 minutes prior to games.
• **Prohibited items:** Bottles and cans (glass or plastic) are not allowed in the stadium. Smoking is prohibited as are video cameras.
• **Ticket tips:** The size of the Olympic Stadium ensures that same-day tickets in all sections are almost always available. The inexpensive general-admission tickets can most likely get you a seat in the Terrace section, but watch out for increased attendance when big teams are in town. NL powerhouses such as the Atlanta Braves and the New York Mets tend to draw bigger crowds, as do the Boston Red Sox and the Toronto Blue Jays.
• **Lost and found:** (514) 253-3434.

Seating Plan

■ VIP	$36	ATM Box 101
▫ Box Seats	$26	♿ Box 109, 110, 113, 114,
■ Terrace	$16	116, 117, 119, 122; Terrace
■ General Admission	$8	201, 204, 205, 208, 209

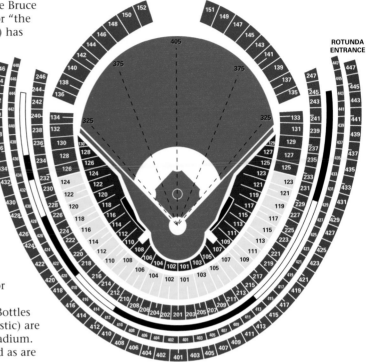

ROTUNDA ENTRANCE

Directions: *Take Rte. 138 (Rue Sherbrooke) to Pie IX, then turn south to Pierre-de-Coubertin. From Hwy. 40, exit at Pie IX. By Metro: Take the Green line to Pie IX. By Bus: Buses are available to and from the stadium. Call the STCUM at AUTOBUS for more information.* **Parking:** *The stadium's 4,000-car underground parking is wheelchair-accessible. There are many unaffiliated outdoor lots in the surrounding area, primarily on Rue Viau, and street parking is available to those who arrive early.*

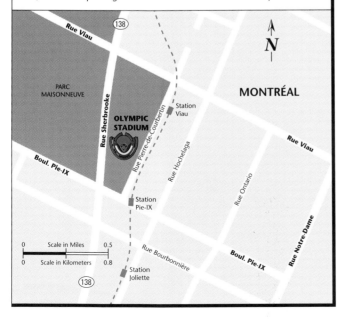

Nearby Hotels

▼▼▼ **Best Western Europa Downtown** *(Hotel)*, 1240 rue Drummond (Montreal), (514) 866-6492, $139-$189
▼▼ **Hotel Auberge Universel Montreal** *(Hotel)*, 5000 rue Sherbrooke est (Montreal), (514) 253-3365, $95-$150
▼▼▼▼ **Hotel Omni Mont-Royal** *(Hotel)*, 1050 rue Sherbrooke ouest (Montreal), (514) 284-1110, $162-$224
▼▼▼▼ **Marriott Chateau Champlain** *(Hotel)*, 1 Place du Canada (Montreal), (514) 878-9000, $186-$241
▼▼ **Motel Le Chablis Le Cadillac** *(Motel)*, 5800 rue Sherbrooke est (Montreal), (514) 259-4691, $70-$150

Nearby Restaurants

▼▼ **Joe's Steak House** *(Steakhouse)*, 1430 rue Stanley (Montreal), (514) 842-4638, $7-$18
▼▼▼ **La Queue de Cheval Bar & Steakhouse** *(Steak & Seafood)*, 1221 boul René-Lévesque ouest (Montreal), (514) 390-0090, $30-$40
▼▼▼▼ **Le Piment Rouge** *(Chinese)*, 1170 rue Peel (Montreal), (514) 866-7816, $19-$30
▼▼ **Mister Steer** *(American)*, 1198 rue Ste-Catherine ouest (Montreal), (514) 866-3233, $6-$15
▼▼ **Montreal Beer Museum** *(Continental)*, 2063 rue Stanley (Montreal), (514) 840-2020, $8-$15

NEW YORK METS

FANS RESPONDED ENTHUSIASTICALLY when the Mets were admitted into the National League in 1962. Despondent over of the defection of the Giants and Dodgers in the late '50s, many New Yorkers were unable to root for the Yankees. The Mets filled the void. For the first years, even while the Mets skimmed the bottom of the ranks, fans poured in to watch the follies of their new team. In 1962 the Mets lost an unbelievable 120 games — still a 20th-century record — but often drew larger crowds than the pennant-bound Yankees. The team began to pick up momentum in 1967 with the signing of pitching ace Tom Seaver. Almost overnight the lovable, but hopeless Mets started winning games. In 1968 the team won more than 70 games for the first time. In 1969 a solid team was assembled around Seaver, including starting pitcher Jerry Koosman, and sluggers Al Weis and Cleon Jones. After a slow start, the team found itself on a roll that wouldn't stop. After catching the Cubs in divisional play, the "Miracle Mets" went on to down Atlanta for the NL pennant and take the World Series from the Orioles, who were considered one of the greatest teams ever. The team showed signs of this brilliance again in 1973, when it overtook the Reds to win the NL crown. The Mets tasted champagne again in 1986, when the All-Star lineup of Darryl Strawberry, Keith Hernandez and Gary Carter brought the pennant back to Shea. In recent years the Mets have experienced a third wave of on-field brilliance. Led by hitters Edgardo Alfonzo and Mike Piazza and pitchers Bobby J. Jones and Mike Hampton, the team took the NL pennant over the Cardinals, only to lose to the crosstown juggernaut Yankees in the 2000 "Subway Series."

Mike Piazza has at least 100 RBIs in his last five seasons.

POSTSEASON
- World Series Titles............2
(1969, '86)
- NL Pennants.....................4
(1969, '73, '86, 2000)

RETIRED NUMBERS
- Gil Hodges (14)
- Casey Stengel (37)
- Tom Seaver (41)

TEAM RECORDS
Hitting Records
- **Edgardo Alfonzo (1995–present)**
Hits (game): 6 (Aug. 30, 1999)
Runs (season): 123 (1999)
- **Roger Cedeno (1999)**
Steals (season): 66 (1999)

The Inside Pitch

- *Shea Stadium was the first ballpark capable of being converted into a football field. With two motor-operated stands that moved on underground tracks, the field shape could be altered to suit both sports.*
- *Look for the Magic Mets Top Hat in center field. When a Met hits a homer, a big, red New York apple rises from the hat.*

- **Todd Hundley (1990–98)**
HRs (season): 41 (1996)
- **Lance Johnson (1996–97)**
At-Bats (season): 682 (1996)
Hits (season): 227 (1996)
3B (season): 21 (1996)
- **Ed Kranepool (1962–79)**
At-Bats (career): 5,436
Hits (career): 1,418
Games (career): 1,853
Pinch-Hits (career): 90
Total Bases (career): 2,047
- **John Olerud (1997–99)**
Batting Avg. (season): .354 (1998)
Batting Avg. (career): .315
Games (season): 162 (1999)
Walks (season): 125 (1999)
- **Mike Piazza (1998–present)**
RBIs (season): 124 (1999)
- **Darryl Strawberry (1983–90)**
HRs (career): 252
RBIs (career): 733
Runs (career): 662
Slugging Pct. (season): .583 (1987)
- **Mookie Wilson (1980–89)**
Steals (career): 281
3B (career): 62

Pitching Records
- **John Franco (1990–present)**
Games (career): 485
Saves (season): 38 (1998)
Saves (career): 268

"To err is human, to forgive is a Mets fan."
— *Banner flown at the Polo Grounds in 1962, epitomizing the love early Mets supporters had for their hard-luck team*

- **Dwight Gooden (1984–94)**
ERA (season): 1.53 (1985)
Shutouts (season): 8 (1985)
- **Tom Seaver (1967–77, '83)**
Complete Games (season): 21 (1971)
Complete Games (career): 171
ERA (career): 2.57
Games Started (career): 395
Shutouts (career): 44
Strikeouts (season): 289 (1971)
Strikeouts (career): 2,541
Wins (season): 25 (1969)
Wins (career): 198
- **Turk Wendell (1997–present)**
Games (season): 80 (1999)

Managing Records
- **Davey Johnson (1984–90)**
Wins (career): 595

LEAGUE HONORS
NL Rookie of the Year
- Tom Seaver (1967)

Vital Stats

Stadium Address:
123–01 Roosevelt Ave., Flushing, N.Y.
Phone: (718) 507-METS
Web: mets.mlb.com
Box Office:
(718) 507-TIXX,
Mon.–Fri. 9–6, Sat.–Sun. 9–5, home games until fifth inning
Media Coverage:
Radio: WFAN (660 AM)
TV: WPIX-TV (Channel 11), Fox Sports NY
Spring Training:
Thomas J. White Stadium, Port St. Lucie, Fla.

- Jon Matlack (1972)
- Darryl Strawberry (1983)
- Dwight Gooden (1984)

NL Cy Young
- Tom Seaver (1969, '73, '75)
- Dwight Gooden (1985)

NL Gold Glove
- Keith Hernandez...............6
- Rey Ordonez.....................3
- Tommie Agee 1
- Ron Darling.......................1
- Doug Flynn 1
- Bud Harrelson...................1
- Robin Ventura...................1

Timeline

52

SHEA STADIUM: THE END APPROACHES

FOLLOWING IN THE FOOTSTEPS of many pro ball teams, the Mets have scheduled the construction of a modern facility, to be opened for the 2004 season. For Shea Stadium, the countdown has begun. The fifth-oldest ballpark in the majors, Shea is a large one, built with the splendor of the Roman Coliseum in mind. Over the years it has seen its share of exhilarating events: the free-for-all that followed the "Miracle Mets" victory in 1969, Tommie Agee's superhuman homer into the upper deck, two Beatles concerts and Bill Clinton's inspiring homage to Jackie Robinson on the 50th anniversary of the breaking of baseball's color barrier are just a few of Shea's momentous events.

CONCESSIONS

Although the food at Shea stadium is not considered to be of the highest quality, there is certainly no shortage of choice. Sausages, hamburgers, chicken, sushi, kosher and vegetarian options are all available. Go for the kosher hot dogs over the regular ones.

Stadium Facts

Opened: April 17, 1964
Cost: $28.5 million
Capacity: 56,521
Type: Outdoor
Surface: Bluegrass
Home Sweet Home:
• Shea Stadium is located along LaGuardia Airport's flight path, which renders it the noisiest ballpark in the majors.
• Visibility for hitters is the worst in MLB.

GAME DAY TIPS

• **Gate hours:** Gate C opens two-and-a-half hours before game time to allow fans in to watch batting practice. All other gates open one hour prior to game time.
• **Weather:** New York's hot and humid weather can be a factor even in early fall. Wear light clothing and a sun hat.
• **Prohibited items:** Cans, coolers, bottles and air horns are not allowed. Smoking is prohibited in the seat areas, but is allowed in designated areas along the concourse.
• **Ticket tips:** The Mets are very popular and they do not reserve any tickets for same-day sale. Seat choices can be quite limited and games against the Met's major rivals — Braves, Red Sox and Yankees — sell out very quickly.
• **Lost and found:** (718) 507-METS.

Directions: *From Grand Central Pkwy. or Whitestone Expwy., exit Northern Blvd./Shea Stadium. From northbound Van Wyck Expwy., exit Northern Blvd. west. By Subway: No. 7 IRT Flushing Line Subway. By Bus: Buses are available to and from the stadium. Call (718) 445-3100 for information.* **Parking:** *Shea's on-site lot holds 6,000 cars, with more spaces available in adjacent lots. Parking for the disabled can be accessed via the entrance on Roosevelt Ave. There is more parking on 126th St.*

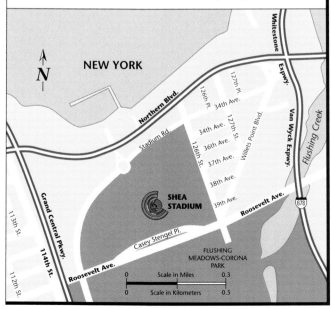

Seating Plan

▨	Inner Field Box	$43	■	Upper Reserved	$12
▨	Inner Loge Box	$43	■	Loge, Mezzanine	
▨	Outer Field Box	$33		Reserved Back Rows	$12
▨	Outer Loge Box	$33	ᴀᴛᴍ	Section 1	
▨	Mezzanine Box	$33	♿	Sections behind home	
■	Loge Reserved	$29		plate, end of left field,	
■	Mezzanine Reserved	$23		end of right field	
▨	Upper Box	$23			

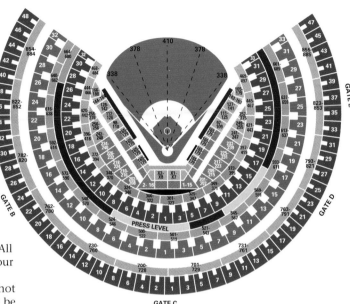

GATE C

Nearby Hotels

▼▼ **Best Western Eden Park** *(Motor Inn)*, 113-10 Corona Ave. (New York), (718) 699-4500, $99-$299
▼▼▼ **Courtyard by Marriott New York/LaGuardia Airport** *(Motor Inn)*, 90-10 Grand Central Pkwy. (New York), (718) 446-4800, $135-$249
▼▼▼ **La Guardia Marriott Hotel** *(Hotel)*, 102-05 Ditmars Blvd. (New York), (718) 565-8900, $165-$300
▼▼ **Pan American Hotel** *(Motor Inn)*, 79-00 Queens Blvd. (New York), (718) 446-7676, $109-$180
▼▼▼ **Wyndham Garden Hotel at La Guardia Airport** *(Motor Inn)*, 100-15 Ditmars Blvd. (New York), (718) 426-1500, $149-$339

Nearby Restaurants

▼ **Carnegie Delicatessen & Restaurant** *(American)*, 854 7th Ave. (New York), (212) 757-2245, $10-$30
▼▼▼ **Chin Chin** *(Chinese)*, 216 E. 49th St. (New York), (212) 888-4555, $12-$21
ESPN Zone *(American)*, 1472 Broadway (New York), (212) 921-3776, $9-$21
▼▼▼ **Fifty-Seven Fifty-Seven Restaurant** *(American)*, 57 E. 57th St. in the Four Seasons Hotel, New York (New York), (212) 758-5757, $28-$34
▼ **Mimi's Macaroni** *(Italian)*, 718 Amsterdam Ave. (New York), (212) 866-6311, $8-$15

NEW YORK YANKEES

THE MOST STORIED TEAM IN BASEBALL, the New York Yankees is also the most successful franchise in all of pro sports, with 26 World Series titles to its credit. Surprisingly, the Bronx Bombers didn't taste championship champagne until 1923, when they were led by the legendary Babe Ruth and his Herculean home-run swing. Ruth was the catalyst for a squad that got better each year, peaking in 1927 with the famed "Murderers' Row" lineup that many experts believe was the greatest team ever assembled. That year Ruth clobbered 60 home runs and Lou Gehrig drove in 175 runs, spurring the team to 110 wins and a World Series sweep of the Pittsburgh Pirates. Each successive generation of Yanks has added names to baseball's Hall of Fame: Phil Rizzuto, Whitey Ford, Joe DiMaggio, Yogi Berra, Mickey Mantle and Reggie Jackson are just a few of the luminaries who have shone their brightest while wearing Yankee pinstripes. And opening the new millennium with another World Series victory in 2000, modern Yankee stars such as Derek Jeter, Paul O'Neill and Bernie Williams promise to continue the tradition of excellence established by Ruth so long ago.

Winners of the 2000 World Series.

POSTSEASON
• World Series Titles.........26
(1923, '27, '28, '32, '36, '37, '38, '39, '41, '43, '47, '49, '50, '51, '52, '53, '56, '58, '61, '62, '77, '78, '96, '98, '99, 2000)

RETIRED NUMBERS
• Billy Martin (1)
• Babe Ruth (3)
• Lou Gehrig (4)
• Joe DiMaggio (5)
• Mickey Mantle (7)
• Yogi Berra (8)
• Bill Dickey (8)
• Roger Maris (9)
• Phil Rizzuto (10)
• Thurman Munson (15)
• Whitey Ford (16)
• Don Mattingly (23)
• Elston Howard (32)
• Casey Stengel (37)
• Reggie Jackson (44)

The Inside Pitch

• Former Yankee greats and a pair of popes are honored in Yankee Stadium's field-level Monument Park, open to ticket holders up to 45 minutes before games.
• In its first 20 years, the team never won a league title. However, the 1923 opening of Yankee Stadium seemed to change the franchise's fortunes. The team responded to its new digs by winning its first World Series that same year.

TEAM RECORDS
Hitting Records
• **Lou Gehrig (1923–39)**
Grand Slams (career): 23
Hits (career): 2,721
HRs (game): 4 (June 3, 1932)
RBIs (season): 184 (1931)
RBIs (career): 1,995
2B (career): 535
• **Rickey Henderson (1985–89)**
Steals (season): 93 (1988)
Steals (career): 326 (1988)
• **Mickey Mantle (1951–68)**
At-Bats: 8,102
Games: 2,401
• **Roger Maris (1960–66)**
HRs (season): 61 (1961)
• **Don Mattingly (1982–95)**
Grand Slams (season): 6 (1987)
Hits (season): 238 (1986)
2B (season): 53 (1986)
• **Babe Ruth (1920–34)**
Batting Avg. (season): .393 (1923)
Batting Avg. (career): .349
HRs (career): 659
Runs (season): 177 (1921)
Runs (career): 1,959

Pitching Records
• **Spud Chandler (1937–47)**
ERA (season): 1.64 (1943)
Winning Pct. (career): .717
• **Jack Chesbro (1903–09)**
Complete Games (season): 48 (1904)
Wins (season): 41 (1904)
• **Russ Ford (1909–13)**
ERA (career): 2.54
• **Whitey Ford (1950, 1953–67)**
Shutouts (career): 45

Strikeouts (career): 1,956
Wins (career): 236
• **Ron Guidry (1975–88)**
Shutouts (season): 9 (1978)
Strikeouts (season): 248 (1978)
Winning Pct. (season): .893 (1978)
• **Dave Righetti (1979, 1981–90)**
Saves (season): 46
Saves (career): 224

Managing Records
• **Joe McCarthy (1931–46)**
Wins (career): 1,460
World Series Titles: 7 (tie)
• **Casey Stengel (1949–60)**
World Series Titles: 7 (tie)
• **Joe Torre (1996–present)**
Wins (season): 114 (1998)

LEAGUE HONORS
AL MVP
• **Lou Gehrig** (1927, '36)
• **Joe DiMaggio** (1939, '41, '47)
• **Joe Gordon** (1942)
• **Spud Chandler** (1943)
• **Phil Rizzuto** (1950)
• **Yogi Berra** (1951, '54, '55)
• **Mickey Mantle**

"To have the chance to play at Yankee Stadium and be on their team — I must be one of the lucky ones."
— 2000 World Series MVP Derek Jeter

(1956, '57, '62)
• **Roger Maris** (1960, '61)
• **Elston Howard** (1963)
• **Thurman Munson** (1976)
• **Don Mattingly** (1985)

AL Rookie of the Year
• Gil McDonald (1951)
• Bob Grim (1954)
• Tony Kubek (1957)
• Tom Tresh (1962)
• Stan Bahnsen (1968)
• Thurman Munson (1970)
• Dave Righetti (1981)
• Derek Jeter (1996)

AL Cy Young
• Bob Turley (1958)
• Whitey Ford (1961)
• Sparky Lyle (1977)
• Ron Guidry (1978)

Vital Stats

Stadium Address:
161st St. & River Ave., New York, N.Y.
Phone: (718) 293-4300
Web: yankees.mlb.com
Box Office:
(718) 293-6000, daily 9–5
Media Coverage:
Radio: WABC (770 AM)
TV: WNYW (Channel 5), Madison Square Garden Network
Spring Training:
Legends Field, Tampa, Fla.

Timeline

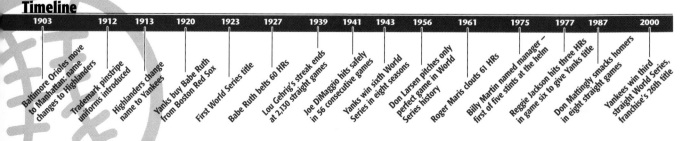

1903	1912	1913	1920	1923	1927	1939	1941	1943	1956	1961	1975	1977	1987	2000
Baltimore Orioles move to Manhattan; name changes to Highlanders	Highlanders change name to Yankees	Trademark pinstripe uniforms introduced	Yanks buy Babe Ruth from Boston Red Sox	First World Series title	Babe Ruth belts 60 HRs	Lou Gehrig's streak ends at 2,130 straight games	Joe DiMaggio hits safely in 56 consecutive games	Yanks win sixth World Series in eight seasons	Don Larsen pitches only perfect game in World Series history	Roger Maris clouts 61 HRs	Billy Martin named manager — first of five stints at the helm	Reggie Jackson hits three HRs in game six to give Yanks title	Don Mattingly smacks homers in eight straight games	Yankees win third straight World Series, franchise's 26th title

54

YANKEE STADIUM: HOME OF CHAMPIONS

OPENED IN 1923 to capitalize on Babe Ruth's incredible draw at the gate, Yankee Stadium stands as one of the world's most famous sporting venues. Over the years, it has been the site of numerous memorable moments, including the tearful retirement of Lou Gehrig, Don Larsen's perfect game in the 1956 World Series, an NFL title game and even a pair of papal addresses. The stadium's colorful history makes it one of the best places in which to watch a game.

CONCESSIONS

Yankees fans won't suffer any lack of options here. Spectators can indulge in pizza, chicken, hamburgers, Mexican food, sausages, kosher, baked goods, vegetarian, ice cream and various sandwiches.

Stadium Facts

Opened: April 18, 1923
Cost: $2.5 million
Capacity: 55,070
Type: Outdoor
Surface: Grass
Home Sweet Home:
• While opposing batters have to stare at a sea of white-shirted fans in the bleachers, a hitter-friendly green screen is lowered when the Yankees bat.
• Catchers love the large foul territory behind home plate.

GAME DAY TIPS

• **Gate hours:** Gates open 90 minutes prior to games on week nights and two hours prior to games on weekends.
• **Weather:** New York can be notoriously humid in the summer and early fall. Light summer clothing is best.
• **Prohibited items:** Cans, bottles (glass or plastic), jugs, coolers and hard containers of any kind are prohibited. Smoking is prohibited.
• **Ticket tips:** Box seats aren't always easy to get, especially when the Yankees play the Boston Red Sox and their crosstown rivals, the New York Mets. The bleachers offer decent views at affordable prices, but be warned: The fans here are very vocal.
• **Lost and found:** (718) 579-4409.

Seating Plan

■ Legends Suites	N/A		■ Tier Boxes	$33
■ Field Championship	$65		■ Main Reserved	$33
■ Loge Championship	$65		■ Tier Reserved	$17
■ Main Championship	$55		■ Bleachers	$8
■ Field Boxes	$42			
■ Main Boxes	$47		**PREMIUM SEATING**	
■ Loge Boxes	$42		■ Club Level	N/A
■ Main Reserved Level	$37		■ Loge Suites	N/A
■ Main Boxes	$37		ATM Sections 229/235, 280/288	
■ Loge Boxes	$37		♿ Throughout	

55

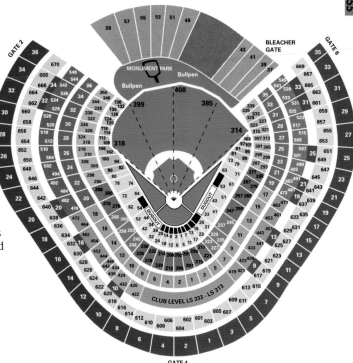

Directions: *Exits from Major Deegan Expwy. (I-87) are at 149th St. and 155th St. northbound and at 161st St. southbound. By Subway: On IND 6th Ave. line, take D train of CC local; on IRT Lexington Ave. line, take No. 4 Woodlawn. By Bus: Buses are available to and from the stadium. Call NYC Transit Authority at (718) 330-1234 for information. **Parking:** There are numerous parking lots on Jerome and River Aves. and E. 153rd and E. 161st Sts. Many have wheelchair parking spots.*

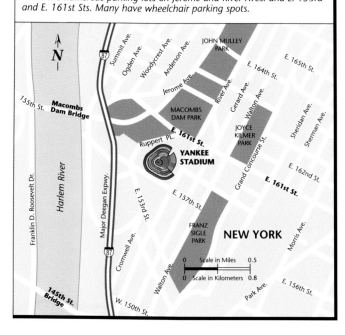

Nearby Hotels

▼▼▼▼▼ **Four Seasons Hotel, New York** (*Hotel*), 57 E. 57th St. (New York), (212) 785-5700, $595-$990
▼ **Hotel Newton** (*Motel*), 2528 Broadway (New York), (212) 678-6500, $95-$175
▼▼▼▼ **Omni Berkshire Place** (*Hotel*), 21 E. 52nd St. (New York), (212) 753-5800, $215-$368
▼▼▼ **Ramada Plaza Hotel** (*Hotel*), 1 Ramada Plaza (New Rochelle), (914) 576-3700, $169-$179
▼▼▼▼ **The Waldorf-Astoria** (*Classic Hotel*), 301 Park Ave. (New York), (212) 872-4800, $205-$765

Nearby Restaurants

▼ **Carnegie Delicatessen & Restaurant** (*American*), 854 7th Ave. (New York), (212) 757-2245, $10-$30
▼▼▼ **Chin Chin** (*Chinese*), 216 E. 49th St. (New York), (212) 888-4555, $12-$21
▼▼▼ **Fifty-Seven Fifty-Seven Restaurant** (*American*), 57 E. 57th St. in the Four Seasons Hotel, New York (New York), (212) 758-5757, $28-$34
▼ **Mimi's Macaroni** (*Italian*), 718 Amsterdam Ave. (New York), (212) 866-6311, $8-$15
Serendipity (*American*), 225 E. 60th St. (New York), (212) 838-3531, $6-$20

OAKLAND ATHLETICS

THE STORY OF THE ATHLETICS is one of big wins and desperate losses. The A's have won 15 American League titles — second only to the Yankees — but have also finished last a whopping 27 times. Started in Philadelphia in 1901 with manager Connie Mack at the helm, the franchise matured fast, capturing six league pennants by 1914. Led by early stars such as Eddie Collins, Frank "Home Run" Barry and pitching legend Jack Coombs, the Athletics ruled the field until 1915, when Mack began to sell off his winning team. Setting a record for managerial longevity, Mack continued to guide the Athletics through a series of wins and slumps until 1950, when he passed ownership to his sons and retired. Without Mack, the Athletics sank fast. After a series of devastating losses and dwindling attendance, the Mack brothers sold their father's legacy and the team was moved to Kansas City in 1954. It wasn't until 1968 that the Athletics arrived in Oakland, a move that proved to be a blessing. In 1969 a young Reggie Jackson blistered 47 homers to carry the team to second place in the AL West — a harbinger of great things to come. With a new manager, Dick Williams, and three great pitchers, Vida Blue, Catfish Hunter and Rollie Fingers, in 1972 the team began a three-year stint as World Series champions. With Rickey Henderson, Dave Stewart and the "Bash Brothers" Jose Canseco and Mark McGwire on the roster, the team won another championship in 1989. After several years of mediocre play, the Athletics won the AL West in 2000. History suggests that a World Series title isn't far off.

Vital Stats

Stadium Address:
7000 Coliseum Wy.,
Oakland, Calif.
Phone: (510) 569-2121
Web: athletics.mlb.com
Box Office:
(510) 638-4627,
Mon.–Fri. 10–6, Sat. 10–4
Media Coverage:
Radio: KABL (960 AM)
TV: KICU (Channel 36),
Fox Sports Net
Spring Training:
Phoenix Municipal
Stadium, Phoenix, Ariz.

POSTSEASON
- World Series Titles...........9
(1910, '11, '13, '29, '30, '72, '73, '74, '89)
- AL Pennants.................15
(1902, '05, '10, '11, '13, '14, '29, '30, '31, '72, '73, '74, '88, '89, '90)
- AL West Titles 11
(1971, '72, '73, '74, '75, '81, '88, '89, '90, '92, 2000)

Jason Giambi is one of base-ball's most powerful sluggers.

RETIRED NUMBERS
- Jim "Catfish" Hunter (27)
- Rollie Fingers (34)

TEAM RECORDS
Hitting Records
- **Bert Campaneris (1964–76)**
At-Bats (career): 7,180
Hits (career): 1,882
- **Jimmy Foxx (1925–35)**
Extra-Base Hits (season): 100 (1932)
HRs (season): 58 (1932)
RBIs (season): 169 (1932)
Slugging Pct. (career): .640
- **Jason Giambi (1995–present)**
Grand Slams (season): 4 (2000)
- **Rickey Henderson (1979–84, 1989–95, '98)**

The Inside Pitch

- *The fan phenomenon known as the "wave" was first seen in 1981 when dugout-hopping "Crazy George" organized the fans to wave together.*
- *The A's nine World Series titles ties them with the Cards for second place on the all-time list. The Yankees are way out in front with 26 championships under their belt.*

"I want to thank you for this honor."
— Part of a full-page ad taken out by Jason Giambi, thanking fans for voting him to the All-Star team

Runs (career): 1,270
Steals (season): 130 (1982)
Steals (career): 867
- **Reggie Jackson (1968–75, '87)**
RBIs (game): 10 (June 14, 1969)
- **Nap Lajoie (1901–02)**
Batting Avg. (season): .426 (1901)
- **Mark McGwire (1986–97)**
HRs (career): 363
- **Al Simmons (1924–32, 1940–41, '44)**
Batting Avg. (career): .356
RBIs (career): 1,178
Runs (season): 152 (1930)
Total Bases (career): 2,998

Pitching Records
- **Dennis Eckersley (1987–95)**
Saves (season): 51 (1992)
Saves (career): 320
- **Jack Coombs (1906–14)**
ERA (season): 1.30 (1910)
Shutouts (season): 13 (1910)
Wins (season): 31 (tie) (1910)
- **Lefty Grove (1925–33)**
Wins (season): 31 (tie) (1931)
Winning Pct. (season):

.886 (1931)
- **Eddie Plank (1901–14)**
Complete Games (career): 362
Shutouts (career): 59
Strikeouts (career): 1,985
Wins (career): 284
- **Rube Waddell (1902–07)**
ERA (career): 1.97
Strikeouts (season): 349 (1904)

LEAGUE HONORS
AL MVP
- Eddie Collins (1914)
- Mickey Cochrane (1928)
- Lefty Grove (1931)
- Jimmy Foxx (1932)
- Bobby Shantz (1952)
- Vida Blue (1971)
- Reggie Jackson (1973)
- José Canseco (1988)
- Rickey Henderson (1990)
- Dennis Eckersley (1992)
- Jason Giambi (2000)

AL Rookie of the Year
- Harry Byrd (1952)
- José Canseco (1986)
- Mark McGwire (1987)
- Walt Weiss (1988)
- Ben Grieve (1998)

AL Cy Young
- Vida Blue (1971)
- Jim "Catfish" Hunter (1974)
- Bob Welch (1990)
- Dennis Eckersley (1992)

Timeline

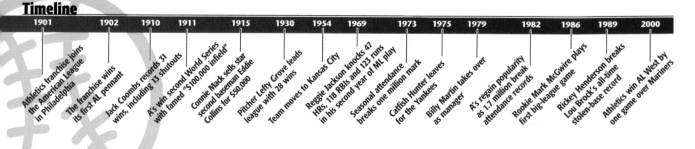

| 1901 | 1902 | 1910 | 1911 | 1915 | 1930 | 1954 | 1969 | 1973 | 1975 | 1979 | 1982 | 1986 | 1989 | 2000 |

Athletics franchise joins the American League in Philadelphia

The franchise wins its first AL pennant

Jack Coombs records 31 wins, including 13 shutouts

A's win second World Series with famed "$100,000 infield"

Connie Mack sells star second baseman Eddie Collins for $50,000

Pitcher Lefty Grove leads league with 28 wins

Team moves to Kansas City

Reggie Jackson knocks 47 HRs, 118 RBIs and 123 runs in his second year of ML play

Seasonal attendance breaks one million mark

Catfish Hunter leaves for the Yankees

Billy Martin takes over as manager

A's regain popularity as 1.7 million break attendance records

Rookie Mark McGwire plays first big-league game

Rickey Henderson breaks Lou Brock's all-time stolen-base record

Athletics win AL West by one game over Mariners

56

NETWORK ASSOCIATES COLISEUM: THE NET

FORMERLY THE OAKLAND-ALAMEDA COUNTY STADIUM, the home of the Athletics is now known affectionately as "the Net." Opened in 1966, it was this sunny new ballpark that lured Kansas City A's owner Charles O. Finley to move his team west two years later. Since then, the Coliseum has hosted 36 postseason games, 22 of which the team has won in front of hometown fans. In some disrepair and with the scoreboard not working during the late 1970s, the ballpark gained the unfortunate nickname "the Mausoleum." The park underwent major reconstructive surgery in the 1990s and is once again viewed fondly by fans.

CONCESSIONS

Food at "the Net" is among the best found in today's baseball parks. The longest lines in the park are usually for the garlic fries. In addition to the usual ballpark offerings, a Black Muslim bakery offers veggie and tofu burgers, as well as carrot and bean pies.

Stadium Facts

Opened: Sept. 18, 1966
Cost: $25.5 million
Capacity: 43,662
Type: Outdoor
Surface: Bluegrass
Home Sweet Home:
• The Coliseum's large foul area reduces batting averages by about five to seven points, making it the best pitcher's park in the AL.

GAME DAY TIPS

• **Gate hours:** Gates open two hours prior to games.
• **Weather:** Summers are usually warm and sunny, with virtually no rain, but occasional heavy fog.
• **Prohibited items:** Cans, bottles, large coolers and alcohol are all prohibited. Umbrellas, video or movie cameras, and poles are also not allowed. Smoking is permitted only in designated areas.
• **Ticket tips:** Tickets for all sections are inexpensive and easy to come by, especially in the upper deck. Spots along the foul poles allow fans to reach out in

Seating Plan

■ Plaza Club	$30		■ Plaza Bleachers	$6
■ MVP Infield	$25		■ Barbecue Plaza	$25
■ Field Level Infield	$19		■ Loge Suites	$500-770
■ Field Level	$19		■ Club Suites	$750-900
■ Plaza Level Infield	$18		■ Plaza Suites	$770
■ Loge Seats	$18		■ Sky View Terrace	$800
■ Plaza Level	$16		ATM Section 120, Gate C, Gate D	
■ Upper Reserved	$8		♿ Sections in 100s	
■ Bleachers	$6			

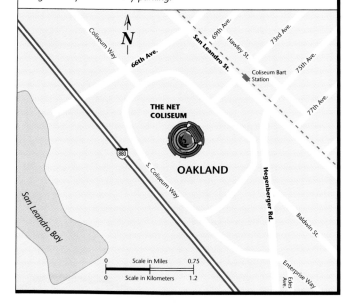

front of the foul screen and catch fair home runs.

• **Lost and found:** (510) 383-4660.

Directions: From I-880, exit at 66th Ave. or Hegenberger Rd. E. and follow east to main entrances. By Bus: Bay Area Rapid Transit arrives near the eastern plaza of the Coliseum. For more information, call BART at (510) 465-2278. **Parking:** There are 11,000 parking spots available at the Coliseum, 143 of which are wheelchair accessible. Signs are posted on game days for auxiliary parking.

Nearby Hotels

▼▼▼ **Best Western Inn at the Square** *(Motel)*, 233 Broadway at entrance to Jack London Square (Oakland), (510) 452-4565, $89-$149
▼▼▼ **Clarion Suites Lake Merritt Hotel** *(Historic Hotel)*, 1800 Madison St. (Oakland), (510) 832-2300, $179-$299
▼▼▼ **Comfort Inn & Suites** *(Motel)*, 8452 Edes Ave. (Oakland), (510) 568-1500, $117-$127
▼▼▼ **Holiday Inn-Oakland Airport/Coliseum** *(Motor Inn)*, 500 Hegenberger Rd. (Oakland), (510) 562-5311, $89-$139
▼▼▼ **Waterfront Plaza Hotel** *(Hotel)*, Ten Washington St. (Oakland), (510) 836-3800, $190-$325

Nearby Restaurants

▼▼▼ **Bay Wolf Restaurant** *(Californian)*, 3853 Piedmont Ave. (Oakland), (510) 655-6004, $30-$34
▼▼▼ **Garibaldi's on College** *(Californian)*, 5356 College Ave. (Oakland), (510) 595-4000, $13-$20
▼▼▼ **Il Pescatore Restaurant** *(Italian)*, 57 Jack London Square (Oakland), (510) 465-2188, $10-$19
▼▼▼ **Oliveto Café & Restaurant** *(Italian)*, 5655 College Ave. (Oakland), (510) 547-5356, $30-$60
▼▼ **Quinn's Lighthouse Restaurant & Pub** *(Seafood)*, 51 Embarcadero Cove (Oakland), (510) 536-2050, $6-$16

PHILADELPHIA PHILLIES

THE PHILADELPHIA PHILLIES BEGAN PLAYING IN 1883 when sporting goods tycoon Al Reach bought the struggling Worcester Brown Stockings and brought them to his hometown. Success was anything but immediate. It took the Phillies 32 years to win the team's first pennant, a 1915 title won largely on the arm of legendary hurler Grover Cleveland Alexander. It took the team another 35 years to capture its second pennant behind "the Whiz Kids," led by young phenoms Robin Roberts and Richie Ashburn. Unfortunately, neither squad attained the ultimate prize of a world championship. That honor would elude the franchise and its perennially frustrated fans until 1980, when a star-studded lineup anchored by future Hall-of-Famers Steve Carlton and Mike Schmidt led Philadelphia to a six-game World Series win over Kansas City. That team, which dominated the National League during much of the 1970s and '80s, set a new tradition of success for the Phillies. The team has been back to the series twice since, in 1983 and '93. While another visit to the fall classic does not appear imminent right now, young stars Scott Rolen and Mike Lieberthal can count on lots of support from the Phillies' vocal fans.

Vital Stats

Stadium Address:
3501 S. Broad St.,
Philadelphia, Pa.
Phone: (215) 685-1500
Web: phillies.mlb.com
Box Office:
(215) 463-1000,
Mon.–Fri. 9–5,
home games 9–8
Media Coverage:
Radio: WPHT (1210 AM)
TV: WPSG (Channel 57),
Comcast SportsNet
Spring Training:
Jack Russell Memorial
Stadium, Clearwater, Fla.

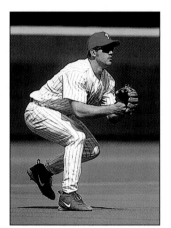

Third baseman Scott Rolen has won two Gold Gloves.

The Inside Pitch

• To mark the opening of Veterans Stadium on April 4, 1971, the ceremonial first pitch was dropped from a helicopter hovering above the field to catcher Mike Ryan, who almost lost the ball, but hung on.
• The Philly Phanatic is one the most recognizable mascots in sport. Named for the team's diehard fans, it debuted in 1978.

POSTSEASON
• World Series Titles 1
(1980)
• NL Pennants.....................5
(1915, '50, '80, '83, '93)
• NL East Titles 6
(1976, '77, '78, '80, '83, '93)

RETIRED NUMBERS
• Rich Ashburn (1)
• Mike Schmidt (20)
• Steve Carlton (32)
• Robin Roberts (36)

TEAM RECORDS
Hitting Records
• **Ed Delahanty**
(1888–89, 1891–1901)
2B (career): 432
3B (career): 151
• **Lenny Dykstra (1989–98)**
Walks (season): 129 (1993)
• **Billy Hamilton (1890–95)**
Batting Avg. (career): .362
Runs (season): 196 (1894)
Steals (season):115 (1891)
• **Chuck Klein (1928–33)**
RBIs (season): 170 (1930)
2B (season): 59 (1930)
• **Sherry Magee (1904–14)**
Steals (career): 387
• **Lefty O'Doul (1929–30)**
Hits (season): 254 (1929)
• **Mike Schmidt (1972–89)**
Grand Slams (career): 7
Hits (career): 2,234

HRs (season): 48 (1980)
HRs (career): 548
RBIs (career): 1,595
Runs (career): 1,506
Strikeouts (career): 1,883
Walks (career): 1,507
• **Sam Thompson (1889–98)**
3B (season): 27 (1894)
• **Tuck Turner (1893–96)**
Batting Avg. (season):
.416 (1894)

Pitching Records
• **Grover Alexander**
(1911–17, '30)
ERA (season): 1.22 (1915)
ERA (career): 2.18
Shutouts (season): 16 (1916)
Shutouts (career): 61
Winning percentage
(career): .676
20-Win Seasons: 6
• **Steve Bedrosian (1986–89)**
Saves (career): 103
• **Steve Carlton (1972–86)**
Starts (career): 499
Strikeouts (career): 3,031
Wins (career): 241
• **Kid Gleason**
(1888–91, 1903–08)
Wins (season): 38 (1890)
• **Al Orth (1895–1901)**
Winning Pct. (season):
.824 (1899)
• **Robin Roberts (1948–61)**
Games (career): 529
Complete Games
(career): 272
• **Curt Schilling (1992–2000)**
Strikeouts (season): 319
(1997)
• **Mitch Williams (1991–93)**
Saves (season): 43 (1993)

Managing Records
• **Gene Mauch (1960–68)**
Wins (career): 645
• **Danny Ozark (1973–1979)**
Wins (season): 101 (1976, '77)

LEAGUE HONORS
NL MVP
• **Chuck Klein (1932)**
• **Jim Konstanty (1950)**
• **Mike Schmidt**
(1980, '81, '86)

NL Rookie of the Year
• **Jack Sanford (1957)**
• **Richie Allen (1964)**
• **Scott Rolen (1997)**

NL Cy Young
• **Steve Carlton**
(1972, '77, '80, '82)
• **John Denny (1983)**
• **Steve Bedrosian (1987)**

NL Gold Glove
• **Mike Schmidt**.................10
• **Garry Maddox**.................8
• **Manny Trillo** 3
• **Bob Boone** 2
• **Larry Bowa**.........................2
• **Jim Kaat**.............................2
• **Scott Rolen** 2
• **Ruben Amaro** 1
• **Steve Carlton** 1
• **Mike Liberthal** 1
• **Bobby Shantz**.....................1
• **Bill White** 1
• **Bobby Wine**.......................1

"I ain't an athlete, lady, I'm a baseball player."
— John Kruk, popular Philly, on being chastised by a fan who thought his off-field carousing was ill-becoming of a professional athlete

Timeline

1883	1887	1915	1938	1932	1950	1957	1971	1976	1980	1989	1993	1997
The Worcester Brown Stockings are moved to Philadelphia and renamed the Phillies	The Phillies move into Baker Bowl	The Phillies win their first NL pennant	Phillies move to Shibe Park, until then exclusive home of the Athletics	Chuck Klein is the Phillies' first NL MVP	Robin Roberts wins 20 games, the first of six straight 20-win seasons	Jack Sanford is the Phillies' first Rookie of the Year	Phillies move into Veterans Stadium	Phillies win the first of three consecutive NL championships	The Phillies win the World Series	Mike Schmidt retires	The Phillies win their fifth NL pennant after beating the favored Atlanta Braves 4-2	Curt Schilling sets team record with 319 strikeouts in season

58

VETERANS STADIUM: THE TOUGHEST FANS IN BASEBALL

OPENED IN 1971 to replace 65-year-old Shibe Park, Veterans Stadium is known more for its irascible fans than for its architecture. The move proved to be good for the team, which won three straight NL East titles beginning in 1976. Located on a 74-acre site in South Philly that also houses CoreStates Arena, home of the NHL's Flyers and the NBA's 76ers, the rounded rectangular stadium has the largest capacity of any major-league ballpark. Inside you'll find comfortable seats, excellent concessions and the loudest boos in all of baseball. Plans for a new stadium are currently underway.

CONCESSIONS

Local Philly favorites are soft pretzels, Italian sandwiches, hoagies and cheese steaks. There are also several fine dining establishments.

Stadium Facts

Opened: *April 4, 1971*
Cost: *$50 million*
Capacity: *62,418*
Type: *Outdoor*
Surface: *AstroTurf*
Home Sweet Home:
• *The turf at Veterans Stadium is notoriously bad. Worn seams can turn routine ground balls into adventures for fielders.*
• *Phillies fans are considered among the loudest in baseball — heckling players to the point of distraction.*

GAME DAY TIPS

• **Gate hours:** Gates open 90 minutes prior to games on weekdays and two hours prior to games on weekends.
• **Weather:** Philadelphia is warm and humid in the summer. Wear light clothing, but be prepared for the occasional rain shower.
• **Prohibited items:** Cans, bottles, alcohol and animals are prohibited. Coolers are permitted if they do not contain alcohol. Smoking is allowed only in designated areas.
• **Ticket tips:** The first base side is exposed to the most sun, which can make it very hot in the summer. Some seats, mainly the 300 level under the balcony, have partially obstructed views.
• **Lost and found:** (215) 685-1534.

Seating Plan

- ■ **Level-Field Box** $24
- ■ **Terrace Box (Outfield)** ... $20
- ■ **300 Level-Terrace Box** .. $20
- ■ **500 Level-Loge Box** $18
- ■ **600 Level-Reserved** $14
- □ **700 Level-Reserved** $8
- □ **General Admission Adult** $8
- □ **General Admission Child** $5
- ᴀᴛᴍ **Section 224**
- ♿ **Outfield 200s; 300s**

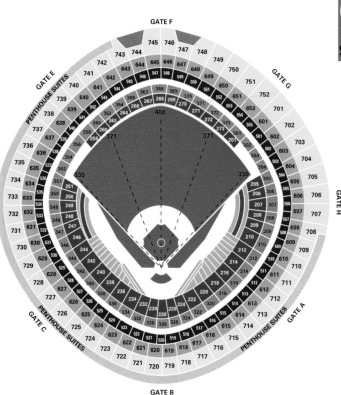

Directions: *From I-95 north, take exit 15 and follow to Packer Ave., then to 10th St. Turn left onto 10th St. to the Sports Complex. From I-95 south, take exit 15 and follow signs to Sports Complex. Turn right at bottom of ramp onto Front St., then right onto Packer Ave. and follow to 10th St. Turn left onto 10th St. to the Sports Complex. By Subway: SEPTA Broad St. Subway Line to Pattison Ave. stop. By Bus: Route C bus southbound to Broad St.* **Parking:** *Lots on S. Darien, S. 11th and S. Broad streets can hold 10,000 cars. Wheelchair-accessible lots are next to gates A, B and F.*

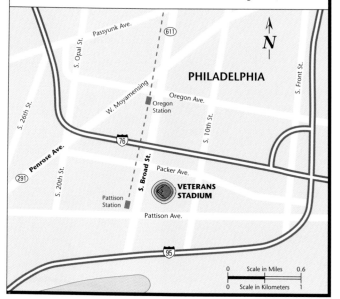

Nearby Hotels

▼▼▼ **Courtyard by Marriott Airport** *(Motor Inn)*, 8900 Bartram Ave. (Philadelphia), (215) 365-2200, $159-$219
▼▼▼ **Hampton Inn-Philadelphia Airport** *(Motel)*, 8600 Bartram Ave. (Philadelphia), (215) 966-1300, $139-$169
▼▼▼ **Hilton Philadelphia Airport** *(Hotel)*, 4509 Island Ave. (Philadelphia), (215) 365-4150, $135-$195
▼▼▼ **Holiday Inn Philadelphia Stadium** *(Hotel)*, 900 Packer Ave. (Philadelphia), (215) 755-9500, $89-$149
▼▼▼ **Philadelphia Fairfield Inn** *(Motel)*, 8800 Bartram Ave. (Philadelphia), (215) 365-2254, $100

Nearby Restaurants

▼▼ **Bistro Romano** *(Italian)*, 120 Lombard St. (Philadelphia), (215) 925-8880, $10-$24
▼▼▼ **The Continental Restaurant & Martini Bar** *(Continental)*, 138 Market St. (Philadelphia), (215) 923-6069, $6-$19
▼▼ **Downey's Restaurant** *(American)*, 526 S. Front St. (Philadelphia), (215) 625-9500, $16-$20
▼ **Engine 46 Steak House** *(American)*, 10 Reed St. (Philadelphia), (215) 462-4646, $5-$19
▼▼▼ **The Plough and the Stars Irish Restaurant & Bar** *(Continental)*, 123 Chestnut St. (Philadelphia), (215) 733-0300, $14-$21

PITTSBURGH PIRATES

THE PIRATES BEGAN as the Pittsburgh Alleghenies in 1876, but switched names in 1890 after Philadelphia Athletics' management accused it of "pirating" A's second baseman Louis Bierbauer. Hapless in the early years, the Pirates' fortunes changed in 1900, when the National League went from 12 teams to eight. As a result, the Pirates were able to add 14 Louisville players to the roster, including future Hall-of-Famers Honus Wagner, Rube Waddell and Fred Clarke. The Pirates won pennants in 1901, '02 and '03 and the World Series in 1909, with Wagner winning seven batting titles over the decade. After languishing near the bottom of the standings for much of the next 15 years, the Pirates surged again in the early 1920s. In '25 a crop of young talent, including Rabbit Maranville and Kiki Cuyler, led the team to the NL title and, with an unlikely 15-hit pounding of Washington's Walter "Big Train" Johnson in game seven, the World Series crown. Pittsburgh didn't reach the fall classic again until 1960, when, led by All-Star Roberto Clemente, the team took on the favored Yankees. With game seven tied in the bottom of the ninth inning, Pirates second baseman Bill Mazeroski struck what may be the most dramatic home run ever to clinch the title for the Bucs. Drama was again high in the team's WS wins in 1971 and '79, both seven-game epics against Baltimore. In '79 the team followed veteran leader Willie Stargell to victory with the team's popular theme song *We Are Family* playing in the background. After narrowly missing visits to the World Series three times in the early '90s, today's Pirates have a new stadium and a talented young team that fans hope can lead them back to baseball's coveted prize.

Jason Kendall led the Pirates with 112 runs, 185 hits and a .320 average in 2000.

POSTSEASON
• World Series Titles 5
(1909, '25, '60, '71, '79)
• NL Pennants.....................9
(1901, '02, '03, '09, '25, '27, '60, '71, '79)
• NL East Titles 9
(1970, '71, '72, '74, '75, '79, '90, '91, '92)

RETIRED NUMBERS
• Billy Meyer (1)
• Ralph Kiner (4)
• Willie Stargell (8)
• Bill Mazeroski (9)
• Pie Traynor (20)
• Roberto Clemente (21)
• Honus Wagner (33)
• Danny Murtaugh (40)

TEAM RECORDS
Hitting Records
• Roberto Clemente
(1955–72)

The Inside Pitch

• The first home run in World Series history was hit by Jimmy Sebring of the Pirates. He swatted an offering from Boston's Cy Young in the first inning of Game 1 at the Huntington Avenue Grounds in 1903.

At-Bats (career): 9,454
Games (career): 2,433
Hits (career): 3,000
Total Bases (career): 4,492
• **Omar Moreno (1975–82)**
Steals (season): 96 (1980)
• **Ralph Kiner (1946–53)**
HRs (season): 54 (1949)
Slugging Pct. (season): .658 (1949)
Walks (season): 137 (1951)
• **Willie Stargell (1962–82)**
Extra-Base Hits (season): 90 (1973)
Extra-Base Hits (career): 953
HRs (career): 475
RBIs (career): 1,540
• **Jake Stenzel (1892–96)**
Runs (season): 148 (1894)
• **Arky Vaughan (1932–41)**
Batting Avg. (season): .385 (1935)
• **Honus Wagner (1900–17)**
Runs (career): 1,521
3B (career): 232
• **Paul Waner (1926–40)**
Batting Avg. (career): .340
Hits (season): 237 (1927)
RBIs (season): 131 (1927)
2B (career): 558
2B (season): 62 (1932)
• **Chief Wilson (1908–13)**
3B (season): 36 (1912)

Pitching Records
• **Howie Camnitz (1904, 1906–13)**
ERA (season): 1.56 (1908)
• **Wilbur Cooper (1912–24)**
Complete Games (career): 263
Starts (season): 48 (1921, '23)
Wins (career): 202
• **Jim Gott (1987–89)**
Saves (season): 34 (1988)
• **Burleigh Grimes (1916–17, 1928–29, '34)**
Innings Pitched (season): 330.2 (1928)
• **Bob Friend (1951–65)**
Innings Pitched (career): 3,480.1
Walks (career): 869
• **Frank Killen (1893–98)**
Starts (season): 48 (1893)
Wins (season): 34 (1893)
• **Ed Morris (1887–89)**
Complete Games (season): 54 (1888)
• **Kent Tekulve (1975–82)**
Games (season): 94 (1979)
Saves (career): 158
• **Bob Veale (1962–72)**
Strikeouts (season): 276 (1965)
• **Vic Willis (1906–09)**
ERA (career): 2.09

"I feel as much a part of this city as the cobblestone streets and the steel mills."
— Willie Stargell, on playing in Pittsburgh

Vital Stats

Stadium Address:
PNC Park at North Shore, 115 Federal St., Pittsburgh, Pa.
Phone: (412) 323-5000
Web: pirates.mlb.com
Box Office:
(412) 321-2827, Mon.–Sat. 8:30–6
Media Coverage:
Radio: KDKA (1020 AM)
TV: WCWB (Channel 12), Fox Sports Net
Spring Training:
McKechnie Field, Bradenton, Fla.

Managing Records
• **Fred Clarke (1900–15)**
Wins (season): 110 (1909)
Wins (career): 1,422
Winning Pct. (career): .595

LEAGUE HONORS
NL MVP
• Dick Groat (1960)
• Roberto Clemente (1966)
• Dave Parker (1978)
• Willie Stargell (tie) (1979)
• Barry Bonds (1992, '93)

NL Cy Young
• Vernon Law (1960)
• Doug Drabek (1990)

NL Manager of the Year
• Jim Leyland (1990, '92)

Timeline

1876	1890	1901	1909	1917	1925	1927	1935	1946	1955	1960	1979	1990	2001

Pittsburgh Alleghenies play first pro baseball game in Pittsburgh

Alleghenies change name to Pirates

Pirates win first NL Pennant, winning 90 games on the season

Pittsburgh wins first World Series title, 4-3 over Detroit

Longtime Pirate star Honus Wagner retires

Pirates come back from a 3-to-1 games deficit to defeat Washington in WS

Babe Ruth slams four homers as Yankees defeat Pirates in WS

Shortston Arky Vaughan wins NL batting title with .385 average

Ralph Kiner begins streak of seven straight seasons in which he wins or shares NL home-run title

Pirates sign outfielder Roberto Clemente

Bill Mazeroski hits ninth-inning home run to win WS

Willie "Pops" Stargell leads Pirates to seven-game World Series win over Orioles

Pirates win first of three consecutive NL East Division titles

Bill Mazeroski is voted into the Hall of Fame

PNC PARK: A COZY GEM

BUILT ON THE ALLEGHENY RIVER a city block from where Three Rivers Stadium used to be, PNC Park is the second-smallest facility in the majors, next to Boston's Fenway Park. In designing PNC, organizers focused on quality of experience rather than capacity. The park holds just over 38,000 spectators, but provides a natural grass surface, seating close to the action (the highest seat is just 88 feet from the field) and perhaps the best city-skyline view in baseball. Players love PNC Park because the give of its grass surface reduces wear and tear on their knees. An outdoor amphitheater houses pre- and post-game events.

CONCESSIONS

Visitors to PNC Park can expect the full range of traditional ballpark favorites, such as pretzels, hot dogs, burgers and pizza. They can also choose from dozens of alternative food choices, including vegetarian, kosher and gourmet. One of the best new features in the new facility is the "Tastes of Pittsburgh," a multi-ethnic cuisine salute to the city's rich cultural heritage.

GAME DAY TIPS

• **Gate hours:** Gates open 90 minutes prior to games on weekdays and two hours prior to games on weekends.
• **Weather:** Summers in Pittsburgh are pleasant enough, with temperatures peaking around July. Bring a light jacket for nighttime games as the temperatures can dip noticeably.
• **Prohibited items:** Cans, glass bottles and alcohol are not allowed. Small snacks and juice boxes may be brought in, along with small coolers. Smoking is permitted only in designated areas.

Stadium Facts

Opened: *April 9, 2001*
Cost: *$228 million*
Capacity: *38,127*
Type: *Outdoor*
Surface: *Grass*
Home Sweet Home:
• *PNC is one of the smallest parks in the major leagues. The narrow foul territory and the lack of space between home plate and the stands makes it difficult for fielders to track down foul balls.*

Directions: *Take I-279 to Fort Duquesne Bridge, then follow signs to PNC Park. By Bus: Several routes stop next to the park. For information, call Port Authority of Allegheny County at (412) 442-2000.* **Parking:** *There are more than 9,800 parking spaces in 60 south shore lots and garages and on S. Commons, River and Martindale on the north shore.*

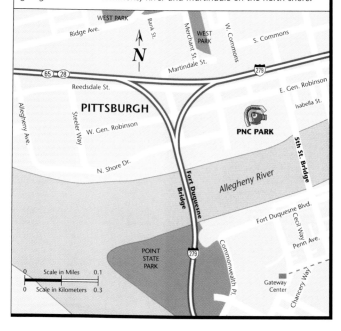

Seating Plan

■ Home Plate Club	N/A	▣ Grandstand	$16
■ Club Level	N/A	■ Club Level/	
■ Dugout Boxes	$35	Group Seating	$25
■ Baseline Boxes	$25	▢ Left/Right Field	
■ Infield Boxes	$25	Grandstand	$9
▢ Left/Right Field Boxes	$23	ATM Sections 105, 114, 119,	
■ Outfield Reserved	$16	125, 131, 134, 313, 319,	
▢ Deck Seating	$16	325; Home Plate Rotunda	
■ Bleachers	$12	♿ Throughout	

• **Ticket tips:** One of the park's great features is that it offers fans views of the city and the field from a restaurant in left field that has a party deck on the roof. There is also a picnic area on top of the right-field stands.
• **Lost and found:** (412) 325-4911.

Nearby Hotels

▼▼▼ **Doubletree Hotel Pittsburgh** (*Hotel*), 1000 Penn Ave. (Pittsburgh), (412) 281-3700, $99-$199
▼▼▼ **Hampton Inn** (*Motel*), 4575 McKnight Rd. (Pittsburgh), (412) 939-3200, $84-$94
▼▼▼ **Hampton Inn-University Center** (*Motel*), 3315 Hamlet St. (Pittsburgh), (412) 681-1000, $99-$109
▼▼▼ **Hilton Pittsburgh** (*Hotel*), in the Gateway Center opposite Point State Park (Pittsburgh), (412) 391-4600, $84-$219
▼▼▼ **Sheraton Station Square Hotel** (*Hotel*), 7 Station Square Dr. (Pittsburgh), (412) 261-2000, $139-$209

Nearby Restaurants

▼▼▼ **Grand Concourse Restaurant** (*Seafood*), 1 Station Square in Pittsburgh and Lake Erie Railroad Terminal Bldg. (Pittsburgh), (412) 261-1717, $17-$25
▼▼ **Kiku's of Japan** (*Japanese*), at Carson and Smithfield Sts. in the Shops at Station Square (Pittsburgh), (412) 765-3200, $15-$20
▼▼ **Pittsburgh Fishmarket Restaurant** (*Seafood*), 1000 Penn Ave., in the Doubletree Hotel Pittsburgh(Pittsburgh), (412) 227-3657, $12-$16
▼▼ **Khalil's II** (*Middle Eastern*), 4757 Baum Blvd. (Pittsburgh), (412) 683-4757, $9-$16
▼▼▼ **Le Mont Restaurant** (*American*), 1114 Grandview Ave. (Pittsburgh), (412) 431-3100, $22-$35 (dinner only)

ST. LOUIS CARDINALS

One of baseball's most feared sluggers, Mark McGwire is also a fan favorite.

St. Louis was a charter member of the National League in 1876, but it took the Cards many years to field a winning team. It wasn't until 1926, with legendary second baseman Rogers Hornsby acting as player/manager, that the team captured its first World Series, a seven-game showdown with the Yankees. That series featured 39-year-old pitcher Grover Cleveland Alexander winning the second and sixth games, and coming on to save the seventh in dramatic fashion. The Cards won two series in the 1930s, bringing life to depression-era St. Louis. The second, in 1934, featured the fun-loving "Gas House Gang." That team featured eccentric brothers Dizzy and Paul Dean, who amassed an incredible 49 wins between them during the season. Then the greatest Cardinal of all arrived in 1941, in the person of Stan "the Man" Musial. He batted .315 that year, the first of 17 consecutive .300 seasons, and the Cards won the World Series. It was a harbinger of things to come, as Musial would lead the team to two more titles in '44 and '46. The 1960s brought a host of baseball greats to St. Louis, most notably base-stealing sensation Lou Brock and fireballer Bob Gibson. Together they would carry the team to three series and two world titles. In the 1980s fielding came to the fore in St. Louis. Led by shortstop Ozzie Smith, the defensive Cardinals appeared in three series that decade, winning in 1982. The Cards had two postseason visits in the '90s and another in 2000, but to a large extent the team's accomplishments have been overshadowed by Mark McGwire's awe-inspiring power and his record-breaking 70 home runs in 1998. With "Big Mac" leading the way, the Cards are flying again.

"It ain't braggin' if you can back it up. "
— Cardinals pitcher Dizzy Dean, on his renowned bravado

POSTSEASON
- **World Series Titles**...........9
(1926, '31, '34, '42, '44, '46, '64, '67, '82)
- **NL Pennants**...................15
(1926, '28, '30, '31, '34, '42, '43, '44, '46, '64, '67, '68, '82, '85, '87)

RETIRED NUMBERS
- Ozzie Smith (1)
- Red Schoendienst (2)
- Stan Musial (6)
- Enos "Country" Slaughter (9)
- Ken Boyer (14)
- Dizzy Dean (17)
- Lou Brock (20)
- Bob Gibson (45)
- August A. Busch Jr. (85)

The Inside Pitch

- St. Louis has fielded some of the greatest defensive players in history. Ozzie Smith's 11 consecutive Gold Glove Awards are followed closely by Bob Gibson's nine straight, Curt Flood's seven and Keith Hernandez' five.

TEAM RECORDS
Hitting Records
- **Lou Brock (1964–79)**
Steals (season): 118 (1974)
Steals (career): 888
- **Rogers Hornsby (1915–26, '33)**
Batting Avg. (season): .424 (1924)
Batting Avg. (career): .359
Hits (season): 250 (1922)
Runs (season): 141 (1922)
- **Mark McGwire (1997–present)**
HRs (season): 70 (1998)
Walks (season): 162 (1998)
- **Joe "Ducky" Medwick (1932–40, 1937–38)**
RBIs (season): 154 (1937)
2B (season): 64 (1936)
- **Stan Musial (1941–44, 1946–63)**
Runs (career): 1,949
HRs (career): 475
Hits (career): 3,630
RBIs (career): 1,951
Total Bases (career): 6,134
2B (career): 725
3B (career): 177

Pitching Records
- **Dizzy Dean (1930, 1932–37)**
Wins (season) 30 (1934)

- **Bob Gibson (1959–75)**
Complete Games (career): 255
ERA (season): 1.12 (1968)
Innings Pitched (career): 3,885
Shutouts (season): 13 (1968)
Shutouts (career): 56
Strikeouts (season): 274 (1970)
Strikeouts (career): 3,117
Wins (career): 251
- **Lee Smith (1990–93)**
Saves (season): 47 (1991)
Saves (career): 160
- **John Tudor (1985–88, '90)**
ERA (career): 2.52
Winning Pct. (career): .705

Managing Records
- **Albert Schoendienst (1965–76, '80, '90)**
Wins (career): 1,041
- **Billy Southworth (1940–45)**
Wins (season): 106 (1942)
Winning Pct. (season): .688 (1942)

LEAGUE HONORS
NL MVP
- Rogers Hornsby (1925)
- Bob O'Farrell (1926)
- Jim Bottomley (1928)
- Frankie Frisch (1931)
- Dizzy Dean (1934)
- Joe Medwick (1937)
- Mort Cooper (1942)
- Stan Musial (1943, '46, '48)
- Marty Marion (1944)
- Ken Boyer (1964)
- Orlando Cepeda (1967)
- Bob Gibson (1968)
- Joe Torre (1971)
- Keith Hernandez (1979)
- Willie McGee (1985)

NL Rookie of the Year
- Wally Moon (1954)
- Bill Virdon (1955)
- Bake McBride (1974)
- Vince Coleman (1985)
- Todd Worrell (1986)

NL Cy Young
- Bob Gibson (1968, '70)

Vital Stats

Stadium Address:
250 Stadium Plaza, St. Louis, Mo.
Phone: (314) 421-3060
Web: cardinals.mlb.com
Box Office:
(314) 421-2400,
Mon.–Sat. 9–5, game days
Sun. 12–4
Media Coverage:
Radio: KMOX (1120 AM)
TV: KLPR (Channel 11),
Fox Sports Net
Spring Training:
Roger Dean Stadium,
Jupiter, Fla.

Timeline

1876	St. Louis becomes charter member of National League, then withdraws after two seasons
1892	Team rejoins NL as Browns
1925	Rogers Hornsby wins his second triple crown
1937	Joe "Ducky" Medwick captures triple crown and records .574 batting average
1944	Cardinals defeat Browns in all-St. Louis World Series
1948	Stan Musial wins third NL MVP Award
1958	Musial collects 3,000th hit
1964	Cardinals defeat Yankees in seven-game World Series
1966	Old Busch Stadium closes
1967	Bob Gibson wins three games to pace Cards over Red Sox in fall classic
1974	Lou Brock sets single-season steals mark with 118 swipes
1982	Shortstop Ozzie Smith wins first of 11 Gold Gloves; Cards beat Brewers in World Series
1985	Willie McGee wins NL Batting title; Cards lose World Series to Royals
1998	St. Louis first-basemen Mark McGwire sets major-league record with 70 home runs
2001	McGwire inks two-year contract extension

62

BUSCH STADIUM: HOME OF THE RED BIRDS

SITUATED NEAR THE Gateway Arch and the banks of the Mississippi River, Busch Stadium was opened in 1966 and immediately spurred a revival in downtown St. Louis. The stadium has two decks that completely surround the diamond. Somewhat sterile at first, the park atmosphere has warmed thanks to several renovations, starting with the 1996 change from artificial to natural turf. Other new features include a family pavilion and a hand-operated scoreboard. A display honors champion Cards teams of the past and statues of the franchise's great players are found outside Gate 6.

CONCESSIONS

Among the wide variety of Busch Stadium food choices are vegetarian and beef burritos, churros, Southwest sausage, foot-long hot dogs and multi-flavored pretzels. There is also a great variety of specialty beers.

Stadium Facts

Opened: May 12, 1966
Cost: $28 million
Capacity: 49,779
Type: Open
Surface: Grass
Home Sweet Home:
• In the 1980s Cards teams were built on speed and defense because their ballpark was so cavernous. Today the power alleys have been shortened, making it more friendly for sluggers such as Mark McGwire.

GAME DAY TIPS

• **Gate hours:** Gates open one hour prior to games on weekday evenings, 90 minutes prior to games on weekends and afternoons.
• **Weather:** Summers are hot and humid. Be prepared for sudden showers.
• **Prohibited items:** Bottles, cans and alcohol are not permitted. Laser pointers are forbidden. Smoking is allowed only in designated areas.
• **Ticket tips:** Fans pack the stadium, so good seats are not easy to find. Because they are so far from the action, avoid outfield upper-deck seats unless you're intent on catching home-run balls.
• **Lost and found:** (314) 421-3060.

Seating Plan

▪ Infield Field Box	$37	▪ Outfield Loge Reserve $21
▪ Infield Loge Box	$34	▪ Terrace Reserve $18
▪ Outfield Field Box	$32	▫ Bleachers $10
▪ Outfield Loge Box	$28	▪ Upper Terrace Reserve $9
▪ Infield Loge Reserve	$25	▫ Standing Room $9
▪ Infield Terrace Box	$23	**ATM** Sections 250, 284, 354
▪ Outfield Terrace Box	$21	♿ Throughout

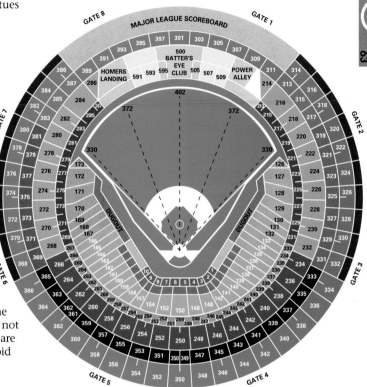

Directions

Directions: From north or south, take I-55 or I-70 to I-64 E., then to Busch Stadium exit. From east or west, take I-64 or I-55/70 to Busch Stadium exit. By Train: Metrolink lightrail has a Busch Stadium stop at 400 S. 8th St. Call St. Louis Regional Transport at (314) 231-2345 for more information. *Parking:* Garages on Spruce, 7th and S. 9th streets and S. Broadway accommodate 6,000 cars. Disabled parking is available in the east garage, the west garage and the stadium bus parking lot.

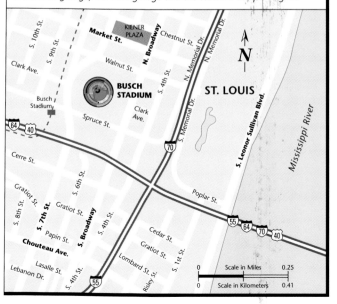

Nearby Hotels

▼▼▼ **Adam's Mark-St. Louis** *(Hotel)*, at 4th and Chestnut Sts. (St. Louis), (314) 241-7400, $129-$235
▼▼ **Best Inns** *(Motel)*, 2423 Old Country Inn Dr. (Caseyville, Ill.), (618) 397-3300, $46-$60
▼▼▼ **Drury Plaza Hotel** *(Historic Motor Inn)*, at 4th and Market Sts. (St. Louis), (314) 231-3003, $135-$165
▼▼▼ **Holiday Inn Downtown Select** *(Hotel)*, 811 N. 9th St. (St. Louis), (314) 421-4000, $109-$159
▼▼▼ **St. Louis Marriott Pavillion Downtown** *(Hotel)*, One Broadway (St. Louis), (314) 421-1776, $179-$194

Nearby Restaurants

▼ **Broadway Oyster Bar** *(Cajun)*, 736 S. Broadway (St. Louis), (314) 621-8811, $8-$14
▼▼▼ **Dierdorf and Hart's** *(Seafood)*, 701 Market St. (St. Louis), (314) 421-1772, $15-$40
▼▼▼ **Mike Shannon's Steaks & Seafood** *(Steak & Seafood)*, 100 N. 7th St. (St. Louis), (314) 421-1540, $16-$35
▼▼▼▼ **Tony's** *(Italian)*, 410 Market St. (St. Louis), (314) 231-7007, $19-$35 (dinner only)
▼▼▼ **Top of The Riverfront Restaurant** *(Regional American)*, 200 S. 4th St. in the Regal Riverfront Hotel (St. Louis), (314) 241-3191, $16-$35 (dinner only)

SAN DIEGO PADRES

Tony Gwynn reached 3,000 hits faster than all but two men.

SINCE BREAKING INTO THE MAJORS IN 1969, the San Diego Padres have experienced significantly more lows than highs. In five of the Padres' first six seasons, the team finished with the worst record in the NL. From 1969 to 1983, the Padres had only one winning season. But in 1984 the team finally gave their hard-luck fans something to cheer: Fleet-footed Alan Wiggins stole a club-record 70 bases and a second-year outfielder named Tony Gwynn took the NL batting crown with a .351 average. In the NLCS against the Cubbies, the Padres came back from a 2-0 deficit in a best-of-five series to win the next three games. Unfortunately, the clock struck midnight for the Cinderella Padres at the World Series, where they fell 4-1 to the powerful Detroit Tigers. The team had a 14-year roller-coaster ride until its next appearance in the fall classic in 1998. Unfortunately, after upsetting the Braves to win the NL Pennant, the Padres suffered a World Series sweep at the hands of the Yankees. Despite the team's many heartbreaks, there has always been a core of Padres heroes. Original Padre and deep-ball threat Nate Colbert paved the way for future franchise stars such as Randy Jones, Rollie Fingers, Gaylord Perry, Dave Winfield, Benito Santiago, Ozzie Smith, Ken Caminiti and Trevor Hoffman. But of all the great players who have come and gone, none is as inextricably linked to the Padres as Gwynn. Having played for no other team since he was drafted by the Padres in 1981, Gwynn has won an incredible nine NL batting titles — giving fans plenty to cheer about even in the lean years.

POSTSEASON
• NL Pennants.....................2
(1984, '98)
• NL West Titles.................3
(1984, '96, '98)

RETIRED NUMBERS
• Randy Jones (35)
• Steve Garvey (6)
• Dave Winfield (31)

TEAM RECORDS
Hitting Records
• **Joe Carter (1990)**
Games (season): 162
(tie) (1990)
• **Ken Caminiti (1995–98)**
RBIs (season): 130 (1996)
• **Jack Clark (1989–90)**
Walks (season): 132 (1989)
• **Nate Colbert (1969–74)**
Grand Slams (career): 5
HRs (career): 163
• **Steve Garvey (1983–87)**
Games (season): 162
(tie) (1985)
• **Tony Gwynn (1982–present)**
At-Bats (career): 9,228

Batting Avg.
(season): .394 (1994)
Batting Avg. (career): .338
Games (career): 2,383
Hits (season): 220 (1997)
Hits (career): 3,122
RBIs (career): 1,127
Runs (career): 1,380
Steals (career): 318
Walks (career): 783
2B (season): 49 (1997)
2B (career): 536
3B (season): 13 (1987)
3B (career): 85
• **Steve Finley (1995–98)**
At-Bats (season): 655 (1996)
Runs (season): 126 (1996)
• **Alan Wiggins (1981–85)**
Steals (season): 70 (1984)
• **Dave Winfield (1973–80)**

Games (season): 162
(tie) (1980)
• **Greg Vaughn (1996–98)**
HRs (season): 50 (1998)

Pitching Records
• **Andy Benes (1989–95)**
Strikeouts (career): 1,036
• **Kevin Brown (1998)**
Strikeouts (season):
257 (1998)
• **Dave Dravecky (1982–87)**
ERA (career): 3.12
• **Trevor Hoffman (1993–present)**
Games (career): 490
Saves (career): 271
Saves (season): 53 (1998)
• **Randy Jones (1973–80)**
Complete Games
(season): 25 (1976)
Complete Games (career): 71
Innings Pitched
(career): 1,766.0
Shutouts (season): 6
(tie) (1975)
Shutouts (career): 18
Starts (season): 40 (1976)
Starts (career): 253
Wins (season): 22 (1976)
• **Craig Lefferts (1984–87, 1990–92)**
Games (season): 83
• **Fred Norman (1971–73)**
Shutouts (season): 6
(tie) (1972)
• **Dave Roberts (1972–75, 1977–78)**
ERA (season): 2.10

The Inside Pitch

• *In 2001 Tony Gwynn became only the 17th player to spend 20 years on the same team.*
• *In 1974 the franchise was on the verge of moving to Washington. New uniforms had been made and front-office files had been boxed. Luckily, Ray Kroc, the founder of McDonald's, stepped in to buy the franchise and keep it in San Diego.*

> *"We play like King Kong one day and Fay Wray the next."*
> — *A frustrated Terry Kennedy during the Padres' up and down 1983 campaign*

Vital Stats

Stadium Address:
9449 Friars Rd.,
San Diego, Calif.
Phone: (619) 641-3100
Web: padres.mlb.com
Box Office:
(619) 283-4494,
Mon.–Sat. 9–6
Media Coverage:
Radio: KOGO (600 AM)
TV: KUSI (Channel 51), Cox
Spring Training:
Peoria Sports Complex,
Peoria, Ariz.

• **Eric Show (1981–90)**
Wins (career): 100

LEAGUE HONORS
NL MVP Award
• Ken Caminiti (1996)

NL Cy Young
• Randy Jones (1976)
• Gaylord Perry (1978)
• Mark Davis (1989)

NL Gold Glove Award
• Tony Gwynn 5
• Ken Caminiti 3
• Benito Santiago 3
• Steve Finley 2
• Ozzie Smith 2
• Dave Winfield 2

NL Manager of the Year
• Bruce Bochy (1996, '98)

Timeline

| 1969 | 1972 | 1974 | 1975 | 1978 | 1981 | 1984 | 1987 | 1991 | 1996 | 1998 | 1999 | 2000 |

Padres beat Astros 2-1 in franchise's first game

Nate Colbert hammers five HRs in doubleheader

Padres finish last in NL West for sixth straight season

Randy Jones is San Diego's first 20-game winner

40-year-old Gaylord Perry wins Cy Young

Padres use their fourth pick to select Tony Gwynn in fourth round of draft

Gwynn wins first batting title and leads team to NL pennant

Benito Santiago wins Rookie of the Year

Fred McGriff belts grand slams in consecutive games

Ken Caminiti cops NL MVP honors while Tony Gwynn takes seventh batting crown

Padres upset Braves to take NL Pennant, but are swept by powerful Yankees in WS

Tony Gwynn collects hit number 3,000 off the Expos' Dan Smith

Gwynn signs on for 20th season in San Diego

QUALCOMM STADIUM: LAST OF A DYING BREED

HOME TO THE PADRES throughout the team's 32-year history, Qualcomm Stadium will host its final major-league season in 2001. Formerly known as San Diego Stadium and later renamed Jack Murphy Stadium in honor of the popular sportswriter who pushed for its construction, "the Q" is a multipurpose facility with a baseball capacity of more than 66,000. That number was approached during recent Padres' postseason runs in 1996 and '98. Not exactly a classic, Qualcomm is nonetheless one of a disappearing generation of parks and worth a visit.

Seating Plan

■ Field Infield	$26
▢ Field Level	$22
▢ Plaza Infield	$22
▨ Plaza Level	$20
■ Club Infield	$24
▢ Club Level	$22
■ Loge Infield	$18
▨ Loge Level	$16
▨ Press Level	$14

▨ Grandstand Plaza	$9
■ Grandstand Club	$8
■ Lower View Infield	$9
▨ View Infield	$8
▨ View Level	$7
▨ Outfield Bleachers	$5
ATM Sections 14 Press, 26 Plaza, 28 Loge	
♿ Throughout	

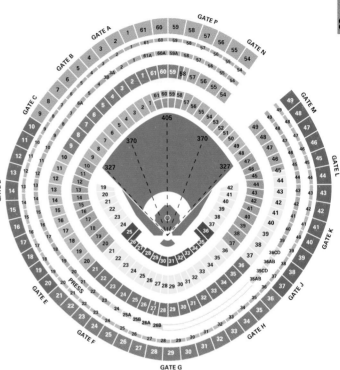

CONCESSIONS

Qualcomm Stadium provides fans with all the standard baseball fare, including pretzels, hot dogs, burgers and pizza. Also available are fish tacos, a San Diego specialty.

Stadium Facts

Opened: Aug. 20, 1967
Cost: $27.75 million
Capacity: 66,307
Type: Outdoor
Surface: Grass
Home Sweet Home:
• For many years, the stadium was one of the most difficult home-run parks in baseball. However, in 1982 the Padres moved the fences forward, making it one of the most hitter-friendly ballparks in the National League.

GAME DAY TIPS

• **Gate hours:** Gates open 90 minutes prior to games on weekdays and two hours prior to games on weekends.
• **Weather:** San Diego is warm in the summer, but rarely very hot. Evenings can turn cool, so pack a light jacket.
• **Prohibited items:** Liquid containers of any kind and alcohol are prohibited. Coolers, however, are permitted. Smoking is allowed only in designated areas. Tailgating is permitted in one's own parking stall.
• **Ticket tips:** Views from rows 1 and 2 on the plaza, loge, club and press levels are partially obstructed because of railings. The back two rows of the plaza level do not have a view of the scoreboard.
• **Lost and found:** (619) 881-6564.

Directions: From I-8 west, take exit I-15 north and follow to Friars Rd. exit. Turn right on Friars Rd. to Stadium exit. From I-15 south, exit at Friars Rd. and turn right, then follow to Stadium exit. By Bus: Padres Express buses stop at five pickup locations (with parking lots) around the city. For information, call NCTD at (619) 685-4900. **Parking:** Lots surrounding the stadium accommodate some 18,500 automobiles. More than 450 spaces are reserved for people with disabilities.

Nearby Hotels

▼▼▼ **Balboa Park Inn** (*Motel*), 3402 Park Blvd. at Balboa Park (San Diego), (619) 298-0823, $89-$219
▼▼▼ **Comfort Suites-Hotel Circle** (*Suite Motel*), 631 Camino Del Rio S. (San Diego), (619) 881-4000, $99-$169
▼▼▼ **Doubletree Hotel-San Diego Mission Valley** (*Hotel*), 7450 Hazard Center Dr. (San Diego), (619) 297-5466, $129-$169
▼▼▼ **Radisson Hotel-San Diego** (*Hotel*), 1433 Camino Del Rio S. (San Diego), (619) 260-0111, $209
▼▼▼ **San Diego Marriott Mission Valley** (*Hotel*), 8757 Rio San Diego Dr. (San Diego), (619) 692-3800, $169-$189

Nearby Restaurants

▼▼▼▼ **Bertrand at Mister A's** (*California*), 2550 Fifth Ave. in the Fifth Avenue Financial Center, top floor (San Diego), (619) 239-1377, $20-$40
▼▼ **City Delicatessen** (*American*), 535 E. University Ave. (San Diego), (619) 295-2747, $4-$16
▼▼ **Islands Restaurant** (*Specialty*), 2270 Hotel Circle in the Hanalei Hotel (San Diego), (619) 297-1101, $14-$25 (dinner only)
▼▼ **Monterey Whaling Company** (*Seafood*), 901 Camino Del Rio S. in the Hilton San Diego Mission Valley (San Diego), (619) 543-9000, $9-$20
▼▼▼ **Prego** (*Italian*), 1370 Frazee Rd. in the Hazard Center (San Diego), (619) 294-4700, $12-$25

SAN FRANCISCO GIANTS

GIANTS

THE HISTORY OF THE GIANTS FRANCHISE is divided into two parts: the early years in New York and the second incarnation of the team in San Francisco. Entering the National League in 1883 as the Gothams, the team played the majority of its first 82 years at the legendary Polo Grounds in North Central Park. These were the glory years for the franchise. Between the early 1900s and the 1940s, the Giants parlayed the play of stars such as Christy Mathewson, Joe McGinnity, George Kelly, Casey Stengel, Mel Ott and Carl Hubbell into four World Series titles. In 1951 the Giants became a part of America's collective imagination when the team fought back from 10 games behind to beat crosstown-rival Brooklyn Dodgers in the National League pennant race. With two out and two strikes against him in the ninth, Bobby Thompson struck a three-run homer known forever as "the shot heard 'round the world" off Ralph Branca to win the game and the pennant. In 1954 the Giants won their last World Series, with the incomparable Willie Mays working his magic. After moving to San Francisco in 1958, the Giants continued to be competitive for a number of years due mainly to the awesome power of Willie Mays, Orlando Cepeda and Willie McCovey and the pitching of Juan Marichal. During the '70s and '80s, the Giants struggled with bad trades, relentless injuries and poor attendance. In 1993 the signing of powerhouse Barry Bonds instigated a turnaround. The slugging left fielder made his impact felt immediately as the Giants won 103 games that year and took the NL West in 1997. The new millennium has not stopped Bonds or the Giants. With manager Dusty Baker at the helm and NL MVP 2000 Jeff Kent providing added offensive punch, the Giants took the NL West in 2000 and show no signs of relinquishing the title in 2001.

Vital Stats

Stadium Address:
24 Willie Mays Plaza,
San Francisco, Calif.
Phone: (415) 972-2000
Web: giants.mlb.com
Box Office:
(415) 972-2000,
Mon.–Sat. 10–5,
during home games
Media Coverage:
Radio: KNBR (680 AM)
TV: KTVU-TV (Channel 2),
Fox Sports Net
Spring Training:
Scottsdale Stadium,
Scottsdale, Ariz.

POSTSEASON
• **World Series Titles**...........5
(1905, '21, '22, '33, '54)
• **NL Pennants**...................17
(1904, '05, '11, '12, '13, '17, '21, '22, '23, '24, '33, '36, '37, '51, '54, '62, '89)
• **NL West Titles**.................5
(1971, '87, '89, '97, 2000)

RETIRED NUMBERS
• **Bill Terry (3)**
• **Mel Ott (4)**
• **Carl Hubbell (11)**
• **Willie Mays (24)**
• **Juan Marichal (27)**
• **Orlando Cepeda (30)**
• **Willie McCovey (44)**

The Inside Pitch

• The Giants have more enshrined members of the National Baseball Hall of Fame than any other franchise in the majors. In all, 49 Cooperstown inductees have worn the Giants uniform.
• The Giants have not been at their best in the month of October. In all, the team has appeared in 16 World Series, winning just five times.

TEAM RECORDS
Hitting Records
• **George Burns (1911–21)**
Steals (career): 334
• **Jack Clark (1975–84)**
2B (season): 46 (1978)
• **Willie Mays (1951–52, 1954–72)**
At-Bats (career): 10, 477
Games (career): 2,857
Hits (career): 3,187
HRs (game): 4 (April 30, 1961)
HRs (season): 52 (1965)
HRs (career): 646
Runs (career): 2,011
2B (career): 504
• **Mel Ott (1926–47)**
RBIs (season): 151 (1929)
RBIs (career): 1,860
• **Bill Terry (1923–36)**
Batting Avg. (season):

Barry Bonds has more homers than any left-handed batter.

.401 (1930)
Hits (season): 254 (1930)
• **Mike Tiernan (1887–99)**
Runs (season): 146 (1893)
• **John Ward (1883–89, 1893–94)**
Steals (season): 111 (1883)

Pitching Records
• **Rod Beck (1991–97)**
Saves (season): 48 (1993)
Saves (career): 199
• **Carl Hubbell (1928–43)**
ERA (season): 1.66 (1933)
• **Gary Lavelle (1974–84)**
Games (career): 647
• **Christy Mathewson (1900–16)**
Complete Games (career): 434
Innings Pitched (career): 4,781
Shutouts (season): 12 (1908)
Shutouts (career): 83
Strikeouts (game): 16 (Oct. 3, 1904)
Strikeouts (season): 267 (1903)
Strikeouts (career): 2,502
Wins (season): 37 (1908)
Wins (career): 372
• **Joe McGinnity (1902–08)**
Complete Games (season): 44 (1903)
• **Julian Tavarez (1997–99)**
Games (season): 89 (1997)

Managing Records
• **John McGraw (1902–32)**
Consecutive NL Pennants: 4

(1921–24)
Games (career): 4,405
Losses (career): 1,808
NL Pennants (career): 10
Wins (career): 2,604
World Series Titles: 3

LEAGUE HONORS
NL MVP
• **Carl Hubbell (1933, '36)**
• **Willie Mays (1954, '65)**
• **Willy McCovey (1969)**
• **Kevin Mitchell (1989)**
• **Barry Bonds (1993)**
• **Jeff Kent (2000)**

NL Rookie of the Year
• **Willie Mays (1951)**
• **Orlando Cepeda (1958)**
• **Willy McCovey (1959)**
• **Gary Matthews (1973)**
• **John Montefusco (1975)**

NL Cy Young
• **Mike McCormick (1967)**

Timeline

1883	1886	1902	1905	1919	1933	1951	1958	1967	1971	1989	2000

The Giants franchise is created in New York City under the name "Gothams"

Manager Jim Mutrie dubs his team "My Giants"

John McGraw is named team manager

The Giants win their first World Series

George Kelly wins home-run title with 23 dingers

Star players Mel Ott, Carl Hubbell and Bill Terry lead the team to World Series win

Willie Mays begins his 22-year career with the Giants

Giants move to San Francisco

Mike McCormick goes 22-10 to win Cy Young Award

Giants skipper Charlie Fox named Manager of the Year

Game three of the World Series between the Giants and the Oakland A's is rocked by an earthquake

Giants capture NL West in first year at Pacific Bell Park

PACIFIC BELL PARK: OVERLOOKING THE BAY

THE OPENING OF PACIFIC BELL PARK was a big event for San Franciscans. After many cold, windy games at the infamous Candlestick Park, fans had been looking forward to more comfortable digs for many years. Much smaller and more intimate than its predecessor, Pacific Bell is situated in the scenic port area of the city. It offers great views of San Francisco Bay and Golden Gate Bridge, and is fitted with a unique waterfront promenade at right field where fans can watch the game for free. This is a great modern facility located in a beautiful natural environment.

CONCESSIONS

Pacific Bell Park offers one of the most diverse menus in all of baseball, including Tex/Mex, Italian and Japanese, as well as more traditional hot dogs and burgers. Try the garlic fries!

GAME DAY TIPS
• **Gate hours:** Gates open two hours prior to games.
• **Tailgating:** Although it's less popular than it was at Candlestick, tailgating still goes on (especially on weekends) in the parking lot next to the right field wall, three to four hours before games.
• **Weather:** The park is located in a sunny spot and is well protected from strong winds, but San Francisco in the summer is quite cool, so take along a sweater.
• **Prohibited items:** Glass bottles and cans as well as laser pointers and air-powered noisemakers are prohibited. Smoking is prohibited, except in a few specially designated areas.
• **Ticket tips:** Five hundred seats in the left-field bleachers are reserved for same-day buyers. For big games (most weekends and anytime against rival L.A.

Stadium Facts

Opened: April 11, 2000
Cost: $319 million
Capacity: 40,800
Type: Outdoor
Surface: Specially designed blend of hybrid bluegrasses
Home Sweet Home:
• The stadium's short right-field fence, just 307 feet from home plate, is a tempting target for left-handed pull hitters such as Barry Bonds. Homers over the left-field fence splash down in the bay.

Seating Plan

■ **Lower Box**	$26	■ **Field Club**	N/A
■ **View Box**	$20	■ **Luxury Suites**	N/A
■ **Arcade**	$20	ATM **Sections 205/207, 217/218,**	
■ **View Reserved**	$16	**230/231**	
■ **Bleachers**	$10	♿ **Throughout**	
■ **AAA Club Level**	N/A		

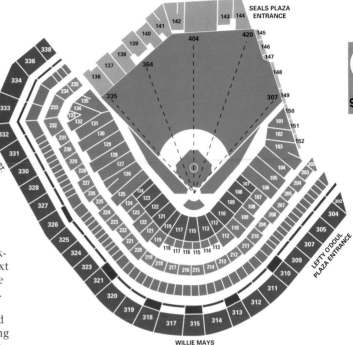

Dodgers), arrive early and expect a lottery. Also, season-ticket holders sell tickets on-line for games that they can't make.
• **Lost and found:** (415) 947-3395.

Directions: From Peninsula/South Bay, take I-280 north to Mariposa St. exit. Turn right on Mariposa, left on Third St. From East Bay, take I-80/Bay Bridge to Fifth St. exit. Turn right on Fifth St., right on Folsom St., right on Fourth St. Merge into left lane and continue on Fourth St. Public Transportation: Streetcars, trains, ferries and buses all go to the park. Call (415) 817-1717 and press 7. **Parking:** There are 4,800 spaces on the south side of China Basin Channel with disabled parking and a shuttle for disabled fans. More parking is on Bryant, 3rd, 4th and Harrison streets.

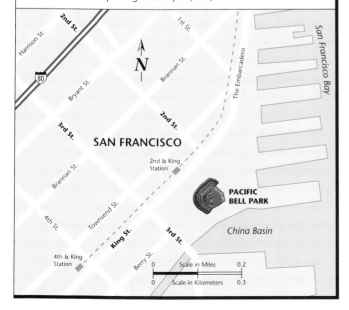

Nearby Hotels

▼▼▼ **Best Western Canterbury Hotel** (*Hotel*), 750 Sutter St. (San Francisco), (415) 474-6464, $125-$375
▼▼▼ **Chancellor Hotel** (*Hotel*), 433 Powell St. (San Francisco), (415) 362-2004, $140-$190
▼▼▼▼ **Hyatt Regency-San Francisco** (*Hotel*), 5 Embarcadero Center (San Francisco), (415) 788-1234, $299-$324
▼▼▼▼▼ **The Ritz-Carlton, San Francisco** (*Hotel*), 600 Stockton St. (San Francisco), (415) 296-7465, $480-$580
▼▼▼ **York Hotel** (*Hotel*), 940 Sutter St. (San Francisco), (415) 885-6800, $129-$179

Nearby Restaurants

▼▼▼ **The Cliff House** (*American*), 1909 Point Lobos at Ocean Beach (San Francisco), (415) 386-3330, $16-$25
▼▼▼ **Dante's** (*Seafood*), on Pier 39 (San Francisco), (415) 421-5778, $17-$24
▼▼▼▼▼ **The Dining Room** (*Nouvelle French*), 600 Stockton St. in The Ritz-Carlton, San Francisco (San Francisco), (415) 296-7465, $61-$87 (dinner only)
▼▼▼ **The Mandarin** (*Northern Chinese*), 900 N. Point St. in the Woolen Mill Bldg., top floor (San Francisco), (415) 673-8812, $10-$20
▼▼▼ **Pompei's Grotto** (*Seafood*), 340 Jefferson St. at Fisherman's Wharf (San Francisco), (415) 776-9265, $10-$20

SEATTLE MARINERS

SEATTLE BASEBALL FANS HAD A TASTE of the big leagues in 1969, but the taste was bitter. The Seattle Pilots played just one season in Seattle, losing 98 games, before being whisked away to Milwaukee the following year. But if there was any doubt about public support when the expansion Mariners took up shop in the Kingdome in '77, it was quickly dispelled as more than one million fans turned out to cheer the new team in its inaugural season. The Mariners' struggle for success on the baseball field would prove a great deal more arduous, as the team finished no better than fourth in the AL West during its first 17 seasons. For most of that time, fans had to content themselves rallying behind slugging stars such as Willie Horton, Alvin Davis and Richie Zisk as they plied their trade in the home-run friendly Kingdome. The arrival of Ken Griffey Jr. in 1990 signalled the beginning of a climb toward legitimacy for the Seattle franchise. The Mariners posted their first-ever winning season in '93, buoyed by Griffey's power, pitcher Randy Johnson's overpowering fastball and the phenomenal hitting of Edgar Martinez. Two years later the team finished on top of its division and entered the postseason for the first time. Seattle swept the Yankees to win its first divisional playoff, but lost to Cleveland in the ALCS. Two years later they were division winners again. Despite losing superstars such as Johnson in 1998 and Griffey in '99, Seattle came one game away from a berth in the 2000 World Series. With continued leadership from veterans such as Martinez and John Olerud, the Mariners look like contenders again.

Edgar Martinez led the Mariners in 2000 with 145 RBIs.

POSTSEASON
- NL West Titles..................2
(1995, '97)
- AL Wild Cards 1
(2000)

TEAM RECORDS
Hitting Records
- **Julio Cruz (1977–83)**
Steals (career): 290
- **Ken Griffey Jr. (1989–99)**
At–Bats (career): 5,832
Extra-Base Hits: (career): 748
Extra-Base Hits (season): 93 (1997)
Hits (career): 1,742
HRs (season): 56 (1997, '98)
HRs (career): 398
RBIs (season): 147 (1997, '98)

RBIs (career): 1,152
Runs (career): 1,063
Total Bases (season): 393
(1997, '98)
Total Bases (career): 3,316
- **Edgar Martinez (1987–present)**
Batting Avg. (career): .320
Games (career): 1,540
Walks (season): 123 (1996)
Walks (career): 973
2B (career): 403
- **Harold Reynolds (1983–92)**
Steals (season): 60 (1987)
3B (career): 48
3B (season): 11 (1988)
- **Alex Rodriguez (1994–2000)**
At-Bats (season): 686 (1998)
Batting Avg. (season): .358 (1996)
Hits (season): 215 (1996)
Runs (season): 141 (1996)
2B (season) 54 (1996)

Pitching Records
- **Norm Charlton (1993, 1995–97)**
ERA (season): 1.51 (1995)
- **Mike Jackson (1988–91, '96)**
ERA (career): 3.38
Games (career): 335
- **Randy Johnson (1989–98)**
Innings (career): 1,838.1
Shutouts (career): 19
Starts (career): 266
Strikeouts (season): 308

Strikeouts (career): 2,162
Wins (season): 20 (1997)
Wins (career): 130
Winning Pct. (season): .900 (1995)
- **Mark Langston (1984–89)**
Complete Games (season): 14 (tie) (1987)
Innings (season): 272 (1987)
- **Mike Moore (1982–88)**
Complete Games (season): 14 (tie) (1985)
Starts (season): 37 (1986)
- **Mike Schooler (1988–92)**
Saves (season): 33 (tie) (1989)
Saves (career): 98

Managing Records
- **Darrell Johnson (1977–80)**
Losses (season): 104 (1978)
- **Lou Piniella (1993–present)**
Wins (career): 631
Wins (season): 91 (2000)

LEAGUE HONORS
AL MVP
- Ken Griffey Jr. (1997)

AL Rookie of the Year
- Alvin Davis (1984)

AL Cy Young
- Randy Johnson (1995)

AL Manager of the Year
- Lou Piniella (1995)

The Inside Pitch

- *The newest Mariners' home-game tradition is the ceremonial closing of the retractable roof. After each game, thousands of fans wait to watch the engineering marvel in action.*
- *The Outside Corner Picnic Patio, directly above the Home Plate Gate entrance, has become the choice hangout spot for fans. Check out the spectacular view of Puget Sound from this spot.*

"The on-the-field adventures of the boys in blue and white have become Seattle's off-the-field addiction."

— Sportswriter Robert L. Jamieson Jr., on the Mariners' popularity

Vital Stats

Stadium Address:
1250 First Ave. S., Seattle, Wash.
Phone: (206) 346-4000
Web: mariners.mlb.com, safeco.com
Box Office:
(206) 622-HITS,
Mon.–Sat. 8:30–7,
Sun. 11–5
Media Coverage:
Radio: KIRO (710 AM)
TV: KIRO-TV (Channel 7),
Fox Sports Net
Spring Training:
Peoria Sports Complex
Peoria, Ariz.

AL Gold Glove
- Ken Griffey Jr 10
- Harold Reynolds..............3
- Mark Langston 2
- Jay Buhner 1
- John Olerud 1
- Omar Vizquel...................1

Timeline

1977	1979	1982	1984	1985	1989	1991	1993	1995	1997	1999	2000

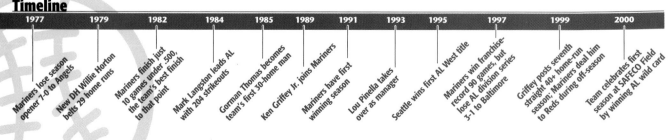

- 1977 Mariners lose season opener 7-0 to Angels
- 1979 New DH Willie Horton belts 29 home runs
- 1982 Mariners finish just 10 games under .500, the team's best finish to that point
- 1984 Mark Langston leads AL with 204 strikeouts
- 1985 Gorman Thomas becomes team's first 30-home man
- 1989 Ken Griffey Jr. joins Mariners
- 1991 Mariners have first winning season
- 1993 Lou Piniella takes over as manager
- 1995 Seattle wins first AL West title
- 1997 Mariners win franchise-record 90 games, but lose AL division series 3-1 to Baltimore
- 1999 Griffey posts seventh straight 40+ home-run season; Mariners deal him to Reds during off-season
- 2000 Team celebrates first season at SAFECO Field by winning AL wild card

SAFECO FIELD: NEW DIGS IN SEATTLE

FEATURING SWEEPING VIEWS both of downtown Seattle and the stunning sunsets over Puget Sound, SAFECO Field is a breathtaking setting for baseball. The beautiful ballpark marks a huge change from the cavernous Kingdome, where the Mariners played until 1999. Fans have been suitably impressed with the new venue; the 31 sellouts in the first season at SAFECO equalled the entire number in 22 years at the Kingdome. Fans can see the field from any point around the main concourse that encircles the field. Other conveniences for spectators include excellent sight lines, ample legroom, plenty of bathrooms, an excellent variety of concessions and, of course, the retractable roof, which keeps out the worst of Seattle's unpredictable weather.

CONCESSIONS

With more than 100 food stands, kiosks, pubs and restaurants, there is plenty of good food at SAFECO. Hot dogs, hamburgers, chicken, seafood, sandwiches, soups, tacos, pizza and Chinese food are all available to the hungry fan. The open-pit grill in the Bullpen Market is a local favorite.

Stadium Facts

Opened: July 15, 1999
Cost: $517.6 million
Capacity: 47,116
Type: Retractable roof
Surface: Grass
Home Sweet Home:
• The asymmetrical outfield fence at SAFECO Field often leads to some strange bounces of balls hit off the wall. This is especially true in the deepest part of right center field, where more than one outfielder has been handcuffed by a ball rattling around back there.

GAME DAY TIPS
• **Gate hours:** Center-field gate opens three hours prior to games (access to Bullpen Market only); others open two hours prior to games.
• **Weather:** Although the roof is closed on very wet days, SAFECO's open-air concept can leave the park somewhat cold and damp. As a rule, dress warmly.
• **Prohibited items:** No glass containers or outside beverages are allowed. Beachballs, balloons, and hard coolers are also prohibited. Smoking is permitted only in designated areas.

Seating Plan

■ Lower Box	$36	
■ Field	$30	
■ AVAYA Terrace Club INF	$36	
■ AVAYA Terrace Club OF	$32	
■ View Box	$20	
■ Lower Outfield Reserved	$20	

■ Lower Outfield Reserved Family	$20
■ View Reserved	$15
■ View Reserved Family	$15
■ Left Field Bleachers	$11
■ Center Field Bleachers	$6
ATM Sections 128, 211, 330	
♿ Throughout	

• **Ticket tips:** Not only are they the cheapest seats in the house, but the center-field bleachers also provide a good view and a great place to catch the afternoon sun. Tickets go quickly for A's, Rangers and Yankees games.
• **Lost and found:** (206) 346-4444.

Directions: From I-5, take exit 164 (south) or 163 (north). From I-90 W., turn right on 4th Ave. S., then right on Royal Brougham Wy. By Bus: Buses are available to and from the stadium. Call Seattle Metro at (206) 553-3000 for more information. **Parking:** SAFECO has a 2,100-space parking garage and there are many lots around the park on S. Jackson St. and Royal Brougham Way. All SAFECO lots have wheelchair-accessible spaces.

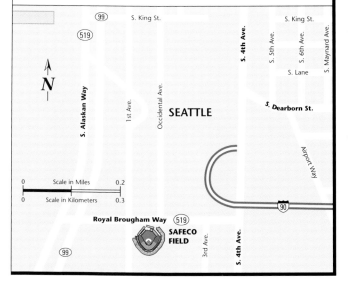

Nearby Hotels

▼▼▼ **Best Western Pioneer Square Hotel** *(Historic Motel)*, 77 Yesler Way (Seattle), (206) 340-1234, $159-$284
▼▼▼ **Georgetown Inn** *(Motel)*, 6100 Corson Ave. S. (Seattle), (206) 762-2233, $64-$169
▼▼▼ **Holiday Inn Express-Downtown Seattle** *(Motel)*, 226 Aurora Ave. N. (Seattle), (206) 441-7222, $89-$119
▼▼▼▼ **Hotel Monaco** *(Hotel)*, 1101 Fourth Ave. (Seattle), (206) 621-1770, $255
▼▼▼ **Mayflower Park Hotel** *(Historic Hotel)*, 405 Olive Way (Seattle), (206) 623-8700, $127-$157

Nearby Restaurants

▼▼▼ **The Brooklyn Seafood, Steak & Oyster House** *(Steak & Seafood)*, 1212 2nd Ave. (Seattle), (206) 224-7000, $18-$33
▼▼ **Bush Garden** *(Japanese)*, 614 Maynard Ave. S. (Seattle), (206) 682-6830, $8-$22
▼▼ **Elliott's Oyster House** *(Seafood)*, Pier 56-Alaskan Way (Seattle), (206) 623-4340, $13-$26
▼▼ **Trattoria Mitchelli** *(Italian)*, 84 Yesler Way in Pioneer Square (Seattle), (206) 623-3883, $8-$15
▼▼▼ **Wild Ginger Asian Restaurant & Satay Bar** *(Asian)*, 1401 Third Ave. (Seattle), (206) 623-4450, $9-$20

TAMPA BAY DEVIL RAYS

IN 1998 THE TAMPA BAY DEVIL RAYS launched its inaugural Major League Baseball season. Baseball's youngest franchise, Tampa is a team still trying to forge an identity. Under the tutelage of first-year manager Larry Rothschild, the 1998 squad focused on the fundamentals with mixed results. Seasonal highlights included a four-game sweep of the Baltimore Orioles, then the defending champions of the AL East, at the O's own ballpark. Although the Rays surprised everyone by finishing second in the AL in defense (.985 fielding pct.) and fourth in pitching (4.35 ERA), the team averaged less than four runs a game. The lack of offense had predictable repercussions, with the team finishing last in the AL East. Enlisting the help of noted long-baller Jose Canseco, the Rays turned things around at the plate in 1999. Canseco's 34 homers, combined with first baseman Fred McGriff's 104 RBIs, spearheaded an offense that scored 152 more runs than it had the previous year — the second-biggest turnaround in AL history. Unfortunately, while Ray bats were ringing, the team's arms lost their zip. In their sophomore season, Tampa pitchers coughed up 162 more runs than they did in the franchise's freshman campaign. Still, there were reasons to cheer: Wade Boggs rapped out career hit number 3,000 and closer Roberto Hernandez notched his 200th save. McGriff has established himself as a leader on and off the field. Playing in 453 of the Rays' first 486 games, "the Crime Dog" has driven in 291 runs and, more importantly, brought 15-years of big-league experience into the young Rays clubhouse.

"We have to do the little things to win games. We can't play selfish baseball."

— *Devil Rays new manager Hal McRae*

Vital Stats

Stadium Address:
1 Tropicana Dr.,
St. Petersburg, Fla.
Phone: (727) 825-3120
Web: devilrays.mlb.com
Box Office:
(727) 825-3250, Mon.–Fri.
9–6, Sat. 9–3, Sun. 12–4
Media Coverage:
Radio: WFLA (970 AM)
TV: WSTP (Channel 10),
WMOR (Channel 32),
Fox Sports Net
Spring Training:
Florida Power Park,
Al Lang Field,
St. Petersburg, Fla.

RETIRED NUMBERS
• Wade Boggs (12)

TEAM RECORDS
Hitting records
• **Miguel Cairo (1998–2000)**
Steals (season): 28 (2000)
Steals (career): 69
3B (career): 12
• **Jose Canseco (1999–2000)**
HRs (season): 34 (1999)
Slugging Pct. (season):
.563 (1999)
• **Quinton McCraken (1998–2000)**
Hits (season): 179 (1998)
2B (season): 38 (1998)
• **Fred McGriff (1998–present)**
At-Bats (career): 1,659

Batting Avg. (season):
.310 (1999)
Extra-Base Hits (season):
63 (1999)
Games (season): 158 (2000)
Games (career): 453
Hits (career): 481
HRs (career): 78
On-Base Pct.
(season): .405 (1999)
RBIs (season): 106 (2000)
RBIs (career): 291
Runs (career): 230
Total Bases (season):
292 (1999)
Total Bases (career): 798
Walks (season): 91 (2000)
2B (career): 81
• **Paul Sorrento (1998–99)**
Grand Slams
(season): 2 (1998)
Pinch-Hit HRs
(season): 2 (1998)
• **Randy Winn (1998–present)**
3B (season): 9 (1998)

Wins (season): 14 (1998)
Wins (career): 21 (tie)
• **Roberto Hernandez (1998–2000)**
Appearances (season):
72 (1999)
Appearances (career): 207
Saves (season): 43 (1999)
Saves (career): 101
• **Albie Lopez (1998–present)**
Complete Games
(season): 4 (2000)
Complete Games
(career): 4 (tie)
Wins (career): 21 (tie)

• **Bryan Rekar (1998–present)**
Innings Pitched (career): 353.5
• **Tony Saunders (1998–99)**
Strikeouts (season):
172 (1998)
• **Bobby Witt (1999)**
Shutouts (season):
2 (tie) (1999)
Starts (season):
32 (tie) (1999)

Managing Records
• **Larry Rothschild (1998–2000)**
Wins (season):
69 (1999, 2000)
Wins (career): 201

LEAGUE HONORS
AL All–Star Game Selections
• Rolando Arrojo (1998)
• Roberto Hernandez (1999)
• Jose Canseco (1999)
• Fred McGriff (2000)

The Inside Pitch

• On April 4, 1999, Frank Thomas of the ChiSox became the first player to belt a homer off the upper catwalk in the left-field corner of Tropicana Field.

• Tampa is the first modern team to conduct spring training in its home city.

• Fred McGriff, Wade Boggs, Gary Sheffield, Dwight Gooden and Hall-of-Famer Al Lopez all come from the Tampa Bay area.

Pitching Records
• **Rolando Arrojo (1998–99)**
Complete Games
(career): 4 (tie)
ERA (season): 3.56 (1998)
Innings (season): 202.0 (1998)
Shutouts (season):
2 (tie) (1998)
Starts (season):
32 (tie) (1998)
Starts (career): 56
Strikeouts (career): 259

Fred McGriff had 100+ RBIs for the Rays in 1999 and 2000.

Timeline

1913	1914	1925	1937	1942	1961	1988	1995	1997	1998	1999	2000
Chicago Cubs move spring training operations from New Orleans to Tampa	Grapefruit League established in Tampa, with Cubs beating St. Louis Browns 3-2	In town with the Yankees, Babe Ruth is scared off Tampa field by alligators	St. Louis Cardinals begin 57-year spring training stint in Tampa	Wartime travel restrictions leave Tampa without spring training teams	Tampa wins Florida State League title, led by Reds farm hand Pete Rose	43,000-seat stadium built in attempts to attract major league team to Tampa	Baseball owners officially approve of the Tampa Bay Devil Rays entry into the major league	Larry Rothschild named manager	Team finishes last in AL East in inaugural season	Jose Canseco hammers 34 homers and earns All-Star selection along with reliever Roberto Hernandez	Fred McGriff drives in 106 runs to break club RBI mark

TROPICANA FIELD: SOMETHING OLD, SOMETHING NEW

TROPICANA FIELD EMBRACES the old and the new. The dimensions of the asymmetrical outfield are very similar to those of the old Ebbets Field. This is also the first major-league park in more than 20 years to feature AstroTurf and all-dirt base paths instead of the dirt cutouts around the bases used in other parks. However, select seats are equipped with touch-screen display units that allow fans to call up one of eight camera angles, watch replays, check stats or visit the team's website. The stadium also boasts a cyber café, a family entertainment center and the major's first in-stadium cigar bar.

CONCESSIONS

In addition to the usual fare of hot dogs, peanuts and burgers, Tropicana Field offers Italian, Japanese and steakhouse food, plus a concession stand geared especially toward kids, featuring child-size menus, portions and prices.

Stadium Facts

Opened: *Mar. 3, 1990*
Cost: *$138 million*
Capacity: *44,027*
Type: *Dome*
Surface: *AstroTurf*
Home Sweet Home:
• *The outfield warning track features a special AstroTurf surface. It is designed to give a different feel from outfield turf for players approaching the fence while tracking a fly.*

GAME DAY TIPS

• **Gate hours:** Gates open 90 minutes prior to games Mon.–Thurs. and two hours prior to games on weekends and holidays.
• **Weather:** St. Petersburg has a semitropical climate, with moderately high summer temperatures and the occasional shower.
• **Prohibited items:** Plastic or glass bottles, coolers and other hard containers are prohibited. Beachballs and frisbees are also prohibited, but bats and brooms are allowed. No animals are allowed, except those trained to help disabled visitors. Tailgating is prohibited.
• **Ticket tips:** The Beach is a uniquely Floridian section of seats at the field, complete with palm trees, sand-colored seats and staff in beachwear.
• **Lost and found:** (727) 825-3488.

Seating Plan

■ Home Plate Box $195	■ Outfield $14
□ Field Box $75	□ The Beach $10
■ Lower Club Box $45	▨ Upper Reserved $10
□ Diamond Club Box $35	■ Upper General
▨ Diamond Club	Admission $8
Reserved $30	■ Southwest Airlines
■ Lower Box $30	Freedom Fan Fare Seats ..$4
▨ Lower Reserved $23	ATM Sections 118, 119, 317;
▨ Terrace Box $23	cyber café
▨ Upper Box $19	♿ Throughout
■ Terrace Reserved $14	

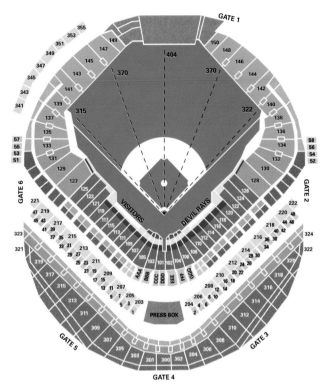

Directions: *From I-275 take exit 9 to I-175. Follow signs to park. By Bus and Trolley: A free motor-coach provides service from six downtown stops. The Central Ave. Trolley also goes to the park.* **Parking:** *Parking lots around Tropicana Field can accommodate 7,000 automobiles. Parking for disabled visitors is available at field lots No. 1, 6a and 7a. Another 25,000 spaces are available on private lots and streets around the park on 1st Ave. S., 2nd Ave. S., 3rd Ave. S. and 4th Ave. S.*

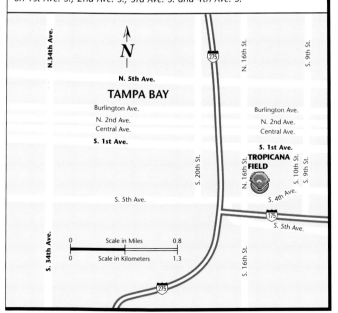

Nearby Hotels

▼▼ **Colonial Bayfront Hotel** *(Historic Motel)*, 126 2nd Ave. NE (St. Petersburg), (727) 896-6400, $55-$150
▼▼ **Grant Motel & Apts** *(Motel)*, 9046 4th St. (St. Petersburg), (727) 576-1369, $35-$50
▼▼ **The Heritage-A Holiday Inn Hotel** *(Historic Motor Inn)*, 234 3rd Ave. N. (St. Petersburg), (727) 822-4814, $80-$150
▼▼▼ **Renaissance Vinoy Resort** *(Classic Resort)*, 501 Fifth Ave. NE (St. Petersburg), (727) 894-1000, $120-$300
▼▼▼ **St. Petersburg Bayfront Hilton** *(Hotel)*, 333 1st St. S. (St. Petersburg), (727) 894-5000, call for rates

Nearby Restaurants

▼▼ **4th Street Shrimp Store** *(Seafood)*, 1006 4th St. N. (St. Petersburg), (727) 822-0325, $4-$21
▼▼ **Columbia Restaurant** *(Spanish)*, 800 2nd Ave. in The Pier, 4th floor (St. Petersburg), (727) 822-8000, $14-$22
▼▼▼ **Marchand's Bar & Grill** *(Continental)*, 501 Fifth Ave. NE in the Renaissance Vinoy Resort (St. Petersburg), (727) 894-1000, $11-$25
▼▼ **Moon Under Water** *(British)*, 332 Beach Dr. NE (St. Petersburg), (727) 896-6160, $7-$17
▼ **Paisano's Pizza & Pasta** *(Italian)*, 6000 4th St. N. (St. Petersburg), (727) 521-2656, $7-$18

TEXAS RANGERS

THE TEXAS RANGERS CAME INTO EXISTENCE when Washington Senators owner Robert E. Short brought the team to Arlington Stadium in 1972. In its 11-year stint in the nation's capital, the team had seen little success, finishing no better than fourth in the American League West. Unfortunately for Texas baseball fans, things did not turn around quickly. For 23 years the Rangers could only flirt with success, finishing second in 1974 under manager Billy Martin and behind the pitching of Comeback Player of the Year Fergie Jenkins. Two more second-place finishes in 1977 and '78 were followed by the franchise's most heartbreaking loss up to that time, when it blew a sixth-inning 3-1 lead over the Brewers to lose the first half of 1981's split season and its best chance at the postseason. Forty-one-year-old Nolan Ryan gave fans something to cheer for when the Texan signed on with his home-state team in 1988. Playing his final five years of baseball with the Rangers, Ryan put an exclamation point on his brilliant Hall-of-Fame career, tossing his sixth and seventh no-hitters. But even he couldn't provide the magic touch to lead the team into the playoffs. That would finally happen in 1996, when the Rangers, blessed with a special combination of power and defensive prowess in superstars such as Juan Gonzalez, Ivan Rodriguez and Will Clark, won the team's first AL West title. The Rangers fell to the Yankees in the division series that year, but returned to the postseason in 1998 and '99, both times to be defeated again by the eventual champion Yankees. In 2001 the Rangers will feature a host of new faces, including Andres Galaragga and, most notably, shortstop Alex Rodriguez. Another shot at postseason success can't be far away.

> *"Now it's time to go pay him back and win him a few championships."*
> — Alex Rodriguez, on being signed by Rangers owner to $252 million contract in 2000

Vital Stats

Stadium Address:
1000 Ballpark Wy., Arlington, Texas
Phone: (817) 3273-5222
Web: rangers.mlb.com
Box Office:
(817) 273-5100,
Mon.–Fri. 9–6, Sat. 10–4
Media Coverage:
Radio: KRLD (1080 AM)
TV: KXAS (Channel 5),
Fox Sports Net
Spring Training:
Charlotte County Stadium,
Port Charlotte, Fla.

AL Manager of the Year
• Johnny Oates (1996)

AL Gold Glove
• Ivan Rodriguez 9
• Jim Sundberg 6
• Buddy Bell 6
• Juan Beniquez 1
• Gary Pettis........................1
• Rafael Palmeiro 1

POSTSEASON
• AL West Titles 3
(1996, '98, '99)

RETIRED NUMBERS
• Nolan Ryan (34)

TEAM RECORDS
Hitting Records
• Juan Gonzalez (1989–98)
HRs (season): 47 (tie) (1996)
HRs (career): 340
RBIs (career): 1,075
Runs (career): 791
2B (season): 50 (1998)
• Toby Harrah
(1972–78, 1985–86)
Walks (season): 113 (1985)

The Inside Pitch

• When Texas hurler Bobby Witt took Ismael Valdes of the Dodgers deep on June 30, 1997, in the first month of interleague play, it was the first home run by an American League pitcher since 1972.
• In 1991 Texas became just the third team in 60 years to have three players with 200 hits in the same season: Rafael Palmeiro, 203; Ruben Sierra, 203; and Julio Franco, 201.

Walks (career): 708
• Al Oliver (1978–81)
Batting Avg. (career): .319
Games (season): 163 (1980)
• Rafael Palmeiro
(1989–93, 1999–present)
HRs (season): 47 (tie) (1999)
Grand Slams (season): 3 (tie) (1999)
Runs (season): 124 (1993)
• Mickey Rivers (1979–84)
Hits (season): 210 (1980)
• Ivan Rodriguez
(1991–present)
At-Bats (career): 4,899
Batting Avg. (season): .347 (2000)
Hits (career): 1,487
2B (career): 293
• Ruben Sierra (1986–92)
3B (season): 14 (1989)
3B (career): 43
• Bump Wills (1977–89)
Steals (season): 52 (1978)
Steals (career): 161

Pitching Records
• Bert Blyleven (1977–78)
ERA (career): 2.74
• Charlie Hough
(1980–90)
Innings Pitched
(career): 2,307.2
Strikeouts (career): 1,452
Wins (career): 139
• Fergie Jenkins
(1974–75, 1978–81)
Complete Games (season):

29 (1974)
Shutouts (season): 6 (1974)
Wins (season): 25
• Jim Kern (1979–81)
ERA (season): 1.57 (1979)
• Jeff Russell
(1985–92, 1995–96)
Games (career): 445
• Nolan Ryan (1989–93)
Strikeouts (season): 301 (1989)
Strikeouts (game): 16
(May 1, 1989);
(April 26, 1990)
• John Wetteland
(1997–present)
Saves (season): 43 (1999)
Saves (career): 150

Managing Records
• Johnny Oates
(1995–present)
Wins (season): 95 (1999)
• Bill Hunter (1977–78)
Winning Pct. (career): .575
• Bobby Valentine
(1985–92)
Wins (career): 581
Losses (career): 605

LEAGUE HONORS
AL MVP
• Jeff Burroughs (1974)
• Juan Gonzalez (1996, '98)
• Ivan Rodriguez (1999)

AL Rookie of the Year
• Mike Hargrove (1974)

Ivan Rodriguez won his ninth straight Gold Glove in 2000.

Timeline

1960	1961	1971	1972	1974	1977	1988	1989	1991	1994	1996	1998	1999	2000
American League awards baseball franchise to Washington, D.C.	President John F. Kennedy throws first pitch in Senators first game	Owner Robert E. Short receives okay to move team to Texas	Rangers lose 1-0 to Angels in first game	Billy Martin named Manager of the Year after leading Texas from last to second in AL West	Bert Blyleven throws Rangers' second no-hitter	Nolan Ryan signs with Texas	Investor group led by George W. Bush buys Rangers	Ryan throws seventh no-hitter of career	Rangers play first game at The Ballpark in Arlington	Rangers enter postseason for first time	Rangers win second AL West title	Rangers clinch third division title; lose to Yankees in AL division series	Rafael Palmeiro leads team with 39 HRs and 120 RBIs

72

THE BALLPARK IN ARLINGTON: BIGGER AND BETTER IN TEXAS

THE BALLPARK IN ARLINGTON is an asymmetrical baseball-only facility that is one of the best in the game. The field is encompassed by a four-story office building containing offices and retail shops and featuring a stunning granite and brick facade. The architecture incorporates many Texas-style details including lone stars at the concourses and seat aisles. The inside is intimate and traditional, with a home run porch in right field, but the complex features many modern treats such as a 12-acre lake and a learning center for kids.

CONCESSIONS
More than 100 concession stands at The Ballpark in Arlington offer standard pizza, nachos, bratwurst, smoked sausage, hand-carved sandwiches, ice cream and desserts.

Stadium Facts

Opened: April 1, 1994
Cost: $191 million
Capacity: 49,178
Type: Outdoor
Surface: Grass
Home Sweet Home:
• To avoid the impact that summer winds can have on fly balls, the field is located 22 feet below street level.
• The numerous corners and angles of the asymmetrical outfield fence can cause strange bounces that handcuff fielders.

GAME DAY TIPS
• **Gate hours:** Gates open three hours prior to evening games and 90 minutes prior to afternoon games.
• **Weather:** Arlington's north Texas location gives it dry, sunny days two-thirds of the year. Thunderstorms occur in spring and summer.
• **Prohibited items:** Cans, glass bottles and alcohol are prohibited. Coolers measuring 16 by 16 by 16 inches or smaller are allowed, provided they do not contain alcohol. Smoking is allowed only in designated areas.
• **Ticket tips:** Fans who want to bask in the sun while watching the game should sit in left field. If you want to stay out of the rain, seats in the 40s, 100s and 240s will give you the most protection.

• **Lost and found:** (817) 273-5131 or (817) 273-5066.

Seating Plan

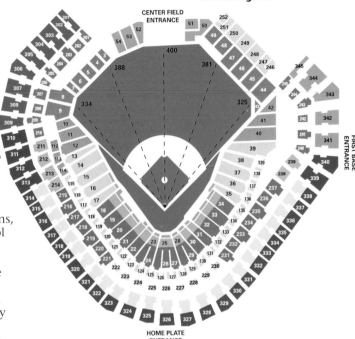

Commissioner's Box	N/A
VIP Infield	N/A
Premium Infield	N/A
Club Infield	N/A
Lower Infield	N/A
Lower Box	$40
Club Box	$40
Club Reserved	$32.50
Corner Box	$28
Terrace Club Box	$22
Lower Home Run Porch	$20
Upper Box	$16
Upper Home Run Porch	$13
Upper Reserved	$12
Bleachers	$12
Grandstand Reserved	$6
Grandstand	$5

ATM Sections 24, 249, 309/310, 326
♿ Throughout

73

Directions: From I-30, take Six Flags Dr. exit. Continue on Six Flags Dr. to Randol Mill Rd. and turn right. From Hwy. 183, take Hwy. 360 south, then exit at Randol Mill Rd. and turn right. **Parking:** There are 13,000 parking spots available around the ballpark, 390 of which are wheelchair-accessible.

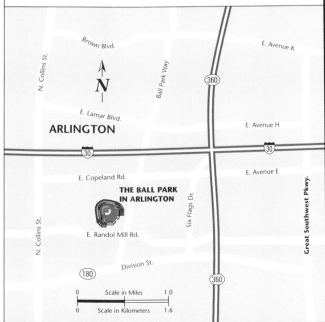

Nearby Hotels
▼▼▼ **Amerisuites (Suite Motel)**, 2380 E Rd. (Arlington) , (817) 649-7676, $119-$144
▼▼ **Baymont Inn & Suites-Arlington (Motel)**, 2401 Diplomacy Dr. (Arlington), (817) 633-2400, $64-$89
▼▼▼ **Fairfield Inn by Marriott (Motor Inn)**, 2500 E. Lamar Blvd. (Arlington), (817) 649-5800, $80
▼▼▼ **La Quinta Inn & Suites South Arlington (Motel)**, 4001 Scott's Legacy (Arlington), (817) 467-7756, $99-$139
▼▼▼ **Wingate Inn (Motel)**, 1024 Brookhollow Plaza Dr. (Arlington), (817) 640-8686, $79-$99

Nearby Restaurants
▼▼ **Arlington Steakhouse (American)**, 1724 E. Division (Arlington), (817) 275-7881, $6-$13
▼▼ **Bobby Valentine's (American)**, 4301 S. Bowen St. (Arlington), (817) 467-9922, $8-$10
▼▼▼ **Cacharel (French)**, 2221 E. Lamar Blvd. (Arlington), (817) 640-9981, $21-$50
▼▼ **Marsala Ristorante (Continental)**, 1618 Hwy. 360 and Ave. K (Arlington), (972) 988-1101, $10-$22

TORONTO BLUE JAYS

IF THERE WAS ANY DOUBT ABOUT potential fan support for Major League Baseball in Toronto, it was quashed on April 7, 1977. That day, in the team's first ever home opener, 44,649 fans braved freezing temperatures and snow to watch their brand new franchise defeat the Chicago White Sox 9-5. With two home runs, Doug Ault became the Jay's first hero, followed closely by the Zamboni driver who cleared snow from the field so the game could be played. The expansion Jays developed quickly into a contender, finishing second in the AL East in 1984, and winning the division in '85 behind solid pitching and a great young outfield anchored by slugger George Bell and speedster Lloyd Moseby. But greater things were to come. In 1990, following a loss to Oakland in the '89 ALCS, Jays GM Pat Gillick orchestrated a blockbuster trade that sent Fred McGriff and Tony Fernandez to the Padres for Roberto Alomar and Joe Carter. After the team came up short again in the '91 ALCS against Minnesota, Gillick added veterans Dave Winfield and Jack Morris. That proved to be a brilliant move, as Morris won 21 games and Winfield delivered the dramatic World Series-winning homer in the six-game triumph over Atlanta in '92. Gillick showed foresight again the next year, signing eventual World Series MVP Paul Molitor, as the team repeated as World Champions in 1993. Denied a chance at a "three-peat" by the strike in '94, the Jays sunk to the AL East basement in '95. Since then Toronto has been climbing steadily. With superstars Carlos Delgado and Shannon Stewart in tow, a return to the top appears imminent.

Carlos Delgado is a perennial run producer for the Jays.

The Inside Pitch

• *Joe Carter was the last player to touch the ball in both of Toronto's World Series wins, catching the final fly out in right field in 1992 and hitting a dramatic ninth-inning home run in 1993.*

• *Catcher Ernie Whitt was the Jays' last connection with its original lineup. He played 23 games in 1977 and was traded following the 1989 season.*

POSTSEASON
• World Series Titles...........2
(1992, '93)
• AL Pennants......................2
(1992, '93)
• AL East Titles 5
(1985, '89, '91, '92, '93)

TEAM RECORDS
Hitting Records
• Roberto Alomar
(1991–95)
Batting Avg. (career): .307
• George Bell
(1981, 1983–90)
HRs (season): 47 (1987)
RBIs (career): 740
• Joe Carter (1991–97)
HRs (career): 203
20-HR Seasons: 7

• Carlos Delgado
(1993–present)
Extra-Base Hits (season):
99 (2000)
RBIs (season): 137 (2000)
Slugging Pct. (season):
.664 (2000)
Total Bases (season):
378 (2000)
Walks (season): 123 (2000)
2Bs (season): 57 (2000)
• Tony Fernandez
(1983–90, '93, 1998–99)
At-Bats (season): 687 (1986)
Games (season): 163 (1986)
Hits (season): 213 (1986)
Hits (career): 1,565
Singles (season): 161 (1986)
2B (career): 287
3B (season): 17 (1990)
3B (career): 72
• Shawn Green (1993–99)
Runs (season): 134 (1999)
• Lloyd Moseby (1980–89)
Steals (career): 255
Walks (career): 547
• John Olerud (1989–96)
Batting Avg. (season):
.363 (1993)
On-Base Pct. (season):
.473 (1993)
On-Base Pct. (career): .395

Pitching Records
• Roger Clemens (1997–98)
ERA (season): 2.05 (1997)
Strikeouts (game):
18 (Aug. 25, 1998)
Strikeouts (season):

292 (1997)
Wins (season): 21 (tie) (1997)
• Tom Henke (1985–92)
Saves (career): 217
• Jimmy Key (1984–92)
Winning Pct. (career): .589
• Jack Morris (1992–93)
Wins (season): 21 (tie) (1992)
• Dave Stieb
(1979–92, '98)
Complete Games (season):
19 (1982)
Complete Games
(career): 103
ERA (career): 3.42
Wins (career): 175
Shutouts (career): 30
Shutouts (season): 5 (1982)
Starts (career): 408
Strikeouts (career): 1,658
• Duane Ward (1986–95)
Saves (season): 45 (1993)

Managing Records
• Cito Gaston (1989–97)
Wins (season): 99 (1985)
Wins (career): 681
• Bobby Cox (1982–85)

"In 16 years, you've gone from the doghouse to the penthouse."

— U.S. President George Bush, congratulating the Jays after their 1992 World Series win

Vital Stats

Stadium Address:
1 Blue Jays Way,
Toronto, Ont.
Phone: (416) 341-3663
Web: bluejays.mlb.com,
skydome.com
Box Office:
(416) 341-1234,
Mon.–Fri. 9–7
Media Coverage:
Radio: CHUM (1050 AM)
TV: CBC (Channel 5), CTV
Sportsnet, TSN
Spring Training:
Dunedin Stadium
at Grant Field,
Dunedin, Fla.

Winning Pct. (season):
.615 (1985)
Winning Pct. (career): .549

LEAGUE HONORS
AL MVP
• George Bell (1987)

AL Rookie of the Year
• Alfredo Griffin (1979)

AL Cy Young
• Pat Hentgen (1996)
• Roger Clemens
(1997, '98)

**AL Manager
of the Year**
• Bobby Cox (1985)

AL Gold Glove
• Roberto Alomar 5
• Devon White.....................5
• Tony Fernandez 4
• Jesse Barfield 2
• Shawn Green 1
• Kelly Gruber......................1

Timeline

1977	1979	1983	1985	1989	1991	1992	1993	1997	1999	2000

Blue Jays win franchise's first game 9-5 over White Sox

Dave Stieb goes 8-8 in rookie season

Jays have first winning season, going 89-73

Toronto wins AL East division; loses to Royals in ALCS

Cito Gaston takes over as manager; Jays win second AL East crown

Jays acquire Joe Carter and Roberto Alomar in trade with Padres

Jays claim first World Series title over Braves

Toronto repeats as WS champions, taking six-game series over Phillies

Jays sign free agent Roger Clemens; he wins 21 games

Carlos Delgado clubs 44 home runs

Jays finish 4.5 games out in AL East race

SKYDOME: AN ENGINEERING FEAT

AT THE TIME OF ITS OPENING in mid-season 1989, the SkyDome was a technological marvel. Built at a cost of more than $500 million, the stadium features a three-panel retractable roof that can be opened or closed in minutes. Another claim to fame is its 110-foot-high video scoreboard — the largest in North America. In 1991 SkyDome's capacity of more 50,000 helped the Jays become the first major-league team to break the four-million attendance mark. A 348-room hotel is located in SkyDome and has some 70 rooms that overlook the field.

CONCESSIONS
The Skydome has a full range of standard stadium food such as pizza, subs and hamburgers. There is also a sushi stand. In addition, three fine restaurants and a bar all face the field.

GAME DAY TIPS
• **Gate hours:** Gates open 90 minutes prior to games on weekdays and two hours prior to games on weekends.
• **Weather:** Toronto is subject to some of the warmest springs and summers in Canada. The city's location by the lake makes July and August especially humid.
• **Prohibited items:** Cans, glass bottles and alcohol can't be brought into the stadium. Coolers and thermos bottles are also prohibited. Banners are allowed, but poles and laser pointers are not. Smoking is allowed only in designated areas.
• **Ticket tips:** The Skydome is rarely sold out for baseball, so same-day tickets are usually easy to get. If there is a sellout, you can still watch the game from the Windows restaurant and the Sightlines bar in the Skydome.
• **Lost and found:** (416) 341-1197.

Stadium Facts

Opened: June 5, 1989
Cost: Approx. $500 million
Capacity: 50,516
Type: Retractable roof
Surface: AstroTurf
Home Sweet Home:
• When the roof is open, the closed end of the stadium becomes a wind scoop, causing a downdraft in the outfield that tends to prevent home runs.

Seating Plan

■ In the Action	$150	■ 100 Level Outfield	$23
■ Club 200 Infield	$44	■ Skydeck Infield	$23
■ Club 200 Baseline	$41	■ Skydeck Bases	$16
■ Premium Dugout Level	$44	■ Skydeck Baseline	$7
■ Field Level Infield	$41	ATM Sections 113A, 130B, 213,
■ Field Level Bases	$35	235, 516, 530
■ Field Level Baseline	$29	♿ Throughout
■ 200 Level Outfield	$23	

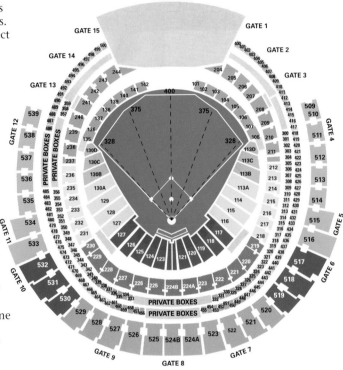

Directions: From Queen Elizabeth Wy./Gardiner Expwy., exit north at Spadina Ave. By Subway/Train: From Union Station, walk west on Front St. or use SkyWalk. Or, take the LRT from Union Station to Spadina, walk north along Rees St. to Gate 7. For more information, call the Toronto Transit Commission at (416) 393-INFO. **Parking:** Lots on Peter, King W., Bay and Blue Jay Way can hold some 17,500 vehicles. Fifty parking spaces are reserved for disabled visitors and are available by reservation.

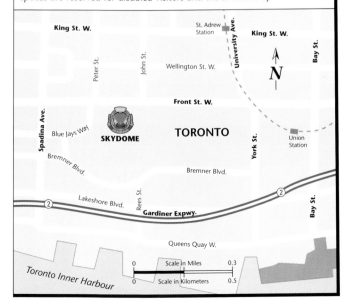

Nearby Hotels

▼▼▼▼ **Crowne Plaza Toronto Centre** (*Hotel*), 225 Front St. W. (Toronto), (416) 597-1400, $189-$239
▼▼▼▼ **The Fairmont Royal York** (*Classic Hotel*), 100 Front St. W. (Toronto), (416) 368-2511, $149-$249
▼▼▼ **Holiday Inn on King** (*Hotel*), 370 King St. W. (Toronto), (416) 599-4000, $219-$259
▼▼▼ **Radisson Plaza Hotel Admiral Toronto-Harbourfront** (*Hotel*), 249 Queen's Quay W. (Toronto), (416) 203-3333, $134-$299
▼▼▼ **Renaissance Toronto Hotel at SkyDome** (*Hotel*), 1 Blue Jays Way (Toronto), (416) 341-7100, $175-$197

Nearby Restaurants

▼▼ **The Bistro** (*American*), 1 Blue Jays Way (Toronto), (416) 341-5045, $10-$25
▼▼ **Joe Badali's Ristorante Italiano** (*Italian*), 156 Front St. W. (Toronto), (416) 977-3064, $9-$17
▼▼ **Shopsy's TV City** (*American*), 284A King St. W. (Toronto), (416) 599-5464, $7-$10
▼ **Wayne Gretzky's Restaurant** (*Canadian*), 99 Blue Jays Way (Toronto), (416) 979-7825, $7-$26
▼▼ **Windows** (*American*), 1 Blue Jay Way (Toronto), (416) 341-2424, $55

BASKE

1

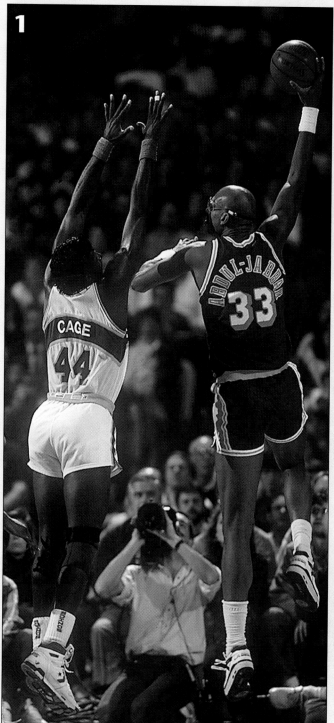

2

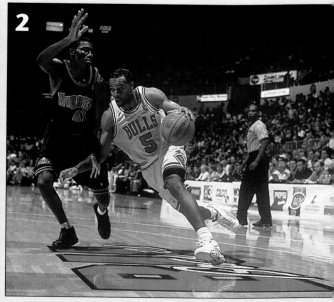

3

TBALL

Atlantic Division
Boston Celtics
Miami Heat
New Jersey Nets
New York Knicks
Orlando Magic
Philadelphia 76ers
Washington Wizards

Central Division
Atlanta Hawks
Charlotte Hornets
Chicago Bulls
Cleveland Cavaliers
Detroit Pistons
Indiana Pacers
Milwaukee Bucks
Toronto Raptors

Midwest Division
Dallas Mavericks
Denver Nuggets
Houston Rockets
Memphis Grizzlies
Minnesota Timberwolves
San Antonio Spurs
Utah Jazz

Pacific Division
Golden State Warriors
Los Angeles Clippers
Los Angeles Lakers
Phoenix Suns
Portland Trail Blazers
Sacramento Kings
Seattle SuperSonics

5

TORONTO

6

THE GAME

BASKETBALL DIFFERS FROM hockey, football and baseball in that it is all about getting vertical. Our most lasting images of the game are of high, arcing shots rainbowing toward the basket and gravity-defying players leaping high above the rim to deliver thunderous slam dunks. The National Basketball Association, basketball's ultimate flying circus, is a land of giants, with many players topping 7 feet. Warning: This is not a place for people who suffer from a fear of heights.

As might be expected from the youngest of the four major North American professional sports leagues, the NBA has been most successful at retaining the youthful zeal we often associate with our own early experiences in sport. Basketball players seem more likely to improvise than they do in the playbook-heavy world of football, importing moves directly from the playground or, better yet, cooking them up in mid-flight. And while other athletes are confined to the boundaries of a rink, a field or a diamond, basketball players are free to soar above the court — and the results are usually spectacular. Even still photos of Connie Hawkins, Michael Jordan, Vince Carter, forever frozen 5 feet off the ground, speak of the incredible vitality and exuberance that form the very core of the game.

At 7 feet 1 inch and 315 pounds, the Lakers' Shaquille O'Neal is one of the NBA's most dominant players.

But basketball wasn't always a thrill-a-minute sport. Before the advent of the 24-second shot clock in 1954, games were often low-scoring yawners in which players passed the ball endlessly, looking for the perfect shot. Once a team had a lead it could kill the clock by playing keep-away — effective, but not very exciting for fans.

Even dunking, although legal, was a rarity, frowned upon by players as grandstanding and insulting to the opposition. Jim Pollard was one of many players in the early 1950s who would unleash his spectacular dunks only in practice. Pollard, who was known as "the Kangaroo Kid," amazed teammates and coaches by taking off from the foul line and slamming home the ball — the same trick that Michael Jordan would amaze the world with decades later.

Even when man-mountains such as Wilt Chamberlain, Bill Russell and Walt Bellamy burst onto the scene and began dunking regularly, they usually did so from directly under the basket. Many people credit the birth and subsequent popularization of the spectacular slam to the old American Basketball Association and its marquee player Julius Erving.

Coming out of the college ranks in which dunking was illegal at the time, Erving, a.k.a. "Dr. J.," said he felt like "the chains had been taken off." Free at last in the ABA, Erving unleashed his unbelievable power and grace on opponents and the world. When the ABA merged with the NBA in 1976, Dr. J. brought along his high-altitude game, pulling fans from their seats and paving the way for future skywalkers.

BOMBERS AND MAGICIANS

The NBA also adopted another ABA innovation: the three-pointer. Not only did the three-point shot add an exciting offensive weapon to a team's arsenal, it also helped unclog the congested area under the basket as players were forced to come out to pressure the shooters.

Since its advent, no player has been as successful at the three-pointer as the Pacers' Reggie Miller. The only man with more than 1,700 career treys, the dead-eyed guard is best known for his last-minute heroics. With his Pacers down by seven with less than nine seconds to go in game one of the 1994–95 Eastern Conference semifinals, Miller nailed two three-pointers and a pair of free throws to win.

And then there are the play makers, ball-handling wizards who fire passes through a forest of arms and legs. Fewer were better than Bob Cousy. "The Houdini of the Hardwood," as he was known, played the point for the Celtics dynasty of the 1950s and '60s, and set a NBA record with 19 assists versus the Lakers — in one half!

"The Big O," Oscar Robertson, was a scoring and defensive whiz renowned for his passing skills, leading the NBA in assists six times and standing third on the all-time list. Magic Johnson may well have been the most creative passer in the game's history. His remarkable no-look dishes were the catalyst for the Lakers flashy offense.

But the game's greatest pure passer is John Stockton. The career leader in assists, Stockton has also racked up the top three single-season performances.

Among the greats on the court in this classic Celtics-Lakers show-down are Larry Bird, Magic Johnson and Kareem Abdul-Jabbar.

STANDING TALL IN THE MIDDLE

In a sport that worships size, no one stands taller than the center. In the early days of basketball, the game was dominated by smaller, quicker players with great ball-handling skills. That all changed when George Mikan lumbered onto the scene in 1946. Taller and stronger than opposing centers, the strategy of 6-foot-10-inch Mikan was simple: stand under the net, pluck high passes out of the air and fill the basket with short, high-percentage shots. Although his repertoire was limited, Mikan was unstoppable. He often scored more points himself than the teams he played against. His impact was immediate and undeniable. During his nine-year career with the Lakers the team won six championships.

Basketball was never the same, with teams sending scouts to scour the collegiate ranks for the newest "Big Man." As the long-arms race escalated, however, so too, centers were forced to evolve. No longer was sheer size a guarantee of success. With teams striving to gain the edge, the demand for centers to be better and better athletes kept growing. Enter Wilton N. Chamberlain.

Hardly a state secret, Chamberlain was a schoolboy legend who in one high-school game scored 60 points in 10 minutes. He was so dominant in college that the powers-that-be effected a number of rule changes, including one that disallowed a player to dunk while taking a free throw. But at 2 inches over 7 feet and 275 pounds, "the Big Dipper" was more than just an immovable object; he was an irresistible force as well. A Big Eight high-jump champion, Chamberlain was a gifted athlete who later played professional volleyball.

But it was on the basketball court that Wilt "the Stilt" truly shone his brightest. The only player ever to record 4,000 points in a season, Chamberlain also has 20 of the NBA's top 30 single-game performances. Although he is most famous for his 100-point night against the Knicks, his versatility set him apart from history's other pure scorers. One of the few men strong enough to block opposing dunks, Chamberlain also led the league in rebounds 11 of his 14 seasons and topped the NBA in assists in 1967–68. When Hall-of-Famer Oscar Robertson was asked if Chamberlain was the best of all time, he just shrugged and said, "The books don't lie."

Great Games in Great Venues

Boston Garden: Many people consider game five of the 1975–76 finals to be the greatest game ever played. With the series between the Celtics and the Suns knotted at two games, the teams battled to a draw at the end of regulation. The first overtime ended with the teams still tied and a turnaround jumper by the Suns' Gar Heard at the end of the second overtime sent the game into a third extra period. The Celtics finally prevailed 128-126, thanks largely to six points by seldom-used Glenn McDonald in the final period.

Madison Square Garden, New York City: After tearing a muscle in game five of the 1969–70 finals, Knicks captain Willis Reed sat out game six. Without Reed guarding him, the Lakers' Wilt Chamberlain poured in 45 points and grabbed 27 rebounds to win the match for his team and send the series to a decisive game seven. Just moments before tip-off, Reed surprised everyone and sent the New York faithful into a frenzy by limping out of the tunnel and taking his place on the court. Inspired by their captain's courage, New York prevailed 113-99 to win the title.

Philadelphia Spectrum: With the team's 7-foot-2-inch colossus Kareem Abdul-Jabbar on the sidelines with a sprained ankle for game six of the 1979–80 NBA finals, things looked bleak for the L.A. Lakers. Facing the Dr. J-led Philadelphia 76ers, L.A. needed someone to step up and play center in Kareem's absence. That someone was rookie guard Magic Johnson, who volunteered to take a stab at playing the post. Winning the opening tip-off, Johnson went on to score 42 points and pull down 15 boards to lead his team to a 123-107 win and the first of his five NBA titles.

Delta Center, Salt Lake City: Looking to finish off the always-tough Utah Jazz in game six of the 1997–98 NBA finals, the Bulls turned to the one and only Michael Jordan. Playing in his last NBA game, Air Jordan was spectacular, racking up 45 points. With his team in trouble, Jordan stole the ball and hit the game-winning jumper with just 5.2 seconds on the clock. Fittingly, Jordan's last career basket gave the Bulls their sixth NBA championship in eight years.

McNichols Arena, Denver: If you like scoring, the Dec. 13, 1983, match between the Detroit Pistons and the Nuggets was the game for you. When the buzzer of the third overtime mercifully ended this shootout, Detroit had outscored Denver 186-184 — a NBA record that may never be broken. Amazingly, the Pistons could have cracked the 200-point barrier had they not made only 37 of 60 free throws.

THE STILT OR AIR?

There is one man who stands between Chamberlain and his coronation as history's greatest hoopster. He is, of course, Michael Jordan. Jordan burst onto the scene like a meteorite in 1984–85, averaging 28.2 points a game and winning Rookie of the Year honors. He went on to lead the league in scoring in 10 seasons, something even Chamberlain could not achieve. When he retired in 1998 his 31.5 career scoring average was another record, edging out Chamberlain once again. Beyond the statistics, however, Jordan had the heart of a champion. Maybe the finest "big game" player to ever take the court, he led his Bulls to six NBA titles in eight years and was named finals MVP each time. But Air Jordan is probably best remembered for the way he soared effortlessly toward the basket, legs splayed, tongue sticking out mischievously, bringing us all back to our childhood when we dreamed of touching the clouds.

KEY MOMENTS

Basketball has changed greatly since it was first created as a sport that could be played during the long winter months. Here's a list of some the major developments that molded the game.

- **1891 Naismith Invents Basketball**

James Naismith creates basketball in a last-ditch effort to come up with an indoor game that can be played in the winter. He sets up peach baskets at each end of the gym 10 feet off the floor, the same height as today's baskets.

- **1895 Backboard Introduced**

With the baskets hung from gymnasium balconies, home-town fans often interfered with opponents' shots. The backboard is developed to curb this, the ultimate expression of home-court advantage.

- **1898 Basketball Goes Pro**

Although called the National Basketball League, the country's first pro league only includes teams from New Jersey and Pennsylvania.

- **1902 First Black Player**

Playing in the New England League, Harry "Buck" Lew is the first black to play side-by-side with whites.

- **1914 Celtics Change Basketball**

The New York Celtics team is formed in Manhattan's west side. Although the team is disbanded when members sign up for World War I, it is reorganized at war's end. The team revolutionizes the game by signing players to year-long contracts, making the center the hub of the offense and developing the zone defense.

- **1925 ABL Paves the Way**

The American Basketball League is formed, placing teams as far east as Boston and as far west as Chicago.

- **1937 Corporations Form New League**

General Electric, Firestone and Goodyear establish the National Basketball League. Current teams, such as the Hawks, Pistons, 76ers and Lakers, can trace their roots to the NBL.

- **1946 BAA Enters the Fray**

The Basketball Association of America is formed. The Knicks, Celtics and Warriors are among the BAA's original 11 teams.

- **1949 Merge Creates NBA**

The NBL merges with the BAA to create the National Basketball Association. The Minneapolis Lakers win the first NBA championship.

- **1950 NBA Integrates**

Chuck Cooper is the first black player drafted by a NBA team. On Oct. 31, Earl Lloyd becomes the first black player in a NBA game.

- **1959 Celtics Begin Streak**

Led by future Hall-of-Famers Bill Russell, Bob Cousy and K.C. Jones, the Boston Celtics win the first of eight straight NBA championships.

- **1962 Wilt Scores 100**

Wilt the Stilt Chamberlain racks up 100 points in a game against the New York Knicks. He finishes the season with an all-time record of 4,029 points.

- **1967 ABA Challenges NBA**

The American Basketball Association begins operations using its trademark red, white and blue basketball.

- **1968 Chamberlain Does It All**

Wilt Chamberlain becomes the only player in history to complete a triple double-double when he gets 22 points, 25 rebounds and 21 assists versus the Pistons.

In the 1992 Olympic Games in Barcelona, Spain, Magic Johnson led the original "Dream Team" to top spot on the medal podium.

- **1974 Dr J. in the House**

The Nets' Julius Erving wins his first of three consecutive ABA MVP Awards.

- **1976 NBA Swallows ABA Survivors**

The ABA folds and four of its teams — Nuggets, Pacers, Nets and Spurs — join the NBA.

- **1984 Kareem Passes Wilt**

The Lakers' Kareem Abdul-Jabbar moves past Wilt Chamberlain as the NBA's all-time leading scorer. When Abdul-Jabbar retires in 1989, he will have racked up 38,387 points.

- **1985 Jordan Arrives on the Scene**

Michael Jordan of the Chicago Bulls wins Rookie of the Year honors.

- **1986 Larry Bird "Three-Peats"**

The Celtics' Larry Bird is the first man since Wilt Chamberlain to win three straight MVP Awards. He tops his season by being named finals MVP as well.

- **1992 Dream Team Brings Home Gold**

Michael Jordan, Larry Bird and Magic Johnson lead the U.S. "Dream Team" to the basketball gold medal at the Barcelona Olympics.

- **1995 Stockton is Mr. Assists**

John Stockton passes Magic Johnson to become NBA's all-time career leader in assists.

- **1998 End of Jordan Era**

Michael Jordan leads his Bulls to a sixth NBA title in eight seasons and wins his sixth finals MVP Award. He retires at the end of the season.

- **2000 Shaq and Kobe Lead Los Angeles**

The Los Angeles Lakers win the NBA finals thanks largely to the stellar play of Shaquille O'Neal and Kobe Bryant. O'Neal has a season to remember, capturing MVP honors for the regular season, the All-Star game and the finals.

Basketball Hall of Fame

FATHER OF BASKETBALL

When James Naismith invented basketball in 1891, he had no idea that it would become one of the world's most popular games. A featured Olympic event since 1936, basketball is currently played in more than 170 countries and has spawned professional leagues everywhere from Australia to Argentina and Israel to Ireland.

The global impact of the game has not been lost on the librarians and historians of the Naismith Memorial Basketball Hall of Fame in Springfield, Mass. The Hall offers visitors wonderful lessons in history and world geography. While many enshrined players, such as Larry Bird and Magic Johnson, are household names, others are not. Players such as Sergei Belov, the magician of Russian basketball and first international-player inductee to the Hall, are given equal importance to their North American counterparts.

PLAYERS, COACHES, PIONEERS

First-time visitors are often struck by the relatively low number of NBA players enshrined here. Of the 238 inductees, only 70 played in the world's premier pro league. Others made their marks in the collegiate ranks or on the international stage. Some player enshrinees predated the NBA. These pioneers include Max "Marty" Friedman, a pro from 1908 to '27, and Ed Krause, whose 6-foot-3-inch stature made him one of the dominant "Big Men" of the 1930s.

Coaches and contributors are also celebrated. The display honoring Red Auerbach, mastermind of the Boston Celtics dynasty of the 1950s and '60s, stands close to those for Antonio Diaz-Miguel and Ernest Blood. Diaz-Manuel was the architect of the Spanish National basketball program, while Blood amassed an incredible 1,268-165 record in his 51 years of coaching, including a 200-1 mark with New Jersey's Passaic High School from 1915 to '24.

Included among contributors is Danny Biasone, the inventor of the NBA's 24-second shot clock; Abe Saperstein, the founder of the Harlem Globetrotters; and Senda Abbott, the "Mother of Women's Basketball." In 1893 Abbott refined the rules so women would not overly exert themselves and upset public sensibilities of the time.

Women are well represented here. Visitors are reminded that two of the game's most successful players were women: Carole Blazejowski finished her collegiate career second only to Pete "Pistol" Maravich in scoring; and Uljana Semjonova, the 7-foot-tall Russian superstar, played 18 seasons of international basketball without ever losing a match.

Four teams have also been enshrined, although not one of them played in the NBA. The so-called "First Team" was comprised of the 18 men who first played James Naismith's new game. The Buffalo Germans, one of the game's first dynasties, rattled off 111 straight wins from 1908 to '11, including a 134-0 shellacking of Hobart College. The original Celtics introduced such innovations as post-play and zone defense. The New York Renaissance, also called the Rens, was a seven-man all-black team that helped bring national attention to the black player. Not allowed to play in "white" leagues, the Rens toured the country taking on all comers in a barnstorming tour that lasted from 1922 to '49. By the time they finally unpacked their bags, the team had posted a 2,588-539 record, often beating some of the best All-Star teams in the land.

BIG SHOES TO FILL

The Hall of Fame is a repository for thousands of basketball artifacts. Not far from the section of the court on which Michael Jordan scored his last points lie the size 22 sneakers worn by Bob Lanier, bronzed like gargantuan baby shoes. Elsewhere Naismith's original handwritten rules, all 13 of them, are on display.

Galleries of award-winning photographs capture the game's color and jaw-dropping athleticism. The images are awesome: Dr. J. in mid-flight, palming a red, white and blue ABA basketball; Chamberlain and Russell fighting for a rebound in the old Boston Garden; the goggled Kareem draining another sky hook; and, of course, Jordan soaring splay-legged above the court, wagging his tongue in defiance of Newton's law. And if photography isn't enough, fans can watch videos of championship games, reliving some of the game's most exhilarating victories and heartrending defeats.

Most importantly, the Hall is true to Naismith's original impetus, which was to get people involved. Interactive exhibits include a shooting gallery in which balls are fed to participants via conveyor belt; a place where visitors can measure their vertical leap against some of the NBA's greatest stars; and a game of one-on-one with a virtual-reality Bill Walton.

Vital Stats

Address:
1150 W. Columbus Ave.
Springfield, Mass.
Phone: (413) 781-6500
Web Site: hoophall.com
Hours: Daily 10–5; closed Thanksgiving Day, Dec. 25, Jan. 1
Admission: Adult $10; youth 7–14 $6; child free (with parent). Adult group (15 or more) $7; youth group (15 or more) $4. Call or write the Hall of Fame for more information on group events.
Directions: The Hall of Fame is one mile off exit 7 on I-91. From Boston and other points east, take Rte. 90 to I-91 south. From Albany and other points west, take Rte. 90. to exit 4 to I-91 south. From New York City and other points south, take I-95 north to I-97 north until Broad St. Turn left at second light. The Hall of Fame is on your right.

Indiana College Basketball display at the Hall of Fame.

THE STARS

CHECK OUT THIS LIST OF NBA RECORDS. Surprised that Michael Jordan appears so infrequently? Remember that steals and blocked shots have been compiled since 1973–74 and three-point field goals since 1979–80. Active players are identified with an asterisk. For all career records, the nearest active players have been included so you can gauge how today's stars rank with the greats of eras past.

BASKETBALL RECORDS

Assists (career):
1. John Stockton* 13,790
2. Magic Johnson 10,141
3. Oscar Robertson 9,887
5. Mark Jackson* 8,574

Blocks (career):
1. Hakeem Olajuwon* 3,652
2. Kareem Abdul-Jabbar 3,189
3. Mark Eaton 3,064

Field Goals (career):
1. Kareem Abdul-Jabbar 15,837
2. Wilt Chamberlain 12,681
3. Karl Malone* 11,435
8. Hakeem Olajuwon* 10,272

Field Goals Pct. (career):
1. Artis Gilmore .599
2. Mark West* .580
3. Shaquille O'Neal* .577

Free Throws (career):
1. Moses Malone 8,531
2. Karl Malone* 8,100
3. Oscar Robertson 7,694

Free Throws Pct. (career):
1. Mark Price .904
2. Rick Barry .900
3. Calvin Murphy .892
7. Reggie Miller* .881
8. Jeff Hornacek* .877

Personal Fouls (career):
1. Kareem Abdul-Jabbar 4,657
2. Robert Parish 4,443
3. Buck Williams 4,267
5. Hakeem Olajuwon* 4,095
7. Otis Thorpe* 4,038

Points (career):
1. Kareem Abdul-Jabbar 38,387
2. Wilt Chamberlain 31,419
3. Karl Malone* 31,041
10. Hakeem Olajuwon* 25,822

Points-Per-Game (career):
1. Michael Jordan 31.5
2. Wilt Chamberlain 30.1
3. Shaquille O'Neal* 27.5
8. Karl Malone* 26.0

Rebounds (career):
1. Wilt Chamberlain 23,924
2. Bill Russell 21,620
3. Kareem Abdul-Jabbar 17,440
12. Hakeem Olajuwon* 12,951
14. Karl Malone* 12,618

Steals (career):
1. John Stockton* 2,844
2. Maurice Cheeks 2,310
3. Michael Jordan 2,306

3-Point Field Goals (career):
1. Reggie Miler* 1,867
2. Dale Ellis* 1,719
3. Glen Rice* 1,353

3-Point Field Goals Pct. (career):
1. Steve Kerr* .464
2. Hubert Davis* .441
3. Drazen Petrovic .437

Assists (season):
1. John Stockton* 1,164 (1990–91)
2. John Stockton* 1,134 (1989–90)
3. John Stockton* 1,128 (1987–88)

Blocks (season):
1. Mark Eaton* 456 (1984–85)
2. Manute Bol 397 (1985–86)
3. Elmore Smith 393 (1973–74)

Field Goals (season):
1. Wilt Chamberlain 1,597 (1961–62)
2. Wilt Chamberlain 1,463 (1962–63)
3. Wilt Chamberlain 1,251 (1960–61)

Field Goals Pct. (season):
1. Wilt Chamberlain .727 (1972–73)
2. Wilt Chamberlain .683 (1966–67)
3. Artis Gilmore .670 (1980–81)

Free Throws (season):
1. Jerry West 840 (1965–66)
2. Wilt Chamberlain 835 (1961–62)
3. Michael Jordan 833 (1986–87)

Free Throws Pct. (season):
1. Calvin Murphy .958 (1980–81)
2. Mahmoud Abdul-Rauf* .956 (1993–94)
3. Jeff Hornacek* .950 (1999–2000)

Points (season):
1. Wilt Chamberlain 4,029 (1961–62)
2. Wilt Chamberlain 3,586 (1962–63)
3. Michael Jordan 3,041 (1986–87)

Points-Per-Game (season):
1. Wilt Chamberlain 50.4 (1961–62)
2. Wilt Chamberlain 44.8 (1962–63)
3. Wilt Chamberlain 38.4 (1960–61)

Personal Fouls (season):
1. Darryl Dawkins 386 (1983–84)
2. Darryl Dawkins 379 (1982–83)
3. Steve Johnson 372 (1981–82)

Rebounds (season):
1. Wilt Chamberlain 2,149 (1960–61)
2. Wilt Chamberlain 2,052 (1961–62)
3. Wilt Chamberlain 1,957 (1966–67)

3-Point Field Goals (season):
1. Dennis Scott 267 (1995–96)
2. George McCloud* 257 (1995–96)
3. Mookie Blaylock* 231 (1995–96)

Wilt Chamberlain notched 118 50-point games and 271 40-point games during his illustrious career.

82

Development of the NBA

THE BIRTH OF BASKETBALL

In 1891 James Naismith was looking to develop an indoor sport that could keep young men occupied and in shape during the long New England winter, one that, unlike football, emphasized skill and agility over brute strength. An instructor at the YMCA in Springfield, Mass., the Canadian-born Naismith asked a janitor to nail two peach baskets to the balconies overlooking both ends of the gym. He then laid out 13 rules for his new game and called it basketball. Amazingly, those original rules, which outlined a somewhat staid activity in which a player could not run once he had the ball, would evolve into the high-octane game of crossover dribbles and tomahawk dunks that is now enjoyed throughout the world.

Basketball enjoyed relatively quick success, with amateur teams springing up in the mid-1890s and one of the first "pro" games (each player was reputedly paid $15) taking place in Trenton, N. J., in 1896.

Despite Naismith's high-minded ideals, early basketball games were just as gladiatorial as football matches. To guard against flying elbows and indiscriminate shoulders, players wore an array of protective gear and courts were often enclosed in a wire cage to keep raucous fans from attacking the opposition.

EARLY LEAGUES

The first professional leagues began popping up in and around the turn of the century. However, with no contracts binding them to a team, players hired themselves out to the highest bidder, playing for one squad on one night and against it the next.

This all changed following World War I, thanks to the New York Celtics, who on top of developing the zone defense began signing players to season-long contracts. Using the Celtics as the model of success and stability, the American Basketball League was formed in 1925, which in turn led to the establishment of the National Basketball League in 1937 and the Basketball Association of America in 1946.

THE NBA IS FORMED

In 1949 the NBL and BAA merged to form the 17-team National Basketball League. While the new league suffered some growing pains — it was down to just eight teams in 1954 — it began to gain in popularity in the late 1950s. This was largely due to the adoption of the 24-second shot clock and the foul-limit rule, both of which helped open up the game and make it more exciting for spectators. Even more important was the emergence of such superstars as Wilt Chamberlain, Bill Russell, Jerry West and Oscar Robertson. Considered among the four best players of all time, this high-flying foursome gave the NBA instant credibility, with the Chamberlain-Russell rivalry thought to be one of the best in all of sport.

ADDED FLOURISH IN THE ABA

The American Basketball Association enjoyed its inaugural season in 1967. The 11-team upstart league spared nothing in its effort to attract fans and bizarre publicity

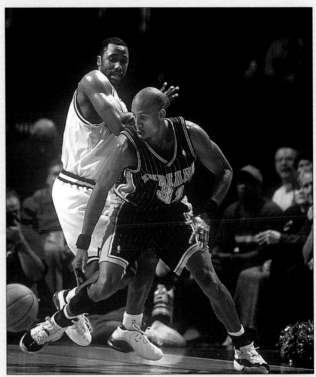

No player in history has made as many three-point field goals as Reggie Miller of the Indiana Pacers.

stunts were the order of the day. The Miami Floridians had ball girls dressed in bikinis and gave away everything from panty hose on Ladies Night and live turkeys on Thanksgiving to 57 pounds of potatoes on Irish Night. The Pacers staged halftime shows that featured cow-milking contests and wrestling matches between a bear and local celebrities. The Kentucky Colonels topped everyone by signing a woman, Penny Ann Early, to a player's contract. Although the 5-foot-3-inch Early played just long enough to fire a single inbound pass, all-important headlines had been made.

But the ABA was also known for some innovations that were eventually adopted by the NBA, most notably the three-point shot. The ABA also played a more free-wheeling type of game, not surprising coming from the league that also gave us the first Slam Dunk Championship. Soaring stars such as Julius "Dr. J." Erving and Connie Hawkins thrilled fans with their imaginative and entertaining above-the-rim acrobatics and their improvised attacks.

THE WORLD JOINS IN

In 1976 the floundering ABA merged with its older, more established cousin, adding the Pacers, Nuggets, Nets and Spurs to the NBA mix. Further expansion in 1980, 1988, 1989 and 1995 has seen the league grow to 29 teams. With two teams currently situated in Canada and a host of players hailing from Europe, Africa, Australia and South America, the NBA has grown into a league of truly international stature, more so than any other of North America's major pro sports. Basketball has come a long way since James Naismith sought a winter diversion for a gym full of rowdy boys.

ATLANTA HAWKS

LIKE A GREAT MANY NBA TEAMS, the Atlanta Hawks franchise has journeyed far to reach its present location. Originally called the Tri-City Blackhawks and located near the city of Moline, Ill., the team moved through Milwaukee and St. Louis before reaching its present home. Success for the early Hawks was limited. The Tri-City team did reach the playoffs in its first season under the leadership of a young coach named Red Auerbach, but it lost its first playoff series. After the season, Auerbach left for greater things in Boston. Following a four-year stint in Milwaukee, the team moved to St. Louis. Success finally arrived in 1954 in the form of a 6-foot-9-inch Louisiana State graduate by the name of Bob Pettit. Gifted with great athletic ability and a fierce competitive nature, Pettit led the Hawks to four consecutive Western Conference titles in the late 1950s and the franchise's only NBA championship in 1958. Pettit retired in 1965 and leadership of the team was taken by ace shooting guard Lou Hudson. The team shocked the city of St. Louis following the 1967–68 season when it announced it was moving to Atlanta under new ownership. Predictions of disaster from those who pointed to Atlanta's lack of a proper venue were silenced when the team went to the Western Conference final in its first two seasons. Since then, the Hawks have had limited playoff success, but Atlanta fans have been able to witness some stunning scorers, including Dominique Wilkins, the NBA's legendary "human highlight reel." Today the team looks to end a long string of early playoff exits.

Guard Jason Terry was named to the NBA All-Rookie second team in 1999–2000.

POSTSEASON
• NBA Championships.......1
(1957–58)
• Western Division Championships 4
(1956–57, 1957–58, 1959–60, 1960–61)
• Central Division Titles....3
(1979–80, 1986–87, 1993–94)

RETIRED NUMBERS
• Bob Pettit (9)
• Lou Hudson (23)

TEAM RECORDS
• Lou Hudson (1968–77)
FG (game): 25
(Nov. 10, 1969)
Points (game): 57
(Nov. 10, 1969)
• Bob Pettit (1954–65)

FG (game): 25 (tie)
(Feb. 8, 1961)
FT (season): 695 (1961–62)
FT Att. (season): 901
(1961–62)
Points (game): 57 (tie)
(Feb. 18, 1961)
Points (season): 2,429
(1961–62)
Points-Per-Game (season): 31.1 (1961–62)
Points-Per-Game (career): 26.4 (tie)
Rebounds (game): 35 (twice)
Rebounds (season): 1,540
(1960–61)
Rebounds (career): 12,851
Rebounds-Per-Game (season): 20.3 (1960–61)
Rebounds-Per-Game (career): 16.2
• Mookie Blaylock (1992–99)
Steals (game): 10
(April 14, 1998)
Steals (season): 212 (twice)
Steals (career): 1,321
3-Point FG (season): 231
(1995–96)
3-Point FG (career): 1,050
• Wayne Rollins (1977–87)
Blocks (season): 343
(1982–83)
Blocks (career): 2,283
• Dominique Wilkins (1982–94)
FG (season): 909 (1987–88)
FG (career): 8,752
Games (career): 882

"I'll always be a Hawk."
— *Team superstar Dominique Wilkins, during the ceremony to retire his number*

Points (game): 57 (tie) (twice)
Points (season): 2,397
(1987–88)
Points (career): 23,292

LEAGUE HONORS
NBA MVP
• Bob Pettit
(1955–56, 1958–59)

Rookie of the Year
• Bob Pettit (1954–55)

Defensive Player of the Year
• Dikembe Mutombo
(1996–97, 1997–98)

Coach of the Year
• Harry Gallatin (1962–63)
• Richie Guerin (1967–68)
• Hubie Brown (1977–78)
• Michael Fratello (1985–86)
• Lenny Wilkens (1993–94)

Basketball Hall of Fame
• Ed Macauley (1960)
• Andy Phillip (1961)
• Bob Pettit (1970)
• Clifford Hagan (1977)
• Slater Martin (1981)
• Red Holzman (1986)
• Bob Houbregs (1987)
• Pete Maravich (1987)
• Clyde Lovellette (1988)
• Lenny Wilkens (1989 as player, 1998 as coach)
• Harry Gallatin (1991)
• Connie Hawkins (1992)
• Walt Bellamy (1993)
• Alex Hannum (1998)

Jump Shot

• The Hawks' Bob Pettit is one of the few players who can legitimately be credited with revolutionizing the game of basketball. Traditionally, men the size of the 6-foot-9-inch forward stayed down low for easy hoops close to the basket. Because of his great conditioning and athletic ability, Pettit was able to take the ball outside and hit a variety of shots.

Vital Stats

Stadium Address:
1 Philips Dr.,
Atlanta, Ga.
Phone: (404) 878-3000
Web: nba.com/hawks,
philipsarena.com
Box Office: (404) 827-3865, Mon.–Fri. 9–5
Media Coverage:
Radio: WSB (750 AM),
WFOX (97.1 FM)
TV: WHOT (Channel 34),
Turner South, Fox
Sports Net
Practice Facility:
Philips Arena, Atlanta, Ga.

Timeline

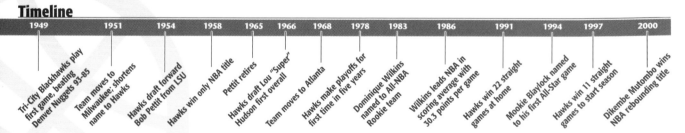

1949	1951	1954	1958	1965	1966	1968	1978	1983	1986	1991	1994	1997	2000

Tri-City Blackhawks play first game, beating Denver Nuggets 93–85

Team moves to Milwaukee; shortens name to Hawks

Hawks draft forward Bob Pettit from LSU

Hawks win only NBA title

Pettit retires

Hawks draft Lou "Super" Hudson first overall

Team moves to Atlanta

Hawks make playoffs for first time in five years

Dominique Wilkins named to All-NBA Rookie team

Wilkins leads NBA in scoring average with 30.3 points per game

Hawks win 22 straight games at home

Mookie Blaylock named to his first All-Star game

Hawks win 11 straight games to start season

Dikembe Mutombo wins NBA rebounding title

PHILIPS ARENA: REVOLUTIONARY BUILDING

PHILIPS ARENA HAS A NUMBER OF FEATURES that make it a special venue. For one, it is connected to the CNN Center and features a 400-foot interior street with numerous food, store and entertainment outlets. This concourse is built with historical architectural elements taken from the demolished Omni, the Hawks' old arena. The seating also represents a bit of a breakthrough, with 60 percent of seats located on the lowest level. The seating actually rises or lowers depending on the event. For basketball, this means extraordinary intimacy and great sight lines.

CONCESSIONS

Most of the concession stands at Philips Arena are located along the Hawk Walk, an indoor street running the length of the stadium. In addition to the standard fare of hamburgers, pizza and hot dogs, hungry fans can feast on calzone, Buffalo wings, Texas chili and various grilled sandwiches.

GAME DAY TIPS

• **Gate hours:** Gates open 90 minutes prior to tip-off.
• **Prohibited items:** Glass bottles, aluminum cans, coolers, thermoses, outside food, alcoholic beverages, sticks, brooms, banners and laser pointers are prohibited. Beachballs and frisbees are also not allowed. Animals are prohibited, except for those that provide service to disabled patrons. Smoking is allowed only in designated areas.
• **Ticket tips:** Single-game tickets are usually easy to come by, although they sell more quickly when one of the league's showcase teams, such as the Knicks or the Lakers, is in town. Tickets can also be hard to get for games against division rivals Utah and San Antonio, especially near the end of the season if the team is in a race for a playoff spot.
• **Lost and found:** (404) 878-3122.

Arena Facts

Opened: *Sept. 24, 1999*
Cost: *$213 million*
Capacity: *19,445*
Home Sweet Home:
• *The closeness of the fans to the court at Philips Arena is a boon to the home team as Hawks players catch the infectious enthusiasm and passion of their crowd.*

Seating Plan

■ VIP	$400	■	$50
■ VIP	$150	■	$40
■ VIP	$110	■	$20
■ VIP	$80	■	$10
■	N/A	ATM Bank of America Club,	
■	N/A	International Entry,	
■	$65	Hawk Walk Entry	
■	$55	♿ Throughout	

CNN ENTRY

INTERNATIONAL ENTRY

HAWK WALK ENTRY

CLUB ENTRY

Club Seats

Premium Seating-Suites

MARTA ENTRY

CLUB ENTRANCE

Nearby Hotels

▼▼▼ **Courtyard by Marriott-Downtown** *(Motor Inn)*, 175 Piedmont Ave. NE (Atlanta), (404) 659-2727, $89-$179
▼▼▼ **Fairfield Inn by Marriott-Downtown** *(Motel)*, 175 Piedmont Ave. NE (Atlanta), (404) 659-7777, $79-$139
▼▼▼ **Hampton Inn & Suites Atlanta Downtown** *(Motel)*, 161 Spring St. (Atlanta), (404) 589-1111, $79-$109
▼▼▼ **Omni Hotel at CNN Center** *(Hotel)*, 100 CNN Center (Atlanta), (404) 659-0000, $99-$224
▼▼ **Travelodge-Downtown** *(Motel)*, 311 Courtland St. NE (Atlanta), (404) 659-4545, $75-$135

Nearby Restaurants

▼▼▼ **The Atlanta Grill** *(Continental)*, 181 Peachtree St. NE in The Ritz-Carlton, Atlanta (Atlanta), (404) 659-0400, $16-$25
▼▼▼ **Hsu's Gourmet Chinese Restaurant** *(Chinese)*, 192 Peachtree Center Ave. (Atlanta), (404) 659-2788, $10-$20
▼▼▼▼ **Nikolai's Roof** *(Continental)*, 255 Courtland St. NE in the Hilton Atlanta & Towers (Atlanta), (404) 221-6362, $67-$116 (dinner only)
▼▼ **Pittypat's Porch** *(Regional American)*, 25 International Blvd. NW (Atlanta), (404) 525-8228, $19-$25 (dinner only)
[FYI] **The Varsity** *(American)*, 61 North Ave. NE (Atlanta), (404) 881-1706, $4-$10

Directions: From I-75/85 south, exit Williams St., right onto International Blvd. to arena. From I-75/85 north, exit International Blvd. to arena. From I-20, exit Windsor/Spring St. to Marietta, turn left and follow signs to arena. *By Public Transportation:* A train station and several bus routes provide quick access to the arena. Call the Metropolitan Atlanta Rapid Transit Authority (MARTA) at (404) 848-4800 for information. *Parking:* There are 4,345 arena spaces (all deck lots have wheelchair-accessible spaces). More lots are on Jones Ave., Marietta St., Techwood Dr. and International Blvd.

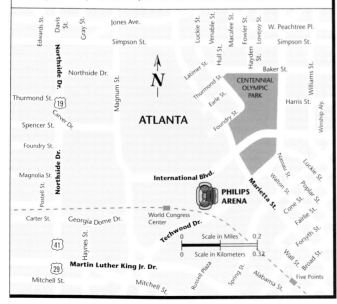

BOSTON CELTICS

NO TEAM IN NBA HISTORY HAS WON with the frequency of the Boston Celtics. Since the franchise's birth in 1946, it has captured 16 NBA titles, all of them coming within a remarkable 30-year stretch between 1956 and '86. The rise of the Celtics corresponds directly to Red Auerbach's first year as coach and to point guard Bob Cousy's first year running the offense. By 1956 the Celtics had added devastating rebounder Bill Russell at center, forward Tom Heinsohn and guards Bill Sharman and Frank Ramsey, all of them future Hall of Famers. With a dream lineup and the cigar-chomping Auerbach as coach, the Celtics won an unparalleled eight straight NBA titles beginning in 1958. Other notables, including gifted scorer John Havlicek, joined the streak in progress and stayed around while the Celtics won four more titles in the next 10 years. The squad experienced a significant slump in the late 1970s, recording below .500 seasons in 1977–78 and 1978–79. But by the following season a crop of standouts, including rookie forward Larry Bird and young post man Cedric Maxwell, was preparing to bring the team back to the top. With the additions of forward Kevin McHale and veteran center Robert Parish in 1980–81, the winning recipe was complete and the Celtics took their 14th NBA finals series 4-2 over Houston. The Celtics would follow that with two more titles in the 1980s and lose two more in dramatic battles with the Lakers. Bird, a three-time league MVP, retired in 1992. The Celtics have yet to recover, reaching the playoffs just once since.

Antoine Walker provides the Celtics with a powerful inside presence and terrific outside shooting.

POSTSEASON
• NBA Championships.....16
(1956–57, 1958–59, 1959–60, 1960–61, 1961–62, 1962–63, 1963–64, 1964–65, 1965–66, 1967–68, 1968–69, 1973–74, 1975–76, 1980–81, 1983–84, 1985–86)

RETIRED NUMBERS
• Walter Brown (1)
• Red Auerbach (2)
• Dennis Johnson (3)
• Bill Russell (6)
• Jo Jo White (10)
• Bob Cousy (14)
• Tom Heinsohn (15)
• Tom Sanders (16)
• John Havlicek (17)
• Dave Cowens (18)
• Don Nelson (19)

Jump Shot
• *One of the most powerful teams in basketball history, Boston owns some staggering records, including a 1959 game in which the team scored 173 points against Minneapolis. Celtics players have also made 114 appearances in the All-Star game, led by Bob Cousy and John Havlicek, both of whom played in 13 matches.*

• Bill Sharman (21)
• Ed Macauley (22)
• Frank Ramsey (23)
• Sam Jones (24)
• K.C. Jones (25)
• Kevin McHale (32)
• Larry Bird (33)
• Reggie Lewis (35)
• Robert Parish (00)
• Jim Loscutoff (LOSCY)

TEAM RECORDS
• **Larry Bird (1979–92)**
FT Pct. (career): .886
Points (game): 60
(March 12, 1985)
Points-Per-Game (career): 24.3
• **Bob Cousy (1950–63)**
Assists (career): 6,945
• **John Havlicek (1962–78)**
Games (career): 1,270
Points (career): 26,395
• **Cedric Maxwell (1977–85)**
FG Pct. (career): .559
• **Robert Parish (1980–94)**
Blocks (season): 214 (1980–81)
• **Bill Russell (1956–69)**
Rebounds (game): 51
(Feb. 5, 1960)
Rebounds (season): 1,930
(1963–64)
Rebounds (career): 21,620

LEAGUE HONORS
NBA MVP
• Bob Cousy (1956–1957)
• Bill Russell (1957–58, 1960–61, 1961–62, 1962–63, 1964–65)

• Dave Cowens (1972–73)
• Larry Bird (1983–84, 1984–85, 1985–86)

Rookie of the Year
• Tom Heinsohn (1956–57)
• Dave Cowens (1970–71)
• Larry Bird (1979–1980)

NBA Finals MVP
• John Havlicek (1974)
• Jo Jo White (1976)
• Cedric Maxwell (1981)
• Larry Bird (1984, '86)

Basketball Hall of Fame
• Ed Macauley (1960)
• Andy Phillip (1961)
• John "Honey" Russell (1964)
• Walter Brown (1965)
• Bill Morkay (1965)
• Alvin "Doggie" Julian (1967)
• Arnold "Red" Auerbach (1968)
• Bob Cousy (1970)
• Bill Russell (1974)
• Bill Sharman (1975)
• Frank Ramsey (1981)
• John Havlicek (1983)
• Sam Jones (1983)
• Tom Heinsohn (1986)
• Bob Houbregs (1987)

"The Boston Celtics are not a basketball team, they're a way of life."
— *Red Auerbach, legendary Celtics coach*

Vital Stats
Stadium Address:
150 Causeway St., Boston, Mass.
Phone: (617) 624-1000
Web: nba.com/celtics, fleetcenter.com
Box Office: (617) 523-3030, Mon.–Sun. 11–7, off-season Mon.–Fri. 11–5
Media Coverage:
Radio: WEEI (850 AM)
TV: Fox Sports Net
Practice Facility: The Sports Authority Training Center, Waltham, Mass.

• Pete Maravich (1987)
• Clyde Lovellette (1988)
• K.C. Jones (1989)
• Dave Bing (1990)
• Nate "Tiny" Archibald (1991)
• Dave Cowens (1991)
• Bill Walton (1993)
• Bailey Howell (1997)
• Larry Bird (1998)
• Arnie Risen (1998)
• Wayne Ebry (1999)
• Kevin McHale (1999)
• John Thompson (1999)

Timeline

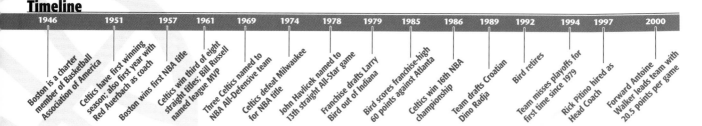

1946	1951	1957	1961	1969	1974	1978	1979	1985	1986	1989	1992	1994	1997	2000

Boston is a charter member of Basketball Association of America

Celtics have first winning season; also first year with Red Auerbach as coach

Boston wins first NBA title

Celtics win third of eight straight titles; Bill Russell named league MVP

Three Celtics named to NBA All-Defensive team

Celtics defeat Milwaukee for NBA title

John Havlicek named to 13th straight All-Star game

Franchise drafts Larry Bird out of Indiana

Bird scores franchise-high 60 points against Atlanta

Celtics win 16th NBA championship

Team drafts Croatian Dino Radja

Bird retires

Team misses playoffs for first time since 1979

Rick Pitino hired as Head Coach

Forward Antoine Walker leads team with 20.5 points per game

FLEETCENTER: BIGGER AND BETTER

OPENED IN 1995 TO REPLACE historic Boston Garden, the FleetCenter increased capacity for Celtics games by more than 3,900 seats. Located behind the former site of the now-demolished Garden, this multisport facility was built in just 27 months and provides fans with such luxuries as air conditioning, a multimillion dollar scoreboard and a pair of in-house restaurants. Although the new arena does not feature decades of tradition, the FleetCenter is still an enjoyable place to cheer.

CONCESSION

The selection of food offered at the FleetCenter is truly dizzying. Aside from the traditional offerings, patrons can have calzone, seasoned fries, lobster rolls and clam chowder. Vegetarians and the health-conscious will enjoy the fresh fruit, sandwiches and wraps, as well as a variety of salads. Beverages include frozen cocktails, microbrew and imported beers, wine and specialty coffees.

GAME DAY TIPS

• **Gate hours:** Gates open one hour prior to tip-off.
• **Prohibited items:** Food, beverages, cameras and recording devices are prohibited. Laser pointers, beachballs and weapons are not permitted. Smoking is not allowed.
• **Ticket tips:** The Celtics tend to sell out only when they are playing such archrivals as the N.Y. Knicks or the L.A. Lakers. Otherwise, it's quite easy to get tickets to games at the last minute. The FleetCenter is known for having far better views than the Boston Garden. Nevertheless, some fans complain that the less expensive seats are too far from the action.
• **Lost and found:** (617) 624-1331.

Arena Facts

Opened: Sept. 30, 1995
Cost: $160 million
Capacity: 18,624
Home Sweet Home:
• With an incredible 16 NBA championship banners and 21 retired jerseys hanging from the rafters, the Fleet Center can be an imposing place to play. Opposing players only need to look up to remember the great teams and players of the Celtics' past.

Seating Plan

		$85			$22
		$72			$18
		$60			$10
		$55			**Club/Premium Seats**
		$44	ATM		**Sections 6, 7**
		$33			**Sections 3, 14, 303, 314,**
		$27			**318, 329**

WEST GATE   EAST GATE

Directions

Directions: Exit I-93 at Storrow Dr. (exit 26) southbound and at Causeway St. (exit 25) northbound. By Subway: Take green or orange line to North Station. By Train: Take purple line to North Station. By Bus: Take Rte. 4 to North Station. Call MBTA at (617) 222-3200 for information. **Parking:** A garage under the stadium for 1,150 cars is accessible via Nashua St. The garage and the lot at nearby Tip O'Neil Federal Building have limited spots for people with disabilities. There are many private lots on Friend, Staniford and Portland Sts. and Lomansey Wy.

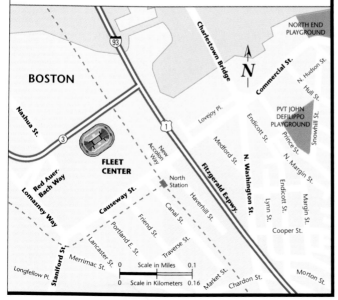

Nearby Hotels

▼▼▼▼ **Boston Harbor Hotel** *(Hotel)*, 70 Rowes Wharf (Boston), (617) 439-7000, $400-$2000
▼▼▼ **Boston Marriott Long Wharf Hotel** *(Hotel)*, 296 State St. (Boston), (617) 227-2867, $425-$600
▼▼▼ **Harborside Inn of Boston** *(Motor Inn)*, 185 State St. (Boston), (617) 723-7500, $145-$310
▼▼▼ **Holiday Inn Select-Boston Government Center** *(Hotel)*, 5 Blossom St. (Boston), (617) 742-7630, $149-$329
▼▼▼ **Millennium Bostonian Hotel** *(Hotel)*, Faneuil Hall Marketplace (Boston), (617) 523-3600, $305-$400

Nearby Restaurants

▼ **Durgin Park** *(Regional American)*, 340 Faneuil Hall Marketplace (Boston), (617) 227-2038, $6-$20
▼▼ **The Kinsale** *(Irish)*, 2 Center Plaza Government Center (Boston), (617) 742-5577, $9-$17
▼ **No Name Restaurant** *(Seafood)*, 17 Fish Pier (Boston), (617) 423-2705, $8-$15
▼▼▼ **Ristorante Davide** *(Northern Italian)*, 326 Commercial St. (Boston), (617) 227-5745, $18-$30
▼▼▼▼ **Rowes Wharf Restaurant** *(Regional American)*, 70 Rowes Wharf in the Boston Harbor Hotel (Boston), (617) 439-3995, $26-$35

CHARLOTTE HORNETS

THE EXPANSION CHARLOTTE HORNETS had an ominous foretaste of the season to come in its very first game in 1988, a 133-93 pasting at the hands of the Cleveland Cavaliers. Spending the majority of their inaugural campaign getting stung by opponents, the Hornets never had more than two wins in a row en route to a dismal 20-62. However, there were some bright spots, notably the sweet scoring touch of Kelly Tripucka and the emergence of 5-foot-3-inch guard Muggsy Bogues as a crowd-pleasing play maker. The diminutive Bogues proved to be the only bright spot in the team's sophomore season, finishing fourth in the league with 10.7 assists per game. Charlotte's turnaround was gradual. In three successive seasons, beginning in 1990, the team drafted shooting guard Kendall Gill, power forward Larry Johnson and 6-foot-10-inch center Alonzo Mourning. The Mourning-Johnson combination proved particularly potent as the duo combined for more than 40 points and 20 rebounds a game. Riding the wave of a 9-3 April, Charlotte enjoyed its first-ever winning season. In its first playoff series, the team knocked off the Boston Celtics on Mourning's 20-foot buzzer beater in game four. However, since 1995 the team has been in transition, with management trading away such stalwarts as Mourning, Johnson and Bogues. Along the way, established players such as Glen Rice, Anthony Mason and Vlade Divac have come and gone. Today's Hornets, led by the likes of David Wesley and Jamal Mashburn, hope that they can get the NBA buzzing again.

Vital Stats

Stadium Address:
100 Paul Buck Blvd.,
Charlotte, N.C.
Phone: (704) 357-4700
Web:
charlottehornets.com,
charlottecoliseum.com
Box Office: (704) 357-4801, Mon.–Fri. 10–5
Media Coverage:
Radio: WBT (1110
AM/99.3 FM)
TV: WAXN (Channel 64),
Fox Sports Net
Training Facility:
Hornets Training Center,
Charlotte, N.C.

Jamal Mashburn provides scoring punch for the Hornets.

Jump Shot

• *The roots of the Hornets name go back to the Revolutionary War. With British Gen. Charles Cornwallis marching northward, his troops encountered unexpectedly fierce resistance outside Charlotte. The greatly outnumbered Americans halted the British advance and Cornwallis was heard to say, "There's a rebel in every bush. It's a veritable nest of hornets."*

POSTSEASON
• **Playoff Appearances**........5
(1992–93, 1994–95, 1996–97, 1997–98, 1999–2000)

RETIRED NUMBERS
• **Fans (6) (Sixth Man)**
• **Bobby Phills (13)**

TEAM RECORDS
• **Muggsy Bogues (1988–98)**
Assists (game): 19 (3 times)
Assists (playoff game): 15
(April 29, 1993)
Assists (season): 867 (1989–90)
Assists (career): 5,557
Starts (career): 501
Steals (career): 1,067
• **Dell Curry (1988–98)**
Consecutive FT: 43
FG (career): 3,951
Games (career): 701
Points (career): 9,839
3-Point FG (game): 7 (tie)
(Dec. 14, 1995)
3-Point FG (career): 929
• **Vlade Divac (1996–98)**
Blocks (game): 12
(Feb. 12, 1997)
• **Kenny Gattison (1989–95)**
FG Pct. (career): .529
• **Dave Hoppen (1999–91)**
FG Pct. (season): .564
(1988–89)
• **Larry Johnson (1991–96)**
Rebounds (game): 23
(Mar. 10, 1992)
Rebounds (season): 899
(1991–92)

Rebounds (career): 3,479
FG (season): 728 (1992–93)
FT (game): 18 (tie)
(Jan. 20, 1991)
FT (career): 1,513
• **Eddie Jones (1998–2000)**
Steals (game): 9 (Nov. 4, 1999)
Steals (season): 192
(1999–2000)
3-Pointers (game): 7 (tie)
(April 14, 2000)
• **Brad Miller (1998–2000)**
Consecutive FG: 14
• **Alonzo Mourning (1992–95)**
Blocks (playoff game): 7
(April 28, 1995)
Blocks (season): 271 (1992–93)
Blocks (career): 684
FT (season): 495 (1994–95)
Rebounds (playoff game): 20
(April 30, 1995)
• **Johnny Newman (1990–94)**
FT (game): 18 (tie)
(Jan. 19, 1991)
• **J.R. Reid (1989–93, 97–99)**
Personal Fouls (season): 292 (1989–90)
• **Glen Rice (1995–99)**
FG (game): 18 (Mar. 6, 1997)
Minutes (season): 3,362
(1996–97)
Points (game): 48 (Mar. 6, '97)

Points (playoff game): 39
(April 26, 1997)
Points (season): 2,115
(1996–97)
Points-Per–Game (season): 26.8 (1996–97)
Points-Per–Game (career): 23.5
3-Point FG (game): 7 (tie)
(Nov. 19, 1998)
3-Point FG (season): 207
(1996–97)
3-Point FG Pct. (season): 470
(1996–97)
3-Point FG Pct. (career): .444
• **Kelly Tripucka (1988–91)**
FT Pct. (season): .910
(1990–91)
FT Pct. (career): .879

LEAGUE HONORS
Rookie of the Year
• **Larry Johnson (1991–92)**

Sixth Man Award
• **Dell Curry (1993–94)**

All-Star MVP
• **Glen Rice (1997)**

NBA Executive of the Year
• **Bob Bass (1996–97)**

"This team belongs to the fans of Charlotte."
— Hornets owner George Shinn, announcing that team was withdrawing its application to relocate to Memphis

Timeline

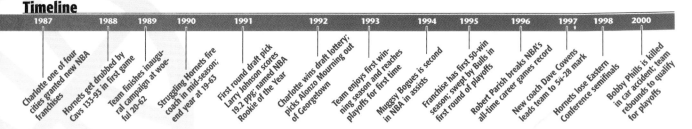

1987 — Charlotte one of four cities granted new NBA franchises

1988 — Hornets get drubbed by Cavs 133-93 in first game

1989 — Team finishes inaugural campaign at woeful 20-62

1990 — Struggling Hornets fire coach in mid-season; end year at 19-63

1991 — First round draft pick Larry Johnson scores 19.2 ppg; named NBA Rookie of the Year

1992 — Charlotte wins draft lottery; picks Alonzo Mourning out of Georgetown

1993 — Team enjoys first winning season and reaches playoffs for first time

1994 — Muggsy Bogues is second in NBA in assists

1995 — Franchise has first 50-win season; swept by Bulls in first round of playoffs

1996 — Robert Parish breaks NBA's all-time career games record

1997 — New coach Dave Cowens leads team to 54-28 mark

1998 — Hornets lose Eastern Conference semifinals

2000 — Bobby Phills is killed in car accident; team rebounds to qualify for playoffs

88

CHARLOTTE COLISEUM: THINGS ARE BUZZING AT THE HIVE

THE CHARLOTTE COLISEUM was designed to make the fans as much a part of the action as possible. Owner George Shinn, the man who spearheaded the push to get a NBA team for Charlotte, has taken this to heart and is usually seen mingling with the crowd. Because of the relatively small fan base, many of the fans seem to know each other, which adds to the friendly ambience. Along with a high-tech scoreboard, the Hive is home to Super Hugo, whose high-flying acrobatics have earned him three NBA mascot slam-dunk titles.

CONCESSIONS

Fans at Charlotte Coliseum can sample the best of everything, from standard arena fare — hot dogs, hamburgers and pizza — to local specialties. Among the latter are baked potatoes served any way you like them, fried chicken, pork barbecue and a variety of local beers.

GAME DAY TIPS

• **Gate hours:** Gates open 90 minutes prior to tip-off.
• **Prohibited items:** Video cameras, audio recorders, weapons and laser pointers are prohibited. Food, alcohol, cans, bottles or coolers may not be brought into the arena. Signs and banners are allowed provided they are inoffensive, non-flammable and small enough for one person to hold. Smoking is allowed only in designated areas.
• **Ticket tips:** Tickets for Hornets games are usually easy to get and prices are lower than the NBA average. However, when Charlotte is playing against such Central Division rivals as the Pacers, it is best to get your tickets in advance. This is especially true toward the end of the season if the Hornets are in the hunt for a playoff spot. The Coliseum is intimate enough that fans in the lower seats are often close enough to the players to get autographs.
• **Lost and found:** (704) 357-4791.

Arena Facts

Opened: Aug. 11, 1988
Cost: $52 million
Capacity: 19,925
Home Sweet Home:
• In 2000 poor fan support was a major factor in pushing Hornets owner George Shinn to apply for relocation to Memphis. But the capacity crowds that turned out for the team's 2001 playoff run prompted Shinn to think again and nix the move.

Seating Plan

■	$85	▨	$21
▨	$60	■	$15
▨	$55	▨	$9
■	$45	ATM Sections 109, 118	
■	$39	♿ Throughout	
▨	$29		

MAIN ENTRANCE

89

Directions: From I-77, take exit 5 (Tyvola Rd.) to Paul Buck Blvd., turn right. From I-85, take exit 33 to Billy Graham Pkwy., turn right on Tyvola Rd. to Paul Buck Blvd., turn left. **By Bus:** Bus No. 10 from Downtown Transportation Center stops about three blocks from the Coliseum. For information, call 704-336-7433. **Parking:** There is parking at the Coliseum for more than 8,000 cars. More than 100 spaces are reserved for handicapped patrons. Extra parking is available at Charlotte Regional Farmers' Market next door.

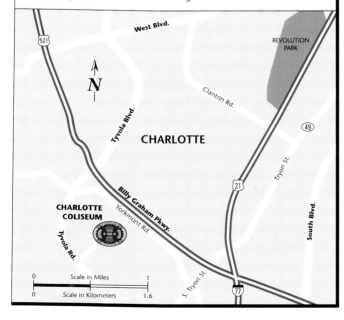

Nearby Hotels

▼▼▼ **Embassy Suites** (*Suite Hotel*), 4800 S. Tryon St. (Charlotte), (704) 527-8400, $109-$239
▼▼▼ **Hampton Inn-Executive Park** (*Motel*), 440 Griffith Rd. (Charlotte), (704) 525-0747, $75-$83
▼▼▼ **La Quinta Inn & Suites-Charlotte Coliseum** (*Motel*), 4900 S. Tryon St. (Charlotte), (704) 523-5599, $82-$112
▼▼ **Red Roof Inn Coliseum** (*Motel*), 131 Red Roof Dr. (Charlotte), (704) 529-1020, $37-$55
▼▼▼ **Wyndham Garden Hotel** (*Motor Inn*), 2600 Yorkmont Rd. (Charlotte), (704) 357-9100, $75-$106

Nearby Restaurants

▼▼ **The Blue Marlin** (*Steak & Seafood*), 1511 East Blvd. (Charlotte), (704) 334-3838, $9-$16 (dinner only)
▼▼ **Koko Chinese Restaurant** (*Chinese*), 1742 Lombardy Cir. (Charlotte), (704) 338-6869, $12-$14
▼▼▼ **La Bibliotheque** (*French*), 1901 Roxborough Rd. in the Roxborough Building, 1st floor (Charlotte), (704) 365-5000, $19-$29
▼▼▼ **The Silver Cricket** (*Regional American*), 4705 South Blvd. (Charlotte), (704) 525-0061, $20-$35 (dinner only)
▼▼▼ **Villa Antonio Fine Italian Ristorante** (*Italian*), 4707 South Blvd. (Charlotte), (704) 523-1594, $15-$35

CHICAGO BULLS

WHILE IT'S TRUE THAT CHICAGO BULLS FANS have been spoiled with success in recent years, that success was a long time in coming. After joining the league for the 1966–67 season, the franchise waited eight years for its first playoff series win. Then things got really bad. Starting in 1975–76, the Bulls missed the playoffs altogether in nine of 11 seasons and didn't enjoy another playoff series win until 1988. During the lean years, fans contented themselves with watching early franchise players such as the hardworking Jerry Sloan and the enormous Artis Gilmore. During this period of ineptness, the Bulls did do something right, however. In 1984 the team drafted a guard by the name of Michael Jordan out of North Carolina. Jordan showed immediate promise, winning NBA Rookie of the Year and astounding fans around the league with his gravity-defying dunks and all-round skills. As gifted on defense as on offense, everyone knew Jordan was the real thing. But success would have to wait until a winning team could be built around him. The Bulls' brain trust, led by Jerry Krause, went to work, drafting key rebounder Horace Grant and defensive whiz Scottie Pippen in 1987 and adding three-point threat B.J. Armstrong along with coach Phil Jackson two years later. By 1990–91 the Bulls were a juggernaut and romped through the playoffs for the first of three straight titles. Jordan collected trophies like they were trading cards and things were good in the Windy City. Jordan retired after the 1993 season to play baseball, but returned triumphantly two years later to lead the Bulls to another trio of championships. His like will not be seen again.

Elton Brand is one of the NBA's fiercest rebounders.

POSTSEASON
• NBA Championships.......6
(1990–91, 1991–92, 1992–93, 1995–96, 1996–97, 1997–98)

RETIRED NUMBERS
• Jerry Sloan (4)
• Bob Love (10)
• Michael Jordan (23)

TEAM RECORDS
• Tony Boerwinkle
(1968–78)
Rebounds (game): 37
(Jan. 8, 1970)
• Elton Brand (1999–present)
Consecutive FG (game): 14
(April 13, 2000)
• Artis Gilmore
(1976–82, 1987–88)
Blocks (season): 221 (1981–82)

Jump Shot

• While Wilt Chamberlain has more NBA records than Michael Jordan, the latter dominates where it counts most: the postseason. Jordan has the record for most career playoff points (5,987), free throws (1,463), steals (376) and points per game (33.4). Not surprisingly, Jordan won six finals MVP awards.

"Best there ever was, best there ever will be."
— *Inscription on statue of Michael Jordan outside United Center*

Blocks-Per-Game (season):
2.7 (1981–82)
Def. Rebounds (game): 25
(Dec. 22, 1978)
FG Pct. (season): .670
(1980–81)
FG Pct. (career): .587
• Craig Hodges (1988–92)
FT Pct. (career): .900
• Michael Jordan
(1984–93, 1995–98)
Assists (career): 5,012
FG (game): 27 (Jan. 16, 1993)
FG (career): 10,962
FG Att. (game): 49
(Jan. 16, 1993)
FG Att. (career): 21,686
FT (game): 26 (Feb. 26, 1987)
FT (career): 6,798
Games (career): 930
Points (game): 69
(Mar. 28, 1990)
Points (season): 3,041
(1986–87)
Points (career): 29,277
Points-Per-Game (season):
37.1 (1986–87)
Rebounds (career): 5,836
Steals (game): 10
(Jan. 29, 1988)

Steals (season): 259 (1987–88)
Steals (career): 2,306
3-Point FG (game): 7
(Jan. 18, 1990)
• Scottie Pippen (1987–98)
Turnovers (game): 12
(Feb. 25, 1990)
• Guy Rodgers (1966–67)
Assists (game): 24
(Dec. 21, 1966)
Assists (season): 908
(1966–67)
Assists-Per-Game (season):
11.2 (1966–67)
• Dennis Rodman (1995–98)
Def. Rebounds (season):
780 (1997–98)
Off. Rebounds (season):
421 (1997–98)
Rebounds (season):
1,201 (1997–98)
Rebounds-Per-Game
(season): 16.1 (1996–97)
• Nate Thurmond (1974–76)
Blocks (game): 12
(Oct. 18, 1974)

LEAGUE HONORS
NBA MVP
• Michael Jordan (1987–88, 1990–91, 1991–92, 1995–96, 1997–98)

Rookie of the Year
• Walt Bellamy (1961–62)
• Terry Dischinger (1962–63)
• Michael Jordan (1984–85)
• Elton Brand (1999–2000)

Vital Stats

Stadium Address:
1901 W. Madison St., Chicago, Ill.
Phone: (312) 455-4500
Web: nba.com/bulls united-center.com
Box Office:
(800) 4NBA-TIX, Mon.–Fri. 11–6, game days until halftime
Media Coverage:
Radio: ESPN (1000 AM)
TV: WGN (Channel 9), WCIU (Channel 26), Fox Sports Net
Practice Facility:
Sheri L. Berto Center, Deerfield, Ill.

Defensive Player of the Year
• Michael Jordan (1987–88)

NBA Sixth Man of the Year
• Toni Kukoc (1995–96)

Coach of the Year
• Johnny Kerr (1966–67)
• Dick Motta (1970–71)
• Phil Jackson (1995–96)

NBA Finals MVP
• Michael Jordan (1991, '92, '93, '96, '97, '98)

Timeline

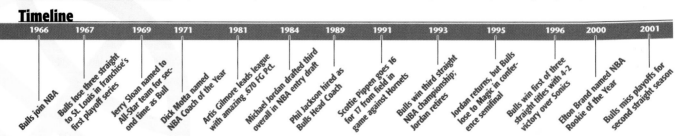

1966 — Bulls join NBA
1967 — Bulls lose three straight to St. Louis in franchise's first playoff series
1969 — Jerry Sloan named to All-Star team for second time as Bull
1971 — Dick Motta named NBA Coach of the Year
1981 — Artis Gilmore leads league with amazing .670 FG Pct.
1984 — Michael Jordan drafted third overall in NBA entry draft
1989 — Phil Jackson hired as Bulls Head Coach
1991 — Scottie Pippen goes 16 for 17 from field in game against Hornets
1993 — Bulls win third straight NBA championship; Jordan retires
1995 — Jordan returns, but Bulls lose to Magic in conference semifinal
1996 — Bulls win first of three straight titles with 4-2 victory over Sonics
2000 — Elton Brand named NBA Rookie of the Year
2001 — Bulls miss playoffs for second straight season

UNITED CENTER: HOME OF CHAMPIONS

WHEN MICHAEL JORDAN RETIRED the first time, he said he didn't have the heart to leave the mystique-filled Chicago Stadium, which he and fans loved, and play across the street at the United Center. Fortunately for Chicago fans, he changed his mind and suitably christened the building with three titles between 1996 and '99. He also discovered improved player facilities, state-of-the-art fan amenities, good sight lines and an increased capacity, important for the legions of Bulls fans who flock there.

CONCESSION

The United Center has a number of must-try Chicago specialties, such as Italian beef sandwiches, thick-crust pizza and foot-long hot dogs with unique toppings. The microbrewery serves a Bulls Pale Ale. Vegetarians have a choice of garden burgers and salads.

Arena Facts

Opened: Aug. 29, 1994
Cost: $175 million
Capacity: 21,711
Home Sweet Home:
• Chicago fans love their Bulls. From the team's first game at the United Center in 1994, every home game was sold out until Nov. 7, 2000 — even though four of those years were without main-draw Michael Jordan.

GAME DAY TIPS

• **Gate hours:** Gates open 90 minutes prior to tip-off.
• **Prohibited items:** Banners, food, beverages and video cameras are prohibited; likewise weapons, beachballs, laser pointers and frisbees. Animals are not allowed in the arena, except those providing service to the disabled. Smoking is allowed only in designated areas.
• **Ticket tips:** Despite the retirement of Michael Jordan, the Bulls are still a very popular team, selling out the majority of their games. Single-game tickets

are available, however, if purchased well in advance. Games against the Pacers are tough to come by. The arena has fairly good sight lines, but fans complain about the large distance from the upper level to the floor.
• **Lost and found:** (312) 455-4500.

Seating Plan

▪ $85	▪ $22
▪ $80	▪ $10
▪ $50	ATM **Sections 106, 116, 309**
▪ $38	♿ **Throughout**
▪ $28	

Directions: From I-90, exit at Madison St. and turn west. From I-55 north, exit at Damen St./Ashland Ave. and head north. From I-290 east, exit at Damen St., turn right on Madison St. By Train: Take Blue Line (Forest Park Train) to Medical Center stop. By Bus: No. 20 Madison Bus and No. 19 Stadium Express go to the center. Call (312) 836-7000 for more information. **Parking:** More than 6,000 parking spots are available at the center. Disabled parking is in lots G and H. Private lots are on W. Harrison, N. Paulina, W. Madison and W. Jackson Sts.

Nearby Hotels

▼▼ **Best Western Grant Park Hotel** (*Hotel*), 1100 S. Michigan Ave. (Chicago), (312) 922-2900, $139-$335
▼▼▼ **Hyatt at University Village** (*Hotel*), 625 S. Ashland Ave. (Chicago), (312) 491-1234, $190-$215
▼▼▼ **Hyatt on Printers Row** (*Hotel*), 500 S. Dearborn St. (Chicago), (312) 986-1234, $205-$230
▼▼ **Quality Inn-Downtown** (*Hotel*), 1 Mid City Plaza (Chicago), (312) 829-5000, $99-$169
▼▼▼ **W Chicago City Center** (*Classic Hotel*), 172 W. Adams St. (Chicago), (312) 332-1200, $290-$464

Nearby Restaurants

▼▼ **Como Inn** (*Northern Italian*), 546 Milwaukee Ave. (Chicago), (312) 421-5222, $12-$25
▼▼ **Harry Caray's Restaurant** (*Steakhouse*), 33 W. Kinzie St. (Chicago), (312) 828-0966, $11-$33
▼▼▼ **Marche** (*French*), 833 W. Randolph St. (Chicago), (312) 226-8399, $14-$34
▼▼▼▼ **OneSixtyBlue,** (*American*), 160 N. Loomis St. (Chicago), (312) 850-0303, $19-$30
▼ **Wishbone** (*American*), 1001 W. Washington Blvd. (Chicago), (312) 850-2663, $7-$14

CLEVELAND CAVALIERS

DESPITE AN ALL-TIME ROSTER that includes some of the game's best players, the Cleveland Cavaliers — or "the Cavs" as fans call them — have had a hard time racking up the big wins. Since their debut in 1970, the Cavs have recorded only 13 winning seasons, most of which came in two bursts: in the mid- to late '70s and the late '80s to early '90s. In the early years, however, the team showed a lot of potential. After four years in the basement of the Central Division, Cleveland became one of the NBA's fastest-maturing teams when it beat out New York in 1976 to take the division crown and advance to the Eastern Conference semifinals. Under coach Bill Fitch's leadership, players such as Austin Carr, Campy Russell, Jim Brewer and Bobby "Bingo" Smith showed that a young team could be capable of good basketball. The Cavaliers qualified for the playoffs in the next two seasons, but failed to live up to their promise and slowly slipped back to the bottom of the division throughout the early 1980s. In 1986 the Cavs began a renaissance of sorts. With Lenny Wilkens as the new Head Coach, the team shrewdly began to assemble a rotation of marquee players: center Brad Daugherty, forward Larry Nance, and guards Ron Harper and Mark Price among them. The team responded immediately, pulling itself out of its losing slump. In 1991 the Cavs put it all together to soar through to the conference finals, where the team finally stumbled in the face of the virtually unbeatable Chicago Bulls. Since then, Cleveland has been a regular playoff participant, but has returned to its habit of failing to advance beyond the early rounds.

"I loved playing here."
— Mark Price, addressing Cavs fans when his jersey was retired

Vital Stats

Stadium Address:
100 Gateway Plaza,
Cleveland, Ohio
Phone: (216)420-2000
Web: cavs.com,
gundarena.com
Box Office:
(216) 420-2200, Mon.–
Sat. 9:30–6, Sun. 12–5
Media Coverage:
Radio: WTAM (1100 AM)
TV: WUAB (Channel 43),
Fox Sports Net
Training Facility:
Gund Arena,
Cleveland, Ohio

Clarence Weatherspoon supplies the Cavs with inside power.

Jump Shot

• To commemorate the 30-year anniversary of the team, the Cavaliers recently honored their five greatest players in a ceremony for the Cavs All-Star starting five. Austin Carr, Brad Daugherty, Shawn Kemp, Larry Nance and Mark Price were voted as the five Cavs players who most influenced the history of basketball in Cleveland, as well as in the NBA.

POSTSEASON
• **Central Division Titles....1**
(1975–76)

RETIRED NUMBERS
• **Bingo Smith (7)**
• **Larry Nance (22)**
• **Mark Price (25)**
• **Austin Carr (34)**
• **Nate Thurmond (42)**
• **Brad Daugherty (43)**

TEAM RECORDS
• **Jim Bagley (1982–87)**
Assists (season): 735 (1985–86)
• **Jim Brewer (1973–79)**
Rebounds (season): 891
(1975–76)
• **Austin Carr (1971–80)**
FG (career): 4,272
FG Att. (career): 9,480
• **Brad Daugherty (1986–96)**
Def. Rebounds (career): 4,020
FT (career): 2,741
FT Att. (career): 3,670
Points (career): 10,389
Rebounds (career): 5,227
Turnovers (career): 1,511
• **Danny Ferry (1990–2000)**
Games (career): 723
• **World B. Free (1982–86)**
Points-Per-Game (career): 23.0
• **Steve Kerr (1989–93)**
3-Point FG Pct. (season):
.507 (1989–90)
3-Point FG Pct. (career): .472
• **Ron Harper (1986–90)**
Steals (game): 10
(Mar. 10, 1987)

Steals (season): 209 (1986–87)
Turnovers (season): 345
(1986–87)
• **Tyrone Hill (1993–97)**
FG Pct. (season): .600
(1996–97)
• **Geoff Huston (1980–85)**
Assists (game): 27
(Jan. 27, 1982)
• **Shawn Kemp (1997–2000)**
FT (season): 493 (1999–2000)
FT Att. (season): 635
(1999–2000)
Personal Fouls (season): 371
(1999–2000)
• **Mike Mitchell (1978–82)**
FG (season): 853 (1981)
FG Att. (season): 1,791
(1980–81)
Points (season): 2,012
(1980–81)
Points-Per-Game (season):
24.5 (1980–81)
• **Larry Nance (1987–94)**
Blocks (game): 11
(Jan. 7, 1989)
Blocks (season): 243
(1991–92)
• **Wesley Person
(1997–present)**
3-Point FG (game): 8
(Feb. 17, 1998)
3-Point FG (season): 192
(1997–98)
3-Point FG Att. (season): 447
(1997–98)
• **Mark Price (1986–1995)**
Assists (career): 4,206
FT (game): 18 (Nov. 17, 1989)

FT Pct. (season): .948
(1992–93)
FT Pct. (career): .906
Steals (career): 734
3-Point FG (career): 802
• **Rick Roberson (1971–73)**
Rebounds (game): 25
(Mar. 4, 1972)
• **Cliff Robinson (1982–84)**
Def. Rebounds (season):
666 (1982–83)
• **Bingo Smith (1978–82)**
Personal Fouls (career): 1,752
• **Walt Wesley (1970–73)**
FG (game): 20 (Feb. 19, 1971)
Points (game): 50
(Feb. 19, 1971)
• **Mark West (1984–88,
1996–97)**
FG Pct. (career): .553
• **John Williams (1986–95)**
Blocks (career): 1,200
Minutes (career): 20,802
Off. Rebounds (career): 1,620

LEAGUE HONORS
Coach of the Year
• **Bill Fitch (1976)**

NBA Sportsman
• **Terrell Brandon (1997)**

Timeline

| 1970 | 1971 | 1974 | 1975 | 1976 | 1981 | 1984 | 1989 | 1991 | 1995 | 1998 | 1999 |

Cavaliers franchise plays its first season

Cavs acquire Irish scoring machine Austin Carr

Cavs come of age with March 24 114-92 win over World Champion New York Knicks

Team records its first winning season

Cavs beat New York to take Central Division; advance to Eastern Conference finals

Mike Mitchell has team record 2,012 buckets in one season

George Karl becomes Head Coach at 33; youngest in team history and in NBA at time

With their 104-96 win over the Knicks on Jan. 7, Cavs tie NBA record with 21 blocked shots

Cavs set NBA record for largest margin of victory with 68-point win over the Miami Heat

Cleveland tops NBA in defense, allowing only 89.8 ppg

Shawn Kemp becomes first Cavalier to start an NBA All-Star game

Kemp scores his 12,000th career point

GUND ARENA: GATEWAY TO B-BALL

BUILT AS PART OF THE GATEWAY DISTRICT rejuvenation program in the mid-1990s, the Gund is situated right in the thick of Cleveland's trendiest downtown area. Suitably, the Gund is a flashy, modern arena that reflects the status the Cavs have in this town. Inside the Gund is fully decked out with all the most up-to-date arena accoutrements: large display screens and scoreboards, a crystal-clear sound system and a viewing intimacy that rivals any in the NBA. Of particular note are the popular extra-wide seats, as well as the legendary Gordon's Sports Bar, where diehard fans congregate faithfully after every game.

CONCESSIONS

Gund Arena offers fans far more than the standard arena fare. Visitors can feast on sandwiches — famously overstuffed with grilled deli meats and vegetables — "skin-on" fries with a variety of toppings, pasta and salad made to order, six unique flavors of chicken wings, and an assortment of international beers and mixed drinks. Fine dining and a sports bar are also available.

Arena Facts

Opened: *Oct. 17, 1994*
Cost: *$152 million*
Capacity: *20,562*
Home Sweet Home:
• *In 1998–99 only 353,000 fans came to watch the Cavs play, a dip of almost 50 percent from the preceding season. However, in 1999–2000, more than 650,000 people came through the turnstiles, making the arena a fun place to play again.*

GAME DAY TIPS

• **Gate hours:** Gates open 90 minutes prior to tip-off.
• **Prohibited items:** Food, cans, bottles and coolers are not permitted inside the arena. Video or professional cameras, laser pointers, and poles, sticks or anything else that could serve as a weapon or a projectile may not be brought into the building. Smoking is allowed only in designated areas.
• **Ticket tips:** Tickets should be easy to get, although games against the Lakers, Philadelphia or Toronto sell more rapidly. Seats in the corner sections are especially close to the action.
• **Lost and found:** (216) 420-2359.

Seating Plan

■	$65	▢	$18
▨	$55	■	$10
▨	$45	**ATM** Sections 106, 128	
▨	$35	♿ **Throughtout**	
■	$30		
■	$26		

Directions: *Exit I-77 north or I-90 west at E. 9th St. and go north. By Public Transportation: Buses and rapid-transit trains go to the stadium. Call RTA at (216) 621-9500 for information. **Parking:** Two on-site garages can accommodate about 3,300 cars, with 72 spaces for the physically disabled. Some 30,000 spaces are available nearby on E. Prospect, Euclid and Summer Aves. and E. 9th and E. 14th Sts.*

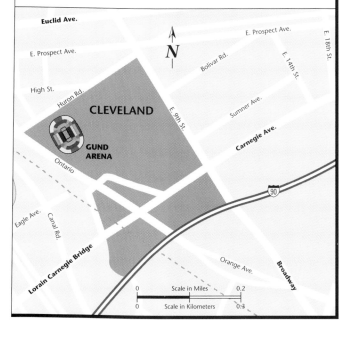

Nearby Hotels

▼▼▼ **Hampton Inn Cleveland-Downtown** *(Motel)*, 1460 E. 9th St. (Cleveland), (216) 241-6600, $99-$179
▼▼▼ **Radisson Hotel at Gateway-Cleveland** *(Hotel)*, 651 Huron Rd. (Cleveland), (216) 377-9000, $129-$149
▼▼▼▼ **The Ritz Carlton, Cleveland** *(Hotel)*, 1515 W. 3rd St. in Tower City Center (Cleveland), (216) 623-1300, $240-$264
▼▼▼ **Sheraton Cleveland City Centre** *(Hotel)*, 777 St. Clair Ave. (Cleveland), (216) 771-7600, $113-$129
▼▼▼ **Wyndham Hotel at Playhouse Square** *(Hotel)*, 1260 Euclid Ave. (Cleveland), (216) 615-7500, $109-$209

Nearby Restaurants

▼▼▼ **Blue Pointe Grille** *(Seafood)*, 700 W. St. Clair Ave. (Cleveland), (216) 875-7827, $15-$30
▼▼ **Café Sausalito** *(American)*, 1301 E. 9th St. in the Galleria at Erieview (Cleveland), (216) 696-2233, $10-$20
▼▼▼ **Johnny's Downtown** *(Northern Italian)*, 1406 W. 6th St. (Cleveland), (216) 623-0055, $18-$34
▼▼ **Li Wah** *(Chinese)*, 2999 Payne Ave. in Asia Plaza (Cleveland), (216) 696-6556, $8-$15
▼▼ **Hyde Park Chop House** *(Steak House)*, 123 Prospect Ave., (Cleveland), (216) 344-2444, $14-$36

DALLAS MAVERICKS

JUDGED BY THE CURRENT OWNER, the Dallas Mavericks may have the most suitable team name in all of sports. That owner, billionaire Mark Cuban, could aptly be called a "maverick." Since taking over in 2000, Cuban has raised the team's profile greatly with his outspoken criticisms of referees and unapologetic boosterism for his team. But the Mavericks have earned a lot of attention all by themselves. Behind the solid play of Michael Finley and three-point sensation Steve Nash, the team has recently begun to show signs of readiness to return to the postseason. It's been a while. The franchise's most recent playoff berth came in 1990, at the tail end of what could be termed the Dallas Mavericks glory years. Of course, what constitutes glory varies among franchises. In this case, it was a string of six playoff appearances in seven seasons from '84 to '90. Those Dallas teams were blessed with gifted scoring from the likes of Mark Aguirre and Rolando Blackman, and featured a solid supporting cast that included center James Donaldson, Sam Perkins, Derek Harper and Brad Davis. Although the team faded through the '90s, Dallas fans still had the opportunity to follow the development of some of the league's young greats, including Jamal Mashburn, Jim Jackson and Detlef Schrempf, each of whom began his career with the Mavs. Dallas fans hope for a return to the team's success of the '80s. Mavericks owner Mark Cuban is sure to make some brash moves to make their hopes come true.

> *"I am very excited to see how far this group of Mavericks can go."*
>
> — *Assistant Coach Del Harris in May 2001, announcing he will remain with the team*

Vital Stats

Stadium Address:
2500 Victory Ave.,
Dallas, Texas
Phone: (214) 303-5535,
(214) 221-8326
Web: nba.com/mavericks,
americanairlinescenter.com
Box Office:
(214) 747-MAVS,
Mon.–Fri. 8:30–5:30
Media Coverage:
Radio: ESPN (103.3 FM)
TV: KTVT (Channel 11),
KTXA (Channel 21)
Practice Facility:
American Airlines Center,
Dallas, Texas

LEAGUE HONORS
Rookie of the Year
• Jason Kidd (tie) (1994–95)

NBA Sixth Man of the Year
• Roy Tarpley (1987–88)

POSTSEASON
• Midwest Division Titles ..1
(1986–87)
• Playoff Appearances........6
(1983–84, 1984–85, 1985–86, 1986–87, 1987–88, 1989–90)

RETIRED NUMBERS
• Brad Davis (15)
• Roland Blackman (22)

TEAM RECORDS
• **Mark Aguirre (1981–89)**
FG (game): 21 (Mar. 24, 1984)
FG (season): 925 (1983–84)
FG Att. (season): 1,765
(1983–84)
FT (season): 465 (1983–84)
FT Att. (season): 621 (1983–84)
Points (season): 2,330
(1983–84)
Points-Per-Game (season):
29.5 (1983–84)
• **Rolando Blackman (1981–92)**
FG (career): 6,487
FG Att. (career): 13,061
FT (career): 3,501
FT Att. (career): 4,166
FT Pct. (season): .898
(1991–92)
Points (career): 16,643
• **Shawn Bradley (1997–present)**
Blocks (game): 13
(April 7, 1998)
Blocks (season): 214
(1997–98)
• **Brad Davis (1980–92)**
Game (career): 883
Personal Fouls (career): 2,040
• **Hubert Davis (1997–2000)**
3-Point FG Pct. (career): .458
• **James Donaldson (1985–92)**
Blocks (career): 615
Def. Rebounds (game): 22
(Dec. 29, 1989)
Def. Rebounds (season): 678
(1986–87)
Def. Rebounds (career): 3,293
FG Pct. (season): .586
(1986–87)
FG Pct. (career): .551
Off. Rebounds (career): 1,296
Rebounds (season): 973
(1986–87)
Rebounds (career): 4,589
Rebounds-Per-Game
(season): 11.9 (1986–87)
• **Derek Harper (1983–94, 1996–97)**
Assists (career): 5,111
Steals (season): 187 (1989–90)
Steals (career): 1,551
Turnovers (career): 1,771
3-Point FG (career): 705
3-Point FG Att. (career): 2,030
• **Jim Jackson (1992–97)**
Points (game): 50 (tie)
(Nov. 26, 1994)
Turnovers (season): 334
(1993–94)
• **Popeye Jones (1993–96)**
Rebounds (game): 28
(Jan. 9, 1996)
• **Jason Kidd (1994–97)**
Assists (game): 25
(Feb. 8, 1996)
Assists (season): 783
(1995–96)
• **Fat Lever (1990–94)**
Steals (game): 9
(Feb. 10, 1994)
• **Jamal Mashburn (1993–97)**
Points (game): 50 (tie)
(Nov. 12, 1994)
• **George McCloud (1994–97)**
3-Point FG (game): 10
(Dec. 16, 1995)
3-Point FG (season): 257
(1995–96)
3-Point FG Att. (season): 678
(1995–96)
• **Jim Spanarkel (1980–84)**
FT Pct. (career): .857
• **Roy Tarpley (1986–91, 1994–95)**
Off. Rebounds (season): 360
(1987–88)
Personal Fouls (season): 313
(1987–88)

Jump Shot
• Mavericks Coach Don Nelson is nothing if not experienced. Only Raptors Coach Lenny Wilkens has more combined games as a player and a coach.
• Mavericks owner Mark Cuban is the most outspoken in the NBA. He was fined $250,000 in January 2001 for taunting officials after he thought they missed a goaltending call.

Steve Nash leads the Mavericks with his accurate three-point shooting.

Timeline

1980	1983	1984	1986	1988	1990	1992	1993	1994	1996	1997	1999	2000

Mavericks join NBA

Mark Aguirre finishes sixth in NBA scoring

Mavs finish 43–39; earn first playoff berth

Dallas eliminates Utah in first round

Roy Tarpley wins NBA Sixth Man Award

Rolando Blackman named to fourth All-Star game

Blackman traded to Knicks for draft choices

Jamal Mashburn drafted fourth overall

Jim Jackson scores 50 points in game against Denver

Mavs set NBA records for three-pointers and three-point attempts

Don Nelson hired as Head Coach

Mavs post 15–10 home record

Michael Finley ends season with four triple-doubles

AMERICAN AIRLINES CENTER: BEAUTY AND COMFORT

OPENED IN JULY 2001, the American Airlines Center is the new-and-improved home of the Mavericks. The arena's beautiful glass exterior offers spectacular views of downtown Dallas. Sweeping rotundas, terrazzo floors, and coffered ceilings are just some of the venue's striking architectural details. The eight-sided scoreboard at the new arena will be almost twice the size of the one at the old Reunion Arena and will offer fans unparalleled views of the game's highlights. Increased concessions and toilets also add to fan comfort.

CONCESSIONS

The American Airline Center offers hungry fans a wide variety of culinary treats, from down-home cooking to four-star food. Standard arena fare such as hot dogs, hamburgers and pizza are available, as well as a host of specialty items, including Southern-style barbecue.

GAME DAY TIPS
• **Gate hours:** Gates open one hour prior to tip-off.
• **Prohibited items:** Food and drinks, pets (except for trained service animals and guide dogs), brooms, sticks, poles, video cameras, flash photography and other recording devices are all prohibited. Patrons may be asked to refrain from using noise-makers if other fans complain. Smoking is permitted in designated outdoor areas.
• **Ticket tips:** Retractable seating means that the arena can be reconfigured to offer optimum sight lines depending on the event. The seating bowl has been specially designed to place fans closer to the action; as a result, there are few bad seats. However, the Mavs draw a lot of fans, so reserve tickets early. Games against division rivals such as the Spurs, the Jazz and the Rockets are particularly popular.
• **Lost and found:** (214) 222-3687.

Arena Facts

Opened: July 28, 2001
Cost: $325 million
Capacity: 19,200
Home Sweet Home:
• *Even though the team has changed venues, its enthusiastic fans remain just as vocal as ever. Architects of the new facility also made sure that the seats are closer to the action, thereby amplifying fan noise.*

Seating Plan

▪ $181		▪ $35
▪ $115		▪ $27
▪ $85		▪ $15
▪ $82		▪ $8
▪ $57		ATM Plaza level, Plaza exterior,
▪ $51		Terrace level
▪ $44		♿ Throughout

WEST ENTRANCE

307 308 309 310 311 312 312
306 313
305 306 307 308 309 310 311 312 313 314
305 314
305 104 105 106 107 108 109 315
304 103 110 316
303 102 111 317
302 101 112 318
301 124 113 319
334 114 320
333 123 115 321
332 122 321
331 121 120 119 118 117 116 322
331 330 323 322
330 329 328 327 326 325 324 323
329 328 327 326 325 324 324

SOUTH ENTRANCE
NORTH ENTRANCE
EAST ENTRANCE

95

Directions: *From Hwy. 35E north or south, take Continental exit. Follow Continental east to N. Houston St. Turn left onto N. Houston St. and follow to arena. By Public Transportation: Buses and light rail service the arena from Union Station. Call Dallas Area Rapid Transit (DART) at 214-979-1111 for information.* **Parking:** *Handicapped parking is located in lots F and S and the Platinum Parking Garage. There is parking on Cedar Springs Rd. and Munger, Field and Akard Sts.*

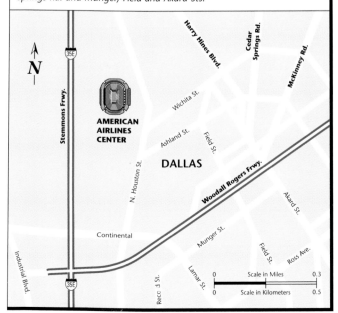

Nearby Hotels

▼▼▼ **Amerisuites-West End** *(Suite Motel)*, 1907 N. Lamar St. (Dallas), (214) 999-0500, $95-$130
▼▼▼ **Courtyard by Marriott-Market Center** *(Motor Inn)*, 2150 Market Center Blvd. (Dallas), (214) 653-1166, $119-$129
▼▼▼ **Fairfield Inn Market Center** *(Motel)*, 2110 Market Center Blvd. (Dallas), (214) 760-8800, $89-$124
▼▼▼ **Holiday Inn-Aristocrat Hotel** *(Historic Hotel)*, 1933 Main St. (Dallas), (214) 741-7700, $189-$199
▼▼▼▼ **Hotel Adolphus** *(Historic Hotel)*, 1321 Commerce St. (Dallas), (214) 742-8200, $355-$455

Nearby Restaurants

▼▼ **Baby Doe's Matchless Mine Restaurant** *(Steakhouse)*, 3305 Harry Hines Blvd. (Dallas), (214) 871-7310, $17-$24
▼▼▼ **Bombay Cricket Club** *(Indian)*, 2508 Maple Ave. (Dallas), (214) 871-1333, $12-$17
▼▼▼▼▼ **The French Room** *(Nouvelle French)*, 1321 Commerce St. in the Hotel Adolphus (Dallas), (214) 742-8200, $52-$70 (dinner only)
▼▼▼ **Pomodoro** *(Italian)*, 2520 Cedar Springs Rd. (Dallas), (214) 871-1924, $12-$26
▼▼ **Queen of Sheba** *(Ethiopian)*, 3527 McKinney Ave. (Dallas), (214) 521-0491, $9-$12

DENVER NUGGETS

DESPITE THE NAME, THE HISTORY OF the Denver Nuggets has been less than golden. After a quarter century of NBA play, the team has appeared in just two conference finals, losing a six-game series to the Seattle Supersonics in 1978 and falling in five to the 1985 Lakers. The Nuggets actually enjoyed their closest brush with success in 1975–76, the last year of the ABA. Then known as the Rockets, the team rode the creative scoring of Rookie-of-the-Year David Thompson to within two games of the championship, as the franchise dropped a tight six-game series to the New York Nets in its one and only finals appearance. Of all the ABA teams that came to the NBA, however, Denver made one of the smoothest transitions, winning 50 games and its division in 1976–77, its first NBA season, and seeing three of its players, Dan Issel, Bobby Jones and David Thompson voted All-Star starters. But playoff success was not to be. Despite that fact, Nuggets fans have had the opportunity to enjoy some of the game's greatest and most consistent scorers. In the early days, it was Thompson, known for his astounding dunks and leaping ability, as well as pure shooter Byron Beck, who provided the thrills. Later, Issel became a league-wide model of durability, missing just 24 games in his 15-year career. In the 1980s Alex English dominated the scoreboard, creatively racking up more points than any other player in the game during that decade. Today the franchise is banking on guard Nick Van Exel and power forward Antonio McDyess to help it finally strike NBA championship gold.

"We have all the right tools."
— Denver guard Nick Van Exel, on the state of the Nuggets

POSTSEASON
- **Midwest Division Titles** ..4
(1976–77, 1977–78, 1984–85, 1987–88)
- **Playoff Appearances** 14
(1976–77, 1977–78, 1978–79, 1981–82, 1982–83, 1983–84, 1984–85, 1985–86, 1986–87, 1987–88, 1988–89, 1989–90, 1993–94, 1994–95)

RETIRED NUMBERS
- Alex English (2)
- David Thompson (33)

Jump Shot

- Denver played in the highest scoring game in NBA history, losing a 1983 triple-overtime marathon to Detroit, 186-184.
- Antonio McDyess is the Nuggets resident franchise player. A member of the U.S. "Dream Team" in the 2000 Olympics, McDyess led the Nuggets in scoring and rebounds during the 2000–01 season.

- Byron Beck (40)
- Dan Issel (44)

TEAM RECORDS
- **Mahmoud Abdul-Rauf (1990–96)**
FT Pct. (season): .956 (1993–94)
FT Pct. (career): .916
3-Point FG (game): 9 (tie) (Dec. 7, 1995)
- **Dale Ellis (1994–97)**
3-Point FG (season): 192 (1996–97)
3-Point FG Pct. (career): .388
- **Alex English (1979–90)**
Assists (career): 3,679
Games (career): 837
FG (season): 965 (1986–87)
FG (career): 8,953
FG Att. (season): 1,920 (1986–87)
FG Att. (career): 17,604
FT (career): 3,721
FT Att. (career): 4,428
Off. Rebounds (career): 2,038
Personal Fouls (career): 2,288
Points (season): 2,414 (1985–86)
Points (career): 21,645
Points-Per-Game (season): 29.8 (1985–86)
Points-Per-Game (career): 25.9
40–Point Games (career): 34
2,000–Point Seasons: 8
- **Dan Issel (1975–85)**
Def. Rebounds (career): 3,536
FT (season): 546 (1981–82)

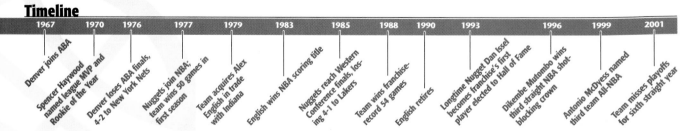

Antonio McDyess is a powerful inside player.

Rebounds (career): 5,011
- **Lafayette Lever (1984–90)**
Steals (game): 10 (Mar. 9, 1985)
Steals (season): 223 (1987–88)
Steals (career): 1,167
- **George McGinnis (1978–80)**
FT Att. (season): 765 (1978–79)
- **Dikembe Mutombo (1991–96)**
Blocks (game): 12 (Apr. 18, 1993)
Blocks (season): 336 (1993–94)

Blocks (career): 1,486
Blocks-Per-Game (season): 4.49 (1995–96)
Blocks-Per-Game (career): 3.81
Defensive Rebounds (season): 726 (1992–93)
Offensive Rebounds (season): 344 (1992–93)
Rebounds (game): 31 (tie) (Mar. 26, 1996)
Rebounds (season): 1,070 (1992–93)
Rebounds-Per-Game (season): 13 (1992–93)
Rebounds-Per-Game (career): 12.3
- **David Thompson (1975–82)**
Points (game): 73 (Apr. 9, 1978)
FG (game): 28 (Apr. 9, 1978)
FG Att. (game): 38 (Apr. 9, 1978)
- **Nick Van Exel (1998–present)**
Assists (season): 714 (1999–2000)
Assists-Per-Game (career): 8.4

LEAGUE HONORS
Defensive Player of the Year
- Dikembe Mutombo (1994–95)

Coach of the Year
- Doug Moe (1987–88)

Basketball Hall of Fame
- Dan Issel (1993)
- David Thompson (1996)
- Alex English (1997)
- Alex Hannum (1998)

Vital Stats

Stadium Address:
1000 Chopper Place, Denver, Colo.
Phone: (303) 405-8555
Web: nba.com/nuggets, pepsicenter.com
Box Office:
(303) 405-1212
Mon.–Fri. 10-6, Sat. 10–3
Media Coverage:
Radio: KKFN (950 AM)
TV: KTVD (Channel 20), Fox Sports Net
Practice Facility:
Pepsi Center, Denver, Colo.

Timeline

1967 — Denver joins ABA
1970 — Spencer Haywood named league MVP and Rookie of the Year
1976 — Denver loses ABA finals, 4-2 to New York Nets
1977 — Nuggets join NBA; team wins 50 games in first season
1979 — Team acquires Alex English in trade with Indiana
1983 — English wins NBA scoring title
1985 — Nuggets reach Western Conference finals, losing 4-1 to Lakers
1988 — Team wins franchise-record 54 games
1990 — English retires
1993 — Longtime Nugget Dan Issel becomes franchise's first player elected to Hall of Fame
1996 — Dikembe Mutombo wins third straight NBA shot-blocking crown
1999 — Antonio McDyess named third team All-NBA
2001 — Team misses playoffs for sixth straight year

PEPSI CENTER: ALMOST PERFECT

SINCE THE PEPSI CENTER first opened its doors in 1999, reviews of the new venue have been mixed. With full training facilities, 95 luxury suites, decent sight lines and excellent sound, no one argues about the facility's technological standing — it's cutting edge all the way. Fans have complained, however, about the too-narrow seats and a lack of convenient bathroom facilities. Whatever is said about the Pepsi Center, it is an improvement over McNichols Arena, the Nuggets' previous venue.

CONCESSIONS

There are many options for those looking for something to eat at the Pepsi Center. Choices include hot dogs, hamburgers, cheese steak sandwiches, chicken wings, fish and chips, pizza, and gyros. There are several on-site bars in which Nuggets patrons can grab a drink before, during or after a game.

GAME DAY TIPS
• **Gate hours:** Gates open 90 minutes prior to tip-off.
• **Prohibited items:** Outside food and drinks, cans, bottles coolers, thermoses, video cameras and laser pointers are prohibited. Beachballs and frisbees cannot be brought into the arena. Smoking is prohibited inside the arena, but guests are allowed to go outside to designated smoking areas.
• **Ticket tips:** The very new Pepsi Center is getting mixed reviews: great sight lines are offset by narrow and uncomfortable seats in the upper deck. In general, Nuggets tickets are readily available, so go for the more expensive seats if comfort is an issue.

Good seats are harder to come by when division rivals such as the Spurs or the Jazz come to town.
• **Lost and found:** (720) 931-1581.

Arena Facts

Opened: Oct. 1, 1999
Cost: $160 million
Capacity: 19,007
Home Sweet Home:
• Like their football counterparts, Denver Nuggets fans can be a loud and boisterous bunch. Even though the team finished second-to-last in the Midwest Division in 2000–01, its 29-12 home record was near the top.

Seating Plan

■	$200	■	$36
■	$143	■	$44
	$100	■	$21
■	$90	■	$16
■	$81	■	$10
■	$80		
■	$67		
■	$65		

ATM Sections 120, 144, 344, 366 and ticket lobby
♿ Throughout

MAIN ENTRANCE

EAST ENTRANCE

Directions: From the I-25 N, exit at Auraria Pkwy. N. From the I-25 S, exit at Speer Blvd. S. By Bus: Buses are available to and from the area near the arena. Call the RTA at (303) 299-6000 for more information.
Parking: The Pepsi Center has 4,700 parking spots, with an additional 2,000 available in a nearby lot. There are 100 wheelchair-accessible spots and these are located immediately beside lot A.

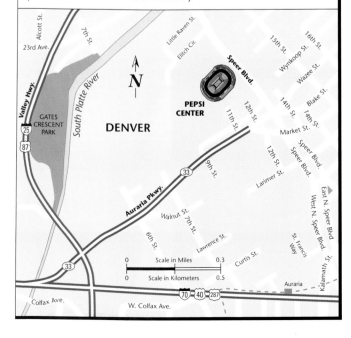

Nearby Hotels

▼▼▼▼ **Brown Palace Hotel** (*Classic Hotel*), 321 17th St. (Denver), (303) 297-3111, $234
▼▼ **Comfort Inn Downtown Denver** (*Hotel*), 401 17th St. (Denver), (303) 296-0400, $129
▼▼▼ **Denver Marriott Hotel City Center** (*Hotel*), 1701 California St. (Denver), (303) 297-1300, $189
▼▼▼ **Holiday Inn Denver Downtown** (*Hotel*), 1450 Glenarm Pl. (Denver), (303) 573-1450, $99-$139
▼▼▼▼ **Hotel Monaco** (*Hotel*), 1717 Champa St. (Denver), (303) 296-1717, $185-$240

Nearby Restaurants

▼▼▼ **McCormick's Fish House & Bar** (*Regional Seafood*), 1659 Wazee St. (Denver), (303) 825-1107, $8-$25
▼▼▼▼ **Palace Arms** (*Continental*), 321 17th St. in the Brown Palace Hotel (Denver), (303) 297-1311, $22-$38
▼▼▼ **Palm Restaurant** (*Steakhouse*), 1201 16th St. in the Westin Tabor Center Denver (Denver), (303) 825-2256, $14-$29
▼▼ **Rocky Mountain Diner** (*American*), 800 18th St. in the Ghost Building (Denver), (303) 293-8383, $9-$18
▼▼ **Rodizio Grill** (*Steakhouse*), 1801 Wynkoop St. (Denver), (303) 294-9277, $18

DETROIT PISTONS

THE DETROIT PISTONS IS ONE OF BASKETBALL'S oldest franchises. Founded in 1941 as part of the old National Basketball League, the team played its first 16 seasons in Fort Wayne, Indiana, before moving to Detroit in 1957. Prior to the. move, the Pistons established themselves as strong contenders; led by George Yardley's offensive brilliance, the Pistons racked up two Western Conference titles in 1955 and '56. After settling in the Motor City, however, the Pistons slid into one of the longest spells of poor performance in the history of pro sports. It took until 1971 for the team to record a winning season and it wasn't until 1983 that the Pistons stumbled on the winning streak that peaked with their 1989 and '90 NBA Championship titles. In spite of this embarrassing record, the Pistons weren't without their superstars. In 1962 the team drafted former Chicago White Sox pitcher Dave DeBusschere, a player who would become legendary as one of the best rebounders in the game. In the the late '60s and early '70s, the duo of Dave Bing and Bob Lanier created one of the most powerful inside-outside teams of the era, and helped steer the Pistons to some of their best results to date. It wasn't until the mid-1980s, though, that the Pistons put together a team that would go down in history. With the acquisition of Indiana Hoosiers guard Isiah Thomas, center Bill Laimbeer, Vinnie "Microwave" Johnson, three-point ace Joe Dumars and rebound wizard Dennis Rodman, the Pistons secured one of the toughest, most physical teams in basketball history — a team that will be known forever as "the Bad Boys." Possessing a solid work ethic, an impenetrable defense and telepathic teamwork, the Bad Boys downed L.A. in '89 and Portland in '90. In the decade since these big wins, the Pistons have struggled to find the magic, but have upheld the tradition of great players over these years with solid superstars Grant Hill and Jerry Stackhouse.

POSTSEASON
- NBA Championships.......2
(1988–89, 1989–90)
- Western Conference Championships 2
(1954–55, 1955–56)
- Eastern Conference Championships 3
(1987–88, 1988–89, 1989–90)
- Central Division Titles....3
(1987–88, 1988–89, 1989–90)

RETIRED NUMBERS
- Chuck Daly (2)
- Joe Dumars (4)
- Isiah Thomas (11)
- Vinnie Johnson (15)
- Bob Lanier (16)
- Dave Bing (21)
- Bill Laimbeer (40)

Jump Shot
- In 1964 Pistons legend Dave DeBusschere set the unusual record of becoming the youngest coach in the history of the NBA. At 24 years of age, DeBusschere coached the Pistons to 29 wins while maintaining his team playing duties.
- On Dec. 13, 1983, the Pistons nipped the Denver Nuggets 186-184 in the highest scoring game in NBA history.

TEAM RECORDS
- Dave Bing (1966–75)
Points (season): 2,213 (1970–71)
FG (season): 836 (1967–68)
FG (game): 22 (Feb. 21, 1971)
- Joe Dumars (1985–99)
3-Point FG (career): 990
3-Point FG (game): 10 (Nov. 8, 1994)
3-Point FG Pct. (season): .432 (1996–97)
FT Pct. (season): .900 (1989–90)
- Allan Houston (1993–96)
3-Point FG (season): 191 (1995–96)
- Bill Laimbeer (1981–94)

"I always thought it was cool to do something and not turn somersaults."

— Joe Dumars, two-time NBA champion and Detroit Pistons legend, on his low-key approach to the game

Rebounds (career): 9,403
- Bob Lanier (1970–80)
Blocks (season): 247 (1973–74)
- Dennis Rodman (1986–93)
FG Pct. (season): .595 (1988–89)
Rebounds (season): 1,530 (1991–92)
Rebounds (game): 34 (Mar. 4, 1992)
- Isiah Thomas (1981–94)
Points (career): 18,822
FG (career): 7,194

Vital Stats
Stadium Address:
Two Championship Dr., Auburn Hills, Mich.
Phone: (248) 377-0100
Web: nba.com/pistons, palacenet.com
Box Office:
(248) 377-8601, Mon.–Fri. 9–6, Sat. 9–4
Media Coverage:
Radio: WWJ (950 AM)
TV: WKBD (Channel 50), Fox Sports Net
Training Facility:
Palace of Auburn Hills, Auburn Hills, Mich.

FT (career): 4,036
Assists (season): 1,123 (1984–85)
Assists (career): 9,061
Steals (season): 204 (1983–84)
Steals (career): 1,861
- Kelly Tripucka (1981–86)
Points (game): 56 (Jan. 29, 1983)
FT (game): 20 (tie) (Jan. 29, 1983)
- Terry Tyler (1978–85)
Blocks (career): 1,070
- George Yardley (1957–59)
FT (season): 655 (1957–58)
FT (game): 20 (tie) (Dec. 26, 1957)

LEAGUE HONORS
Rookie of the Year
- Dave Bing (1966–67)
- Grant Hill (tie) (1994–95)

Defensive Player of the Year
- Dennis Rodman (1989–90, 1990–91)

Coach of the Year
- Ray Scott (1973–74)

Basketball Hall of Fame
- Dave DeBusschere (1982)
- Dave Bing (1989)
- Bob Lanier (1991)
- Chuck Daly (1993)
- George Yardley (1995)

Jerry Stackhouse is a terror for opposing defenses to contain.

Timeline

1941 Pistons magnate Fred Zollner launches the Fort Wayne Zollner Pistons in the National Basketball League

1944 Pistons win NBL Championship

1950 Pistons join newly formed NBA

1957 Pistons move to Detroit

1958 Pistons George Yardley becomes first player to score more than 2,000 points in a season

1961 Pistons move to Cobo Arena

1966 Team acquires guard Dave Bing, who takes NBA Rookie of the Year honors

1970 Pistons draft Bob Lanier No. 1 and post first winning season since moving to Detroit

1974 Long-time Pistons owner Fred Zollner sells team

1981 Pistons scoop Isiah Thomas and Kelly Tripucka in NBA Draft

1983 Tripucka tallies 56 points to set new team record

1989 Pistons win first NBA title in four straight games over Lakers

1994 Pistons acquire Duke University forward Grant Hill

1999 Joe Dumars retires after 14 years as a player with Pistons

The Palace of Auburn Hills:
A House Built for Champions

THE COLLAPSE OF THE PONTIAC SILVERDOME roof in 1986 was a telling event for a host of Pistons fans. After many losing seasons, the team was finally coming into its own; a new, swanky home seemed essential as the Pistons climbed the NBA ranks and tried to distance themselves from their checkered past. The Palace was the answer. Renowned for its warm atmosphere and great sight lines, the Palace is recognized as one of the premier basketball venues in the country: suitable for NBA champions like the Pistons. Also, with many extra features, such as the free virtual-reality game and Pistons memorabilia, the Palace is an all-around fun place to spend an evening.

CONCESSIONS

Visitors to the Palace can enjoy the best in casual arena fare as well as some fancier specialties. Some of the tasty treats include jalapeno poppers, crepes, salmon, kielbasa, frozen daiquiris and a variety of imported, domestic and microbrewery beers.

GAME DAY TIPS

- **Gate hours:** Gates open 90 minutes prior to tip-off.
- **Prohibited items:** Alcohol, bottles, cans or coolers, as well as video and sound recording devices are prohibited. Banners are allowed provided they have no sticks or poles attached, do not contain offensive messages and do not obstruct the views of other patrons. Smoking is allowed only in designated areas.
- **Ticket tips:** Pistons tickets are typically pretty easy to come by at the box office on game day, although the Palace has been known to sell out for games against NBA's more popular teams such as the Lakers and the Trailblazers. The best seats in the house for the money are the ones located along the first and second row of the second level.
- **Lost and found:** (248) 377-8240.

Arena Facts

Opened: Aug. 13, 1988
Cost: $70 million
Capacity: 22,076
Home Sweet Home:
- When the 22,000-seat Palace of Auburn Hills is filled to capacity, the decibel level can drive opposing players to distraction. With Detroit having won back-to-back championships to close out the 1980s, the team's fans are basketball savvy. Their vocal support bolsters the team.

Directions: Take I-75 to exit 79, 81 or 83. Follow signs to the Palace.
Parking: The parking lot at the Palace has space for 8,400 automobiles and is rarely full. About 100 spots are reserved for the disabled.

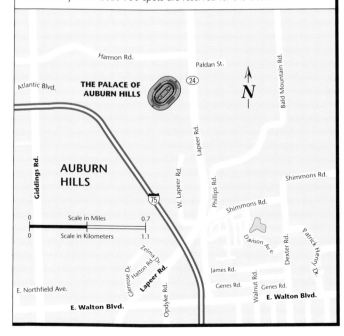

Nearby Hotels

▼▼▼ **AmeriSuites** *(Motel)*, 1545 Opdyke Rd. (Auburn Hills), (248) 475-9393, $89-$179
▼▼▼ **Fairfield Inn by Marriott-Auburn Hills** *(Motel)*, 1294 Opdyke Rd. (Auburn Hills), (248) 373-2228, $89-$99
▼▼▼ **Hilton Suites Auburn Hills** *(Suite Hotel)*, 2300 Featherstone Rd. (Auburn Hills), (248) 334-2222, $99-$199
▼▼▼ **Wellesley Inn & Suites** *(Motel)*, 2100 Featherstone Rd. (Auburn Hills), (248) 335-5200, $69-$199
▼▼▼ **Wingate Inn** *(Motel)*, 2200 Featherstone Rd. (Auburn Hills), (248) 334-3324, $129-$179

Nearby Restaurants

▼▼ **Beau Jack's Food & Spirits** *(American)*, 4108 W. Maple Rd. (Bloomfield Hills), (248) 626-2630, $7-$17
▼▼ **Big Buck Brewery** *(Steakhouse)*, 2550 Takata Dr. (Auburn Hills), (248) 276-2337, $7-$29
▼▼▼ **Fox & Hounds Restaurant** *(Steak & Seafood)*, 39560 N. Woodward Ave. (Bloomfield Hills), (248) 644-4800, $14-$30
▼▼ **The Main Event Restaurant** *(American)*, 1200 Featherstone Rd. (Auburn Hills), (248) 858-7888, $15-$20
▼▼ **Northern Lakes Seafood Company** *(Seafood)*, 1475 N. Woodward Ave. in the Kingsley Hotel & Suites (Bloomfield Hills), (248) 646-7900, $19-$30

GOLDEN STATE WARRIORS

JUDGING BY THE TEAM'S PERFORMANCE in recent years, you'd probably rank the Golden State Warriors among the most snake-bit franchises in sport. But a look in the record books shows that this is a team with a long and proud history. Playing out of Philadelphia between 1946 and '62, the Warriors served as the launching pad for the man many consider to be basketball's greatest player: Wilt Chamberlain. A Philadelphia native, Chamberlain stunned the league with his play from the very start of his legendary career and single-handedly raised the profile of the NBA to a vast national audience. With the team from 1959 to '65, the 7-foot center also made the Warriors a perennial threat and led the team to its second title in '56. Chamberlain's career with the Warriors peaked with his astounding 50.4-point scoring average in 1961–62. The following season the team moved to San Francisco and two years after that, in 1965, Chamberlain was traded back to his home town of Philadelphia to join the Sixers. Warrior pride runs deeper than the Stilt, though. With sharp-shooting Rick Barry, another future Hall of Famer, leading the charge, the Warriors picked up more NBA hardware with a four-game finals sweep of the Washington Bullets in '75. Since then, playoff success has been elusive, despite the influx of such stars as Bernard King, Robert Parish, Tim Hardaway, Joe Barry Carroll and Chris Mullin. Now fans look to young stars Antawn Jamison and Larry Hughes to end the seven-year playoff drought.

> *"Some night he's really going to explode. He might hit 90 points in some game sometime."*
> — Fuzzy Levane, Knicks coach, following Wilt Chamberlain's pro debut in 1959; Levane underestimated the Stilt, who would have a 100-point game in 1962

POSTSEASON
- **BAA Championships** 1
(1946–47)
- **NBA Championships** 2
(1955–56, 1974–75)
- **Eastern Conference Titles** 1
(1955–56)
- **Western Conference Titles** 3
(1963–64, 1966–67, 1974–75)

RETIRED NUMBERS
- Wilt Chamberlain (13)
- Tom Meschery (14)
- Alvin Attles (16)
- Rick Barry (24)
- Nate Thurmond (42)

TEAM RECORDS
- **Rick Barry**
(1965–67, 1972–78)
FT (season): 753 (1966–67)
FT Pct. (season): .924 (1977–78)
- **Joe Barry Carroll (1980–88)**

Jump Shot
- *Perhaps more astounding than his 100-point game is Chamberlain's average of 50.4 points per game in 1961–62. Neither record has ever been approached. A further measure of his dominance, he recorded 65 consecutive games with 30 points or more that season.*

Blocks (career): 837
- **Wilt Chamberlain (1959–65)**
FG (season): 1,463 (1962–63)
FG (career): 7,216
FT (game): 28 (Mar. 2, 1962)
Points (game): 100 (Mar. 2, 1962)
Points (season): 3,586 (1962–63)
Points (career): 17,783
Points-Per-Game (season): 50.4 (1961–62)
Points-Per-Game (career): 41.5
Rebounds (game): 55 (Nov. 24, 1960)
Rebounds (season): 1,946 (1962–63)
Rebounds-Per-Game (season): 24.3 (1962–63)
- **Tim Hardaway (1989–96)**
3-Point FG (season): 168 (1994–95)
- **Bernard King (1980–82)**
FG Pct. (season): .588 (1980–81)
- **Chris Mullin (1985–97, 2000–present)**
Games (career): 787
3-Point FG (game): 7 (tie) (Dec. 22, 1992)
- **Robert Parish (1976–80)**
Def. Rebounds (game): 25 (Mar. 30, 1979)
Def. Rebounds (season): 651 (1978–79)
- **Guy Rodgers (1958–66)**
Assists (game): 28 (Mar. 14, 1963)
Assists (career): 4,855

- **Nate Thurmond (1963–74)**
Rebounds (career): 12,771

LEAGUE HONORS
NBA MVP
- **Wilt Chamberlain (1959–60)**

Rookie of the Year
- **Woody Sauldsberry (1957–58)**
- **Wilt Chamberlain (1959–60)**
- **Rick Barry (1965–66)**
- **Keith Wilkes (1974–75)**
- **Mitch Richmond (1988–89)**
- **Chris Webber (1993–94)**

Coach of the Year
- **Alex Hannum (1963–64)**
- **Don Nelson (1991–92)**

Basketball Hall of Fame
- Andy Phillip (1961)
- Tom Gola (1975)
- Eddie Gottlieb (1971)
- Harry Litwack (1975)
- Bill Sharman (1975)
- Frank McGuire (1976)
- Paul Arizin (1977)
- Joe Fulks (1977)
- Wilt Chamberlain (1978)
- Pete Newell (1978)
- Jerry Lucas (1979)
- Al Cervi (1984)
- Nate Thurmond (1984)
- Rick Barry (1986)
- Neil Johnston (1989)
- Bob Lanier (1992)

Antawn Jamison gives the Warriors hope for the future.

Vital Stats
Stadium Address:
7000 Coliseum Wy., Oakland, Calif.
Phone: (510) 569-2121
Web: nba.com/warriors
Box Office:
(888) GSW-HOOP, Mon.–Fri. 10–6
Media Coverage:
Radio: KNBR (680 AM)
TV: KICU (Channel 36), Fox Sports Net
Practice Facility:
Warriors Practice Facility, Oakland, Calif.

Timeline

1946	1949	1955	1956	1959	1962	1963	1965	1967	1971	1975	1987	1994	1999
Philadelphia Warriors win Basketball Association of America title	BAA becomes NBA	Warriors finish last in Eastern Division	Team goes worst to first, winning second title	Philadelphia native Wilt Chamberlain joins Warriors	Chamberlain records 100-point game	Warriors relocate to San Francisco	Chamberlain traded to Philadelphia 76ers for three players plus cash	Warriors lose NBA finals 4-2 to 76ers	Team changes name to Golden State Warriors	Warriors sweep Bullets for NBA championship	Team reaches playoffs for first time since 1977	Chris Webber named Rookie of the Year	Antawn Jamison named to second All-Rookie team

THE ARENA IN OAKLAND: WELCOME RENOVATIONS

THE WARRIORS PLAYED THEIR 1996 home games at the San Jose Arena to allow time for renovations to the Arena in Oakland. By all accounts, the wait was worth it. Along with adding 4,000 seats, 72 luxury suites and an all-new scoreboard and sound system, the Arena was completely refurbished, right down to the plumbing, increasing restroom capacity by 2.5 times. Fans have generally given the building the stamp of approval—the main complaint seems to be the Warriors, who simply don't win enough games.

Seating Plan

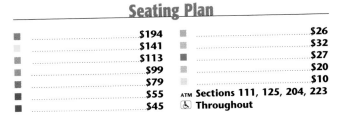

■	$194	■	$26
▫	$141	▨	$32
■	$113	■	$27
▨	$99	■	$20
■	$79	■	$10
■	$55	**ATM** Sections 111, 125, 204, 223
■	$45	♿ Throughout

CONCESSION

The choices offered at the Arena in Oakland are fairly standard. Fans can chow down on burgers, hot dogs, chili cheese fries, sausages, nachos, fish and fajitas. Healthier options — sandwiches, salads and pasta are offered in club level seating.

Arena Facts

Opened: *Nov. 9, 1966*
Cost: *$25.5 million (arena and coliseum)*
Capacity: *19,596*
Home Sweet Home:
• *In the team's renovation of the Arena, it added a significant number of discount club seats at each end of the facility, adding significant noise and activity to distract opposing players at the charity stripe.*

GAME DAY TIPS

• **Gate hours:** Gates open 90 minutes prior to tip-off.
• **Prohibited items:** Food, beverages, coolers, video cameras and audio recorders, as well as digital cameras and laser pointers are prohibited. Smoking is not allowed anywhere inside the stadium, but patrons are permitted to smoke outside gate entrances.
• **Ticket tips:** In general, tickets for Warriors games are easy to come by. The toughest tickets to get are for games with the Lakers. The arena has excellent sight lines so good views are available from all seats.
• **Lost and found:** (510) 383-4660.

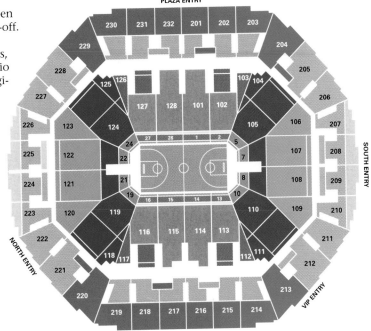

PLAZA ENTRY

SOUTH ENTRY

NORTH ENTRY

VIP ENTRY

Directions: *From I-880, exit at 66th Ave. or Hegenberger Rd. east. By Train: Take BART to Coliseum/Oakland Airport Station. Call (510) 465-2278 for information. By Bus: From downtown Oakland, the No. 58 bus goes to Coliseum/Oakland Airport Station.* **Parking:** *More than 10,000 spots are available at the arena; 143 are reserved for patrons with disabilities. Signs are posted on game days for auxiliary parking.*

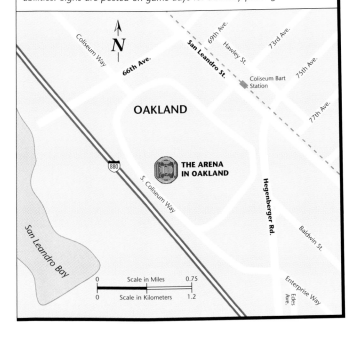

Nearby Hotels

▼▼▼ **Best Western Inn at the Square** *(Motel)*, 233 Broadway at entrance to Jack London Square (Oakland), (510) 452-4565, $89-$149
▼▼▼ **Clarion Suites Lake Merritt Hotel** *(Historic Hotel)*, 1800 Madison St. (Oakland), (510) 832-2300, $179-$299
▼▼▼ **Comfort Inn & Suites** *(Motel)*, 8452 Edes Ave. (Oakland), (510) 568-1500, $117-$127
▼▼▼ **Holiday Inn-Oakland Airport/Coliseum** *(Motor Inn)*, 500 Hegenberger Rd. (Oakland), (510) 562-5311, $89-$139
▼▼▼ **Waterfront Plaza Hotel** *(Hotel)*, Ten Washington St. (Oakland), (510) 836-3800, $190-$325

Nearby Restaurants

▼▼▼ **Bay Wolf Restaurant** *(Californian)*, 3853 Piedmont Ave. (Oakland), (510) 655-6004, $30-$34
▼▼▼ **Garibaldi's on College** *(Californian)*, 5356 College Ave. (Oakland), (510) 595-4000, $13-$20
▼▼▼ **Il Pescatore Restaurant** *(Italian)*, 57 Jack London Square (Oakland), (510) 465-2188, $10-$19
▼▼▼ **Oliveto Café & Restaurant** *(Italian)*, 5655 College Ave. (Oakland), (510) 547-5356, $30-$60
▼▼ **Quinn's Lighthouse Restaurant & Pub** *(Seafood)*, 51 Embarcadero Cove (Oakland), (510) 536-2050, $6-$16

HOUSTON ROCKETS

BASKETBALL IS A GAME OF BIG MEN and few teams stock them bigger than the Houston Rockets. The team's first superstar was Elvin "Big E" Hayes, who as a rookie in 1968–69 led the league in scoring and won MVP honors. Next came Moses Malone, a 6-foot-10-inch 260-pounder who had turned pro out of high school. From 1977 to '82, Malone patrolled the paint for Houston, combining ferocious rebounding with a deft scoring touch. But although Malone would win two MVP trophies, even his powerful shoulders could not carry the team to the NBA summit. In 1984 Houston drafted Hakeem Olajuwon, passing over such future luminaries as John Stockton, Charles Barkley and Michael Jordan. The 7-foot Olajuwon teamed up with 7-foot-4-inch Ralph Sampson to create the "Twin Towers" one of the tallest front courts in history. Olajuwon emerged as both a gifted player and gritty competitor as evidenced by his 1995 showdown with the Knicks' Patrick Ewing in the NBA finals. The leading scorer in all seven games of the hotly contested series, he became the only player ever to win Defensive Player of the Year, NBA MVP and NBA finals MVP in the same season. The following year an injury-plagued Houston squad limped into the playoffs as only the sixth seed. But the team kept fighting, dispatching three teams with better records en route to the finals. Squaring off against Orlando's Shaquille O'Neal, Olajuwon dug deep again, led all scorers and drove Houston to its second NBA crown. Only the fifth squad to win back-to-back titles, the Rockets were flying in a whole different stratosphere.

102

Vital Stats

Stadium Address:
10 E. Greenway Plaza, Houston, Texas
Phone: (713) 843-3995
Web: nba.com/rockets, compaqcenter.com
Box Office:
(713) 843-3900,
Mon.–Sat. 10–6
Media Coverage:
Radio: KPRC (950 AM)
TV: KTBU (Channel 55), Fox Sports Net
Training Facility:
Westside Tennis Club, Houston, Texas

Steve Francis logs lots of quality minutes for the Rockets.

Jump Shot

• Born and raised in Nigeria, Hakeem Olajuwon didn't start playing basketball until 1978, when he was 15. Just five years later, Olajuwon was named MVP of the NCAA Division I Tournament. In 1997 the big center was selected as one of the 50 greatest players in NBA history.

POSTSEASON
• **NBA Championships**.......2
(1993–94, 1994–95)
• **Western Conference Championships** 4
(1980–81, 1985–86, 1993–94, 1994–95)
• **Central Division Titles**....1
(1976–77)
• **Midwest Division Titles**..3
(1985–86, 1992–93, 1993–94)

RETIRED NUMBERS
• Clyde Drexler (22)
• Calvin Murphy (23)
• Moses Malone (24)
• Rudy Tomjanovich (45)

TEAM RECORDS
• **Rick Barry (1978–80)**
FT Pct. (career): .941
• **Matt Bullard (1990–94, 1996–present)**
3-Point Pct. (season): .446 (1999–2000)
• **Clyde Drexler (1995–98)**
Steals (game): 10 (Nov. 1, 1996)
• **Elvin Hayes (1968–72, 1981–84)**
Blocks (game): 13 (tie) (twice)
FG (season): 948 (1970–71)
• **Allen Leavell (1979–89)**
Assists (game): 22 (tie) (Jan. 23, 1983)
• **Moses Malone (1976–82)**
Rebounds (game): 37 (Feb. 9, 1979)
Rebounds (season): 1,444

(1978–79)
Points (season): 2,520 (1981–82)
Points-Per-Game (season): 31.1 (1981–82)
Points-Per-Game (career): 24.0
• **Vernon Maxwell (1989–95)**
3-Pointers (season): 172
3-Pointers (career): 730
• **Calvin Murphy (1970–83)**
Assists (career): 4,402
FT Pct. (season): .958 (1980–81)
Points (game): 57 (Mar. 18, 1978)
• **Hakeem Olajuwon (1984–present)**
Blocks (season): 376 (1989–90)
Blocks (career): 3,652
FT (career): 5,253
Games: 1,119
Rebounds (career): 12,951
Points (career): 25,822
Steals (season): 213 (1988–89)
Steals (career): 2,018
40-Point Games (career): 32

> *"He's not 'the Dream' for nothing."*
> — Kevin Garnett of Minnesota, on an aging Hakeem Olajuwon running roughshod over the Timberwolves

• **Ralph Sampson (1990–96)**
Blocks (game): 13 (tie) (Dec. 12, 1983)
• **Kenny Smith (1990–96)**
3-Point Pct. (career): .407 (tie)
• **Otis Thorpe (1988–94)**
FG Pct. (season): .592 (1991–92)
FG Pct. (career): .559

LEAGUE HONORS
NBA MVP
• Moses Malone (1978–79, 1981–82)
• Hakeem Olajuwon (1993–94)

Rookie of the Year
• Ralph Sampson (1983–84)
• Steve Francis (1999–2000)

Defensive Player of the Year
• Hakeem Olajuwon (1992–93, 1993–94)

Coach of the Year
• Tom Nissalke (1976–77)
• Don Chaney (1990–91)

NBA Finals MVP
• Hakeem Olajuwon (1994, '95)

Basketball Hall of Fame
• Rick Barry (1986)
• Elvin Hayes (1990)
• Calvin Murphy (1993)
• Alex Hannum (1998)

Timeline

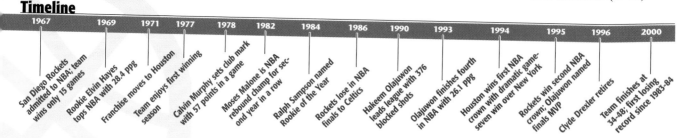

1967	1969	1971	1977	1978	1982	1984	1986	1990	1993	1994	1995	1996	2000
San Diego Rockets admitted to NBA, team wins only 15 games	Rookie Elvin Hayes tops NBA with 28.4 ppg	Franchise moves to Houston	Team enjoys first winning season	Calvin Murphy sets club mark with 57 points in a game	Moses Malone is NBA rebound champ for second year in a row	Ralph Sampson named Rookie of the Year	Rockets lose in NBA finals to Celtics	Hakeem Olajuwon leads league with 376 blocked shots	Olajuwon finishes fourth in NBA with 26.1 ppg	Houston wins first NBA crown with dramatic game-seven win over New York	Rockets win second NBA crown; Olajuwon named finals MVP	Clyde Drexler retires	Team finishes at 34-48; first losing record since 1983-84

COMPAQ CENTER: A CENTER OF ACTIVITY

WITH SOME TWO MILLION PEOPLE going through its turnstiles each year, the Compaq Center is one of the nation's busiest arenas. Concerts, circuses and sporting events such as boxing, figure skating and pro wrestling are regularly staged here. In fact, the Rockets is just one of five professional sports teams that call the Compaq Center home. The arena is part of the Greenway Plaza, a mixed-use commercial, residential and entertainment development, and is linked to underground parking and one of the city's finest hotels.

CONCESSIONS

In addition to arena favorites such as burgers, hot dogs, pizza and popcorn, Compaq Center offers Mexican, seafood, barbecue and fresh-cut fries. There are local and international beers, as well as some microbrewery brands.

Arena Facts

Opened: Nov. 2, 1975
Cost: $27 million
Capacity: 16,285
Home Sweet Home:
• Houston fans know their basketball. Their vocal support has helped the Rockets take back-to-back NBA titles and the Houston Comets have won four Women's National Basketball Association crowns in a row.

GAME DAY TIPS

• **Gate hours:** Gates open 90 minutes prior to tip-off.
• **Prohibited items:** Food, beverages, bottles, cans, alcohol and coolers are prohibited. Laser pointers, beachballs, frisbees, fireworks, compressed air noisemaking devices or anything else that can be used as a weapon may not be brought in. Still cameras without flash are permitted, but video cameras and audio recording devices are not. Smoking is not allowed in the arena, although there is a designated smoking area outside Compaq Center.

TIMMONS ENTRANCE

Seating Plan

■ $112	■ $26.50
■ $84	■ $13
░ $59	■ $10
▒ $46	**ATM** Section 108
░ $34	♿ Sections 105–125, 111–119

LOWER EDLOE ENTRANCE

• **Ticket tips:** As befits a new arena, Compaq Center has great sight lines everywhere, even in the top rows. Tickets are usually fairly easy to get, although seats get snapped up more quickly when popular teams such as Los Angeles and Portland roll into town.
• **Lost and found:** (713) 843-3930.

Directions: Exit Hwy. 59 (SW Frwy.) at Edloe/Weslayan. Follow signs to Compaq Center. By Bus: Several buses arrive at the center from downtown Houston. Call the Metropolitan Transit Authority (MTA) of Harris County at (713) 635-4000 for information. **Parking:** There are about 9,000 spots at Greenway Plaza Parking Garage; 240 are reserved for the disabled. Parking is also available on Circle Drwy., Westheimer Rd. and E. Greenway Plaza.

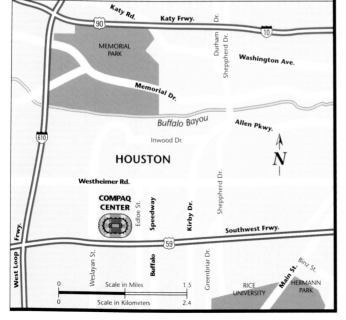

Nearby Hotels

▼▼▼ **Doubletree Club Houston near Greenway Plaza** *(Hotel)*, 2828 Southwest Fwy. (Houston), (713) 942-2111, $59-$109
▼▼▼ **Fairfield Inn by Marriott Galleria** *(Motel)*, 3131 W. Loop Fwy. S. (Houston), (713) 961-1690, $89
▼▼▼ **Holiday Inn Select-Greenway Plaza** *(Hotel)*, 2712 Southwest Fwy. (Houston), (713) 523-8448, $59-$89
▼▼▼ **La Quinta Inn-Greenway Plaza** *(Motel)*, 4015 Southwest Fwy. (Houston), (713) 623-4750, $55-$72
FYI Renaissance Houston Hotel, 6 Greenway Plaza E. (Houston), (713) 629-1200, call for rates

Nearby Restaurants

▼▼▼▼ **The Brownstone** *(Continental)*, 2736 Virginia St. (Houston), (713) 520-5666, $21-$32
▼▼ **Cafe Express** *(American)*, 3200 Kirby Dr. (Houston), (713) 522-3994, $5-$8
▼▼ **Goode Co. Seafood** *(Regional American)*, 2621 Westpark (Houston), (713) 523-7154, $7-$24
▼▼ **Maxim's** *(French)*, 3755 Richmond Ave. (Houston), (713) 877-8899, $17-$30
▼▼ **Prego Restaurant** *(Italian)*, 2520 Amherst in University Village (Houston), (713) 529-2420, $11-$23

INDIANA PACERS

WHAT BETTER PLACE FOR A PROFESSIONAL basketball franchise than Indiana? Nowhere could the fledgling ABA find a more dedicated basketball audience than in the state where university ball is revered. Predictions for the success of the franchise proved, for the most part, remarkably accurate. A playoff team in its first year of existence, the Pacers won the team's first ABA title in 1970 behind the scoring of Roger Brown and the rebounding strength of Mel Daniels. When the team added offensive powerhouse George McGinnis in 1971, it again rose to the top and captured back-to-back titles in 1972 and '73. By the time the league merged with the NBA in 1976, the Pacers franchise owned three titles in just nine seasons and a place in history as arguably the ABA's most successful franchise. But the true proving ground for professional basketball is the NBA and it took the Pacers five seasons to earn its first NBA playoff berth, another six to earn its second. But since the turn of the 1990s, the Pacers have been a consistent contender. With a balanced attack that featured big Rik Smits at center, Dale Davis at forward pulling down the lion's share of the rebounds, and the outside shooting of guard Reggie Miller, the Pacers became a perennial playoff threat in the 1990s. They reached the Eastern Conference finals three times in the decade and came close to an NBA title with a 4-2 finals defeat in 2000. For fans the Pacers promise excitement, thanks in large part to Miller's late-game heroics. His clutch shooting is so well known around the NBA, in fact, that the dying seconds are often referred to as "Miller time."

Vital Stats

Stadium Address:
One Conseco Court,
125 S. Pennsylvania St.,
Indianapolis, Ind.
Phone: (317) 917-2500
Web: nba.com/pacers,
consecofieldhouse.com
Box Office:
(317) 917-2727
Mon.–Fri. 9–6, Sat. 10–5
Media Coverage:
Radio: WIBC (1070 AM)
TV: WTTV (Channel 4),
Fox Sports Net
Practice Facility:
Conseco Fieldhouse,
Indianapolis, Ind.

POSTSEASON
- **Eastern Conference Championships** 1
(1999–2000)
- **ABA Championships** 3
(1969–70, 1971–72, 1972–73)

RETIRED NUMBERS
- George McGinnis (30)
- Mel Daniels (34)
- Roger Brown (35)
- Bob "Slick" Leonard (529)

TEAM RECORDS
- **Dale Davis (1991–2000)**
FG Pct. (season): .568
(1992–93)
FG Pct. (career): .543
Off. Rebounds (career): 2,185
Rebounds (career): 5,784
- **Vern Fleming (1984–95)**
Assists (career): 4,038

The Inside Pitch

- Fans watching the Pacers can expect lots of long-range shots. Pacer Reggie Miller holds the NBA records for both three-pointers and three-point attempts.
- The Pacers' name honors the state's long history of harness racing, where the horses are called pacers; and the Indy 500, with its pace car.

- **Mark Jackson (1994–2000)**
Assists (game): 19 (twice)
Assists (season): 713 (1997–98)
Assists-Per-Game (season): 8.7 (1997–98)
- **Clark Kellogg (1982–87)**
Off. Rebounds (season): 340 (1982–83)
Rebounds (season): 860 (1982–83)
- **Billy Knight (1974–83)**
FG (season): 831 (1976–77)
Points (season): 2,075 (1976–77)
Points-Per-Game (season): 26.6 (1976–77)
- **Reggie Miller (1987–present)**
FG (career): 6,455
FG Att. (career): 13,460
FT (season): 551 (1990–91)
FT (career): 5,015
FT Att. (career): 5,690
Games (career): 1,013
Points (game): 57 (Nov. 28, 1992)
Points (career): 19,792
Points-Per-Game (career): 19.5
Seasons (career): 13
Steals (career): 1,159

Turnovers (career): 1,945
3-Point FG (game): 8 (twice)
3-Point FG (season): 229 (1996–97)
3-Point FG (career): 1,867
3-Point FG Att (game): 16 (April 18, 1993)
3-Point Att. (season): 536 (1996–97)
3-Point FG Att (career): 4,629
- **Chris Mullin (1997–2000)**
FT Pct. (season): .939 (1997–98)
FT Pct. (career): .912
3-Point Fg Pct (career): .441
3-Point FG Pct (season): .465 (1998–99)
- **Detlef Schrempf (1988–93)**
Def. Rebounds (season) 570 (1992–93)
FT Att. (season): 653 (1992–93)
- **Rik Smits (1988–2000)**
Blocks (career): 1,111
Def. Rebounds (career): 3,746
Disqualifications (career): 73
Personal Fouls (career): 3,011
- **Herb Williams (1981–89)**
Blocks (game): 9 (three times) (tie)
Blocks (season): 184

Reggie Miller is one of the NBA's most consistent scorers.

(1985–86)
Rebounds (game): 29 (Jan. 23, 1989)

LEAGUE HONORS
Rookie of the Year
- Chuck Person (1986–87)

NBA Sixth Man of the Year
- Detlef Schrempf (1990–91, 1991–92)

Coach of the Year
- Jack McKinney (1980–81)
- Larry Bird (1997–98)

> *"When I look back on our franchise, the most important decision ever made was drafting Reggie Miller."*
> — Pacers President Donnie Walsh at the end of the 2000–01 season

Timeline

1967	1969	1973	1975	1976	1983	1987	1990	1992	1994	1996	1997	2000
Pacers join ABA	Indiana reaches ABA finals, losing 4-1 to the Oakland Oaks	Pacers win second of two straight ABA titles	Pacers move into Market Square Arena	Pacers join NBA	Clark Kellogg named to All-Rookies team	Chuck Person named NBA Rookie of the Year	Reggie Miller named to first All-Star game	Miller scores career-high 57 points vs. Charlotte	Indiana reaches Eastern Conference finals, losing 4-3 to Knicks	Guard Mark Jackson traded to Nuggets only to be reacquired through trade a year later	Native son Larry Bird named head coach	Pacers play in first NBA Finals, losing 4-2 to Lakers

CONSECO FIELDHOUSE: BASKETBALL CATHEDRAL

IN INDIANA, BASKETBALL is like a religion and in Conseco Fieldhouse, the Pacers have an appropriate cathedral. Despite possessing all the modern amenities fans have come to expect, Conseco has the feel of a 1940s-style field house, thanks largely to its spacious entry hall, grand staircase, memorabilia cases and carefully selected architectural appointments. The view of the stadium from the outside is also memorable. Two large glass curtains on the east and west are visible on the Indianapolis skyline as you approach.

CONCESSIONS

The array of treats available at Conseco Fieldhouse includes a selection of deli, grilled meat sandwiches, Tex-Mex, fried shrimp baskets and healthier options such as wraps, soups and salads. For an authentic Indianapolis experience, try the French Velvet soup. Traditionalists shouldn't be alarmed, there are plenty of hot dog, hamburger and pizza outlets as well.

GAME DAY TIPS

• **Gate hours:** Gates open 90 minutes prior to tip-off.
• **Prohibited items:** Food and beverages, coolers, cans, and bottles, as well as cameras and video recorders, laser pointers, cowbells, and whistles are prohibited. Signs are permitted, provided they aren't offensive and don't block people's view. Smoking is allowed on six designated terraces. The terraces are heated in the winter and are equipped with televisions so smokers can follow the action.
• **Ticket tips:** The Pacers' new venue, combined with their good record, has made the team very popular. Sellouts are common, especially against the Knicks or the Lakers. Fortunately, virtually every seat in the house is a good one.
• **Lost and found:** (317) 917-2500.

Arena Facts

Opened: Nov. 6, 1999
Cost: $183 million
Capacity: 18,500
Home Sweet Home:
• Indiana is probably the most basketball-crazy state in the union. Hence, Pacer fans are among the NBA's most devoted, vocal and knowledgeable, an irritating combination for opposing teams.

Directions: Take I-65 N to Market St. exit. Turn left onto Market St., left onto East St., right onto South St. Off I-65 S or I-70 W, take Fletcher Ave. exit. Turn right onto Fletcher Ave., then right onto Delaware St. By Bus: A number of buses go to and from Conseco. Call IndyGo at (317) 635-3344 for information. **Parking:** A parking garage, located east of the arena and connected to it via a skywalk, holds 2,700 cars. There are about 55 spots reserved for people with disabilities, located on each level of the garage. There are also private lots on Market, Washington, Maryland, Meridian and South Sts.

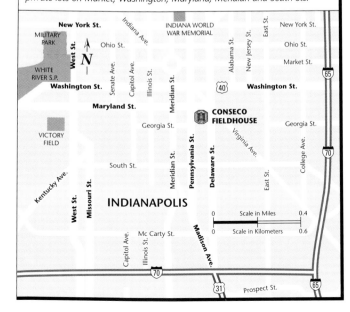

Seating Plan

■ Courtside	$115-$315	■	$32
■	$85	■	$21
■	$65	■	$16
■	$55	▦	$10
■	$54	ATM Sections 18/19, 1/20, 222
■	$48	♿ Throughout
■	$45	

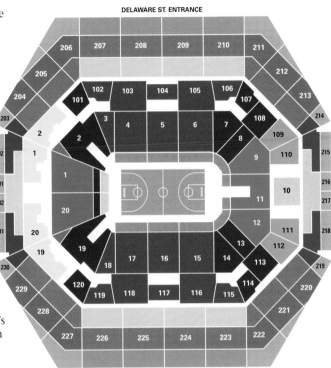

DELAWARE ST. ENTRANCE

PENNSYLVANIA ST. ENTRANCE

Nearby Hotels

▼▼▼▼ **Canterbury Hotel (Classic Hotel)**, 123 S. Illinois St. (Indianapolis), (317) 634-3000, $250-$1550
▼▼▼ **Comfort Inn & Suites City Centre (Motel)**, 530 S. Capitol Ave. (Indianapolis), (317) 631-9000, $100-$350
▼▼▼ **Courtyard by Marriott-Downtown (Hotel)**, 501 W. Washington St. (Indianapolis), (317) 635-4443, $159
▼▼ **Days Inn Downtown (Motel)**, 401 E. Washington St. (Indianapolis), (317) 637-6464, $50-$255
▼▼▼ **Hampton Inn Downtown at Circle Center (Motor Inn)**, 105 S. Meridian St. (Indianapolis), (317) 261-1200, $104-$114

Nearby Restaurants

▼▼ **40 West Coffee Café (American)**, 40 W. Jackson Pl. in the Omni Severin Hotel (Indianapolis), (317) 686-1414, $3-$10 (lunch only)
▼▼ **The California Cafe Bar & Grill (West American)**, 49 W. Maryland St. in Circle Centre Mall (Indianapolis), (317) 488-8686, $12-$25
▼▼▼ **The Majestic Restaurant (Seafood)**, 47 S. Pennsylvania St. (Indianapolis), (317) 636-5418, $13-$39
▼▼▼ **Palomino (Continental)**, 49 W. Maryland St. #189 (Indianapolis), (317) 974-0400, $14-$30
▼▼▼▼ **The Restaurant at the Canterbury Hotel (Continental)**, 123 S. Illinois St. in the Canterbury Hotel (Indianapolis), (317) 634-3000, $15-$25

LOS ANGELES CLIPPERS

IT ISN'T EASY BEING A FAN of the Los Angeles Clippers. For one thing, the franchise has only had five winning seasons in 30 years. Four of those years came in the 1970s, when Bob McAdoo anchored the squad. At 6 feet 9 inches and just 225 pounds, McAdoo certainly wasn't the league's biggest forward, but he was one of the best. Combining a guard's grace and a center's toughness, McAdoo led the league in scoring in his first three seasons and was always among the top rebounders. His brilliant play earned him Rookie of the Year honors in 1972–73 and the league MVP award in 1974–75. But while the offense was always among the league's best, a porous defense proved to be an Achilles heel. Sometimes the team's woes have just been a case of bad luck: Bill Walton spent most of his days as a Clipper out of action with injuries. The year he was traded to the Celtics, however, he won the NBA's Sixth Man Award and helped the team win the 1985–86 championship. When the team drafted Danny Manning number one overall in 1988, things were looking up. That was until Manning blew his knee out just 26 games into the season. The present-day Clippers also have the misfortune of sharing a city with one of the game's greatest franchises, the Lakers. Since the Clippers first arrived in Los Angeles in 1984, they haven't won a single title and have only made the playoffs three times, never advancing past the first round. During that same span, the Lakers have won seven division titles, six conference championships and four NBA crowns. It's enough to make a Clippers fan weep.

POSTSEASON
• NBA Playoff
Appearances........................6
(1973–74, 1974–75, 1975–76, 1991–92, 1992–93, 1996–97)

TEAM RECORDS
• **Benoit Benjamin (1985–91)**
Blocks (game): 10 (twice)
Blocks (career): 1,117
• **Tom Chambers (1981–83)**
Personal Fouls (season): 341 (1982–83)
• **Terry Dehere (1993–97)**
3-Point FG Pct. (season): .440 (1995–96)
3-Point FG (season): 139 (1995–96)
• **Ernie DiGregorio (1973–77)**
Assists (game): 25 (Jan. 1, '74)
FT Pct. (season): .945 (1976–77)
FT Pct. (career): .906
• **James Donaldson (1983–85)**
FG Pct. (season): .637 (1984–85)

Jump Shot
• Since the team first joined the NBA in 1970, it has called three cities home, played in eight different arenas, had four owners and 16 coaches. Appearing in 32 playoff games, the Clippers have won just two postseason series.

• **World B. Free (1978–80)**
FT (game): 22 (Jan. 13, '79)
FT (season): 654 (1978–79)
Points-Per-Game (career): 29.4
• **Bob McAdoo (1972–76)**
Blocks (season): 246 (1973–74)
FG (game): 22 (twice) (tied)
FG (season): 1,095 (1974–75)
Minutes (season): 3,539 (1974–75)
Points (game): 52 (twice) (tied)
Points (season): 2,831 (1974–75)
• **Swen Nater (1977–83)**
FG Pct. (career): .542
Rebounds (game): 32 (Dec. 14, '79)
Rebounds (season): 1,216 (1979–80)
• **Norm Nixon (1983–89)**
Assists (season): 914 (1983–84)
• **Eric Piatkowski (1994–present)**
3-Point FG Pct. (career): .389
3-Point FG (game): 7 (Mar. 9, '98)
3-Point FG (career): 427
• **Doc Rivers (1991–92)**
Steals (game): 9 (Nov. 6, '91)
• **Charles Smith (1988–92)**
Points (game): 52 (tie) (Dec. 1, '90)
• **Randy Smith (1971–79, 1982–83)**
Assists (career): 3,498
Games (career): 715
FG (career): 5,214
FT (career): 2,304

Personal Fouls (career): 2,018
Points (career): 12,735
Steals (season): 203 (1973–74)
Steals (career): 1,072
• **Loy Vaught (1990–98)**
Rebounds (career): 4,471
• **Freeman Williams (1978–82)**
FG (game): 22 (tied) (Jan. 19, '90)

LEAGUE HONORS
NBA MVP
• Bob McAdoo (1974–75)

Rookie of the Year
• Bob McAdoo (1972–73)
• Ernie DiGregorio (1973–74)
• Adrian Dantley (1976–77)
• Terry Cummings (1982–83)

All-Star Game Selections
• Bob Kaufman (1971, '72, '73)
• Bob McAdoo (1974, '75, '76)
• Randy Smith (1976, '78)
• World B. Free (1980)
• Norm Nixon (1985)
• Marques Johnson (1986)
• Danny Manning (1993, '94)

All-Star Game MVP
• Randy Smith (1978)

Basketball Hall of Fame
• Bob McAdoo (2000)

"To see how Los Angeles has rallied behind the Clippers is amazing."
— Sportswriter Lonnie White, on growing fan support for the Clippers

Lamar Odom has emerged as an offensive force in the NBA.

Timeline

1970	1973	1974	1975	1978	1980	1984	1988	1991	1994	1998	1999	2000
Expansion Buffalo Braves join NBA	Bob McAdoo wins Rookie of the Year	Team enjoys first winning season and first playoff game	McAdoo wins scoring title and MVP award	Team moves to San Diego; changes name to Clippers	World B. Free finishes second in league scoring for second straight season	Franchise moves to Los Angeles	Team drafts Danny Manning first overall; Manning blows out knee	Clippers suffer 12th consecutive losing season	Team trades for superstar Dominique Wilkins	Coach Bill Fitch records win number 939; second most in league history	Clippers win just nine games in lockout-shortened season	Team's 15-67 record is worst in NBA

106

STAPLES CENTER:
FLASHY DIGS

SINCE BRUCE SPRINGSTEEN'S SPLASHY opening concert at STAPLES Center in 1999, Los Angeles' latest jewel has established itself as one of the world's premier entertainment venues. Complete with 1,200 TV monitors, a 675-speaker sound system and a $2-million light show, STAPLES Center helps to imbue all Clippers games with carnivalesque flair. The arena was designed as a venue for everyone, from families to movie stars. Fans can expect great sight lines in all sections or, for an annual fee of $10,500, they can watch the game and sip wine from the Grand Reserved Club, an exclusive restaurant with only 200 memberships.

CONCESSIONS

STAPLES Center's 23 refreshment stands feature a wide variety of foods, including hot dogs, pretzels, Chinese food, pizza, hamburgers, Mexican food, and standard deli fare. The City View Grill offers diners a unique outdoor setting and spectacular views of downtown Los Angeles. There are a number of bars on the premises that provide patrons with a relaxed setting to enjoy a drink.

GAME DAY TIPS

• **Gate hours:** Gates open one hour prior to tip-off.
• **Prohibited items:** Bottles, cans, coolers, outside food or beverages, recording devices of any sort, weapons, frisbees, beachballs, banners and balloons are all prohibited. Animals are not allowed, except for those providing assistance for people with disabilities.

• **Ticket tips:** The Clippers sold out just nine times in the 1999–2000 season, so tickets should still be available for most games. However, one of the biggest draws is when the Clippers square off against Los Angeles' other, more successful team, the Lakers.
• **Lost and found:** (213) 742-7444.

Arena Facts

Opened: *Oct. 17, 1999*
Cost: *$400 million*
Capacity: *18,997*
Home Sweet Home:
• *The Clippers enjoy superb fan support. Although the team was more than 20 games out of a playoff spot, a STAPLES Center sell-out treated the team to a five-minute standing ovation after the final game of the 2000–01 season.*

Seating Plan

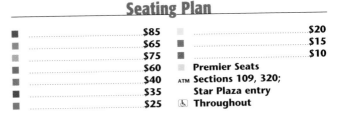

■	$85	▫	$20
▦	$65	■	$15
▨	$75	■	$10
■	$60		**Premier Seats**
■	$40	**ATM**	**Sections 109, 320;**
■	$35		**Star Plaza entry**
■	$25	♿	**Throughout**

11TH ST. ENTRY

FIGUEROA ST. ENTRY

STAR PLAZA ENTRY

Nearby Hotels

▼▼ **Best Western Dragon Gate Inn** *(Motor Inn)*, 818 N. Hill St. (Los Angeles), (213) 617-3077, $79-$189
▼▼▼▼ **Hyatt Regency Los Angeles** *(Hotel)*, 711 S. Hope St. (Los Angeles), (213) 683-1234, $210-$235
▼▼▼ **Los Angeles Downtown Marriott Hotel** *(Hotel)*, 333 S. Figueroa St. (Los Angeles), (213) 617-1133, $190-$149
▼▼▼ **The Millennium Biltmore Los Angeles** *(Classic Hotel)*, 506 S. Grand St. at 5th St. (Los Angeles), (213) 624-1011, $135-$155
▼▼▼ **Wyndham Checkers Hotel** *(Hotel)*, 535 S. Grand Ave. (Los Angeles), (213) 624-0000, $99-$199

Nearby Restaurants

▼▼▼ **A Thousand Cranes Restaurant** *(Japanese)*, 120 S. Los Angeles St. in the New Otani Hotel (Los Angeles), (213) 253-9255, $35-$90
▼▼▼ **Checkers Restaurant** *(Continental)*, 535 S. Grand Ave. in the Wyndham Checkers Hotel (Los Angeles), (213) 891-0519, $16-32 (dinner only)
▼▼ **Engine Company No. 28** *(American)*, 644 S. Figueroa St. (Los Angeles), (213) 624-6996, $10-$20
▼▼ **McCormick & Schmick's** *(Seafood)*, 633 W. 5th St. in the First Interstate World Center Bldg., 4th floor (Los Angeles), (213) 629-1929, $9-$20
▼▼▼ **The Tower** *(Continental)*, 1150 S. Olive St. in the Transamerica Center Bldg., 32nd floor (Los Angeles), (213) 746-1554, $35-$45

Directions: *Take I-405, I-105 or I-10 to I-110 north. Exit right onto Adams Blvd., then left onto Figueroa St. and left onto 11th St. By Public Transportation: Many buses go to the arena. The Metro Blue Line and Red Line also pass nearby. Call the Metropolitan Transportation Authority (MTA) at 1-800-COMMUTE for information.* **Parking:** *Parking lots around the arena can hold about 6,000 cars; all are wheelchair-accessible. More parking is available on 8th, 9th, 11th and 12th Sts. and Olympic Blvd.*

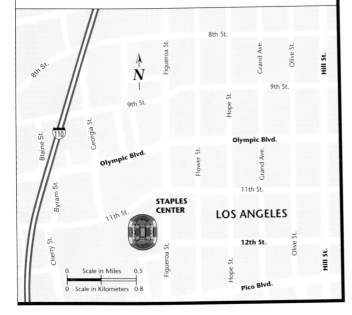

LOS ANGELES LAKERS

THE LAKERS ARE THE QUINTESSENTIAL L.A. team. Glitzy, glamorous and always ready to perform for their fans, they have worked hard to foster a showbiz image that would best represent the entertainment-hungry City of Angels. This effort has paid off. Over the last 25 years, Lakers players have become as famous as the movie stars and celebrities who congregate courtside to watch the latest installment of "Showtime," a nickname given to Lakers games during the team's reign of dominance in the 1980s. The key to the squad's popularity — and success — has always been its superstars. Founded in Minneapolis in 1947, the franchise found its first star in "Big George" Mikan, a 6-foot-10-inch center, whose unmatched scoring prowess was instrumental in the team's five NBA titles between 1949 and 1954. On moving to L.A. in 1960 the team maintained a roster of scoring heroes and crowd-pleasers, including Elgin Baylor and Jerry West. Baylor's showy acrobatics and West's perfectionism won the admiration of Angelinos who followed the Lakers' saga as they battled the unstoppable Celtics in six classic NBA finals throughout the 1960s. The signing of the mythic Wilt Chamberlain in 1968 only added to this fervor. By the time the Lakers won their first NBA crown in Los Angeles in 1972, thanks to Chamberlain's MVP-winning performance, the legacy was set — only the best would suffice for the Lakers. The team's 30-year history since this win has been dominated by some the biggest names in the game: Kareem Abdul-Jabbar, Earvin "Magic" Johnson and a supporting cast that ranks the team with the greatest in history. With Shaquille O'Neal and Kobe Bryant leading the charge, the Lakers won two straight NBA titles in 2000 and 2001.

Vital Stats

Stadium Address:
1111 S. Figueroa St.,
Los Angeles, Calif.
Phone: (213) 742-7100
Web: nba.com/lakers,
staplescenter.com
Box Office: (213) 742-7340, Mon.–Sat. 10–7
Media Coverage:
Radio: KLAC (570 AM)
TV: KCAL (Channel 9),
Fox Sports Net
Practice Facility:
HealthSouth Training
Center, El Segundo, Calif.

Kobe Bryant is one of the premier guards in the game.

Jump Shot

• In the 1950s George Mikan's dominance was so great that the NBA decided to change the game rules and widen the foul lane in order to give other teams a fighting chance against Mikan's scoring onslaught.
• In 1992 "Magic" Johnson added the esteemed J. Walter Kennedy Citizenship Award to his trophy case for his tireless crusade for HIV research funds and AIDS awareness.

POSTSEASON
• NBA Championships.....13
(1948–49, 1949–50, 1951–52, 1952–53, 1953–54, 1971–72, 1979–80, 1981–82, 1984–85, 1986–87, 1987–88, 1999–2000, 2000–2001)

RETIRED NUMBERS
• Wilt Chamberlain (13)
• Elgin Baylor (22)
• Gail Goodrich (25)
• "Magic" Johnson (32)
• Kareem Abdul-Jabbar (33)
• James Worthy (42)
• Jerry West (44)

TEAM RECORDS
• **Kareem Abdul-Jabbar (1975–89)**
Blocks (career): 2,694
Def. Rebounds (game): 29 (Dec. 14, 1975)
FG (career): 9,935
• **Elgin Baylor (1958–72)**
FG (season): 1,029 (1962–63)
Points (game): 71 (Nov. 15, '60)
Points (season): 2,719 (1962–63)
Rebounds (career): 11,463
• **Wilt Chamberlain (1968–73)**
FG (game): 29 (Feb. 9, 1969)
Rebounds (game): 42 (Mar. 7, 1969)
Rebounds (season): 1,712 (1968–69)
• **Earvin "Magic" Johnson**

"You have to do it in front of your home fans."
— *Veteran Ron Harper, on taking 1999–2000 NBA crown in L.A.*

(1979–91, '96)
Assists (game): 24 (twice)
Assists (season): 989 (1990–91)
Assists (career): 10,141
FT (half): 14 (twice)
Steals (season): 208 (1981–82)
Steals (career): 1,724
• **Elmore Smith (1973–75)**
Blocks (game): 17 (Oct. 28, '73)
Blocks (season): 393 (1973–74)
• **Nick Van Exel (1993–98)**
3-Point FG (game): 8 (tie) (three times)
3-Point FG (season): 183 (1994–95)
3-Point FG (career): 750
• **Jerry West (1961–74)**
FT (half): 14 (Dec. 21, 1966)
FT (season): 840 (1995–96)
FT (career): 7,160
FT Att. (career): 8,801
Points (career): 25,192
Steals (game): 10 (Dec. 7, 1973)

LEAGUE HONORS
NBA MVP
• **Kareem Abdul-Jabbar** (1975–76, 1976–77, 1979–80)
• **"Magic" Johnson** (1986–87, 1988–89, 1989–90)

• Shaquille O'Neal (1999–2000)

Rookie of the Year
• Elgin Baylor (1958–59)

Defensive Player of the Year
• Michael Cooper (1986–87)

Coach of the Year
• Bill Sharman (1971–72)
• Pat Riley (1989–90)
• Del Harris (1994–95)

NBA Finals MVP
• Jerry West (1969)
• Wilt Chamberlain (1972)
• "Magic" Johnson (1980, '82, '87)
• Kareem Abdul-Jabbar (1985)
• James Worthy (1988)
• Shaquille O'Neal (2000)

Basketball Hall of Fame
• George Mikan (1959)
• Bill Sharman (1975)
• Elgin Baylor (1977)
• Jim Pollard (1977)
• Wilt Chamberlain (1979)
• Pete Newell (1979)
• Jerry West (1980)
• Slater Martin (1981)
• John Kundla (1995)
• Vern Mikkelsen (1995)
• Kareem Abdul-Jabbar (1995)
• Gail Goodrich (1996)

Timeline

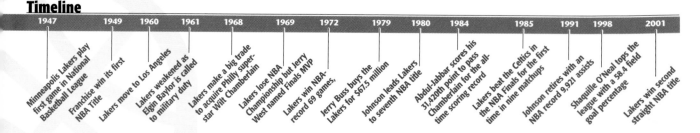

1947	1949	1960	1961	1968	1969	1972	1979	1980	1984	1985	1991	1998	2001
Minneapolis Lakers play first game in National Basketball League	Franchise win its first NBA Title	Lakers move to Los Angeles	Lakers weakened as Elgin Baylor is called to military duty	Lakers make a big trade to acquire Philly super-star Wilt Chamberlain	Lakers lose NBA Championship but Jerry West named Finals MVP	Lakers win NBA-record 69 games,	Jerry Buss buys the Lakers for $67.5 million	Johnson leads Lakers to seventh NBA title	Abdul-Jabbar scores his 31,420th point to pass Chamberlain for the all-time scoring record	Lakers beat the Celtics in the NBA Finals for the first time in nine matchups	Johnson retires with an NBA record 9,921 assists	Shaquille O'Neal tops the league with a 58.4 field goal percentage	Lakers win second straight NBA title

STAPLES CENTER: WELCOME TO SHOWTIME

SINCE BRUCE SPRINGSTEEN'S SPLASHY, Hollywood-style opening concert at STAPLES Center, L.A.'s latest jewel has been established as one of the world's premier entertainment venues. Complete with 1,200 TV monitors, a $1.5-million 675-speaker sound system, a $2-million light show and a futuristic design, the center helps to imbue all Lakers games with a carnivalesque flair suitable for L.A.'s superstar team. Moreover, STAPLES Center prides itself on being a venue for everyone, from families to movie stars. Fans can expect great sight lines and comfortable seats in all sections, while, for an annual fee of $10,500, fans can watch the game and sip wine at the Grand Reserved Club, an exclusive restaurant with only 200 memberships.

CONCESSIONS

STAPLES Center's 23 refreshment stands feature a wide variety of foods, including hot dogs, pretzels, Chinese food, pizza, hamburgers, Mexican food and standard deli fare.

GAME DAY TIPS

• **Gate hours:** Gates open one hour prior to tip-off.
• **Prohibited items:** Bottles, cans, coolers and outside food or beverages are prohibited. Recording devices of any sort, banners and balloons are also prohibited.
• **Ticket tips:** Lakers tickets are among the most sought-after in the NBA and all but a small handful of games are usually sold out. Traditional rivalries against the Knicks and the Celtics don't really affect ticket sales, although games against those teams always have a special appeal. The team directs fans to Ticketmaster for ticket purchases, but a limited number of tickets are available at the Box Office only on game days.
• **Lost and found:** (213) 742-7444.

Arena Facts

Opened: Oct. 17, 1999
Cost: $400 million
Capacity: 18,997
Home Sweet Home:
• *Jack Nicholson and Steven Spielberg are just a few of the celebrities who sit at courtside during Lakers games. The star-studded atmosphere, along with the support of Lakers faithful, has helped the franchise become one of the NBA's most successful.*

Seating Plan

▪ $21	▪ $160
▪ $31	▪ Premier ....N/A
▪ $55	ATM Sections 109, 320;
▫ $70	Star Plaza entry
▪ $100	♿ Throughout
▪ $140	

11TH ST. ENTRY

FIGUEROA ST. ENTRY

STAR PLAZA ENTRY

Nearby Hotels

▼▼ **Best Western Dragon Gate Inn** (*Motor Inn*), 818 N. Hill St. (Los Angeles), (213) 617-3077, $79-$189
▼▼▼▼ **Hyatt Regency Los Angeles** (*Hotel*), 711 S. Hope St. (Los Angeles), (213) 683-1234, $210-$235
▼▼▼ **Los Angeles Downtown Marriott Hotel** (*Hotel*), 333 S. Figueroa St. (Los Angeles), (213) 617-1133, $190-$149
▼▼▼ **The Millennium Biltmore Los Angeles** (*Classic Hotel*), 506 S. Grand St. at 5th St. (Los Angeles), (213) 624-1011, $135-$155
▼▼▼ **Wyndham Checkers Hotel** (*Hotel*), 535 S. Grand Ave. (Los Angeles), (213) 624-0000, $99-$199

Nearby Restaurants

▼▼▼ **A Thousand Cranes Restaurant** (*Japanese*), 120 S. Los Angeles St. in the New Otani Hotel (Los Angeles), (213) 253-9255, $35-$90
▼▼▼ **Checkers Restaurant** (*Continental*), 535 S. Grand Ave. in the Wyndham Checkers Hotel (Los Angeles), (213) 891-0519, $16-32 (dinner only)
▼▼ **Engine Company No. 28** (*American*), 644 S. Figueroa St. (Los Angeles), (213) 624-6996, $10-$20
▼▼ **McCormick & Schmick's** (*Seafood*), 633 W. 5th St. in the First Interstate World Center Bldg., 4th floor (Los Angeles), (213) 629-1929, $9-$20
▼▼ **The Tower** (*Continental*), 1150 S. Olive St. in the Transamerica Center Bldg., 32nd floor (Los Angeles), (213) 746-1554, $35-$45

Directions: *Take I-405, I-105 or I-10 to I-110 north. Exit right onto Adams Blvd., then left onto Figueroa St., left onto 11th St. By Public Transportation: Many buses go to the arena. The Metro Blue Line and Red Line also pass nearby. Call the Metropolitan Transportation Authority (MTA) at 1-800-COMMUTE for information.* **Parking:** *Parking lots around the arena can accommodate about 6,000 cars; all are wheelchair-accessible. More parking is available on 8th, 9th, 11th and 12th Sts. and Olympic Blvd.*

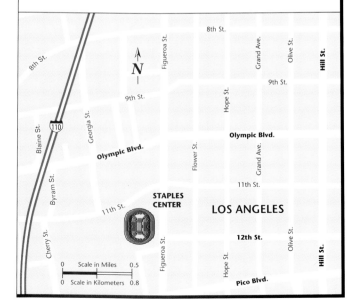

MEMPHIS GRIZZLIES

THE 2001–2002 SEASON will mark the first time the people of Memphis will be able to cheer their very own NBA team. But the Grizzlies franchise was born a long way from Memphis in Vancouver. The team was admitted to the NBA in 1994 as the league's 29th franchise and began play a year later. Along with the Toronto Raptors, who also joined the league for the 1995 season, the birth of the Vancouver team marked an experiment in Canadian pro basketball — an experiment that many basketball experts predicted was doomed to failure. The troubles for the Grizzlies began before the team even had its first official tipoff; unable to sell enough season tickets to guarantee NBA support, a number of major Canadian companies had to band together to pick up the majority of the unsold tickets. And then there were problems with the team itself. In spite of the imposing presence of Oklahoma State's 7-foot, 300-pound center, Bryant "Big Country" Reeves, and forward Shareef Abdur-Rahim — one of the league's top scorers and rebounders — the inexperienced squad never established itself. Fan support dwindled as the Grizzlies won only four games in 72 during the 1996–97 season and eight out of 50 in 1998–99, a winning percentage of just .160. During the 1999–2000 season, things were beginning to look up for the Grizzlies; they set a club record of 22 wins and enjoyed additional great performances by Mike Bibby and Dennis Scott. Unfortunately, it was too little, too late. With fan support at its all-time low — the Grizzlies played to only one sellout crowd that year — Michael Heisley Sr., the team's owner, made it clear that the Vancouver basketball experiment was over. Heisley began looking at other cities as viable homes for his team. Early frontrunners included Las Vegas, Anaheim, St. Louis, New Orleans and Louisville. However, the enthusiastic contingent from Memphis eventually won over Heisley and the other NBA owners, giving the city on the Mississippi its first taste of the big time.

Vital Stats

Stadium Address:
One Auction Ave.,
Memphis, Tenn.
Phone: (901) 521-9675
Web: nba.com/grizzlies,
pyramidarena.com
Box Office: (901)
521-9675 ext. 333,
Mon.–Fri. 10–5
Media Coverage:
Radio: To be determined
TV: To be determined
Training Facility:
To be determined

"This is an exciting day for the city of Memphis."

— J.R. Hyde, minority owner of the Grizzlies, after the NBA sanctioned the move to Memphis

Michael Dickerson is one of the Grizzlies' top scorers.

TEAM RECORDS

• **Shareef Abdur-Rahim (1996–present)**
Blocks (career): 297
Def. Rebounds (season): 607 (1999–2000)
FG (season): 653 (1997–98)
FG (career): 2,183
FT (game): 16 (23/2/99)
FT (season): 502 (1997–98)
FT (career): 1,704
FT Pct. (season): .841

Jump Shot

• *In spite of the team's tough times, the Grizzlies have had some moments of brilliance. In 1996–97 "Big Country" Reeves and Shareef Abdur-Rahim were one of the NBA's highest scoring frontcourt duos. In 1998–99 Abdur-Rahim was fourth overall in scoring, pouring in 23 points a game average, while Mike Bibby was on top of the rookie charts with his 13.2 point and 6.5 assist game average.*

(1998–99)
Minutes (season): 3,223 (1999–2000)
Minutes (career): 10,996
Off. Rebounds (season): 227 (1997–98)
Off. Rebounds (career): 775
Points (season): 1,829 (1997–98)
Points (career): 6,138
Points-Per-Game Avg. (career): 20.9
Rebounds (season): 825 (1999–2000)
Rebounds (career): 2,335
Steals (career): 326
Turnovers (season): 257 (1997–98)
• **Greg Anthony (1995–97)**
3-Pointers (career): 178
• **Mike Bibby (1998–present)**
Assists (game): 16 (Nov. 6, 1999)
Assists (season): 665 (1999–2000)
Assists (career): 990
Steals (season): 132 (1999–2000)
• **Michael Dickerson (1999–present)**
3-Point Pct. (career): .409
• **Sam Mack (1997–99)**

3-Pointers (game): 8 (Feb. 14, 1999)
FT Pct. (career): .841
• **Bryant "Big Country" Reeves (1995–present)**
Def. Rebounds (career): 1,569
Disqualifications (career): 22
FG (game): 18 (April 19, 1997)
FG Pct. (season): .523 (1997–98)
Games (career): 320
Personal Fouls (career): 1,122
Points (game): 41 (Jan. 15, 1998)
• **Roy Rogers (1996–97)**
Blocks (season): 163 (1996–97)
Blocks-Per-Game (career): 1.99
• **Michael Smith (1998–99)**
FG Pct. (career): .520

LEAGUE HONORS
NBA All-Rookie Team
• **Bryant Reeves (1995–96)**
• **Shareef Abdur-Rahim (1996–97)**
• **Mike Bibby (1998–99)**

NBA Rookie of the Month
• **Shareef Abdur-Rahim** (Dec. 1996, Feb. 1997)

Timeline

1993	1994	1995	1996	1997	1998	1999	2000	2001
Sports magnate Arthur Griffiths reveals plans to promote a Vancouver NBA franchise	The NBA approves league expansion and sets franchise fees at $125 million	Grizzlies draft Greg Anthony and Bryant "Big Country" Reeves	Grizzlies lose an unprecedented 23 consecutive games, a NBA record	Bryant Reeves and Shareef Abdur-Rahim establish themselves as the Grizzlies scoring duo	Abdur-Rahim finishes season with a 22.3 scoring average — sixth-highest in NBA	Mike Bibby makes the All-Rookie First Team as the Grizzlies suffer an abysmal 8-42 season	Team rounds out the season with 22-60 (.268); its best season to date	Grizzlies move to Memphis

THE PYRAMID: GRIZZLIES' NEW DEN

THE NEW HOME OF THE GRIZZLIES is one of North America's most unique sporting venues. The 32-story stainless steel pyramid is the third-largest pyramid in the world, standing taller than both India's Taj Mahal and New York City's Statue of Liberty. The design was chosen as a tribute to the original Memphis on the Nile River. At its base, the massive structure covers more space than six football fields. Located on the banks of the Mississippi River, the Pyramid is equipped with a giant, state-of-the-art video display scoreboard that allows fans to watch replays from the game in progress.

CONCESSIONS

Fans at the Pyramid can enjoy all the best in Southern cuisine, including award-winning barbecue. All the traditional arena favorites are also here, along with a wide selection of beers.

GAME DAY TIPS

• **Gate hours:** Gates open 90 minutes prior to tipoff.
• **Prohibited items:** Oversized signs and banners, fireworks or noisemaking devices and laser pointers are prohibited. Bottles and cans, as well as coolers, outside food and beverages are not allowed. Illegal drugs, firearms, projectiles and dangerous devices of any kind may not be brought into the arena. Smoking is allowed only in designated areas outside the pyramid.
• **Ticket tips:** Because of the arena's unique shape, two-thirds of the seats are located in the lower level, with great sight lines as a result. For the same reason, though, leg room in the upper level tends to be cramped.
• **Lost and found:** (901) 521-9675

Arena Facts

Opened: Nov. 9, 1991
Cost: $65 million
Capacity: 20,142
Home Sweet Home:
• Over its last few years in Vancouver, the team played in front of sparse crowds. The response in Memphis has been overwhelming and the Grizzlies will enjoy a large and raucous fan base. This is especially true seeing as how this is the only pro team in the city.

111

Directions: *From I-40 west or east, take exit 1 (Riverside Dr.) or exit 2 (2nd and 3rd Sts.) and go north to arena. By Public Transportation: The Memphis Trolley and several buses stop at the Pyramid. Call Memphis Area Transit Authority at (901) 274-6282.* **Parking:** *There are 2,000 spaces available at the Pyramid, of which 160 are reserved for the disabled. Additional parking is available in lots on Auction Ave. and N. Center, N. Main and N. 2nd Sts.*

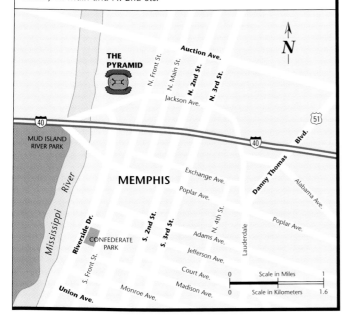

Nearby Hotels

▼▼▼ **Comfort Inn Downtown** *(Motor Inn)*, 100 N. Front St. (Memphis), (901) 526-0538, $89-$129
▼▼▼ **Holiday Inn Select-Downtown** *(Hotel)*, 160 Union Ave. (Memphis), (901) 525-5491, $139-$149
▼▼▼▼ **Peabody Memphis** *(Historic Hotel)*, 149 Union Ave. (Memphis), (901) 529-4000, $180-$270
▼▼ **Sleep Inn at Court Square** *(Hotel)*, 40 N. Front St. (Memphis), (901) 522-9700, $79-$124
▼▼▼ **Wyndham Garden Hotel** *(Hotel)*, 300 N. Second St. (Memphis), (901) 525-1800, $75-$93

Nearby Restaurants

▼▼▼▼ **Chez Philippe** *(Continental)*, 149 Union Ave. in Peabody Memphis (Memphis), (901) 529-4188, $20-$30 (dinner only)
▼▼▼ **Dux** *(American)*, 149 Union Ave. in Peabody Memphis (Memphis), (901) 529-4000, $10-$30
▼▼▼ **Folk's Folly Prime Steak House** *(Steak & Seafood)*, 551 S. Mendenhall (Memphis), (901) 762-8200, $40-$45
▼▼ **The Pier** *(Seafood)*, 100 Wagner Pl. (Memphis), (901) 526-7381, $18-$22
▼▼ **Paulette's** *(Regional American)*, 2110 Madison (Memphis), (901) 726-5128, $9-$19

MIAMI HEAT

MIAMI HEAT

WHEN THE EXPANSION MIAMI HEAT first took the court in 1988, expectations were tempered by the knowledge that all new teams suffer growing pains. Nobody warned the players, however, how painful growth could be. After an opening game loss to the Clippers, Miami lost again. And again. And again. In all, the Heat dropped its first 17 games, setting a dubious record for the worst-ever start by an NBA team. Even after the Heat broke the spell with an 89-88 victory over the Clippers, it quickly slipped back into its old patterns, including a 10-game losing streak in January and a 1-13 skid in February. When the season mercifully ended, Miami's record was a woeful 15-67, worst in the NBA. Although the squad would have only two winning seasons over the next six campaigns, the situation gradually improved. Young players such as Rony Seikaly, Grant Long, Glen Rice and Sherman Douglas took their lumps early and quickly developed into experienced veterans. In 1995 Pat Riley was named Head Coach of the Heat and began laying the foundations for a winning team. Rice, who had emerged as one of the league's top scorers, was traded away in a blockbuster deal that reeled in Alonzo Mourning, a scowling, hardworking center. Riley also orchestrated the deal that brought guard Tim Hardaway to Miami. The move paid instant dividends, with Mourning's ferocious defense and surprising scoring touch complemented by Hardaway's deft passing and lethal three-point bombs. Since 1997 the duo has led the team to four consecutive Atlantic Division Titles. Can an NBA crown be far behind?

Anthony Mason is a talented scorer and a fierce rebounder.

POSTSEASON
• **Atlantic Division Titles...4**
(1997, '98, '99, 2000)

TEAM RECORDS
• **Keith Askins (1990–99)**
Games (career): 486
• **Anthony Carter (1999–present)**
Assists (playoff game): 13
(April 25, 2000)
• **Tim Hardaway (1996–present)**
Assists (game): 19
(April 19, 1996)
Assists (season): 695 (1996–97)
Assists (career): 2,384

Jump Shot

• *Miami's coach Pat Riley is a proven winner. As head coach of the Lakers from 1981–90, Riley led his team to the Pacific Division Title a remarkable nine straight years. He didn't miss a beat when he joined the Knicks in 1991, coaching the squad to three consecutive Atlantic Division titles and a second place finish. In 1995–96, Riley's first year in Miami, the Heat finished third in the division. The team has won four straight titles since.*

FG (playoff game): 12
(three times) (tie)
Minutes (season): 3,136
(1996–97)
Points (playoff game): 38
(May 18, 1997)
Steals (game): 8 (Dec. 20, 1997)
Steals (playoff game): 5
(May 18, 1997)
Steals (season): 151
(1996–97)
3-Pointers (playoff game): 6
(twice) (tie)
3-Pointers (season): 203
(1996–97)
• **Grant Long (1989–95)**
Personal Fouls (season): 337
(1988–89)
Personal Fouls
(career): 1,699
Steals (career): 666
• **Alonzo Mourning (1995–present)**
Blocks (game): 9 (five times)
Blocks (playoff game): 9
(April 22, 2000)
Blocks (season): 294
(1999–2000)
Blocks (career): 982
FG (playoff game): 12
(May 21, 2000)
FG Pct. (career): 53.5
FT (game): 17 (Feb. 23, 2000)
FT (season): 488 (1995–96)
FT (career): 1,850
• **Glen Rice (1989–95)**
FG (game): 20 (April 15, 1995)
FG (season): 672 (1991–92)
FG (career): 3,604

FT Pct. (season): 88.0
(1993–94)
FT Pct. (career): 83.5
Minutes (career): 17,059
Points (game): 56
(April 15, 1995)
Points (season): 1,831
(1994–95)
Points (career): 9,248
3-Pointers (career): 708
• **Rony Seikaly (1988–94)**
FT (playoff game): 14
(April 29, 1992)
Rebounds (game):
34 (Mar. 3, 1993)
Rebounds (playoff game):
20 (May 3, 1994)
Rebounds (season): 934
(1991–92)
Rebounds (career): 4,544
• **Brian Shaw (1991–94)**
3-Pointers (game): 10
(Mar. 8, 1993)
• **John Sunvold (1988–92)**
3-Point Pct. (season): 52.2
(1988–89)
3-Point Pct. (career): 47.4

LEAGUE HONORS
All-NBA First Team
• **Tim Hardaway**
(1996–97)
• **Alonzo Mourning**

"You can't stop because you're afraid of failure."

— *Alonzo Mourning, on his return to action after a kidney ailment.*

Vital Stats

Stadium Address:
601 Biscayne Blvd.,
Miami, Fla.
Phone: (786) 777-1000
Web: nba.com/heat,
aaarena.com
Box Office:
(786) 777-1240,
Mon.–Fri. 10–4
Media Coverage:
Radio: WIOD (610 AM)
TV: WAMI (Channel 69),
Sunshine Network
Training Facility:
AmericanAirlines Arena,
Miami, Fla.

(1998–99)
Defensive Player of the Year
• **Alonzo Mourning**
(1998–99, 1999–2000)

All-Rookie First Team
• **Sherman Douglas**
(1989–90)
• **Steve Smith** (1991–92)

Coach of the Year
• **Pat Riley**
(1996–97)

Timeline

1987	1988	1989	1990	1991	1992	1993	1994	1995	1996	1997	1998	1999	2000

- NBA grants Miami new franchise
- Team loses first game 101-80 to Clippers
- Heat drafts Glen Rice out of University of Michigan
- Rony Seikaly has franchise's first 40-point game
- Sherman Douglas leads team with 18.5 ppg
- Miami makes playoffs for first time; swept by Bulls in opening round
- Harold Miner wins Slam Dunk competition at All-Star game
- Heat enjoys first playoff game win in its history
- Glen Rice scores 56 points against Orlando
- Alonzo Mourning in top 10 for points, rebounds and blocked shots
- Heat wins first Atlantic Division title
- Pat Riley becomes winningest coach in Heat history
- Team wins third straight Atlantic Division title
- Heat loses to Knicks in Eastern Conference semifinals

AMERICANAIRLINES ARENA: THE HEAT IS ON

HOME TO THE HEAT and the Miami Sol of the WNBA, the AmericanAirlines Arena is one of the best places to watch a basketball game. To begin with, the steep configuration of the lower bowl brings fans closer to the action, especially with 42 percent of the seats located at sidecourt. Adjustable seats behind the baskets ensure the best possible sight lines. All concourses afford beautiful views of the skyline and Biscayne Bay and the arena's tropical-themed restaurant offers some of South Florida's hottest salsa dancing.

CONCESSIONS

AmericanAirlines Arena offers a wide variety of standard fare such as hot dogs and pizza. There are also Cuban delicacies, conch fritters, bratwursts and grilled chicken sandwiches. Kosher food is also available, as are some vegetarian selections.

Arena Facts

Opened: *Dec. 31, 1999*
Cost: *$175 million*
Capacity: *19,600*
Home Sweet Home:
• *Miami's fans are known to be a loud and enthusiastic group and it is obvious that the team gets pumped up by the support. The Heat's 29-12 home record in 2000-01 was tied for third best in the 15-team Eastern Conference.*

GAME DAY TIPS

• **Gate hours:** Arena gates open from one hour to 90 minutes prior to tip-off.
• **Prohibited items:** Food, beverages, coolers and alcohol are prohibited. Noisemakers, laser pointers and weapons of any kind are also prohibited. No flash or video cameras are permitted. Signs are allowed provided they do not block people's views of the game. Smoking is generally prohibited throughout the arena, except for a few designated areas. Shoes and shirts are required.
• **Ticket tips:** Tickets are almost always available for Heat games, though the Lakers and Knicks sometimes help sell out the arena when they're in town. There are no obstructed views anywhere in the stadium, so if price is a concern, you'll still see the game well from the higher seats.
• **Lost and found:** (786) 777-1400.

Seating Plan

Lower Bowl (100 Level)

	N/A
	$200
	$100
	$80
	$60

	$35
	$20
	$8-10
	$30

ATM Sections 111, 123, 313
♿ Sections 104–109, 116–121, 124, Level 300 corners

Upper Bowl (300 Level)

	$60

Directions:

Directions: Take I-95 to exit 5A; follow N.E. 8th St. to arena. Or, take Rte. 836/I-395 W to exit 5 (N.E. 2nd Ave.). Go south to N.E. 8th St. and turn left; follow to arena. **By Public Transit:** Several buses and trains go to the AmericanAirlines Arena. Call the Miami-Dade Transit Agency at (305) 770-3131 for information. **Parking:** There are 208 parking spaces at the arena; 26 are reserved for the disabled. There are also 900 spaces at the Miami-Dade Community College lot two blocks west of the arena. There is parking on Biscayne Blvd., N.E. 2nd, N.W. 7th and N.W. 8th Sts.

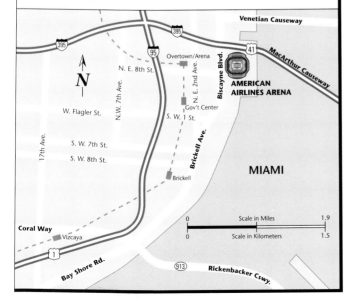

Nearby Hotels

▼▼▼ **Clarion Hotel & Suites** *(Hotel)*, 100 SE 4th St. (Miami), (305) 374-5100, $69-$179
▼▼ **Holiday Inn-Downtown** *(Motor Inn)*, 200 SE 2nd Ave. (Miami), (305) 374-3000, $99-$149
▼▼▼▼ **Hotel Inter-Continental Miami** *(Hotel)*, 100 Chopin Plaza (Miami), (305) 577-1000, $159-$450
▼▼▼▼ **Hyatt Regency Miami** *(Hotel)*, 400 SE Second Ave. (Miami), (305) 358-1234, $169-$234
▼▼▼ **Wyndham Hotel Miami Biscayne Bay** *(Hotel)*, 1601 Biscayne Blvd. (Miami), (305) 374-0000, $139-$399

Nearby Restaurants

▼▼ **Cardoza Cafe** *(Cuban)*, 1300 Ocean Dr. (Miami Beach), (305) 538-0553, $6-$25
▼▼▼ **China Grill** *(Asian)*, 404 Washington Ave. (Miami Beach), (305) 534-2211, $21-$35
▼▼▼▼ **Crystal Cafe** *(Continental)*, 726 Arthur Godfrey Rd. (Miami Beach), (305) 673-8266, $13-$25 (dinner only)
▼▼▼ **The Fish Market** *(Seafood)*, 1601 Biscayne Blvd. in the Wyndham Hotel Miami Biscayne Bay (Miami), (305) 374-4399, $20-$35 (dinner only)
▼▼ **Joe's Stone Crab Restaurant** *(Seafood)*, 11 Washington Ave. (Miami Beach), (305) 673-0365, $5-$60

MILWAUKEE BUCKS

IT MIGHT HAVE BEEN THE MOST fortuitous coin toss in sports history. Coming off a last place finish in its inaugural 1968–69 season, the Milwaukee Bucks won the coin toss to determine which team got first pick in the upcoming college draft. The choice was obvious: 7-foot 2-inch Lew Alcindor out of UCLA. Alcindor, who would change his name to Kareem Abdul-Jabbar in 1971, made an instant impact, finishing second in the league in scoring as a rookie. The 1970 acquisition of superstar Oscar "The Big O" Robertson gave Milwaukee a potent one-two punch. With Abdul-Jabbar leading the league with 31.7 points a game and Robertson's veteran wiles acting as a catalyst for the young Bucks, the team posted a league-best 66–16 record. In the playoffs, the Milwaukee juggernaut lost only two games en route to its first title — just three years after entering the NBA. Although the Bucks set a record in 1973–74 by becoming the first team to have three straight 60-win seasons, the squad would not win another title. When Robertson retired in 1974 and Abdul-Jabbar was traded the following year, Milwaukee fell into a four-year tail spin. But the 1980 arrival of big Bob Lanier helped plug the gap at center and the Bucks began a 12-year string of playoff appearances. As successful as the 1980s were for the Bucks, the 1990s proved disastrous. The team struggled through seven seasons below .500. In 1999, however, the drought was broken as the Bucks fought their way back into the postseason. It's been a long time between titles and both the players and fans in Milwaukee are getting impatient for another one.

Vital Stats

Stadium Address:
1001 N. Fourth St.,
Milwaukee, Wis.
Phone: (414) 227-0797
Web: nba.com/bucks
bradleycenter.com
Box Office:
(414) 227-0893, Mon.–Fri.
9–5:30, Sat. 10–4
Media Coverage:
Radio: WTMJ (620 AM)
TV: WCGV (Channel 24)
and Midwest Sports
Channel (cable)
Training Facility:
Milwaukee Bucks Training
Center, Archbishop Cousins
Center, St. Francis, Wis.

"Their fans were terrific. They were all over us."

— *Doc Rivers, coach of the Magic, on Bucks fans in the 2001 playoffs*

POSTSEASON
• NBA Championships.......1
(1970–71)
• Western Conference
Championships 2
(1970–71, 1973–74)
• Midwest Division
Titles 6
(1971–74, 1975–76, 1979–80)
• Central Division Titles....6
(1981–86)

RETIRED NUMBERS
• Oscar Robertson (1)
• Junior Bridgeman (2)
• Sidney Moncrief (4)

Jump Shot

• *For Bucks fans, Jun. 16, 1975 stands out as a day of infamy. It was on that date that Kareem Abdul-Jabbar and Walt Wesley were traded to Los Angeles for four players. Abdul-Jabbar, who had won three MVP trophies in Milwaukee, went on to win five NBA titles with the Lakers and retire with a league-high 38,387 points.*

• Jon McGlocklin (14)
• Bob Lanier (16)
• Brian Winters (32)
• Kareem Abdul-Jabbar (33)

TEAM RECORDS
• **Kareem Abdul-Jabbar**
(1969–75)
Blocks (season):
283(1973–74) (tie)
FG Pct. (season): .574
(1971–72)
Points (game): 55
(Dec. 10, 1971)
Points (season): 2,822
(1971–72)
Points-Per-Game (season):
34.8 (1971–72)
Rebounds (season): 1,346
(1971–72)
FG (game): 24 (Jan. 25, 1973)
FG (season): 1,159 (1971–72)
FG (career): 5,902
FG Pct. (career): .547
Rebounds (career): 7,161
Points (career): 14,211
Points-Per-Game (career): 30.4
• **Ray Allen (1996–present)**
3-Point FG (season):
172 (1999–2000)
3-Point FG (career): 497
• **Quinn Buckner (1976–82)**
Steals (career): 1,042
• **Sam Cassell (1999–present)**

Assists (season): 729
(1999–2000)
• **Alton Lister**
(1981–86, 1994–96)
Blocks (career): 804
• **Sydney Moncrief (1979–89)**
FT (career): 3,505
• **Alvin Robinson (1989–93)**
Steals (game): 10 (Nov. 19, '90)
Steals (season): 246 (1990–91)
• **Paul Pressey (1982–90)**
Assists (career): 3,272
• **Jack Sikma (1986–91)**
FT Pct. (season): .922 (1987–88)
FT Pct. (career): .884
Personal Fouls (season):
328 (1986–87) (tie)

Ray Allen is one of the NBA's most accurate three-point shooters.

LEAGUE HONORS
NBA MVP
• Kareem Abdul-Jabbar
(1970–71, 1971–72, 1973–74)

Rookie of the Year
• Kareem Abdul-Jabbar
(1969–70)

**Defensive Player
of the Year**
• Sidney Moncrief
(1982–83, 1983–84)

Sixth Man Award
• Ricky Pierce (1986–87,
1989–90)

Coach of the Year
• Don Nelson
(1982–83,
1984–85)

NBA Finals MVP
• Kareem Abdul-
Jabbar (1970–71)

**Basketball Hall
of Fame**
• Oscar
Robertson (1980)
• Bob Lanier
(1992)
• Kareem
Abdul-Jabbar
(1995)
• Alex English
(1997)

Timeline

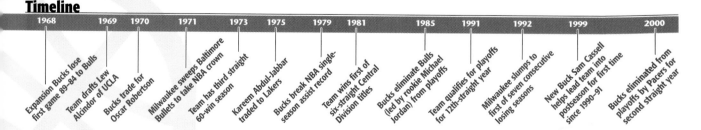

1968 Expansion Bucks lose first game 89–94 to Bulls
1969 Team drafts Lew Alcindor of UCLA
1970 Bucks trade for Oscar Robertson
1971 Milwaukee sweeps Baltimore Bullets to take NBA crown
1973 Team has third straight 60-win season
1975 Kareem Abdul-Jabbar traded to Lakers
1979 Bucks break NBA single-season assist record
1981 Team wins first of six-straight Central Division titles
1985 Bucks eliminate Bulls (led by rookie Michael Jordan) from playoffs
1991 Team qualifies for playoffs for 12th-straight year
1992 Milwaukee slumps to first of seven consecutive losing seasons
1999 New Buck Sam Cassell helps lead team into postseason for first time since 1990–91
2000 Bucks eliminated from playoffs by Pacers for second straight year

BRADLEY CENTER: GIFT TO MILWAUKEE

THE $91 MILLION BRADLEY CENTER opened on Oct. 1, 1988. Unlike so many stadiums and arenas in the country, the Bradley Center was built using private funds, namely those of Jane and Lloyd Pettit. The Pettits donated the money as a gift to Milwaukee and the state of Wisconsin. One of finest sports and entertainment complexes in the country, the Bradley Center is a beautiful piece of architecture, with glass-enclosed lobbies, spectacular skylights and an exterior constructed of polished South Dakota granite.

CONCESSIONS

The Bradley Center offers visitors all the old arena favorites, including hot dogs, burgers, pizza and chili. Fans will also find chicken tenders, jumbo pretzels, Polish sausage, BBQ pork and smoothies. For thirsty visitors, Bradley offers a good selection of local and imported beers.

GAME DAY TIPS

• **Gate hours:** Gates open one hour prior to tip-off time.
• **Prohibited items:** Food, cans, bottles and beverages of any kind. Video cameras and audio recording devices are also prohibited in the arena. Large signs that may obstruct the views of other patrons, air horns, laser pointers and weapons are also not permitted. Smoking is allowed in designated areas only.
• **Ticket tips:** As an increasingly successful franchise, Milwaukee has been selling out more and more frequently in recent years. Games against the Lakers, Toronto and Philadelphia are guaranteed to sell well. If these teams are in town, make certain to buy tickets well in advance, and if possible, try for a weekday game.
• **Lost and Found:** (414) 227-0797.

Arena Facts

Opened: *Oct. 1, 1988*
Cost: *$91 million*
Capacity: *20,000*
Home Sweet Home:
• *The recent resurgence of the Bucks has been boosted in part by the renewed enthusiasm of Milwaukee fans. During the 2000–01 postseason, one reporter referred to the Bradley Center as a "boiling cauldron of playoff emotion."*

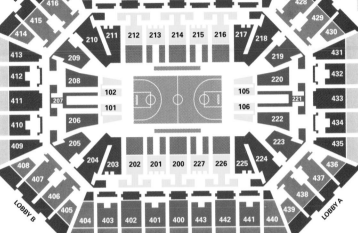

■ $80		■ $23	
☐ $70		■ $18	
■ $47			$10
■ $40	ATM **Sections 212, 223**		
■ $30	♿ **Throughout**		

Directions: Take I-94 to exit 1H. Go north to Wells St., then right. Continue to 6th St., turn left and follow to arena. Or, take the I-43 north to exit 72C. Go left at 6th St. and follow to arena. By Bus: The Milwaukee County Transit System (MCTS) offers bus service to the Bradley Center. Call (414) 344-6711. *Parking:* The center's garage has 760 spaces, with 15 reserved for the disabled. There are also 12,000 more spaces within a six-block radius in lots and on the street.

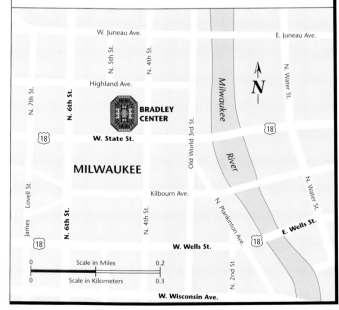

Nearby Hotels

▼▼▼ **Comfort Suites** (*Motel*), 6362 S. 13th St. (Oak Creek), (414) 570-1111, $89-$229
▼▼▼ **Hilton Milwaukee City Center** (*Hotel*), 509 W. Wisconsin Ave. (Milwaukee), (414) 271-7250, $89-$139
▼▼▼ **Hotel Metro-Milwaukee** (*Hotel*), 411 E. Mason St. (Milwaukee), (414) 272-1937, $180-$190
▼▼▼ **Hyatt Regency Milwaukee** (*Hotel*), 333 W. Kilbourn Ave. (Milwaukee), (414) 276-1234, $149-$174
▼▼▼▼ **The Pfister Hotel** (*Classic Hotel*), 424 E. Wisconsin Ave. (Milwaukee), (414) 273-8222, $244-$314

Nearby Restaurants

▼▼▼ **Bartolotta's Lake Park Bistro** (*French*), 3133 E. Newberry Blvd. (Milwaukee), (414) 962-6300, $8-$29
▼▼ **Benson's Steak House** (*Steakhouse*), 509 W. Wisconsin Ave. in Hilton Milwaukee City Center(Milwaukee), (414) 271-7684, $18-$39
▼▼▼ **Eddie Martini's** (*Traditional American*), 8612 W. Watertown Plank Rd. (Wauwatosa), (414) 771-6680, $15-$30
▼▼▼ **Ristorante Bartolotta** (*Northern Italian*), 7616 W. State St. (Wauwatosa), (414) 771-7910, $13-$26
▼▼▼▼ **Sanford Restaurant** (*American*), 1547 N. Jackson St. (Milwaukee), (414) 276-9608, $42-$69

MINNESOTA TIMBERWOLVES

IN MANY WAYS, THE MINNESOTA TIMBERWOLVES' early years were typical for an expansion team. There was the initial fan support; in its very first season, 1989–90, the team set a new NBA single-season attendance record. Good players came and went. Pooh Richardson, Isaiah Rider, Christian Laettner and Luc Longley all began their careers in Minnesota before moving on. Most predominantly, however, there was a string of poor seasons. The team endured eight-straight losing seasons, including a dismal 15–67 campaign in 1991–92, before it finally turned the corner in 1997–98. The 'Wolves savior came in an unexpected package. In 1995 management raised eyebrows by drafting Kevin Garnett, a skinny 19-year-old 7-footer who had jumped to the pros directly from high school. The team also traded away Christian Laettner in 1996, giving Garnett the chance to play every day and begin his NBA apprenticeship. Garnett was a quick learner. Improving every year, he ended 1998–99 by leading the team in scoring, blocks and rebounds. He turned it up a notch the next season, finishing 10th in the league with 22.9 ppg and third in rebounds with 956 boards. He also was runner-up to Shaquille O'Neal in MVP voting. More important than his numbers, Garnett's attitude has helped forge a winner in Minnesota. A selfless team player, he inspires teammates with his tireless work ethic. With their lanky center leading the charge, the 'Wolves have made it to the postseason every year since 1996–97. With a few more lessons under his belt, Garnett might be able to take his team to the top.

As well as being an offensive threat, Kevin Garnett is a also a ferocious defender.

POSTSEASON
• Playoff appearances 4
(1996–97, 1997–98, 1998–99, 1999–2000)

TEAM RECORDS
• **Terrell Brandon (1999–present)**
FT Pct. (career): .886
Steals (game): 8 (tie)
(Mar. 24, 2000)
3-Point FG Pct. (career): .384
• **Randy Breuer (1989–92)**
Blocks (game): 9 (Apr. 13, '90)
• **Tony Campbell (1989–92)**
Points (game): 44 (Feb. 2, '90)

Jump Shot
• *In 1999–2000, Kevin Garnett became only the ninth player in NBA history to average 20 ppg, 10 rpg and 5 apg in a season — further testimony to his incredible overall ability.*
• *The bold move to pick Garnett fifth overall in the 1995 draft was made by the team's shrewd VP of basketball operations, Hall-of-Famer Kevin McHale.*
• *Despite playing forward at just 6 feet 7 inches and 215 pounds, Sam Mitchell is the Timberwolves' all-time leading scorer.*

Points (season): 1,903
(1989–90)
• **Tyrone Corbin (1989–92)**
Steals (game): 8 (tie)
(Mar. 30, 1990)
• **Dean Garrett (1996–97, 1998–present)**
FG Pct. (season): .573
(1996–97)
FG Pct. (career): .532
• **Kevin Garnett (1995–present)**
Blocks (season): 163
(1996–97)
Blocks (career): 653
Consecutive FG: 13 (tie)
FG (game): 16 (tie)
(Mar. 22, 2000)
FG (season): 759 (1999–00)
FG (career): 2,718
Minutes (season): 3,243
(1999–2000)
Rebounds (game): 23
(Dec. 27, 1999)
Rebounds (season): 956
(1999–00)
Rebounds (career): 3,350
Steals (career): 528
• **Tom Gugliotta (1994–98)**
FT (season): 464 (1996–97
• **Christian Laettner (1992–96)**
FT (game): 18 (Feb. 18, 1993)
• **Stephon Marbury**

(1996–99)
Assists (game): 17 (tie)
(April 18, 1997)
3-Pointers (game): 8
Dec. 23, 1997)
• **Sam Mitchell (1989–92, 1995–present)**
FT (career): 1,695
Minutes (career): 16,685
Personal Fouls (season): 338
(1990–91)
Personal Fouls (career): 1,748
Points (career): 6,632
• **Anthony Peeler (1998–present)**
3-Point Pct. (season): .453
(1997–98)
• **Pooh Richardson (1989–92)**
Assists (season): 734
(1990–91)
Assists (career): 1,973
• **Isaiah Rider (1993–96)**
3-Point FG (season): 139
(1994–95)
3-Point FG (career): 295
• **Michael Williams (1992–98)**
Consecutive FT: 97
FT Pct. (season): .907
(1992–93)
• **Doug West (1989–98)**
Games (career): 609
Starts (career): 371

"I know the boos are a love-hate thing. That's why it doesn't bother me."
— Former Timberwolf Stephon Marbury, on his reception in Minnesota

Vital Stats
Stadium Address:
600 First Ave. N.,
Minneapolis, Minn.
Phone: (612) 673-1300
Web:
nba.com/timberwolves,
targetcenter.com
Box Office:
(612) 673-0900,
Mon.–Fri. 10–6, Sat. four
hours prior to events
Media Coverage:
Radio: KFAN (1130 AM)
TV: KARE (Channel 11),
KMWB (Channel 23)
Practice Facility:
Target Center,
Minneapolis, Minn.

LEAGUE HONORS
Sportsmanship
• Kevin Garnett (1999)

All-NBA First Team
• Kevin Garnett (2000)

All-Rookie First Team
• Pooh Richardson (1990)
• Christian Laettner (1993)
• Isaiah Rider (1994)
• Stephon Marbury (1997)
• Wally Szczerbiak (2000)

Slam Dunk Champion
• Isaiah Rider (1994)

Timeline
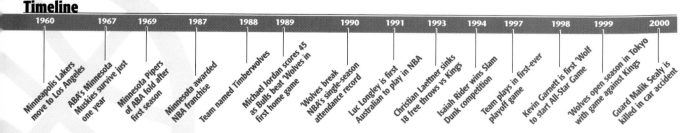

| 1960 | 1967 | 1969 | 1987 | 1988 | 1989 | 1990 | 1991 | 1993 | 1994 | 1997 | 1998 | 1999 | 2000 |

Minneapolis Lakers move to Los Angeles | ABA's Minnesota Muskies survive just one year | Minnesota Pipers of ABA fold after first season | Minnesota awarded NBA franchise | Team named Timberwolves | Michael Jordan scores 45 as Bulls beat 'Wolves in first home game | 'Wolves break NBA's single-season attendance record | Luc Longley is first Australian to play in NBA | Christian Laettner sinks 18 free throws vs Kings | Isaiah Rider wins Slam Dunk competition | Team plays in first-ever playoff game | Kevin Garnett is first 'Wolf to start All-Star Game | 'Wolves open season in Tokyo with game against Kings | Guard Malik Sealy is killed in car accident

TARGET CENTER: THE COMFORT ZONE

LOCATED IN THE HEART of downtown Minneapolis, the Target Center is home to the NBA's Timberwolves and the WNBA's Lynx. Opened in 1990, the arena has been designed with fan comfort in mind. Good sight lines are enhanced by the giant color video replay board and the theater-style cushioned seats give more leg room than traditional arena seating. The venue is also equipped with almost four times as many washroom facilities as would be found in most arenas and has a 160,000-square-foot health club.

CONCESSIONS
The Target Center has concessions to suit all tastes and palates. Visitors can munch on old standards such as hot dogs, hamburgers and pizza, as well as Polish sausage, Wolf wings, fajita wraps and taco puffs. Beverages include soft drinks, juices, beers and margaritas. Prices are fairly reasonable for arena fare.

GAME DAY TIPS
• **Gate hours:** Arena gates open 90 minutes prior to tip-off.
• **Prohibited items:** Food, beverages, and containers of any kind are prohibited. Banners, flags and signs are also not permitted. Cameras are allowed, but video cameras are prohibited. Smoking is allowed only in the restaurant on the corner of 6th St. and 1st Ave. and outside the building on 2nd Ave.
• **Ticket tips:** Timberwolves tickets are generally pretty easy to get at the box office or through Ticketmaster. Games against the Lakers obviously sell well, as do weekend games. Even so, there were only a handful of sellouts in the 1999–2000 season.
• **Lost and found:** (612) 673-1333.

Arena Facts
Opened: *Oct. 13, 1990*
Cost: *$104 million*
Capacity: *19,006*
Home Sweet Home:
• *The team hands out "howl towels" before play-off games. Fans whip them around over their head and howl to rile up their team. 'Wolves fans are enthusiastic; in 1989–90, the team drew 1,072,572 — a league record.*

Directions: *Take I-94 W. to the 5th St. exit. Proceed to 1st Ave. N and follow to stadium. Or, take I-394 E. to 7th St. or 5th St exits. Or, take I-35 N. and exit at Washington Ave. Follow to First Ave. and turn left.* **By Bus:** *Numerous buses go to the Target Center. Call Metro Transit at (612) 373-3333 for information.* **Parking:** *Two city-owned parking ramps near the center can hold about 11,000 cars. There are disabled spaces on every level. There's more parking on 4th, 5th, 7th and 8th Sts.*

Seating Plan

▪	$250	▪	$42
▪	$135	▪	$34
▪	$125	▪	$27
▪	$115	▪	$20
▪	$90	▪	$10
▪	$67	ATM	**Section 138**
▪	$49	♿	**Throughout**

SKYWAY ENTRANCE

1ST AVE. ENTRANCE

Nearby Hotels
▼▼▼ **Best Western Downtown (*Motel*)**, 405 S. 8th St. (Minneapolis), (612) 370-1400, $89-$104
▼▼▼ **Crowne Plaza Northstar Hotel (*Hotel*)**, 618 S. 2nd Ave. S. (Minneapolis), (612) 338-2288, $89-$149
▼▼▼▼ **The Marquette Hotel (*Hotel*)**, 710 Marquette Ave. (Minneapolis), (612) 333-4545, $189-$209
▼▼ **Quality Inn & Suites (*Motel*)**, 41 N. 10th St. (Minneapolis), (612) 339-9311, $99-$250
▼▼▼ **Radisson Plaza Hotel Minneapolis (*Hotel*)**, 35 S. 7th St. (Minneapolis), (612) 339-4900, $89-$239

Nearby Restaurants
▼▼▼ **Basil's (*American*)**, 710 Marquette Ave. in the Marquette Hotel (Minneapolis), (612) 376-7404, $10-$30
▼▼▼ **Cafe Brenda (*American*)**, 300 1st Ave. N. (Minneapolis), (612) 342-9230, $7-$12
▼▼▼▼ **Goodfellow's (*American*)**, 40 S. 7th St. in the City Center Shopping Complex (Minneapolis), (612) 332-4800, $25-$35
▼▼▼ **Murray's Restaurant (*American*)**, 26 S. 6th St. (Minneapolis), (612) 339-0909, $11-$49
▼▼▼ **Palomino Euro-Bistro (*American*)**, 825 Hennepin Ave. on the Skyway level of Lasalle Plaza (Minneapolis), (612) 339-3800, $9-$27

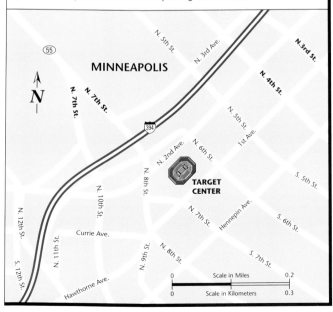

NEW JERSEY NETS

IN THE MIND OF EVERY LONGTIME NETS FAN, there are two very distinct images of the team. The first is one of the hopeful team in the 1970s, a time when the Nets were playing in Long Island and climbing the ranks of the very competitive American Basketball Association. When fans remember this era, they think of skywalking Julius Erving, the great "Dr. J," who was rewriting the way the game is played with his midair spins and blistering slam-dunks. They remember two incredible ABA Championships, in 1974 and '76, and the feelings of pride when their team prepared to take on all comers in the NBA. The second image Nets fans carry is of the hapless team in the years that followed this golden age, a team that could only muster seven winning seasons in the last 23 and posted one of the lowest single-season winning percentages in the history of the sport — a wretched .207 in 1989–90. Nets fans have continued to rally around their players, however, opting to place blame on a series of bad trades, successive short-term coaches and poor managerial decisions. Many fans view the team as a symbol of potential, a good team that, because of unfortunate circumstances, has never really had its chance to shine. With pride, they recall the scoring sprees of Bernard King in the late 1970s, the ascension of rebound king Buck Williams during the '80s, the one-two punch of Derrick Coleman and Drazen Petrovic in the early '90s, and the brilliant plays of Kenny Anderson. These days Nets fans place their hopes on the play of guards Kelly Kittles and Kendall Gill, among others, as they wait for their team to break the spell of bad luck.

> "We are going to plant some seeds, throw water on it and watch it grow."
> — Coach Byron Scott, on the efforts to rebuild the Nets

The Nets' Kenyon Martin is a powerful presence in the paint.

POSTSEASON
• NBA Playoff Appearances.....................10
(1978–79, 1981–82, 1982–83, 1983–84, 1984–85, 1985–86, 1991–92, 1992–93, 1993–94, 1997–98)
• ABA Championships.......2
(1973–74, 1975–76)

RETIRED NUMBERS
• Drazen Petrovic (3)
• Wendell Ladner (4)
• John Williamson (23)
• Bill Melchionni (25)
• Julius Erving (32)
• Charles "Buck" Williams (52)

Jump Shot

• The 2000–01 season marked Byron Scott's first as Head Coach for the Nets. Management hopes that Scott's winning ways as a player — he won three NBA titles as a member of the Lakers — will rub off on the players.
• At the end of his first season at the Nets' helm, Scott said one of the highlights was watching rookie Kenyon Martin develop into a solid everyday player.

TEAM RECORDS
• **Kenny Anderson** (1991–96)
Assists (career): 2,363
• **Derrick Coleman** (1990–95)
FT (season): 439 (1993–94)
• **Darwin Cook** (1980–86)
Steals (career): 875
• **Darryl Dawkins** (1982–87)
Blocks (game): 13 (Nov. 5, 1983)
• **Kendall Gill** (1995–present)
Steals (game): 11 (Apr. 3, 1999)
• **George Johnson** (1977–80, 1984–85)
Blocks (season): 274 (1977–78)
Blocks (career): 863
• **Bernard King** (1977–79, 1992–93)
Points (season): 1,909 (1977–78)
FG (season): 798 (1977–78)
• **Kerry Kittles** (1996–present)
3-Point FG (season): 158 (1996–97)
3-Point FG (career): 414
• **Kevin Porter (1977–78)**
Assists (season): 801 (1977–78)
Assists (game): 29 (Feb. 24, 1978)
• **M.R. Richardson** (1982–86)

Steals (season): 243 (1984–85)
• **Buck Williams** (1981–89)
Points (career): 10,440
FG (career): 3,981
FT (career): 2,476
Rebounds (season): 1027 (1982–83)
Rebounds (career): 7,576
Rebounds (game): 27 (Feb. 1, 1987)
• **Ray Williams** (1981–82, 1885–87)
Points (game): 52 (tie) (Apr. 17, 1982)
FG (game): 21 (Apr. 17, 1982)

Vital Stats

Stadium Address:
50 Rte. 120,
East Rutherford, N.J.
Phone: (201) 935-8500
Web: nba.com/nets, meadowlands.com
Box Office:
(201) 935-3900
Mon.–Fri. 9–6, Sat. 10–6, Sun. 12–5
Media Coverage:
Radio: WOR (710 AM)
TV: Fox Sports Net
Practice Facility:
The Champion Center, East Rutherford, N.J.

• John Williamson (1973–80)
Free Throws (game): 22 (Dec. 9, 1978)

LEAGUE HONORS
Rookie of the Year
• Buck Williams (1981–82)
• Derrick Coleman (1990–91)

Basketball Hall of Fame
• Julius Erving (1993)

NBA All-Stars
• Buck Williams (1982, '83, '86)
• Otis Birdsong (1984)
• M.R. Richardson (1985)
• Derrick Coleman (1994)
• Kenny Anderson (1994)
• Jayson Williams (1998)

Timeline

1967 The New Jersey Americans commence play in the American Basketball Association

1969 Team moves to Long Island and is renamed the New York Nets

1973 Nets acquire Julius Erving

1974 Nets win first ABA title

1976 Nets join the NBA

1977 Franchise moves to New Jersey; Team goes to NBA playoffs for the first time; George Johnson places second in league for blocked shots

1979 Buck Williams captures Rookie of the Year

1982 Darryl Dawkins leads team to franchise-record 11 straight wins

1983 Nets win first ever playoff game

1984 M.R. Richardson becomes first forward to record 1,000 rebounds in four seasons

1985 Richardson banned from the NBA after a third drug violation

1986 Nets set dubious NBA record of losing 346 games to injury

1988 Bill Fitch coaches his 800th NBA win, the fourth highest total in history

1991

1998 Nets lose three straight to Bulls in opening round of playoffs

118

CONTINENTAL AIRLINES ARENA
B-BALL AT THE MEADOWLANDS

SINCE BRUCE SPRINGSTEEN ROCKED the Meadowlands Sports Complex on the opening day of the Brendan Byrne Arena 20 years ago, this venue has remained a favorite. Renamed the Continental Airlines Arena in 1996, the space offers fans great sight lines and a homey environment, but it was disgraced a few years ago when it was discovered that the management was amplifying artificial cheers and whistles to boost morale. In 1999 the Nets announced plans to build a new arena in Newark in 2003, so check out a Nets game at the Meadowlands soon — time is running out.

CONCESSIONS

The food at the Continental is quite varied. Choices include the more traditional hot dogs, nachos, hamburgers and fries, as well as more exciting options such as sausages, hand-carved meat sandwiches, and soup and chili in bread bowls. Vegetarians will enjoy a variety of salads, knishes and baked potatoes with assorted toppings.

GAME DAY TIPS

• **Gate hours:** Gates open 90 minutes prior to tip-off.
• **Prohibited items:** Video cameras, air horns, megaphones, bottles, signs, banners and posters are all forbidden at the Continental Airlines Arena. Smoking is allowed only in the designated areas located outside gates B and D.
• **Ticket tips:** There are usually lots of tickets available in a wide variety of sections for Nets games. The tickets are quite reasonably priced and most seats, even those in the upper level, offer a good view of the court. Games against the rival Knicks bring out many more fans.
• **Lost and found:** (201) 460-4343.

Arena Facts

Opened: July 2, 1981
Cost: $85 million
Capacity: 20,049
Home Sweet Home:
• As with other NBA fans, Nets supporters can be vocal. But the Continental Airlines Arena management has been known to bolster the home team's support a little by playing dance music during opponents' free throws just to disconcert the rival shooters.

Seating Plan

■	$175	■	$40
■	$125	■	$30
■	$100	■	$25
■	$80	**ATM** Section 101	
■	$65	**♿** 100 Level end zones	
■	$50		

GATE C GATE D

230 231 232 233 234 235 236 237 238
229   239
228   240
227 119 120 121 122 123 124 125 241
226 118   126 242
225 117   127 243
224 116   9   1   128 244
223 115   101 201
222 114   7   3   102 202
221 113   103 203
220 112   104 204
219 111 110 109 108 107 106 105 205
218   206
217   207
216 215 214 213 212 211 210 209 208

GATE B GATE A

Directions

Directions: Take the New Jersey Turnpike to exit 16W (Sports Complex); follow signs to the Sports Complex. By Bus: Buses are available from the Port Authority in NYC. Call (212) 564-8484 for more information.
Parking: Arena parking can hold 4,000 cars and there are 22,000 more spots available in the complex. Parking for people with disabilities is available in lots 21 and 23.

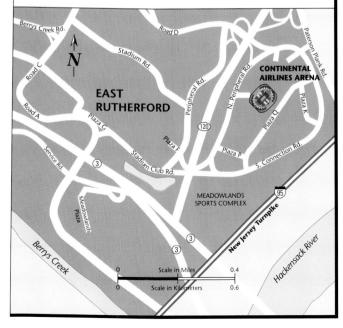

Nearby Hotels

▼▼▼ **Amerisuites** *(Motel)*, 41-01 Broadway (Fair Lawn), (201) 475-3888, $119-$199
▼▼▼ **Courtyard by Marriott** *(Motel)*, 455 Harmon Meadow Blvd. (Secaucus), (201) 617-8888, $180-$209
▼▼▼ **Fairfield Inn by Marriott** *(Motel)*, 850 SR 120 S. (East Rutherford), (201) 507-5222, $129
▼▼▼ **Hampton Inn** *(Motel)*, 250 Harmon Meadow Blvd. (Secaucus), (201) 867-4400, $135-$185
▼▼▼ **The Holiday Inn Harmon Meadow** *(Hotel)*, 300 Plaza Dr. (Secaucus), (201) 348-2000, $149-$209

Nearby Restaurants

▼▼ **Harold's New York Deli Restaurant** *(American)*, 10 Polito Ave. in the Quality Inn-Meadowlands (Lyndhurst), (201) 935-2600, $6-$20
▼▼ **La Dolce Vita** *(Italian)*, 316 Valley Brook Ave. (Lyndhurst), (201) 935-4260, $11-$25
▼▼ **Park & Orchard** *(American)*, 240 Hackensack St., (201) 939-9292 (East Rutherford), $13-$24
▼▼▼ **The River Palm Terrace** *(Steak & Seafood)*, 41-11 Broadway (Fair Lawn), (201) 703-3500, $19-$36
▼▼▼ **Sonoma Grill** *(American)*, 64 Hoboken Rd. (East Rutherford), (201) 507-8989, $17-$27

NEW YORK KNICKS

BY MANY STANDARDS, THE NEW YORK KNICKS has been a successful franchise. Since first jogging out onto the court as a charter member of the old American Basketball Association in 1946, the team has reached the playoffs an incredible 37 times. But in the Big Apple, success is measured only one way: titles. In that regard, the team has come up short. From 1951–53, New York made three trips to the NBA finals, all of which ended in bitter defeat. Those early squads were led by the dead-eye shooting of Carl Braun and the passing of "Tricky" Dick McGuire. When the team failed to make the playoffs in 1957, breaking its 10-year streak, it was a sign of the hard times to come. From 1958–66, the Knicks would see postseason action only once. But in 1967 Red Holzman took the coaching reigns and breathed new life into the faltering club. Reaching the NBA finals in 1970, the Knicks defeated the Lakers in an emotional Game Seven, inspired by Willis Reed who took the court despite a severe leg injury. New York reached the NBA pinnacle again in 1973 with a lineup that included Reed, Walt Frazier, Bill Bradley, Earl "the Pearl" Munroe, Dave DeBusschere and Jerry Lucas — all future Hall of Famers. Since those heady days, however, New York has failed to win another crown. Even the 1985 arrival of Patrick Ewing failed to give the team its third title. Despite his incredible career numbers, Ewing and the Knicks reached the finals twice, in 1994 and '99, only to lose both times. Now with Ewing playing in Seattle, Knicks fans will have to pin their hopes on someone else.

Latrell Sprewell is one of the league's pure scorers.

POSTSEASON
- **NBA Championships**.......2
(1969–70, 1972–73)
- **Eastern Conference Championships** 4
(1971–72, 1972–73, 1993–94, 1998–99)
- **Eastern Division Championships** 4
(1950–51, 1951–52, 1952–53, 1969–70)
- **Atlantic Division Titles**...3
(1988–89, 1992–93, 1993–94)

RETIRED NUMBERS
- **Walt Frazier** (10)
- **Dick Barnett** (12)
- **Earl Monroe** (15)
- **Dick McGuire** (15)
- **Willis Reed** (19)
- **Dave DeBusschere** (22)
- **Bill Bradley** (24)
- **Red Holzman** (613)

TEAM RECORDS
- **Patrick Ewing** (1985–00)
Blocks (season): 327 (1989–90)
Blocks (career): 2,758
Games (career): 1,039
FG (season): 922 (1989–90)
FG (career): 9,260
FT (career): 5,126
Points (season): 2,347 (1989–90)
Points (career): 23,665
Rebounds (career): 10,759
Steals (career): 1,061
- **Walt Frazier** (1967–77)
Assists (career): 4,791

- **Richie Guerin** (1956–64)
Assists (game): 21 (Dec. 12, '58)
FG (game): 23 (tie)
(Feb. 14, 1962)
- **Mark Jackson** (1987–92)
Assists (season): 363 (1987–88)
- **Bernard King** (1982–87)
FG Pct. (season): .572 (1983–84)
Points (game): 60 (Dec. 25, '84)
Points-Per-Game (season): 32.9 (1984–85)
- **Bob McAdoo** (1977–79)
Points-Per-Game (career): 26.7
- **Willis Reed** (1964–74)
Rebounds (game): 33 (tie) (Feb. 2, 1971)
Rebounds (season): 1,191 (1968–69)
- **Michael Ray Richardson**

Jump Shot

- *In honor of coach Red Holzman, the Knicks retired the number of his regular season wins, 613.*
- *The duo of Walt Frazier and Earl Monroe is considered one of the best backcourt tandems of all time.*
- *At the time of his trade in 2000, Patrick Ewing was one of 12 NBA players to have amassed 20,000 points and 10,000 rebounds.*

"Pat-rick Ew-ing! Pat-rick Ew-ing!"
— Notoriously tough New York fans showing a soft spot when former Knicks Patrick Ewing returned home as a Sonic to face his old squad

(1978–82)
Steals (season): 265 (1979–80)
- **John Starks** (1990–98)
3-Pointers (season): 217 (1994–95)
3-Pointers (career): 982

LEAGUE HONORS
NBA MVP
- **Willis Reed** (1969–70)

Rookie of the Year
- **Willis Reed** (1964–65)
- **Patrick Ewing** (1985–86)
- **Mark Jackson** (1987–88)

Sixth Man Award
- **Anthony Mason** (1994–95)
- **John Starks** (1996–97)

Coach of the Year
- **Red Holzman** (1969–70)
- **Pat Riley** (1992–93)

NBA Finals MVP
- **Willis Reed** (1970, '73)

Basketball Hall of Fame
- **Ned Irish** (1964)
- **Joe Lapchick** (1966)
- **Tom Gola** (1975)
- **Jerry Lucas** (1979)

Vital Stats

Stadium Address:
2 Pennsylvania Plaza, New York, N.Y.
Phone: *(212) 465-6000*
Web: *nba.com/knicks, thegarden.com*
Box Office: *(212) 465-6741, Mon.–Sat. 12–6; opens at 9 on morning of event days and at 10 on matinee event days*
Media Coverage:
*Radio: WFAN (660 AM)
TV: MSG Network*
Practice Facility:
State University of New York, Purchase, N.Y.

- **Willis Reed** (1981)
- **Slater Martin** (1981)
- **Bill Bradley** (1982)
- **Dave DeBusschere** (1982)
- **Red Holzman** (1985)
- **Walt Frazier** (1987)
- **Earl Monroe** (1990)
- **Harry Gallatin** (1991)
- **Al McGuire** (1992)
- **Dick McGuire** (1993)
- **Walt Bellamy** (1993)
- **Bob McAdoo** (2000)

Timeline

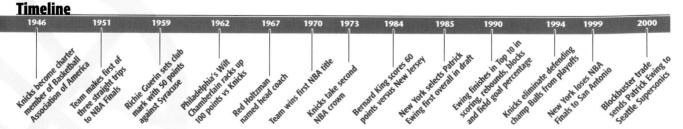

1946	1951	1959	1962	1967	1970	1973	1984	1985	1990	1994	1999	2000

Knicks become charter member of Basketball Association of America • Team makes first of three straight trips to NBA Finals • Richie Guerin sets club mark with 50 points against Syracuse • Philadelphia's Wilt Chamberlain racks up 100 points vs Knicks • Red Holtzman named head coach • Team wins first NBA title • Knicks take second NBA crown • Bernard King scores 60 points versus New Jersey • New York selects Patrick Ewing first overall in draft • Ewing finishes in Top 10 in scoring, rebounds, blocks and field goal percentage • Knicks eliminate defending champ Bulls from playoffs • New York loses NBA Finals to San Antonio • Blockbuster trade sends Patrick Ewing to Seattle Supersonics

MADISON SQUARE GARDEN: WORLD'S MOST FAMOUS ARENA

WITH TYPICAL NEW YORK BRAVADO, Madison Square Garden is billed as "the world's most famous arena." It certainly is one of the most storied, hosting everything from championship boxing, basketball, hockey and dog shows to singers ranging from Bing Crosby to Elvis. The current structure is actually the fourth incarnation of MSG, with the first being built in 1874 by P.T. Barnum for his circus. Built in 1968, the current structure is as much a New York landmark as the Statue of Liberty and the Empire State Building.

CONCESSIONS

Madison Square Garden offers fans all the best in New York delicacies. There are burgers, hot dogs and pizza, as well as traditional snacks like crackerjacks, popcorn, giant pretzels and cotton candy. A selection of imported and local beers complement the selection of food.

Arena Facts

Opened: Feb. 11, 1968
Cost: $43 million
Capacity: 19,763
Home Sweet Home:
• New York fans are always among the loudest and most brash — regardless of the sporting event. The Knicks' most famous fan is director Spike Lee, whose trash talk wars with the Pacers' Reggie Miller are now a part of legend.

GAME DAY TIPS
• **Gate hours:** Gates open 90 minutes prior to tip-off.
• **Prohibited items:** Food, beverages, alcohol and any kind of containers are prohibited. Noisemakers and air horns are also forbidden, as are weapons or projectiles. Signs and banners are allowed as long as they are not offensive and do not obstruct views. Video and flash cameras are not allowed. Smoking is allowed only in designated areas.
• **Ticket tips:** The Knicks have sold out every home game since 1992, so tickets will be hard to get. There are three interior concourses in the lower level, so for those seated in the first few rows, the view may be partially obstructed by passersby.
• **Lost and found:** (212) 465-6299

Seating Plan

■ ....Call for info
■ ....Call for info
■ ....Call for info
■ ....Call for info
■ ....Call for info
■ ....Call for info

■ ....Call for info
■ ....Call for info
■ ....Call for info
ATM Box Office lobby, 6th floor Tower A
♿ Throughout

Directions: Located on 7th Ave. between 33rd and 31st Sts. By Bus: Several buses go to the Garden. Call NYC Transit Authority at (718) 330-1234 for information. By Subway: Lines 1, 2, 3 or 9 or A, C or E to 34th St./Penn Station. Or, line B, D, F, N, Q, R or PATH to 34th St./Ave. of the Americas. **Parking:** Ten private lots and garages surround the arena; all have disabled parking. There is also some street parking on 7th, 8th, 9th and 10th Aves. and W. 35th St.

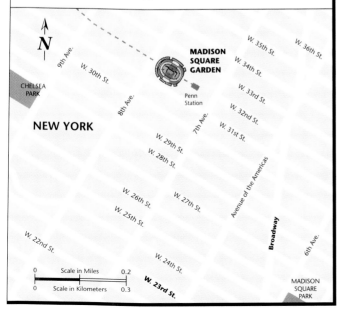

Nearby Hotels

▼▼▼ **The Avalon (Hotel)**, 16 E. 32nd St. (New York), (212) 299-7000, $175-$400
▼▼ **The Best Western Manhattan Hotel (Hotel)**, 17 W. 32nd St. (New York), (212) 736-1600, $109-$799
▼▼▼ **Courtyard by Marriott/Manhattan-Times Square South (Motel)**, 114 W. 40th St. (New York), (212) 391-0088, call for rates
▼▼▼ **Martinique on Broadway (Motor Inn)**, 49 W. 32nd St. (New York), (212) 736-3800, $199-$399
▼▼▼ **Southgate Tower Suite Hotel (Extended Stay Hotel)**, 371 7th Ave. (New York), (212) 563-1800, $229-$335

Nearby Restaurants

▼ **Carnegie Delicatessen & Restaurant (American)**, 854 7th Ave. (New York), (212) 757-2245, $10-$30
▼▼▼ **Chin Chin (Chinese)**, 216 E. 49th St. (New York), (212) 888-4555, $12-$21
▼▼▼▼ **Fifty-Seven Fifty-Seven Restaurant (American)**, 57 E. 57th St. in the Four Seasons Hotel, New York (New York), (212) 758-5757, $28-$34
▼ **Mimi's Macaroni (Italian)**, 718 Amsterdam Ave. (New York), (212) 866-6311, $8-$15
ESPN Zone (American), 1472 Broadway (New York), (212) 921-3776, $9-$21

ORLANDO MAGIC

INSPIRED BY THE MAGIC of Central Florida — the sun-drenched landscapes, the lush citrus groves, surreal theme parks and dripping Spanish moss — the Orlando Magic is a team that has worked hard to forge a strong relationship with its state and its community. In just 14 short years, the Orlando franchise has become one of the more successful programs in the NBA; with consistent, gutsy performances and a long string of winning seasons, the team has struck a rapport with fans that is the envy of many, more successful teams. Early on, the Magic showed that it had what it takes to play great basketball and entertain the fans. In 1990, Scott Skiles' NBA record 30 assists in one game showed that a new team was capable of great things. When Shaquille O'Neal signed aboard in 1992, however, the team quickly came of age. Within a year's time, the Magic had qualified for its first NBA playoffs, by rounding out the season in second place in the Atlantic Division. For his part, O'Neal was nothing short of fabulous; with each game he shattered team records and helped create the sense that there was indeed something magical happening in Orlando. In 1995, the team could do little wrong. After riding the wave of success throughout the regular season, the Magic nipped Washington 111-110 to take the Atlantic Division and then walloped Indiana to become the second-youngest team in history to make it to the NBA Finals. In 1995–96 season, Orlando continued its winning ways. Led by Shaq, Anfernee Hardaway and the uncanny three-point brilliance of Dennis Scott, who broke both the NBA season and the NBA game records, the Magic topped the Atlantic Division for the second consecutive year. In the last few years, Orlando has developed another great lineup that is loaded with potential; with Tracy McGrady, Darrell Armstrong and Grant Hill on the current roster, great things are expected of Orlando's favorite team.

Vital Stats

Stadium Address:
600 W. Amelia St., Orlando, Fla.
Phone: (407) 849-2000
Web: nba.com/magic, orlandocentroplex.com/tdwaterhouse.shtml
Box Office:
(407) 849-2020,
Mon.–Fri. 10–5, game days 3 hours before tip-off
Media Coverage:
Radio: WDBO (580 AM)
TV: WRBW (Channel 65),
Sunshine Network
Practice Facility:
RDV Sportsplex,
Orlando, Fla.

POSTSEASON
• **Eastern Conference Championships** 1
(1994–95)
• **Division Titles**..................2
(1994–95, 1995–96)
• **NBA Playoff Appearances**.........................5
(1993–94, 1994–95, 1995–96, 1996–97, 1998–99)

TEAM RECORDS
• **Nick Anderson (1989–99)**
FG (career): 4,075
FT (career): 1,614
Points (career): 10,650
Steals (career): 1,004

Jump Shot

Steals (game): 8 (Nov. 11, 1991)
Turnovers (career): 1,241
• **Darrell Armstrong (1995–present)**
FT Pct. (season): .911 (1999–2000)
• **Anfernee Hardaway (1993–99)**
Steals (season): 190 (1993–94)
• **Shaquille O'Neal (1992–96)**
FG (season): 953 (1993–94)
FG (game): 22 (April 20, 1994)
FG Pct. (season): .599 (1993–94)
FG Pct. (career): .581
FT (season): 471 (1993–94)
Points (game): 53 (April 20, '94)
Points (season): 2,377 (1993–94)
Rebounds (game): 28 (Nov. 20, 1993)
Rebounds (season): 1,122 (1992–93)
Rebounds (career): 3,691
Blocks (game): 15 (Nov. 20, '93)
Blocks (season): 286 (1992–93)
Blocks (career): 824
Turnovers (season): 307 (1992–93)
• **Dennis Scott (1990–97)**
3-Point FG (game): 11 (April 18, 1996)
3-Point FG (season): 267 (1995–96)

3-Point FG (career): 981
• **Scott Skiles (1989–94)**
Assists (game): 30 (Dec. 30, '90)
Assists (season): 735 (1992–93)
Assists (career): 2,776
FT Pct. (career): .895

LEAGUE HONORS
Rookie of the Year
• Shaquille O'Neal (1992–93)

NBA Sixth Man of the Year
• Darrell Armstrong (1998–99)

All–NBA First Team
• Anfernee Hardaway (1994–95, 1995–96)

Coach of the Year
• Glenn "Doc" Rivers (1999–2000)

Tracy McGrady has many of the characteristics of a future NBA superstar.

Timeline

1986	1987	1990	1991	1992	1994	1995	1995	1996	1997	1999	2000
Spearheaded by local businessman Jim Hewitt, Orlando enters the NBA expansion race	NBA accepts the Orlando franchise bid	Scott Skiles sets NBA record with 30 assists vs Denver	Rich DeVos purchases the Magic	Orlando drafts Shaquille O'Neal first overall	Magic earns first-ever playoff berth	April 17: Team clinches its first Atlantic Division title	June 4: Orlando whips Indiana 105-81 to advance to NBA finals	Ground is broken for the new RDV Sportsplex in Orlando	Former Pistons coach Chuck Daly takes over coaching reins	Glenn "Doc" Rivers begins tenure as head coach	Rivers is fifth first-season coach to win NBA Coach of the Year Award

TD WATERHOUSE CENTRE: FIND THE MAGIC

ORIGINALLY NAMED THE ORLANDO ARENA, the TD Waterhouse Centre opened in 1989 as the crown jewel of the Orlando Centroplex. Distinguished by its square, modernist design, distinctive curved glass walls and terrazzo floors, the Waterhouse epitomizes Florida-style architecture. Light and airy, the building's interior is often cited as one of the most aesthetically pleasing environments in pro sports; in 1991 the Waterhouse won the prestigious Arena of the Year Award. A multipurpose facility, the "O-Rena" also hosts the finest in entertainment, and is home to the Orlando Predators of the very popular Arena Football league.

CONCESSIONS

Every kind of concession is available at TD Waterhouse Centre, and then some. Fans can choose from barbecue, Italian, subs, burgers, hot dogs and more. For lighter snacks, there are glaze-roasted nuts, frozen yogurt and cotton candy. A full-service bar also serves a variety of imported and national beers.

Arena Facts

Opened: Jan. 29, 1989
Cost: $100 million
Capacity: 17,248
Home Sweet Home:
• Although more seats were added to the Waterhouse a few years ago, it is still one of the most intimate arenas in the NBA. With the fans right on top of the action, the arena is also extremely loud. The always vocal Magic fans usually leave the arena with their ears ringing.

GAME DAY TIPS

• **Gate hours:** Gates open one hour prior to tip-off.
• **Prohibited items:** Food, cans, bottles and alcohol are prohibited. Professional cameras and any recording devices are also not permitted. Banners and signs are allowed as long as they are in good taste. Umbrellas are not allowed. Smoking is not permitted anywhere in the arena.

Directions: Take I-4 to Amelia Ave. exit. Turn left at the bottom of the off-ramp. Drive one block, turn right and follow signs to the arena. By Bus: The free Limo bus service from the Downtown Terminal on Church St. and Orange Ave. goes to the arena. There is also regular bus service. Call Lynx at (407) 841-8240 for information. **Parking:** There are 4,000 spaces on-site with 144 reserved for the disabled. There are another 7,570 spaces nearby on Robinson, Washington, Amelia and Church Sts.

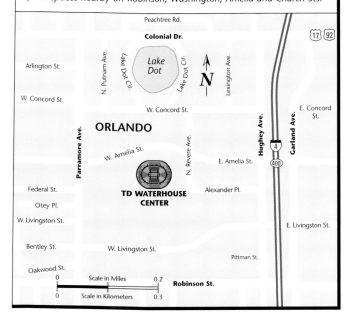

Seating Plan

$132	$44
$77	$34
$69	$24
$54	$18
$44	$10
$44	ATM **Section 106**
$34	♿ **Sections 102–104, 109–114,**
$24	**121, 122**
$18	

NORTH SIDE ENTRANCE

221 222 220 219 218 217 216 215 214 223 224 225 213 212 211 226 227 228 229 230 231 232 233 234 235 236 201 202 203 204 205 206 207 208 209 210

114 113 112 111 110 109 108 107 106 105 104 115 116 117 118 119 120 121 122 101 102 103

113S 112S 111S
122S 101S 102S
F1 F2 F3 F4

EAST SIDE ENTRANCE

SOUTH SIDE ENTRANCE

• **Ticket tips:** Magic tickets are still easy to get, although increasingly less so. As can be expected, games against the Lakers and Toronto are especially popular, as are weekend games. This arena is intimate and many fans like the seats in the upper bowl between the sidelines.
• **Lost and found:** (407) 849-2000.

Nearby Hotels

▼▼ **Best Western Orlando West** (*Motel*), 2014 W. Colonial Dr. (Orlando), (407) 841-8600, $49-$99
▼▼▼ **Holiday Inn at the Orlando Arena** (*Hotel*), 304 W. Colonial Dr. (Orlando), (407) 996-0100, $84-$114
▼▼▼ **Orlando Marriott Downtown** (*Hotel*), 400 W. Livingston St. (Orlando), (407) 843-6664, $85
▼▼▼ **Portofino Bay Hotel** (*Hotel*), 5601 Universal Blvd. (Orlando), (407) 503-1000, $235-$445
▼▼▼ **Radisson Plaza Hotel Orlando** (*Hotel*), 60 S. Ivanhoe Blvd. (Orlando), (407) 425-4455, $82

Nearby Restaurants

▼▼ **Johny Rivers Smokehouse & BBQ Co.** (*Steakhouse*), 5370 W. Colonial Dr. (Orlando), (407) 293-5803, $9-$14
ESPN® Club (*American*), Disney's Boardwalk, (Lake Buena Vista), (407) 939-1177, $10-$20
▼▼▼ **Manuel's on the 28th** (*International*), 390 N. Orange Ave. in the Bank of America Building, 28th floor (Orlando), (407) 246-6580, $27-$39 (dinner only)
▼▼ **Straub's Fine Seafood Restaurant** (*Seafood*), 5101 E. Colonial Dr. (Orlando), (407) 273-9330, $12-$25 (dinner only)
▼▼ **Vivaldi Italian Restaurant** (*Italian*), 107 W. Pine St. (Orlando), (407) 423-2335, $12-$24

PHILADELPHIA 76ERS

WHEN THE SYRACUSE NATIONALS FRANCHISE arrived in Philadelphia in 1963, it came with three NBA finals appearances and a host of experience. The City of Brotherly love didn't have to wait long for the team, renamed the 76ers, to find success again, thanks largely to a 1965 trade that brought center Wilt Chamberlain to town. With Chamberlain making a stunning imprint on the record books and guard Hal Greer supplying backcourt savvy, the Sixers won three straight Eastern Division titles and the 1967 NBA championship. Chamberlain was traded to the Lakers following the 1968 season and the team slowly sank in the standings, hitting an all-time low in 1972–73, when it won just nine games. Steady improvement throughout the mid-1970s was capped with the acquisition of Julius Erving in 1976. "Dr. J" amazed fans with his offensive moves as the Sixers racked up a 50-32 record. The team lost the NBA finals that year to the Portland Trail Blazers and continued to come up short of a title until the 1982–83 season and the arrival of center Moses Malone. As good as Malone was during the season, he was even better in the playoffs, averaging 26 points and almost 16 rebounds per game and leading the Sixers to a 4-0 sweep of the Lakers and the NBA championship. A year later the 76ers' next franchise player arrived in surly power forward Charles Barkley. Barkley's power inside kept the team respectable throughout the 1980s, but with his departure came another lull. Now it is the scoring of gifted guard Allen Iverson that promises to bring the team back to the top. Although Iverson is about a foot shorter than Chamberlain, he has the skills to do it.

Vital Stats

Stadium Address:
3601 S. Broad St.,
Philadelphia, Penn.
Phone: (215) 336-3600
Web: sixers.com,
comcast-spectacor.com
Box Office:
(215) 952-7000
Mon.–Fri. 9–6,
Sat. event days 10–4
Media Coverage:
Radio: WIP (610 AM)
TV: WPSG (Channel 57),
Comcast SportsNet
Practice Facility:
76ers Practice Facility,
Philadelphia, Penn.

POSTSEASON
- NBA Championships.......3
(1954–55, 1966–67, 1982–83)
- **Eastern Conference
Championships** 4
(1976–77, 1979–80, 1981–82,
1982–83)
- **Eastern Division
Championships** 4
(1949–50, 1953–54, 1954–55,
1966–67)

RETIRED NUMBERS
- Julius Erving (6)
- Maurice Cheeks (10)
- Wilt Chamberlain (13)

Jump Shot

- *Wilt Chamberlain's name is etched in many places in the record book. Perhaps his most notable record during his Philadelphia years came against Detroit on Feb. 2, 1968. That night he had 22 points, 25 rebounds and 21 assists for the only double-triple-double in NBA history.*
- *Sixers President Pat Croce made his original connection to the pro sports world as conditioning coach for the Philadelphia Flyers.*

- Hal Greer (15)
- Bobby Jones (24)
- Billy Cunningham (32)

TEAM RECORDS
- **Charles Barkley (1984–92)**
Def. Rebounds. (career): 4,391
Off. Rebounds. (career): 2,688
- **Dana Barros (1993–95)**
3-Point FGs (season) 197
(1994–95)
3-Point FG Pct. (season):
46.4 (1994–95)
- **Shawn Bradley (1993–95)**
Blocks (season): 274 (1994–95)
- **Wilt Chamberlain
(1965–68)**
FGs (season): 1,074 (1965–66)
FG Pct. (season): 68.3
(1966–67)
Points (game): 68
(Dec. 16, 1967)
Points (season): 2,649
(1965–66)
Points-Per-Game (season):
33.5 (1965–66)
Rebounds (game): 43
(Mar. 6, 1965)

> *"That's special to have teammates like that, who lay it on the line."*
> — Allen Iverson, on Eric Snow playing with a fractured ankle

Rebounds (season): 1,957
(1966–67)
- **Maurice Cheeks (1978–89)**
Assists (game): 21 (tie)
(Oct. 30, 1982)
Assists (season): 753 (1985–86)
Assists (career): 6,212
Steals (career): 1,942
- **Julius Erving (1976–87)**
Blocked Shots (career): 1,293
- **Hal Greer (1963–73)**
FGs (career): 8,504
Points (career): 21,586
- **Hersey Hawkins (1988–93)**
3-Point FGs (career): 476
- **Allen Iverson
(1996–present)**
Points (rookie season): 1,787
(1996–97)
- **Moses Malone
(1982–86, 1993–94)**
Def. Rebounds. (season): 749
(1982–83)
Off. Rebounds. (season): 445
(1982–83)

LEAGUE HONORS
NBA MVP
- **Wilt Chamberlain**
(1965–66, 1966–67, 1967–68)
- **Julius Erving** (1980–81)
- **Moses Malone** (1982–83)

Rookie of the Year
- Allen Iverson (1996–97)

NBA Sixth Man of the Year
- Bobby Jones (1982–83)

Talented guard Allen Iverson is bringing new life to the 76ers.

Coach of the Year
- Dolph Schayes (1965–66)

NBA Finals MVP
- Moses Malone (1983)

Basketball Hall of Fame
- Alex Hannum (1972)
- Wilt Chamberlain (1978)
- Hal Greer (1981)
- Billy Cunningham (1986)
- Jack Ramsay (1992)
- Julius Erving (1993)
- Chuck Daly (1994)
- Bailey Howell (1997)
- Dolph Schayes (1998)

Timeline

1949	1963	1965	1967	1968	1977	1981	1983	1986	1990	1992	1994	1996	1998	2000

- Syracuse Nationals become one of original NBA teams
- Nationals move to Philadelphia; change name to 76ers
- Sixers acquire Wilt Chamberlain in trade
- Philadelphia wins NBA title
- Chamberlain traded to Los Angeles
- Sixers reach NBA finals; lose to Portland
- Julius Erving named to third of five straight All-NBA teams
- Sixers sweep Lakers in NBA finals
- Maurice Cheeks named to fourth straight NBA All-Defense team
- Sixers win Atlantic Division
- Charles Barkley traded to Phoenix
- Moses Malone plays last season as Sixer
- Team drafts Georgetown guard Allen Iverson
- Sixers make playoffs for first time in seven years
- Iverson finishes second in NBA scoring race

FIRST UNION CENTER: SOMETHING SPECIAL INSIDE

OPENED IN 1996, FIRST UNION CENTER offers spectators everything they would expect in a new venue — and a few things they wouldn't. Along with top-notch sight lines, seating and facilities, the stadium also features the only microbrewery and cigar club — the Red Bell Brewery and Pub — in all of sports. Artworks of various types can be found on the walls and in the halls of First Union. The arena also offers many interactive exhibits, including touch-screen video kiosks that recount some of the Sixers' history.

CONCESSIONS

Given how popular they are in Philadelphia, it is no surprise that hoagies are a main attraction at the First Union Center. If the tuna, roast beef or cheese steak hoagies don't appeal, other options include hot dogs, gourmet pretzels, popcorn, pizza and microbrewery beer.

Arena Facts

Opened: Aug. 31, 1996
Cost: $210 million
Capacity: 21,000
Home Sweet Home:
With 2,000 more seats than the old Spectrum, First Union Center also has a much higher decibel level. The 76ers' notoriously loud fans helped spur the team to the best record in the east in 2000–01.

GAME DAY TIPS

• **Gate hours:** Gates open 90 minutes prior to tip-off.
• **Prohibited items:** Video and audio recorders, laser pointers, noise-makers, brooms, weapons, sticks, bats, food, beverages, coolers, cans, bottles and hard containers are all prohibited. Smoking is forbidden inside the stadium, but patrons are allowed to smoke in a designated area outside the building.
• **Ticket tips:** First Union Center is considered one of the best arenas in which to watch a basketball game. The sight lines are excellent in all of the pricing areas. Although the 76ers don't regularly sell out games, they tend to draw far larger crowds when any of the league's marquee teams, such as the Los Angeles Lakers or the New York Knicks, roll into town.
• **Lost and found:** (215) 389-9529.

Seating Plan

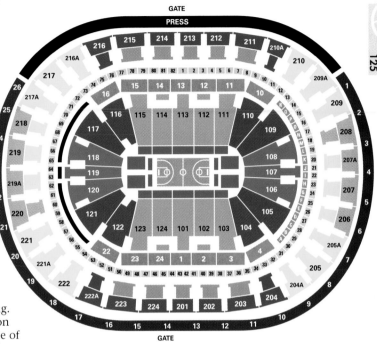

■	Call for info	
▨	$75	
■	$55	
■	$40	
■	Call for info	
▨	Call for info	
■	$50	
■	$35	
▨	$25	
▨	$10-14	
■	Call for info	

ATM **Sections 103, 219A**
♿ **Sections 112, 114, 121, 124, 202, 204A, 222**

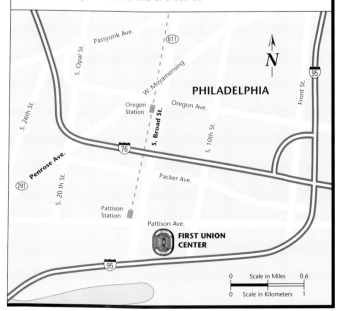

Directions: *From I-95 north or south, exit Broad St. First Union Center is on the left. By Subway: Take Broad St. Line to Pattison Ave./Broad St. stop. By Bus: Various buses go to and from the arena. Call (215) 580-7800 for more information.* **Parking:** *There are 6,100 spots in the lot surrounding the First Union Center. Spots for patrons with disabilities are located in lots C and D. Overflow parking is accommodated by lots on S. Darien St., S. 11th St. and S. Broad St.*

Nearby Hotels

▼▼▼ **Courtyard by Marriott Airport** *(Motor Inn)*, 8900 Bartram Ave. (Philadelphia), (215) 365-2200, $159-$219
▼▼▼ **Hampton Inn-Philadelphia Airport** *(Motel)*, 8600 Bartram Ave. (Philadelphia), (215) 966-1300, $139-$169
▼▼▼ **Hilton Philadelphia Airport** *(Hotel)*, 4509 Island Ave. (Philadelphia), (215) 365-4150, $135-$195
▼▼▼ **Holiday Inn Philadelphia Stadium** *(Hotel)*, 900 Packer Ave. (Philadelphia), (215) 755-9500, $89-$149
▼▼▼ **Philadelphia Fairfield Inn** *(Motel)*, 8800 Bartram Ave. (Philadelphia), (215) 365-2254, $100

Nearby Restaurants

▼▼ **Bistro Romano** *(Italian)*, 120 Lombard St. (Philadelphia), (215) 925-8880, $10-$24
▼▼▼ **The Continental Restaurant & Martini Bar** *(Continental)*, 138 Market St. (Philadelphia), (215) 923-6069, $6-$19
▼▼ **Downey's Restaurant** *(American)*, 526 S. Front St. (Philadelphia), (215) 625-9500, $16-$20
▼ **Engine 46 Steak House** *(American)*, 10 Reed St. (Philadelphia), (215) 462-4646, $5-$19
▼▼▼ **The Plough and the Stars Irish Restaurant & Bar** *(Continental)*, 123 Chestnut St. (Philadelphia), (215) 733-0300, $14-$21

PHOENIX SUNS

WITH AN OWNERSHIP INVESTORS GROUP THAT INCLUDED such entertainment luminaries as Tony Curtis, Henry Mancini, Andy Williams and Bobby Gentry, the Phoenix Suns certainly had stars in their eyes when they joined the NBA in 1968. But glitterati don't win ball games and things weren't easy in those early years. Finishing with a Western Conference worst 16-66 record in its first season, the franchise participated in a coin toss with the Eastern cellar-dwelling Milwaukee Bucks to determine who would have the first draft pick the following year. The Suns lost the toss, the Bucks drafted Lew Alcindor, later known as Kareem Abdul-Jabbar, and won the NBA title two years later. But the Phoenix franchise would come to enjoy many days in the sun, the first of which came with the team's unlikely run to the NBA finals in 1976. The Boston Celtics captured the series 4-2, but with the dramatic, triple-overtime game five, often called "the greatest game ever played," the "Sunderella" Suns blazed into national prominence. There they have remained since, thanks largely to an incredible 21 playoff appearances. Many of the NBA's best and brightest have scorched a trail across the Phoenix sky, including early greats Connie Hawkins and Paul Silas, creative guard Walter Davis, brutish big man Larry Nance and the never-boring Charles Barkley, who brought the team to its second finals appearance, a 4-2 loss to the Bulls in 1993. Today with the dream backcourt tandem of Jason Kidd and Penny Hardaway lighting it up nightly, the Suns' future looks bright indeed.

Guard Jason Kidd is always among the league leaders in assists.

"When the fans are behind you and they're making a lot of noise, it brings you more energy."

— Suns guard Tony Delk

POSTSEASON
• Western Conference Championships 2
(1975–76, 1992–93)
• Pacific Division Titles 3
(1980–81, 1992–93, 1994–95)

RING OF HONOR
• Dick Van Arsdale (5)
• Walter Davis (6)
• Tom Chambers (24)
• Alvan Adams (33)
• Connie Hawkins (42)
• Paul Westphal (44)

Jump Shot

• Current Suns owner Jerry Colangelo has been at the helm of the team since its first season, first as general manager, since 1987 as owner. His tenure is eclipsed only by that of Red Auerbach in Boston. Colangelo has been named NBA Executive of the Year four times.

TEAM RECORDS
• Alvan Adams (1975–88)
Games (career): 988
Rebounds (career): 6,937
Steals (career): 1,289
• Tom Chambers (1988–93)
FG (season): 810 (1989–90)
Points (season): 2,201 (1989–90)
Points-Per-Game (season): 27.2 (1989–90)
• Walter Davis (1977–88)
FG (career): 6,497
FG Att. (career): 12,497
Points (career): 15,666
• Connie Hawkins (1969–74)
FT (season): 577 (1969–70)
FT Att. (season): 741 (1969–70)
• Jeff Hornacek (1986–92)
3-Point FG Pct. (season): .439 (tie) (1991–92)
• Kevin Johnson (1987–2000)
Assists (season): 991 (1988–89)
Assists (career): 6,518
Assists-Per-Game (season): 12.2 (1988–89)
FT (career): 3,851
FT Att. (career): 4,579
• Ron Lee (1976–79)
Steals (season): 1977–78

• Kyle Macy (1980–1985)
FT Pct. (career): .884
• Dan Majerle (1988–95)
3-Point FG (season): 199 (1994–95)
3-Point FG (career): 721
3-Point FG Att (career): 1,965
• Larry Nance (1981–88)
Blocks (season): 217
Blocks (career): 939
• Rodney Rogers (1993–present)
3-Point FG Pct. (season): .439 (tie)
• Charlie Scott (1971–75)
FG Att. (season): 1,809 (1972–73)
Points-Per-Game (career): 24.8
• Paul Silas (1969–72)
Rebounds (season): 1,015 (1970–71)
Rebounds-Per-Game (season): 12.5 (1970–71)
• Neal Walk (1969–74)
Personal Fouls (season): 323 (1972–73)
• Mark West (1987–2000)
FG Pct. (season): .653 (1988–89)
FG Pct. (career): .613

LEAGUE HONORS
NBA MVP
• Charles Barkley (1992–93)

Rookie of the Year
• Alvan Adams (1975–76)
• Walter Davis (1977–78)

Sixth Man Award
• Eddie Johnson (1988–89)
• Danny Manning (1997–98)
• Rodney Rogers (1999–2000)

Most Improved Player
• Kevin Johnson (1988–89)

Coach of the Year
• Cotton Fitzsimmons (1988–89)

Vital Stats

Stadium Address:
201 E. Jefferson St., Phoenix, Ariz.
Phone: (602) 379-2000
Web: nba.com/suns, americawestarena.com
Box Office:
(602) 379-7800, Mon.–Fri. 10–5
Media Coverage:
Radio: KTAR (620 AM)
TV: KUTP (Channel 45), KPNX (Channel 12), COX
Practice Facility:
America West Arena, Phoenix, Ariz.

Timeline

1968 — Phoenix granted NBA franchise
1969 — Gail Goodrich leads team with 23.8 points per game
1971 — First winning season, at 48-34
1976 — Team reaches NBA finals, losing 4-2 to Celtics
1977 — Suns retire jersey of former star Connie Hawkins
1984 — Suns lose Western Conference finals 4-2 to Lakers
1987 — Suns acquire guard Kevin Johnson from Cleveland
1989 — Forward Tom Chambers leads team to 55-27 record
1992 — Suns acquire Charles Barkley from Sixers
1993 — Phoenix loses finals to Bulls
1997 — Franchise falls below .500 for first time in 10 years
1999 — Jason Kidd named first team All-NBA
2000 — Rodney Rogers named Sixth Man of the Year as Suns win 53 games
2001 — Suns reach playoffs for 13th consecutive season

AMERICA WEST ARENA: MODELED AFTER THE BEST

THE 1992–93 SEASON WAS an exciting one for the Phoenix Suns and their fans. The team got a new star, Charles Barkley, a new coach in Paul Westphal and a brand new venue, the America West Arena. America West is an excellent venue and that is no accident. The Suns hired retired star Alvan Adams to tour the world's best arenas. The team then incorporated the best of these designs into America West. Fans enjoy the downtown location and the great sight lines, concessions and design at this facility. Players like the on-site practice gym.

CONCESSIONS

Fans coming to America West Arena can expect all the old arena favorites: hamburgers, hot dogs, sausages, popcorn, corn on the cob and ice cream. Several local and national restaurant chains have franchises in the arena. Some regional beers are available.

Arena Facts

Opened: June 1, 1992
Cost: $90 million
Capacity: 19,023
Home Sweet Home:
• Phoenix fans are renowned as among the most enthusiastic in the league. The team once drew 18,000 people — to a practice — with another 4,000 turned away at the door.

GAME DAY TIPS

• **Gate hours:** Gates open one hour prior to tip-off.
• **Prohibited items:** Bottles, cans, food or alcohol, video cameras, professional cameras, signs, banners, and laser pointers or projectiles of any kind are prohibited. Smoking is allowed only in designated areas.
• **Ticket tips:** The Suns sold out just two games last season, meaning tickets for most home games are usually readily available. However, for contests against such popular opponents as the Lakers, the 76ers or the Trail Blazers, the selection of good seats may be significantly smaller. There are very few bad seats in America West Arena. In fact, seats in the upper bowl are an especially good value for the money.
• **Lost and found:** (602) 379-7776.

Seating Plan

■	N/A	■	$29
■	$95	■	$25
■	$85	■	$10
■	$85		
■	$70	**ATM** Sections 116, 117	
■	$60	♿ Sections 105, 106, 110,	
■	$36	111, 117, 118, 122, 123,	
■	$32	203, 211, 219, 227	

Directions: Take I-10 to Washington St./Jefferson St. Follow Washington St. to 3rd St. and turn left. Follow to arena. By Bus: Several buses from downtown Phoenix arrive at the arena. Call ValleyMetro at (602) 253-5000 for information. **Parking:** The arena has a 900-space parking garage; 45 spaces are reserved for the disabled. There are more than 30,000 spots available in downtown Phoenix lots within a 15-minute walk on 1st, 2nd, 3rd, 4th, 5th and 7th Sts.

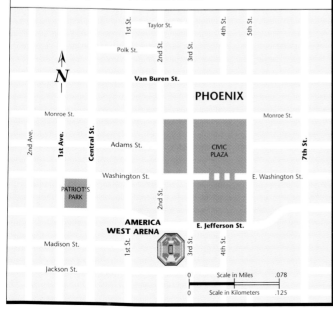

Nearby Hotels

▼▼▼ **Best Western Executive Park Hotel (Hotel)**, 1100 N. Central Ave. (Phoenix), (602) 252-2100, $61-$91
▼▼▼ **Embassy Suites Hotel Airport West (Suite Hotel)**, 2333 E. Thomas Rd. (Phoenix), (602) 957-1910, $69-$139
▼▼▼ **Hilton Suites-Phoenix (Suite Hotel)**, 10 E. Thomas Rd. in Phoenix Plaza (Phoenix), (602) 222-1111, $59-$239
▼▼▼ **Hyatt Regency Phoenix (Hotel)**, 122 N. 2nd St. (Phoenix), (602) 252-1234, $224-$249
▼▼▼ **La Quinta Inn Thomas Rd (Motel)**, 2725 N. Black Canyon Hwy. (Phoenix), (602) 258-6271, $49-$99

Nearby Restaurants

▼▼▼ **Eddie Matney's (French)**, 2398 E. Camelback Rd. in Northern Trust Bank Tower (Phoenix), (602) 957-3214, $17-$25
▼▼ **Omaha Steakhouse (Southwest American)**, 2630 E. Camelback Rd. in Embassy Suites-Biltmore (Phoenix), (602) 955-3992, $11-$34
▼▼ **Rennicks (American)**, 2435 S. 47th St. (Phoenix), (480) 894-1600, $10-$19
▼▼ **Rose's (American)**, 1100 N. Central Ave. in Best Western Executive Park Hotel (Phoenix), (602) 252-2100, $9-$18
▼ **Stockyards Restaurant (American)**, 5001 E. Washington Ave. (Phoenix), (602) 273-7378, $14-$32

PORTLAND TRAIL BLAZERS

BLAZERS FEW PRO SPORTS TEAMS CAN BOAST the fervent fan loyalty of the Trail Blazers. Beginning with their meteoric rise to success in the 1976–77 season, Portland fans began pouring in to see their team and have never stopped. To date the Blazers have played almost 1,000 sold-out games, believed to be a record for any pro sport. The key to this "Blazermania" has always been strong team unity. Although Portland has always had its share of stars, the Blazers have built their fan allegiance around great teamwork, intelligent plays and a well-known hard-work ethic; with each game, fans leave feeling like the team has played just for them. The Blazers' strong team approach has also been valuable in winning games. In 30 seasons of play, the Blazers have struck up one of the most consistent playoff-appearance records in the league, having missed the postseason only seven times. In 1977 the team rallied around "Big Bill" Walton to take the Philadelphia 76ers in six games. Although Walton, with his intense, smart playing style, charismatic personality, and public counterculture leanings, was the most famous Blazer of the era, the NBA crown was the result of incredible team syncopation. Again in the early 1990s, it was this strong collective spirit that brought Portland to the cream of the NBA. Under Coach Rick Adelman, the Blazers assembled a rotation of great players who thrived on telepathic teamwork. With Clyde Drexler, Buck Williams, Terry Porter, Kevin Duckworth and Danny Ainge working the courts, Portland — or "Rip City" as it was becoming known — took three major playoff titles and made it to the NBA finals twice. More recently the team of Sean Elliot, Isaiah Rider, Brian Grant and Rasheed Wallace gave the Blazers their fourth Pacific Division title and secured the team's reputation as a major contender for the upcoming seasons.

128

Vital Stats

Stadium Address:
One Center Court,
Portland, Ore.
Phone: (503) 235-8771
Web: nba.com/blazers,
rosegarden.com
Box Office:
(503) 797-9619,
Mon.–Fri. 9–5:30,
Sat. 10–5, event days
Media Coverage:
Radio: KXL (750 AM)
TV: BlazersCable,
KGW (Channel 8)
Practice Facility:
Blazers Practice Facility,
Portland, Ore.

"These fans are deserving."

— Clyde Drexler, on the Trail Blazers tremendous fan support despite the team's failings in winning championships

POSTSEASON
- **NBA Championships**.......1
(1976–77)
- **Western Conference Championships** 3
(1976–77, 1989–90, 1991–92)
- **Pacific Division Titles** 4
(1977–78, 1990–91, 1991–92, 1998–99)

Jump Shot

- *Blazers power forward Rasheed Wallace is known as a fierce competitor and he often challenges referee calls. During the 2000–01 season, this resulted in his setting a NBA record with 40 (CK) technical fouls.*
- *In May 1988 the Trail Blazers were purchased by Microsoft co-founder Paul Allen. Allen, with a fortune worth an estimated $40 billion, is a hands-on owner, arranging his business itinerary each year around the team's schedule.*

- **NBA Playoff Appearances**......................23
(1976–77, 1977–78, 1978–79, 1979–80, 1980–81, 1982–83, 1983–84, 1984–85, 1985–86, 1986–87, 1987–88, 1988–89, 1989–90, 1990–91, 1991–92, 1992–93, 1993–94, 1994–95, 1995–96, 1996–97, 1997–98, 1998–99, 1999–2000)

RETIRED NUMBERS
- **Larry Weinberg (1)**
- **Dave Twardzik (13)**
- **Larry Steele (15)**
- **Maurice Lucas (20)**
- **Bill Walton (33)**
- **Lloyd Neal (36)**
- **Geoff Petrie (45)**
- **Jack Ramsay (77)**

TEAM RECORDS
- **Clyde Drexler (1983–95)**
Games (career): 867
FG (season) 849 (1987–88)
FG (career): 6,889
FT (career): 3,798
Personal Fouls
(career): 2,699
Points (career): 18,040
Points-Per-Game (season):

27.2 (1988–89)
Rebounds (career): 5,339
Steals (career): 1,795
- **Lloyd Neal (1972–79)**
Rebounds (season): 967
(1972–73)
- **Terry Porter (1985–95)**
Assists (career): 5,319
3-Point FG (career): 773
- **Clifford Robinson (1989–97)**
3-Point FG (season): 178
(1995–96)
- **Mychal Thompson (1978–86)**
Blocks (career): 768
Def. Rebounds
(career): 3,389
- **Kiki Vandeweghe (1984–89)**
FT (season): 523 (1985–86)
- **Bill Walton (1974–79)**
Blocks (season): 211 (1976–77)
Def. Rebounds (season): 723
(1976–77)

LEAGUE HONORS
NBA MVP
- **Bill Walton (1977–78)**

Rookie of the Year
- **Geoff Petrie (1970–71)**
- **Sidney Wicks (1971–72)**

Sixth Man of the Year
- **Clifford Robinson (1992–93)**

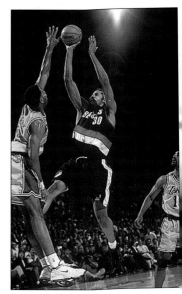

Rasheed Wallace scores, rebounds and blocks shots with the league's best.

Coach of the Year
- **Mike Schuler (1986–87)**
- **Mike Dunleavy (1998–99)**

NBA Finals MVP
- **Bill Walton (1977)**

NBA Hall of Fame
- **Jack Ramsay (1992)**
- **Bill Walton (1993)**

Timeline

1970	1972	1977	1978	1986	1988	1990	1991	1992	1995	1999
Portland wins first ever NBA game over the Cavs	Sidney Wicks wins NBA Rookie of the Year	Blazers win NBA championship in first playoff appearance	Bill Walton becomes the only Trail Blazer to win NBA MVP	The long-time tenure of coach Jack Ramsay comes to an end	Clyde Drexler sets team record: 2,185 points in a season	Blazers make their second NBA finals appearance, but lose to Detroit Pistons	Blazers break the L.A. Lakers nine-year lock on the Pacific Division	Team loses NBA finals to Michael Jordan and the Bulls	Two eras end in Portland: Drexler is traded to Houston and Memorial Coliseum closes	Mike Dunleavy wins Coach of the Year as team takes its fourth division title

THE ROSE GARDEN: DOWNTOWN GEM

THE ROSE GARDEN HAS BECOME the cornerstone of Portland's scenic downtown. Considered one of the most majestic arenas in the NBA, the Garden features a beautiful outdoor courtyard, fountain and beer garden, as well as a cheerful, airy interior. The Rose Garden is also one of the most hi-tech venues in pro sports. With the only adjustable "acoustic cloud" in the country, the Garden can alter the sound quality to best fit the event — whether it's sports, music or something else. Furthermore, the Rose Garden Command Center seamlessly controls all aspects of the arena's functions — lighting, sound, air quality, traffic flow and security monitors — so the environment remains optimal at all times.

CONCESSIONS

Fans at the Rose Garden are guaranteed the full range of concessions. In addition to standard fare such as hamburgers, hot dogs and pizza, there are several sit-down restaurants and bars. There are also desserts and a wide selection of beers.

GAME DAY TIPS
- **Gate hours:** Gates open two hours prior to tip-off.
- **Prohibited items:** Food, beverages and containers of any kind are prohibited. Professional, flash or video cameras are strictly forbidden. Banners and signs are allowed, but poles and sticks are not. No weapons or projectiles are permitted. Smoking is allowed in outdoor designated areas.
- **Ticket tips:** The Blazers currently have a 98-game sellout streak, but tickets are still available for most games up until game day. Tickets tend to go quickly for games against the likes of the Lakers, Spurs or Sacramento. There are no bad views, but seats in end zone sections 208, 209, 223 and 224 are partly obstructed by the backboard.
- **Lost and found:** (503) 797-9995.

Arena Facts

Opened: Oct. 13, 1995
Cost: $262 million
Capacity: 19,980
Home Sweet Home:
- As Portland's only major-league professional sports franchise, the Trail Blazers enjoy the undivided attention and the unchallenged support of sports fans in that city. Blazers fans are renowned as being among the most loyal in the NBA.

Directions: Take I-5 to Rose Quarter exit. Follow signs to the parking garages. Or, take I-405 to I-5 south. Get off at Rose Quarter exit and follow signs to parking garages. Or, cross Broadway Bridge or Steel Bridge and follow signs to parking garages. By Public Transit: Several buses and a MAX train arrive at the Rose Quarter. Call Tri-Met at (503) 238-7433 for more information. **Parking:** There are 2,317 spaces in four garages available on the Rose Quarter Campus, with 56 reserved for the disabled. There are 3,000 more spaces at the shuttle lots in Lloyd District on 7th Ave. and Multnomah St. Call (503) 797-9831 for shuttle information.

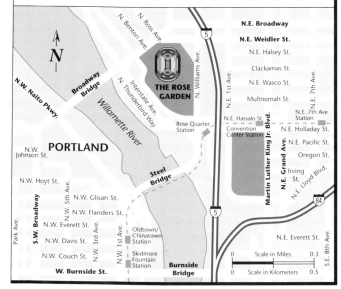

Seating Plan

$127	$16
$102	$16
$69	$10
$47	**Suites** N/A
$36	ATM **Sections 103, 118, 219, 320,**
$27	**outside box office lobby**
$23	♿ **Throughout**

Nearby Hotels

▼▼ **Best Western Rose Garden Hotel** *(Motor Inn)*, 10 N. Weidler St. (Portland), (503) 287-9900, $69-$89

▼▼▼ **Courtyard by Marriott-Portland Lloyd Center** *(Motor Inn)*, 435 NE Wasco St. (Portland), (503) 234-3200, $79-$109

▼▼▼ **Doubletree Hotel-Lloyd Center** *(Hotel)*, 1000 NE Multnomah St. (Portland), (503) 281-6111, $89-$119

▼▼ **Holiday Inn Convention Center** *(Hotel)*, 1021 NE Grand Ave. (Portland), (503) 235-2100, $109-$155

▼▼▼ **Radisson Hotel Portland** *(Hotel)*, 1441 NE 2nd Ave. (Portland), (503) 233-2401, $119-$129

Nearby Restaurants

▼▼▼ **Jake's Famous Crawfish Restaurant** *(Seafood)*, 401 SW 12th Ave. (Portland), (503) 226-1419, $10-$23

▼▼ **Metronome** *(American)*, 1426 NE Broadway (Portland), (503) 288-4300, $9-$22 (dinner only)

▼▼ **Ringside Steakhouse** *(Steakhouse)*, 2165 W. Burnside St. (Portland), (503) 223-1513, $14-$40 (dinner only)

▼▼ **Rustica Italian Caffe** *(Italian)*, 1700 NE Broadway (Portland), (503) 288-0990, $9-$13

▼▼ **Typhoon! On Broadway** *(Thai)*, 400 SW Broadway (Portland), (503) 224-8285, $6-$20

SACRAMENTO KINGS

WITH A FRANCHISE THAT IS OLDER than the NBA itself, you'd think the Sacramento Kings would garner a little respect. Beginning as the Rochester Royals in 1945, the team earned its respect the old fashioned way: It whipped everyone else en route to a championship in the now-defunct National Basketball League. As charter members of the new NBA in 1949, the Royals continued their winning ways and steamrolled their way to the postseason six years in a row. Led by future Hall-of-Famer Arnie Risen, the 1950–51 squad defeated the Knicks in a gritty game seven of the finals to take its first NBA title. Unfortunately, since its blazing start, the team has had trouble keeping the momentum going. In fact, it hasn't made it to a NBA championship series since. Maybe it was an identity crisis: The team became the Kings in 1972. Maybe it was all the moving: Since its founding, the franchise has played in three different leagues and four different cities, finally landing in Sacramento in 1985. The team has certainly not lacked opportunity. Since its championship in 1952, Sacramento has reached the playoffs no less than 20 times, but has always come up short. And the lack of success can't be traced back to a dearth of talent. Some of basketball's greatest luminaries have worn the franchise's ever-changing colors, including Oscar Robertson, Jerry Lucas and Nate "Tiny" Archibald. Whatever the reason, today's crop of Kings, such as forward Chris Webber and slick-passing guard Jason Williams, hope that they can solve the mystery and put the Kings back atop the NBA throne.

A solid scorer and rebounder, Chris Webber is also a strong leader for the Kings.

POSTSEASON
- NBA Championships.......1
(1950–51)
- Western Division
Championships 1
(1950–51)
- Western Division
Titles 2
(1948–49, 1951–52)
- Midwest Division
Titles 1
(1978–79)

RETIRED NUMBERS
- Nate Archibald (1)
- Fans (6) (Sixth Man)
- Bob Davies (11)
- Maurice Stokes (12)
- Oscar Robertson (14)
- Jack Twyman (27)
- Sam Lacey (44)

Jump Shot

- *In the 1972–73 season Nate "Tiny" Archibald became the first player in NBA history to lead the league in scoring (34 ppg) and assists (11.4 asp). Despite Archibald's heroics, the MVP award went to Boston's Dave Cowens, who was out of the top 10 in every major category except for rebounds, in which he finished third.*

TEAM RECORDS
- **Nate Archibald (1970–76)**
Assists (season): 910
(1972–73)
FT (game): 23 (Jan. 21, 1975)
Minutes (season): 3,681
(1972–73)
Points (season): 2,719
(1972–73)
Points-Per-Game (season):
34.0 (1972–73)
- **Duane Causwell (1990–97)**
Blocks (season): 215
(1991–92)
- **Steve Johnson (1981–84)**
FG Pct. (season): .624
(1982–83)
FG Pct. (career): .604
- **Sam Lacey (1970–82)**
Blocks (career): 1,098
Games (career): 888
Rebounds (career): 9,353
Steals (career): 950
- **Jerry Lucas (1963–70)**
Rebounds (game):
40 (Feb. 29, 1964)
Rebounds (season): 1,668
(1965–66)
- **Oscar Robertson (1960–70)**
Assists (game): 22
(tie) (Oct. 29, 1961)
Assists (career): 7,731
FG (career): 7,713
FT (career): 6,583
Minutes (career): 33,088
Points (career): 22,009
- **Mitch Richmond**

(1991–98)
3-Point FG (game): 8
(Feb. 25, 1994)
3-Point FG (career): 993
- **Brian Taylor (1976–77)**
Steals (season): 199
(1976–77)
- **Jack Twyman (1955–66)**
Points (game):
59 (tie) (Jan. 15, 1960)
- **Spud Webb (1991–95)**
FT Pct. (season): .934
(1994–95)
- **Chris Webber (1998–present)**
Blocks (game): 9
(tie) (Feb. 7, 1999)

LEAGUE HONORS
NBA MVP
- Oscar Robertson
(1963–64)

Rookie of the Year
- Maurice Stokes (1955–56)
- Oscar Robertson
(1960–61)
- Jerry Lucas (1963–64)
- Phil Ford (1978–79)

Coach of the Year
- Phil Johnson (1974–75)
- Cotton Fitzsimmons
(1978–79)

"When we win, we all benefit; it's not one individual."

— *Sacramento guard Nick Anderson*

Vital Stats

Stadium Address:
One Sports Pkwy.,
Sacramento, Calif.
Phone: (916) 928-3650
Web: nba.com/kings,
arcoarena.com
Box Office:
(916) 928-6900,
Mon.–Sat. 10–6
Media Coverage:
Radio: KHTK (1140 AM)
TV: KMAX (Channel 31),
Fox Sports Net
Training Facility:
ARCO Arena,
Sacramento, Calif.

Basketball Hall of Fame
- Bob Davies (1969)
- Jerry Lucas (1979)
- Oscar Robertson (1979)
- Jack Twyman (1982)
- Al Cervi (1984)
- Red Holzman (1985)
- Bobby Wanzer (1986)
- Clyde Lovellette (1987)
- Nate Archibald (1990)
- Alex Hannum (1998)
- Arnie Risen (1998)
- Wayne Embry (1999)

Timeline

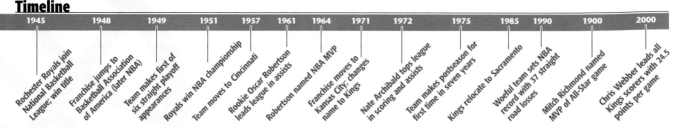

1945	1948	1949	1951	1957	1961	1964	1971	1972	1975	1985	1990	1900	2000
Rochester Royals join National Basketball League; win title	Franchise jumps to Basketball Association of America (later NBA)	Team makes first of six straight playoff appearances	Royals win NBA championship	Team moves to Cincinnati	Rookie Oscar Robertson leads league in assists	Robertson named NBA MVP	Franchise moves to Kansas City; changes name to Kings	Nate Archibald tops league in scoring and assists	Team makes postseason for first time in seven years	Kings relocate to Sacramento	Woeful team sets NBA record with 37 straight road losses	Mitch Richmond named MVP of All-Star game	Chris Webber leads all Kings scorers with 24.5 points per game

130

ARCO ARENA:
BIG SHOW IN A SMALL MARKET

AS THE ONLY MAJOR sports team in Sacramento, the Kings are a popular draw, making ARCO Arena one of the most rollicking places to see a NBA game. Even when the team is struggling, a visit is an event in and of itself. The large, tan arena looks inauspicious from the outside, plunked in the middle of a large undeveloped lot. But once inside, visitors get their money's worth. Many fans come to the game early in order to watch the Kings' in-house pregame show on one of the numerous monitors around the building.

Seating Plan

■	$99.50	■	$29.50
	$89.50	■	$19.50
■	$75.50	■	$10
■	$60.50	**ATM**	**Sections 106, 123**
■	$43.50	♿	**Throughout**

CONCESSIONS

No fan need go hungry at ARCO Arena. All the standard stadium munchies — hot dogs, pizza, etc. — are found here, as well as a few extras. Try a smoked turkey leg, teriyaki chicken or an enchilada plate. There are also sopaipillas (a Mexican dessert) and sushi.

Arena Facts

Opened: Nov. 8, 1988
Cost: $40 million
Capacity: 17,317
Home Sweet Home:
• *Despite going through some difficult times, the Kings have great fans, with 497 consecutive sellouts from 1985 to '98. When the fans start stomping on the wooden floors in the stands, the arena becomes one of the NBA's loudest.*

GAME DAY TIPS

• **Gate hours:** Gates open 90 minutes prior to tip-off.
• **Prohibited items:** Food, beverages, alcohol and containers are prohibited. Video or audio recording equipment of any sort is not permitted. Weapons and projectiles are also forbidden, as are animals, with the exception of seeing-eye dogs. Smoking is not allowed.
• **Ticket tips:** The Kings sell out virtually all their home games, so tickets will be nearly impossible to get at short notice. This is true regardless of who their opponents are or the day of the week and now

that the team is a contender again, tickets are even harder to come by. Sight lines are perfect all around the court.
• **Lost and found:** (916) 928-6931.

Directions: Take I-5 north or south to Del Paso Rd. exit. Follow Del Paso Rd. east to Natomas Blvd./ARCO Arena Blvd. and turn right. ARCO Arena is on right. **Parking:** The arena has 12,000 parking spaces on-site and the lots open two-and-a-half hours before each game. There are 151 disabled spaces in lot H, which can be reached by entering the parking lot through Toll Plaza 5.

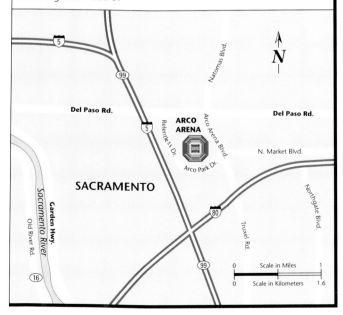

Nearby Hotels

▼▼ **Delta King River Boat Hotel (*Historic Hotel*)**, 1000 Front St. (Sacramento), (916) 444-5464, $149-$179
▼▼▼ **Governors Inn (*Motel*)**, 210 Richards Blvd. (Sacramento), (916) 448-7224, $79-$119
▼▼▼ **Hilton Garden Inn (*Motor Inn*)**, 2540 Venture Oaks Way (Sacramento), (916) 568-5400, $79-$149
▼▼▼▼ **Hyatt Regency (*Hotel*)**, 1209 L St. (Sacramento), (916) 443-1234, $209-$234
▼▼▼ **Residence Inn by Marriott (*Motel*)**, 2410 W. El Camino (Sacramento), (916) 649-1300, $139-$169

Nearby Restaurants

▼▼ **Bradshaws Restaurant (*American*)**, 9647 Micron Ave. (Sacramento), (916) 362-3274, $7-$14
▼▼ **California Fats (*Chinese*)**, 1015 Front St. (Sacramento), (916) 441-7966, $12-$19
▼▼▼ **Chanterelle (*Continental*)**, 1300 H St. in The Sterling Hotel (Sacramento), (916) 442-0451, $16-$24
▼▼▼ **Delta King Pilothouse Restaurant (*Continental*)**, 1000 Front St. in the Delta King River Boat Hotel (Sacramento), (916) 441-4440, $17-$29
▼▼ **Fat City Bar & Café (*American*)**, 1001 Front St. (Sacramento), (916) 446-6768, $9-$19

SAN ANTONIO SPURS

THERE'S NOTHING LIKE A STORY with a happy ending. San Antonio fans know that only too well. From the early years of the franchise the Spurs had all the makings of a champion. Going into the 1998–99 season, the franchise had the third-best all-time record in the league, behind the Celtics and Lakers, and owned a slew of division titles to prove it. The team had enjoyed tremendous offensive weapons, including George "Ice Man" Gervin, who racked up four scoring titles, James Silas and more recently the twin towers of David "the Admiral" Robinson and Tim Duncan. The Spurs featured feared rebounders in the forms of early greats Swen Nater and Artis Gilmore and the current duo of Robinson and Duncan. Gervin and Robinson highlighted a capable crew of leaders for the squad, while players such as Johnny Moore and Avery Johnson provided solid play at guard. And with Robinson and Duncan both making repeated appearances on the NBA's All-Defensive team, the Spurs have not lacked at the defensive end of the court for some time. And last, but surely not least, the Spurs enjoy great fan support in San Antonio. Even though the Spurs have had all the makings of a champion since their earliest days as an ABA franchise, the team always had a less than stellar postseason record and no title to show for all its greatness. But in the strike-shortened season of 1998–99, the Spurs would right that wrong for once and for all. Led by Duncan's outstanding play at both ends, Robinson's character and Sean Elliot's scoring, the Spurs went 15-2 in the postseason, culminating in a 4-1 series win in the finals over the Knicks. The Spurs had its happy ending at last and the fans had something to cheer about.

Vital Stats

Stadium Address:
100 Montana St.,
San Antonio, Texas
Phone: (210) 207-3600
Web: nba.com/spurs,
alamodome.com
Box Office:
(210) 554-7787,
Mon.–Fri. 8–6, game days
Media Coverage:
Radio: WOAI (1200 AM)
TV: KBEJ (Channel 2),
KENS (Channel 5),
Fox Sports Net
Practice Facility:
Alamodome,
San Antonio, Texas

POSTSEASON
- **NBA Championships**.......1
(1998–99)
- **Western Conference Championships** 1
(1998–99)
- **Central Division Titles**....2
(1977–78, 1978–79)
- **Midwest Division Titles** 8
(1980–81, 1981–82, 1982–83, 1989–90, 1990–91, 1994–95, 1995–96, 1998–99)

RETIRED NUMBERS
- **Johnny Moore (00)**
- **James Silas (13)**
- **George Gervin (44)**

TEAM RECORDS
- **Johnny Dawkins (1986–89)**
FT Pct. (career): .861
- **Tim Duncan (1997–present)**
Rebounds-Per-Game (career): 12

Jump Shot
- *Since Greg Popovich took over as Spurs GM in May 1994, he has totally remodeled the team. In fact, the only player left from before his arrival is star center David Robinson.*

- **Sean Elliot (1989–93, 1994–present)**
3-Point FG (career): 508
3-Point FG Att. (career): 1,356
- **George Gervin (1974–85)**
Disqualifications (career): 36
FG (career): 7,526
FG Att. (career): 14,647
Points (season): 2,585 (1979–80)
Points (career): 19,383
Points-Per-Game (season): 33.1 (1979–80)
Points-Per-Game (career): 26.3
- **Artis Gilmore (1982–87)**
FG Pct. (career): .620
- **Avery Johnson (1990–present)**
Assists (career): 4,237
- **Johnny Moore (1980–90)**
Assists-Per-Game (career): 7.9
- **Terry Porter (1999–present)**
3-Point FG Pct. (season): .435 (1999–2000)
3-Point FG Pct. (career): .435
- **David Robinson (1989–present)**
Blocks (career): 2,506
Blocks (season): 320 (1990–91)
Blocks-Per-Game (career): 3.28
FT (career): 5,263
FT Att. (career): 7,122
Games (career): 765

"We're a small town like Portland and Salt Lake City, and this is a thrill for us and our fans."

— Coach Gregg Popovich, following Spurs NBA finals win in 1999–2000

Minutes (season): 3,241 (1993–94)
Personal Fouls (career): 2,304
Rebounds (career): 8,651

Steals (career): 1,170
Turnovers (career): 2,108
- **Dennis Rodman (1993–95)**
Rebounds (season): 1,367 (1993–94)
Rebounds-Per-Game (season): 17.3 (1993–94)

LEAGUE HONORS
NBA MVP
- David Robinson (1994–95)

Rookie of the Year
- David Robinson (1989–90)
- Tim Duncan (1997–98)

Defensive Player of the Year
- Alvin Robertson (1985–86)
- David Robinson (1991–92)

NBA Finals MVP
- Tim Duncan (1999)

Basketball Hall of Fame
- George Gervin (1995)

Tim Duncan has become the Spurs main offensive weapon.

Timeline

1973	1975	1976	1977	1980	1983	1985	1988	1990	1994	1997	1998	1999
Team moves to San Antonio, renamed Spurs	Swen Nater leads ABA in rebounding with 16.4 boards a game	Spurs jump to NBA	Team clinches playoff berth in first NBA season	George Gervin wins third straight NBA scoring title	Spurs lose conference finals to Lakers	Gervin plays in 12th and final NBA All-Star Game	Larry Brown named head coach	David Robinson named NBA Rookie of the Year	Dennis Rodman wins third straight NBA rebounding title	Spurs record 20-62 record, worst in franchise history	Tim Duncan voted Rookie of the Year and named to All-NBA First Team	Spurs capture first NBA title

ALAMODOME:
AS BIG AS IT WANTS TO BE

OPENED AT THE START OF THE 1993–94 season, the Alamodome instantly propelled San Antonio to the leading edge of stadium technology. With a cable-suspended roof and a retractable seating system, the dome still has flexibility features that are rare in sport. For selected games, capacity of the venue can be raised from 20,557 to more than 34,000, a boon when the Spurs go deep into the playoffs. The facility, which has excellent sight lines and an extensive food court area, was paid for by a half-cent tax levied on residents from 1989 to '94.

CONCESSIONS

Hungry fans at the Alamodome can sample the best in Texan specialties. All the traditional favorites are available, including hamburgers, hot dogs, pizza and peanuts, as well as Mexican, Tex/Mex and barbecue, all with a variety of the spiciest and reddest sauces this side of the Mississippi.

Arena Facts

Opened: *May 15, 1993*
Cost: *$186 million*
Capacity: *20,557*
Home Sweet Home:
• *The ability of the Alamodome to increase capacity to more than 34,000 for selected games means enormous crowds and lots of noise for opponents in big games.*

GAME DAY TIPS

• **Gate hours:** Gates open one hour and 15 minutes prior to tip-off.
• **Prohibited items:** Food, beverages, alcohol and containers are prohibited. Professional cameras and video cameras are strictly forbidden. Noisemakers, beachballs, frisbees and laser pointers are not allowed. The only animals permitted in the arena are those that provide assistance to the disabled. Smoking is not allowed anywhere inside the arena.
• **Ticket tips:** Tickets should be easy to get, although there may be more demand for games against division

rivals such as Utah and Houston and the ever-popular Lakers. In general, the crowds are larger for weekend games, especially if the Spurs are in the playoff

hunt toward the end of the season. Sometimes the upper level is opened to increase the arena's capacity.
• **Lost and found:** (210) 207-3680.

Seating Plan

▪ Baseline & Corner Prime **$55**
▪ Sideline Prime **$50**
▪ Lower Level Corners & Baseline **$37**
▪ Lower Level Corners & Baseline **$25**
▪ Lower Baseline **$17**
▫ Courtside Lower Prime .. **N/A**
▪ Courtside Prime .... **N/A**
ATM Sections 101, 123; Northside entrance
♿ Throughout

Directions: *Take I-37/Rte.281 to Durango Blvd./Alamodome exit. Follow signs to the arena. By Bus: Buses 24, 25 and 26 go to the arena. Call VIA Metropolitan Transit at (210) 362-2020 for information.* **Parking:** *There are 2,810 spaces on-site, with 35 reserved for the disabled. About 12,000 more spaces are within a half-mile radius on Market and St. Mary's Sts.*

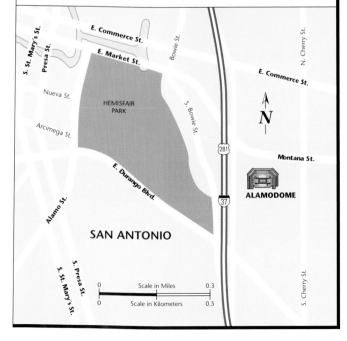

Nearby Hotels

▼▼ **Alamo Inn** *(Motel)*, 2203 E. Commerce St. (San Antonio), (210) 227-2203, $50-$110
▼▼▼ **Arbor House Inn & Suites** *(Historic Bed & Breakfast)*, 540 S. St. Mary's St. (San Antonio), (210) 472-2005, $95-$195
▼ **Days Inn-Downtown Laredo St** *(Motel)*, 1500 IH-35 S/IH-10 (San Antonio), (210) 271-3334, $40-$99
▼▼▼ **Riverwalk Inn** *(Bed & Breakfast)*, 329 Old Guilbeau (San Antonio), (210) 212-8300, $125-$180
▼▼▼▼ **San Antonio Marriott RiverCenter** *(Hotel)*, 101 Bowie St. (San Antonio), (210) 223-1000, $259-$279

Nearby Restaurants

▼▼ **The Bayous Riverside,** *(Seafood)*, 517 N. Presa (San Antonio), (210) 223-6403, $12-$26
▼▼▼▼ **Fig Tree Restaurant** *(Continental)*, 515 Villita St. in La Villita Historic Complex (San Antonio), (210) 224-1976, $24-$38 (dinner only)
▼▼ **Little Rhein Steakhouse** *(Steakhouse)*, 231 S. Alamo St. (San Antonio), (210) 225-2111, $28-$33 (dinner only)
▼ **Mi Tierra Cafe Y Panaderia** *(Mexican)*, 218 Produce Row (San Antonio), (210) 225-1262, $6-$17
▼▼ **Tower of the Americas Restaurant** *(American)*, 222 Hemisfair Plaza (San Antonio), (210) 223-3101, $16-$30

SINCE THE SUPERSONICS JOINED THE NBA in 1967, Seattle has experienced two distinct "Sonic Booms" — one in the late 1970s and another more recently in the mid-1990s. The tremors of this first blast were felt in 1975, when the Sonics advanced to the playoffs for the first time. As a young team, the Sonics had been struggling to find the magic despite a number of good players such as Fred "Downtown" Brown and the controversial Spencer Haywood, a 6-foot-9-inch forward whose brilliant plays and off-court problems kept him in the news. By the mid-1970s, however, all the elements began to come together and the team started winning games. With the 1977 acquisition of center Jack Sikma and rebound wizard Paul Silas, the Sonics were poised for greatness. The newcomers added depth to the squad and helped the Sonics take their first conference title. In the NBA finals, the team fell to Washington in seven games and vowed revenge. The following season the Sonics blasted to division and conference title wins and made easy work of the Bullets in five games of the NBA finals. After an inconsistent stretch in the 1980s, Seattle made a strong resurgence in the '90s. Led by Shawn Kemp, one of the most innovative slam-dunkers of his era, point guard Gary Payton and the brash and creative coach George Karl, the Sonics developed an inexhaustible and unconventional playbook. In the 1995–96 season the team shined once again; after big wins against the Houston Rockets and Utah Jazz, Seattle advanced to the finals for the second time. Unfortunately, the team was no match for a Bulls' squad led by Michael Jordan.

Vital Stats

Stadium Address:
305 Harrison St.,
Seattle, Wash.
Phone: (206) 684-7200
Web: nba.com/sonics,
seattlecenter.com
Box Office:
(206) 283-DUNK,
Mon.–Sat. 10–6
Media Coverage:
Radio: KJR (950 AM)
TV: KONG (Channel 6),
Fox Sports Net
Practice Facility:
Furtado Center,
Seattle, Wash.

Most Improved Player
• Dale Ellis (1986–87)

Coach of the Year
• Bernie Bickerstaff
(1986–87)

Sportsmanship
• Hersey Hawkins
(1998–99)

NBA Finals MVP
• Dennis Johnson (1979)

POSTSEASON
• **NBA Championships**.......1
(1978–79)
• **Western Conference Championships** 3
(1977–78, 1978–79, 1995–96)

RETIRED NUMBERS
• Nate McMillan (10)
• Lenny Wilkens (19)
• Fred Brown (32)
• Jack Sikma (43)

TEAM RECORDS
• **Fred Brown (1971–84)**
FG (game): 24 (Mar. 23, 1974)
FG (career): 6,006
Games (career): 963
Points (game): 58
(Mar. 23, 1974)
Points (career): 14,018

Jump Shot

• When the three-pointer was introduced to the NBA for the 1979–80 season, the Sonics Fred Brown led all NBA shooters with a .443 percentage.
• A Hall of Famer both as a player and a coach, Lenny Wilkens has strong ties to the Sonics. His first coaching stint came in Seattle in 1968–70 when he was a player/coach for the team.

• **James Donaldson (1980–83)**
FG Pct. (season): .609 (1981–82)
FG Pct. (career): .584
• **Dale Ellis (1986–99)**
Points (season): 2,253 (1988–89)
3-Pointers (game): 9 (April 20, 1990)
• **Jim Fox (1972–75)**
Rebounds (game): 30 (Dec. 26, 1973)
• **Spencer Haywood (1970–75)**
FG (season): 889 (1972–73)
Points-Per-Game (season): 29.2 (1972–73)
Points-Per-Game (career): 24.9
• **Shawn Kemp (1989–97)**
Blocks (game): 10 (Jan. 18, 1991)
Blocks (career): 959
• **Alton Lister (1986–89)**
Blocks (season): 180 (twice)
• **Nate McMillan (1986–98)**
Assists (game): 25 (Feb. 23, 1987)
• **Gary Payton (1990–present)**

"Sometimes people boo because they know you're good."
— Former Sonics Shawn Kemp, on playing at KeyArena as a Cavalier

Assists (career): 5,548
Steals (career): 1,756
3-Pointers (season): 177 (1999–2000)
3-Pointers (career): 707
• **Ricky Pierce (1990–94)**
FT Pct. (season): .925 (1990–91)
FT Pct. (career): .906
• **Detlef Schrempf (1993–99)**
3-Point Pct. (season): .514 (1994–95)
• **Jack Sikma (1977–86)**
Def. Rebounds (season): 815 (1981–82)
FT (game): 21 (Nov. 14, 1980)
FT (career): 3,044
Rebounds (season): 1,038 (1981–82)
Rebounds (career): 7,729
• **Don "Slick" Watts (1973–78)**
Steals (season): 261 (1975–76)
• **Marvin Webster (1977–78)**
Off. Rebounds (season): 361 (1977–78)
• **Lenny Wilkens (1968–72)**
Assists (season): 766 (1971–72)
Free Throws (season): 547 (1968–69)
• **Gus Williams (1977–84)**
Steals (game): 10 (Feb. 22, 1978)

LEAGUE HONORS
Defensive Player of the Year
• Gary Payton (1995–96)

Gary Payton is a force both on offense and defense.

Timeline

1966	1967	1970	1971	1974	1979	1983	1986	1992	1994	1996	1998	2000

- 1966: Seattle is granted NBA franchise
- 1967: Rookie Bob Rule pours in 47 points on Nov. 21 to set an early franchise record
- 1970: Lenny Wilkens tops NBA in assists with an average of 9.1 assists-per-game
- 1971: After lawsuits, NBA alters rules to allow Spencer Haywood to play for the Sonics before graduating from college
- 1974: Fred Brown sets a team scoring record with 58 points in a game
- 1979: Sonics win NBA crown
- 1983: Barry Ackerly buys the team
- 1986: Sonics acquire 3-point ace Dale Ellis from Dallas
- 1992: Team hires George Karl to rebuild team
- 1994: Sonics become the first No. 1 seed to lose to No. 8 seed in the playoffs
- 1996: Team loses the finals to the Bulls; Gary Payton named Defensive Player of the Year
- 1998: Nate McMillan retires after 12 seasons
- 2000: Gary Payton sinks 177 3-pointers, a team record

134

KeyArena:
Preserving the Tradition

SITUATED UNDER THE SHADOW of the famous Space Needle, the recently constructed KeyArena prides itself on its strong connection to Seattle's rich past. To preserve the tradition of the old Seattle Center Arena — the Sonics' first home — the architects of KeyArena decided to maintain the outer shell of the previous building and completely refurbish the interior with materials recycled from the Seattle 1962 World's Fair. The result is a fascinating architectural montage: The cobblestone inside the building comes from the former International Fountain, while the hi-tech concrete walls come from the NASA pavilion. It is this mixture of state-of-the-art technology and historical materials that makes KeyArena one of the NBA's most unique venues.

CONCESSIONS

KeyArena offers all the arena classics, along with a few extras such as clam chowder, sausages, stir-fry, Tex/Mex, fish and chips, frozen yogurt, specialty coffees and microbrewery beer. Vegetarians will find many options, including veggie hot dogs and salads.

GAME DAY TIPS

• **Gate hours:** Gates open one hour prior to tip-off.
• **Prohibited items:** Food and beverages, cameras, video and audio recorders, coolers, cans, bottles, pets, fireworks, laser pointers and dangerous projectiles are prohibited. Smoking is forbidden inside the arena, but is permitted in designated outdoor areas.
• **Ticket tips:** Since KeyArena is one of the NBA's smallest venues, it's no surprise that even the cheapest seats offer a good view of the court. Tickets are usually easy to come by, except for Lakers and Trail Blazers games.
• **Lost and found:** (206) 684-7200.

Arena Facts

Opened: Oct. 26, 1995
Cost: $101.2 million
Capacity: 17,072
Home Sweet Home:
• One of the NBA's smallest venues, KeyArena puts fans right on top of the action. This added intimacy has helped spur the Sonics to an impressive 171-59 home record, or .743 winning percentage, since the arena opened in 1995.

Seating Plan

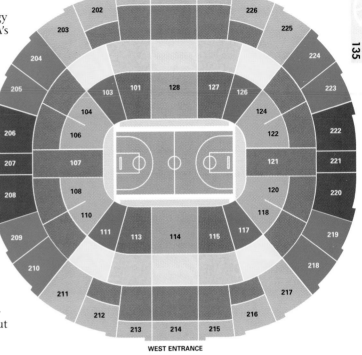

▢ Courtside	
▢ Club Seats	
▢ Club Seats	
▢ $110	
▢ $95	
▢ $90	
▢ $65	
▢ $60
▢ $40
▢ $25
▢ $15
▢ $9

ATM Sections 106, 126
♿ Sections 22, 125, 209, 224

EAST ENTRANCE

WEST ENTRANCE

Directions: Take I-5 to Mercer St. exit and follow signs to Seattle Center. KeyArena is on the northwest corner of the grounds, accessible via N. 1st Ave. By Public Transportation: The Seattle Center Monorail departs regularly from Westlake Center in downtown Seattle. Fifteen bus routes go to the Seattle Center. Call (206) 684-7200 for information. **Parking:** The Seattle Center has several lots and garages for a total of some 4,000 spots. Patrons with disabilities are best accommodated in Lot 6. There are also private lots in the area on Elliot, Westlake and 7th Aves.

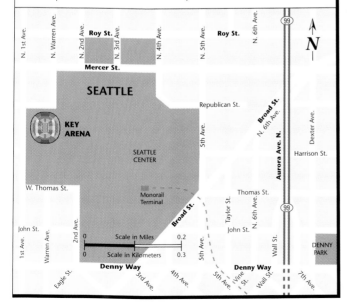

Nearby Hotels

▼▼▼ **Best Western Executive Inn/Seattle** (*Motor Inn*), 200 Taylor Ave. N. (Seattle), (206) 448-9444, $80-$170
▼▼▼ **Hampton Inn & Suites-Downtown/Seattle Center** (*Motel*), 700 5th Ave. N. (Seattle), (206) 282-7700, $94-$149
▼▼▼ **Holiday Inn Express-Downtown Seattle** (*Motel*), 226 Aurora Ave. N. (Seattle), (206) 441-7222, $89-$119
▼▼▼ **Travelodge by the Space Needle** (*Motel*), 200 6th Ave. N. (Seattle), (206) 441-7878, $89-$179
▼▼▼▼ **The Westin Seattle** (*Hotel*), 1900 5th Ave. (Seattle), (206) 728-1000, $139-$305

Nearby Restaurants

▼▼▼ **Brasa** (*Mediterranean*), 2107 Third Ave. (Seattle), (206) 728-4220, $17-$23 (dinner only)
▼▼▼ **Kaspar's** (*Seafood*), 19 W. Harrison St. (Seattle), (206) 298-0123, $15-$21 (dinner only)
▼▼▼ **Nikko Restaurant** (*Ethnic*), 1900 5th Ave. in The Westin Seattle (Seattle), (206) 322-4641, $11-$25
▼▼▼ **Roy St. Bistro** (*Continental*), 174 Roy St. (Seattle), (206) 284-9093, $11-$15 (dinner only)
▼▼▼ **Sky City Restaurant** (*American*), 219 4th Ave. N. (Seattle), (206) 443-2100, $24-$42

TORONTO RAPTORS

THE ARRIVAL OF THE TORONTO RAPTORS franchise did not mark the beginning of NBA basketball in Toronto, but rather, the return. The long-forgotten Toronto Huskies, were charter members of the NBA in 1946 and had actually played in the new league's first game, a 68-66 loss in Toronto. That team folded after the 1947–48 season, and NBA basketball did not return until the Raptors tipped off against Vancouver in November 1995. The Raptors won that game easily, and that early result seems to have been a glimpse of the future for both franchises. While the Grizzlies have continually struggled, the Raptors, after a few years of obligatory expansion woes, have become as fierce as their name suggests. The early days of the Raptors are dominated by a couple of names — Isiah Thomas and Damon Stoudamire. The two are linked. Stoudamire, the stand-out point guard from Arizona, was Thomas' first draft pick as head of Raptors' basketball operations. But after two losing seasons, Thomas resigned. Less than a year later, Stoudamire was dealt to Portland. Fortunes turned for the franchise with the acquisition of guard Vince Carter in 1998. Carter quickly caught the league's attention, scoring 18.3 points per game as a rookie, and leading the team to its best-ever finish. A year later, he emerged as a bona fide superstar, earning an all-star nod for his amazing scoring ability and leading the Raptors to the playoffs in just their fifth year of existence. Now the Raptors hope to follow in the tradition of another Toronto franchise, the Blue Jays, and take basketball's ultimate prize; a championship.

Stadium Address:
40 Bay St.,
Toronto, Ont.
Phone: (416) 815-5500
Web: nba.com/raptors,
theaircanadacentre.com
Box Office:
(416) 366-DUNK,
Mon.–Fri. 9:30–5,
game days until halftime
Media Coverage:
Radio: The FAN (590 AM)
TV: CTV Sportsnet, TSN
Practice Facility:
Air Canada Center,
Toronto, Ont.

POSTSEASON
• **Playoff Appearances**........1
(1999–2000)

TEAM RECORDS
• **Dee Brown (1998–2000)**
3-Point FG (game): 9
(Apr. 28, 1999)
• **Marcus Camby (1996–98)**
Blocks (game): 11
(Apr. 14, 1998)
Blocks (season): 230 (1997–98)
Blocks (career): 360
Def. Rebounds (game): 15
(Mar. 21, 1997)
• **Vince Carter (1998–present)**
FG (game): 20 (Jan. 14, 2000)
FG (season): 788 (1999–2000)
FG Att. (season): 1,696
(1999–2000)
FT (game): 14 (tie) (Feb. 9, 2000)

Jump Shot

• *In his 75 regular season games in 2000–01, Vince Carter led the team in scoring 66 times. In the seven-game Eastern Conference finals, Carter topped all Raptors' shooters six times.*
• *The Raptors have the shortest player in NBA history: Muggsy Bogues stands just 5 feet 3 inches, but has scored more than 6,000 points in his career.*

FT (season): 436 (1999–2000)
Points (game): 51
(Feb. 27, 2000)
Points (season): 2,107
(1999–2000)
Points-Per-Game (season):
25.7 (1999–2000)
Points-Per-Game (career): 22.9
30+ Points Games (season):
25 (1999–2000)
30+ Points Games (career): 28
• **Doug Christie (1996–2000)**
Def. Rebounds (career): 1,121
Disqualifications (career): 15
FG (career): 1,532
FG Att. (career): 3,698
FT (career): 953
Games (career): 314
Minutes (career): 10,916
Off. Rebounds (career): 413
Personal Fouls (career) 821
Points (career): 4,448
Rebounds (career): 1,448
Steals (game): 9 (Feb. 25, 1997)
Steals (season): 201 (1996–97)
Steals (career): 664
Steals-Per-Game (season):
2.48 (1996–97)
Turnovers (career): 767
3-Point FGs (career): 431
• **Antonio Davis (1999–present)**
Def. Rebounds (season): 461
Rebounds (season): 696
(1999–2000)
Rebounds-Per-Game
(season): 8.8 (1999–2000)
Rebounds-Per-Game
(career): 8.8

Vince Carter is one of the NBA's most electrifying players.

• **Popeye Jones (1996–98)**
Off. Rebounds (season): 270
(1996–97)
Rebounds (game): 21
(Dec. 11, 1996)
• **Tracy McGrady (1997–2000)**
Off. Rebounds (career): 413
• **Tracy Murray (1995–96)**
FT Pct. (career): .831
3-Point FG Pct. (season):
.422 (1995–96)

"I'd like to have everyone stick together because I think we can build something great here."

— *Raptors superstar Vince Carter following the 2000–01 season*

3-Point FG Pct. (career): .422
• **Charles Oakley (1998–present)**
Personal Fouls (season): 294
(1999–2000)
• **Carlos Rogers (1995–98)**
FG Pct. (career): .521
• **Damon Stoudamire (1995–98)**
Assists (game): 19
(Feb. 27, 1996)
Assists (season): 709 (1996–97)
Assists (career): 1,761
Assists-Per-Game (season):
9.3 (1995–96)
Assists-Per-Game (career): 8.8
Minutes (season): 3,311
(1996–97)
Turnovers (game) 12
(Jan. 25, 1997)
Turnovers (season): 288
(1996–97)
3-Point FGs (season): 176
(1996–97)
• **Zan Tabak (1995–98)**
FG Pct (season): .543 (1995–96)

LEAGUE HONORS
Rookie of the Year
• **Damon Stoudamire (1995–96)**
• **Vince Carter (1998–99)**

Timeline

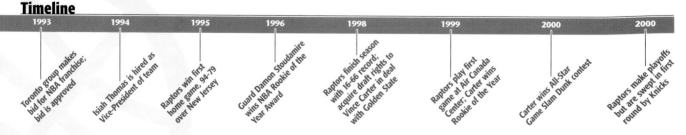

1993 — Toronto group makes bid for NBA franchise; bid is approved

1994 — Isiah Thomas is hired as Vice-President of team

1995 — Raptors win first home game, 94-79 over New Jersey

1996 — Guard Damon Stoudamire wins NBA Rookie of the Year Award

1998 — Raptors finish season with 16-66 record; acquire draft rights to Vince Carter in deal with Golden State

1999 — Raptors play first game at Air Canada Center; Carter wins Rookie of the Year

2000 — Carter wins All-Star Game Slam Dunk contest

2000 — Raptors make playoffs but are swept in first round by Knicks

AIR CANADA CENTRE:
ONE OF THE NBA'S BEST

OPENED IN 1999, the Air Canada Centre is widely acknowledged as one of best arenas in the NBA. Set spectacularly in the heart of downtown Toronto, it contains, along with a top-notch game court, a full practice court and team offices. It also features wide upholstered seats and excellent concessions. The top-flight sound system and television monitors make sure that you don't miss any action. The Air Canada Centre is one of the few facilities in the NBA to be wholly owned by the team. The entire venture was privately funded.

CONCESSIONS

The Air Canada Centre offers food ranging from traditional hot dogs and hamburgers to sushi, chicken wings, pizza, submarines and deli. Vegetarians can choose from a variety of wraps, sanwiches and salads. There is also a pasta bar. The stadium has an in-house brewery.

Arena Facts

Opened: *Feb. 20, 1999*
Cost: *$265 million*
Capacity: *19,800*
Home Sweet Home:
• *Known more as a hockey town, Toronto has proven it has a large and raucous basketball fan base as well. During the 2000–01 season, vocal Raptors fans helped their team amass a stalwart 27-14 record.*

GAME DAY TIPS

• **Gate hours:** Gates open one hour prior to tip-off.
• **Prohibited items:** Bottles, cans, coolers, sticks, weapons, fireworks, skateboards, rollerblades, video cameras, helium balloons, outside food and beverages are prohibited. Smoking is allowed outside Gates 4 and 5A.
• **Ticket tips:** The Raptors are becoming increasingly popular and tickets to the see them are getting difficult to come by. Fortunately, the newly built Air Canada Center offers great views

from any section.
• **Lost and found:** (416)

815-5958 to speak to a fan advocate.

Seating Plan

■ Side Prime	$130		■ Balcony Baseline	$20
■ Side	$110		■ Sprite Zone	$10.50
■ Air Canada Club	$110		ATM Sections 105/106, 116/117
■ Baseline Prime	$95		323/324
■ Lower Bowl Endzone	$66		♿ Sections 104–106, 115–117,
■ Balcony Prime	$38		309, 317, 319
■ Balcony	$27			

Directions: *Take Gardiner Expwy. to York St. exit, then continue one block north.* By Subway: *Yonge-University-Spadina Line to Union Station. Call the Toronto Transit Commission at (416) 369-INFO for information.* By Train: *The GO Train to Union Station. Call (416) 869-3200 for schedules.* **Parking:** *The center's underground parking is not public, but there are 13,000 spaces within walking distance on King St. W., York St., Lakeshore Blvd., and Queen's Quay W. Disabled patrons can call (416) 815-5743 to reserve an underground spot. A drop-off point is located on the west side of the arena.*

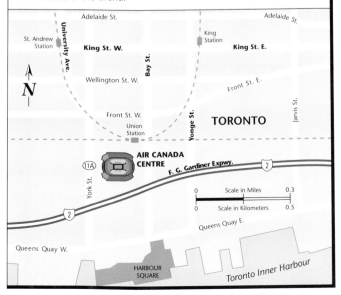

Nearby Hotels

▼▼▼▼ **Crowne Plaza Toronto Centre** (*Hotel*), 225 Front St. W. (Toronto), (416) 597-1400, $189-$239
▼▼▼▼ **The Fairmont Royal York** (*Classic Hotel*), 100 Front St. W. (Toronto), (416) 368-2511, $149-$249
▼▼▼ **Novotel Toronto Centre** (*Hotel*), 45 The Esplanade (Toronto), (416) 367-8900, $225-$250
▼▼ **The Strathcona Hotel** (*Hotel*), 60 York St. (Toronto), (416) 363-3321, $99-$149
▼▼▼▼ **The Westin Harbour Castle** (*Hotel*), One Harbour Square (Toronto), (416) 869-1600, $149-$239

Nearby Restaurants

▼▼ **Hothouse Cafe Inc** (*American*), 35 Church St. (Toronto), (416) 366-7800, $11-$13
▼▼ **Joe Badali's Ristorante Italiano** (*Italian*), 156 Front St. W. (Toronto), (416) 977-3064, $9-$17
▼▼ **Shopsy's Delicatessen Restaurant** (*American*), 33 Yonge St. (Toronto), (416) 365-3333, $8-$10
▼▼ **Tom Jones Steakhouse & Seafood** (*Steak & Seafood*), 17 Leader Ln. (Toronto), (416) 366-6583, $21-$45
▼ **Wayne Gretzky's Restaurant** (*Canadian*), 99 Blue Jays Way (Toronto), (416) 979-7825, $7-$26

UTAH JAZZ

IF THERE WERE AN AWARD FOR THE BEST TEAM never to have won a championship, the Utah Jazz might just take the crown. With an amazing 19 consecutive trips to the playoffs and two visits to the finals in 1997 and '98, the Jazz franchise has established itself as one of the game's elite. But it wasn't always that way. Playing out of New Orleans for its first five seasons, the team went nine years without even a taste of the postseason. The problem wasn't a lack of scoring. Early Jazz superstars such as Pete Maravich and Adrian Dantley provided that particular commodity, each winning a NBA scoring title along the way. But it wasn't until the arrival of a pair of draft picks, John Stockton in 1984 and Karl Malone in 1985, that the Utah Jazz became a team to be feared. With a slight 6-foot-1-inch frame, Stockton doesn't appear to be a franchise player. But appearances can be deceiving. With exceptional court vision, Stockton has developed into perhaps the greatest passer the game has known. When he teamed up with Malone, a devastating power forward, it was pure magic. With these two superstars at its core for more than 15 seasons, the Jazz has performed like a well-oiled machine. The team reached a pinnacle with two trips to the finals in the late 1990s. Unfortunately for Jazz fans, Michael Jordan was also on top of his game and Utah lost both series. But although they have made an indelible print in the basketball record book, Utah's future Hall of Famers show no sign of slowing down. And that is music to every Jazz fan's ears.

Jazz guard John Stockton holds the NBA record for career assists.

POSTSEASON
- **Western Conference Championships** 2
(1996–97, 1997–98)

RETIRED NUMBERS
- **Frank Layden (1)**
- **Pete Maravich (7)**
- **Darrell Griffith (35)**
- **Mark Eaton (53)**

TEAM RECORDS
- **Adrian Dantley (1979–86)**
FG Pct. (career): .562
FT (season): 813 (1983–84)
FT Att. (season): 946 (1983–84)
Points-Per-Game (career): 29.6
- **Mark Eaton (1982–94)**
Blocks (season): 456
(1984–85)
Blocks (career): 3,064

Jump Shot

- *Jazz coach Jerry Sloan is one of the most successful in NBA history. He stands in the top 10 all-time in winning percentage, playoff wins and consecutive playoff appearances.*
- *When the All-Star game came to Utah in 1993, Karl Malone and John Stockton put on a show, leading the West to victory and collecting co-MVP awards.*

Blocks-Per-Game (season): 5.56 (1984–85)
- **Jeff Hornacek (1994–2000)**
Ft Pct. (season): .950
(1999–2000)
FT Pct. (career): .897
3-Point FG Pct. (season): .478
(1999–2000)
3-Point FG Pct. (career): .428
- **Adam Keefe (1994–2000)**
FG Pct. (season): .577
(1994–95)
- **Karl Malone (1985–present)**
Def. Rebounds (career): 9,486
FG (season): 914 (1989–90)
FG (career): 11,435
FG Att. (career): 21,777
FT (career): 8,100
FT Att. (career): 11,027
Off. Rebounds (career): 3,132
Personal Fouls (career): 3,813
Points (season): 2,540
(1989–90)
Points (career): 31,041
Rebounds (career): 12, 618
Turnovers (season): 325
(1987–88)
Turnovers (career): 3,704
- **Pete Maravich (1974–80)**
Points-Per-Game (season):

31.1 (1976–77)
FG Att. (season): 2,047
(1976–77)
- **Len "Truck" Robinson (1977–79)**
Rebounds (season): 1,288
(1977–78)
Rebounds-Per-Game (season): 15.8 (1977–78)
- **Byron Russell (1993–present)**
3-Point FG (season): 108
(1996–97)
3-Point FG Att. (season): 268
(1999–2000)
- **John Stockton (1984–present)**
Assists (season): 1,164
(1990–91)
Assists-Per-Game (season): 14.5 (1990–91)
Assists (career): 13,790
Games (career): 1,258
Steals (season): 263
(1988–89)
Steals (career): 2,701
Steals-Per-Game (season): 3.21 (1988–89)
3-Point FG (career): 730
3-Point FG Att. (career): 1,912

> *"[Malone's] combination of durability and productivity may never again be duplicated in the NBA."*
>
> — *Brad Greenberg, former 76ers GM*

Vital Stats

Stadium Address:
301 W. S. Temple St., Salt Lake City, Utah
Phone: (801) 325-2000
Web: nba.com/jazz, deltacenter.com
Box Office:
(801) 355-DUNK, Mon.–Fri. 9–6, Sat. game days until halftime
Media Coverage:
Radio: KFAN 1320 AM
TV: KJZZ (Channel 14), Fox Sports Net
Practice Facility:
Franklin Covey Wellness Center, Salt Lake City, Utah

LEAGUE HONORS
NBA MVP
- Karl Malone (1996–97, 1998–99)

Rookie of the Year
- Darrell Griffith (1980–81)

Defensive Player of the Year
- Mark Eaton (1984–85, 1988–89)

Coach of the Year
- Frank Layden (1983–84)

Basketball Hall of Fame
- Pete Maravich (1987)

Timeline

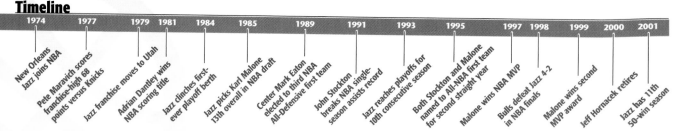

| 1974 | 1977 | 1979 | 1981 | 1984 | 1985 | 1989 | 1991 | 1993 | 1995 | 1997 | 1998 | 1999 | 2000 | 2001 |

New Orleans Jazz joins NBA / Pete Maravich scores franchise-high 68 points versus Knicks / Jazz franchise moves to Utah / Adrian Dantley wins NBA scoring title / Jazz clinches first-ever playoff berth / Jazz picks Karl Malone 13th overall in NBA draft / Center Mark Eaton elected to third NBA All-Defensive first team / John Stockton breaks NBA single-season assists record / Jazz reaches playoffs for 10th consecutive season / Both Stockton and Malone named to All-NBA first team for second straight year / Malone wins NBA MVP / Bulls defeat Jazz 4-2 in NBA finals / Malone wins second MVP award / Jeff Hornacek retires / Jazz has 11th 50-win season

138

DELTA CENTER:
HITTIN' HIGH NOTES WITH THE JAZZ

THE DELTA CENTER'S exterior appearance might lead you to think it was a large office building rather than the home of a NBA franchise. But the large, silver, cube-shaped building, which opened in 1991, is home to one of the league's most successful franchises. Located in downtown Salt Lake City near such attractions as the Mormon Tabernacle and Temple Square, the Delta Center is ultramodern with great sight lines and fan amenities. Look for the 18-wheel truck in the parking lot painted with western scenes. It belongs to Karl Malone.

CONCESSIONS
The concessions at the Delta Center offer standard items such as hot dogs, popcorn, ice cream, hamburgers, subs, Philly cheese steaks, pizza and a selection of domestic beers, including some less common local varieties. Vegetarian choices include baked potatoes and salads.

GAME DAY TIPS
• **Gate hours:** Gates open one hour prior to tip-off.
• **Prohibited items:** Video cameras, laser pointers, food and beverages, including outside alcohol, weapons, beachballs, and frisbees are prohibited. No smoking is allowed inside the facility, but smoking is permitted outside in designated areas.
• **Ticket tips:** The Utah Jazz is a popular team and although its games rarely sell out, don't expect to get a wide selection of seating options if you buy tickets at the last minute. The Jazz is a perennial playoff team and once the postseason starts, seats are significantly tougher to come by. Sight lines at the Delta Center are good, even from the "nosebleed" sections.
• **Lost and found:** (801) 325-2033.

Arena Facts

Opened: Oct. 9, 1991
Cost: $64 million
Capacity: 19,911
Home Sweet Home:
• Jazz fans are renowned as some of the NBA's most vocal and supportive. How much do they love their Jazz? In February 2001, 93 couples were married at the Delta Center during a game halftime. One bride wore a Jazz warm-up suit.

Seating Plan

- ■ **$82.50**
- ■ **$77**
- ■ **$72**
- ■ **$66**
- ■ **$50.50**
- ■ **$32.50**
- ■ **$25**
- ■ **$17**
- □ **$10**
- ATM **Concourse sections 7, 18**
- ♿ **Throughout**

ENTRANCE

ENTRANCE

Directions: Take I-15 to 6th S. St. off-ramp. Turn left on 300 W. St., left onto 100 S. St. **By Train:** The new TRAX train will get you closer to the arena than any of the parking lots and is free from within the downtown core. Get off at Delta Center stop. Call UTA at (801) 743-3882 for more information. **Parking:** The Delta Center has no on-site lot, but ample parking is available at private lots in the area on Main, S. W. Temple, 200 W., and W. Broadway Sts. Many lots reserve spots for people with disabilities. Guests with disabilities may be dropped off on S. Temple St.

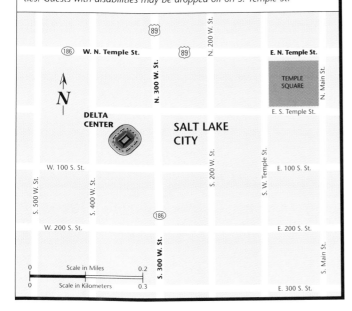

Nearby Hotels
▼▼▼ **Best Western Salt Lake Plaza** *(Hotel)*, 122 W. S. Temple St. (Salt Lake City), (801) 521-0130, $69-$250
▼▼▼ **Howard Johnson Express Inn** *(Motel)*, 121 N. 300 W. St. (Salt Lake City), (801) 521-3450, $59-$89
▼▼▼ **The Inn at Temple Square** *(Hotel)*, 225 N. State St. (Salt Lake City), (801) 575-1112, $119-$229
▼▼▼▼ **Salt Lake City Marriott Downtown** *(Hotel)*, 75 S. W. Temple St. (Salt Lake City), (801) 531-0800, $75-$179
▼▼▼ **Wyndham Salt Lake City** *(Hotel)*, 215 W. S. Temple St. (Salt Lake City), (801) 531-7500, $109-$129

Nearby Restaurants
▼▼▼ **Christophers Seafood & Steakhouse** *(Steak & Seafood)*, 110 W. Broadway in the Peery Hotel (Salt Lake City), (801) 519-8515, $12-$24
▼▼▼ **JW's Steak House** *(Steak & Seafood)*, 75 S. W. Temple St. in the Salt Lake City Marriott Downtown (Salt Lake City), (801) 531-0800, $18-$27 (dinner only)
▼▼ **Lamb's Restaurant** *(American)*, 169 S. Main St. (Salt Lake City), (801) 364-7166, $13-$19
▼▼▼ **Market Street Grill** *(Seafood)*, 48 W. Market St. (Salt Lake City), (801) 322-4669, $11-$30
▼▼▼▼ **Metropolitan** *(American)*, 173 W. Broadway S. (Salt Lake City), (801) 364-3472, $18-$32 (dinner only)

WASHINGTON WIZARDS

THE CHICAGO PACKERS, the earliest incarnation of the Wizards franchise, played its first game on October 19, 1961, suffering a 120-103 loss to the Knicks. As with most expansion teams, it took the franchise eight years to put together its first winning season. But luckily for fans of the team, the Packers' first season was also Walt Bellamy's rookie campaign. Bellamy, a gifted player, set franchise records for scoring and rebounding that year that still stand today. The team moved to Baltimore in 1963 and was renamed the Baltimore Bullets. Five years later the arrival of Wes Unseld marked the beginning of the glory years for the franchise. Not only was that the team's first winning season, but Unseld, a fearsome rebounder, had the unlikely honor of winning both Rookie of the Year and league MVP awards. The team let some talent pass through its hands, most notably Earl "the Pearl" Monroe, who was traded to New York after four brilliant seasons. But the team also picked up some greats, including Elvin Hayes. Together Hayes and Unseld would carry the franchise, located out of Washington since 1973, to its only NBA championship, a four-game sweep of Seattle in 1978. Following the 1980–81 season, Unseld retired and Hayes was traded to the Rockets and a golden era in Bullets' basketball was over. Since then success has been hard to come by. Despite some great talent powering the team, including Moses Malone, Jeff Malone, Bernard King and Chris Webber, Washington has made just six playoff appearances since. Renamed the Wizards in 1997, the team has hired Michael Jordan as president to help find the magic.

"He has stepped up like he has been playing this game for years."
— Juwan Howard, on young teammate Richard Hamilton, considered a top NBA sixth man.

Richard Hamilton is one of the NBA's promising young players.

Jump Shot

- Wizards GM Wes Unseld has enjoyed a remarkably long tenure with the team. He first donned a Bullets jersey in 1968 and was hired immediately after retiring as a player in 1981. His years of service stands at 34 years and counting.
- In 1997 as part of an anti-violence campaign, the team changed its name from Bullets to Wizards.

POSTSEASON
- NBA Championships.......1
(1977–1978)
- Eastern Conference Championships 4
(1970–71, 1974–75, 1977–78, 1978–79)
- Eastern Division Titles.....1
(1968–69)
- Central Division Titles.....5
(1970–71, 1971–72, 1972–73, 1973–74, 1974–75)
- Atlantic Division Titles 1
(1978–79)

RETIRED NUMBERS
- Elvin Hayes (11)
- Gus Johnson (25)
- Wes Unseld (41)

TEAM RECORDS
- **Michael Adams (1986–87, 1991–94)**
Steals (game): 9 (Nov. 1, 1991)
- **Greg Ballard (1977–85)**
Steals (career): 762
- **Walt Bellamy (1961–65)**
Points (season): 2,495 (1961–62)
Points-Per-Game (season): 31.6 (1961–62)
Points-Per-Game (career): 27.6
Rebounds (season): 1,500 (1961–62)
Rebounds-Per-Game (career): 16.7
- **Manute Bol (1985–88)**
Blocks (game): 15 (Jan. 25, 1986)
- **Rex Chapman (1991–95)**
3-Point FG (game): 8 (Nov. 12, 1994)
- **Bob Dandridge (1977–81)**
Turnovers (game): 11 (Feb. 7, 1978)
- **Elvin Hayes (1972–81)**
Blocks (career): 1,558
FG (game): 20 (Mar. 13, 1977)
FG (career): 6,251
FG Att. (career): 13,658
FT (career): 3,046
FT Att. (career): 4,499
Points (career): 15,551
- **Juwan Howard (1994–2000)**
Turnovers (career): 1,220
- **Bernard King (1987–91)**
Points (game): 52 (Dec. 29, 1990)

- **Tim Legler (1995–99)**
3-Point FG Pct. (career): .476
- **Jeff Malone (1983–90)**
FT Pct. (career): .869
- **Moses Malone (1986–88)**
FT (game): 21 (Dec. 29, 1986)
- **Gheorghe Muresan (1993–98)**
FG Pct. (career): .578
- **Tracy Murray (1996–99)**
3-Point FG (career): 410
3-Point FG Att. (career): 1,069
- **Kevin Porter (1972–75, 1979–83)**
Assists (game): 24 (Mar. 23, 1980)
- **Rod Strickland (1996–2000)**
Assists-Per-Game (career): 9.2

Vital Stats

Stadium Address:
601 F St. NW, Washington, D.C.
Phone: (202) 628-3200
Web: nba.com/wizards, mcicenter.com
Box Office: (202) 628-3200, Mon.–Sat. 10–5:30, event days
Media Coverage:
Radio: WTEM (980 AM)
TV: WBDC (Channel 50), Home Team Sports
Training Facility: MCI Center, Washington, D.C.

- **Wes Unseld (1968–81)**
Assists (career): 3,822
Games (career): 984
Personal Fouls (career): 2,762
Rebounds (game): 30 (April 6, 1975)
Rebounds (career): 13,769

LEAGUE HONORS
NBA MVP
- Wes Unseld (1968–69)

Rookie of the Year
- Earl Monroe (1967–68)
- Wes Unseld (1968–69)

Coach of the Year
- Gene Shue (1968–69, 1981–82)

NBA Finals MVP
- Wes Unseld (1978)

Basketball Hall of Fame
- Wes Unseld (1988)
- Dave Bing (1990)
- Elvin Hayes (1990)
- Earl Monroe (1990)
- Walt Bellamy (1993)
- Bailey Howell (1997)

Timeline

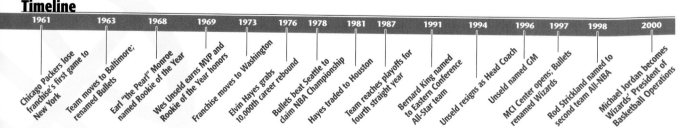

1961	1963	1968	1969	1973	1976	1978	1981	1987	1991	1994	1996	1997	1998	2000
Chicago Packers lose franchise's first game to New York	Team moves to Baltimore; renamed Bullets	Earl "the Pearl" Monroe named Rookie of the Year	Wes Unseld earns MVP and Rookie of the Year honors	Franchise moves to Washington	Elvin Hayes grabs 10,000th career rebound	Bullets beat Seattle to claim NBA Championship	Hayes traded to Houston	Team reaches playoffs for fourth straight year	Bernard King named to Eastern Conference All-Star team	Unseld resigns as Head Coach	Unseld named GM	MCI Center opens, Bullets renamed Wizards	Rod Strickland named to second team All-NBA	Michael Jordan becomes Wizards' President of Basketball Operations

140

MCI CENTER: A CAPITAL VENUE

THE WASHINGTON WIZARDS HOPED its first game in the new MCI Center in 1997 might be a sign of things to come. It was a rare home win before a sellout crowd. The Washington, D.C., arena features a restrained exterior that blends in well with the neighborhood and a colorful interior that is meant to build excitement as fans near the entrances to the seating bowl. The ultramodern facility includes restaurants and shops and is connected to a light rail station, which makes travel to the games easy and inexpensive.

CONCESSIONS

MCI Center offers fans standard concessions (hamburgers, hot dogs, pizza and the like) with a few extra treats. Visitors should try soft pretzels prepared in front of their eyes, food from a local Chinese restaurant and a wide assortment of fun desserts for the kids.

For vegetarians, one of the stands offers a variety of wraps.

GAME DAY TIPS
• **Gate hours:** Gates open one hour prior to tip-off.
• **Prohibited items:** Food, beverages and alcohol are prohibited. Laser pointers, video cameras and flash cameras also are not permitted. Banners and signs are allowed provided they are not offensive and do obstruct people's views. With the exception of animals that provide service to the disabled, animals are not permitted in the arena. Smoking is allowed only in designated areas.
• **Ticket tips:** The Wizards sold out only seven games

Arena Facts

Opened: Dec. 2, 1997
Cost: $260 million
Capacity: 20,674
Home Sweet Home:
• *The Wizards fans are notoriously tough on their hard-luck team. In recent years there has been little home-court advantage as the fans have regularly jeered the team and even owner Michael Jordan.*

Seating Plan

⬜ .... N/A	⬛ $40
⬛ .... N/A	⬛ $40
▨ .... N/A	⬜ $32
⬜ $77	⬜ $19
⬛ $67	**ATM** Section 112, F St. entrance,
⬛ $67	Discovery Store
⬛ $67	♿ Throughout
▨ $67	

F ST. ENTRANCE

in the 1999–2000 season. Tickets are usually available for most games, although some of the big teams such as the Lakers, New York and Portland tend to be more popular with the Washington faithful.
• **Lost and found:** (202) 661-5678.

Directions: *Take I-66 to Constitution Ave., left on 7th St. SW. Or, I-395 north, bear right and follow to 12 St. exit, right on Constitution Ave., left on 7th St. SW. Or, Rte. 50/New York Ave. to 7th St. NW and turn left. By Subway: Metrorail Red, Yellow or Green line to Gallery Place/Chinatown station. For more information, call Washington Metropolitan Area Transit Authority (WMATA) at (202) 637-7000* **Parking:** *About 2,500 spots are available to the public at the MCI Center garage; 24 spots are for the disabled. Extra parking can be found on D, E, F, H, I, 4th, 5th and 6th Sts.*

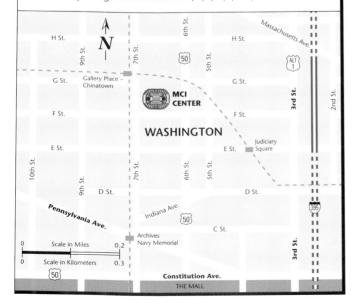

Nearby Hotels

▼▼▼ **Channel Inn Hotel** *(Motor Inn)*, 650 Water St. SW (Washington, D.C.), (202) 554-2400, $135-$150
▼▼▼ **Courtyard by Marriott-Convention Center** *(Hotel)*, 900 F St. NW (Washington, D.C.), (202) 638-4600, $79-$231
▼▼▼ **Grand Hyatt Washington at Washington Center** *(Hotel)*, 1000 H St. NW (Washington, D.C.), (202) 582-1234, $265-$290
▼▼▼ **Henley Park Hotel** *(Historic Hotel)*, 926 Massachusetts Ave. NW (Washington, D.C.), (202) 638-5200, $205-$265
▼▼ **Red Roof Inn Downtown** *(Motel)*, 500 H St. NW (Washington, D.C.), (202) 289-5959, $115-$175

Nearby Restaurants

▼▼▼ **701 Pennsylvania Avenue** *(Continental)*, 701 Pennsylvania Ave. NW (Washington, D.C.), (202) 393-0701, $15-$23
▼▼ **District Chophouse & Brewery** *(American)*, 509 7th St. NW (Washington, D.C.), (202) 347-3434, $19-$28
▼▼ **Hunan Chinatown** *(Chinese)*, 624 H St. NW (Washington, D.C.), (202) 783-5858, $10-$20
▼▼ **Les Halles** *(French)*, 1201 Pennsylvania Ave. NW (Washington, D.C.), (202) 347-6848, $14-$21
▼▼▼▼ **The Willard Room** *(American)*, 1401 Pennsylvania Ave. NW in The Willard Inter-Continental (Washington, D.C.), (202) 637-7440, $23-$29

FOOT

1

2

3

BALL

AFC East
Buffalo Bills
Indianapolis Colts
Miami Dolphins
New England Patriots
New York Jets

AFC Central
Baltimore Ravens
Cincinnati Bengals
Cleveland Browns
Jacksonville Jaguars
Pittsburgh Steelers
Tennessee Titans

AFC West
Denver Broncos
Kansas City Chiefs
Oakland Raiders
San Diego Chargers
Seattle Seahawks

NFC East
Arizona Cardinals
Dallas Cowboys
Philadelphia Eagles
New York Giants
Washington Redskins

NFC Central
Chicago Bears
Detroit Lions
Green Bay Packers
Minnesota Vikings
Tampa Bay Buccaneers

NFC West
Atlanta Falcons
Carolina Panthers
New Orleans Saints
St. Louis Rams
San Francisco 49ers

6

THE GAME

THE PARALLELS BETWEEN war and football are obvious, built into the very language of the game. In the struggle for territory, measured one yard at a time, defenses blitz and offenses march, all while huge linemen battle it out in the trenches. Quarterbacks, sometimes referred to as field generals, lead air attacks from shotgun formations, opting for quick strikes or a devastating long bomb to swing the momentum in the favor of their team. On the other side of the ball, a defensive end can turn the tide by swooping in and sacking the quarterback, much like a marauding army sacks an unsuspecting town.

There is no denying that football is a violent sport. Each play is designed as a series of collisions between men who, as the years go by, are getting bigger. Ironically, despite the huge difference in size and speed of today's players compared to football's pioneers, the modern game is relatively tame. In the 1905 college season alone, there were 18 deaths and 149 serious injuries during the college football season. The public was so horrified by the carnage that President Theodore Roosevelt considered banning football forever unless officials made it safer.

The violence is inescapable, an integral part of the game's lore. In a 1914 game against the Akron Indians, a team that was led by star George "Peggy" Parratt, Canton's captain Harry Turner broke his back and died just hours later. Legend has it that Turner's last words were, "I know I must go, but I am satisfied, for we beat Peggy Parratt."

People still talk about Chuck Bednarik's devastating hit on the Giants' star RB Frank Gifford in 1960, forcing Gifford out of the sport for more than a year with head injuries. And will anyone forget the sight and sound of Joe Theisman's leg snapping mid-shin as he was hit by Lawrence Taylor in 1985?

DEFINING MOMENTS

Some players are defined by the violence. Legendary linebackers such as Joe Schmidt, Dick Butkus and Ray Nitschke hurled themselves into each fray, covering themselves in mud, blood and glory. In one season alone, LB Fred Naumetz split nine helmets as a result of collisions. During a match at Wrigley Field in the 1930s, the fearsome Bronko Nagurski took the ball, lowered his head and bowled over half the opposing defense en route to a score. Head still down, Nagurski rammed into the brick wall on the other side of the end zone, cracking it. Getting up with a grin on his face, Nagurski said to his teammates, "That last guy hit me pretty good."

Other players rise above the mayhem, displaying impossible courage and grace under fire: Gale Sayers creating daylight where only darkness existed; Lynn Swann leaping high to pluck another scoring pass from the sky; and nimble Barry Sanders waterbugging his way downfield and making defenders miss with moves that will never again be duplicated.

The best quarterbacks are often those who are coolest. Once Johnny Unitas dropped back to pass, only to be laid out by a vicious hit. Baltimore's OL Jim Parker looked down at a dazed Unitas and apologized for missing his block. Jamming a clod of turf in his nose to staunch the bleeding, Unitas called the exact same play and threw a perfect strike to his receiver streaking downfield for a TD.

In the 1986 AFC title game, the Denver Broncos found themselves down by seven with 5:32 to go and the ball on their own two yard line. Reveling in the moment rather than crumbling under the pressure, a smiling John Elway joined the Denver huddle. Elway proceeded to march his team 98 yards for the score in what is now referred to in mythical terms as "the Drive."

Ravens standout ML Ray Lewis is a frightening combination of power, speed and size.

THE HUNTERS AND THE HUNTED

Intimidation plays a huge role in football. Defenses, in particular, are measured by the fear they inspire. Included among the NFL's most frightening defensive units are Chicago's legendary "Monsters of the Midway" of the 1940s and '50s, the Rams' "Fearsome Foursome" of the 1960s, and in the 1970s, Minnesota's "Purple People Eaters" and Pittsburgh's notorious "Steel Curtain."

But often the tables are turned and the hunted becomes the hunter. Along with Nagurski, the Browns' Marion Motley was a prototype power back who relished nothing more than bowling over a defender. Motley paved the way for Jim Brown, considered by many to be the greatest player to ever buckle up a chin strap. A lethal combination of speed and power, Brown won eight rushing titles in his nine-year career. Despite amassing 58 100-yard games, Brown is often best remembered for his short-yardage runs, in which he plowed into linemen with obvious glee. Brown retired suddenly in 1966, when he was still at the top of his game, and it is safe to say that among NFL defenders, nary a tear was shed.

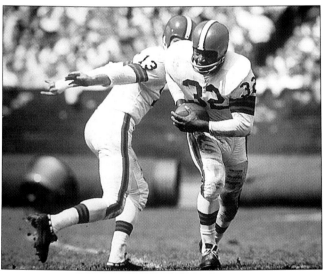

One of the greatest backs of all time, Jim Brown also played varsity basketball and lacrosse while at Syracuse University.

THE SPECIALISTS ENTER THE FRAY

There was a distinctly gladiatorial quality to early NFL games. Thousands of people would fill coliseums, cheering the primordial battle that raged in the mud below. Raw-boned men such as Bruiser Kinard and Tuffy Leemans played a very different style of football. Participants wore little, if any, protective clothing and played on offense and defense. Sammy Baugh epitomized this versatility. A quarterback, safety and punter for the Redskins in 1943, "the Texas Tornado" completed a rare triple crown, leading the league in pass completions, punting average and interceptions. One of the NFL's last two-way stars was Chuck Bednarik. A gunner on a bomber in World War II, Bednarik played with the Eagles on his return stateside. Filling the gruelling positions of center and linebacker, Philadelphia's "Iron Man" missed just three games between 1949 and '62, and was All-Pro on both sides of the ball.

Aside from a few exceptions (such as DT William "the Refrigerator" Perry coming in to score a TD in Super Bowl XX from the fullback position), today's players are specialists. Not only are they divided into offensive, defensive and special team units, modern players are regularly

Great Games in Great Venues

Yankee Stadium: Experts believe that the 1958 NFL championship game between the Giants and the Colts was instrumental in establishing pro football as a major spectator sport. The two star-studded teams fought to a 17-17 draw after regulation, sending the game into the NFL's first overtime period. The national TV audience was captivated as it watched QB Johnny Unitas drive the Colts 80 yards to give Baltimore the win.

Lambeau Field: The 1967 NFL championship between the Packers and the Cowboys will forever be remembered as "the Ice Bowl." Lambeau's underground heating system had broken down in the frigid -13°F. weather, transforming the field into a jagged skating rink. Facing a wind chill of -46°F., the two teams waged an epic seesaw struggle that was won on Bart Starr's quarterback sneak with 13 seconds remaining. With the win, the Pack moved on to Super Bowl II, where it scored a 33-14 victory over the Raiders.

Three Rivers Stadium: With 22 seconds left in the 1972 AFC divisional playoff game, the Steelers were trailing the Raiders 7-6 and faced a fourth-and-10 from their own 40. They needed a miracle — and they got one. Terry Bradshaw's desperation pass bounced off the helmet of an Oakland defender and into the hands of rookie RB Franco Harris, who scampered all the way for the winning score.

Orange Bowl Stadium: The 1981 AFC divisional playoff game between the Chargers and the Dolphins is considered to be one of the greatest ever. After San Diego jumped to a 24-0 lead, Miami battled back to tie the game in the third quarter. The Dolphins took the lead in the fourth quarter, but the Chargers' Dan Fouts marched his team 82 yards for the tying TD with 58 seconds to go. San Diego won on a 29-yard field goal by Rolf Benirschke in overtime, but the real hero was TE Kellen Winslow, who overcame two injured shoulders to make 13 catches for 166 yards and a TD. Winslow also blocked what would have been the winning field goal with four seconds to go in regulation time.

Tampa Stadium: The 1991 seesaw battle in Super Bowl XXV saw Buffalo take the lead on Thurman Thomas' 31-yard scamper to open the fourth quarter, but a Giants' field goal put New York up 20-19. With four seconds on the clock, the Bills' Scott Norwood attempted a 47-yard field goal to win the game, but the kick sailed just wide.

substituted in and out of a game depending on the situation. Speedy pass rushers will come in on obvious passing downs and extra tight ends are added to block for the running backs on short yardage plays.

This kind of specialization has raised football's skill level. Gone are the days when an offense would go whole quarters, even whole games, without throwing a pass, content just to grind opponents into dust under the feet of thick-legged backs. Today's game is epitomized by stars such as the Titans' Jevon Kearse and the Vikings' wideout Randy Moss, both incredibly gifted athletes who are capable, it seems, of doing the impossible on any given play.

Although the game has changed, one thing remains the same: Football players give no quarter. Men still play injured and quarterbacks still stand in the pocket looking for a receiver, seemingly oblivious to the massive linemen swooping down on them with absolute malice. Ronnie Lott, the Hall-of-Fame free safety, had his badly broken little finger amputated rather than miss any games while it healed. Yes, football players will always be warriors.

KEY MOMENTS

Football's roots can be traced to two sources: soccer and rugby. The game has taken more than a century to evolve into the sport we enjoy today. The following is a list of some the major developments that molded the game.

• 1869 First College Game
Rutgers beats Princeton in the first college football game. Modern fans wouldn't recognize the sport, however, as each team had 25 men using their heads and feet to advance the ball.

• 1880 Walter Camp Changes the Game
Walter Camp, regarded as "the father of American football," begins laying down the foundations of the modern game. Camp's innovations include 11 men per side and a system of downs to maintain ball possession.

• 1892 First Pro Player
William "Pudge" Heffelfinger is paid $500 to play a game for the Allegheny Athletic Association.

• 1902 Pro League Established
A three-team pro league in Pennsylvania ends indecisively, with the trio of teams finishing at 2-2.

• 1906 Forward Pass
The forward pass is legalized. A short toss from George "Peggy" Parratt of the Massillon Tigers to Dan "Bullet" Riley is the first completed pass in pro football history.

• 1912 Rules Refined
Officials shorten the field to 100 yards, add a fourth down and make each touchdown worth six points.

• 1920 APFA is Formed
Jim Thorpe leads the group that forms the 14-team American Professional Football Association. The league will be renamed the National Football League in 1922.

• 1933 First NFL Championship Game
Officials divide the NFL into two divisions. The Chicago Bears beat the New York Giants 23-21 in NFL's first championship game between division winners.

• 1937 Slingin' Sammy Revolutionizes Game
Rookie QB Sammy Baugh popularizes the forward pass by leading his Redskins to the NFL championship. In the title game, Baugh passes for 354 yards and three TDs.

• 1942 Hutson Rewrites Record Books
Green Bay's Don Hutson is the first player to have 1,000 receiving yards in a single season.

• 1943 Helmets Mandatory
The NFL rules that all players must wear helmets, although by then most had already taken to using them voluntarily.

• 1946 NFL Challenged by AAFC
The All-American Football Conference becomes the nation's "other" football league. Although the AAFC will last only four years, three of its teams (Cleveland Browns, Baltimore Colts and San Francisco 49ers) will join the NFL in 1950.

• 1958 The Greatest Game Ever Played
A national television audience watches as the Giants and Colts square off for the NFL championship. The game goes into sudden-death overtime, the NFL's first, and the Giants' dramatic 23-17 win puts pro football on the map.

• 1960 Upstart AFL Enters Fray
Blocked from buying the Chicago Cardinals in 1958, Lamar Hunt forms the American Football League.

• 1967 Super Bowl I
Green Bay whips Kansas City 35-10 in the first AFL–NFL title game, dubbed "the Super Bowl."

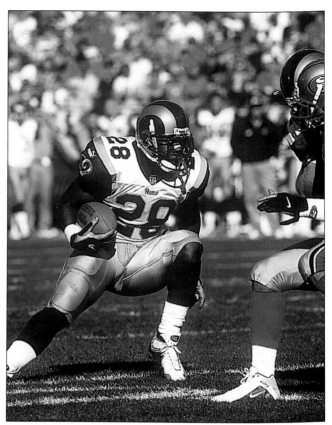

Marshall Faulk of St. Louis set a single-season touchdown record after striking pay dirt 26 times in 2000.

• 1969 The AFL's Revenge
The Jets' brash young QB Joe Namath guarantees a win over the heavily favored Colts in Super Bowl III — and delivers. New York's 16-7 victory gives the AFL its first crown in three tries.

• 1970 AFL–NFL Merge
The AFL and NFL officially ratify an agreement to merge. The new NFL is divided into the National Football Conference and the American Football Conference.

• 1972 Dolphins Perfect
The Dolphins go 17-0 (14 regular-season wins, two playoff wins and a victory in Super Bowl VII) to become the only unbeaten team in NFL history.

• 1977 Payton Runs Wild
RB Walter Payton of the Bears sets single-game rushing mark with 275 yards against the Vikings.

• 1980 Steelers Dynasty
The Steelers win Super Bowl XIV over the Rams, the team's fourth title in six years. QB Terry Bradshaw earns second Super Bowl MVP award in a row.

• 1984 Dickerson Has Season to Remember
The Rams' Eric Dickerson charges his way into the record book with 2,105 rushing yards in a single season.

• 1993 Shula Eclipses Halas
Miami's Don Shula passes George Halas to become the winningest coach in NFL history when his team defeats the Eagles for victory number 325.

• 1995 Jerry Rice: San Francisco Treat
The 49ers' Jerry Rice breaks NFL's single-season record with 1,848 receiving yards. Along the way, Rice becomes the game's career leader in receptions and receiving yards.

• 2001 Ravens Soar to New Heights
The Baltimore Ravens defense throttles the Giants en route to a 34-7 win in Super Bowl XXXV.

Pro Football Hall of Fame

FOOTBALL'S ROOTS

It is only fitting that the Pro Football Hall of Fame is located in Canton, Ohio. The direct forerunner of the NFL, the American Professional Football Association was founded in a Canton car showroom in 1920. One of the men present that day was Jim Thorpe, star of the Canton Bulldogs football team. The Bulldogs were one of pro football's earliest powerhouses, champions of the old Ohio League and winners of NFL titles in 1922 and '23. Three of Canton's sons (Marion Motley, Alan Page and Dan Dierdorf) have been enshrined in the Hall of Fame and of all the states, only Texas and Pennsylvania can boast more enshrinees than Ohio. This, quite simply, is "Football Country."

The road to Canton is not an easy one. The Hall of Fame is one of pro sport's most exclusive clubs, with a membership of just over 200.

Interestingly, not all Hall of Famers were born in the United States. LB Ted "the Mad Stork" Hendricks, a mainstay in the middle for the Raiders, was born in Guatemala. Gritty DT Ernie Stautner is a native of Bavaria, while the legendary Bronko Nagurski hailed from Canada. Other countries represented in the Hall of Fame include Honduras, Italy, Mexico and Norway.

Regardless of their nationality, all the men found in the Hall of Fame have one thing in common: They excelled at football, whether it was as a player, a coach, an owner, an administrator or a league official.

Vital Stats

Address:
2121 George Halas Dr. NW, Canton, Ohio
Phone: *(303) 456-8207*
Web Site:
profootballhof.com
Hours: *Daily 9–8, Memorial Day–Labor Day; daily 9–5, rest of year. Closed Dec. 25.*
Admission: *Adult $12; senior citizen (over 62) $8; child (14 and under) $6; family (parents and all dependent children) $30. Substantial reductions are offered for groups. Call or write for information.*
Directions: *The Hall of Fame is located at exit 107A (Fulton Rd.) off I-77. From Pittsburgh and Philadelphia, take I-76 west to I-77 south. From New York, take I-80 west to I–77 south. From Chicago, take I-94 south to I-80 east to I-77 south. From Detroit, take I-75 south to I-80 east to I-77 south.*

HONORING THE PAST

Visitors to the five-building complex are greeted by a seven-foot bronze statue of Thorpe, one of the game's earliest stars and box-office attractions. Considered by many to be the greatest American-born athlete of all time, Thorpe was an accomplished baseball player, an Olympic decathlon gold medalist and, of course, a brilliant two-way football player.

The Hall's first exhibition rotunda outlines the evolution of the game from its earliest days to the present, underscoring key moments both on and off the field. Action photographs, antique equipment and historical mementos help bring to life the game's bygone eras. Appetites sufficiently whetted, visitors will find themselves in the Pro Football Today display, in which detailed histories of each of the NFL's teams are presented.

THE HALL'S CENTERPIECE

Located in the second and third buildings, the Hall's twin enshrinement galleries are its true centerpieces. Each member is honored with a bronze bust and a mural of him in action. Although each brief biography gives the pertinent details of a man's career, it is often his statue that brings back a flood of memories. Looking on the bust of Vince Lombardi, visitors have visions of the great coach patrolling the sidelines of Lambeau Field in December, barking out orders in white puffs of breath. One can almost hear the legendary coach's famous words, "Winning isn't everything, it's the only thing." Walking by Walter Payton's display, people can't help but have flashbacks of "Sweetness" running around, over and through defenders, en route to the all-time rushing records. But the memories are also tinged with sadness, as both men died of illness far too young.

The Pro Football Photo-Art Gallery is a favorite among fans. Winning photos from the Hall's annual photography contest capture football's color and drama. High-quality shots depict the game in all its high-impact glory as well as more reflective sideline portraits of players and coaches. Elsewhere the Pro Football Adventure Room tells the stories of the various other pro leagues that both laid the groundwork for and challenged the NFL. Exhibit booths display equipment and mementos of contemporary record holders. As new marks are established, the displays are updated.

More artifacts are on display in the Enshrinees' Mementos room. Blocky cleats, scarred leather helmets and flimsy shoulder pads give an indication as to just how vulnerable players were in football's early years, especially when compared to the space-age design of today's state-of-the-art equipment.

One of the most popular draws is the Championship Chase video that is played on a giant screen. Created in conjunction with NFL Films, the video chronicles an entire NFL season, from the first day of training camp right through to the moment the Super Bowl trophy is held aloft.

Although the Hall of Fame was built to commemorate football's brightest luminaries, the celebration belongs to the fans. When parents pose their children next to the busts of Johnny "Blood" McNally, Gino Marchetti, Mike Ditka or Eric Dickerson, they may very well be remembering their own childhood, when life was simpler and giants played the game.

The Pro Football Hall of Fame entrance in Canton, Ohio.

THE STARS

HERE ARE SOME OF THE NFL'S most hallowed records. Remember that sacks only became an official stat in 1982, even though some teams had been recording them long before. Also, tackles are compiled by each team, but are not recognized as an official stat by the NFL. Active players are identified with an asterisk. For all career records, the nearest active players have been included so you can gauge how today's stars rank with the greats of eras past.

Passing Records
Completions (career):
1. Dan Marino 4,967
2. John Elway 4,123
3. Warren Moon 3,988
8. Brett Favre* 2,997
10. Vinny Testaverde* 2,897

Passing Yards (career):
1. Dan Marino 61,361
2. John Elway 51,475
3. Warren Moon 49,325
10. Vinny Testaverde* 36,307
13. Brett Favre* 34,706

TD Passes (career):
1. Dan Marino 420
2. Fran Tarkenton 342
3. John Elway 300
8. Brett Favre* 255 (tie)
17. Vinny Testaverde* 226

Completions (season):
1. Warren Moon 404 (1991)
2. Drew Bledsoe* 400 (1994)
3. Dan Marino 385 (1994)

Passing Yards (season):
1. Dan Marino 5,084 (1984)
2. Dan Fouts 4,802 (1981)
3. Dan Marino 4,746 (1986)

TD Passes (season):
1. Dan Marino 48 (1984)
2. Dan Marino 44 (1986)
3. Kurt Warner* 41 (1999)

Receiving Records
Receiving Yards (career):
1. Jerry Rice* 19,247
2. James Lofton 14,004
3. Henry Ellard 13,777

Receptions (career):
1. Jerry Rice* 1,281
2. Cris Carter* 1,020
3. Andre Reed 951

TD Receptions (career):
1. Jerry Rice* 176
2. Cris Carter* 123
3. Steve Largent 100

Receiving Yards (season):
1. Jerry Rice* 1,848 (1995)
2. Isaac Bruce* 1,781 (1995)
3. Charley Hennigan, 1,746 (1961)

Receptions (season):
1. Herman Moore* 123 (1995)
2. Cris Carter* 122 (1994, '95)
   Jerry Rice* 122 (1995)

TD Receptions (season):
1. Jerry Rice* 22 (1987)
2. Mark Clayton 18 (1984)
   Sterling Sharpe 18 (1994)

Rushing Records
Rushing Yards (career):
1. Walter Payton 16,726
2. Barry Sanders 15,269
3. Emmitt Smith* 15,166
12. Thurman Thomas* 12,074

Rushing TDs (career):
1. Emmitt Smith* 144
2. Marcus Allen 123
3. Walter Payton 110
15. Ricky Watters* 72

Rushing Yards (season):
1. Eric Dickerson 2,105 (1984)
2. Barry Sanders, 2,053 (1997)
3. Terrell Davis 2,008 (1998)

Rushing TDs (season):
1. Emmitt Smith* 25 (1995)
2. John Riggins 24 (1983)
3. Joe Morris 21 (1985)
   Emmitt Smith* 21 (1994)
   Terry Allen 21 (1996)
   Terrell Davis 21 (1998)

Scoring Records
Field Goals (career):
1. Gary Anderson* 461
2. Morten Anderson* 441
3. Nick Lowery 383

Points (career):
1. Gary Anderson* 2,059
2. George Blanda 2,002
3. Morten Anderson* 1,938

TDs (career):
1. Jerry Rice* 187
2. Emmitt Smith* 156
3. Marcus Allen 145

Field Goals (season):
1. Olindo Mare* 39 (1999)
2. John Kasay 37 (1996)
3. Cary Blanchard* 36 (1996)
   Al Del Greco* 36 (1998)

Points (season):
1. Paul Hornung 176 (1960)
2. Gary Anderson* 164 (1998)
3. Mark Moseley 161 (1983)

TDs (season):
1. Marshall Faulk*, 26 (2000)
2. Emmitt Smith* 25 (1995)
3. John Riggins 24 (1983)

Defensive Records
Int. (career):
1. Paul Krause 81
2. Emlen Tunnell 79
3. Dick Lane 68
8. Eugene Robinson* 58
   Rod Woodson* 58

Int. (season):
1. Dick Lane 14 (1952)
2. Dan Sandifer 13 (1948)
   Orban Sanders 13 (1950)
4. By nine players

Sacks (career):
1. Reggie White 192.5
2. Bruce Smith* 181
3. Kevin Greene 160

Sacks (season):
1. Mark Gastineau 22 (1984)
2. Reggie White 21 (1987)
   Chris Doleman 21 (1989)
4. Lawrence Taylor 20.5 (1986)

Miami Dolphin Dan Marino holds the majority of single-season and career passing records.

Leagues and Divisions

FOOTBALL'S ROOTS
On Nov. 6, 1869, Princeton and Rutgers squared off in what is considered to be the first-ever college football game. Had modern fans been present that day, they would have scratched their head at the sight of 50 players jabbing at the ball with their feet and head. The result looked more like a huge soccer match than a football game.

In fact, football has its roots in both soccer and rugby, with the game evolving gradually over the years. In 1876 football's first official rules were drawn up and adopted. During the 1880s Yale University coach Walter Camp laid down the blueprint for the modern game. Eleven-man squads, playbooks, a system of downs, point values for different types of scoring plays and set blocking formations were just some of the innovations Camp is credited with implementing.

BIRTH OF THE NFL
Americans had been playing football for some 50 years by the time the American Professional Football Association was formed in 1920. Although there had been pro leagues in the past, scandals, financial problems and the ever-growing popularity of the college game had hampered these early efforts.

From its very outset, the APFA set itself apart from its regional predecessors, such as the Ohio League, because its founders envisioned it as a league for the entire country. By the 1922 season, officials had changed its name to the National Football League.

CHALLENGE FROM A NEW CONFERENCE
The NFL gained popularity through the 1930s, with such teams as Green Bay, Chicago and the Giants dominating play. But the NFL's monopoly on the pro game was broken, however briefly, in 1946, with the birth of the All-American Football Conference. Following World War II, football's popularity was on the rise again and there was a glut of talented players graduating from colleges and returning from overseas. More importantly, a number of wealthy people had been rejected by the NFL when they had expressed interest in purchasing a team. These elements paved the way for the new league.

Although the AAFC lasted just four seasons, it had a huge influence on the NFL. Three of the NFL's most storied franchises, the Cleveland Browns, the San Francisco 49ers and the Baltimore Colts were charter members of the AAFC. A number of future Hall of Famers began their career in the upstart league, including Lou Groza, Marion Motley, Y.A. Tittle, Elroy "Crazy Legs" Hirsch and Otto Graham. Also, many of the innovations implemented by the Browns' coach Paul Brown, including playbooks, timing patterns by receivers and the two-minute offense, were copied by his NFL contemporaries.

NEW KIDS ON THE BLOCK
Snubbed by the NFL in 1958 when he tried to buy the Chicago Cardinals franchise, Texan Lamar Hunt went one step better and formed his own league. In 1960 the eight-team American Football League kicked off its inaugural season. The new league struggled initially, playing in front of sparse crowds at high school stadiums and having one of its teams, the Minnesota Vikings, defect to the NFL in 1961.

Relations between the two leagues worsened, with each one vying for college football's top prospects, often using underhanded techniques to sign a star. By the mid-1960s, established AFL and NFL stars were being lured to the rival league. In 1965 the AFL pulled a major coup when its New York Jets signed QB Joe Namath out of Alabama. "Broadway" Joe was a high-octane talent on the field and a high-profile playboy off the field — just the media relations boost the AFL needed. In 1967 Namath lived up to his billing and became the first pro quarterback to pass for over 4,000 yards in a single season. People began flocking to AFL games.

Traditionalists were feeling very smug after the NFL's mighty Green Bay Packers easily won the first two Super Bowl games over the AFL's top teams. But when the Namath-led Jets upset the Baltimore Colts in Super Bowl III, people were forced to take the AFL seriously. Looking to strengthen both their products and consolidate the huge fan base, the two leagues merged in 1970. The majority of the old AFL teams formed the American Football Conference and the original NFL squads made up the National Football Conference.

THE NFC: KING OF THE HILL
Since the merger, the NFC holds a 18-15 edge over the AFC in Super Bowl crowns. It's been a streaky race, with the AFC winning nine championships from 1970 to '80 and the NFC roaring back with an impressive string of 13-straight titles from 1984 to '96. Following the Ravens' win in Super Bowl XXXV, however, the AFC has a 1-0 edge in the new millennium.

In 2000 DE Jevon Kearse set a rookie record with 14.5 sacks.

TAILGATING

ALTHOUGH TAILGATING HAS its roots in football, today it is enjoyed by fans of auto racing, baseball, hockey and basketball. Basically anywhere there's both a sporting event and a parking lot, people will gather, cook food, drink beer and share some laughs. A chance to get together with old friends and new ones, tailgating has become an integral part of game day.

THE BEGINNINGS

Although the origins of tailgating are sketchy at best, they appear to have been devised by Ivy League football fans in the late 1800s. One general explanation for the practice is that whenever two Ivy League teams would square off, there would be a ceremonial meeting between supporters from both schools during which they would discuss the upcoming match and feast on everything from fish to wild game. This camaraderie between rivals remains an important part of modern tailgating.

Of course, the competition to be recognized as the originator of tailgating is almost as fierce as the football games themselves. Officials at Rutgers and Princeton maintain that tailgating can be traced back to the very beginning of college football itself. Fans traveling to the historic game between the two schools (said to be college football's first) by horse and buggy stopped to cook sausages at the back of their carriage, or the "tail end" of the horse.

Not to be outdone, Yale officials were quick to claim tailgating as an invention of their venerable institute. As the story goes, groups of fans who took trains to the games would work up an appetite during the long walk from the station to the stadium. The more farsighted among them began packing picnic hampers so they could grab a quick nosh and a drink just before game time.

COMMON COURTESY

Regardless of its origins, modern tailgating has grown into as much a tradition as football and turkey on Thanksgiving. As with all public events, tailgating has its own set of unwritten rules of etiquette. One of the keys to having a great time while tailgating is to remember these few simple pointers:

• **Greet people**
Tailgating is all about having fun with friends, family and total strangers. Once you've set up your spot, go over and meet the neighbors. Often the best way to break the ice is to offer them a cup of coffee or a soda. Chances are they'll sling you a tasty bratwurst.

• **Don't be a lout**
A common element in many tailgating parties is an impromptu game of pick-up football. Watch out for little kids and elderly people. If you happen to launch a long bomb into someone's chili pot, apologize and make a peace offering, such as a nice cold drink.

• **Really, don't be a lout**
Many participants regard beer as the official drink of a good tailgate party. That's all fine, as long as moderation is exercised and you have a designated driver.

• **Theme parties are "in"**
Tailgaters love a good theme party. Thanksgiving means turkey, Christmas means decorations, trees and cooks dressed like Santa. Another favorite trick is to tailor menus to poke fun at the opposing team. Fish, especially mahi-mahi, is a favorite whenever the Dolphins are in town, as is poultry for the Eagles, Ravens and Seahawks.

• **Wear team colors**
Tailgate aficionados consider themselves to be the home team's "12th man." This means wearing any and everything with a team logo on it. The serious ones fly team flags, pitch tents in team colors and decorate their spot with pennants.

• **Keep it clean**
Remember, tailgating is a family affair and, as such, people should refrain from swearing around the kids.

• **Keep it cleaner**
Real tailgaters are as serious about cleaning up as they are about stocking their grill. When possible, leave your spot in better shape than it was when you arrived. This means cleaning up any of the refuse left behind by previous, poorly trained partyers.

Veteran tailgaters will tell you that not all parking spots are created equal. Avoid spots on the outskirts or you run the risk of isolating yourself from the rest of the party.

The Ultimate Tailgating Checklist

BE PREPARED

Nothing is worse than arriving at your stadium lot only to find out that you are missing a vital component to your tailgate party (tongs, lawn chairs, beverages, etc.). Make a list of everything you want to take and check each item off as you pack your car. Although it might sound like a time-consuming process, you'll soon find that the routine will become second nature after a couple of weekends. One of the keys to smart packing is to take versatile items that have more than one use. The following is a list of essentials, not including food, that you should have at your party. The list is fairly extensive, so you might want to tailor it to your needs.

• Cooking utensils
Pots, pans, spatulas, cooking forks, etc. A good set of tongs are a cook's best friend as they can be used to turn meat and sausages (fork punctures allow the juices to drip out) and stir coals. Some tailgaters come equipped with large storage containers in which they carry all their utensils. It keeps them all in one place and is a tidy way to cart them home for post-party washing.

• Grill or propane stove
Clean your grill or stove as soon as possible after the cooking is done and prepare it for the coming weekend (check your propane level, too). Make sure you have enough charcoal or propane. Serious grillers burn seasoned hickory or oak wood chips to add flavor to food.

• Table and chairs
Good folding chairs are less bulky, but tables can take up a large amount of space. If you don't have room for a table in your vehicle, consider buying small lap trays. Some of the higher-end chairs come equipped with trays that attach to the chair arms.

• Condiments
It's amazing how many people prepare wonderful meals, only to realize they forgot the condiments. You can save time by chopping your onions and tomatoes and other toppings the night before. Also, buy cheap plastic bottles for mustard and ketchup.

• Garbage bags
You can never have too many garbage bags, and the bigger the better. As well as being an essential component in the clean-up phase of a tailgate, bags can be used to take dirty plates, cutlery and cooking utensils back home at the end of the day. They can also keep things dry during a shower and, in a pinch, they make a rudimentary, though functional, poncho.

• Resealable bags
Resealable, watertight plastic bags are perfect for packing items in coolers. Veteran tailgaters will fill these with water and freeze them the night before to use as ice bags in their coolers. At the end of the day, the ice can be emptied and the bags used to pack leftovers. Remember, never reuse a bag that has been carrying raw meat, fish or poultry until it has been thoroughly washed.

• Aluminum foil
Another multipurpose tool: Grillers will tell you that you can cook just about everything on a grill if you wrap it in foil first, and that includes meats, fish, potatoes and corn. Foil can also double as pot covers and wraps for leftover food.

• Paper plates and plastic utensils
It's your call: They don't break and are great in terms of speeding the clean up afterward, but they aren't very friendly to the environment. Some partyers buy inexpensive plastic plates because although they still have to be washed at the end of the day, they don't break and they are reusable.

• Water
An often overlooked item on game day. You won't have access to much running water in a parking lot, so plan to pack a few gallons of your own. You'll need it for drinking and washing. In an emergency, you can always use the melted ice in your cooler.

• Miscellaneous items
Paper towels: Can serve as everything from napkins to — in an emergency — toilet paper. Premoistened towels: Essential if you are serving sticky finger foods such as ribs and chicken. Old towels: These are great for cleaning up major spills, but can also be used as pot holders or bibs for messy eaters.

Tailgaters in Baltimore have had plenty to celebrate, starting with Johnny Unitas and the Colts, right through to the Ravens' victory in Super Bowl XXXV.

GREAT GRUB

YOU MAY FIND YOURSELF the center of attention when your parking lot tailgating neighbors catch a whiff of what you've got going on the grill. We've gathered these recipes from around football country to raise your grilling skills a notch or two. Give them a try and remember to pay special attention to the food-handling advice in the box on the opposite page. Now fire up that grill!

Bacon-Wrapped Tequila Lime Shrimp

1	pound shrimp, shelled and deveined
12	slices bacon, halved
1/2	cup oil
1/4	cup tequila
2/3	cup lime juice
1	teaspoon garlic, chopped
1	teaspoon kosher salt
1/2	teaspoon cracked black pepper
4	tablespoons cilantro, chopped fine
1	teaspoon jalapeno sauce
1	cup white onions, chopped

• Place all ingredients (except bacon and shrimp) in a glass bowl and mix well.
• Add shrimp to mixture and marinate in the refrigerator 30 to 45 minutes.
• Remove shrimp from marinade and reserve marinade.
• Wrap each shrimp in one half slice bacon and thread on a skewer.
• Place on hot grill and grill over medium heat for 8 to 10 minutes. Baste with reserved marinade during grilling.

Serves 4

Merrill's (Must-Try) Cheesy Roasted Wisconsin Potatoes

4	Wisconsin baking potatoes
2	cups Italian dressing
4	tablespoons grated parmesan cheese

• Bake or microwave baking potatoes at home until three-quarters done.
• Cut potatoes lengthwise into quarters.
• Marinate in Italian dressing for 1 hour.
• Roll quartered potatoes in parmesan cheese and grill over indirect heat for approximately 20 minutes or until golden brown.

Serves 4

Mad Dog's Grilled Wisconsin Potato Slices

Wisconsin baking potatoes
Italian dressing
Grated cheese of choice

• Slice bakers lengthwise into several 1/4-inch-thick slices.
• Marinate for 2 hours in Italian dressing.
• Grill over direct medium heat for 5 to 7 minutes each side, basting occasionally.
• Top with grated cheese 1 minute before removing from grill.

One potato per person

Mexican Corn on the Cob

8	slices bacon
8	ears corn on the cob
1/4	cup chili powder

• Wrap a bacon slice around each ear of corn.
• Place on a sheet of heavy-duty aluminum foil.
• Sprinkle with chili powder and wrap in foil.
• Cook, covered with grill lid, over medium-hot coals (350-400°F.) 15 to 20 minutes, turning once.

Serves 8

Twice-Dunked Yaki Hot Wings

5	pounds chicken wings, rinsed and patted dry

Hot 'n' Tangy Marinade:

2	cups cider vinegar
4	tablespoons crushed red pepper flakes
1	tablespoon salt
2	teaspoons black pepper
1	teaspoon cayenne pepper
1/2	teaspoon sugar
2	12-ounce bottles teriyaki sauce

• Combine all six ingredients for marinade and mix well.
• Put chicken wings into large resealable freezer bag and pour in marinade.
• Refrigerate up to 3 days (longer marinating time equals hotter wings).
• Grill directly over low-medium heat 15 minutes or until done.
• Pour teriyaki sauce into large non-reactive bowl.
• Remove wings from grill and put in bowl with teriyaki sauce and toss until wings are covered.
• Serve promptly right from bowl.

Serves 6-8

Suggestion: The wings can be marinated and cooked ahead of time, then reheated and dunked in the teriyaki sauce just before serving.

Drunken Grilled Brats

8   bratwurst sausages
2   bottles dark beer

• Pierce each bratwurst several times with a fork.
• Grill sausages directly over a low fire until shriveled and wrinkly.
• When the brats go on the grill, pour the beer into a shallow metal baking dish or disposable aluminum drip tray and heat to just below a boil.
• Put the grilled sausages into the beer and continue heating until they have absorbed the beer and plumped back up.

Serves 4-8

Suggestion: Serve on sesame seed rolls with mustard, grilled onions, sauerkraut and shredded sharp cheddar cheese. Onions and sauerkraut can be wrapped in foil to reheat on the grill.

Kansas City-Style Pork Ribs

4   racks baby-back ribs
    Kansas City Rub (recipe follows)
    Kansas City Sauce (recipe follows)

• Remove membrane from back of ribs. Combine all rub ingredients and rub about two-thirds of mixture well into the ribs. Wrap in plastic and refrigerate overnight.
• The next day rub remaining mixture well into the ribs. Slow-smoke for about 3 hours until rub is fully caramelized onto outside of ribs.
• Brush the ribs with sauce and continue to smoke for at least 1 more hour.

Kansas City Barbecue Rub:

3/4   cup dark brown sugar
1/4   cup mild New Mexico red chile powder
1/4   cup mild paprika
2 1/2   tablespoons kosher salt
2 1/2   tablespoons fresh-ground black pepper
1   tablespoon granulated onion
1/2   tablespoon granulated garlic
1/2   teaspoon cayenne pepper

• Mix and store in covered container.
• Rub into ribs.

Kansas City Barbecue Sauce:

1   cup Pepsi Cola®
1   cup tomato sauce
1/2   cup dark brown sugar
1/2   cup dark molasses
1/2   cup white vinegar
1   6-ounce can tomato paste
1/4   cup sweet butter
1/4   cup Worcestershire sauce
2   tablespoons balsamic vinegar
2   tablespoons maple syrup
1   tablespoon dry mustard
1   tablespoon mild New Mexico chili powder
1/2   tablespoon kosher salt
1/2   tablespoon fresh-ground black pepper
1   teaspoon wasabi powder
1   teaspoon summer savory
1   teaspoon marjoram
1   teaspoon granulated garlic
1   teaspoon onion powder
2   dashes Tabasco® habanero sauce

• Mix all ingredients together and simmer over low heat until thick enough to coat the back of a metal spoon.

Serves 4-6

Germ Warfare

TAKE PRECAUTIONS

Fresh air and good food can add up to a memorable afternoon, provided you take certain precautions to make sure everything stays fresh and safe to eat.

• **Wash your hands**
Dirty hands are prime culprits for spreading germs. Always wash your hands thoroughly with soap and water after going to the bathroom or preparing raw meats. Waterless hand sanitizer is an easy solution.

• **Put it on ice**
Harmful organisms can start growing long before tell-tale bad smells send out signals. Poultry and eggs always carry salmonella and must be cooked thoroughly. Keep all raw meat and eggs packed on ice. NEVER use the raw meat ice as cubes in your drinks; keep a separate stash instead.

• **Cook it properly**
The best defense is to make sure that things are cooked to a safe internal temperature. Carry a small meat thermometer with you to gauge internal temperatures. Whole chicken breasts should reach 180°F; 160-170°F will do for pork; ground beef should reach 160°F; and beef will need to reach 160-170°F.

• **Beware of the sun**
Even cooked food can become contaminated, especially in sunny climes. Set up ice stations in which you nestle smaller bowls of food in larger containers of ice, especially for meats and perishable foods such as eggs, dairy products and potato salad. The safest system is to keep food in a cooler until guests arrive.

• **When in doubt, throw it out**
A good rule of thumb is to throw out anything that's been outside for more than an hour in 90°F weather or more than two hours in cooler temperatures. When taking food home, never use ice or wrappings that have held raw meat.

ARIZONA CARDINALS

FOUNDED IN 1899 AS THE Morgan Athletic Club of Chicago, the Cardinals are the NFL's oldest franchise, predating even the league itself. Unfortunately, longevity hasn't translated into a wealth of championships for the Cardinals. Since entering the American Professional Football Association (forerunner to the NFL) in 1920, the team has managed just two league titles, no Super Bowls and only a few playoff appearances. Fittingly, the Cardinals' 1925 NFL Championship was controversial, with the league-leading Pottsville Maroons suspended for playing an illegal exhibition game. As if being punished by a higher power, the Cardinals languished for the next 21 years, enjoying winning seasons in just three of them. This isn't to say that the team lacked talent. In a 1929 contest versus Chicago, future Canton-enshrinee Ernie Nevers scored 40 points on six TDs and four point-after conversions — a record that still stands. The long championship drought ended in 1947, when the team's "Million-Dollar Backfield" drove it to a 28-21 win over the Eagles in the title match. Tough times returned in 1949 and the Cardinals, who moved to St. Louis in 1960, did not make it back to the playoffs until 1974 and '75. Although he never won a major title in his 13 seasons with the franchise, Hall-of-Fame OT Dan Dierdorf played during this time, making him one of the rare Cardinals to participate in postseason play. Hard times returned, however, and the Cards closed out the century with a dismal 151-235-2 record. In Arizona since 1988, the team hopes the change of scenery will do it good.

David Boston has emerged as the Cards "go-to" receiver.

POSTSEASON
- NFL Championships ....2 (1925, '47)
- NFC East Titles ....2 (1974, '75)
- NFC Wild Card Berths 1 (1998)

RETIRED NUMBERS
- Larry Wilson (8)
- Stan Mauldin (77)
- J.V. Cain (88)
- Marshall Goldberg (99)

TEAM RECORDS
Offense
- **Otis Anderson (1979–86)**
Rushing Yards (season): 1,605 (1979)
Rushing Yards (career): 7,999
Rushing TDs (career): 46

Extra Point
- *In 80 NFL seasons, the Cardinals have won 10 or more games in a single season just five times. The team has lost 10 or more games in 19 seasons, including back-to-back 0-10 campaigns in 1943 and '44.*
- *On Oct. 2, 1950, WR Bob Shaw caught a NFL-record five TD passes in a game against Baltimore.*

100-Yard Games (season): 9 (1979)
100-Yard Games (career): 34
- **Jim Bakken (1962–78)**
Field Goals (career): 282
Points (career): 1,380
- **Larry Centers (1990–98)**
Receptions (season): 101 (1995)
Receptions (career): 535
- **John David Crow (1958–64)**
TDs (season): 17 (1966)
- **Boomer Esiason (1996)**
Passing Yards (game): 522 (Nov. 10, 1996)
- **Greg Davis (1991–96)**
Field Goals (season): 30 (1995)
- **Roy Green (1979–90)**
Receiving Yards (career): 8,497
TDs (career): 69
- **Jim Hart (1966–83)**
Comp. (career): 2,590
Pass Att. (career): 5,096
Passing Yards (career): 34,639
TD Passes (career): 209
- **Charley Johnson (1961–69)**
TD Passes (season): 28 (tie) (1963)
- **Neil Lomax (1981–89)**
Comp. (season): 345 (1984)
Passing Yards (season): 4,614 (1984)

"We're going to be an offense that comes out and hits you."
— *RB Michael Pittman, on the 2001 Cardinals*

- **Rob Moore (1995–present)**
Receiving Yards (season): 1,584 (1997)
- **Ernie Nevers (1929–31)**
Points (game): 40 (Nov. 28, 1929)
TDs (game): 6 (Nov. 28, 1929)
- **Neil O'Donoghue (1980–85)**
Points (season): 117 (1984)

Defense
- **Mark Arneson (1972–80)**
Fumble Recoveries (career): 19 (tie)
- **Bob Nussbaumer (1949–50)**
Int. (season): 12 (1949)
- **Larry Wilson (1960–72)**
Int. (career): 52

LEAGUE HONORS
NFC Player of the Year
- Jim Hart (1974)
- Ottis Anderson (1979)

NFC Rookie of the Year
- Ottis Anderson (1979)
- Simeon Rice (1996)

Vital Stats
Stadium Address: Fifth St., Tempe, Ariz.
Phone: (480) 965-3933
Web: azcardinals.com
Box Office: (602) 379-0102, Mon.–Fri. 8:30–5, Sat. 9–1
Media Coverage:
Radio: KDUS (1060 AM), KSLX (100.7 FM)
TV: KSAZ (Channel 10), Fox Sports Net
Training Facility: Tempe, Ariz.

NFL Coach of the Year
- Don Coryell (1974)

Pro Football Hall of Fame
- Ernie Nevers (1963)
- Jim Thorpe (1963)
- Jimmy Conzelman (1964)
- Guy Chamberlin (1965)
- John "Paddy" Driscoll (1965)
- Walt Kiesling (1966)
- Charles Bidwill (1967)
- Charley Trippi (1968)
- Ollie Matson (1972)
- Dick "Night Train" Lane (1974)
- Larry Wilson (1978)
- Don Maynard (1987)
- Jackie Smith (1994)
- Dan Dierdorf (1996)

Timeline

1898	1901	1920	1925	1929	1947	1960	1963	1974	1975	1980	1988	1994	1998	2000
Morgan Athletic Club founded in Chicago	Faded maroon jerseys dubbed "cardinal red;" team gets new name	Cards are charter members of APFA (forerunner of NFL)	Team wins its first NFL Championship	RB Ernie Nevers scores NFL-record 40 points in one game	Charley Trippi's 75-yard punt return for TD sparks Cards second NFL crown	Franchise moves to St. Louis	Charley Johnson throws 28 TD passes	Cards make playoffs for first time in 25 years	Team repeats as NFC East champs	OT Dan Dierdorf selected for sixth Pro Bowl	Team moves to Phoenix where it never finishes higher than fourth in NFC East	Cornerback Aeneas Williams named All-Pro for first time	Wild-card berth puts team in playoffs for first time since 1982	Cards have dismal 3-13 season; finish last in NFC East

SUN DEVIL STADIUM: BETWEEN THE BUTTES

CONSTRUCTED IN 1958 as home of Arizona State football, Sun Devil Stadium is situated between two mountain buttes in Tempe. The large open-air stadium has undergone a series of renovations geared toward improving fans' enjoyment of the games. Unlike many venues that try to increase capacity at all cost, Sun Devil's 1992 renovations eliminated some 1,300 seats. As a result, sight line problems experienced by people sitting in the lower rows were rectified.

CONCESSIONS

The food selection at Sun Devil Stadium includes the usual hot dogs, burgers, chicken breast sandwiches, popcorn and pretzels, but there is a popular Mexican food stand as well. A few other snacks are available at vendor stands throughout the stadium.

Stadium Facts

Opened: Oct. 4, 1958
Cost: $1 million
Capacity: 73,273
Type: Open
Surface: Grass
Home Sweet Home:
Temperatures can climb to well over 100° F. under the relentless sun. Players who are not used to the heat, especially those on northern teams, often wilt in the fourth quarter.

GAME DAY TIPS

• **Gate hours:** Gates open 90 minutes prior to kickoff.
• **Tailgating:** Parking lots reserved for tailgating open 3.5 hours prior to kickoff.
• **Weather:** Phoenix is dry and ranges from hot to mild. Rain is rare and minimal. Bring sunscreen and drink a lot of water.
• **Prohibited items:** Bottles, cans, hard coolers and alcohol are prohibited. Smoking is allowed only in designated areas.
• **Ticket tips:** Sun Devil Stadium is a university installation, so bench seating is what you get. The stadium gets extremely hot at times and air circulation is minimal, so some fans may prefer the upper-level seats. Tickets are plentiful, and priced well below NFL standards.
• **Lost and found:** (480) 965-3933.

Seating Plan

▪	$220	▪	$35
▫	$135	▪	$25
▨	$80	▫	N/A
▪	$55	**ATM** Field level behind section 37	
▪	$45	♿ Throughout lower stands	

Directions: From I-10 east, exit onto Loop 202 toward Tempe. Turn right on Scottsdale Ave., right on University Dr., right on Stadium Dr. From Hwy. 60 west, exit at Mill Ave. and turn right. Turn right on University Dr., left on Stadium Dr. By Bus: Bus No. 72 goes to the stadium. Call Tempe in Motion at (480) 350-2739 for information. **Parking:** Some 3,500 parking spots are available in lots around the stadium. There are 383 disabled parking spaces in the lot outside the northeast stadium gates. There is additional parking on Mill and Ash Aves. and 5th St.

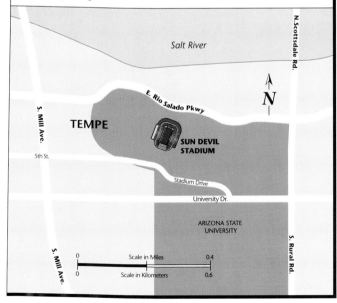

Nearby Hotels

▼▼▼ **Hilton Phoenix Airport (Hotel)**, 2435 S. 47th St. (Phoenix), (480) 894-1600, $59-$244
▼▼▼ **Holiday Inn Express Hotel & Suites (Motor Inn)**, 3401 E. University Dr. (Phoenix), (602) 453-9900, $79-$149
▼▼▼ **Quality Inn-South Mountain (Motor Inn)**, 5121 E. La Puenta Ave. (Phoenix), (480) 893-3900, $60-$100
▼▼▼ **Radisson Phoenix Airport Hotel (Hotel)**, 3333 E. University Dr. (Phoenix), (602) 437-8400, $59-$179
▼▼ **Red Roof Inn (Motel)**, 5215 W. Willetta St. (Phoenix), (602) 233-8004, $49-$99

Nearby Restaurants

▼▼ **Havana Cafe (Cuban)**, 4225 E. Camelback Rd. (Phoenix), (602) 952-1991, $10-$17
▼▼ **Macayo Depot Cantina (Mexican)**, 300 S. Ash Ave. (Tempe), (480) 966-6677, $6-$12
▼ **Rusty Pelican (Seafood)**, 1606 W. Baseline Rd. (Phoenix), (480) 345-0972, $12-$21
▼▼ **Tarbell's (Continental)**, 3213 E. Camelback Rd. (Tempe), (602) 955-8100, $13-$29 (dinner only)
▼▼▼ **Top of the Rock Restaurant (American)**, 2000 Westcourt Way in Wyndham Buttes Resort (Tempe), (602) 225-9000, $21-$32 (dinner only)

ATLANTA FALCONS

WHEN RANKIN SMITH FINALLY BROUGHT professional football to Atlanta, he filled a huge void in the southeast, which had never been home to a NFL franchise. The largely unknown Smith endeared himself to fans with savvy early team decisions, hiring Norb Hecker, one of Vince Lombardi's assistants at Green Bay, as Head Coach, and signing Texas linebacker Tommy Nobis, the country's number one college prospect. The early years of the franchise were marked by streaks of brilliance among long stretches of mediocrity. But early stars such as Nobis, RB Dave Hampton and WR Ken Burrow gave fans something to cheer about as the losses mounted. Things turned for the team with the drafting of QB Steve Bartkowski in 1975. Combined with the team's stingy defense, Barkowski led the team to its first playoff appearance in 1978, in a dramatic 14-13 win over the Eagles. The Falcons made a pair of playoff appearances in the early 1980s and then again in the early 1990s, but it was in 1998 that the franchise's high-water mark came. Led by veteran QB Chris Chandler and paced by the electrifying running of Jamal Anderson, "the Dirty Birds" finished the season 14-2 and then marched through the playoffs, winning the NFC title over Minnesota with an overtime field goal. Less than two months after quadruple bypass surgery, Head Coach Dan Reeves was leading his Falcons to a Super Bowl showdown with his former team, the Denver Broncos. Atlanta lost the game 34-19 to the powerhouse Broncos, but once again the team had scored a significant blow for football in the American southeast.

Kicker Morten Andersen has played 20 NFL seasons.

"There's a lot of enthusiasm around here."
— *Falcons WR Terrance Mathis*

POSTSEASON
- NFC Championships 1 (1998)
- NFC West Titles 1 (1980)
- NFC Wild Card Berths .....2 (1978, '95)

RETIRED NUMBERS
- William Andrews (31)
- Jeff Van Note (57)
- Tommy Nobis (60)

Extra Point

- *After a lengthy contract holdout in 1989, Deion Sanders finally suited up for an Oct. 8 game against the Rams and proceeded to run a punt back for a TD in the first quarter.*
- *After the 1998 Falcons dubbed themselves "the Dirty Birds," RB Jamal Anderson developed a touchdown dance to fit the name.*

TEAM RECORDS
Offense
- **Jamal Anderson (1994–present)**
Carries (season): 410 (1998)
Rushing Yards (season): 1,846 (1998)
TDs (season): 16 (1998)
100-Yard Games (season): 12 (1998)
- **Morten Andersen (1995–present)**
Field Goals (season): 31 (1995)
Field Goals (career): 139
Longest Field Goal: 59 yards (Dec. 24, 1995)
Points (season): 122 (1995)
Points (career): 620
- **William Andrews (1979–86)**
Yards-Per-Carry (season): 4.94 (1980)
Yards-Per-Carry (career): 4.55
- **Steve Bartkowski (1975–85)**
Comp. (career): 1,870
Passing Yards (season): 23,468
TD Passes (season): 31 (1980)
TD Passes (career): 154
- **Jeff George (1994–96)**
Comp. (season): 336 (1995)
Comp. Pct. (career): 60.5
Pass Att. (season): 557 (1995)
Passing Yards (season): 4,143 (1995)
- **Alfred Jenkins (1975–83)**
Receiving Yards (season): 1,358 (1981)

- Norm Johnson (1975–83)
Field Goals (game): 6 (Nov. 13, 1994)
- **Terrence Mathis (1994–present)**
Receiving Yards (career): 6,785
Receptions (season): 111 (1994)
Receptions (career): 522
- **Gerald Riggs (1982–88)**
Carries (career): 1,587
Rushing Yards (career): 6,631
Rushing TDs (career): 48
- **Andre Rison (1990–94)**
Receiving TDs (season): 15 (1993)
TDs (career): 56
100-Yard Games (career): 25

Special Teams
- **Billy Johnson (1982–87)**
Punt-Return Yards (career): 1,251
- **Deion Sanders (1989–93)**
Combined Kickoff/Punt-Return Yards (career): 4,177
Longest Punt Return: 79 Yards (Oct. 28, 1990)

Defense
- **Scott Case (1984–94)**
Int. (season): 10 (1988)
- **Claude Humphrey (1968–78)**
Sacks (career): 62.5
- **Rolland Lawrence (1973–81)**
Int. (career): 39
- **Joel Williams (1979–82, 1986–89)**
Sacks (season): 16 (1980)

LEAGUE HONORS
NFL Rookie of the Year
- Steve Bartkowski (1975)

NFL Defensive Rookie of the Year
- Buddy Curry (1980)
- Al Richardson (1980)

NFL Coach of the Year
- Dan Reeves (1998)

NFC Coach of the Year
- Leeman Bennett (1977, '80)

Vital Stats

Stadium Address:
1 Georgia Dome Dr., Atlanta, Ga.
Phone: (404) 223-9200
Web: atlantafalcons.com
Box Office:
(404) 223-8000
Mon.–Fri. 9–5
Media Coverage:
Radio: WGST (640 AM)
TV: Fox (WAGA, Channel 5)
Training Facility:
Flowery Branch, Ga.

Timeline

1965 — NFL awards franchise to Georgia banker Rankin M. Smith

1966 — Falcons lose first game 9-7 to Philadelphia

1971 — Rookie Ken Burrow sets NFC record with 190 receiving yards in game against Detroit

1975 — RB Dave Hampton becomes Falcons' first 1,000-yard rusher

1978 — Falcons defeat Eagles in the franchise's first playoff game

1979 — QB Steve Bartkowski sets team record with 2,502 passing yards

1984 — RB Gerald Riggs sets team record with 202 rushing yards against Saints

1986 — Longtime Falcons center Jeff Van Note honored after final game

1989 — Deion Sanders returns a punt for a TD in first game with Atlanta

1992 — Georgia Dome opens

1995 — NFL-record four Falcons gain 1,000 yards: Eric Metcalf, Terrance Mathis, Bert Emmanuel and Craig Heyward

1997 — Dan Reeves hired as Head Coach

1998 — Falcons win first NFC championship

1999 — Falcons fall to Broncos in Super Bowl XXXIII

156

GEORGIA DOME: THE NFL'S BEST INDOOR VENUE

THE CONCEPT OF THE INDOOR FOOTBALL STADIUM has been questioned for years, often with just cause since few are very good for football. But the Georgia Dome finally has it right. With huge windows that allow in plenty of natural light and a roof that is supported by cables, not pillars, so as not to obstruct views, the Dome is one of the best venues in the league. The field is AstroTurf and the fan and player amenities are state-of-the-art. The Georgia Dome also hosted the gymnastics and basketball events during the 1996 Olympics.

Seating Plan

$41	ATM Sections 109, 129
$37	♿ Throughout 100s, end zone
$25	200s

CONCESSIONS

Hungry football fans will find a wide selection of food at the Georgia Dome. Fare includes traditional hot dogs, sandwiches, pretzels, popcorn and pizza, as well more exciting options such as barbecue beef and turkey, wings, Chinese food, microbrewed beer and smoothies.

Stadium Facts

Opened: Aug. 23, 1992
Cost: $210 million
Capacity: 71,228
Type: Domed
Surface: AstroTurf
Home Sweet Home:
• When the Falcons are playing well, Atlanta's vocal fans, combined with the stadium's dome can create a noise problem for opposing teams.

GAME DAY TIPS

• **Gate hours:** Gates open 90 minutes prior to kickoff.
• **Tailgating:** Although the stadium has no on-site lot, there is no shortage of pre-game fun. The Birdsnest, held in the International Plaza (between Philips Arena and Georgia Dome), begins 2.5 hours before each home game and features live music, games, food, cheerleaders and more. Traditional tailgating also takes place in private lots in the area.
• **Prohibited items:** Items prohibited from the Georgia Dome include cans, bottles, alcoholic beverages, food and helium balloons. Smoking is forbidden in seating areas, but it is permitted in designated outer concourses.
• **Ticket tips:** The Falcons are a popular team, but they do not regularly sell out. Expect bigger crowds when their rivals, the New Orleans Saints, are in town. The seats in the corners of the Georgia Dome are angled so spectators don't need to turn their heads to see the action on the field.
• **Lost and found:** (404) 223-8900.

Directions: From I-75/85 south, exit 248A (Martin Luther King Jr. Dr.), right on Northside Dr. From I-75/85 north, exit 246 (Central Ave.), left on Martin Luther King Jr. Dr., right on Northside Dr. From I-20 east, exit 56B (Spring St.), left on Martin Luther King Jr. Dr., right on Northside Dr. From I-20 west, exit 58A (Spring St.), left on Martin Luther King Jr. Dr., right on Northside Dr. By Train: Omni/Dome/GWCC Station. Call MARTA at (404) 848-4711.
Parking: Few on-site spots, but private lots are on Techwood Dr., Spring, Marietta and Mitchell streets. Disabled patrons may park at the stadium.

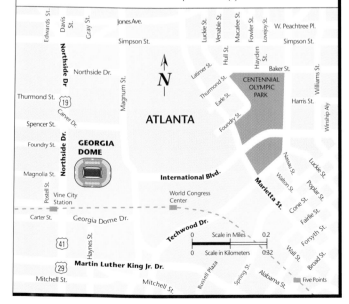

Nearby Hotels

▼▼▼ **Courtyard by Marriott-Downtown** *(Motor Inn)*, 175 Piedmont Ave. NE (Atlanta), (404) 659-2727, $89-$179
▼▼▼ **Fairfield Inn by Marriott-Downtown** *(Motel)*, 175 Piedmont Ave. NE (Atlanta), (404) 659-7777, $79-$139
▼▼▼ **Hampton Inn & Suites Atlanta Downtown** *(Motel)*, 161 Spring St. (Atlanta), (404) 589-1111, $79-$109
▼▼▼ **Omni Hotel at CNN Center** *(Hotel)*, 100 CNN Center (Atlanta), (404) 659-0000, $99-$224
▼▼ **Travelodge-Downtown** *(Motel)*, 311 Courtland St. NE (Atlanta), (404) 659-4545, $75-$135

Nearby Restaurants

▼▼▼ **The Atlanta Grill** *(Continental)*, 181 Peachtree St. NE in The Ritz-Carlton, Atlanta (Atlanta), (404) 659-0400, $16-$25
▼▼▼ **Hsu's Gourmet Chinese Restaurant** *(Chinese)*, 192 Peachtree Center Ave. (Atlanta), (404) 659-2788, $10-$20
▼▼▼▼ **Nikolai's Roof** *(Continental)*, 255 Courtland St. NE in the Hilton Atlanta & Towers (Atlanta), (404) 221-6362, $67-$116 (dinner only)
▼▼ **Pittypat's Porch** *(Regional American)*, 25 International Blvd. NW (Atlanta), (404) 525-8228, $19-$25 (dinner only)
FYI **The Varsity** *(American)*, 61 North Ave. NE (Atlanta), (404) 881-1706, $4-$10

BALTIMORE RAVENS

THE BALTIMORE RAVENS HAVE SHOCKED THE SPORTS WORLD on a couple of occasions. The first came at the sudden birth of the franchise. In November 1995 Cleveland Browns owner Art Modell announced his intention to move the decades-old team to Baltimore. Two months later the NFL approved the move and the Browns were history. As upset as Cleveland supporters were, fans in Baltimore, starved for football since their beloved Colts bolted for Indianapolis in 1984, were thrilled. With his selection of LB Ray Lewis in the 1996 draft, director of pro personnel Ozzie Newsome put in place the centerpiece of what would become one of the greatest defenses in football history. Even as the Ravens endured losing seasons in 1996, '97 and '98, the team was improving steadily on defense, helped by the drafting of linebacker Peter Boulware in 1997 and the signings of free agents Tony Siragusa in '97 and veteran free safety Rod Woodson in '98. With new Head Coach Brian Billick at the helm in 1999, the Ravens won their final four games of the season to finish at 8-8. More impressive than the record was the team's defense, which ranked number two in the NFL. In 2000 that defense was even more dominating. The Ravens set a NFL record for fewest points allowed in a season on the way to a 12-4 season. In the playoffs, Baltimore limited its opponents to 23 points over four games, smothering high-flying Tennessee and Oakland squads before ripping the Giants 34-7 in Super Bowl XXXV. Ray Lewis, the clear leader of a devastating defense, was name Super Bowl MVP.

"We didn't do anything different today. We just came out and proved that we're the best defense in NFL history."
— *Super Bowl XXXV MVP Ray Lewis*

Vital Stats

Stadium Address:
1101 Russell St., Baltimore, Md.
Phone: (410) 230-8000
Web: ravenszone.net
Box Office:
(410) 261-RAVE, Mon.–Sat. 9–5, three hours before kickoff
Media Coverage:
Radio: WLIF (102 FM), WJFK (1300 AM)
TV: CBS (WJZ Channel 13)
Training Facility:
Owings Mills Training Facility, Baltimore, Md.

POST SEASON
• **Super Bowl Championships** 1 (2000)
• **AFC Titles** 1 (2000)
• **AFC Wild Card Berth** 1 (2000)

RING OF HONOR
• Earnest Byner (21)

TEAM RECORDS
Offense
• **Matt Stover (1996–present)**
Field Goal Pct. (career): 80.8
Field Goals (season): 35 (2000)
Field Goals (career): 129
Points (game): 18 (tie) (Sept. 21, 1997)

Points (season): 135
Points (career): 539
• **Priest Holmes (1997–2001)**
Carries (career): 459
Longest Run From Scrimmage: 72 Yards (Dec. 5, 1999)
Receptions (game): 13 (Oct. 11, 1998)
Rushing TDs (season): 7 (1998)
Rushing TDs (career): 10
Rushing Yards (game): 227 (Nov. 22, 1998)
Rushing Yards (career): 2,102
Yards-Per-Carry (career): 4.6
• **Qadry Ismail (1999-present)**
Receiving Yards (game): 258 (Dec. 12, 1999)
TD Receptions (game): 3 (tie) (Dec. 12, 1999)
• **Michael Jackson (1996–98)**

Receiving Yards (season): 1,201 (1996)
Receiving Yards (career): 2,596
Receptions (season): 76 (1996)
Receptions (career): 183
TD Receptions (game): 3 (tie) (Dec. 22, 1996)
TD Receptions (season): 14 (1996)
TD Receptions (career): 18 (tie)
• **Jamal Lewis (2000–present)**
Carries (season): 309 (2000)
Rushing Yards (season): 1,364 (2000)
Yards-Per-Carry: (season): 4.4 (2000)
• **Vinny Testaverde (1996–97)**
QB Rating (season): 88.7 (1996)

QB Rating (career): 82.8
Pass Att. (game): 51 (Oct. 27, 1996)
Pass Att. (season) 549 (1996)
Pass Att. (career): 1,019
Passing Yards (game): 429 (Oct. 27, 1996)
Passing Yards (season): 4,177 (1996)
Passing Yards (career): 7,148

Defense
• **Ray Lewis (1996–present)**
Tackles (game): 22 (Sept. 14, 1997)
Tackles (season): 210 (1997)
Tackles (career): 891
• **Michael McCrary (1997–present)**
Sacks (game): 4 (Nov. 8, 1998)
Sacks (season): 14.5 (1998)
Sacks (career): 41.5
• **Rod Woodson (1998–present)**
Int. (season): 7 (1999)
Int. (career): 17

LEAGUE HONORS
Super Bowl MVP
• Ray Lewis (2000)

AFC Defensive Player of the Year
• Ray Lewis (2000)

Extra Point

• *The name Ravens was chosen as a tribute to Baltimore native Edgar Allen Poe, whose most famous poem is titled "The Raven."*
• *In four games during the 2000 playoffs, the Ravens allowed just one offensive touchdown, a two-yard run by the Titans' Eddie George in Baltimore's 24-10 win over Tennessee.*

LB Ray Lewis is the linchpin of the Ravens defense.

Timeline

1995	1996	1997	1998	1999	2000	2001
Cleveland Browns announce plans to move to Baltimore for 1996 season	Ravens win first game in Baltimore, 19-14 over Raiders	Linebacker Ray Lewis named to his first Pro Bowl	Ravens win 38-31 over Indy in Colts first game in Baltimore since leaving in 1983	Brian Billick takes over as Head Coach	Ravens win last seven games of regular season to finish with 12-4 record; earn wild-card berth	Ravens crush Giants 34-7 in Super Bowl XXXV; LB Ray Lewis named MVP

PSINET STADIUM:
ANOTHER SUCCESS IN BALTIMORE

THE ADDITION OF PSINET STADIUM to the Camden Yards complex created perhaps the world's premier dual stadium facility. Baltimore's football stadium features a brick archway exterior similar to that of adjacent Oriole Park and an innovative interior design. The upper deck is divided into four sections by V-shaped notches, eliminating unpopular end-zone corner seats and providing fans views outside the stadium. With all modern amenities, excellent sight lines and three unique plaza areas, this is a top-notch football facility.

CONCESSIONS

• PSINet Stadium offers a variety of food, including pizza, subs, sausages and kosher food (hot dogs, knishes and sandwiches), as well as salads and sandwiches for vegetarians. The crab cakes and crab soup are not-to-be-missed local specialties.

Stadium Facts

Opened: Sept. 6, 1998
Cost: $220 million
Capacity: 69,084
Type: Outdoor
Surface: SportGrass
Home Sweet Home:
• *The city of Baltimore has a long history in professional football. Fans are knowledgeable and very vocal, especially those in the lower corner section called "the Chain Gang."*

GAME DAY TIPS

• **Gate hours:** Gates open two hours prior to kickoff.
• **Tailgating:** Tailgating begins five hours prior to kickoff in all stadium lots. Only season ticket holders can get into those lots, but other non-stadium lots in the area also host tailgating.
• **Weather:** Baltimore in the fall can be cool and rainy. Wear layers and bring rain gear.
• **Prohibited items:** Cans, coolers, glass and water bottles, thermoses, and umbrellas are all prohibited. Smoking is allowed, but only in the open concourses and ramps.
• **Ticket tips:** The front row seats at PSINet Stadium,

raised six feet above the field and only 50 feet from the sidelines, are a great place to watch a game. The upper-level end zone seats are fairly close to the field.
• **Lost and found:** (410) 230-8014.

Seating Plan

Zone A	$75		Club I	$302.50
Zone B	$65		Club II	$242.50
Zone C	$46		Club III	$172.50
Zone D	$66		Club IV	$112.50
Zone E	$56		ATM Sections 118, 217, 243, 245, 502, 529	
Zone F	$46			
Zone G	$41		♿ Throughout	
Zone H	$31			

Directions: *From I-83 south, take Lombard St. From I-95 north toward Baltimore, take exit 52. From I-95 south, go through Ft. McHenry Tunnel, take I-395 north toward Baltimore, then take exit 53. By Train: The Light Rail system stops at the stadium (Hamburg Station) on game days. Bus service is available; call (410) 539-5000.* **Parking:** *Stadium parking is reserved for season ticket holders, but there are lots on Greene, Howard and Pratt streets. Disabled parking can be found in lower lots B, C and R.*

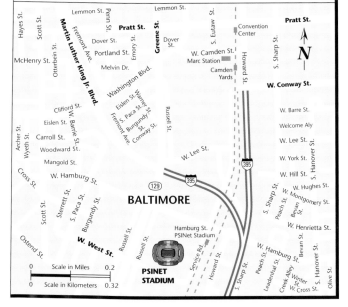

Nearby Hotels

▼▼▼ **Best Western Hotel & Conference Center** *(Motor Inn)*, 5625 O'Donnell St. (Baltimore), (410) 633-9500, $99-$119
▼▼ **Holiday Inn-Inner Harbor** *(Hotel)*, 301 W. Lombard St. (Baltimore), (410) 685-3500, $139-$189
▼▼▼ **Hyatt Regency Baltimore** *(Hotel)*, 300 Light St. (Baltimore), (410) 528-1234, $215-$240
▼▼▼ **Sheraton Inner Harbor Hotel** *(Hotel)*, 300 S. Charles St. (Baltimore), (410) 962-8300, $119-$264
▼▼▼ **Tremont Plaza Hotel** *(Apartment)*, 222 St. Paul Pl. (Baltimore), (410) 727-2222, $109-$129

Nearby Restaurants

▼▼▼ **Della Notte Ristorante** *(Italian)*, 801 Eastern Ave. (Baltimore), 410/837-5500, $11-$20
▼▼ **Germano's Trattoria** *(Regional Italian)*, 300 S. High St. (Baltimore), 410/752-4515, $13-$25
▼▼ **Obrycki's Crab House and Seafood Restaurant** *(Seafood)*, 1727 E. Pratt St. (Baltimore), 410/732-6399, $16-$28
▼▼▼ **Pisces** *(Seafood)*, 300 E. Light St. in the Hyatt Regency Baltimore (Baltimore), 410/605-2835, $22-$32 (dinner only)
▼▼▼ **Windows** *(American)*, 202 E. Pratt St. in the Renaissance Harborplace Hotel (Baltimore), 410/685-8439, $14-$30

BUFFALO BILLS

EVER THE BRIDESMAID and never the bride, the Buffalo Bills have been court-ing the Super Bowl crown since they joined the NFL in 1970. The only team in history to enjoy four straight Super Bowl appearances, the Bills also are notorious for losing all four. Early on, however, there was little to indicate that the team would ever be in a position to vie for any championship. Buffalo struggled in its first two AFL seasons, finishing with losing records in both 1960 and '61. But an administrative error allowed the Bills to snatch QB Jack Kemp off waivers from the rival Chargers for a mere $100. In his initial season at the helm, Kemp spurred the team to its first winning record. The fol-lowing year he led the Bills to the AFL championship game, which was salted away when a jarring tackle by Buffalo linebacker Mike Stratton broke the ribs of the Chargers' star fullback. Defense ruled the day again a year later when the Bills shut out San Diego to win its second-straight AFL crown. But defense was not on the minds of Bills' management when they draft-ed RB O.J. Simpson in 1969. Simpson's meteoric career peaked in 1973, when he became the first player to rush for over 2,000 yards in a single season. Buffalo's greatest — and most painful — years, however, are from 1988 to '93. Led by superstars Jim Kelly, Thurman Thomas, Bruce Smith and Cornelius Bennett, the Bills won five division titles and four AFC crowns, but they never came home with the Super Bowl. Today Bills fans hope young bloods such as Rob Johnson and Eric Moulds can finally deliver the championship they've long been awaiting.

> *"Count me in with Buffalo."*
> — Bills owner Ralph C. Wilson, during 1959 phone call to Lamar Hunt, founder of fledgling AFL

Vital Stats

Stadium Address:
One Bills Dr.,
Orchard Park, N.Y.
Phone: (716) 648-1800
Web: buffalobills.com
Box Office: (877) BBTICKS
Mon.–Fri. 8–6, Sat. and game days 9–4
Media Coverage:
Radio: WGRF (96.9 FM)
TV: WIVB (Channel 4),
Fox (Channel 29)
Training Facility:
Buffalo Bills Fieldhouse,
Orchard Park, N.Y.

POSTSEASON
- AFL Championships........2 (1964, '65)
- AFC Championships ....4 (1990, '91, '92, '93)
- AFC East Titles ....7 (1980, '88, '89, '90, '91, '93, '95)
- AFC Wild Card Berths.....6 (1974, '81, '92, '96, '98, '99)

BILLS WALL OF FAME
- Joe Ferguson (12)
- Jack Kemp (15)
- Robert James (20)
- George Saimes (26)
- O.J. Simpson (32)
- Elbert Dubenion (44)
- Mike Stratton (58)
- Billy Shaw (66)
- Joe Delamielleure (68)
- Bob Kalsu (68)
- Tom Sestak (70)

Extra Point
- *QB Jim Kelly's favorite target was WR Andre Reed. The duo connected for 65 scoring passes, good enough for third on the all-time QB-to-receiver TD list. Only San Francisco's Steve Young and Jerry Rice (85 TDs) and Miami's Dan Marino and Mark Clayton (79 TDs) rank higher.*

- Eddie Abramoski (Trainer)
- Marv Levy (Head Coach)
- Patrick J. McGroder (Administrator)
- Ralph C. Wilson Jr. (Founder / Club President)
- The 12th Man (Bills fans)

TEAM RECORDS
Offense
- **Steve Christie (1992–present)**
Field Goals (career): 234
Longest Field Goal: 59 yards (Sept. 26, 1993)
Points (season): 140 (1998)
Points (career): 1,011
- **Joe Ferguson (1973–84)**
Pass Att. (season): 508 (1983)
- **Cookie Gilchrist (1962–64)**
Points (game): 30 (Dec. 8, 1963)
- **Jim Kelly (1986–96)**
Comp. (season): 304 (1991)
Comp. (career): 2,874
Passing Yards (season): 3,844 (1991)
Passing Yards (career): 35,467
TD Passes (season): 33 (1991)
TD Passes (career): 237
- **Eric Moulds (1996–present)**
Receiving Yards (season): 1,368 (1998)
Receptions (season): 94 (2000)
- **Andre Reed (1985–99)**
Receiving Yards (career): 13,095
Receptions (career): 941
TDs (career): 87

- O.J. Simpson (1969–77)
Rushing Yards (game): 273 (Nov. 25, 1976)
Rushing Yards (season): 2,003 (1973)
TDs (season): 23 (1975)
- **Thurman Thomas (1988–99)**
Carries (season): 355 (1993)
Carries (career): 2,849
Rushing Yards (career): 11,938
Rushing TDs (career): 65

Defense
- **Butch Byrd (1964–70)**
Int. (career): 40
- **Bruce Smith (1985–99)**
Sacks (season): 19 (1990)
Sacks (career): 171
- **Chris Spielman (1996–98)**
Tackles (season): 206 (1996)

LEAGUE HONORS
AFL MVP
- Cookie Gilchrist (1962)
- Jack Kemp (1965)

NFL MVP
- O.J. Simpson (1973)
- Thurman Thomas (1991)

NFL Defensive Player of the Year
- Bruce Smith (1990, '93, '96)

AFC Defensive Player of the Year
- Bruce Smith (1987, 88)

- Cornelius Bennett (1988, '91)

AFL Rookie of the Year
- Bobby Burnett (1966)

NFL Rookie of the Year
- Shane Conlan (1987)

Pro Football Hall of Fame
- O.J. Simpson (1985)
- Billy Shaw (1999)
- Marv Levy (2001)

Rob Johnson is the Bills QB.

Timeline
1960	1963	1964	1965	1969	1973	1980	1985	1988	1990	1993	1994	2000	2001
Bills are seventh of eight charter members of the AFL	Team claims QB Jack Kemp off NFL waivers for $100	Buffalo leads AFL in rushing yards and TDs; wins first AFL Championship	Bills shutout Chargers to win second-straight AFL crown	O.J. Simpson drafted No. 1 out of USC	Simpson is first to gain 2,000 yards on the ground	Bills go 11-5 and win first AFC East title	Bills draft DE Bruce Smith and WR Andre Reed	Defense allows fewest points in AFC; team wins division	Bills popularize "no-huddle" offense; win first AFC crown	QB Frank Reich comes off bench to spearhead 38-point comeback win in AFC wild-card game	Bills become first team to go to four-straight Super Bowls; team loses all four	QB Rob Johnson gets sur-prise nod over Flutie for AFC wild-card game; Bills lose	Flutie released; Johnson is undisputed No. 1 QB

RALPH WILSON STADIUM: MOST POPULAR PLACE IN TOWN

DESPITE THE OFTEN FRIGID temperatures and the fact that the hard-luck Bills just can't seem to win a Super Bowl, Ralph Wilson Stadium is almost always a full house. Built in 1973, the stadium has undergone two major facelifts — the most recent in 1999. On top of improving the sound system and bringing some seats closer to the action, the old playing surface was replaced with a new and improved AstroTurf. The absorption layer underneath has been specially designed to provide a softer landing when the weather gets cold.

CONCESSIONS

• The Ralph Wilson Stadium has a wide variety of food options. Choices include barbecue, chili, Italian sausages, pizza and kosher hot dogs. Limited vegetarian options.

GAME DAY TIPS

• **Gate hours:** Gates open two hours prior to kickoff.

Stadium Facts

Opened: *Aug. 17, 1973*
Cost: *$22 million*
Capacity: *75,339*
Type: *Outdoor*
Surface: *AstroTurf*
Home Sweet Home:
• *"The Hawk" (cold wind blowing off Lake Erie late in the season) makes it hard for warm-weather teams to put together an effective passing game.*

• **Tailgating:** Tailgating begins four hours prior to game time in all stadium lots. The Buffalo Bills Fieldhouse, located next to the stadium, holds the largest indoor tailgating party in the league.
• **Weather:** The weather in Buffalo can be extreme — the summer months are hot and sunny, but after October dress for chilly and often snowy weather.
• **Prohibited items:** Cans, bottles, coolers, whistles, horns, fireworks, laser pointers, strollers, umbrellas and video cameras are forbidden.

Seating Plan

■ **Tunnel Entrance End Zone - 100 Level** Scoreboard End Zone **$35**
■ **Tunnel Entrance End Zone -200 Level Upper Deck Rows 21-38** **$40**
■ **Lower Level, Upper Decks Rows 1-20** **$42**
■ ......**N/A**
■ ......**N/A**
▨ ......**N/A**
ATM Locations not permanent
♿ Throughout 100s

Smoking is prohibited in the stadium.
• **Ticket tips:** Tickets for individual games are often available in advance, although games against division rivals such as New England and Miami sell out quickly.
• **Lost and found:** (716) 648-1800.

Directions: *From I-90 west, take exit 55 (Rte. 219 S.), then exit at Mile Strip Rd. W. and turn left on Abbott Rd. From Rte. 219 north, take exit 20A W. (Big Tree Rd.) and turn right onto Abbott Rd. From I-90 east, take exit 56 and turn left onto Rte. 179, then proceed to Abbot Rd. By Bus: NFTA offers bus service to and from the stadium. Call (716) 855-7211 for more information.* **Parking:** *There are 14 lots surrounding the stadium. Parking for the disabled is offered in all the "suite" lots closest to the stadium.*

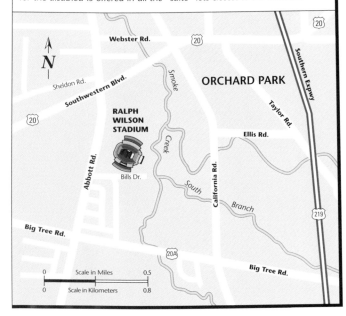

Nearby Hotels

▼▼ **Econo Lodge South** *(Motel)*, 4344 Milestrip Rd. (Blasdell), (716) 825-7530, $40-$99
▼▼▼ **Holiday Inn Hamburg** *(Motor Inn)*, 5440 Camp Rd. (Hamburg), (716) 649-0500, $79-$109
▼▼ **McKinley Park Inn** *(Motor Inn)*, 3950 McKinley Pkwy. (Blasdell), (716) 648-5700, $52-$106
▼▼ **Red Roof Inn** *(Motel)*, 5370 Camp Rd. (Hamburg), (716) 648-7222, $42-$84
▼▼ **Tallyho-tel** *(Motel)*, 5245 Camp Rd. (Hamburg), (716) 648-2000, $30-$99

Nearby Restaurants

▼▼▼ **Daniel's** *(American)*, 174 Buffalo St. (Hamburg), (716) 648-6554, $15-$22 (dinner only)
▼▼ **Ilio DiPaolo's Restaurant** *(Italian)*, 3785 S. Park Ave. (Blasdell), (716) 825-3675, $7-$18
▼▼ **Romanello's South** *(Italian)*, 5793 S. Park Ave. (Hamburg), (716) 649-0450, $12-$25 (dinner only)
Seven's Corners Restaurant *(American)*, 4536 Big Tree Rd. (Hamburg), (716) 649-9728, $8-$12
Zebb's Deluxe Grill & Bar *(American)*, 3349 Southwestern Blvd. (Orchard Park), (716) 674-3700, $7-$12

CAROLINA PANTHERS

THE CAROLINA PANTHERS COULD SERVE AS A MODEL for professional expansion teams everywhere. From its administration and stadium to its performance on the field, Carolina has been first class all the way. The tone for the franchise was set immediately when team officials made their final presentation before the NFL expansion committee who would decide where to locate new franchises. At the time, through permanent seat licenses, the Panthers had already effectively sold out their yet to be constructed stadium and had more than $140 million pledged for its construction. This great start translated right away to success on the field. After an expansion record seven wins in its inaugural campaign, the Panthers put together one of the most unlikely seasons in NFL history, posting a 12-4 record and winning the 1996 NFC West division title. On offense, young quarterback Kerry Collins and tight end Wesley Walls led the charge. At the same time, the defense, anchored by veteran linebacker Sam Mills, emerged as one of the league's stingiest. The upstart Panthers strode into Texas Stadium and defeated the defending Super Bowl champion Dallas Cowboys 26-17 in the divisional playoff game. The Panthers lost the NFC championship game 30-13 to Green Bay, but Carolina pride was high. The team fell back to Earth the following season, finishing at 7-9, and dropped to 4-12 in 1998. In 1999 Coach Dom Capers was out and former 49er head coach George Siefert was in. Siefert has led the Panthers to respectable records in 1999 and 2000, but loyal Carolina fans are still waiting for the team's second playoff appearance.

Vital Stats

Stadium Address:
800 South Mint St.,
Charlotte, N.C.
Phone: (704) 358-7000
Web: cpanthers.com
Box Office:
(704) 358-7800
Mon.–Fri. 8:30–5:30,
game days
Media Coverage:
Radio: WRFX (99.7 FM)
TV: WSOC (Channel 9),
WAXN (Channel 64)
Training Facility:
Ericsson Stadium,
Charlotte, N.C.

POSTSEASON
• NFC West Titles 1
(1996)

RING OF HONOR
• Mike McCormack (1997)
• Sam Mills (1998)

TEAM RECORDS
Offense
• Steve Beuerlein
(1996–2000)
Comp. Pct. (season):
62.97 (1998)
Comp. Pct. (career): 60.41
Pass Att. (season): 571 (1999)
Pass Att. (career): 1,723
Pass Comp. (season):
343 (1999)
Pass Comp. (career): 1,041
Passing Yards (game):

373 (Dec. 12, 1999)
Passing Yards (season):
4,436 (1999)
Passing Yards (career): 12,960
TD Passes (game): 5
(Jan. 2, 2000)
TD Passes (season): 36 (1999)
TD Passes (career): 86
• Tshimanga Biakabutuka
(1996–present)
Carries (career): 558
Longest Run From
Scrimmage: 67 yards
(Sept. 26, 1999)
Rushing TDs (career): 13 (tie)
Rushing Yards (career): 2,300
Yards-Per-Carry (season):
5.2 (1999)
• Kerry Collins (1995–98)
Pass Att. (game): 53
(Sept. 27, 1998)
Int. (season): 21 (1997)
Int. (career): 54
• John Kasay (1995–99)
Points (season): 145 (1996)
Points (career): 532
Field Goals (game): 5 (Sept.
1, 1996) (Sept. 8, 1996)
Field Goals (season): 37 (1996)
Field Goals (career): 126
• Fred Lane (1996–99)
Rushing Yards (game):

Muhsin Muhammad displays great speed at wide receiver.

147 (Nov. 2, 1997)
Rushing TDs (season):
7 (1997)
Rushing TDs (career): 13 (tie)
• Muhsin Muhammed
(1996–present)
Receiving Yards (season):
1,253 (1999)
Receiving Yards (career): 4,101
Receptions (game):

11 (Dec. 18, 1999)
Receptions (season):
102 (2000)
Receptions (career): 318
TD Receptions (game): 3
(Dec. 18, 1999)
• Wesley Walls
(1996–present)
TD Receptions (season):
12 (1999) (tie)
TD Receptions (career) 35
• Patrick Jeffers (1999)
TD Receptions (season):
12 (1999) (tie)
Yards-Per-Reception (season):
17.17 (1999)

Defense
• Michael Barrow (1997–99)
Tackles (game): 18
(Sept. 6, 1998)
Tackles (season): 158 (1998)
Tackles (career): 394
• Eric Davis (1996–2000)
Int. (career): 25
Int. Return Yards
(career): 223
• Kevin Greene
(1996, 1998–99)
Sacks (game): 3.0
(Sept. 6, 1998)
Sacks (season): 15.0 (1998)
Sacks (career): 41.5
• Brett Maxie (1995–96)
Int. (season): 6 (1995)

LEAGUE HONORS
NFL Coach of the Year
• Dom Capers (1996)

Extra Point

• Eight-year vet Michael Bates holds the Panther record for longest kickoff return, a 100-yard TD scamper against Atlanta in 1999. His speed is definitely world class — Bates won bronze in the 200-meter at the Barcelona Olympics.
• The 1996 Panthers defense allowed only 56 points in the second half of the season, a NFL record.

"They were there for us and I wanted to thank them."

— Offensive lineman Blake Brockermeyer, explaining why he'd run across the field to high-five Panther fans after playoff win

Timeline

1987	1989	1990	1992	1993	1994	1995	1996	1997	1998	1999	2000	2001

- Former Colt receiver Jerry Richardson announces intention to bring NFL to Carolinas
- Richardson selects site in uptown Charlotte for new football venue
- Exhibition game between Atlanta and Washington sells out in Chapel Hill, NC
- Richardson presents private funding plans for new stadium
- NFL selects Carolina as 29th NFL franchise
- First Panther players are signed
- Panthers go 7-9 in first season, setting record for first year teams
- Ericsson Stadium opens
- Panthers defeat defending Super Bowl champion Cowboys in team's first playoff game
- Sam Mills inducted into Panthers Hall of Honor
- George Siefert hired as Head Coach
- Carolina goes 7-9, missing playoffs
- Panthers release QB Steve Beuerlein, who had started team's previous 44 games

ERICSSON STADIUM: A MODEL FACILITY

WIDELY ACKNOWLEDGED AS one of the NFL's finest facilities, Ericsson Stadium is a huge complex that occupies a prominent site in uptown Charlotte. One hundred percent privately funded, partially through the sale of personal seat licenses, Ericsson is the ideal self-contained team headquarters, complete with training facilities, practice fields and team offices. It is also a great place to see football. Open-air and with a natural-grass surface, it has great atmosphere and some of the best sight lines and fan amenities in the league.

CONCESSIONS

By and large, the concessions offered at Ericsson Stadium are standard: hamburgers, bratwurst, hot dogs, pizza, fries, nachos and ice cream. Club level seating gives hungry spectators access to a wider variety of food, including lobster, crab cakes, ribs and chicken.

Stadium Facts

Opened: *Aug. 3, 1996*
Cost: *$187 million*
Capacity: *73,258*
Type: *Outdoor*
Surface: *Grass*
Home Sweet Home:
• *Ericsson's enormous size and intense fan noise along with its interior design, which echos the team colors, make it an intimidating place for visiting teams.*

GAME DAY TIPS

• **Gate hours:** Gates open two hours prior to kickoff.
• **Tailgating:** Although Ericsson does not have a lot open to the public, tailgating does take place and begins about three hours before kickoff in the private lots around the stadium.
• **Weather:** Charlotte is known for its wonderful weather and the football season is no exception. Expect warm and sunny days.
• **Prohibited items:** Items not allowed at Ericsson Stadium include coolers, containers, bottles, cans, umbrellas, video cameras and tape recorders. As well, strollers, baby seats, folding chairs, noisemakers, horns, and beachballs are not allowed. Smoking is permitted only in designated areas.
• **Ticket tips:** About 10 percent of available tickets are reserved for single-game purchases. These sell out quickly, especially if rivals such as the 49ers or the Packers are in town.
• **Lost and found:** (704) 358-7407.

163

Seating Plan

☐	$50	☐	N/A
☐	$38	☐	N/A
☐	N/A	☐	N/A
☐	N/A	☐	N/A
☐	N/A	**ATM Sections 345/346, 516/517**	
☐	N/A	♿ **Throughout**	
☐	N/A		

Directions: Take Fifth St., Trade St. or John Belk Frwy. exit off I-77 north. From I-85 west, take Brookshire Frwy. E. (exit 36) to Graham St. From I-85 south, take Graham St. (exit 40). By Bus: Call Charlotte Transit at (704) 336-3366 for information. *Parking:* There is no parking at the stadium but there are private lots on S. Tryon, Graham, 2nd, 3rd and 4th streets. A drop-off spot for the disabled is located on Morehead St. between Church and Mint. Carolinas Medical Center runs park and shuttle service for people with disabilities. Call (704) 358-7000 ext. 5656.

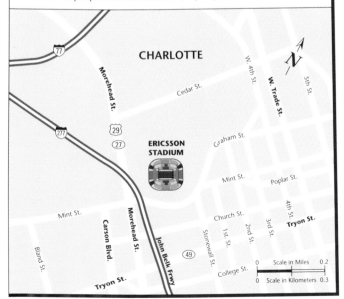

Nearby Hotels

▼▼▼ **DoubleTree Hotel Charlotte at Gateway Village** *(Motor Inn)*, 895 W. Trade St. (Charlotte), (704) 347-0070, $71-$165
▼▼▼▼ **Hilton Charlotte & Towers** *(Hotel)*, 222 E. Third St. (Charlotte), (704) 377-1500, $95-$185
▼▼▼ **La Quinta Inn-Airport** *(Motel)*, 3100 I-85 S. Service Rd. (Charlotte), (704) 393-5306, $49-$65
▼▼▼ **Morgan Hotel and Suites** *(Suite Motel)*, 315 E. Woodlawn Rd. (Charlotte), (704) 522-0852, $79-$189
▼▼ **Red Roof Inn-Airport** *(Motel)*, 3300 I-85 S. Service Rd. (Charlotte), (704) 392-2316, $42-$57

Nearby Restaurants

▼▼▼ **Bravo Ristorante** *(Northern Italian)*, 555 S. McDowell St. in the Adam's Mark Charlotte (Charlotte), (704) 372-5440, $16-$26 (dinner only)
▼▼ **India Palace** *(Indian)*, 4515 E. Independence Blvd. (Charlotte), (704) 568-7176, $8-$16
▼▼▼▼ **McNinch House** *(Continental)*, 511 N. Church St. (Charlotte), (704) 332-6159, $85 (dinner only)
▼▼ **Ranch House** *(Steakhouse)*, 5614 Wilkinson Blvd. (Charlotte), (704) 399-5411, $10-$22 (dinner only)
▼▼ **Sonoma** *(Regional American)*, 129 W. Trade St. (Charlotte), (704) 377-1333, $18-$24

CHICAGO BEARS

RICH IN HISTORY AND SUPPORTED by some of the rowdiest, most loyal fans in all of sport, the Chicago Bears are a national institution. Started as the Decatur Staleys in 1920 by legendary founder and head coach George Halas, the franchise first came to prominence when it signed college superstar Red Grange in 1925. That year the Bears' nationwide barnstorming tour with Grange was instrumental in selling professional football to a national audience. Although Halas retired from coaching four times over his career, he always seemed to come back. He was at the helm for the team's 23-21 win over the New York Giants in the first official NFL championship game in 1933 and still there 30 years later for the last of his five titles in 1963. But no coach wins by himself. The history of the Bears is littered with players whose bios read more like myths. There is RB Bronko Nagurski, who was said to have cracked a brick wall at the back end of the end zone after he ran into it; QB Sid Luckman, winner of four NFL titles and the leader of the Bears' revolutionary T-formation; kicker George Blanda, the NFL's paragon of longevity who began his record 26-season career in Chicago; TE Mike Ditka, the man who changed "third tackle" into a receiving position; fearsome LB Dick Butkus, who played, and hit, with unmatched ferocity; and RB Walter "Sweetness" Payton, who combined power and grace like no other back and holds the all-time rushing yards record to prove it. Chicago hasn't won a championship since 1985, when its defense destroyed all comers. But with a couple of upsets in the 2000 season, the current Bears have shown signs of coming out of hibernation.

Vital Stats

Stadium Address:
425 E. McFetridge Dr.,
Chicago, Ill.
Phone: (312) 747-1285
Web: chicagobears.com,
soldierfield.net
Box Office:
(847) 615-2327
Mon.–Fri. 9–4
Media Coverage:
Radio: WBBM (780 AM)
TV: WFLD-FOX (Channel 3)
Training Facility:
Halas Hall, Lake Forest, Ill.

• Gary Fencik (1976–87)
Int. (career): 38

LEAGUE HONORS
Pro Football Hall of Fame
• Harold "Red" Grange (1963)
• George Halas (1963)
• Bronko Nagurski (1963)
• Ed Healey (1964)
• Roy "Link" Lyman (1964)
• George Trafton (1964)
• John "Paddy" Driscoll (1965)
• Danny Fortmann (1965)
• Sid Luckman (1965)
• George McAfee (1966)
• Clyde "Bulldog" Turner (1966)
• Joe Stydahar (1967)
• Bill Hewitt (1971)
• Bill George (1974)
• George Connor (1975)
• Gale Sayers (1977)
• Dick Butkus (1979)
• George Blanda (1981)
• Doug Atkins (1982)
• George Musso (1982)
• Mike Ditka (1988)
• Stan Jones (1991)
• Walter Payton (1993)
• Mike Singletary (1998)

NFL Rookie of the Year
• Mike Ditka (1961)
• Ronnie Bull (1962)
• Gale Sayers (1965)
• Mark Carrier (1990)

NFL MVP
• Sid Luckman (1943)
• Walter Payton (1977, '85)

POSTSEASON
• Super Bowl
• Championships 1
(1985)
• NFL Championships 6
(1933, '40, '41, '43, '46, '63)
• NFC Central Titles 6
(1984 ,'85, '86, '87, '88, '90)

RETIRED NUMBERS:
• Bronko Nagurski (3)
• George McAfee (5)
• George Halas (7)
• Willie Galimore (28)
• Walter Payton (34)
• Gale Sayers (40)
• Brian Piccolo (41)
• Sid Luckman (42)
• Dick Butkus (51)

Extra Point
• George Halas named the team the Bears as a tribute to Chicago Cubs owner Bill Veeck. Noting that football players are bigger than baseball players, Halas quipped, "If baseball players are cubs, then football players must be bears."
• With a 617-439-42 all-time win-loss record, the Bears have won more games than any other franchise in NFL history.

"I enjoyed playing in Soldier Field and I'm very excited that Soldier Field will not be torn down."
— Former Bear Mike Singletary

• Bill Hewitt (56)
• Bill George (61)
• Clyde "Bulldog" Turner (66)
• Harold "Red" Grange (77)

TEAM RECORDS
Offense
• Jim Harbaugh (1987–93)
Comp. (career): 1,023
Comp. Pct. (game): 90.0 (Jan. 2, 1994)
• Erik Kramer (1994–98)
Comp. (season): 315 (1995)
Comp. Pct. (career): 58.6
Pass Att. (game): 60 (Nov. 16, 1997)
QB Rating (career): 80.7
TD Passes (season): 29 (1995)
• Sid Luckman (1939–50)
Passing Yards (career): 14,686
TD Passes (game): 7 (Nov. 14, 1943)
TD Passes (career): 137
• Johnny Lujack (1948–51)
Passing Yards (game):

468 (Dec. 11, 1949)
• Walter Payton (1975–87)
Receptions (career): 492
Rushing Yards (game): 275 (Nov. 20, 1977)
Rushing Yards (season): 1,852 (1977)
Rushing Yards (career): 16,726
1,000-yard Seasons: 10
100-yard Games (career): 77
Rushing TDs (career): 110

Defense
• Richard Dent (1983–93, '95)
Sacks (season): 17.5 (1984)
Sacks (career): 124.5

Glyn Milburn provides Chicago with a solid return game.

Timeline

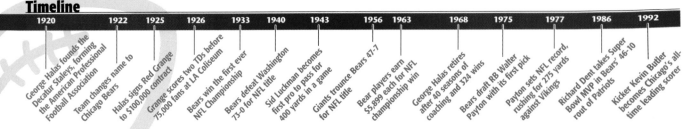

| 1920 | 1922 | 1925 | 1926 | 1933 | 1940 | 1943 | 1956 | 1963 | 1968 | 1975 | 1977 | 1986 | 1992 |

George Halas founds the Decatur Staleys, forming the American Professional Football Association

Team changes name to Chicago Bears

Halas signs Red Grange to $100,000 contract

Grange scores two TDs before 75,000 fans at LA Coliseum

Bears win the first ever NFL Championship

Bears defeat Washington 73-0 for NFL title

Sid Luckman becomes first pro to pass for 400 yards in a game

Giants trounce Bears 47-7 for NFL title

Bear players earn $5,899 each for NFL championship win

George Halas retires after 40 seasons of coaching and 324 wins

Bears draft RB Walter Payton with its first pick

Payton sets NFL record, rushing for 275 yards against Vikings

Richard Dent takes Super Bowl MVP in Bears 46-10 rout of Patriots

Kicker Kevin Butler becomes Chicago's all-time leading scorer

SOLDIER FIELD: A PILLAR OF THE COMMUNITY

BUILT AS A MEMORIAL TO THE SOLDIERS of the World War I, Soldier Field hosted its first football game in 1924, when Notre Dame edged Northwestern 13-6. The Bears didn't arrive until 1971, ending the team's 50-year residence at Wrigley Field. The stadium was renovated extensively in 1979 to improve sight lines, lighting and the playing surface. But with its age showing, it has been officially confirmed that the Bears will rebuild Soldier Field, keeping the original pillars but knocking down the rest. In the meantime, the team will play in a not-yet-determined location.

CONCESSIONS

• Soldier Field offers a few specialty foods such as ribs, Tex/Mex and Italian. Other concessions include pro sports basics such as hot dogs, beer and nachos. Vegetarians looking for a meal have few choices.

Stadium Facts

Opened: Oct. 9, 1924
Cost: $13 million
Capacity: 66,950
Type: Outdoor
Surface: Grass
Home Sweet Home:
• Situated on the banks of Lake Michigan in the Windy City, Soldier Field can be an inhospitable venue for players unaccustomed to cold weather and strong breezes.

GAME DAY TIPS

• **Gate hours:** Gates open two hours prior to kickoff.
• **Tailgating:** Tailgating takes place in all on-site lots and those in the surrounding area. Festivities start four hours before kickoff.
• **Weather:** Low temperatures and wind whipping off Lake Michigan mean games after October can be cold.
• **Prohibited items:** Umbrellas, poles, coolers, cans, bottles and video cameras are prohibited. Smoking is allowed only in the concourse area.
• **Ticket tips:** The Bears are regularly sold out, mostly to season ticket holders. A few tickets are reserved for single-game sales, but these disappear very quickly after they go on sale (June 1 by mail). Demand is lower for preseason and late-season due to the colder weather. Games against Bears rival the Packers sell out especially quickly.
Lost and found: (312) 747-1285.

Seating Plan

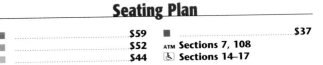

■ ....$59   ■ $37
■ ....$52   ATM **Sections 7, 108**
■ ....$44   ♿ **Sections 14–17**

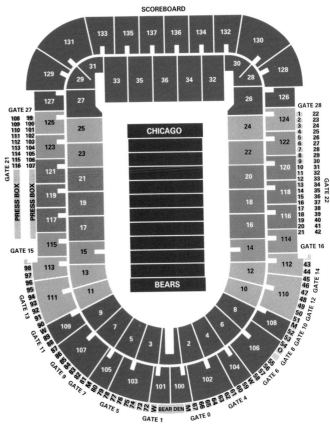

Directions: Take I-55 north to Lakeshore Dr. (Hwy. 41 N.), exit McFetridge Dr. From I-290 east or I-94 south, take Congress Pkwy. exit, turn right onto Columbus Dr. and turn onto McFetridge Dr. **Public Transportation:** Trains, buses and subways go to Soldier Field. Call the Regional Transit Authority at (312) 836-7000 for information. **Parking:** On-site lots are reserved for season ticket holders, but there are 18,000 spots nearby on McFetridge Dr., E. 18th and Lakeshore and 31st St. The disabled can get a reserved spot in the stadium lot or be dropped off on Waldron near Lot 4.

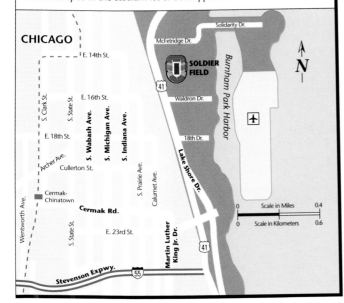

Nearby Hotels

▼▼ **Best Western Grant Park Hotel** *(Hotel)*, 1100 S. Michigan Ave. (Chicago), (312) 922-2900, $139-$335
▼▼ **The Congress Plaza Hotel & Convention Center** *(Hotel)*, 520 S. Michigan Ave. (Chicago), (312) 427-3800, $99-$205
▼▼▼▼ **Hilton Chicago** *(Classic Hotel)*, 720 S. Michigan Ave. (Chicago), (312) 922-4400, $129-$354
▼▼▼ **Hyatt on Printers Row** *(Hotel)*, 500 S. Dearborn St. (Chicago), (312) 986-1234, $205-$230
▼▼▼▼ **Hyatt Regency McCormick Place Chicago** *(Hotel)*, 2233 S. Martin Luther King Dr. (Chicago), (312) 567-1234, $219-$244

Nearby Restaurants

▼▼ **Emperor's Choice,** *(Chinese)*, 2238 S. Wentworth Ave. (Chicago), (312) 225-8800, $7-$20
▼▼▼▼▼ **Everest** *(French)*, 440 S. LaSalle St. at One Financial Place (Chicago), (312) 663-8920, $28-$34 (dinner only)
▼▼ **Harry Caray's Restaurant** *(Steakhouse)*, 33 W. Kinzie St. (Chicago), (312) 828-0966, $11-$33
▼▼ **The Italian Village** *(Italian)*, 71 W. Monroe St. (Chicago), (312) 332-7005, $11-$22
▼▼▼ **Russian Tea Time** *(Russian)*, 77 E. Adams St. (Chicago), (312) 360-0000, $15-$26

CINCINNATI BENGALS

IN THE MID-1960S FORMER CLEVELAND BROWNS coach Paul Brown had the urge to get back into football. He considered the possibility of a second professional franchise in Ohio. His son Mike did some research and suggested Cincinnati as a good site. The legendary coach went to Ohio Governor James Rhodes with the idea and in 1967 Brown's group was awarded an AFL franchise. Having compiled a 115-49-6 record as head coach of Cleveland, Brown was unaccustomed to losing — and it showed. In just its third season, and the first following the AFL–NFL merger, the Bengals won their division and a trip to the playoffs. At the time, this stood as the quickest ascent by an expansion team in league history. With the drafting of Ken Anderson in 1971, Cincinnati secured the quarterback position for many years to come. By 1975 Anderson was collecting his second NFL passing title and leading the Bengals back into the postseason. But it was in 1981 that the franchise really hit the big time. Riding Anderson's arm and Pete Johnson's power rushing, the Bengals made it all the way to Super Bowl XVI, but lost the game 26-21 to the 49ers. Seven years later, with NFL MVP Boomer Esiason barking the signals and feeding the ball to receiving sensation Eddie Brown and rusher James Brooks, the franchise made it to the title game again. The Bengals lost again, this time on a heartbreaking last-minute Joe Montana touchdown pass. With the current squad in the midst of a long rebuilding process, Bengals' fans are left speculating when they'll get their next chance at glory.

Corey Dillon's rushing is a bright spot for the Bengals.

POSTSEASON
- AFC Championships ....2 (1981, '88)
- AFC Central Titles ....5 (1970, '73, '81, '88, '90)
- AFC Wild Card Berths.....1 (1975)

RETIRED NUMBERS
- Bob Johnson (54)

TEAM RECORDS
Offense
- **Ken Anderson (1971–86)**
Comp. (game): 40 (Dec. 20, 1982)
Comp. (career): 2,654
Pass Att. (career): 4,475
Passing Yards (career): 32,838
QB Rating (season): 98.4 (1981)
TD Passes (season) 29 (1981)
TD Passes (career): 197
Yards-Per-Carry (career): 5.6
- **Jeff Blake (1994–99)**
Pass Att. (season): 567 (1995)
Comp. (season): 326 (1995)
- **Jim Breech (1980–92)**
Points (career): 1,151
Field Goals (career): 225
- **James Brooks (1984–91)**
Rushing Yards (career): 6,447
Yards-Per-Carry (season): 5.6 (1989)
- **Eddie Brown (1992–99)**
Receiving Yards (season): 1,273 (1988)
Yards-Per-Reception (season): 24.0 (1988)
- **Isaac Curtis (1973–84)**
Receiving Yards (career): 7,101
- **Corey Dillon (1994–present)**
Rushing Yards (season): 1,435 (2000)
- **Boomer Esiason (1984–92, '97)**
Passing Yards (game): 490 (Oct. 7, 1990)
Passing Yards (season): 3,959 (1986)
- **Pete Johnson (1977–83)**
Carries (season): 274 (1981)
Carries (career): 1,402
Rushing TDs (career): 64
- **Tremain Mack (1992–present)**
Kickoff Return TDs (career): 2
Kickoff Return Yards (season): 1,382 (1999)
- **Doug Pelfrey (1992–2000)**
Field Goals (season): 29 (1995)
Points (season): 121 (1995)
- **Carl Pickens (1992–99)**
Receptions (season) 100 (1996)
Receptions (career): 530
Receiving TDs (season): 17 (1995)
- **Ickey Woods (1992–99)**
Rushing TDs (season): 15 (1988)

Defense
- **Coy Bacon (1976–77)**
Sacks (season): 22 (1976)
- **Eddie Edwards (1977–88)**
Sacks (game): 5 (tie) (Dec. 21, 1981)
Sacks (career): 83.5
- **Mike Reid (1970–74)**
Sacks (game): 5 (tie) (Oct. 15, 1972)
- **Ken Riley (1969–83)**
Int. (season): 9 (1978)
Int. (career): 65
Int. TDs (career): 5

LEAGUE HONORS
Pro Football Hall of Fame
- Anthony Munoz (1998)

NFL MVP
- Ken Anderson (1981)
- Boomer Esiason (1988)

NFL Rookie of the Year
- Eddie Brown (1985)
- Carl Pickens (1992)

AFL Rookie of the Year
- Greg Cook (1969)

Vital Stats

Stadium Address:
One Paul Brown Stadium, Cincinnati, Ohio
Phone: (513) 621-3550
Web: bengals.com
Box Office:
(513) 621-8383, Mon.–Fri. 9–5, game week Sat. 12–5
Media Coverage:
Radio: WCKY (1360 AM), WOFX (92.5 FM)
TV: CBS (WKRC Channel 12)
Training Facility:
Paul Brown Stadium, Cincinnati, Ohio

Extra Point

- *The Bengals have an impressive 13-7 record in regular season games that go into overtime.*
- *On Aug. 1, 1998, former Bengal OT Anthony Munoz became the franchise's first career player to be elected to the Pro Football Hall of Fame. Munoz, a perennial Pro Bowler, was elected in his first year of eligibility.*

Timeline

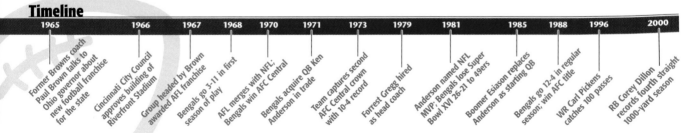

1965	1966	1967	1968	1970	1971	1973	1979	1981	1985	1988	1996	2000
Former Browns coach Paul Brown talks to Ohio governor about new football franchise for the state	Cincinnati City Council approves building of Riverfront Stadium	Group headed by Brown awarded AFL franchise	Bengals go 3-11 in first season of play	AFL merges with NFL; Bengals win AFC Central	Bengals acquire QB Ken Anderson in trade	Team captures second AFC Central crown with 10-4 record	Forrest Gregg hired as head coach	Anderson named NFL MVP; Bengals lose Super Bowl XVI 26-21 to 49ers	Boomer Esiason replaces Anderson as starting QB	Bengals go 12-4 in regular season; win AFC title	WR Carl Pickens catches 100 passes	RB Corey Dillon records fourth straight 1000-yard season

PAUL BROWN STADIUM: MONUMENT TO A FOOTBALL ICON

SITUATED ON THE CINCINNATI WATERFRONT, Paul Brown Stadium provides a dramatic setting for football and is a fitting homage to the Bengals' first coach and founder. The facility sits on the west end of a Cincinnati waterfront project that will also include a new ballpark for the Reds to the east and parkland in between the two buildings. The stadium features low-tiered end zones, which allow fans a look at the city skyline and the Ohio River. The facility has excellent sight lines and fan amenities.

CONCESSIONS

As well as traditional options, Paul Brown Stadium offers steak sandwiches, barbecue, shrimp and Cincinnati specialties such as chili and coney dogs. Vegetarians can enjoy a choice of sandwiches and salads.

Stadium Facts

Opened: Aug. 20, 2000
Cost: $453.2 million
Capacity: 65,600
Type: Outdoor
Surface: Grass
Home Sweet Home:
• Despite controversies over team management and lawsuits against the team over seat licenses, the Bengals still drew more fans than ever in 2000. And Bengals fans are renowned as being among the game's loudest.

GAME DAY TIPS

• **Gate hours:** Gates open two hours prior to kickoff.
• **Tailgating:** Tailgating takes place in the lots at Paul Brown Stadium beginning four hours before kickoff. There is also tailgating at many of the private lots in the surrounding area.
• **Weather:** Although local weather is usually fairly temperate early in the football season, Cincinnati can be cool in November and subject to rain showers. To stay dry and warm, make sure to wear several layers and bring along rain gear.
• **Prohibited items:** Bottles, cans, thermoses, hard coolers, alcoholic beverages, chairs, fireworks, frisbees, weapons, laser pointers, strollers, noisemakers, umbrellas, sticks and bats, video cameras and audio recorders are prohibited. Smoking is allowed only at designated areas in the stair landings and ramps.
• **Ticket tips:** The very new Paul Brown Stadium was carefully designed to ensure that there's not a bad seat in the house. Single-game tickets are usually not too hard to get. The Bengals' biggest rival is Ohio's other team, the Browns; games between the two sell out very quickly.
• **Lost and found:** (513) 455-4850.

Seating Plan

■ **Club**
Sold As Season Tickets Only
■ **$50**
■ **$45**
■ **$40**
■ **$35**
ATM **Sections 114, 317, 333; lounges; plaza pro shop**
♿ **Throughout**

GATE D

GATE C · GATE B · GATE A · GATE E

BENGALS · CINCINNATI

Directions: From I-71 south, exit 3rd St., left onto Central. From I-71/I-75 north, exit 2nd St., right onto Elm. By Public Transportation: A new transit center is scheduled to open in late 2001. **Parking:** The stadium lot is for season ticket holders, but there are over 14,000 spaces available within walking distance of the stadium on 3rd, 4th, 6th and 7th streets. Disabled parking is available in the Smith St. lot at Central Ave. and Pete Rose Way.

Nearby Hotels

▼▼▼ **Amos Shinkle Townhouse Bed & Breakfast** (*Historic Bed & Breakfast*), 215 Garrard St. (Covington, Ky.), (859) 431-2118, $79-$150
▼▼▼▼ **The Cincinnatian Hotel** (*Hotel*), 601 Vine St. (Cincinnati), (513) 381-3000, $225-$1500
▼▼▼ **Cincinnati's Weller Haus Bed & Breakfast** (*Historic Bed & Breakfast*), 319 Poplar St. (Bellevue, Ky.), (859) 431-6829, $89-$158
▼▼▼ **Hampton Inn Cincinnati Riverfront** (*Motel*), 200 Crescent Ave. (Covington, Ky.), (859) 581-7800, $84-$109
▼▼▼ **Holiday Inn-Riverfront** (*Motor Inn*), 600 W. 3rd St. (Covington, Ky.), (859) 291-4300, $79-$109

Nearby Restaurants

▼▼▼ **J's Fresh Seafood Restaurant** (*Seafood*), 2444 Madison Rd. (Cincinnati), (513) 871-2888, $14-$25
▼▼▼▼ **Maisonette** (*French*), 114 E. 6th St. (Cincinnati), (513) 721-2260, $22-$44
▼▼ **Montgomery Inn** (*American*), 9440 Montgomery Rd. (Cincinnati), (513) 791-3482, $12-$23
▼▼ **Montgomery Inn at the Boathouse** (*American*), 925 Eastern Ave. (Cincinnati), (513) 721-7427, $11-$24
▼▼▼ **Riverview Restaurant** (*Seafood*), 668 5th St. in the Clarion Hotel Riverview (Covington, Ky.), (859) 491-5300, $17-$25

CLEVELAND BROWNS

WHEN LONGTIME BROWNS OWNER Art Modell announced plans to move the team to Baltimore, Cleveland fans were livid. Founded in 1946, the team had established itself as one of the city's most beloved institutions. From the outset, the Browns franchise had established itself as a winner. With an original lineup that included All-Stars Otto Graham, Lou "the Toe" Groza and Marion Motley, the Browns dominated the All-America Football Conference for four years. In 1950 — the year the Browns joined the NFL — the team easily trounced all comers to take the NFL championship. Then, in 1957, the Browns signed a 6-foot-2-inch, 230-pound fullback by the name of Jim Brown. For nine seasons, Brown rewrote the record books and redefined offensive greatness, leading the NFL rushing stats eight times, amassing 106 rushing TDs and a whopping 756 career points. To this day he is known as perhaps the greatest runner in the history of the game. Following Brown's retirement in 1965, the team kept the magic alive for a few years, riding a winning streak that peaked with two AFC titles in the late 1960s. By the 1990s, however, the Browns were lagging; even a series of division wins in the 1980s seemed like a distant memory to Modell and the Browns management. So, in spite of the outpouring of emotion from "the Dawgs," Cleveland's most notorious fans, the team relocated to Baltimore as planned. Fortunately for Browns fans, a group headed by Carmen A. Policy was awarded a new franchise in 1998. The new Browns took the field in their rightful home in 1999.

> *"When you've got the biggest cannon, you shoot it."*
> — *Cleveland coach Paul Brown, on Browns' superstar Jim Brown*

In 1999 Tim Couch led all rookie QBs in passing yards.

POSTSEASON
- NFL Championships........4
(1950, '54, '55, '64)
- AFC Titles 3
(1950, '68, '69)
- AFC Central Titles 3
(1986, '87, '89)
- AFC Wild Card Berths.....1
(1994)

RETIRED NUMBERS
- Otto Graham (14)
- Jim Brown (32)
- Ernie Davis (45)
- Don Fleming (46)
- Lou Groza (76)

Extra Point
- *Named after their first coach and general manager, Paul Brown, the Cleveland Browns is the only pro sports team that carries a person's name.*

TEAM RECORDS
Offense
- **Jim Brown (1957–65)**
Rushing Yards (season): 1,863 (1963)
Rushing Yards (career): 12,312
TDs (season): 21 (1965)
TDs (career): 126
Rushing TDs (season): 17 (1965)
Rushing TDs (career): 106
Points (season): 126 (1965)
Yards-Per-Carry (career): 5.22
- **Gary Collins (1962–71)**
Receiving TDs (season): 13 (1963)
Receiving TDs (career): 70
- **Otto Graham (1950–55)**
Comp. Pct. (season): 64.73 (1953)
Highest QB rating (game): 158.33 (Oct. 10, 1954)
- **Lou Groza (1950–59, 1961–67)**
Points (career): 1,349
FGs (career): 233
- **Bernie Kosar (1985–93)**
Comp. Pct. (career): 58.83
Lowest Int. Pct. (season): 1.82 (1991)
- **Ozzie Newsome (1978–90)**
Receptions (season): 89 (1984)
Receptions (career): 662
Yards (career): 7,980
Yards (game): 191 (Oct. 14, 1984)
- **Brian Sipe (1973–83)**
Passing TDs (season): 30 (1980)
Passing TDs (career): 154

Comp. (season): 337 (1980)
Comp. (career): 1,944
Yards (season): 4,132 (1980)
Yards (career): 23,713
- **Matt Stover (1991–95)**
FGs (season): 29 (1995)
- **Webster Slaughter (1986–91)**
Receiving Yards (season): 1,236 (1989)

Defense
- **Thom Darden (1972–74, 1976–81)**
Int. (season): 10 (1978)
Int. (career): 45
- **Bill Glass (1962–68)**
Sacks (season): 14.5 (1965)
- **Warren Lahr (1950–59)**
Int. TDs (career): 5
- **Clay Mathews (1978–93)**
Sacks (career): 76.5

Special Teams
- **Don Cockroft (1968–80)**
Punts (career): 651
Punt Yards (career): 26,262
- **Chris Gardocki (1999–present)**
Punts (season): 106 (1999)
Punt Yards (season): 4,645 (1999)
- **Gerald Mcneil (1986–89)**
Punt Returns (season): 49 (1989)
Punt Returns (career): 161
Punt Return Yards (season): 496 (1989)
Punt Return Yards (career): 1,545

- **Eric Metcalf (1989–94)**
Punt Return TDs (season): 2 (1994)
Punt Return TDs (career): 5

LEAGUE HONORS
NFL MVP
- **Jim Brown** (1957, '58, '63, '65)
- **Otto Graham** (1951, '53, '55)
- **Leroy Kelly** (1968)
- **Brian Sipe** (1980)

NFL Rookie of the Year
- **Jim Brown** (1957)

NFL Coach of the Year
- **Paul Brown** (1951, '53, '57)

Pro Football Hall of Fame
- Otto Graham (1965)
- Paul Brown (1967)
- Marion Motley (1968)
- Jim Brown (1971)
- Lou Groza (1974)
- Dante Lavelli (1975)
- Len Ford (1976)
- Bill Willis (1977)
- Bobby Mitchell (1983)
- Paul Warfield (1983)
- Mike McCormack (1984)
- Frank Gatski (1985)
- Leroy Kelly (1994)
- Ozzie Newsome (1999)

Vital Stats
Stadium Address:
1085 W. 3rd St., Cleveland, Ohio
Phone: (440) 891-5000
Web: clevelandbrowns.com
Box Office:
(888) 891-1999 (toll free), Mon.–Fri. 9–5, Sat. 11–5
Media Coverage:
Radio: WMJI (105.7 FM)
TV: WKYC (Channel 3)
Training Facility:
Browns Training Complex, Berea, Ohio

Timeline
1946	1950	1955	1957	1961	1965	1970	1971	1977	1980	1984	1985	1995	1999
Otto Graham becomes the first player signed to the Browns	Browns win the NFL title against Los Angeles	Browns win third NFL title	Jim Brown signed to team; wins Rookie of the Year	Art Modell buys Browns for the then unheard of sum of $4 million	Jim Brown wins MVP in his last year of play	Browns join AFC Central Division; team beats Jets on first-ever TV broadcast of Monday Night Football	Browns wins first AFC Central crown	Greg Pruitt completes third consecutive 1,000-yard rushing seasons	QB Brian Sipe named MVP	Ozzie Newsome sets season record with 89 receptions	Teammates Kevin Mack and Earnest Byner both rush over 1,000 yards	Browns go 5-11 in last season before franchise moves to Baltimore	New Cleveland Browns Stadium opens

168

CLEVELAND BROWNS STADIUM: A NEW POUND FOR THE DAWGS

CONSTRUCTED ON THE GROUNDS of the old Cleveland Municipal Stadium, this new arena maintains a strong link to the rich historical past of the Browns. There is plenty of Browns memorabilia in the Hall of Fame Museum and many images of the beloved, but worn-out Municipal Stadium to remind people of the old days. The new stadium, however, is undeniably modern, with many stores, restaurants and game areas. The stadium has also been designed to blend with the nearby Science Center and Rock n' Roll Hall of Fame to help create a grand entertainment village.

Seating Plan

■ A	$69		■ Club-4	$106
■ B	$59		▨ G	$59
■ C	$42		▢ H	$42.50
■ D	$32		▢ I	$37
■ Dawg Pound	$32		■ J	$32
■ E	$42.50			$25
■ F	$32		**ATM** Suites 109/309, 132/332;	
▨ Club-1	$249		end zone 320, 347	
▨ Club-2	$175		♿ Throughout	
■ Club-3	$106			

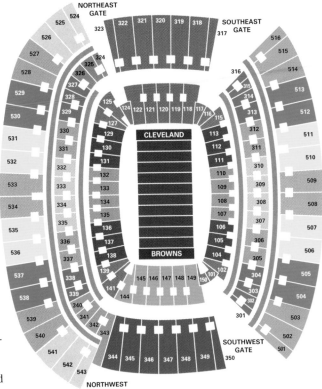

CONCESSIONS

All the great sporting delicacies can be found at the Cleveland Browns Stadium: chicken, pizza, hamburgers, Mexican, sandwiches, baked goods, ice cream and snacks. There is also a number of vegetarian items.

Stadium Facts

Opened: *Aug. 21, 1999*
Cost: *$290 million*
Capacity: *Over 73,200*
Type: *Outdoor*
Surface: *Grass*
Home Sweet Home:
• *Cleveland boasts the only sand/soil-based field in the NFL, making it a great surface in poor weather.*
• *The infamous "Dawgs" are some of the noisiest fans in the game. Wearing flea collars and dog masks, they are known for giving opponents a hard time.*

GAME DAY TIPS

• **Gate hours:** Gates open two hours prior to kickoff.
Weather: Browns Stadium is known to be windy. Dress warmly for all seasons.
• **Tailgating:** Tailgating festivities commence a few hours before the game and go on after the game as well. It all happens at "the Barking Lot" on the north side of the stadium.
• **Prohibited items:** No outside food or beverages are allowed in the stadium. Also, no glass or metal containers are allowed. Smoking is permitted in designated sections.
• **Ticket tips:** The loud and boisterous Dawg Pound is the favorite section of diehard fans. The Browns have rivalries with many AFC Central teams, particularly the Bengals. Tickets to these games go quickly.

• **Lost and found:** (440) 891-5000.

Directions: *Exit Cleveland Memorial Shoreway (Hwy. 2) at 3rd St. W. or Erieside Ave. By Bus: Buses are available to and from the stadium. Call the Regional Transit Authority at (216) 621-9500 for information.* **Parking:** *There are four large wheelchair-accessible parking lots around the stadium. Be warned: At peak times, spots go fast and can be pricey. Extra spots can be found on W. 3rd St., Erieside Ave., W. 9th St. and E. Lakeside Ave.*

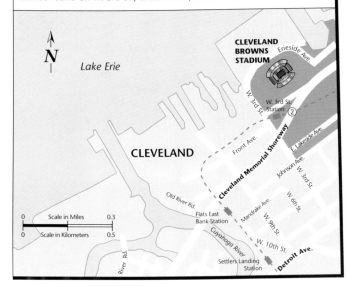

Nearby Hotels

▼▼▼ **Hampton Inn Cleveland-Downtown** (*Motel*), 1460 E. 9th St. (Cleveland), (216) 241-6600, $99-$179
▼▼▼ **Radisson Hotel at Gateway-Cleveland** (*Hotel*), 651 Huron Rd. (Cleveland), (216) 377-9000, $129-$149
▼▼▼▼ **The Ritz Carlton, Cleveland** (*Hotel*), 1515 W. 3rd St. in Tower City Center (Cleveland), (216) 623-1300, $240-$264
▼▼▼ **Sheraton Cleveland City Centre** (*Hotel*), 777 St. Clair Ave. (Cleveland), (216) 771-7600, $113-$129
▼▼▼ **Wyndham Hotel at Playhouse Square** (*Hotel*), 1260 Euclid Ave. (Cleveland), (216) 615-7500, $109-$209

Nearby Restaurants

▼▼▼ **Blue Pointe Grille** (*Seafood*), 700 W. St. Clair Ave. (Cleveland), (216) 875-7827, $15-$30
▼▼ **Café Sausalito** (*American*), 1301 E. 9th St. in the Galleria at Erieview (Cleveland), (216) 696-2233, $10-$20
▼▼▼ **Johnny's Downtown** (*Northern Italian*), 1406 W. 6th St. (Cleveland), (216) 623-0055, $18-$34
▼▼ **Li Wah** (*Chinese*), 2999 Payne Ave. in Asia Plaza (Cleveland), (216) 696-6556, $8-$15
▼▼ **Hyde Park Chop House** (*Steak House*), 123 Prospect Ave., (Cleveland), (216) 344-2444, $14-$36

DALLAS COWBOYS

THERE IS A JOKE ABOUT TEXAS STADIUM that aptly describes the importance and allure of the Dallas Cowboys for football fans across the nation. "Why does Texas Stadium have a hole in the roof?" The response: "So God can watch His favorite team." Whether by divine intervention or just great football, over the last 40 years the squad has been the NFL's most successful franchise. With 15 NFC East titles, eight conference championships and five Super Bowls, there can be little argument about that fact, or about the Cowboys' right to the moniker "America's team." Football icons populate the Cowboys' history like stars in the night sky. The list has to start with legendary Head Coach Tom Landry, whose unmistakable sartorial figure could be seen at the Dallas sidelines from its first season in 1960 to 1988. Landry's partner was team President and GM Tex Schramm, who was in charge of filling the Dallas lineup. And what a lineup it has been. Early stars such as QB "Dandy" Don Meredith and "Doomsday Defense" members Bob Lilly, Mel Renfro and Chuck Howley set a standard of offensive and defensive greatness that successive generations of Dallas players have tried to meet. In the 1970s QB Roger Staubach and RB Tony Dorsett drove the offense, while Randy White and Harvey Martin continued to make the Dallas defense one of the NFL's most feared. After an uncharacteristic lapse in the late 1980s, the Cowboys rebounded, riding Troy Aikman's arm and Emmitt Smith's rushing to three more Super Bowls in the 1990s. Now rebuilding once again, it won't be long before America's team gives its legion of fans across the nation a reason to cheer again.

"Never once in my heart did I ever see myself playing . . . for any fans other than Cowboys fans."
— Former Cowboy Michael Irvin, on his appreciation of fans

Vital Stats

Stadium Address:
2401 E. Airport Frwy., Irving, Texas
Phone: (972) 785-4000
Web: dallascowboys.com
Box Office: (972) 785-5000, Mon.–Fri. 9–5, two hours before games
Media Coverage:
Radio: KVIL (103.7 FM)
TV: KTVT (Channel 11), WFAA (Channel 8), KDFW (Channel 4)
Training Facility:
Valley Ranch Training Facility, Wichita Falls, Texas

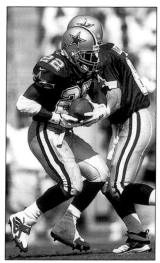

Emmitt Smith is the NFL's all-time leader in rushing TDs.

Extra Point

• With his 10th 1,000-yard rushing season in 2000, Cowboys running back Emmitt Smith equalled the NFL record set by former Detroit Tiger Barry Saunders.
• During the 1990s the Dallas Cowboy Cheerleaders made more international entertainment trips to U.S. military bases than any other performers.

POSTSEASON
• **Super Bowl Championships** 5
(1971, '77, '92, '93, '95)
• **NFC Championships**........8
(1970, '71, '75, '77, '78, '92, '93, '95)
• **NFC East Titles** 15
(1970, '71, '73, '76, '77, '78, '79, '81, '85, '92, '93, '94, '95, '96, '98)

RING OF HONOR
• Tony Dorsett
• Chuck Howley
• Lee Roy Jordan
• Tom Landry
• Bob Lilly
• Don Meredith
• Don Perkins
• Mel Renfro
• Roger Staubach
• Randy White

TEAM RECORDS
Offense
• **Troy Aikman (1989–2000)**
Pass Comp. (career): 2,898
Passing Yards (career): 32,942
TD Passes (career): 165
• **Tony Dorsett (1977–87)**
Yards-Per-Carry (career): 4.37 Yards
Longest Run (career): 99 Yards (Mar. 1, 1983)
• **Bob Hayes (1965–74)**
Receiving Yards (game): 246 (Nov. 13, 1966)

TD Receptions (career): 71
• **Michael Irvin (1989–99)**
Receptions (season): 111 (1995)
Receptions (career): 750
Receiving Yards (career): 11,904
Receiving Yards (season): 1,603 (1995)
• **Emmitt Smith (1990–present)**
Points (season): 150 (1995)
Points (career): 938
Rushing Yards (game): 237 (Oct. 31, 1993)
Rushing Yards (season): 1,773 (1995)
Rushing Yards (career): 15,166
TDs (season): 25 (1995)
TDs (career): 156
• **Roger Staubach (1969–79)**
QB Rating (season): 104.8 (1971)
QB Rating (career): 83.42

Defense
• **Lee Roy Jordan (1963–76)**
Tackles (career): 1,236
• **Bob Lilly (1961–74)**
Sacks (game): 5 (tie) (Nov. 20, 1966)
• **Eugene Lockhart (1984–90)**
Tackles (season): 222 (1989)
• **Harvey Martin (1973–83)**
Sacks (season): 20 (1977)
Sacks (career): 113
• **Mel Renfro (1964–77)**
Int. (career): 52

• **Everson Walls (1981–89)**
Int. (season): 11 (1981)

LEAGUE HONORS
NFL MVP
• Don Meredith (1966)
• Roger Staubach (1971)
• Emmitt Smith (1993)

Super Bowl MVP
• Chuck Howley (1970)
• Roger Staubach (1971)
• Randy White (1977)
• Harvey Martin (1977)
• Troy Aikman (1992)
• Emmitt Smith (1993)
• Larry Brown (1995)

Pro Football Hall of Fame
• Bob Lilly (1980)
• Roger Staubach (1985)
• Tom Landry (1990)
• Tex Schramm (1991)
• Tony Dorsett (1994)
• Randy White (1994)
• Mel Renfro (1996)

Timeline

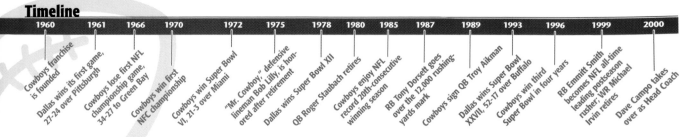

1960	1961	1966	1970	1972	1975	1978	1980	1985	1987	1989	1993	1996	1999	2000

Cowboys franchise is founded

Dallas wins its first game, 27-24 over Pittsburgh

Cowboys lose first NFL championship game, 34-27 to Green Bay

Cowboys win first NFC championship

Cowboys win Super Bowl VI, 21-3 over Miami

"Mr. Cowboy," defensive lineman Bob Lilly, is honored after retirement

Dallas wins Super Bowl XII

QB Roger Staubach retires

Cowboys enjoy NFL record 20th-consecutive winning season

RB Tony Dorsett goes over the 12,000 rushing-yards mark

Cowboys sign QB Troy Aikman

Dallas wins Super Bowl XXVII, 52-17 over Buffalo

Cowboys win third Super Bowl in four years

RB Emmitt Smith becomes NFL all-time leading postseason rusher; WR Michael Irvin retires

Dave Campo takes over as Head Coach

TEXAS STADIUM: SHOWCASE FOR AMERICA'S TEAM

LOCATED IN THE DALLAS SUBURB OF IRVING, Texas Stadium should feel familiar to all who visit it — certainly no stadium has enjoyed more national television time. The facility's most unique feature is its overhanging roof, which covers fans from inclement weather but keeps the game outdoors. Texas Stadium is first-rate all around, with very few bad seats and a wealth of fan amenities. With its devoted, vocal fans, the Ring of Honor and the internationally famous Dallas Cowboy Cheerleaders, it offers an unmatched atmosphere to appreciate a football game.

CONCESSIONS

Texas Stadium boasts dozens of concession stands, serving everything from standard stadium fare to Texas specialties. One local favorite is "Superbowl nachos," crispy treats served with cheese, chili and jalapenos.

Stadium Facts

Opened: Oct. 24, 1971
Cost: $35 million
Capacity: 65,675
Type: Outdoor
Surface: Sportfield turf
Home Sweet Home:
• With their team known as "America's Team," Cowboy fans are among the proudest and most supportive in sport. With Texas Stadium partially enclosed, noise can make play-calling tough on opposing quarterbacks.

GAME DAY TIPS

• **Gate hours:** Gates open two hours prior to kickoff.
• **Tailgating:** Tailgating is allowed in stadium parking lots. To accommodate tailgaters, Gate 1 and Gate 6 open four hours before game time.
• **Weather:** Dallas is warm throughout the year. However, severe weather is not uncommon, including rains, lightning storms, hail, floods and tornados.
• **Prohibited items:** Coolers, bottles and cans are prohibited. Alcohol cannot be taken into the stadium. Smoking is allowed on the concourse.
• **Ticket tips:** Cowboys seats are a hot commodity, so tickets are hard to come by. Games against the Redskins are particularly popular. Your best bet is to look into pre-season games or a ticket broker for single tickets.
• **Lost and found:** (972) 785-4000.

Seating Plan

■ .... $61   ■ $36
■ .... $58   ATM **Sections 20, 27/28, 35**
■ .... $52   ♿ **Sections 13, 20, 21, 24**
□ $37

Directions: Take Rte. 114 to the stadium or Rte. 183 to Rte. 12 north. By Bus: There is bus service to the stadium from 12 locations in Dallas and Fort Worth. Buses leave for the stadium two hours before kickoff and leave the stadium no later than 45 minutes after the game. For more information call (972) 979-1111. **Parking:** Parking lots surrounding the stadium can accommodate some 16,800 cars. However, the lots closest to the gates are reserved for season ticket holders. Wheelchair-accessible parking spaces total 111.

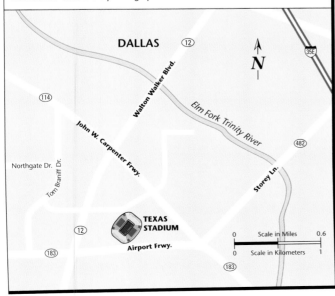

Nearby Hotels

▼▼▼ **Comfort Suites (Motel),** 2287 W. Northwest Hwy. (Dallas), (214) 350-4011, $74-$94
▼▼ **Drury Inn & Suites-Dallas North (Motel),** 2421 Walnut Hill Ln. (Dallas), (972) 484-3330, $58-$78
▼▼▼▼ **Four Seasons Resort & Club (Resort),** 4150 N. MacArthur Blvd. (Irving), (972) 717-0700, $320-$450
▼▼▼ **Hampton Inn-Dallas North I-35 at Walnut Hill (Motel),** 11069 Composite Dr. (Dallas), (972) 484-6557, $74-$89
▼▼ **Red Roof Inn-Northwest (Motel),** 10335 Gardner Rd. (Dallas), (972) 506-8100, $40-$50

Nearby Restaurants

▼▼ **Celebration (American),** 4503 W. Lovers Ln. (Dallas), (214) 351-5681, $8-$14
▼▼ **Mercado Juarez (Regional Mexican),** 1901 W. Northwest Hwy. (Dallas), (972) 556-0796, $8-$14
▼▼ **Ninfa's (Mexican),** 2701 Stemonns Fwy. (Dallas), (214) 638-6865, $7-$14
▼▼▼ **Old San Francisco Steak House (Steakhouse),** 10965 Composite Dr. (Dallas), (214) 357-0484, $10-$28
▼▼▼▼ **Star Canyon (American),** 3102 Oak Lawn Ave., Ste. 144 (Dallas), (214) 520-7827, $20-$28

DENVER BRONCOS

THE DENVER BRONCOS are living proof that good things will come to those who wait — eventually. An AFL original team, Denver kicked off operations in 1960, quickly establishing itself as an underachiever. With the exception of a 7-7 season in 1962, the hapless Broncos managed to post a losing record every year from '60 to '72. During that time the team finished last in its division no less than 10 times. One of Denver's few light moments occurred during a 1962 intrasquad game when the team burned all its much-hated vertically striped socks in a huge bonfire just prior to unveiling its new orange and blue uniforms. Denver's fortunes changed in 1977, when its vaunted "Orange Crush" defense paced the team to its first division crown with a gaudy 12-2 record. But in Super Bowl XII, the Broncos lost to Dallas. The inability to perform well in the big game became the team's unfortunate trademark during the 1980s. From 1986 to '89, the Broncos reached the Super Bowl three times, only to come away empty-handed on each occasion. People began to wonder if John Elway, already establishing himself as one of the game's greatest quarterbacks, was doomed to go his whole career without winning a championship. But Elway and the Broncos kept striving toward their goal and in 1997 their hard work finally paid off. Going 12-4 during the regular season, the wild-card Broncos won Super Bowl XXXII by defeating the favored Packers. Not satisfied, the 38-year-old Elway returned in 1999 to lead the team to another Super Bowl victory and earn himself MVP honors.

Sure-handed Ed McCaffrey is Denver's top receiver.

POSTSEASON
- Super Bowl Championships ....2 (1997, '98)
- AFC Championships ....6 (1977, '86, '87, '89, '97, '98)
- AFC West Titles..............10 (1977, '78, '84, '86, '87, '89, '91, '96, '97, '98)
- AFC Wild Card Berths.....1 (1993)

RETIRED NUMBERS
- John Elway (7)
- Frank Tripucka (18)
- Floyd Little (44)

RING OF FAME
- John Elway
- Austin Gonsoulin

Extra Point

- The Broncos franchise made its greatest trade in 1983, sending two players and a first-round draft pick to the Colts for rookie QB John Elway. During his career, Elway engineered 40 game-winning drives in the fourth quarter or in overtime. When Elway retired in 1999, he was second only to Dan Marino in career passing yards and pass completions.

- Randy Gradishar
- Rich Jackson
- Tom Jackson
- Charley Johnson
- Floyd Little
- Craig Morton
- Haven Moses
- Gerald Phipps (owner)
- Paul Smith
- Lionel Taylor
- Billy Thompson
- Frank Tripucka
- Jim Turner
- Louis Wright

TEAM RECORDS
Offense
- **Terrell Davis (1995–present)**
Points (season): 138 (1998)
Rushing Yards (season): 2,008 (1998)
Rushing Yards (career): 6,906
TDs (season): 23 (1998)
TDs (career): 63
- **Jason Elam (1993–present)**
Points (career): 949

"It was so loud in Mile High all the time. I can't imagine being on the other side of the ball."

— *John Elway, former Broncos QB*

- **John Elway (1983–98)**
Comp. (season): 348 (1993)
Comp. (career): 4,123
Passing Yards (season): 4,030 (1993)
Passing Yards (career): 51,475
TD Passes (season): 27 (1997)
TD Passes (career): 300
- **Ed McCaffrey (1995–present)**
Receiving Yards (season): 1,317 (2000)
Receptions (season): 101 (2000)
- **Shannon Sharpe (1990–99)**
Receiving Yards (career): 6,983
Receptions (career): 552

Defense
- **Simon Fletcher (1985–95)**
Sacks (career): 97.5
- **Steve Foley (1976–86)**
Int. (career): 44
- **Goose Gonsoulin (1960–66)**
Int. (season): 11 (1960)

Special Teams
- **Rick Upchurch (1975–83)**
Punt Return Yards (season): 653 (1977)
Punt Return Yards (career): 3,008

LEAGUE HONORS
NFL MVP
- Terrell Davis (1998)

Vital Stats

Stadium Address:
1701 Bryant St., Denver, Colo.
Phone: (720) 258-3000
Web: denverbroncos.com
Box Office: (720) 258-3333, Mon.–Fri. 8–5, call for game-day hours
Media Coverage:
Radio: KOA (850 AM)
TV: KUSA-9NEWS, ESPN
Training Facility:
Dove Valley Headquarters, Englewood, Colo.

- John Elway (1987)

Super Bowl MVP
- Terrell Davis (1997)
- John Elway (1998)

Defensive Player of the Year
- Paul Smith (1973)
- Lyle Alzado (1977)
- Randy Gradishar (1978)
- Rulon Jones (1986)

NFL Rookie of the Year
- Mike Croel (1991)

AFL Rookie of the Year
- Billy Joe (1963)

Pro Football Hall of Fame
- Willie Brown (1984)

Timeline

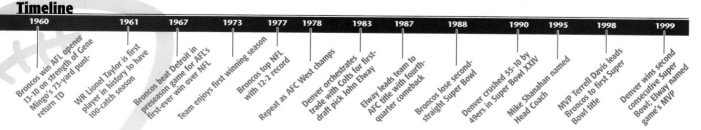

| 1960 | 1961 | 1967 | 1973 | 1977 | 1978 | 1983 | 1987 | 1988 | 1990 | 1995 | 1998 | 1999 |

- **1960** Broncos win AFL opener 13-10 on strength of Gene Mingo's 73-yard punt-return TD
- **1961** WR Lionel Taylor is first player in history to have 100-catch season
- **1967** Broncos beat Detroit in preseason game for AFL's first-ever win over NFL
- **1973** Team enjoys first winning season
- **1977** Broncos top NFL with 12-2 record
- **1978** Repeat as AFC West champs
- **1983** Denver orchestrates trade with Colts for first-draft pick John Elway
- **1987** Elway leads team to AFC title with fourth-quarter comeback
- **1988** Broncos lose second-straight Super Bowl
- **1990** Denver crushed 55-10 by 49ers in Super Bowl XXIV
- **1995** Mike Shanahan named Head Coach
- **1998** MVP Terrell Davis leads Broncos to first Super Bowl title
- **1999** Denver wins second consecutive Super Bowl, Elway named game's MVP

INVESCO FIELD AT MILE HIGH: REPLACING A LEGENDARY VENUE

THE BRONCOS OPENED their 2001 season at a new stadium, INVESCO Field at Mile High. While many Broncos fans have maintained that the old Mile High Stadium was perfectly good, they will find that the new venue is vastly improved. Wider seats offer more leg- and elbow-room as well as improved sight lines. Extra restrooms and concession stands will mean fewer lineups. However, architects have taken great pains to replicate some of the old stadium's elements, including its distinctive horseshoe shape.

CONCESSIONS

Fans will find Southwestern fare such as tamales, burritos, green chiles and even buffalo meat at the new stadium. Colorado microbrews will also be on tap.

GAME DAY TIPS

• **Gate hours:** Gates open two hours prior to kickoff.

• **Tailgating:** The permanent site for tailgating will be ready in 2002. Until then, tailgating takes place due east of the stadium across I-25.

• **Weather:** During the course of the football season, Denver's weather can change drastically, from hot in August and September to cold and snowy in November and December.

• **Prohibited items:** Glass bottles, cans, alcoholic beverages, drugs, firearms, and signs that use sticks or poles are prohibited. Coolers must be soft and able to fit under the seat. Smoking is allowed only in designated areas.

• **Ticket tips:** Tickets are tough to get. The team has sold out every home game for the last 24 years. Call well in advance or try for same-day tickets at the box office. Monday night games and games against division rivals are the most popular.

Stadium Facts

Opened: Aug. 25, 2001
Cost: $350 million
Capacity: 76,125
Type: Open
Surface: Grass
Home Sweet Home:
• Although the Broncos are acclimatized to Denver's high altitude, opposing players often find it difficult. And noise from fans bounces off the steel rafters, adding to the intensity.

Seating Plan

■ Field Level	$68	■ Upper Level	$48
□ Field Level	$65	■ Upper Level	$46
▨ Field Level	$50	■ Upper Level	$30
■ Plaza Level	$50	■ Various .... (Prices relative
■ Club Level	$300	to location)
■ Club Level	$275	ATM Sections 105, 122, 134,
■ Club Level	$225	508, 534
■ Club Level	$55	♿ Throughout

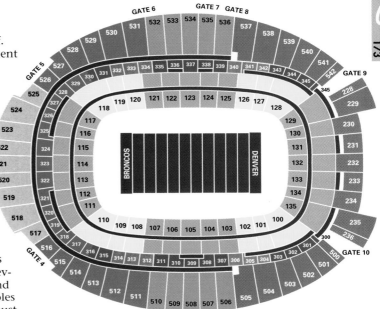

Directions: From I-25, take Hwy. 40/287 west (Colfax Ave.). Follow Hwy. 40/287 to Federal Blvd. north (Hwy. 287 N). The stadium is on the right. By Bus: The No. 20 and No. 31 have stops near the stadium. Call the RTD at (303) 299-6000. **Parking:** On-site parking is for permit holders, but several hundred spaces for the disabled are available. Shuttles run from the Pepsi Center and Auraria Campus lots east of the Platte River as well as 28 other locations. There is more parking on Speer Blvd. and Auraria Pkwy.

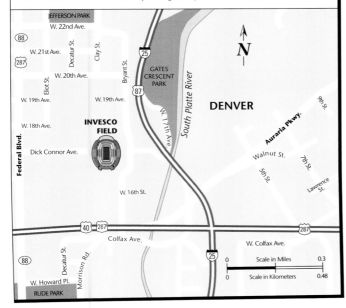

Nearby Hotels

▼▼▼▼ **Brown Palace Hotel** (*Classic Hotel*), 321 17th St. (Denver), (303) 297-3111, $234
▼▼ **Comfort Inn Downtown Denver** (*Hotel*), 401 17th St. (Denver), (303) 296-0400, $129
▼▼▼ **Denver Marriott Hotel City Center** (*Hotel*), 1701 California St. (Denver), (303) 297-1300, $189
▼▼▼ **Holiday Inn Denver Downtown** (*Hotel*), 1450 Glenarm Pl. (Denver), (303) 573-1450, $99-$139
▼▼▼▼ **Hotel Monaco** (*Hotel*), 1717 Champa St. (Denver), (303) 296-1717, $185-$240

Nearby Restaurants

▼▼▼ **McCormick's Fish House & Bar** (*Regional Seafood*), 1659 Wazee St. (Denver), (303) 825-1107, $8-$25
▼▼▼▼ **Palace Arms** (*Continental*), 321 17th St. in the Brown Palace Hotel (Denver), (303) 297-1311, $22-$38
▼▼▼ **Palm Restaurant** (*Steakhouse*), 1201 16th St. in the Westin Tabor Center Denver (Denver), (303) 825-2256, $14-$29
▼▼ **Rocky Mountain Diner** (*American*), 800 18th St. in the Ghost Building (Denver), (303) 293-8383, $9-$18
▼▼ **Rodizio Grill** (*Steakhouse*), 1801 Wynkoop St. (Denver), (303) 294-9277, $18

DETROIT LIONS

THE PEOPLE OF DETROIT were somewhat spoiled in 1935 when their Lions won the NFL championship just two years after having moved there from Portsmouth, Ohio. With All-Pro linemen George Christiansen and Ox Emerson opening gaping holes, Detroit's backs gained 2,885 yards on the ground — a league record that would last until 1972. While the team remained competitive through the 1930s, it faced stiff competition from Green Bay and Chicago. It wasn't until 1952 that the Lions roared back to the NFL's top spot, this time riding in on the backs of an intimidating defense and the fiery leadership of QB Bobby Layne. The team continued its winning ways the following season, with another win over Cleveland in the title game. His team trailing by six points with four minutes to go, Layne ignored a play sent in from the sidelines and improvised a new one in the huddle. His 33-yard scoring strike to Jim Doran provided the winning points in Detroit's 17-16 win. Just missing a "three-peat" the following year, the Lions won again in 1957. After the heady 1950s ended, however, Detroit would make only sporadic trips to the playoffs. From 1960 to '89, the team made only three postseason appearances. But with the 1989 arrival of Heisman Trophy-winner Barry Sanders, Detroit's fortunes changed. The diminutive Sanders, one of the most elusive backs of all time, went on a rampage, stringing together 10 consecutive 1,000-yard seasons and carrying Detroit into the playoffs five times. Just like the old days, the ground game was back and so were the Lions' winning ways.

Vital Stats

Stadium Address:
1200 Featherstone Rd.,
Pontiac, Mich.
Phone: (248) 858-7358
Web: detroitlions.com
Box Office:
(248) 335-4151,
Mon.–Fri. 10–6
Media Coverage:
Radio: WXYT (1270 AM)
TV: Fox (WJVK Channel 2),
CBS (WWJ Channel 62)
Training Facility:
Pontiac Silverdome,
Pontiac, Mich.

"Barry Sanders is unbelievable. His ability is unparalleled and he transcends time."
— Jim Brown, Hall-of-Fame RB

POSTSEASON
• NFL Championships 4
(1935, '52, '53, '57)
• NFC Central Titles 3
(1983, '91, '93)
• NFC Wild Card Berths.....5
(1970, '94, '95, '97, '99)

TEAM RECORDS
Offense
• Cloyce Box
(1949–50, 1952–54)
Receiving Yards (game):
302 (Dec. 3, 1950)
TD Receptions (game):
4 (Dec. 3, 1950)
TD Receptions (season):

15 (1952)
• Jason Hanson
(1992–present)
Field Goals (season): 34 (1993)
Points (season): 132 (1995)
• Bobby Layne (1950–58)
Comp. (career): 1,074
Pass Att. (career): 2,193
Passing Yards (career): 15,710
TD Passes (career): 118
• Scott Mitchell (1994–98)
Comp. (season): 346 (1995)
Passing Yards (season):
4,338 (1995)
TD Passes (season): 32 (1995)
• Herman Moore
(1991–present)
Receiving Yards (season):
1,686 (1995)
Receiving Yards (career): 9,098
Receptions (game):
14 (Dec. 4, 1995)
Receptions (season):
123 (1995)
Receptions (career): 646
TD Receptions (career): 62
• Eddie Murray (1980–91)
Field Goals (career): 244
Points (career): 1,113
• Barry Sanders (1989–98)
Carries (season): 343 (198)
Carries (career): 3,062
Rushing TDs (career): 99
Rushing Yards (game):

237 (Nov. 13, 1994)
Rushing Yards (season):
2,053 (1997)
Rushing Yards (career): 15,269
TDs (career): 109

Defense
• Bubba Baker (1978–82)
Sacks (season): 23 (1978)
Sacks (career): 75.5
• Don Doll (1949–52)
Int. (season): 12 (1950)
• Dick LeBeau (1959–72)
Int. (game): 4 (Oct. 23, 1949)
Int. (career): 62
• Chris Spielman (1988–95)
Tackles (season): 195 (1994)
Tackles (career): 1,138

LEAGUE HONORS
NFL MVP
• Frank Sinkwich (1944)
• Joe Schmidt (1960)
• Barry Sanders (1991, '97)

NFL Rookie of the Year
• Mel Farr (1967)
• Earl McCullouch (1968)
• Billy Sims (1980)
• Barry Sanders (1989)

NFL Coach of the Year
• Wayne Fontes (1991)

Pro Football Hall of Fame
• Earl "Dutch" Clark (1963)
• Bill Dudley (1966)
• Bobby Layne (1967)
• Alex Wojciechowicz (1968)
• Jack Christiansen (1970)
• Hugh McElhenny (1970)
• Ollie Matson (1972)
• Joe Schmidt (1973)
• Dick "Night Train" Lane (1974)
• Yale Lary (1979)
• Frank Gatski (1985)
• Doak Walker (1986)
• John Henry Johnson (1987)
• Lem Barney (1992)
• Lou Creekmur (1996)

Extra Point

• Looking to boost interest in the Lions, owner G.A. Richards convinced the NBC Radio Network to broadcast the 1934 Thanksgiving Day match between Detroit and the Bears. The response was so overwhelming that Detroit has played a game every Thanksgiving Day since. The team's record on "Turkey" Day is 32-27-2.

James Stewart filled the hole made by Barry Sanders' retirement.

Timeline

1930	1934	1935	1940	1950	1953	1962	1971	1983	1989	1991	1997	1999	2000
Portsmouth Spartans play first NFL season	Team moves to Detroit; changes name to Lions	Lions beat Giants for first NFL Championship	Whizzer White leads all NFL rushers	Future Hall-of-Famers Doak Walker and Bobby Layne join team	Lions take second straight NFL crown	LB Joe Schmidt selected to ninth-straight Pro Bowl	WR Chuck Hughes dies of heart attack during a game	Lions win first NFC Central crown	Rookie Barry Sanders leads all NFC running backs	Wayne Fontes named NFL Coach of the Year	Sanders rushes for 2,053 yards — second-best season in history	Lions land wild-card spot; Sanders retires	James Stewart leads team with 1,184 rushing yards

PONTIAC SILVERDOME: THE LIONS DEN

IN THE YEAR 2000 the Lions celebrated a quarter century in the Pontiac Silverdome. With one of the largest seating capacities in the NFL, the Silverdome is also one of the biggest structures of its type in the world. The stadium also boasts a series of firsts, including the first structure to use a fiberglass fabric roof system and the first northern U.S. city to host a Super Bowl (Super Bowl XVI). In 1994 the venue added to this list by hosting the first World Cup Soccer match to be staged in a domed stadium.

CONCESSIONS

Choices at the Silverdome include traditional hot dogs, burgers, nachos, pizza and pretzels, as well as a specialty sausage stand that serves Italian sausage and fresh kielbasa. A vegetarian pita is one of the few meat-free options available.

Stadium Facts

Opened: Aug. 23, 1975
Cost: $55.7 million
Capacity: 80,311
Type: Domed
Surface: AstroTurf
Home Sweet Home:
• *The crowd noise in the Silverdome can be deafening for opposing quarterbacks. During the '90s, Detroit was 23-8 when it played before a sellout crowd.*

GAME DAY TIPS

• **Gate hours:** Gates open two hours prior to kickoff.
• **Tailgating:** Tailgating generally begins six hours before kickoff in the stadium and auxiliary lots. Only propane grills are allowed; no charcoal or log fires.
• **Prohibited items:** Bottles, cans, hard-case containers, laser pointers, flashlights, alcoholic beverages, weapons and video cameras are all prohibited. Smoking is not allowed on the premises, but patrons are allowed to smoke between turnstiles and at stadium exits.
• **Ticket tips:** Tickets to the Thanksgiving game as well as games against the Packers sell out quickly. When choosing seats at the Silverdome, avoid the first few rows of seats.
• **Lost and found:** (248) 456-1650.

Directions: Take I-75 (Chrysler Frwy.) to 59 W, then exit at Opdyke Rd. and turn left. **By Public Transportation:** SMART shuttle service is offered from downtown Pontiac. Call (248) 456-1600 for more information. **Parking:** The main lot is usually filled by season ticket holders; an auxiliary lot takes overflow. A free shuttle runs from the Phoenix Center on Saginaw St. and Water St. Disabled patrons without season tickets may find a free spot in the stadium lot; otherwise drop-offs are usually allowed.

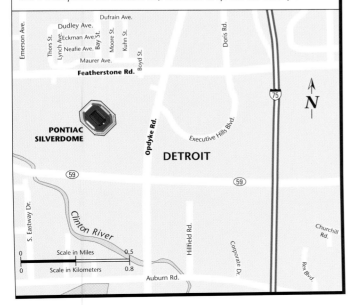

Seating Plan

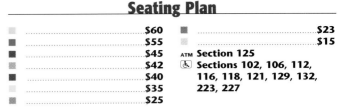

- $60
- $55
- $45
- $42
- $40
- $35
- $25
- $23
- $15

ATM Section 125

♿ **Sections 102, 106, 112, 116, 118, 121, 129, 132, 223, 227**

Nearby Hotels

▼▼▼ **AmeriSuites** *(Motel)*, 1545 Opdyke Rd. (Auburn Hills), (248) 475-9393, $89-$179
▼▼▼ **Fairfield Inn by Marriott-Auburn Hills** *(Motel)*, 1294 Opdyke Rd. (Auburn Hills), (248) 373-2228, $89-$99
▼▼▼ **Hilton Suites Auburn Hills** *(Suite Hotel)*, 2300 Featherstone Rd. (Auburn Hills), (248) 334-2222, $99-$199
▼▼▼ **Wellesley Inn & Suites** *(Motel)*, 2100 Featherstone Rd. (Auburn Hills), (248) 335-5200, $69-$199
▼▼▼ **Wingate Inn** *(Motel)*, 2200 Featherstone Rd. (Auburn Hills), (248) 334-3324, $129-$179

Nearby Restaurants

▼▼ **Beau Jack's Food & Spirits** *(American)*, 4108 W. Maple Rd. (Bloomfield Hills), (248) 626-2630, $7-$17
▼▼ **Big Buck Brewery** *(Steakhouse)*, 2550 Takata Dr. (Auburn Hills), (248) 276-2337, $7-$29
▼▼▼ **Fox & Hounds Restaurant** *(Steak & Seafood)*, 39560 N. Woodward Ave. (Bloomfield Hills), (248) 644-4800, $14-$30
▼▼ **The Main Event Restaurant** *(American)*, 1200 Featherstone Rd. (Auburn Hills), (248) 858-7888, $15-$20
▼▼ **Northern Lakes Seafood Company** *(Seafood)*, 1475 N. Woodward Ave. in the Kingsley Hotel & Suites (Bloomfield Hills), (248) 646-7900, $19-$30

GREEN BAY PACKERS

THE ONLY SURVIVING "TOWN" TEAM in a league that was originally only comprised of such franchises, the Green Bay Packers occupy a special place in the NFL. Founded in 1919 with a sponsorship investment from the Acme Packing Company (hence the name), the Packers were the brainchild of Earl "Curly" Lambeau, a former Notre Dame football star who functioned as general manager, coach, player and key marketing man for the team during its early years. Dominant in the 1920s and early '30s with future Hall-of-Famers Cal Hubbard and Mike Michalske anchoring an impenetrable defensive line, the Pack got its first bona fide offensive star in 1935, when it drafted wide receiver Don Hutson out of Alabama. In the next 10 years, Hutson would come to own the receiving portion of the NFL record book and lead the team to 11 straight winning seasons. Lambeau resigned as coach in 1950 and the franchise floundered until Vince Lombardi arrived in 1959. Lombardi molded the talent in Green Bay into one of the dominant teams of all time. With Bart Starr at QB, Paul Hornung and Jim Taylor running the ball, and a defense that included Forrest Gregg, Ray Nitschke, Willie Davis and Willie Wood, the Pack would win five NFL titles in the next nine seasons, as well as Super Bowls I and II. As difficult as that success has been to live up to, QB Brett Favre brought the Packers to another Super Bowl title following the 1996 season and has kept Wisconsin's fans — including the ubiquitous "cheeseheads" — happy with his exceptional passing prowess and gutsy leadership.

Vital Stats

Stadium Address:
1265 Lombardi Ave.,
Green Bay, Wis.
Phone: (920) 496-5700
Web: packers.com
Box Office: (920) 496-5719, Mon.–Fri. 8–5
Media Coverage:
Radio: WTMJ (620 AM)
TV: WLUK (Channel 11),
WFRB (Channel 5), Fox Sports Net
Training Ground:
Don Hutson Center,
Green Bay, Wis.

Extra Point

• Vince Lombardi had a stellar tenure as Packers coach, leading the team to five NFL titles in seven years. But perhaps his most glittering stat is that he never coached a losing season.
• Brett Favre is one of the most durable players in NFL history. His streak of 141 consecutive starts is an all-time NFL record for quarterbacks.

Brett Favre was named NFL MVP three straight years.

POSTSEASON
• Super Bowl Championships 3
(1966, '67, '96)
• NFL Championships 8
(1936, '39, '44, '61, '62, '65, '66, '67)
• NFC Championships 2
(1996, '97)
• NFC Central Titles 4
(1972, '95, '96, '97)
• NFC Wild Card Berths.....3
(1993, '94, '98)

RETIRED NUMBERS
• Tony Canadeo (3)
• Don Hutson (14)
• Bart Starr (15)
• Ray Nitschke (66)

TEAM RECORDS
Offense
• Lynn Dickey
(1976–77, 1979–85)
Passing Yards (season):
4,458 (1983)
• Brett Favre (1992–present)
Comp. (season): 363 (1994)
Comp. (career): 2,997
Passing Yards (career): 34,706
TD Passes (season): 39 (1996)
TD Passes (career): 255
• Paul Hornung
(1957–62, 1964–66)
Points (game): 33
(Oct. 8, 1961)
Points (season): 176 (1960)
TDs (game): 5 (Dec. 12, 1965)
• Don Hutson (1935–45)

"Winning isn't everything, it's the only thing."
— Former Packers coach Lombardi

Points (career): 823
TD Receptions (career): 99
• James Lofton (1978–86)
Receiving Yards (career): 9,656
• Sterling Sharpe (1988–94)
Receptions (season): 112 (1993)
Receptions (career): 595
TD Receptions (game): 4 (tie)
(Oct. 24, 1993, Nov. 24, 1994)
TD Receptions (season): 18 (1994)
• Bart Starr (1956–71)
Fewest Int. (season): 3 (1966)
Games (career): 196
• Jim Taylor (1958–66)
Rushing Yards (season): 1,474 (1962)
Rushing Yards (career): 8,207
Rushing TD (season): 19 (1962)
Rushing TDs (career): 81

Defense
• Bobby Dillon (1952–59)
Int. (game): 4 (tie)
(Nov. 26, 1953)
Int. (career): 52

LEAGUE HONORS
NFL MVP
• Don Hutson (1941, '42)

• Paul Hornung (1961)
• Jim Taylor (1962)
• Bart Starr (1966)
• Brett Favre (1995–97)

Super Bowl MVP
• Bart Starr (1966–67)
• Desmond Howard (1996)

NFL Rookie of the Year
• John Brockington (1971)
• Chester Marcol (1972)
• Willie Buchanon (1972)

NFL Coach of the Year
• Vince Lombardi (1959, '61)
• Lindy Infante (1989)

Pro Football Hall of Fame
• Robert "Cal" Hubbard (1963)
• Don Hutson (1963)
• Earl L. "Curly" Lambeau (1963)
• Johnny "Blood" McNally (1963)
• Clarke Hinkle (1964)
• Mike Michalske (1964)
• Arnie Herber (1966)
• Vince Lombardi (1971)
• Tony Canadeo (1974)
• Jim Taylor (1976)
• Forrest Gregg (1977)
• Bart Starr (1977)
• Ray Nitschke (1978)
• Herb Adderley (1980)
• Willie Davis (1981)
• Jim Ringo (1981)
• Paul Hornung (1986)
• Willie Wood (1989)
• Henry Jordan (1995)

Timeline

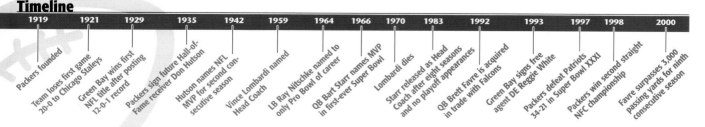

1919 — Packers founded
1921 — Team loses first game 20-0 to Chicago Staleys
1929 — Green Bay wins first NFL title after posting 12-0-1 record
1935 — Packers sign future Hall-of-Fame receiver Don Hutson
1942 — Hutson names NFL MVP for second consecutive season
1959 — Vince Lombardi named Head Coach
1964 — LB Ray Nitschke named to only Pro Bowl of career
1966 — QB Bart Starr names MVP in first-ever Super Bowl
1970 — Lombardi dies
1983 — Starr released as Head Coach after eight seasons and no playoff appearances
1992 — QB Brett Favre is acquired in trade with Falcons
1993 — Green Bay signs free agent DE Reggie White
1997 — Packers defeat Patriots 34-21 in Super Bowl XXXI
1998 — Packers win second straight NFC championship
2000 — Favre surpasses 3,000 passing yards for ninth consecutive season

LAMBEAU FIELD: FOOTBALL'S SHRINE

OPENED IN 1957 AS CITY FIELD, Green Bay's football stadium was renamed in 1965 following the death of Packers founder Curly Lambeau. Regarded as a shrine by football fans, Lambeau Field has been home to dozens of legendary players, coaches and games including four NFL title games in the 1960s. The natural-grass field is often referred to as "the frozen tundra" because of the inclement conditions there. Renovations are currently underway to add more seats and an atrium, which will house the pro shop, offices and the team Hall of Fame.

CONCESSIONS

Lambeau Field offers fans the best in stadium fare, with an unusual touch. All the concession stands in the stadium are staffed by volunteers from non-profit organizations and churches in the community. In return, they get a 12 percent share of the profits from sales.

GAME DAY TIPS
- **Gate hours:** Gates open two hours prior to kickoff.
- **Tailgating:** Parking lots open four hours prior to kickoff.
- **Weather:** Green Bay's climate is moderately cold in late fall and early winter. However, the team has a history of playing in bitterly cold December games. Check the forecast and make sure to dress warmly.
- **Prohibited items:** Alcohol, cans, bottles, ice chests, coolers and jugs are prohibited. Banners are permitted as long as they are not offensive and do not obstruct people's view. Smoking is allowed only in designated areas.
- **Ticket tips:** The Packers

Stadium Facts

Opened: *Sept. 29, 1957*
Cost: *$960,000*
Capacity: *60,890*
Type: *Open*
Surface: *Grass*
Home Sweet Home:
- *Lambeau Field is infamous for being one of the coldest places to play late in the year. Warm-weather teams or those that play in domed stadiums often succumb to Green Bay's inhospitable climes.*

Seating Plan

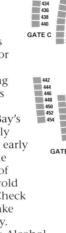

have sold out every home game dating back to 1960 and there is a waiting list of more than 50,000 for season tickets. However, Packers Fan Tours sells single-game tour packages. Call (800) 851-7225 for more information.
- **Lost and found:** (920) 496-5700.

Directions: Take Hwy. 41 or 172 to Lombardi Ave. exit. Turn right and follow Lombardi Ave. to stadium. By Bus: From the Transit Center, take the No. 9 bus and ride to Liberty St. and Oneida Ave. Call Green Bay Transit at (920) 448-3450 for more information. Parking: There are about 5,800 spots around Lambeau Field, including on Ridge Rd., with another 1,000 behind nearby Brown County Arena. Residents offer parking on their front lawn. Disabled parking is available in lots A and B.

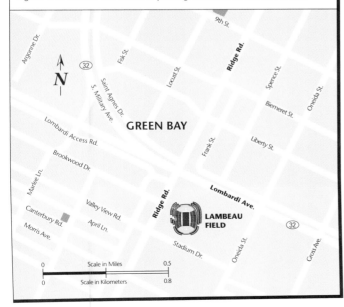

Nearby Hotels
▼▼▼ **AmericInn** *(Motel)*, 2032 Velp Ave. (Green Bay), (920) 434-9790, $65-$99
▼▼▼ **The Astor House** *(Historic Bed & Breakfast)*, 637 S. Monroe Ave. (Green Bay), (920) 432-3585, $85-$152
▼▼ **Bay Motel** *(Motor Inn)*, 1301 S. Military Ave. (Green Bay), (920) 494-3441, $40-$70
▼▼▼ **Country Inn & Suites by Carlson** *(Motel)*, 2945 Allied St. (Green Bay), (920) 336-6600, $68-$109
▼▼▼ **Radisson Hotel & Conference Center** *(Hotel)*, 2040 Airport Dr. (Green Bay), (920) 494-7300, $89-$99

Nearby Restaurants
▼ **Bay Motel Restaurant** *(American)*, 1301 S. Military Ave. in the Bay Motel (Green Bay), (920) 494-3441, $5-$9
▼▼▼ **Bistro John Paul** *(American)*, 1244 Main St. (Green Bay), (920) 432-2897, $17-$22 (dinner only)
▼▼ **Eves Supper Club** *(American)*, 2020 Riverside Dr. (Green Bay), (920) 435-1571, $10-$50
▼▼ **Titletown Brewing Company** *(American)*, 200 Dousman St. (Green Bay), (920) 437-2337, $6-$15
▼▼▼ **The Wellington Restaurant** *(American)*, 1060 Hansen Rd. (Green Bay), (920) 499-2000, $16-$28

HOUSTON TEXANS

WHEN THE HOUSTON TEXANS charge onto the field to start the 2002 NFL season, it will mark the beginning of a new era for the football-mad city. Texas itself has long been a bastion of the game, with high school teams serving as the focal point for many small communities. Houston has a rich tradition of professional football, beginning in 1960 when the Houston Oilers became charter members of the upstart American Football League. Led by the legendary George Blanda, the Oilers stormed from the blocks and won the first two AFL championships. The team joined the NFL in 1970 and over the next 26 years it enjoyed its share of ups and downs. Houston's many high points included the stalwart play of QB Warren Moon and Texas-born RB Earl Campbell. But in 1997, the team relocated to Nashville and became the Titans and, for the first time in 37 years, Houston was without pro football. However, the same year that the team moved to Tennessee, Bob McNair began working on plans to secure a new franchise for the city. Despite some tense moments along the way, McNair's hard work paid off when NFL owners voted unanimously in October 1999 to award Houston the league's 32nd franchise. Playing in AFC South, the Texans will find themselves in tough against three of the NFL's strongest teams: the Titans, the Colts and the Jaguars. Both head coach Dom Capers and GM Charlie Casserly are seasoned NFL veterans, and football fans in Houston are banking on their collective savvy to bring the good times back to the Houston gridiron as soon as possible.

Coach Dom Capers brings years of experience to Houston.

Extra Point

• *How important is football to Texans? The Texas State Legislature has only four people listed as official "Texas State Heroes." The first three, Davey Crockett, Sam Houston and Stephen F. Austin all were key players in the settlement and formation of the state. The fourth is Earl Campbell, the Houston Oilers' Hall of Fame running back.*

• *Texas boasts six Heisman Trophy winners, tying it with California and Ohio as the most produced by a state. The winners include Davey O'Brien (1938), Doak Walker (1948), John David Crow (1956), Earl Campbell (1977), Andre Ware (1989) and Ricky Williams (1998).*

• *The Houston Texans will become the NFL's 10th expansion team, excluding the clubs that joined the league as part of the AFL–NFL merger.*

NFL Realignment

The addition of the Texans to the NFL in 2002, forced the league to realign itself.

Both conferences will be composed of four divisions. One look at the new AFC East, where the Dolphins, Bills, Jets and Patriots will fight it out, and it is clear to see that the NFL tried to maintain as many natural rivalries as possible.

That being said, the league was unable to fulfill the Texans' request of slotting the team in the AFC, where Houston could renew its old rivalries with Cincinnati, Pittsburgh and Cleveland.

However, Texans team officials should be happy with at least one of their division mates, the Tennessee Titans. As most football fans know, the Titans spent 37 years as the Houston Oilers before pulling up the stakes and moving to Nashville in 1997. No doubt, Texans fans will be chomping at the bit to see the two teams square off beginning in 2002.

Here is the NFL as it will appear for the 2002 season.

> *"At night the building will glow like the crown jewel of the NFL."*
>
> – Texans owner Bob McNair on Reliant Stadium's translucent roof

• **AFC EAST**
Buffalo Bills
Miami Dolphins
New England Patriots
New York Jets

• **AFC WEST**
Denver Broncos
Kansas City Chiefs
Oakland Raiders
San Diego Chargers

• **AFC NORTH**
Baltimore Ravens
Cincinnati Bengals
Cleveland Browns
Pittsburgh Steelers

• **AFC SOUTH**
Houston Texans
Indianapolis Colts
Jacksonville Jaguars
Tennessee Titans

• **NFC EAST**
Dallas Cowboys
New York Giants
Philadelphia Eagles
Washington Redskins

• **NFC WEST**
Arizona Cardinals
St. Louis Rams
San Francisco 49ers
Seattle Seahawks

• **NFC NORTH**
Chicago Bears
Detroit Lions
Green Bay Packers
Minnesota Vikings

• **NFC SOUTH**
Atlanta Falcons
Carolina Panthers
New Orleans Saints
Tampa Bay Buccaneers

Vital Stats

Stadium Address:
8400 Kirby Dr.,
Houston, Texas
Phone:
(713) 799-9500
Web:
houstontexans.com
Box Office:
(713) 799-9500
Mon.-Sat. 10-5:30
Media Coverage:
Radio: KILT (100.3 FM),
SportsRadio (610 AM)
TV: KTRK (Channel 13, ABC)
Training Facility:
Texans Practice Facility,
Houston, Texas

Timeline

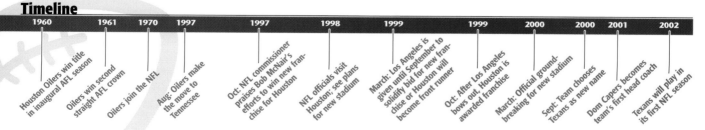

1960 — Houston Oilers win title in inaugural AFL season

1961 — Oilers win second straight AFL crown

1970 — Oilers join the NFL

1997 — Aug: Oilers make the move to Tennessee

1997 — Oct: NFL commissioner praises Bob McNair's efforts to win new franchise for Houston

1998 — NFL officials visit Houston; see plans for new stadium

1999 — March: Los Angeles is given until September to solidify bid for new franchise or Houston will become front runner

1999 — Oct: After Los Angeles bows out, Houston is awarded franchise

2000 — March: Official ground-breaking for new stadium

2000 — Sept: Team chooses Texans as new name

2001 — Dom Capers becomes team's first head coach

2002 — Texans will play in its first NFL season

RELIANT STADIUM:
SOMETHING FOR EVERYONE

OPENING IN AUGUST 2002, Reliant Stadium is Texas big, with a capacity of almost 70,000. It is also a versatile architectural design, built to host everything from football and soccer to the Olympic Games and, that most Texan of events, rodeo. The fully retractable roof, the first in the NFL, is unique in that it will be made of a translucent fabric in order to let in the natural light. Football fans are in for a treat, as the first row of luxury suites will be closer to the action than in any other NFL stadium.

CONCESSIONS

Although, as of this printing, the exact nature of Reliant's concessions is unknown, it is a safe bet that there will be a good mix of standard stadium food and more traditional Texas fare.

Stadium Facts

Projected Opening:
August 2002
Projected Cost:
$300 million
Capacity: *69,500*
Type: *Retractable roof*
Surface: *Grass*
Home Sweet Home:
• *Houston fans are among football's most enthusiastic and knowledgeable. With the new stadium designed to put them closer to the action, Texans fans promise to be a noisy bunch.*

GAME DAY TIPS

• **Gate hours:** Gates open two hours prior to games.
• **Tailgating:** Details are not yet determined.
• **Prohibited items:** Weapons, glass containers and illegal substances are prohibited. Smoking is allowed in designated areas.
• **Ticket tips:** Reliant Stadium promises good seats for just about everyone, with 44,000 to be located on the sideline as opposed to just 28,200 in the Astrodome. Tickets will probably be hard to come by, especially against the new AFC South rivals, as well as traditional

Seating Plan

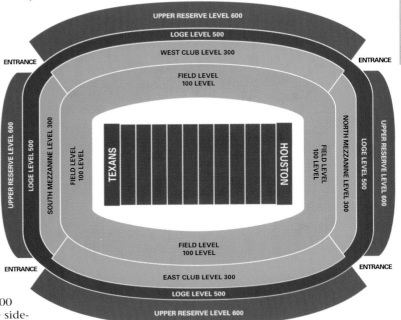

Houston foes, Pittsburgh, Cleveland and Cincinnati.

• **Lost and found:** (713) 799-9500

Directions: *Take Hwy. 288 south to the I-610 west and exit at Kirby Dr. From Hwy. 59 north take the I-610 south to the I-610 east and exit at Kirby Dr. By Bus: Several bus routes stop at Reliant Park and a METRO-RAIL system is planned for 2004. For route and schedule information call METRO at (713) 635-4000.* **Parking:** *There are 25,000 parking spaces available around the stadium with 227 spots reserved for the disabled.*

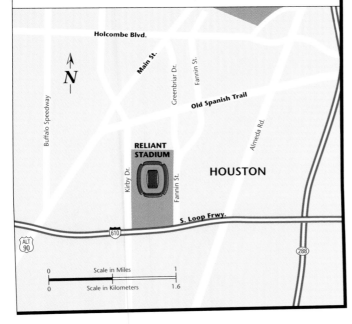

Nearby Hotels

▼▼▼ **Holiday Inn Astrodome** *(Hotel)*, 8111 Kirby Dr. (Houston), (713) 790-1900, $130-$170
▼▼▼ **Homestead Village Guest Studios Galleria** *(Extended Stay Motel)*, 2300 W. Loop Fwy. S. (Houston), (713) 960-9660, $69-$129
▼▼▼ **La Quinta Inn-Houston-Astrodome** *(Motel)*, 9911 Buffalo Speedway (Houston), (713) 668-8082, $55-$102
▼▼▼▼▼ **Omni Houston Hotel** *(Hotel)*, Four Riverway (Houston), (713) 871-8181, $269-$1295
▼▼ **Wellesley Inn & Suites** *(Extended Stay Motel)*, 1301 S. Braeswood Blvd. (Houston), (713) 794-0800, $98-$108

Nearby Restaurants

▼▼ **Benjy's** *(American)*, 2424 Dunstan (Houston), (712) 522-7602, $8-$24
▼▼▼▼ **The Brownstone** *(Continental)*, 2736 Virginia St. (Houston), 520-5666, $21-$32
▼▼ **Goode Co. Seafood** *(Regional American)*, 2621 Westpark (Houston), (713) 523-7154, $7-$24
▼▼ **Shanghai River** *(Chinese)*, 520 N. Post Oak Rd. (Houston), (713) 528-5528, $8-$26
▼▼ **Trattoria De Velio** *(Italian)*, 2325 University Blvd. (Houston), (713) 529-2002, $10-$25

INDIANAPOLIS COLTS

Peyton Manning ranks among the NFL's top signal callers.

THE INDIANAPOLIS COLTS FRANCHISE IS STEEPED IN HISTORY. The Colts first stormed onto the gridiron in Baltimore in 1947 as part of the All-American Football Conference — a rival to the NFL. The team struggled at the box office and was dissolved in January 1951. After two football-free years, Baltimore was awarded a NFL franchise for the 1953 season. Under the leadership of legendary coach Weeb Ewbank, the new Colts built a juggernaut through shrewd acquisitions. None was more pivotal than the 1956 signing of a skinny quarterback named Johnny Unitas, who had been released by the Steelers. Unitas established himself as one of the game's greatest gunslingers. Setting a host of records, including 47 straight games with a touchdown pass, Unitas led the team to three NFL championships and a victory in Super Bowl V in 1971. In 1984 the Colts were relocated to Indianapolis where, after several lean years, the team electrified fans again by signing such superstars as Eric Dickerson and Marshall Faulk. Today the Colts are armed to the teeth with the likes of running back Edgerrin James, wide receiver Marvin Harrison and quarterback Peyton Manning, already on his way to becoming the best Colts' QB since Unitas himself.

POSTSEASON
- **Super Bowl Championships** 1 (1970)
- **NFL Championships** ....3 (1958, '59, '68)
- **AFC Championships** 1 (1970)
- **AFC East Titles** ....6 (1970, '75, '76, '77, '87, '99)

RETIRED NUMBERS
- **Johnny Unitas (19)**
- **Buddy Young (22)**
- **Lenny Moore (24)**
- **Art Donovan (70)**
- **Jim Parker (77)**
- **Raymond Berry (82)**
- **Gino Marchetti (89)**

TEAM RECORDS
Offense
- **Raymond Berry (1955–67)**
Receiving Yards (game): 224 (Nov. 10, 1957)
Receiving Yards (career): 9,275
Receptions (career): 631
TD Receptions (career): 68
- **Dean Biasucci (1984, 1986–94)**
Field Goals (career): 176
Points (career): 783
- **Cary Blanchard (1995–97)**
Field Goals (season): 36 (1996)
- **Eric Dickerson (1987–91)**
Rushing TDs (game): 4 (Oct. 31, 1988)
- **Jeff George (1990–93)**
Comp. (game): 37 (Nov. 7, 1993)
- **Marvin Harrison (1996–present)**
Receiving Yards (season): 1,663 (1999)
Receptions (season): 115 (1999)
Receptions (game): 14 (Dec. 26, 1999)
TD Receptions (season): 14 (tie) (2000)
- **Gary Hogeboom (1986–88)**
TD Passes (game): 5 (tie) (Oct. 4, 1987)
- **Edgerrin James (1999–present)**
Rushing Yards (game): 219 (Oct. 15, 2000)
Rushing Yards (season):
1,709 (2000)
100-Yard Games (season): 10 (1999)
- **Peyton Manning (1998–present)**
Comp. (season): 357 (2000)
Passing Yards (game): 440 (Sept. 25, 2000)
Passing Yards (season): 4,413 (2000)
TD Passes (season): 33 (2000)
- **Lydell Mitchell (1972–77)**
Rushing Yards (career): 5,487
- **Lenny Moore (1956–67)**
Rushing TDs (season): 16 (1964)
Rushing TDs (career): 63
TDs (career): 113
- **Mike Vanderjagt (1998–present)**
Points (season): 145 (1999)
- **Johnny Unitas (1956–72)**
Comp. (career): 2,796
Games (career): 206
Passing Yards (career): 39,768
TD Passes (career): 287

Defense
- **Bob Boyd (1960–68)**
Int. (career): 57
- **Chad Bratzke (1999–present)**
Sacks (season): 12 (1999)
- **Tom Keane (1953–54)**
Int. (season): 11 (1953)

Extra Point
- *In 1958 the Colts won the NFL championship by beating the New York Giants 23-17. The nationally televised game, called "the greatest ever played," is credited with putting the NFL on the map.*
- *After posting a dismal 3-13 record in 1998, the Colts rebounded with a 13-3 record the following year — the greatest single-season turnaround in NFL history.*

> *"It was dusk. The lights were on. Banners were flying. We were champions of the world and I was in such awe."*
> — *Colts DE Don Joyce, after winning the 1958 NFL championship, often called "the greatest game ever played"*

Vital Stats
Stadium Address:
100 South Capitol Ave., Indianapolis, Ind.
Phone: *(317) 262-3410*
Web: *www.colts.com*
Box Office: *(317) 297-7000, Mon.–Fri. 9–5, home games Sat. 10–4*
Media Coverage:
Radio: WFBQ 94.7 FM
TV: WISH (Channel 8)
Training Facility:
Football Center, Indianapolis, Ind.

LEAGUE HONORS
NFL MVP
- **Johnny Unitas** (1957, '58, '59, '64, '67)
- **Lenny Moore** (1964)
- **Earl Morrall** (1968)
- **Bert Jones** (1976)

NFL Rookie of the Year
- **Alan Ameche** (1955)
- **Lenny Moore** (1956)
- **Jimmy Orr** (1958)
- **Marshall Faulk** (1994)
- **Edgerrin James** (1999)

Pro Football Hall of Fame
- **Art Donovan** (1968)
- **Gino Marchetti** (1972)
- **Raymond Berry** (1973)
- **Jim Parker** (1973)
- **Lenny Moore** (1975)
- **Weeb Ewbank** (1978)
- **Johnny Unitas** (1979)
- **Ted Hendricks** (1990)
- **John Mackey** (1992)
- **Don Shula** (1997)
- **Eric Dickerson** (1999)

Timeline

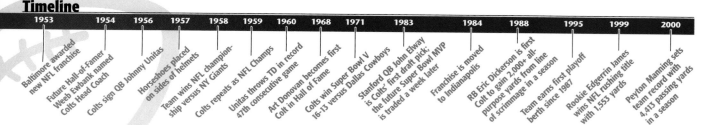

1953 Baltimore awarded new NFL franchise
1954 Future Hall-of-Famer Weeb Ewbank named Colts Head Coach
1956 Colts sign QB Johnny Unitas
1957 Horseshoes placed on sides of helmets
1958 Team wins NFL championship versus NY Giants
1959 Colts repeats as NFL Champs
1960 Unitas throws TD in record 47th consecutive game
1968 Art Donovan becomes first Colt in Hall of Fame
1971 Colts win Super Bowl V 16-13 versus Dallas Cowboys
1983 Stanford QB John Elway is Colts' first draft pick; the future Super Bowl MVP is traded a week later
1984 Franchise is moved to Indianapolis
1988 RB Eric Dickerson is first Colt to gain 2,000+ all-purpose yards from line of scrimmage in a season
1995 Team earns first playoff berth since 1987
1999 Rookie Edgerrin James wins NFL rushing title with 1,553 yards
2000 Peyton Manning sets team record with 4,413 passing yards in a season

RCA DOME: ALL-PURPOSE VENUE

INDIANAPOLIS' RCA DOME is one of only four major air-supported stadiums in the U.S. A central part of the city's downtown core, the stadium was designed to accommodate a host of events. As such, the Dome has been the site of everything from rock concerts and trade shows to NCAA Final Four Tournaments, the Pan Am Games and the World Gymnastic Championships. Tours of the facilities (including the playing field and the players' locker room) are conducted throughout the week.

CONCESSIONS

Vegetarians be warned. This is a meat-lover's haven. Hot dogs and burgers as well as Cajun specialities, barbecue pork and beef sandwiches, and domestic and imported beers are available.

Stadium Facts

Opened: May 3, 1984
Cost: $77 million
Capacity: 56,127
Type: Dome
Surface: AstroTurf 12
Home Sweet Home:
• Football-savvy Indy fans give their Colts a huge boost with their vocal support. Buoyed by the crowd, the team's winning percentage of .812 at home over the 1999 and 2000 seasons was among the best in the NFL.

GAME DAY TIPS

• **Gate hours:** Gates open 90 minutes prior to kickoff.
• **Tailgating:** Tailgating begins at the crack of dawn on game days in the south lot (immediately south of the stadium). There are also tailgating parties at the entrance of the stadium featuring live music.
• **Prohibited items:** Video cameras, cans and bottles are prohibited. Banners are welcome provided they are not offensive or commercial in nature. Also, banners cannot obscure the view of other fans.
• **Ticket tips:** Plan to buy your tickets well in advance

Seating Plan

■	$125	■	$49
■	$39	■	$10
■	$59	ATM **Sections 109, 145**
■	$34	♿ **Throughout**
■	$29		

181

as the Colts sold out all their home games in both 1999 and 2000. Tickets for games against AFC rivals, notably the Miami Dolphins and New York Jets, are particularly hard to come by.
• **Lost and found:** (317) 262-3350 (ask specifically for Lost and Found).

Nearby Hotels

▼▼▼▼ **Canterbury Hotel (Classic Hotel)**, 123 S. Illinois St. (Indianapolis), (317) 634-3000, $250-$1550
▼▼▼ **Comfort Inn & Suites City Centre (Motel)**, 530 S. Capitol Ave. (Indianapolis), (317) 631-9000, $100-$350
▼▼▼ **Courtyard by Marriott-Downtown (Hotel)**, 501 W. Washington St. (Indianapolis), (317) 635-4443, $159
▼▼ **Days Inn Downtown (Motel)**, 401 E. Washington St. (Indianapolis), (317) 637-6464, $50-$255
▼▼ **Hampton Inn Downtown at Circle Center (Motor Inn)**, 105 S. Meridian St. (Indianapolis), (317) 261-1200, $104-$114

Nearby Restaurants

▼▼ **40 West Coffee Café (American)**, 40 W. Jackson Pl. in the Omni Severin Hotel (Indianapolis), (317) 686-1414, $3-$10 (lunch only)
▼▼ **The California Cafe Bar & Grill (West American)**, 49 W. Maryland St. in Circle Centre Mall (Indianapolis), (317) 488-8686, $12-$25
▼▼▼ **The Majestic Restaurant (Seafood)**, 47 S. Pennsylvania St. (Indianapolis), (317) 636-5418, $13-$39
▼▼▼ **Palomino (Continental)**, 49 W. Maryland St. #189 (Indianapolis), (317) 974-0400, $14-$30
▼▼▼▼ **The Restaurant at the Canterbury Hotel (Continental)**, 123 S. Illinois St. in the Canterbury Hotel (Indianapolis), (317) 634-3000, $15-$25

Directions: From south, take I-65 to I-70 west to West St. (exit 79A), right to Maryland St. From north, take I-65 to West St. (exit 114), south to Maryland St. From west, take 1-70 to West St. (exit 79A), left to Maryland St. From east, take I-70 to I-65 north to West St. (exit 114), south to Maryland St. **By Bus:** Several buses go to the RCA Dome. Call IndyGo at (317) 635-3344. **Parking:** More than 40,000 spaces are within a 10-minute walk; extra parking is available on Washington, South and Illinois Sts. and Capitol Ave.

JACKSONVILLE JAGUARS

SINCE ENTERING THE NFL in 1995, the Jacksonville Jaguars have never had a player win a major award at the end of the season. They've had no MVPs, no Defensive Players of the Year and no Rookies of the Year. But the players don't seem to mind the lack of individual hardware in the team's trophy case. They'll content themselves with these numbers instead: six years in the league, two AFC Central titles, four trips to the playoffs. Although success has come quickly to Jacksonville, it hasn't come easily. At the first training camp in Wisconsin in the summer of 1995, Head Coach Tom Coughlin put the team through such rigorous paces that it became national news. While cattle were dying in the midst of a mid-West heat wave, Jacksonville players were training twice a day, often in full gear. While the Jags went 4-12 in the team's first season, the players earned a reputation for never quitting. Most importantly, young QB Mark Brunell emerged as a threat as both a passer and a runner. Winning their last game of 1995, the Jags kept the momentum going in '96. With Brunell's 4,367 passing yards leading the NFL, the second-year Jacksonville squad copped a wild-card spot. In the playoffs the upstart Jags knocked off Buffalo and Denver, the AFC's top team, before losing to the Patriots in the AFC final. After another wild-card year in 1997, the Jags won the AFC Central outright in 1998, largely on the strength of rookie RB Fred Taylor's 18 TDs. The team built on this success in 1999, winning 11 consecutive games down the stretch and finishing with a 14-2 record, best in the NFL.

Vital Stats

Stadium Address:
One Alltel Stadium Pl., Jacksonville, Fla.
Phone: (904) 633-6000
Web: jaguars.com
Box Office:
(904) 633-2000,
Mon.–Fri. 9–5,
weekend home-game days 10–3
Media Coverage:
Radio: WOKV (690 AM),
WBWL (600 AM),
WKQL (96.9 FM),
TV: CBS (WJXT Channel 4),
WAWS (Channel 30), Fox
(interconference games)
Training Facility:
Ferrell Fields,
Jacksonville, Fla.

POST SEASON
• AFC Central Titles 2
(1998, '99)
• AFC Wild Card Berths 2
(1996, '97)

TEAM RECORDS
Offense
• **Mark Brunell**
(1995–present)
Comp. (season): 353 (1996)
Comp. (career): 1,596
Comp. Pct. (season):
63.4 (1996)
Comp. Pct. (career): 60.3
Passing Att. (season):
557 (1996)

Extra Point

• In 1995 OT Tony Boselli became the first draft pick in franchise history. The massive lineman has proved worthy of the first-round pick. Touted by many as being one of the best offensive linemen in the NFL, Boselli has been selected to five straight Pro Bowls. In the 1996 play-offs, Boselli, in just his second year, lined up against 1996 Defensive Player of the Year Bruce Smith. Smith managed just three tackles and no sacks.

Passing Att. (career): 2,645
Passing Yards (season):
4,367 (1996)
Passing Yards (career): 19,117
QB Rating (season):
91.2 (1997)
TD Passes (career): 106
TD Passes (season):
20 (1998, 2000)
• **Mike Hollis (1995–present)**
Extra Points (season):
45 (1998)
Extra Points (career): 210
Field Goals (career): 157
Field Goals (season): 31
(1997, '99)
Field Goal Pct. (career): 83.0
Points (season): 134 (1997)
Points (career): 681
• **Jimmy Smith**
(1995–present)
Receiving Yards (season):
1,636 (1999)
Receiving Yards (career): 6,887
Receptions (career): 472
TD Receptions (career): 36
TD Receptions (season):
8 (1998, 2000)
• **James Stewart (1995–2000)**
Rushing TDs (career): 33
TDs (game): 5 (Oct. 12, 1997)
TDs (career): 38
• **Fred Taylor (1998–present)**
Carries (season): 292 (2000)
Carries (career): 1,057
Rushing Yards (career): 3,354
Rushing Yards (season):
1,223 (1998)
TDs (season): 17 (1998)

Defense
• **Aaron Beasley**
(1996–present)
Int. (season): 6 (1999)
Int. (career): 12
• **Tony Brackens**
(1996–present)
Fumble Recoveries (career): 11
Sacks (season): 12 (1999)
Sacks (career): 37
• **Kevin Hardy**
(1996–present)
Tackles (season): 186 (1998)
Tackles (career): 628

LEAGUE HONORS
AFC Coach of the Year
• Tom Coughlin (1996)

Pro Bowl Selections
• Tony Boselli (1996, '97, '98, '99, 2000)
• Mark Brunell (1996, '97, '99)
• Keenan McCardell (1996)
• Bryan Barker (1997)
• Mike Hollis (1997)
• Jimmy Smith (1997, '98, '99, 2000)
• Tony Brackens (1999)
• Kevin Hardy (1999)
• Carnell Lake (1999)
• Leon Searcy (1999)

Big and quick, OT Tony Boselli is a perennial Pro Bowler.

"The toughest team I ever played on. The team never backed down."
— DE Jeff Lageman, on the 1995 Jags, a team that went 4-12

Timeline

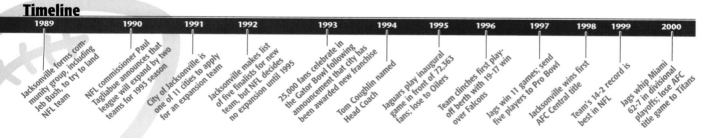

| 1989 | 1990 | 1991 | 1992 | 1993 | 1994 | 1995 | 1996 | 1997 | 1998 | 1999 | 2000 |

Jacksonville forms community group, including Jeb Bush, to try to land NFL team.

NFL commissioner Paul Tagliabue announces that league will expand by two teams for 1993 season

City of Jacksonville is one of 11 cities to apply for an expansion team

Jacksonville makes list of five finalists for new team, but NFL decides no expansion until 1995

25,000 fans celebrate in the Gator Bowl following announcement that city has been awarded new franchise

Tom Coughlin named Head Coach

Jaguars play inaugural game in front of 72,363 fans; lose to Oilers

Team clinches first play-off berth with 19-17 win over Falcons

Jags win 11 games; send five players to Pro Bowl

Jacksonville wins first AFC Central title

Team's 14-2 record is best in NFL

Jags whip Miami 62-7 in divisional playoffs; lose AFC title game to Titans

ALLTEL STADIUM: EVERYBODY'S HAPPY

On Aug. 18, 1995, the Jacksonville Jaguars became the first expansion team in sports history to play its first game in a brand new stadium. The amazing thing is that construction of the open-air masterpiece had begun less than 20 months earlier, making it the fastest construction of a North American major-league stadium. The reviews of the venue were favorable right from the start, with fans enjoying the stadium's aesthetics, sight lines and twin JumboTron screens and players raving about the condition of the grass field.

CONCESSIONS
Options include sausages, burgers, cheese steak sandwiches, clam chowder and the popular spicy Buffalo chicken tenders. Vegetarians will enjoy the spicy red beans and rice. Everyone loves the catfish strips, a local specialty.

Stadium Facts

Opened: *Aug. 18, 1995*
Cost: *$138 million*
Capacity: *73,000*
Type: *Outdoor*
Surface: *Grass*
Home Sweet Home:
• *Because the Jags play half their games on their home grass field, the team's players suffer fewer injuries of the kind generally attributed to unforgiving artificial surfaces.*

GAME DAY TIPS
• **Gate hours:** Touchdown Club doors open two hours prior to kickoff. Other gates open 30 minutes later.
• **Tailgating:** Tailgating begins four hours before games in all stadium lots. Other lots in the area also host tailgating.
• **Weather:** Florida in the fall is pleasantly warm. The west side of the stadium will be sunnier during early afternoon games.
• **Prohibited items:** Cans, coolers, bottles, umbrellas, strollers, laser pointers, video cameras and tape recorders, and outside food and beverages are prohibited. Smoking is allowed only in designated ramp areas.
• **Ticket tips:** Alltel Stadium is known for having great sight lines. The majority of

seats (75 percent) are located on the sides. Tickets are generally available, but watch for early sellouts when rivals Tennessee or Baltimore are in town.
• **Lost and found:** (904) 630-6114.

Seating Plan

		$50			$40
		$50			$40
		$65			$50
		$65			$65
		$95			$65
		$95			$65
		$50			$40
		$65	**ATM**	**Sections 123, 435**	
		$50	♿	**Throughout**	

Directions: *From I-95 south, take Main St. exit, cross Main St. Bridge, exit Ocean St. From I-95 north, take Union St. exit. From Arlington Expwy/Matthews Bridge, take Stadium exit. From Hart Bridge, take Stadium exit. By Bus: The JTA offers bus shuttle service from various locations. Call (904) 630-3100 for details.* **Parking:** *The stadium's 8,500 spaces are mostly reserved for season ticket holders. Overflow parking is accommodated by surrounding lots. Extra parking is available on Georgia St., Tallyrand Ave. and Haines St. There is no disabled parking reserved for non-season ticket holders, but passengers can be dropped off at the stadium driveway or Gate 2 on Duval St. up to one hour prior to kickoff.*

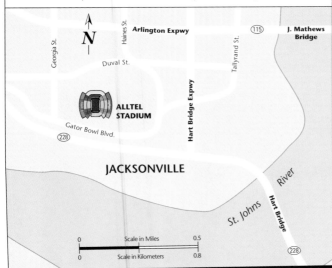

Nearby Hotels

▼▼ **Best Inns of America** *(Motel)*, 8220 Dix Ellis Tr. (Jacksonville), (904) 739-3323, $45-$48
▼▼▼ **Hampton Inn Central** *(Motel)*, 1331 Prudential Dr. (Jacksonville), (904) 396-7770, $69-$115
▼▼▼ **La Quinta Inn & Suites** *(Motel)*, 4868 Lenoir Ave. S. (Jacksonville), (904) 296-0703, $79-$99
▼▼▼ **Omni Jacksonville Hotel** *(Hotel)*, 245 Water St. (Jacksonville), (904) 355-6664, $134
▼▼ **Red Roof Inn** *(Motel)*, 6969 Lenoir Ave. E. (Jacksonville), (904) 296-1006, $50-$87

Nearby Restaurants

▼▼▼▼ **Matthew's** *(Continental)*, 2107 Hendricks Ave. (Jacksonville), (904) 396-9922, $20-$60 (dinner only)
▼▼ **Pattaya Thai Restaurant** *(Thai)*, 10916 Atlantic Blvd. (Jacksonville), (904) 646-9506, $6-$18
▼▼ **River City Brewing Company** *(American)*, 835 Museum Cir. (Jacksonville), (904) 398-2299, $12-$20
▼▼ **Siboney Cafe** *(Cuban)*, 2777-1 University Blvd. (Jacksonville), (904) 733-8300, $3-$17
▼▼▼ **Wilfried's 24 Miramar** *(American)*, 4446 Hendricks Ave. (Jacksonville), (904) 448-2424, $23-$28 (dinner only)

KANSAS CITY CHIEFS

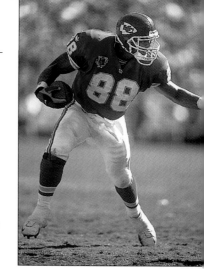

AN AFL ORIGINAL, the Kansas City Chiefs began as the Dallas Texans in 1960. Success came quickly, with a victory in the 1962 AFL championship. But the celebration was short-lived. The following year, with the team playing out of Kansas City, rookie RB Stone Johnson suffered a broken neck in a preseason game and died 10 days later. Reeling from the loss, the Chiefs stumbled to a 5-7 record. Tragedy struck again in 1965, when RB Mack Lee Hill died during a routine knee operation. This time the team rebounded to win the AFL title. Three years later the franchise enjoyed one of its greatest moments when it eliminated the defending Super Bowl champ New York Jets from the play-offs, a win highlighted by the Chiefs' dramatic fourth-quarter goal-line stand. Three weeks later Kansas City took the field for Super Bowl IV wearing a patch that read "AFL-10," a testament to the decade-old league. Playing for AFL pride, the underdog Chiefs stunned experts by dismantling the NFL's Vikings 23-7. The 1970s and '80s were tough on the Chiefs. From 1974 to '88, the team had only four winning seasons. Tragedy revisited the Chiefs again in '83, with the drowning of running back Joe Delaney. The team turned the corner in '89, when punishing RB Christian Okoye, aka "the Nigerian Nightmare," battered his way to 1,480 yards. The defense was buoyed by rookie LB Derrick Thomas, who led the squad with 10 sacks. The heart and soul of the team throughout the '90s, Thomas passed away following a horrible car accident in 2000. Only time will tell how the team will fare without its inspirational leader.

Tony Gonzales is a marvel of athleticism at tight end.

POSTSEASON
- Super Bowl Championships.................1 (1969)
- AFL Championships........2 (1962, '66)
- AFC West Titles ....4 (1971, '93, '95, '97)
- AFC Wild Card Berths.....4 (1986, '90, '91, '94)

RETIRED NUMBERS
- Jan Stenerud (3)
- Len Dawson (16)
- Abner Haynes (28)
- Stone Johnson (33)
- Mack Lee Hill (36)
- Willie Lanier (63)
- Bobby Bell (78)
- Buck Buchanan (86)

Extra Point

- *On June 29, 1983, Chiefs RB Joe Delaney saw three boys drowning in a water hole. Without a second's hesitation, he jumped in and pulled one boy ashore. Going back in to try and save the other two, Delaney drowned. What makes Delaney's act all that more heroic is the fact that he entered the water twice, even though he couldn't swim.*

TEAM RECORDS
Offense
- **Marcus Allen (1993–97)** Rushing TDs (career): 44
- **Derrick Alexander (1998–present)** Receiving Yards (season): 1,391 (2000)
- **Chris Buford (1960–67)** TD Receptions (season): 12 (1962)
- **Len Dawson (1962–75)** Comp. (career): 2,115 Passing Yards (career): 28,507 TD Passes (game): 6 (Nov. 1, 1964) TD Passes (season): 30 (1964) TD Passes (career): 237
- **Tony Gonzales (1997–present)** Receptions (season): 93 (2000)
- **Abner Hayes (1960–64)** Points (game): 30 (Nov. 26, 1961) TDs (season): 19 (1962)
- **Bill Kenney (1979–88)** Comp. (season): 346 (1983) Passing Yards (season): 4,348 (1983)
- **Nick Lowery (1980–93)** Field Goals (season): 34 (1990) Field Goals (career): 329 Longest Field Goal: 58 yards (Sept. 18, 1983, Sept. 12, 1985) Points (season): 139 (1990) Points (career): 1,466
- **Henry Marshall (1976–87)** Receptions (career): 415
- **Christian Okoye (1987–92)** Rushing Yards (season): 1,480 (1989) Rushing Yards (career): 4,897
- **Otis Taylor (1965–75)** Receiving Yards (career): 7,306 TDs (career): 60

Defense
- **Gary Spani (1978–86)** Tackles (season): 157 (1979) Tackles (career): 999
- **Derrick Thomas (1989–99)** Sacks (game): 7 (Nov. 11, 1990) Sacks (season): 20 (1990) Sacks (career): 126.5
- **Emmitt Thomas (1966–78)** Int. (season): 12 (1974) Int. (career): 58

LEAGUE HONORS
Super Bowl MVP
- Len Dawson (1969)

NFL Rookie of the Year
- Dale Carter (1992)

NFL Defensive Rookie of the Year
- Bill Maas (1984)

"It's the football capital of this country. This is an all-out hell hole to come into."
— Gunther Cunningham, on what visiting teams face in Kansas City

Vital Stats

Stadium Address: One Arrowhead Dr., Kansas City, Mo.
Phone: (816) 920-9300
Web: kcchiefs.com
Box Office: (816) 920-9400, Mon.–Fri. 8:30–5
Media Coverage: Radio: KCFX (101.1 FM) TV: Fox (Channel 4), CBS (Channel 5)
Training Facility: Arrowhead Stadium, Kansas City, Mo.

- Derrick Thomas (1989)
- Dale Carter (1992)

AFC Rookie of the Year
- Joe Delaney (1981)
- Dale Carter (1992)

Pro Football Hall of Fame
- Lamar Hunt (1972)
- Bobby Bell (1983)
- Willie Lanier (1986)
- Len Dawson (1987)
- Buck Buchanan (1990)
- Jan Stenerud (1991)

Timeline

1959	1962	1963	1965	1970	1980	1983	1987	1989	1990	1993	1994	1997	2000
Lamar Hunt establishes AFL; is owner of league's Dallas Texans	QB Len Dawson wooed from NFL; team wins AFL's Western Division	Franchise moved to Kansas City and renamed Chiefs	RB Mack Lee Hill dies during routine knee surgery	Chiefs shock football world by beating Vikings in Super Bowl IV	Club releases Jan Stenerud; signs journeyman kicker Nick Lowery	RB Joe Delaney drowns trying to save three youngsters	Chiefs draft Christian Okoye in second round	Okoye tops NFL rushers; LB Derrick Thomas named NFL's Defensive Rookie MVP	Thomas sets NFL record with seven sacks in a single game	Chiefs add QB Joe Montana and RB Marcus Allen to roster	Montana engineers two playoff comebacks; Chiefs bow out in AFC title game	Kansas City wins AFC West	Derrick Thomas dies of injuries related to car accident

ARROWHEAD STADIUM: THREE DECADES OF FOOTBALL

THE 2001 NFL SEASON marks the 30th campaign for the Kansas City Chiefs in Arrowhead Stadium. Original plans called for the stadium to be equipped with a revolutionary roof that could be rolled into place. Cost overruns scrapped that ambitious phase of the project. After toying with the idea of putting the stadium under a dome, officials decided to stick to an open-air policy. The result is a beautiful venue that hearkens back to football's glory years, especially since 1994, when the artificial turf was replaced by grass.

CONCESSIONS

Regular visitors to Arrowhead Stadium look forward to the pizza or the classic Polish sausage, bratwurst or quarter-pound hot dog. Try the chicken fajita pitas, with a hot chocolate or schnapps on the side. Vegetarian food is also available.

Stadium Facts

Opened: *Aug. 12, 1972*
Cost: *$14 million*
Capacity: *79,451*
Type: *Open*
Surface: *Grass*
Home Sweet Home:
• *The Chiefs are supported by some of the league's loudest fans. Dressed in red and banging on tom-toms, they helped the team set a NFL-best .813 winning percentage in the 1990s.*

GAME DAY TIPS

• **Gate hours:** Gates open two hours prior to kickoff.
• **Tailgating:** Parking lot gates open three hours prior to kickoff.
• **Weather:** Kansas City is generally warm and mild, even in late fall and winter.
• **Prohibited items:** Cans, coolers, noisemakers and video cameras are prohibited. Unopened plastic and cardboard beverage containers are allowed, as are umbrellas and banners and outside food. Smoking is allowed only in designated areas.
• **Ticket tips:** The Chiefs have been sold out for some 80 or more straight games, so tickets are very hard to come by, especially when the Oakland Raiders are in town. Any single-game tickets are usually made available in July.
• **Lost and found:** (816) 920-4201.

Seating Plan

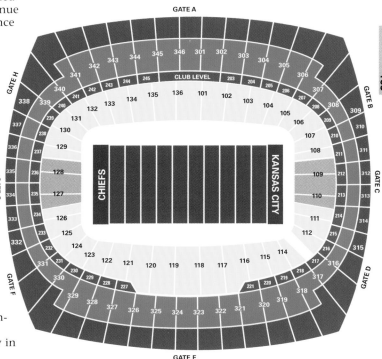

■ Upper Reserved	$45	■ Club Level	$61
▦ Field Reserved	$48	ATM Sections 101, 118	
■ Upper Box	$51	♿ Field Reserved, Field Box	
▢ Field Box	$55		

Directions: *Take I-29/35 to I-70. Head east on I-70 and exit at Blue Ridge cutoff. Arrowhead Stadium is on right. From north or south, take I-43 south to exit 63 C (Sports Complex). By Bus: Bus service is available to the stadium. Call Kansas City Transportation Authority (KCTA) at (816) 346-0200 for information.* **Parking:** *Lots at the stadium can accommodate 26,000 automobiles. Disabled parking is available in lots A, B, C, F, G, H and J. There are additional parking spots around the complex.*

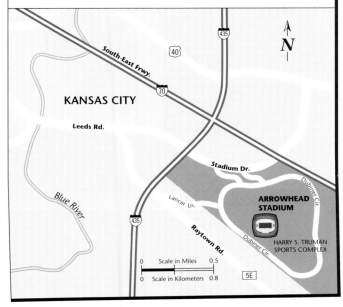

Nearby Hotels

▼▼▼ **Adams Mark-Kansas City** *(Hotel)*, 9103 E. 39th St. (Kansas City), (816) 737-0200, $99-$129
▼▼▼ **Drury Inn-Stadium** *(Motel)*, 3830 Blue Ridge Cutoff (Kansas City), (816) 923-3000, $69-$95
▼▼▼ **Holiday Inn-Sports Complex** *(Motor Inn)*, 4011 Blue Ridge Cutoff (Kansas City), (816) 353-5300, $72-$109
▼▼ **Red Roof Inn-Independence** *(Motel)*, 13712 E. 42nd Terr. (Independence), (816) 373-2800, $42-$60
▼▼ **Shoney's Inn-Independence** *(Motel)*, 4048 S. Lynn Court Dr. (Independence), (816) 254-0100, $49-$79

Nearby Restaurants

▼▼ **Michael Forbes Grill** *(American)*, 7539 Wornall Rd. (Kansas City), (816) 444-5445, $8-$15
▼▼▼ **Remington's** *(American)*, 9103 E. 39th St. in Adams Mark-Kansas City (Kansas City), (816) 737-4760, $15-$35
▼▼▼ **Stephenson's Apple Farm Restaurant** *(American)*, 16401 Hwy. 40E (Independence), (816) 373-5400, $9-$20
▼▼ **Stephenson's Red Mule Restaurant** *(American)*, 16506 Hwy. 40E (Independence), (816) 478-1810, $6-$13
▼▼▼ **V's Italiano Ristorante** *(Italian)*, 10819 Hwy. 40E (Independence), (816) 353-1241, $13-$18

Miami Dolphins

THE MIAMI DOLPHINS ARE PROOF of how a team can become a success via the draft. How successful have the Dolphins been? Since the NFL–AFL merger in 1970 the team's overall record of 304-166-2 is the best in the NFL. But things didn't start out so well for the franchise. In its first four years in the AFL, from 1966 to '69, the Dolphins posted a dismal 15-39-2 record. During this time, however, management was laying the groundwork for the future. Drafting Bob Griese in 1967, Larry Csonka and Jim Kiick in '68, and Mercury Morris and sack specialist Bob Stanfill in '69, the Dolphins armed themselves to take on the big boys of the NFL. With Griese emerging as one of the AFC's premier signal callers and Csonka bulldozing his way to 1,000 yards on the ground, Miami won the 1971 AFC East. In 1972 the Dolphins were undefeated in all 14 regular season games and two playoff contests, before capping their perfect season with a 14-7 victory over the Redskins in Super Bowl VII. Although they weren't perfect in 1973, Miami repeated as Super Bowl champions, with Csonka earning MVP honors. Ten years later the team made its greatest draft pick when it selected QB Dan Marino. As a rookie, Marino led the AFC in passing and in 1984 he set records for TD passes (48) and yards passing (5,084). Breaking record after record with each passing season, the strong-armed Marino carried the Dolphins into the post-season in 10 of his 17 years. When Marino retired in 1999, QB Jay Fiedler took the keys and drove the squad to the AFC East crown, continuing the Dolphins' winning tradition.

"When he goes on safari, the lions roll up their windows."

— *Former offensive coordinator Monte Clark, on Miami's bruising fullback Larry Csonka*

POSTSEASON
- **Super Bowl Championships**..................2 (1972, '73)
- **AFC Championships**.......5 (1971, '72, '73, '82, '84)
- **AFC East Titles**...............12 (1971, '72, '73, '74, '78, '81, '83, '84, '85, '92, '94, 2000)
- **AFC Wild Card Berths**.....7 (1970, '78, '90, '95, '97, '98, '99)

RETIRED NUMBERS
- **Bob Griese (12)**
- **Dan Marino (13)**

DOLPHIN HONOR ROLL
- **Nick Buoniconti**

Extra Point
- *When Dan Marino retired following the 1999 season, he had established himself as one of the NFL's greatest quarterbacks. His name sits atop the NFL record book for pass attempts (8,358), completions (4,967), passing yards (61,361) and TD passes (420).*

- **Larry Csonka**
- **Bob Griese**
- **Bob Kuechenberg**
- **Jim Langer**
- **Larry Little**
- **Dan Marino**
- **Nat Moore**
- **Joe Robbie**
- **Don Shula**
- **Dwight Stephenson**
- **Paul Warfield**
- **1972 Undefeated Team**

TEAM RECORDS
Offense
- **Mark Clayton (1983–92)** Receiving Yards (season): 1,389 Receptions (career): 550 TDs (season): 18 (1984) TD Receptions (career): 81
- **Larry Csonka (1968–74, '79)** Rushing TDs (career): 53 Rushing Yards (career): 6,737
- **Mark Duper (1982–92)** Receiving Yards (career): 8,869
- **Bob Griese (1967–80)** TD Passes (game): 6 (tie) (Nov. 24, 1977)
- **Dan Marino (1983–99)** Comp. (season): 385 (1994) Comp. (career): 4,967

Passing Yards (season): 5,084 (1984) Passing Yards (career): 61,361 TD Passes (season): 48 (1984) TD Passes (career): 420
- **Mercury Morris (1969–75)** Rushing Yards (game): 197 (Sept. 30, 1973)
- **Pete Stoyanovich (1989–95)** Field Goals (career): 176 Longest Field Goal: 59 yards (Nov. 12, 1989)
- **Garo Yepremian (1970–78)** Points (career): 830

Vital Stats

Stadium Address: 2269 Dan Marino Blvd. (NW 199th St.), Miami, Fla.

Phone: (305) 623-6100

Web: dolphinsendzone.com, pro-player-stadium.com

Box Office: (888) FINS-TIX, Mon.–Fri. 8:30–6, Sat. 10–4

Media Coverage: Radio: WQAM (560 AM) TV: CBS (WFOR Channel 4), Fox (WSVN Channel 7)

Training Facility: Nova University, Davie, Fla.

Defense
- **Jake Scott (1970–75)** Interceptions (career): 35
- **Bill Stanfill (1969–76)** Sacks (game) 5 (Oct. 7, 1973) Sacks (season) 18.5 (1973) Sacks (career) 67.5

LEAGUE HONORS
NFL MVP
- **Bob Griese (1977)**
- **Dan Marino (1984)**

Super Bowl MVP
- **Jake Scott (1972)**
- **Larry Csonka (1973)**

NFL Rookie of the Year
- **Dan Marino (1983)**
- **Richmond Webb (1990)**

NFL Coach of the Year
- **Don Shula (1970, '72)**

Pro Football Hall of Fame
- **Paul Warfield (1983)**
- **Larry Csonka (1987)**
- **Jim Langer (1987)**
- **Bob Griese (1990)**
- **Larry Little (1993)**
- **Don Shula (1997)**
- **Dwight Stephenson (1998)**
- **Nick Buoniconti (2001)**

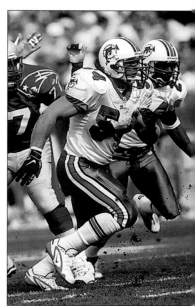

LB Zach Thomas is one of the NFL's hardest workers and surest tacklers.

Timeline

1965	1966	1967	1970	1971	1973	1974	1981	1983	1984	1993	2000
Actor Danny Thomas and lawyer Joe Robbie awarded expansion team in Miami	Joe Auer returns opening kickoff 95 yards for a Dolphins' TD in franchise's first game	Future Hall-of-Famer QB Bob Griese selected in first round	Don Shula named Head Coach; leads team to playoffs for first time	FB Larry Csonka is club's first 1,000-yard rusher	Dolphins cap undefeated 1972 season with 14-7 win over Redskins in Super Bowl VII	Miami repeats as Super Bowl champs	Griese retires after 14 years with Dolphins	Team selects QB Dan Marino in first round of draft	Marino becomes first QB to pass for 5,000 in a season; named league MVP	Marino surpasses the 40,000-yard passing mark in just 153 games – fastest man to do so	QB Dan Marino retires after 17 years with the Dolphins; his 61,361 career passing yards is all-time NFL record

PRO PLAYER STADIUM: HOME OF THE FINS

IN 1987 JOE ROBBIE BUILT a state-of-the-art home for his team. Joe Robbie Stadium was built almost entirely with private funding, much of it raised through season ticket holders' making long-term agreements and in turn benefiting from the new venue's first-class amenities. The stadium has no obstructed views and excellent scoreboards and TV monitors at concession stands. In 1996 the facility was renamed Pro Player Stadium. Domed stadium plans have been shelved.

CONCESSIONS

Hamburgers, hot dogs, chicken, ice cream, cookies and the like are sold here. The choice for vegetarians is limited to pretzels, nachos or desserts. In all, the stadium has 43 concession stands.

GAME DAY TIPS

• **Gate hours:** Stadium

Stadium Facts

Opened: *Aug. 16, 1987*
Cost: *$115 million*
Capacity: *75,540*
Type: *Outdoor*
Surface: *Grass*
Home Sweet Home:
• *The crowd noise at Pro Player Stadium can be deafening. When the fans try to drown out the opposing QB's signals, Dolphin defensive backs use hand signals to communicate.*

gates open two hours prior to kickoff.
• **Tailgating:** Tailgating takes place in all stadium lots. Permit holders can get in four hours before kickoff; others are allowed in one hour later. In addition, the Dolphins host a pre-game event called Sports Town, which features a pair of large tents, local bands and food.
• **Weather:** South Florida is usually quite warm in the fall and can be rainy. The Club Level seats are protected from the sun, but people sitting in other areas will have to go to the concourse for shade.
• **Prohibited items:** Coolers, bottles, cans, jugs and thermoses, strollers, laser pointers, beachballs and food not purchased within the stadium are prohibited. Smoking

Seating Plan

■ **Club Level** $140	■ **Upper End Zones** $39
■ **Lower Sidelines** $55	■ **Economy Sections** $27
▢ **Upper Sidelines** $49	■ **TD's Touchdown Zone** .. $20
■ **Lower Corners** $46	ATM **Sections 149, 150, 456**
■ **Lower End Zones** $44	♿ **Throughout**
■ **Upper Corners** $40	

is permitted only on the ramps of each level.
• **Ticket tips:** Single-game tickets are available if purchased well in advance.

Traditional rivals — and typical sellouts — include the Bills and the Patriots.
• **Lost and found:** (305) 626-7275.

Directions: *From I-95, take Ives Dairy Rd. and proceed west for five miles to stadium. From Florida Tpk. Interchange, take exit 2X (NW 199th St./Stadium exit). By Bus: The No. 27 bus will take you to the stadium. Call (305) 770-3131 for schedules and information.* **Parking:** *The stadium lot accommodates 14,970 cars. There are 262 spots reserved for people with disabilities and these are located in lots A, C, E and G.*

Nearby Hotels

▼▼▼ **Don Shula's Hotel & Golf Club** *(Resort)*, 15255 Bull Run Rd. (Miami Lakes), (305) 821-1150, $99-$129
▼▼ **El Palacio Resort Hotel & Suites** *(Motor Inn)*, 16805 NW 12th Ave. (Miami), (305) 624-8401, $98-$170
▼▼▼ **Holiday Inn-Calder/Pro Player Stadium** *(Motor Inn)*, 21485 NW 27th Ave. (Miami), (305) 621-5801, $82-$1000
▼▼▼ **TownePlace Suites by Marriott** *(Extended Stay Motel)*, 10505 NW 36th St. (Miami), (305) 718-4144, $69-$139
▼▼▼▼ **Turnberry Isle Resort & Club** *(Resort)*, 19999 W. Country Club Dr. (Aventura), (305) 932-6200, $275-$485

Nearby Restaurants

▼▼▼▼ **Chef Allen's** *(American)*, 19088 NE 29th Ave. (Aventura), (305) 935-2900, $26-$38 (dinner only)
▼▼ **Mike Gordon Seafood Restaurant** *(Seafood)*, 1201 NE 79th St. (Miami), (305) 751-4429, $12-$25
▼▼▼ **Shula's Steakhouse** *(Steakhouse)*, 7601 NW 154th St. in Don Shula's Hotel & Golf Club (Miami Lakes), (305) 820-8102, $18-$33
▼▼ **Shula's Steak 2** *(Sports Bar)*, 7601 NW 154th St. in Don Shula's Hotel & Golf Club (Miami Lakes), (305) 820-8047, $6-$20
▼▼ **Tuna's Waterfront Grille** *(Seafood)*, 17201 Biscayne Blvd. (North Miami Beach), (305) 945-2567, $10-$25

MINNESOTA VIKINGS

HOW MINNESOTA HAS FARED SINCE it joined the NFL in 1961 depends to a great extent on how you measure success. Reaching the playoffs 23 times in 40 seasons is no mean feat. In fact, on that scale, the Vikings franchise has been among the most successful in sports history. But the team's ability to get to the postseason year in and year out has been offset by its inability to win the big game. In four Super Bowl appearances, all losses, the team was outscored by a combined 98-37. Still, since its earliest days, the Vikings' wealth of talent has provided Minnesota football fans with many reasons to cheer. Some names are inextricably linked to the franchise: Fran Tarkenton, a prodigious passer and elusive scrambler who quarterbacked the team in its inaugural season and returned in the 1970s to lead the Vikes to three NFC championships; defensive lineman Alan Page, a constant sack-threat who played in 236 consecutive NFL games and blocked 28 kicks; Paul Krause, the eight-time Pro-Bowl free safety who picked off 53 passes for the Vikes; Head Coach Bud Grant, who in 18 seasons at the helm guided the team to 11 division titles. Recent years have seen the emergence of a new crop of talent. With WR Cris Carter, second only to Jerry Rice in career receptions, and the exceptionally talented wideout Randy Moss, the Vikes are blessed with one of the best air attacks in football. Mammoth young QB Daunte Culpepper stepped up in 2000 and showed he can get the ball to his explosive receiving corps. Minnesota fans want to know if he can lead the squad to the one big win it has never enjoyed: a Super Bowl.

> *"I would hate to have to come here . . . and not be able to hear the quarterback."*
> — Viking Korey Stringer, on fan noise at the Metrodome

Vital Stats

Stadium Address:
900 S. 5th St.,
Minneapolis, Minn.
Phone: (612) 332-0386
Web: vikings.com
Box Office:
(612) 33-VIKES, Mon.–Fri.
and game days 8:30–5,
Sat. 9–1 during season
Media Coverage:
Radio: WCCO (830 AM)
TV: Fox (WFTC Channel
29), CBS (WCCO Channel
4), ABC (KSTP Channel 5)
Training Facility:
Winter Park,
Eden Prairie, Minn.

POSTSEASON
- NFL Championship 1 (1969)
- NFC Championship.........3 (1973, '74, '76)
- NFC Central Titles ....14 (1970, '71, '73, '74, '75, '76, '77, '78, '80, '89, '92, '94, '98 2000)
- NFC Wild Card Berths.....6 (1987, '88, '93, '96, '97, '99)

RETIRED NUMBERS
- Fran Tarkenton (10)
- Paul Krause (22)
- Jim Marshall (70)
- Alan Page (88)

TEAM RECORDS
Offense
- Gary Anderson

Extra Point
- With a fourth-quarter field goal against Buffalo on Oct. 22, 2000, Vikings kicker Gary Anderson became the leading scorer in NFL history, passing Hall-of-Famer George Blanda.
- Going into his 10th season at the helm of the Vikings, Dennis Green is tied with Bill Cowher for the longest tenure of any NFL head coach.

(1998–present)
Points (season): 164 (1998)
Field Goals (season): 35 (1998)
- **Cris Carter (1990–present)**
Receiving Yards (career): 11,512
Receptions (season): 122 (1994, '95)
Receptions (career): 931
TD Receptions (season): 17 (tie) (1995)
TD Receptions (career): 104
- **Fred Cox (1963–77)**
Field Goals (career): 282
Points (career): 1,365
- **Chuck Foreman (1973–79)**
Rushing Yards (game): 200 (Oct. 24, 1976)
TDs (season): 13 (tie) (1975, '76)
TDs (career): 52 (tie)
- **Randy Moss (1998–present)**
Receiving Yards (season): 1,437 (2000)
TD Receptions (season): 17 (tie) (1998)
- **Robert Smith (1993–2000)**
Rushing Yards (season): 1,521 (2000)
Rushing Yards (career): 6,818
Yards-per-Carry (season): 5.5 (1997)
100-Yard Games (career): 29
1,000-Yard Seasons: 4
- **Fran Tarkenton (1961–66, 1972–78)**

Comp. (career): 2,635
Comp. Pct. (career): 57.6
Pass Att. (career): 4,569
Passing Yards (career): 33,098
QB Rating (career): 80.2
TD Passes (career): 239

Defense
- **Chris Doleman (1985–93, '99)**
Sacks (season): 21 (1989)
- **Carl Eller (1964–78)**
Sacks (career): 130
- **Paul Krause (1968–79)**
Int. (season): 10 (1975)

Int. (career): 53
- **Alan Page (1967–78)**
Sacks (rookie season): 8.5 (1967)
- **Scott Studwell (1977–90)**
Tackles (season): 230 (1981)
Tackles (career): 1,981

LEAGUE HONORS
NFL MVP
- Alan Page (1971)
- Fran Tarkenton (1975)
- Randall Cunningham (1998)

NFL Rookie of the Year
- Paul Flatley (1963)
- Chuck Foreman (1973)
- Sammy White (1976)
- Randy Moss (1998)

Pro Football Hall of Fame
- Fran Tarkenton (1986)
- Alan Page (1988)
- Bud Grant (1994)
- Jim Finks (1995)
- Paul Krause (1998)

Daunte Culpepper led the Vikings to the NFC title game in 2000.

Timeline

1960	1961	1964	1967	1969	1971	1975	1979	1985	1989	1992	1994	1998	1999	2000

- 1960 — Vikings founded
- 1961 — Team plays first game, losing 38-13 to Cowboys
- 1964 — Minnesota records first winning season
- 1967 — Bud Grant named Head Coach
- 1969 — Vikings win NFL championship game 27-7 over Browns
- 1971 — Defensive lineman Alan Page named NFL MVP
- 1975 — Vikings lose to Steelers in team's third Super Bowl appearance
- 1979 — Construction begins on Metrodome
- 1985 — Bud Grant returns as coach for 1985 season after one-year retirement
- 1989 — Vikings win 12th division title since 1968
- 1992 — Dennis Green named Head Coach
- 1994 — Vikings acquire QB Warren Moon in trade with Houston Oilers
- 1998 — Vikings go 15-1, the best regular season record in team history
- 1999 — Team drafts QB Dante Culpepper in first round
- 2000 — Vikings lose to Giants in NFC championship game

HUBERT H. HUMPHREY METRODOME: THE GREAT INDOORS

THE VIKINGS MOVED inside in 1982 after playing its first 22 seasons outdoors at the Metropolitan Stadium. Although baseball fans generally dislike the dome, football patrons are more forgiving, maybe due to the Vikings' 106-58 win-loss record since moving inside or because the dome keeps out Minnesota's harsh winter weather. Two Sony JumboTron replay screens follow the action. Although the seats are angled for excellent sight lines, the atmosphere tends to be tame. Commercials on the big screens can be very loud.

CONCESSIONS

The Metrodome has specialty sausages, ranging from bratwurst to Italian. There are also a number of choices for the health conscious and vegetarians, including salads, yogurt smoothies and sandwiches. The "Walkaway Sundae" is a fan favorite.

Stadium Facts

Opened: *April 3, 1982*
Cost: *$83 million*
Capacity: *64,121*
Type: *Enclosed*
Surface: *AstroTurf*
Home Sweet Home:
• *Noise in the Metrodome often reaches 130 decibels, making snap counts almost inaudible. When the Vikings are on offense, the team is forced to post a sign on the scoreboard requesting quiet.*

GAME DAY TIPS

• **Gate hours:** Gates open 90 minutes prior to kickoff.
• **Tailgating:** Although the stadium does not have its own lot, tailgating takes place three to four hours before kickoff in public lots on Washington St. between Portland St. and 10th St.. The Vikings also host a pre-game party in the plaza area before each home game.
• **Prohibited items:** Cans, bottles, beachballs, helium balloons, plastic containers, beverages, laser pointers, bats and brooms are prohibited. Alcohol cannot be brought into the stadium. Signs are permitted provided they are not on sticks or poles and do not obstruct people's view.
• **Ticket tips:** The majority of seats at the Metrodome are sold to season ticket holders.

Seating Plan

.................$32		.................$76
.................$37		.................$83
.................$51	**ATM** **Sections 106, 116, 123, 136**
.................$58	♿ **Throughout**
.................$61	

Single-game tickets are available, but sell out quickly. Games against NFC Central rivals such as Green Bay and the Buccaneers sell out quickest.
• **Lost and found:** (651) 631-1981.

Directions: *From I-94, take 5th St. exit. From I-394 north, take 4th St. exit. From I-35W south, take Washington Ave. exit. From I-35W north, take 3rd St. exit. By Bus: There are bus routes to the Metrodome from various points in town. Call (612) 373-3333 for routes and schedules.*
Parking: *Get to the park early to get one of the eight-hour meters nearby. The Metrodome has no private lot, but there are public lots on S. 3rd, S. Park, S. 5th, S. 11th and S. Washington Sts. A lot reserved for people with disabilities is found on Chicago Ave. between S. 3rd St. and S. 4th St.*

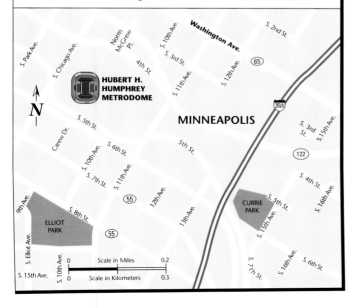

Nearby Hotels

▼▼▼ **Best Western Downtown** *(Motel)*, 405 S. 8th St. (Minneapolis), (612) 370-1400, $89-$104
▼▼▼ **Crowne Plaza Northstar Hotel** *(Hotel)*, 618 S. 2nd Ave. S. (Minneapolis), (612) 338-2288, $89-$149
▼▼▼ **Embassy Suites Minneapolis Downtown,** *(Suite Hotel)*, 425 S. 7th St. (Minneapolis), (612) 333-3111, $170-$199
▼▼▼ **Holiday Inn Metrodome** *(Hotel)*, 1500 Washington Ave. S. (Minneapolis), (612) 333-4646, $115-$209
▼▼▼ **Hyatt Whitney** *(Hotel)*, 150 Portland Ave. (Minneapolis), (612) 375-1234, $155-$210

Nearby Restaurants

▼▼▼ **Basil's** *(American)*, 710 Marquette Ave. in the Marquette Hotel (Minneapolis), (612) 376-7404, $10-$30
▼▼▼ **Cafe Brenda** *(American)*, 300 1st Ave. N. (Minneapolis), (612) 342-9230, $7-$12
▼▼▼ **Goodfellow's** *(American)*, 40 S. 7th St. in the City Center Shopping Complex (Minneapolis), (612) 332-4800, $25-$35
▼▼▼ **Murray's Restaurant** *(American)*, 26 S. 6th St. (Minneapolis), (612) 339-0909, $11-$49
▼▼▼ **Palomino Euro-Bistro** *(American)*, 825 Hennepin Ave. on the Skyway level of Lasalle Plaza (Minneapolis), (612) 339-3800, $9-$27

NEW ENGLAND PATRIOTS

FOUNDED IN NOVEMBER 1959, the then Boston Patriots were the eighth and final franchise awarded by the fledgling AFL. Drawing on a large, heavily populated region that was already known for its college football prowess, the Pats garnered large attention and fan support — despite the team's lack of success and somewhat nomadic home-field situation (the Pats played out of four different area stadiums in the first 12 seasons). The franchise's early years were nonetheless filled with excitement, thanks largely to the play of wide receiver and kicker Gino Cappelletti, quarterback Babe Parilli and running back Jim Nance. The Pats managed to win just one division title in the team's first decade of existence, that coming in 1963. By the late 1970s, however, New England had assembled a capable group led by future Hall-of-Famers offensive guard John Hannah and cornerback Mike Haynes. But playoff births in 1976 and '79 failed to yield the desired result — a crack at the Super Bowl. That day would come in 1986, when with Tony Eason at QB and Stanley Morgan catching passes, the Pats parlayed a wild-card playoff spot into a berth in the Super Bowl. Facing a Bears team that boasted one of the greatest defenses of all time, the Pats took it on the chin 46-10. QB Drew Bledsoe's arrival in 1993 signaled another new era for New England. His prodigious air attack brought the franchise back to the ultimate game again in 1997. This time the Packers won a hard-fought battle. It hasn't been easy for the Pats, but their fans are patient and loyal. And if the hard-nosed Bledsoe has anything to say about it, fortune may shine on them yet.

"Bill Belichick is a defensive genius."
— *Hall-of-Fame RB Jim Brown, on Patriots head coach*

Vital Stats

Stadium Address:
60 Washington St.,
Foxboro, Mass.
Phone: (508) 543-8200
Web: patriots.com
Box Office:
(800) 543-1776,
Mon.–Sat. 9–5
Media Coverage:
Radio: WBCN (104.1 FM)
TV: FOX (WFXT Channel 25), CBS (WBZ Channel 4), ABC (WCVB Channel 5)
Training Facility:
Foxboro Stadium,
Foxboro, Mass.

POSTSEASON
• AFC Championships 2
(1985, '96)
• AFC East Titles 4
(1978, '86, '96, '97)
• AFC Wild Card Berths 3
(1985, '94, '98)
• AFL East Titles..................1
(1963)

RETIRED NUMBERS
• Gino Cappelletti (20)
• Mike Haynes (40)
• Steve Nelson (57)
• John Hannah (73)
• Jim Lee Hunt (79)
• Bob Dee (89)

HALL OF FAME
• Nick Buoniconti

Extra Point

• When Tony Franklin hit a field goal to put the Pats up 3-0 in the team's first Super Bowl in 1986, New England fans had hope. It was dashed very soon as the Bears went on to score the next 44 points in the 46-10 Chicago victory.
• Hope springs eternal for New England fans. The Pats sold out every regular-season home game in 1999 in just 90 minutes.

Drew Bledsoe's passing led the Pats to the 1996 Super Bowl.

• Gino Cappelletti
• Bob Dee
• Steve Grogan
• John Hannah
• Mike Haynes
• Jim Lee Hunt
• Steve Nelson
• Vito Parilli
• Andre Tippett

TEAM RECORDS
Offense
• **Drew Bledsoe**
(1993–present)
Pass Att. (season): 691 (1994)
Pass Att.: (career): 4,452
Pass Comp. (game):
45 (Nov. 13, 1994)
Pass Comp. (season):
400 (1994)
Pass Comp. (career): 2,504
Passing Yards (game):
426 (Nov. 13, 1994)
Passing Yards (season): 4,555 (1994)
Passing Yards (career): 29,257
• **Gino Cappelletti (1960–70)**
Points (game): 28
(Dec. 18, 1965)
Points (season): 155 (1964)
Points (career): 1,130
• **Ben Coates (1991–99)**
Receptions (season): 96 (1994)
• **Sam Cunningham**
(1973–79, 1981–82)
Carries (career): 1,385
Rushing Yards (career): 5,453
• **Terry Glenn**
(1996–present)
Receptions (game):
13 (Oct. 3, 1999)
Receiving Yards (game):
214 (Sept. 3, 1999)
• **Steve Grogan (1975–90)**
TD Passes (game): 5
(tie) (Sept. 9, 1979)
TD Passes (career): 182
• **Curtis Martin (1995–97)**
Rushing Yards (season):
1,487 (1995)
Rushing TDs (season):
14 (1995, '96)
• **Stanley Morgan (1977–89)**
Receiving Yards
(season): 1,491
Receiving Yards
(career): 10,352

Receptions (career): 534
TD Receptions (season):
12 (1979)
TD Receptions (career): 67
• **Vito Parilli (1961–67)**
TD Passes (game) 5 (tie) (Nov. 15, 1964, Oct. 10, 1967)
TD Passes (season): 31 (1964)

Defense
• **Raymond Clayborn**
(1977–89)
Int. (career): 36
• **Andre Tippett**
(1982–88, 1990–93)
Sacks (career): 100
Sacks (season): 18.5 (1984)

LEAGUE HONORS
Pro Football Hall of Fame
• John Hannah (1991)
• Michael Haynes (1994)
• Nick Buoniconti (2001)

NFL Rookie of the Year
• John Stephens (1988)
• Curtis Martin (1995)

AFL MVP
• Gino Cappelletti (1964)
• Jim Nance (1966)

Timeline

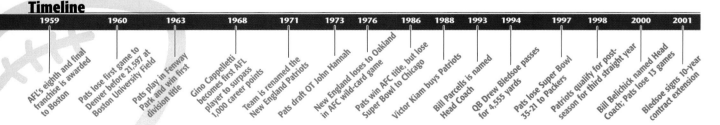

1959 — AFL's eighth and final franchise is awarded to Boston
1960 — Pats lose first game to Denver before 21,597 at Boston University Field
1963 — Pats play in Fenway Park and win first division title
1968 — Gino Cappelletti becomes first AFL player to surpass 1,000 career points
1971 — Team is renamed the New England Patriots
1973 — Pats draft OT John Hannah
1976 — New England loses to Oakland in AFC wild-card game
1986 — Pats win AFC title, but lose Super Bowl to Chicago
1988 — Victor Kiam buys Patriots
1993 — Bill Parcells is named Head Coach
1994 — QB Drew Bledsoe passes for 4,555 yards
1997 — Pats lose Super Bowl 35-21 to Packers
1998 — Patriots qualify for post-season for third straight year
2000 — Bill Belichick named Head Coach; Pats lose 13 games
2001 — Bledsoe signs 10-year contract extension

FOXBORO STADIUM: PROFITABLE VENUE

BUILT FOR $61 MILLION IN 1971, Foxboro Stadium has been one of the most profitable sports venues in history. Since the first game, more than 15 million spectators have passed through the turnstiles to see their Patriots. The stadium is very basic with few frills, but it does have excellent sight lines and there are few bad seats. It's also quite open to the elements and can be very cold. The 2001 season is scheduled to be the Pats' last at Foxboro. The new CMGI Field is set to open in 2002.

CONCESSIONS

Foxboro Stadium has a wide variety of traditional food options, including pizza, subs, hamburgers and hot dogs, as well as less standard fare such as fried dough, buffalo fingers, Italian sausages and Italian ices.

Stadium Facts

Opened: Aug. 15, 1971
Cost: $61 million
Capacity: 60,293
Type: Outdoor
Surface: Grass
Home Sweet Home:
• The Pats' gaudy 45-26 home record since 1994 is partially attributable to amazing fan support. New England has enjoyed a remarkable string of 71 consecutive sellouts since that year.

GAME DAY TIPS

• **Gate hours:** Gates open two hours prior to kickoff.
• **Tailgating:** Tailgating begins four hours prior to a game and ends two hours after the final whistle.
• **Weather:** Early season games are usually comfortable, but temperatures drop in November and December. Rain is not uncommon in the fall and you might even see snow late in the season.
• **Prohibited items:** Weapons, coolers, cans, bottles, umbrellas, fireworks, cameras, video recorders, strollers or baby seats, folding chairs, noisemakers, bull horns, helium balloons and beachballs are prohibited. Food and beverages cannot be brought into the stadium.

Seating Plan

- ■ $75
- ■ $51
- ■ $47
- ▫ $34
- ■ $31
- **ATM** Sections 207, 220
- ♿ Sections 22–24, 106, 108

• **Ticket tips:** Foxboro is known for having great sight lines from almost any spot in the stadium, which is important as there is not a wide variety of seats available for single games. A small number of tickets are reserved for individual ticket sales, but they go quickly.
• **Lost and found:** (508) 543-0350.

Directions: From I-95 south, exit 9 to Rte. 1 S. From I-95 north, exit to I-495 N., take exit 14A to Rte. 1. From I-90 east, exit to I-495 S., take exit 14A to Rte. 1. Follow Rte.1 to stadium. By Train: MBTA runs train service from Boston to Foxboro on game days. Call (508) 543-3900 for schedule information. **Parking:** Parking is available in nine lots on the stadium site. There are 187 spots available for people with disabilities, all of which are located in the south end zone and can be accessed by the P6 entrance. Extra parking is available at 20 lots along Hwy. 1.

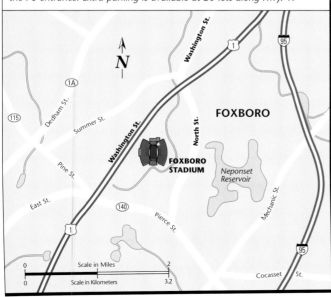

Nearby Hotels

▼▼ **Comfort Inn Foxboro** *(Motel)*, 4 Fisher St. (Foxboro), (508) 543-1000, $79-$199
▼▼▼ **Courtyard by Marriott** *(Motel)*, 35 Foxboro Blvd. (Foxboro), (508) 543-5222, $94-$150
▼ **EndZone Motor Inn** *(Motel)*, 105 Washington St. (Foxboro), (508) 543-4000, $65-$80
▼▼▼ **Sharon Inn** *(Motel)*, 775 Providence Hwy. (Sharon), (781) 784-5800, $99-$119
▼▼ **Super 8 Motel** *(Motel)*, 395 Old Post Rd. (Sharon), (781) 784-1000, $75-$145

Nearby Restaurants

The Commons Eatery & Café *(American)*, 20 Central St. (Foxboro), (508) 543-4432, $8-$12
▼▼ **Lafayette House** *(Continental)*, 109 Washington St. (Foxboro), (508) 543-5344, $16-$23
Luciano's Restaurant *(Northern Italian)*, 800 Washington St. (Wrentham), (508) 384-3050, $17-$26
Ninety Nine Restaurant and Pub *(Steakhouse)*, 4 Fisher St. (Foxboro), (508) 543-1199, $8-$12
▼▼ **Piccadilly Pub** *(American)*, 25 Foxborough Blvd. (Foxboro), (508) 543-0535, $6-$14

NEW ORLEANS SAINTS

IT WOULD BE HARD TO SCRIPT a more electrifying beginning for a new football franchise. Before many of the 80,000 hometown fans had settled in their seats for New Orleans' 1967 NFL debut, speedy John Gilliam took the opening kickoff 94 yards for a touchdown. Unfortunately, the Saints lost the game. It was a harbinger of things to come — lots of individual highlights, but not much team success. In 1967 Danny Abramowicz emerged as the league's top receiver, gaining 1,015 yards on 73 catches, but the team finished at 4-9. One year later, while New Orleans was floundering en route to a 2-11 record, Tom Dempsey drilled a 63-yard field goal — the longest in history — to beat the Lions. QB Archie Manning was named 1978 NFC MVP, but the team suffered through its 12th straight losing season. When New Orleans stumbled to 1-15 in 1980, disgruntled fans started wearing paper bags on their head and calling themselves "the Aints." The team turned the corner in 1987, closing out the season with nine straight wins and earning its first playoff spot. The Saints' postseason ended quickly, however, when they got pasted by the Vikings 44-10 in the wild-card game. New Orleans reached the playoffs again from 1990 to '92, but all three postseasons ended with first-round losses. However, the team's 34 years of playoff futility ended in 2000. The team won the NFC West, thanks to record-setting years by WR Joe Horn and DT La'Roi Glover. Facing the defending Super Bowl champion Rams in the first round, the Saints won the game and, more important, finally silenced their critics.

Joe Horn is a force both on special teams and as a receiver.

POSTSEASON
- NFC West Titles 2
(1991, 2000)
- NFC Wild Card Berths 3
(1987, '90, '92)

RETIRED NUMBERS
- Jim Taylor (31)
- Doug Atkins (81)

TEAM RECORDS
Offense
- **Morten Anderson (1982–94)**
Field Goals (season): 31 (1985)
Field Goals (career): 302
Points (season): 121 (1987)
Points (career): 1,318

Extra Point

- *His team down 16-14 with just three seconds left in a 1970 game against the Lions, kicker Tom Dempsey trotted onto the field to the sound of laughter from Detroit's linemen. Dempsey, who was born with only half his kicking foot, was about to try a 63-yard field goal — an astounding seven yards longer than the existing NFL record. Paying no heed, Dempsey nailed the kick and won the game.*

"Losing was never an option."

— LB Keith Mitchell, after the Saints defense held off a furious Rams comeback in New Orlean's 2000 playoff victory

- **Tom Dempsey (1969–70)**
Longest Field Goal:
63 Yards (Nov. 8, 1970)
- **Jim Everett (1994–96)**
Comp (season): 346 (1995)
Pass Att. (season): 567 (1995)
Passing Pct. (season):
64.1 (1994)
Passing Pct. (career): 61.0
Passing Yards (season):
3,970 (1995)
TD Passes (season): 26 (1995)
- **Dalton Hilliard (1986–93)**
Carries (career): 1,126
TDs (season): 18 (1989)
TDs (career): 53
- **Joe Horn (2000–present)**
Receiving Yards (season):
1,332 (2000)
Receptions (season):
94 (2000)
- **Billy Kilmer (1967–70)**
TD Passes (game):
6 (Nov. 2, 1969)
- **Archie Manning (1971–75. 1977–82)**
Comp (career): 1,849
Pass Att. (career): 3,335
Passing Yards (game):
377 (Dec. 7, 1980)

Passing Yards
(career): 21,734
TD Passes (career): 115
- **Eric Martin (1985–93)**
Receiving Yards
(career): 7,844
Receptions (career): 532
- **George Rogers (1981–84)**
Carries (season): 378 (1981)
Rushing Yards (game):
206 (Sept. 4, 1983)
Rushing Yards (season):
1,674 (1981)
Rushing Yards (career): 4,267
100-Yard Games (career): 16

Defense
- **La'Roi Glover (1997–present)**
Sacks (season): 18 (2000)
- **Rickey Jackson (1981–93)**
Fumble Recoveries
(career): 26
Sacks (career): 123
- **Dave Waymer (1980–89)**
Int. (career): 37
- **Dave Whitsell (1967–69)**
Int. (season): 10 (1967)

Special Teams
- **Tyrone Hughes (1993–96)**
Kickoff Return Yards
(season): 1,791
Kickoff Return Yards
(career): 5,717
Punt Return Yards
(career): 1,060
Punt Return Yards (season):
503 (1993)

Vital Stats

Stadium Address:
1500 Poydras St.,
New Orleans, La.
Phone: (504) 587-3663
Web: superdome.com
neworleanssaints.com
Box Office: (504) 587-3822, Mon.–Fri. 9–4:30
Media Coverage:
Radio: WWL Newsradio
(870 AM)
TV: WWL (Channel 4),
WVUE (Channel 8)
Training Facility:
New Orleans Saints Facility,
Metairie, La.

LEAGUE HONORS
NFL Rookie of the Year
- George Rogers (1981)

Coach of the Year
- Jim Mora (1987)

Pro Football Hall of Fame
- Jim Taylor (1976)
- Doug Atkins (1982)
- Jim Finks (1995)

Timeline

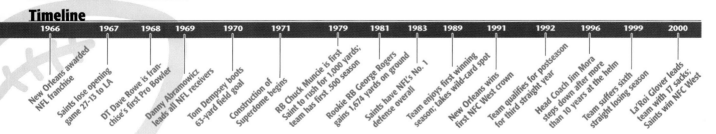

1966	1967	1968	1969	1970	1971	1979	1981	1983	1989	1991	1992	1996	1999	2000
New Orleans awarded NFL franchise	Saints lose opening game 27-13 to LA	DT Dave Rowe is franchise's first Pro Bowler	Danny Abramowicz leads all NFL receivers	Tom Dempsey boots 63-yard field goal	Construction of Superdome begins	RB Chuck Muncie is first Saint to rush for 1,000 yards; team has first .500 season	Rookie RB George Rogers gains 1,674 yards on ground	Saints have NFL's No. 1 defense overall	Team enjoys first winning season, takes wild-card spot	New Orleans wins first NFC West crown	Team qualifies for postseason for third straight year	Head Coach Jim Mora steps down after more than 10 years at the helm	Team suffers sixth straight losing season	La'Roi Glover leads team with 17 sacks; Saints win NFC West

LOUISIANA SUPERDOME: BIG STADIUM IN THE BIG EASY

THE LOUISIANA SUPERDOME is so big that the Houston Astrodome could fit inside it. As it is this 25-year-old facility is often the focal point of New Orleans' exuberant social scene. The venue for one of the city's most rollicking Mardi Gras parties, the Superdome has also hosted the world's largest indoor rock concert — 87,500 ecstatic fans for the Rolling Stones in 1981 — and a record five Super Bowls. Saints football fans like the Superdome for two reasons: no obstructed views in the house and a powerful air-conditioning system to beat the New Orleans heat.

CONCESSIONS

Visitors to the Louisiana Superdome can sample the best of the state's distinctive cuisine. In addition to standard stadium fare such as peanuts, popcorn, hot dogs and pizza, you can enjoy frozen daiquiris, gumbo, muffaletta and, for the truly adventurous, alligator sausages.

GAME DAY TIPS
• **Gate hours:** Gates open two hours prior to kickoff.
• **Tailgating:** Tailgating is prohibited by city ordinance.
• **Prohibited items:** Cans, bottles or containers, weapons, missiles, fireworks and video cameras are prohibited. Hand-held still cameras without tripods are allowed. Small hand-held signs are permitted. Smoking is allowed in designated areas.
• **Ticket tips:** With the Saints' recent successes, tickets have become harder to get, especially when the Atlanta Falcons are in town. Seven out of eight games in the 2000 season were sold out. There is no need to bring seat cushions — all seating is comfortable.
• **Lost and found:** (504) 587-3900.

Stadium Facts

Opened: Aug. 3, 1975
Cost: $163 million
Capacity: 72,675
Type: Dome
Surface: Artificial turf
Home Sweet Home:
• A full house of screaming Saints fans can disrupt opposing offenses by making it impossible for the other players to hear the quarterback's snap count or his audibles.

Directions: Take I-10 to Tulane Ave./Superdome exit. Or, take Hwy. 90 to Superdome exit. By Bus: Several buses go to the Superdome. Call the New Orleans Regional Transit Authority (RTA) at (504) 827-7802. **Parking:** The Superdome has parking garages with spaces for some 5,000 cars; 10,000-plus spaces are within walking distance. Extra parking is available on Loyola Ave., Gravier St., O'Keefe St., Poydras St. and Rampart St. Season parking for the disabled is available in lots E-1, E-11 and Graves/IMA.

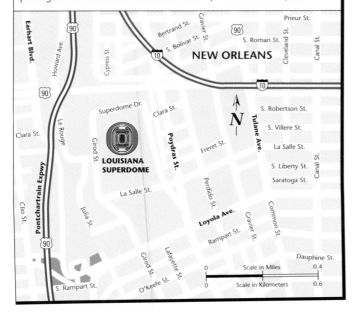

Seating Plan

- Plaza Sideline $50
- Plaza End Zone $45
- Club Sideline .... N/A
- Club End Zone $50
- Upper Box Sideline $50
- Upper Box End Zone $45
- Terrace Sideline, Terrace Upper Sideline and Terrace End Zone ... $40
- ATM Sections 115/116, 155/156
- Plaza, Terrace levels

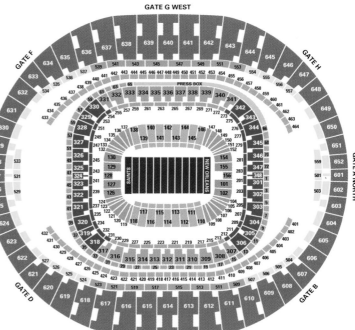

193

Nearby Hotels

▼▼▼ **Baronne Plaza Travelodge** (*Motel*), 201 Baronne St. (New Orleans) , (504) 522-0083, $79-$249
▼▼▼ **Courtyard by Marriott-New Orleans** (*Hotel*), 124 St. Charles Ave. (New Orleans), (504) 581-9005, call for rates
▼▼▼ **Hampton Inn Downtown-New Orleans** (*Hotel*), 226 Carondelet St. (New Orleans), (504) 529-9990, $89-$159
▼▼▼ **Holiday Inn Downtown-Superdome** (*Hotel*), 330 Loyola Ave. (New Orleans), (504) 581-1600, $79-$219
▼▼▼▼ **Windsor Court Hotel** (*Hotel*), 300 Gravier St. (New Orleans), (504) 523-6000, $430-$470

Nearby Restaurants

▼▼▼ **Bizou** (*French*), 701 St. Charles Ave. (New Orleans), (504) 524-4114, $15-$23
▼▼▼ **Christino's** (*Greek*), 228 Camp St. in the Omni Royal Crescent Hotel (New Orleans), (504) 571-7500, $16-$23
▼▼▼▼ **Emeril's** (*Creole*), 800 Tchoupitoulas St. (New Orleans), (504) 528-9393, $18-$32
▼▼ **Michaul's Live Cajun Music Restaurant** (*Regional American*), 840 St. Charles Ave. (New Orleans), (504) 522-5517, $10-$25 (dinner only)
▼▼ **Tony Angello Ristorante** (*Italian*), 6262 Fleur de Lis Dr. (New Orleans), (504) 488-0888, $12-$25 (dinner only)

NEW YORK GIANTS

Michael Strahan is one of the Giants' best pass rushers.

ALTHOUGH THE NFL WAS BORN in the mid-West, nothing helped bolster the game's stature more than the inclusion of the New York Giants to the league in 1925. Just months into the season 70,000 people came out to the Polo Grounds to watch the new boys play the Chicago Bears. Buoyed by the enthusiasm, the Giants posted the NFL's best record just two years later, thanks largely to a marauding defense led by Cal Hubbard and Steve Owen. In 1934 the squad squared off against the undefeated Chicago Bears in the NFL title game. With the Giants trailing and the field iced over, the Giants' coach sent his equipment manager to find shoes with better traction. At halftime he returned with bags of basketball shoes. The improved traction helped New York take the famous "Sneakers Game" and its first NFL crown. After their second title in 1938, the Giants found the going tough. Even in the '50s, with great players such as Kyle Rote and Frank Gifford on the roster, the team added only one more championship trophy to its collection. After decades of struggling, glory returned to the franchise in the 1980s. Drafting young stars such as Phil Simms, Lawrence Taylor, Joe Morris and Mark Bavaro, the Giants began winning games again. In 1986 the team rolled over Denver to take Super Bowl XXI and in 1990 QB Jeff Hostler and RB O.J. Anderson led the team to its second Super Bowl victory. Although the 2000 squad came up short in Super Bowl XXXV, it's clear that the Giants are once again among the NFL's big boys.

Extra Point

• *In 1930 Giants owner Tim Mara handed the team over to his two sons, Jack and Wellington. At 14 years of age, Wellington became the youngest owner in the history of football and began his long, influential career with the team.*

POSTSEASON
• **Super Bowl Wins** 2
(1986, '90)
• **NFL Championships** 4
(1927, '34, '38, '56)
• **NFC Championships** 3
(1986, '90, 2000)
• **NFC East Titles** 4
(1986, '90, '97, 2000)

RETIRED NUMBERS
• Ray Flaherty (1)
• Tuffy Leemans (4)
• Mel Hein (7)
• Phil Simms (11)
• Y.A. Tittle (14)
• Al Blozis (32)
• Joe Morrison (40)
• Charlie Conerly (42)
• Ken Strong (50)
• Lawrence Taylor (56)

TEAM RECORDS
Offense
• **Frank Gifford**
(1952–60, 1962–64)
Receiving Yards (career): 5,434
TDs (career): 78
• **Pete Gogolak (1966–74)**
Field Goals (career): 126
Points (career): 646
• **Ali Haji-Sheikh (1983–85)**
Points (season): 127 (1983)
• **Rodney Hampton**
(1990–97)
Rushing Yards (career): 6,897
• **Homer Jones (1964–69)**
Receiving Yards (season):
1,209 (1967)
• **Joe Morris (1982–89)**
TDs (season): 21 (1985)
Rushing Yards (season):
1,516 (1986)
• **Joe Morrison (1959–72)**
Receptions (career): 395
• **Kyle Rote (1951–61)**
Receiving TDs (career): 48
• **Phil Simms (1979–93)**
Comp. (season): 286 (1984)
Comp. (career): 2,576
Passing Yards (season):
4,044 (1984)
Passing Yards (career): 33,462
TD Passes (career): 199
• **Y.A. Tittle (1961–64)**
TD Passes (season): 36 (1963)
• **Amani Toomer**
(1996–present)
Receptions (season): 79 (1999)

Defense
• **Jimmy Patton**
(1955–66)
Int. (season): 11 (1958)
• **Lawrence Taylor**
(1955–66)
Sacks (season): 20.5 (1986)
Sacks (career): 132.5
• **Emlen Tunnell**
(1948–58)
Int. (career): 74

LEAGUE HONORS
NFL MVP
• **Mel Hein (1938)**
• **Frank Gifford (1956)**
• **Charley Conerly (1959)**
• **Y.A. Tittle (1961, '62, '63)**
• **Andy Robustelli (1962)**
• **Phil Simms (1986)**
• **Lawrence Taylor (1986)**

NFL Defensive
Player of the Year
• **Lawrence Taylor**
(1981, '82, '86)

NFL Rookie of the Year
• **Lawrence Taylor (1981)**

Super Bowl MVP
• **Phil Simms (1986)**
• **Ottis Anderson (1990)**

Pro Football Hall of Fame
• **Tim Mara (1963)**
• **Mel Hein (1963)**
• **Steve Owen (1966)**
• **Ken Strong (1967)**
• **Emlen Tunnell (1967)**
• **Cal Hubbard (1963)**
• **Y.A. Tittle (1971)**
• **Andy Robustelli (1971)**
• **Roosevelt Brown (1975)**
• **Frank Gifford (1977)**
• **Alphonse Leemans (1978)**
• **Morris Badgro (1981)**
• **Sam Huff (1982)**
• **Arnold Weinmeister**
(1984)
• **Wellington Mara (1997)**
• **Lawrence Taylor (1999)**

Vital Stats

Stadium Address:
*50 State Rte. 120,
East Rutherford, N.J.*
Phone:
(201) 935-8500
Web: *giants.com
giantsstadium.com*
Box Office:
*(201) 935-3900, Mon.–Fri.
9–6, Sat. 10–6, Sun. 12–5*
Media Coverage:
*Radio: WFAN (660 AM)
TV: Fox (Channel 5)*
Training Facility:
*Giants Practice Dome,
East Rutherford, N.J.*

"We're playing football on it, not golf. It's not going to look like your lawn."
— *John Mara, Giants Executive Vice President,
on the rough state of the new real turf playing surface*

Timeline

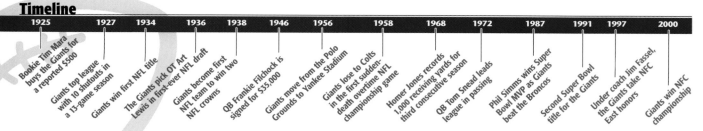

1925	1927	1934	1936	1938	1946	1956	1958	1968	1972	1987	1991	1997	2000
Bookie Tim Mara buys the Giants for a reported $500	Giants top league with 10 shutouts in a 13-game season	Giants win first NFL title	The Giants pick OT Art Lewis in first-ever NFL draft	Giants become first NFL team to win two NFL crowns	QB Frankie Filchock is signed for $35,000	Giants move from the Polo Grounds to Yankee Stadium	Giants lose to Colts in the first sudden-death overtime NFL championship game	Homer Jones records 1,000 receiving yards for third consecutive season	QB Tom Snead leads league in passing	Phil Simms wins Super Bowl MVP as Giants beat the Broncos	Second Super Bowl title for the Giants	Under coach Jim Fassel, the Giants take NFC East honors	Giants win NFC championship

GIANTS STADIUM: FIRST-RATE FACILITY

GIANTS STADIUM IS PART of the Meadowlands Sports Complex, one of the world's great entertainment facilities. Located in New Jersey less than seven miles from Times Square, Giants Stadium attracted the New York team with its ample seating and relative proximity to the Big Apple. Although New Yorkers were initially hesitant to see their team leave the city, Giants fans have made a tradition of crossing the Hudson River to see their team in action on Sundays. Also, as the home to many rock concerts and entertainment spectacles, Giants Stadium has become known as one of the best "New York" night spots.

CONCESSIONS

Giants Stadium offers a large selection of food, from hot dogs, hamburgers and pizza to submarines, turkey legs and potato knishes. Try the chili-covered New York hot dog or the Jersey hot dog with cheese and onions.

GAME DAY TIPS
• **Gate hours:** Gates open two hours prior to kickoff.
• **Tailgating:** Parking lots open for tailgating four hours before game time. Visitors are allowed to occupy only one parking space per party.
• **Weather:** Fall in New York is cool and winters often can be cold. Wear several layers of clothing.
• **Prohibited items:** Bottles, cans, coolers, fireworks, laser pointers, and video cameras or recording equipment of any kind is prohibited. Signs are allowed if they are not offensive and do not obstruct people's view. Smoking is allowed in designated areas.
• **Ticket tips:** The few available single-game tickets for Giants games are usually found through ticket brokers. The best seats are in the Mezzanine.
• **Lost and found:** (201) 935-8500 ext. 2240 or 2241.

Stadium Facts

Opened: Oct. 10, 1976
Cost: $75 million
Capacity: 79,466
Type: Open
Surface: Grass
Home Sweet Home:
• Fans here are a raucous group, famous for hurling insults at foes and whipping up support for their team. As a result, the Giants are home-game winners.

Seating Plan

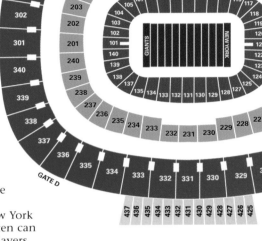

- ■ Mezzanine $50
- ■ Lower Levels $45
- ■ Upper Levels $45
- ▫ Suites .... Call for info

ATM **Upper level Gate B / Gate D**
Lower level Gate A / Gate C
♿ **Sections 117–125**

Directions: From Rte. 3 west, exit Rte. 120 north and follow to stadium. From Rte. 80, exit 64 (east) or 64B (west) and follow Rte. 17 south to Paterson Plank Rd., then left to stadium. By Bus: Buses leave from the Port Authority Bus Terminal in New York City. For more information, call (718) 330-1234. **Parking:** Parking lots surrounding the stadium can accommodate 25,000 vehicles. Handicapped parking is available in Lots 4, 7, 8 and 18.

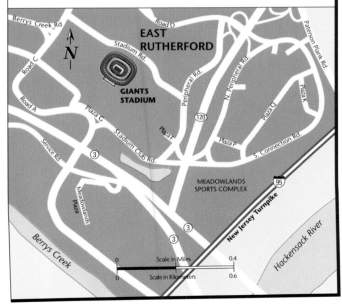

Nearby Hotels

▼▼▼ **Amerisuites** *(Motel)*, 41-01 Broadway (Fair Lawn), (201) 475-3888, $119-$199
▼▼▼ **Courtyard by Marriott** *(Motel)*, 455 Harmon Meadow Blvd. (Secaucus), (201) 617-8888, $180-$209
▼▼▼ **Fairfield Inn by Marriott** *(Motel)*, 850 SR 120 S. (East Rutherford), (201) 507-5222, $129
▼▼▼ **Hampton Inn** *(Motel)*, 250 Harmon Meadow Blvd. (Secaucus), (201) 867-4400, $135-$185
▼▼▼ **The Holiday Inn Harmon Meadow** *(Hotel)*, 300 Plaza Dr. (Secaucus), (201) 348-2000, $149-$209

Nearby Restaurants

▼▼ **Harold's New York Deli Restaurant** *(American)*, 10 Polito Ave. in the Quality Inn-Meadowlands (Lyndhurst), (201) 935-2600, $6-$20
▼▼ **La Dolce Vita** *(Italian)*, 316 Valley Brook Ave. (Lyndhurst), (201) 935-4260, $11-$25
▼▼ **Park & Orchard** *(American)*, 240 Hackensack St., (201) 939-9292 (East Rutherford), $13-$24
▼▼▼ **The River Palm Terrace** *(Steak & Seafood)*, 41-11 Broadway (Fair Lawn), (201) 703-3500, $19-$36
▼▼▼ **Sonoma Grill** *(American)*, 64 Hoboken Rd. (East Rutherford), (201) 507-8989, $17-$27

NEW YORK JETS

WHEN THE NEW YORK FRANCHISE joined the AFL in 1959, owner Harry Wismer christened his team the Titans. Noting that in mythology Titans were the only beings more powerful than giants, Wismer issued a direct challenge to his cross-town NFL rival New York Giants. Unfortunately, the Titans had a hard time living up to their name. Despite finishing second in their inaugural AFL campaign, the Titans plummeted to last place in 1962. The following year the team was sold and renamed the Jets, and legendary coach Weeb Ewbank was recruited to revive the floundering franchise. Ewbank began the rebuilding process by making some shrewd draft picks, including FB Matt Snell and LB Edward McDaniel. But Ewbank's greatest move was drafting college superstar Joe Namath in 1965. "Broadway Joe" quickly established himself as the AFL's marquee player — a brilliant leader on game day and a smiling ladies' man off the field. In 1967, with Namath on his way to becoming the first QB to pass for 4,000 yards in a season, the team set AFL attendance records. Namath topped himself the next year, leading the team to its first Eastern Division title and brashly predicting a win over the favored Colts in Super Bowl III. Piloting his Jets to a 16-7 victory in the title game, Namath was named MVP in what is regarded as one of football's greatest upsets. The team slumped horribly after the win, going 12 years without a winning season. The skid ended in the 1980s when the Jets' marauding defensive line, led by Mark Gastineau and Joe Klecko and dubbed the "New York Sack Exchange," spurred the team to four playoff spots. The Jets have been inconsistent since, often riding the bottom of the AFC ranks. In 1998 QB Vinnie Testaverde led the team to its first AFC East title, giving fans reason to hope that the Jets are getting ready to fly again.

Vital Stats

Stadium Address:
50 State Rte. 120,
East Rutherford, N.J.
Phone: (201) 935-8500
Web: newyorkjets.com,
meadowlands.com
Box Office: (201) 935-3900, Mon.–Fri. 9–6,
Sat. 10–6, Sun. 12–5
Media Coverage:
Radio: WABC (770 AM)
TV: CBS (Channel 2),
ABC (Channel 7),
Fox (Channel 5)
Training Facility:
Weeb Ewbank Hall,
Hempstead, N.Y.

POSTSEASON
• **Super Bowl Championships**..................1
(1968)
• **AFL Championships** 1
(1968)
• **AFC East Titles**.................1
(1998)
• **AFC Wild Card Berths**.....4
(1981, '85, '86, '91)

RETIRED NUMBERS
• Joe Namath (12)
• Don Maynard (13)

TEAM RECORDS
Offense
• **Emerson Boozer (1966–75)**

Extra Point

• The Jets were part of the now infamous "Heidi Game" in 1969. Leading the Raiders 32-29 with 1:05 left to play, New York gave up two quick TDs and lost the match 43-32. The only problem was that TV viewers missed the comeback because the network pulled the plug in order to show the previously-scheduled movie "Heidi."

Rushing TDs (season):
11 (1972)
Rushing TDs (career): 52
• **Pat Leahy (1974–91)**
Points (career): 1470
Field Goals (career): 304
• **Curtis Martin (1998–present)**
Carries (season): 369 (1998)
Rushing Yards (season):
1,465 (1999)
• **Don Maynard (1960–72)**
Receiving Yards (season):
1,434 (1967)
Receiving Yards (career): 11,732
Receptions (career): 627
TDs (season): 14 (tie) (1965)
TDs (career): 88
• **Freeman McNeil (1981–92)**
Carries (career): 1,798
Rushing Yards (career): 8,074
• **Joe Namath (1965–76)**
TD Passes (game):
6 (Sept. 24, 1972)
TD Passes (career): 170
Passing Yards (season):
4,007 (1967)

"The greatest athlete I ever coached."
— Paul Bryant, Joe Namath's college coach, on Namath

Passing Yards (career): 27,057
• **Richard Todd (1976–83)**
Comp. (game): 42
(Sept. 21, 1980)
Comp. (season): 308 (1983)
Passing Att. (season):
518 (1983)
• **Jim Turner (1964–70)**
Field Goals (season):
34 (1968)
Points (season): 145 (1968)

Defense
• **Bill Baird (1963–69)**
Int. (career): 34
• **Mark Gastineau (1979–88)**
Sacks (season): 22 (1984)
• **Dainard Paulson (1961–66)**
Int. (season): 12 (1964)

Special Teams
• **Brian Hansen (1963–69)**
Punts (season): 99 (1995)
• **Bruce Harper (1977–84)**
Kickoff Return Yards
(season): 1,280 (1978)
Kickoff Return Yards
(career): 5,407
Punt Return Yards
(career): 1,784
• **Chuck Ramsey (1977–84)**
Punts (career): 553

League Honors
AFL MVP
• Joe Namath (1968, '69)

NFL Defensive Player of the Year
• Joe Klecko (1981)
• Mark Gastineau (1982)

AFL Rookie of the Year
• Joe Namath (1965)

Super Bowl MVP
• Joe Namath (1968)

Pro Football Hall of Fame
• Weeb Ewbank (1978)
• Joe Namath (1985)
• Don Maynard (1987)
• John Riggins (1992)

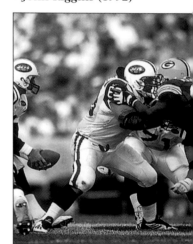

Kevin Mawae has emerged as one of the league's top centers.

Timeline

1959 The New York franchise – the Titans – joins the American Football League

1960 Don Maynard signs contract with the team

1963 Weeb Ewbank takes over as Head Coach and General Manager; team renamed the Jets

1965 Rookie QB Joe Namath signs a $427,000 contract

1968 Namath leads Jets to upset Super Bowl win over the Colts

1970 Jets lose to Browns in first-ever Monday Night Football broadcast

1972 Namath throws for 496 yards and six TDs in game against Colts

1974 Ewbank retires; Charlie Winner takes over as Head Coach

1980 QB Richard Todd puts name in the NFL record books with 42 completions versus 49ers

1984 Team moves to the Meadowlands

1991 Pat Leahy ties the all-time FG record with No. 304

1998 Jets win their first AFC East title

GIANTS STADIUM: NOT JUST FOR GIANTS

FROM THE BEGINNING THE JETS have been in the unfortunate position of never really having a place to call their own. After stints at the Polo Grounds and Shea Stadium, the Jets have been secondary tenants to their rivals, the Giants, since 1984. As such, the team has to play in a stadium decorated in Giants colors and, of course, under their enemy's name. In spite of this, Jets fans flock to the Meadowlands in droves to watch their team in action. As a home to many sports teams, Giants Stadium is considered one of the best multi-purpose arenas in North America. From rock concerts to group weddings, papal visits to soccer games, the stadium can provide something for almost anyone.

CONCESSIONS

Giants Stadium offers fans a large selection of food, from hot dogs, hamburgers and pizza to submarines, turkey legs and potato knishes. Try the chili-covered New York hot dog or the Jersey hot dog with cheese and onions.

Stadium Facts

Opened: Oct. 10, 1976
Cost: $75 million
Capacity: 79,466
Type: Open
Surface: Grass
Home Sweet Home:
• Jets fans try to intimidate opponents. In 1988 some fans set fire to their seats in an attempt to distract the Buffalo Bills, who were winning the game at the time.
• Unfortunately, the Jets lose their home-field advantage when they play the Giants, with whom they share the stadium.

GAME DAY TIPS

• **Gate hours:** Gates open two hours prior to kickoff.
• **Tailgating:** Parking lots open for tailgating four hours before kickoff. Visitors may take up no more than one parking space per party.
• **Weather:** Fall in New York is cool and often winters can be cold. Wear several layers of clothing and on very cold days be prepared for snow.
• **Prohibited items:** Bottles, cans and coolers are prohibited. Fireworks, laser pointers and video cameras or recording equipment of any kind are not permitted in the stadium. Smoking is allowed only in designated areas.
• **Ticket tips:** There are no single-game tickets available for Jets games. In fact, there is a 10-15 year waiting list to obtain season tickets, although tickets may be available through ticket brokers. Contact the team or consult its website for more information.
• **Lost and found:** (201) 935-8500 ext. 2240 or 2241.

Directions: From Rte. 3 west, exit Rte. 120 north and follow to stadium. From Rte. 80, exit 64 (east) or 64B (west) and follow Rte. 17 south to Paterson Plank Rd., then left to stadium. By Bus: Buses leave from the Port Authority Bus Terminal in New York City. For more information, call (718) 330-1234. **Parking:** Parking lots surrounding the stadium can accommodate 25,000 vehicles. Handicapped parking is available in Lots 4, 7, 8 and 18.

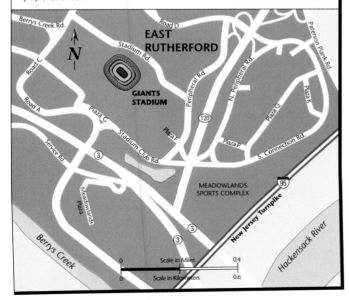

Seating Plan

- ■ **Mezzanine** $70
- ■ **Upper Levels** $55
- □ **Lower Levels** $55

ATM Upper level Gate B / Gate D
Lower level Gate A / Gate C
♿ **Sections 117–125**

Nearby Hotels

▽▽▽ **Amerisuites** (*Motel*), 41-01 Broadway (Fair Lawn), (201) 475-3888, $119-$199
▽▽▽ **Courtyard by Marriott** (*Motel*), 455 Harmon Meadow Blvd. (Secaucus), (201) 617-8888, $180-$209
▽▽▽ **Fairfield Inn by Marriott** (*Motel*), 850 SR 120 S. (East Rutherford), (201) 507-5222, $129
▽▽▽ **Hampton Inn** (*Motel*), 250 Harmon Meadow Blvd. (Secaucus), (201) 867-4400, $135-$185
▽▽▽ **The Holiday Inn Harmon Meadow** (*Hotel*), 300 Plaza Dr. (Secaucus), (201) 348-2000, $149-$209

Nearby Restaurants

▽▽ **Harold's New York Deli Restaurant** (*American*), 10 Polito Ave. in the Quality Inn-Meadowlands (Lyndhurst), (201) 935-2600, $6-$20
▽▽ **La Dolce Vita** (*Italian*), 316 Valley Brook Ave. (Lyndhurst), (201) 935-4260, $11-$25
▽▽ **Park & Orchard** (*American*), 240 Hackensack St., (201) 939-9292 (East Rutherford), $13-$24
▽▽▽ **The River Palm Terrace** (*Steak & Seafood*), 41-11 Broadway (Fair Lawn), (201) 703-3500, $19-$36
▽▽▽ **Sonoma Grill** (*American*), 64 Hoboken Rd. (East Rutherford), (201) 507-8989, $17-$27

OAKLAND RAIDERS

WHEN THE MINNEAPOLIS FRANCHISE left the newly formed AFL in 1960, a spot was freed up for another team to take its place. An Oakland group, led by businessman Chet Soda, was eventually awarded the eighth league franchise. After a couple of rough years, the Raiders enlisted the help of maverick coach Al Davis and by the end of 1963 the team had climbed to second place in the Western Division. By 1967 Davis was acting as General Manager and was instrumental in the acquisition of Daryle Lamonica, George Blanda, Willie Brown and Gene Upshaw. This infusion of new talent propelled Oakland to an AFL-record 13 wins and the team's first Super Bowl appearance, which it lost to Green Bay. Once in the NFL, the Silver and Black asserted itself as a dominant force, winning the AFC West every year from 1972 to '75. In 1976 the team turned it up a notch. Led by southpaw QB Ken Stabler and sure-handed WR Fred Biletnikoff on offense and hard-nosed Jack Tatum on defense, the team earned its first Super Bowl win with a 32-14 massacre of the Vikings. Taking another NFL crown in 1980, the team broke the hearts of Oakland residents when it moved to Los Angeles in 1982. The team's subsequent Super Bowl win in 1983, thanks largely to RB Marcus Allen's record-setting 191 rushing yards, only rubbed salt in the wounds of the fans back in Oakland. The city remained without a team until 1995, when Al Davis, now the team's owner, brought the Raiders home. At first, postseason pickings were slim until 2000, when the Raiders added yet another AFC West title to their trophy case.

Vital Stats

Stadium Address:
7000 Coliseum Wy.,
Oakland, Calif.
Phone: (510) 569-2121
Web: raiders.com
Box Office:
(510) 569-2121, Mon.–Fri.
10–6, Sat. 10–4
Media Coverage:
Radio: KTCT (1050 AM)
TV: KPIX (Channel 5),
KICU (Channel 36), KRON
(Channel 4), Fox Sports Net
Training Facility:
Oakland Raiders Facility,
Alameda, Calif.

"Just win, baby, win."

– Raiders owner Al Davis

POSTSEASON
• **Super Bowl Championships** 3
(1976, '80, '83)
• **AFL Championships** 1
(1967)
• **AFC Championships** 3
(1976, '80, '83)
• **AFC West Titles** 10
(1970, '72, '73, '74, '75, '76, '83, '85, '90, 2000)

TEAM RECORDS
Offense
• **Marcus Allen (1982–92)**
Carries (season): 380 (1985)
Carries (career): 2,090
Rushing Yards (season): 1,759 (1985)
Rushing Yards (career): 8,545
TDs (season): 18 (1984)
TDs (career): 98

Extra Point

• *The Raiders are pro football's most winning team. From 1963 to 2000, the Silver and Black amassed a winning percentage of .624, nipping the .621 of the Cowboys.*

Tyrone Wheatley is one of the NFL's most powerful backs.

• **Chris Bahr (1980–88)**
Field Goals (career): 162
TDs (season): 18 (1984)
• **Pete Banaszak (1966–78)**
Rushing TDs (season): 16 (1975)
• **George Blanda (1967–75)**
Extra Points (career): 395
Points (career): 863
• **Tim Brown (1988–present)**
Receptions (season): 104 (1997)
Receptions (career): 770
Receiving Yards (season): 1,408 (1995)
Receiving TDs (career): 86
Receiving Yards

(career): 12,072
• **Jeff George (1997–98)**
Passing Yards (season): 3,917 (1997)
• **Jeff Jaeger (1989–95)**
Points (season): 132 (1993)
Field Goals (season): 35 (1993)
• **Daryle Lamonica (1967–74)**
TD Passes (season): 34 (1969)
• **Art Powell (1963–66)**
Receiving TDs (season): 16 (1964)
• **Ken Stabler (1970–79)**
Comp. (season): 304 (tie) (1979)
Comp. (career): 1,146
Passing Yards (career): 19,078
TD Passes (career): 150

Defense
• **Lester Hayes (1977–86)**
Int. (season): 13 (1980)
Int. (career): 39
• **Terry McDaniel (1988–97)**
Int. for TDs (career): 5
• **Jack Tatum (1971–79)**
Fumble Return Yards (game): 104 (Sept. 24, 1972)

Special Teams
• **Tim Brown (1988–present)**
Punt Return Yards (career): 3,106
• **Desmond Howard (1997–98)**
Kickoff Returns (season): 61 (1997)

• **Bo Roberson (1962–65)**
Kickoff Returns (career): 113
• **Fulton Walker (1985–86)**
Punt Return Yards (season): 692 (1985)

LEAGUE HONORS
NFL MVP
• George Blanda (1970)
• Ken Stabler (1974, '76)
• Marcus Allen (1985)

AFL MVP
• Daryle Lamonica (1967, '69)

NFL Rookie of the Year
• Raymond Chester (1970)
• Marcus Allen (1982)
• Bo Jackson (1987)

Super Bowl MVP
• Fred Biletnikoff (1976)
• Jim Plunkett (1980)
• Marcus Allen (1983)

Pro Football Hall of Fame
• Jim Otto (1980)
• George Blanda (1981)
• Willie Brown (1984)
• Gene Upshaw (1987)
• Fred Biletnikoff (1988)
• Art Shell (1989)
• Ted Hendricks (1990)
• Al Davis (1992)
• Mike Haynes (1997)
• Eric Dickerson (1998)
• Howie Long (2000)
• Ronnie Lott (2000)

Timeline

1959	1960	1961	1963	1967	1969	1977	1981	1982	1984	1989	1995	2000
AFL formed	Oakland Raiders enter the AFL; QB Tom Flores leads league with a 54 percent completion rate	Raiders set up temporary residence at Candlestick Park	Under new coach Al Davis, Oakland takes second place in the AFL West	Raiders win AFL title, but lose to Green Bay in Super Bowl II	John Madden signs on as coach	Oakland trounces Vikings in Super Bowl XI	Raiders are first wild-card team to win Super Bowl	Raiders move to Los Angeles	Marcus Allen rushes for record 191 yards in Raiders' Super Bowl win	Art Shell is NFL's first African-American coach	Raiders return to Oakland	Team wins AFC West

NETWORK ASSOCIATES COLISEUM: A.K.A. "THE NET"

KNOWN THESE DAYS AS "THE NET," the old Oakland-Alameda County Coliseum was constructed in 1966 as a multipurpose sporting venue. Since then, the stadium has seen more than 100 million people pass through its turnstiles and still remains one of the most popular arenas in pro sports. Considered a warm and sunny stadium, the Net also boasts some of the driest conditions around, rarely seeing rain during the peak seasons. Now, with its recently completed $100 million renovation, the Net prides itself on being one of the most comfortable stadiums in North America.

CONCESSIONS

Food at the Net is among the NFL's best. Traditionalists will find the staples such as hot dogs, hamburgers and pizza. But the more adventurous might sample the Black Muslim bakery, which offers veggie and tofu burgers, as well as carrot and bean pies. The longest lines are usually for the garlic fries.

Stadium Facts

Opened: Sept. 18, 1966
Cost: $25.5 million
Capacity: 63,142
Type: Outdoor
Surface: Grass
Home Sweet Home:
• Raiders fans dress in outlandish costumes and are among the most vocal in all of football.

GAME DAY TIPS

• **Gate hours:** Gates open two hours prior to kickoff.
• **Tailgating:** Parking lot gates open four hours before kickoff.
• **Weather:** Summers are usually warm and sunny, with virtually no rain. However, there is heavy fog on occasion.
• **Prohibited items:** Cans, bottles, large coolers and alcohol, umbrellas, video or movie cameras, and poles are not allowed. Smoking is permitted only in designated areas.
• **Ticket tips:** You can almost always get single-game tickets from the box office the week of the game (and often on game day). If the Kansas City Chiefs, traditional rivals of the Raiders, are in town, the selection may be somewhat more limited.

• **Lost and found:** (510) 383-4660.

Seating Plan

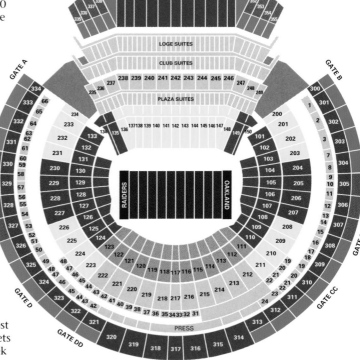

$81
$71
$61
$51
$41
Club PSL Seating Only
ATM Sections 105, 125, 231, 301, 316, 321, 331,
Sections 117–125

Directions: Take I-880 to 66th Ave. exit and follow east to the main entrance. By Bus: Bay Area Rapid Transit (BART) arrives near the eastern plaza. For information, call BART at (510) 465-2278. **Parking:** There are 11,000 parking spots available at the stadium, 143 of which are wheelchair-accessible. Signs are posted game days for auxiliary parking.

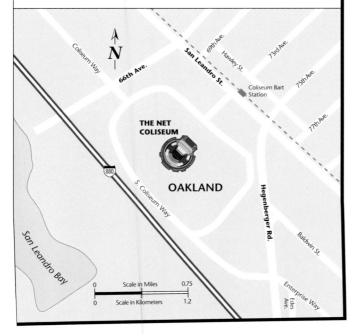

Nearby Hotels

▼▼▼ **Best Western Inn at the Square** *(Motel)*, 233 Broadway at entrance to Jack London Square (Oakland), (510) 452-4565, $89-$149
▼▼▼ **Clarion Suites Lake Merritt Hotel** *(Historic Hotel)*, 1800 Madison St. (Oakland), (510) 832-2300, $179-$299
▼▼▼ **Comfort Inn & Suites** *(Motel)*, 8452 Edes Ave. (Oakland), (510) 568-1500, $117-$127
▼▼▼ **Holiday Inn-Oakland Airport/Coliseum** *(Motor Inn)*, 500 Hegenberger Rd. (Oakland), (510) 562-5311, $89-$139
▼▼▼ **Waterfront Plaza Hotel** *(Hotel)*, Ten Washington St. (Oakland), (510) 836-3800, $190-$325

Nearby Restaurants

▼▼▼ **Bay Wolf Restaurant** *(Californian)*, 3853 Piedmont Ave. (Oakland), (510) 655-6004, $30-$34
▼▼▼ **Garibaldi's on College** *(Californian)*, 5356 College Ave. (Oakland), (510) 595-4000, $13-$20
▼▼▼ **Il Pescatore Restaurant** *(Italian)*, 57 Jack London Square (Oakland), (510) 465-2188, $10-$19
▼▼▼ **Oliveto Café & Restaurant** *(Italian)*, 5655 College Ave. (Oakland), (510) 547-5356, $30-$60
▼▼ **Quinn's Lighthouse Restaurant & Pub** *(Seafood)*, 51 Embarcadero Cove (Oakland), (510) 536-2050, $6-$16

PHILADELPHIA EAGLES

ONE OF THE OLDEST FOOTBALL TEAMS in the NFL, the Eagles took flight in 1933. Although the team didn't post a winning season until 1943, it managed to develop a strong fan base around players such as Don Looney, Tommy Thompson and Heisman Trophy-winner Davey O'Brien. In 1944 things began to turn around for "the Birds." The main difference was the acquisition of Louisiana State graduate Steve Van Buren, whose blinding speed and nose for pay dirt injected new life into the squad. Van Buren proved to be indispensable, topping the NFL in scoring and rushing in 1945, while leading Philadelphia to a second-place finish in the East. In 1947 he became the second man in history to crack 1,000 rushing yards in a season. One year later in a bitter snowstorm at Chicago's Shibe Park, the Eagles shut out the Cardinals 7-0 to take the NFL crown. They repeated as champs in 1949 with a 14-0 win over Los Angeles — the only time in NFL history a team has posted back-to-back championship game shutouts. It wasn't until 1960 that the Eagles could muster that sort of magic again. Led by Norm "the Dutchman" Van Brocklin and Chuck Bednarik, one of the game's greatest two-way players, the Birds came from behind to beat Green Bay for their third NFL title. Since then, the Eagles have had their share of stars — Harold Carmichael, Wilbert Montgomery, Ron Jaworski, Mike Quick and Randall Cunningham among them — but have come up short in the big games. However, the squad's 11-5 showing in 2000 could mean the Eagles are ready to soar once again.

Vital Stats

Stadium Address:
3501 S. Broad St.,
Philadelphia, Pa.
Phone: (215) 685-1500
Web:
philadelphiaeagles.com
Box Office:
(215) 463-5500,
Mon.–Fri. 9–5
Media Coverage:
Radio: WYSP (94.1 FM)
TV: FOX (WTFX Channel 29), ETN (Channel 17)
Training Facilities:
NovaCare Complex,
Philadelphia, Pa.

POSTSEASON
• **NFL Championships** 3
(1948, '49, '60)
• **NFC Championships** 1
(1980)
• **NFC East Titles** 2
(1980, '88)
• **NFC Wild Card Berths** 9
(1978, '79, '81, '89, '90, '92, '95, '96, 2000)

RETIRED NUMBERS
• Steve Van Buren (15)
• Tom Brookshier (40)
• Pete Retzlaff (44)
• Chuck Bednarik (60)
• Al Wistert (70)
• Jerome Brown (99)

Extra Point

• The Philadelphia Eagles were named after the triumphant eagle symbol in Franklin Roosevelt's National Recovery Act, a major part of his New Deal.
• In 1943, with many players off fighting in WW II, the Eagles and the Steelers joined forces to create a team that journalists loved to call "the Steagles." This move contributed to the first winning season for the Eagles.

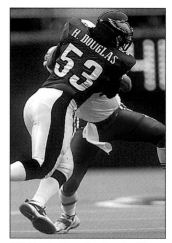
DE Hugh Douglas is relentless in his pursuit of ball carriers.

TEAM RECORDS
Offense
• **David Akers (1999–present)**
Points (season): 121 (2000)
• **Harold Carmichael (1971–83)**
Receptions (career): 589
Receiving Yards (career): 8,978
TDs (career): 79
• **Randall Cunningham (1985–95)**
Passing Yards (season): 3,808 (1988)
• **Irving Fryar (1996–98)**
Receptions (season): 88 (1996)
• **Ron Jaworski (1977–86)**
Comp. (career): 2,088
Passing Yards (career): 26,963

TD Passes (career): 175
• **Sonny Jurgensen (1957–63)**
TD Passes (season): 32 (1961)
• **Paul McFadden (1984–87)**
FGs (season): 30 (1984)
FGs (career): 91
• **Donovan McNabb (1999–present)**
Comp. (season): 330 (2000)
• **Wilbert Montgomery (1977–84)**
Rushing Yards (season): 1,512 (1979)
Rushing Yards (career): 6,538
• **Mike Quick (1982–90)**
Receiving Yards (season): 1,409 (1983)
• **Steve Van Buren (1944–51)**
TDs (season): 18 (1945)
Rushing TDs (career): 69
• **Bobby Walston (1951–62)**
Points (career): 881

Defense
• **Eric Allen (1988–94)**
Int. (career): 34 (tie)
Int. for TDs (career): 5
• **Bill Bradley (1969–76)**
Int. (season): 11 (1971)
Int. (career): 34 (tie)
• **Reggie White (1985–92)**
Sacks (season): 21 (1987)
Sacks (career): 124

Special Teams
• **Timmy Brown (1960–67)**
Kickoff Return Yards (career): 4,483

"No one played quarterback like the Dutchman."
— Alex Karras, former Detroit Lions tackle, on Eagle QB Norm Van Brocklin

• **Vai Sikahema (1992–93)**
Punt Return Yards (season): 503 (1992)

LEAGUE HONORS
NFL MVP
• Norm Van Brocklin (1960)
• Pete Retzlaff (1965)
• Ron Jaworski (1980)
• Randall Cunningham (1988, '90)

NFL Rookie of the Year
• Keith Jackson (1988)

Pro Football Hall of Fame
• Bert Bell (1963)
• Steve Van Buren (1965)
• Chuck Bednarik (1967)
• Alex Wojciechowicz (1968)
• Earl "Greasy" Neale (1969)
• Pete Pihos (1970)
• Bill Hewitt (1971)
• Norm Van Brocklin (1971)
• Ollie Matson (1972)
• Jim Ringo (1981)
• Sonny Jurgensen (1983)
• Tommy McDonald (1998)

Timeline

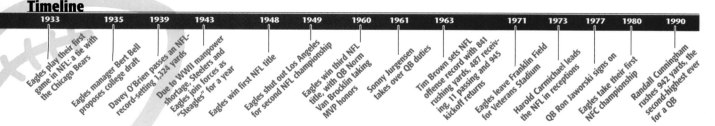

| 1933 | 1935 | 1939 | 1943 | 1948 | 1949 | 1960 | 1961 | 1963 | 1971 | 1973 | 1977 | 1980 | 1990 |

Eagles play their first game in NFL; a tie with the Chicago Bears

Eagles manager Bert Bell proposes college draft

Davey O'Brien passes an NFL-record-setting 1,324 yards

Due to WWII manpower shortage, Steelers and Eagles join forces as "Steagles" for a year

Eagles win first NFL title

Eagles shut out Los Angeles for second NFL championship

Eagles win third NFL title, with QB Norm Van Brocklin taking MVP honors

Sonny Jurgensen takes over QB duties

Tim Brown sets NFL offense record with 841 rushing yards, 487 receiving, 11 passing and 945 kickoff returns

Eagles leave Franklin Field for Veterans Stadium

Harold Carmichael leads the NFL in receptions

QB Ron Jaworski signs on

Eagles take their first NFC championship

Randall Cunningham rushes 942 yards, the second-highest ever for a QB

VETERANS STADIUM: THE END IS NEAR

KNOWN AS "THE VET," the home of the the Eagles has been a well-used, much-storied stadium for 30 years. Many great football and baseball games have been played here and the Vet still remains the favorite venue of the popular Army-Navy Classic. These days Veterans Stadium is showing its age. In spite of a slew of renovations and facelifts, the Vet is now considered by many to be cold, shabby and outdated. As a result, the Eagles have announced plans for a new stadium to be built over the next few years. Visitors take note: Philly fans are among the most abrasive in North America.

CONCESSIONS
The stadium has food for all tastes. Local favorites are soft pretzels, Italian sandwiches, hoagies and cheese steaks. There are also several fine dining establishments.

GAME DAY TIPS
• **Gate hours:** Gates open two hours prior to kickoff.

• **Tailgating:** Tailgating is a little complex since the City of Philadelphia does not allow it. However, cars parked south of the stadium are allowed limited tailgating. The Eagles host an indoor party in the nearby First Union Center before every home game.

• **Weather:** Philadelphia can be fairly cool in the fall. Wear warm clothes and always be prepared for the possibility of snow later in the season.

• **Prohibited items:** Cans, bottles, alcohol and animals are prohibited. Coolers are allowed if they do not contain alcohol. Smoking is allowed in designated areas.

Stadium Facts

Opened: *April 4, 1971*
Cost: *$50 million*
Capacity: *65,352*
Type: *Outdoor*
Surface: *AstroTurf*
Home Sweet Home:
• *The fans at Veterans Stadium are relentless in their disapproval of their foes. They've been known to boo opposing players as they lie injured on the field.*

▪	....	$55
▫	....	$55
▪	....	$55
▪	....	$55
▪	....	$45
▪	....	N/A

ATM **Section 224**
♿ **Outfield 200s; 300s**

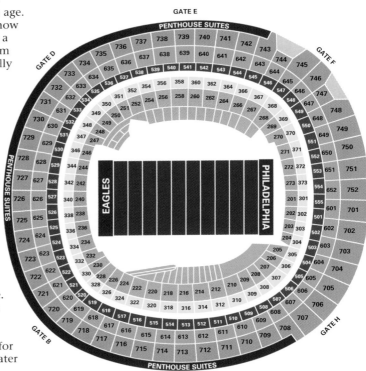

• **Tickets tips:** The Eagles reserve tickets for single-game purchase, but they sell out quickly, especially for games against the Cowboys.

Some seats, mainly the 300s under the balcony, have obstructed views.
• **Lost and found:** (215) 463-6000.

Directions: From I-95 north, take exit 15. Follow signs to Packer Ave., then follow and turn left onto 10th St. From I-95 south, take exit 15. Follow signs to Sports Complex. Turn right at bottom of ramp onto Front St., then right onto Packer Ave., left onto 10th St. to Sports Complex. By Subway: SEPTA Broad Street Subway Line to Pattison Avenue stop. By Bus: Route C southbound to Broad St. *Parking:* Lots on S. Darien, S. 11th and S. Broad Sts. can hold 10,000 cars. Wheelchair-accessible lots are next to gates A, B and F.

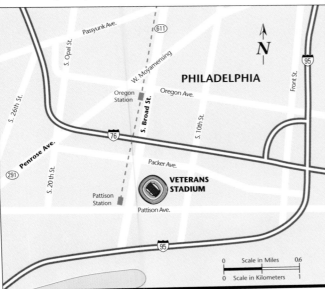

Nearby Hotels

▼▼▼ **Courtyard by Marriott Airport** *(Motor Inn)*, 8900 Bartram Ave. (Philadelphia), (215) 365-2200, $159-$219
▼▼▼ **Hampton Inn-Philadelphia Airport** *(Motel)*, 8600 Bartram Ave. (Philadelphia), (215) 966-1300, $139-$169
▼▼▼ **Hilton Philadelphia Airport** *(Hotel)*, 4509 Island Ave. (Philadelphia), (215) 365-4150, $135-$195
▼▼▼ **Holiday Inn Philadelphia Stadium** *(Hotel)*, 900 Packer Ave. (Philadelphia), (215) 755-9500, $89-$149
▼▼▼ **Philadelphia Fairfield Inn** *(Motel)*, 8800 Bartram Ave. (Philadelphia), (215) 365-2254, $100

Nearby Restaurants

▼▼ **Bistro Romano** *(Italian)*, 120 Lombard St. (Philadelphia), (215) 925-8880, $10-$24
▼▼▼ **The Continental Restaurant & Martini Bar** *(Continental)*, 138 Market St. (Philadelphia), (215) 923-6069, $6-$19
▼▼ **Downey's Restaurant** *(American)*, 526 S. Front St. (Philadelphia), (215) 625-9500, $16-$20
▼ **Engine 46 Steak House** *(American)*, 10 Reed St. (Philadelphia), (215) 462-4646, $5-$19
▼▼▼ **The Plough and the Stars Irish Restaurant & Bar** *(Continental)*, 123 Chestnut St. (Philadelphia), (215) 733-0300, $14-$21

PITTSBURGH STEELERS

IT TOOK THE PITTSBURGH STEELERS a long time to taste championship champagne, but once the players got a sip they kept coming back for more. The team had an inauspicious beginning in 1933, when Art Rooney bought the rights for an NFL franchise with money he had won at the horse track. It was the last time Rooney's team was associated with winning for a very long time. From 1933 to '71, the club managed to make the postseason just once, in '47, getting whitewashed 21-0 by the Eagles in its only playoff game. The tide began to turn, however, in 1969, when Rooney hired 37-year-old Chuck Noll as Head Coach. Not only a great football strategist, Noll also proved to be a brilliant judge of talent. From 1969 to '74, the former assistant with the Colts and Chargers drafted no fewer than eight future Hall of Famers, including QB Terry Bradshaw, DT "Mean" Joe Greene, WR Lynn Swann, and LBs Jack Ham and Jack Lambert. Pittsburgh's breakout year came in 1974. Led by its intimidating "Steel Curtain" defense, the team won the AFC Central and beat the Vikings in Super Bowl IX. This was the beginning of a veritable dynasty, with the Steelers repeating in '75 and winning another two Super Bowl crowns in 1978 and '79. Although Pittsburgh has yet to relive the glory years of the '70s, the team always seems playoff bound; it had six straight postseason appearances in the '90s. With bruising RB Jerome Bettis leading the charge, Pittsburgh fans are hoping for another taste of greatness.

Vital Stats

Stadium Address:
100 Art Rooney Ave.,
Pittsburgh, Pa.
Phone: (412) 323-1200
Web: steelers.com
Box Office:
(412) 323-1200, Mon.–Fri.
9–5, call for weekend hours
Media Coverage:
Radio: WBGG (970 AM),
WDVE (102.5 FM)
TV: KDKA (Channel 2), ESPN
Practice Facility:
UPMC Sports Performance
Complex, Pittsburgh, Pa.

POSTSEASON

- **Super Bowl Championships** 4
(1974, '75, '78, '79)
- **AFC Championships** 5
(1974, '75, '78, '79, '95)
- **AFC Central Titles** 14
(1972, '74, '75, '76, '77, '78, '79, '83, '84, '92, '94, '95, '96, '97)
- **AFC Wild Card Berths** 3
(1973, '89, '93)

TEAM RECORDS
Offense

- **Gary Anderson (1982–94)**
Field Goals (career): 309
Points (career): 1,343
- **Terry Bradshaw (1970–83)**
Comp. (career): 2,025
Passing Yards (season): 3,724 (1979)
Passing Yards (career): 27,989
TD Passes (season): 28 (1978)
TD Passes (career): 212
- **Buddy Dial (1959–63)**
Receiving Yards (game): 235 (Oct. 22, 1961)

TD Receptions (season): 12 (tie) (1961)
- **Barry Foster (1990–94)**
Rushing Yards (season): 1,690 (1992)
- **Franco Harris (1972–83)**
Rushing Yards (career): 11,950
TDs (career): 100
100-Yard Games (career): 47
- **Norm Johnson (1995–97)**
Points (season): 141 (1995)
- **Bobby Layne (1958–62)**
Passing Yards (game): 409 (Dec. 13, 1958)
- **Louis Lipps (1984–91)**
TDs (season): 15 (1985)
- **Neil O'Donnell (1990–95)**
Comp. (season): 270 (1993)
Pass Att. (game): 55 (Dec. 24, 1995)
- **John Stallworth (1974–87)**
Receiving Yards (career): 8,723
Receptions (career): 537
TD Receptions (career): 63
- **Yancy Thigpen (1992–97)**
Receiving Yards (season): 1,398 (1997)
Receptions (season): 85 (1995)

Defense

- **Mel Blount (1970–83)**
Int. (season): 11 (1975)
Int. (career): 57
- **L.C. Greenwood (1969–81)**
Sacks (career): 73.5
- **Mike Merriweather**

(1982–87)
Sacks (season): 15 (1987)

LEAGUE HONORS
NFL MVP

- Bill Dudley (1946)
- Terry Bradshaw (1978)

Super Bowl MVP

- Franco Harris (1974)
- Lynn Swann (1975)
- Terry Bradshaw (1978, '79)

Defensive Player of the Year

- Joe Greene (1972, '74)
- Mel Blount (1975)
- Jack Ham (1975)
- Jack Lambert (1976, '83)
- Rod Woodson (1993)
- Greg Lloyd (1994)

NFL Rookie of the Year

- Jimmy Orr (1958)
- Franco Harris (1972)
- Louis Lipps (1984)

Pro Football Hall of Fame

- Bert Bell (1963)
- Johnny McNally (1963)
- Art Rooney (1964)
- Bill Dudley (1966)
- Walt Kiesling (1966)
- Bobby Layne (1967)

- Ernie Stautner (1969)
- "Mean" Joe Greene (1987)
- John Henry Johnson (1987)
- Jack Ham (1988)
- Mel Blount (1989)
- Terry Bradshaw (1989)
- Franco Harris (1990)
- Jack Lambert (1990)
- Chuck Noll (1993)
- Mike Webster (1997)
- Dan Rooney (2000)

Kordell Stewart is one of the NFL's most versatile athletes.

Extra Point

- During his career, Terry Bradshaw never passed for 400 yards in a game and had only four 300-yard games. But Bradshaw knew how to win, earning four Super Bowl rings and a pair of Super Bowl MVP trophies.

"You can go to the bank and borrow money, but you can't go to the bank and borrow a Super Bowl ring."
— Steelers DT "Mean" Joe Greene, owner of four Super Bowl rings

Timeline

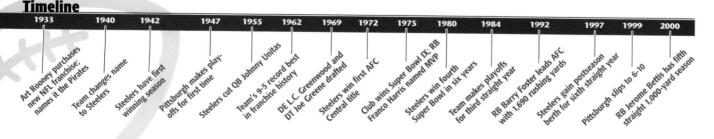

| 1933 | 1940 | 1942 | 1947 | 1955 | 1962 | 1969 | 1972 | 1975 | 1980 | 1984 | 1992 | 1997 | 1999 | 2000 |

- Art Rooney purchases new NFL franchise; names it the Pirates
- Team changes name to Steelers
- Steelers have first winning season
- Pittsburgh makes playoffs for first time
- Steelers cut QB Johnny Unitas
- Team's 9-5 record best in franchise history
- DE L.C. Greenwood and DT Joe Greene drafted
- Steelers win first AFC Central title
- Club wins Super Bowl IX; RB Franco Harris named MVP
- Steelers win fourth Super Bowl in six years
- Team makes playoffs for third straight year
- RB Barry Foster leads AFC with 1,690 rushing yards
- Steelers gain postseason berth for sixth straight year
- Pittsburgh slips to 6-10
- RB Jerome Bettis has fifth straight 1,000-yard season

HEINZ FIELD: IN WITH THE NEW

ALTHOUGH MANY STEELERS FANS had a strong attachment to Three Rivers Stadium, the team's new home, one of the league's newest structures, is a definite step up. There are many more seats between the end zones and at the lower levels, bringing the boisterous Pittsburgh fans that much closer to the action. Also, a cutting-edge scoreboard and sound system have been added. The striking horseshoe design offers a beautiful view of the downtown area and is a stunning addition to the North Shore riverfront.

CONCESSIONS

In addition to the the regular hot dogs and hamburgers, several vendors serve local specialities

GAME DAY TIPS

• **Gate hours:** Gates open two hours before the game.
• **Tailgating:** Tailgating

Stadium Facts

Opened: Aug. 18, 2001
Cost: $250 million
Capacity: 65,000
Type: Outdoor
Surface: Grass
Home Sweet Home:
• Few fans in the NFL combine the dual qualities of rowdiness and football savvy as the Steelers faithful. Their unflinching vocal support has always given the team an added edge.

takes place throughout the parking lot and begins as soon as the lots open up.
• **Weather:** During the football season Pittsburgh's weather can run the gamut from hot and humid to snowy and cold. Only fans in the upper seating bowl are protected from the rain.
• **Prohibited items:** Glass bottles, cans, weapons and alcohol. Coolers must fit under the seat. Banners must not be offensive and cannot block views or cover existing ads. Smoking is permitted in designated areas only
• **Ticket tips:** The Steelers have been selling out for virtually every game for

Seating Plan

■ $190
■ $145
■ $52
□ $46

ATM Ask Information for locations
♿ Call stadium for information

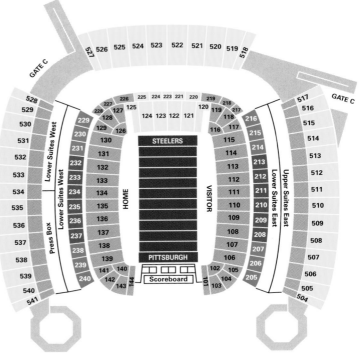

years on end. Don't wait until the last minute to buy a ticket. Games against longtime rivals such as the Cleveland Browns are snapped up very quickly.
• **Lost and found:** (412) 323-1200.

Nearby Hotels

▼▼▼ **Doubletree Hotel Pittsburgh** *(Hotel)*, 1000 Penn Ave. (Pittsburgh), (412) 281-3700, $99-$199
▼▼▼ **Hampton Inn** *(Motel)*, 4575 McKnight Rd. (Pittsburgh), (412) 939-3200, $84-$94
▼▼▼ **Hampton Inn-University Center** *(Motel)*, 3315 Hamlet St. (Pittsburgh), (412) 681-1000, $99-$109
▼▼▼ **Hilton Pittsburgh** *(Hotel)*, in the Gateway Center opposite Point State Park (Pittsburgh), (412) 391-4600, $84-$219
▼▼▼ **Sheraton Station Square Hotel** *(Hotel)*, 7 Station Square Dr. (Pittsburgh), (412) 261-2000, $139-$209

Nearby Restaurants

▼▼▼ **Grand Concourse Restaurant** *(Seafood)*, 1 Station Square in Pittsburgh and Lake Erie Railroad Terminal Bldg. (Pittsburgh), (412) 261-1717, $17-$25
▼▼ **Kiku's of Japan** *(Japanese)*, at Carson and Smithfield Sts. in the Shops at Station Square (Pittsburgh), (412) 765-3200, $15-$20
▼▼▼ **Pittsburgh Fishmarket Restaurant** *(Seafood)*, 1000 Penn Ave., in the Doubletree Hotel Pittsburgh(Pittsburgh), (412) 227-3657, $12-$16
▼▼ **Khalil's II** *(Middle Eastern)*, 4757 Baum Blvd. (Pittsburgh), (412) 683-4757, $9-$16
▼▼▼▼ **Le Mont Restaurant** *(American)*, 1114 Grandview Ave. (Pittsburgh), (412) 431-3100, $22-$35 (dinner only)

Directions: From I-279 north, take exit 11B and follow the signs to the stadium. **By Bus:** Several bus routes provide service to the stadium. For more information, call Port Authority of Allegheny County at (412) 442-2000. **Parking:** There are more than 9,800 parking spaces available in private lots and garages around Heinz Field. In addition to 60 lots on the south shore, there are also lots on S. Commons, Martindale St. and River Ave. on the north shore.

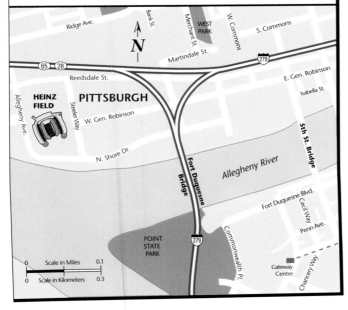

ST. LOUIS RAMS

WHILE THE ST. LOUIS RAMS have played in three different cities, they've won a championship for each set of hometown fans. The first incarnation of the Rams appeared in 1937 in Cleveland, where it struggled for its first seven seasons. The arrival of rookie QB Bob Waterfield in 1945 changed the Rams' fortunes. With Waterfield finishing third among league passers, the Rams won their first NFL championship. Success couldn't keep the team in Cleveland, however, and immediately following the season the team moved west to Los Angeles. There, fans had to wait until 1951 for the Rams to bring home the top prize. That year, the Rams' quarterbacking tandem of Waterfield and Norm Van Brocklin finished first and second in league passing and wide-out Elroy "Crazy Legs" Hirsch topped the NFL in scoring and receptions. In the title game, the Rams upset the heavily favored Browns on a fourth-quarter bomb from Van Brocklin to Tom Fears. In the late 1960s the Rams reemerged as a force in the West. Led by their "Fearsome Foursome" defensive line, the team went 32-7-3 from 1967 to '70. But despite making the playoffs 14 times from 1973 to '89, the team couldn't win a Super Bowl. That would have to wait until 1999. Backup QB Kurt Warner, who went undrafted out of Northern Iowa before toiling in the Arena League, was thrust into action when the Rams' starter went down in the preseason. Warner earned MVP honors by becoming only the second player to pass for more than 40 TDs in a season. More unbelievably, he ended his Cinderella story by leading the team to a Super Bowl victory.

> " I want to win today. I don't want to wait for tomorrow."
>
> — George Allen, Rams Head Coach 1966-70

Vital Stats

Stadium Address:
901 N. Broadway, St. Louis, Mo.
Phone: (314) 342-5201
Web: stlouisrams.com
Box Office: (314) 425-8830, Mon.–Fri. 9–5
Media Coverage:
Radio: KLOU (103.3 FM)
TV: KTVI (Channel 2), KDNL (Channel 30), Fox SportsNet
Training Facility:
Rams Park, St. Louis, Mo.

Kurt Warner was both league and Super Bowl MVP in 1999.

Extra Point

• Before he joined the Rams, Kurt Warner played in the Arena Football League and also worked stocking shelves at a local grocery store.
• In 1999 RB Marshall Faulk set the NFL record for most yards from scrimmage, amassing 2,429 yards.

POSTSEASON
• **Super Bowl Championships** 1
(1999)
• **NFL Championships** 2
(1945, '51)

• **NFC Championships** 2
(1979, '99)
• **NFC West Titles** 8
(1973, '74, '75, '76, '77, '78, '85, '99)
• **NFC Wild Card Berths** 7
(1980, 1983–84, '86, 1988–89, 2000)

RETIRED NUMBERS
• Bob Waterfield (7)
• Eric Dickerson (29)
• Merlin Olsen (74)
• Jackie Slater (78)

RAMS RING OF FAME
• Norm Van Brocklin
• Deacon Jones
• Eric Dickerson
• Tom Fears
• Elroy "Crazy Legs" Hirsch
• Tom Mack
• Merlin Olson
• Bob Waterfield

TEAM RECORDS
Offense
• **Isaac Bruce (1994–present)**
Receptions (season): 119 (1995)
Receiving Yards (season): 1,781 (1995)
• **Eric Dickerson (1983–87)**
Rushing Yards (season): 2,105 (1984)
Rushing Yards (career): 7,245
TDs (career): 58
• **Jim Everett (1986–93)**
Comp. (career): 1,847

Passing Yards (career): 23,758
• **Henry Ellard (1983–93)**
Receptions (career): 593
Receiving Yards (career): 9,761
• **Marshall Faulk (1999–present)**
Points (season): 160 (2000)
TDs (season): 26 (2000)
• **Roman Gabriel (1962–72)**
TD Passes (career): 154
• **Elroy Hirsch (1949–57)**
TD Receptions (career): 53
• **Mike Lansford (1982–90)**
Points (career): 789
• **Norm Van Brocklin (1949–57)**
Passing Yards (game): 554 (Sept. 28, 1951)
• **Kurt Warner (1998–present)**
Comp. (season): 325 (1999)
Passing Yards (season): 4,353 (1999)
TD Passes (season): 41 (1999)

Defense
• **Deacon Jones (1961–71)**
Sacks (season): 22 (1964)
Sacks (career): 159.5
• **Dick Lane (1952–53)**
Interceptions (season): 14 (1952)
• **Ed Meador (1959–70)**
Interceptions (career): 46
• **Merlin Olsen (1962–76)**
Tackles (career): 915

LEAGUE HONORS
NFL MVP
• Parker Hall (1939)

• Bob Waterfield (1945)
• Roman Gabriel (1969)
• Merlin Olsen (1974)
• Kurt Warner (1999)
• Marshall Faulk (2000)

NFL Rookie of the Year
• Eric Dickerson (1983)
• Jerome Betis (1993)

Super Bowl MVP
• Kurt Warner (1999)

Pro Football Hall of Fame
• Bob Waterfield (1965)
• Daniel Reeves (1967)
• Elroy Hirsch (1968)
• Tom Fears (1970)
• Andy Robustelli (1971)
• Norm Van Brocklin (1971)
• Dick Lane (1974)
• Deacon Jones (1980)
• Merlin Olsen (1982)
• Sid Gillman (1983)
• Pete Rozelle (1985)
• Tex Schramm (1991)
• Eric Dickerson (1999)
• Tom Mack (1999)
• Jackie Slater (2001)
• Jack Youngblood (2001)

Timeline

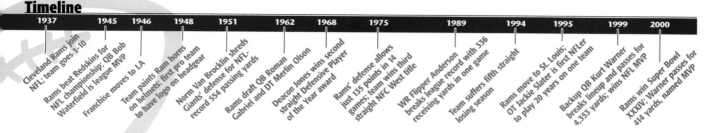

1937	1945	1946	1948	1951	1962	1968	1975	1989	1994	1995	1999	2000
Cleveland Rams join NFL; team goes 1-10	Rams beat Redskins for NFL championship; QB Bob Waterfield is league MVP	Franchise moves to LA	Team paints Ram horns on helmets; first pro team to have logo on headgear	Norm Van Brocklin shreds Giants' defense for NFL-record 554 passing yards	Rams draft QB Roman Gabriel and DT Merlin Olson	Deacon Jones wins second straight Defensive Player of the Year award	Rams' defense allows just 135 points in 14 games; team wins third straight NFC West title	WR Flipper Anderson breaks league record with 336 receiving yards in one game	Team suffers fifth straight losing season	Rams move to St. Louis; OT Jackie Slater is first NFLer to play 20 years on one team	Backup QB Kurt Warner breaks lineup and passes for 4,353 yards; wins NFL MVP	Rams win Super Bowl XXXIV; Warner passes for 414 yards, named MVP

204

The Dome at America's Center: On Top of the Action

THE STADIUM opened Nov. 12, 1995, for the Rams' 10th game of the season. Designed as a multi-use complex, the Dome is an integral part of the America's Center complex as well as being the state-of-the-art home of the Rams. The stadium's "Magic Turf" system allows the playing surface to be rolled into place in about one hour. The stadium is constructed so that most of the 66,000 seats enjoy good sight lines and have that "on top of the action" feel. Once called the Trans World Dome, the venue is seeking a new corporate identity.

CONCESSIONS

The Dome offers fans the full array of stadium food, from burgers and hot dogs to nachos, pizza and peanuts. For something a little less ordinary, try the specialty concession stands, offering everything from steaks to gourmet ice cream and vegetarian food.

GAME DAY TIPS

• **Gate hours:** Gates open 90 minutes prior to kickoff.
• **Tailgating:** The Rams organize a tailgate party at Bayer Plaza across from the Dome before every game. Private lots around the Dome also allow tailgating.
• **Weather:** The temperature in the Dome is kept at a constant comfortable 72°F.
• **Prohibited items:** Food, beverages, bottles or cans, strollers, peanuts in the shell, poles, laser pointers and noisemakers are prohibited. Smoking is not permitted in the stadium.
• **Ticket tips:** Single-game Rams' tickets are hard to get, especially since the team's 1999 Super Bowl victory. Pre-season games are a better bet for tickets. Keep in mind that seats near the top of the Dome are more vulnerable to the notoriously bad sound.
• **Lost and found:** (314) 342-5036.

Stadium Facts

Opened: *Nov. 12, 1995*
Cost: *$280 million*
Capacity: *66,000*
Type: *Dome*
Surface: *AstroTurf*
Home Sweet Home:
• *Used to the losing ways of the old St. Louis Cardinals, hometown fans have come alive with the emergence of the Rams as one of the NFL's most exciting teams.*

Seating Plan

■	N/A	■		$44
■	N/A	■		$37
■	N/A	▫	Club Level	
■	$44	ATM	Sections 118, 421	
■	$44	♿	Throughout	

Directions: *Take I-44 or I-270 to I-55/70. Exit at Memorial Dr. Turn on Washington Ave., right on 9th St. Follow to Cole St., right on Cole. Or, exit I-70 at Broadway and follow to stadium.* **By Public Transportation:** *Several buses and the MetroLink light rail system stop at the Dome. Call St. Louis Regional Transit at (314) 231-2345 for information.* **Parking:** *More than 30,000 parking spaces are available within a 10-minute walk, including on 1st, 2nd, Carr and Morgan Sts. and Lacledes Landing Blvd..*

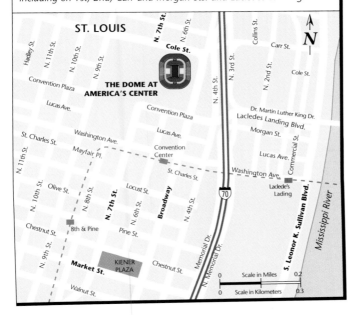

Nearby Hotels

▼▼▼ **Adam's Mark-St. Louis (Hotel)**, at 4th and Chestnut Sts. (St. Louis), (314) 241-7400, $129-$235
▼▼ **Best Inns (Motel)**, 2423 Old Country Inn Dr. (Caseyville, Ill.), (618) 397-3300, $46-$60
▼▼▼ **Drury Inn & Suites (Motor Inn)**, 711 N. Broadway (St. Louis), (314) 231-8100, $82-$104
▼▼▼ **Holiday Inn Downtown Select (Hotel)**, 811 N. 9th St. (St. Louis), (314) 421-4000, $109-$159
▼▼▼ **Omni Majestic Hotel (Historic Hotel)**, 1019 Pine St. (St. Louis), (314) 436-2355, $187-$197

Nearby Restaurants

▼▼▼ **Al's Restaurant (Continental)**, 1200 N. 1st St. (St. Louis), (314) 421-6399, $20-$50 (dinner only)
▼▼▼▼ **Cafe De France (French)**, 410 Olive St. (St. Louis), (314) 231-2204, $20-$25 (dinner only)
▼▼▼ **Dierdorf and Hart's (Seafood)**, 701 Market St. (St. Louis), (314) 421-1772, $15-$40
▼▼ **Hannegan's (American)**, 719 N. 2nd St. in Laclede's Landing (St. Louis), (314) 241-8877, $12-$18
▼▼▼ **Kemoll's Italian Restaurant (Italian)**, 1 Metropolitan Sq. in the Metropolitan Square Building (St. Louis), (314) 421-0555, $12-$40 (dinner only)

SAN DIEGO CHARGERS

PERHAPS NO TEAM IN NFL HISTORY suits its logo as well as the San Diego Chargers. When the team first took the field in 1960 as part of the AFL's inaugural season, its players sported lightning bolts on their helmets and down the legs of their pants. Those early teams were known for their wide-open offense, with such electrifying performers as Lance Alworth and Keith Lincoln hauling down Jack Kemp bombs. On defense the Chargers were equally explosive. Time and time again, opposing teams were dropped dead in their tracks after another bone-jarring sack by Earl Faison or Ernie "Big Cat" Ladd. From 1960 to '65, the Chargers won four AFL Western Division crowns and one AFL Championship. But the Bolts fell to Earth quickly after that, unable to finish higher than third in the division over the next 13 seasons. The Chargers' fortunes turned for the better in 1979, when Don Coryell installed his famous "Air Coryell" passing attack. Modeling his current squad on those exciting teams of the '60s, Coryell built his offense around the strong arm and stout heart of QB Dan Fouts. Fouts, who understudied for Johnny Unitas when he became the first man in NFL history to pass for 40,000 yards, excelled, leading the NFL in passing yards from 1979 to '82. Not surprisingly, the team flourished, making the playoffs all four years, including a 41-38 overtime victory over Miami that many consider the greatest game ever played. With today's Chargers led by linebacker Junior Seau on defense and Doug Flutie on offense, fans are waiting for lightning to strike again.

Junior Seau is one of the NFL's most dominant linebackers.

POSTSEASON
- AFL Championships........1
(1963)
- AFC Titles 1
(1994)
- AFC West Titles................5
(1979, '80, '81, '92, '94)
- AFC Wild Card Berths.....1
(1995)

RETIRED NUMBERS
- Dan Fouts (14)

TEAM HALL OF FAME
- Chuck Allen
- Lance Alworth
- Frank Buncom
- Rolf Benirschke
- Don Coryell (Head Coach)
- Speedy Duncan
- Earl Faison

Extra Point
- *In his second season with the Chargers, kicker Rolf Benirschke was diagnosed with ulcerative colitis. After four surgeries in 1979, his weight dropped to 127 pounds. Remarkably, he returned the next year and played another seven seasons. When he retired in 1986, Benirschke's 766 career points was a Charger record.*

- Dan Fouts
- Gary Garrison
- Sid Gilman (Head Coach)
- John Hadl
- Barron Hilton (Owner)
- Gary Johnson
- Charlie Joiner
- Emil Karas
- Ernie Ladd
- Bob Laraba
- Keith Lincoln
- Paul Lowe
- Jacque MacKinnon
- Ron Mix
- George Pernicano (Owner)
- Walt Sweeney
- Russ Washington
- Doug Wilckerson
- Kellen Winslow

TEAM RECORDS
Offense
- **Lance Alworth (1962–70)**
Receiving Yards (season): 1,602 (1965)
Receiving Yards (career): 9,585
TD Receptions (career): 81
- **John Carney (1990–present)**
Points (season): 135 (1994)
Points (career): 1,076
- **Dan Fouts (1973–87)**
Pass Comp. (career): 3,297
Passing Yards (season): 4,802 (1981)
Passing Yards (career): 43,040
TD Passes (season): 33 (1981)
TD Passes (career): 254
- **Charlie Joiner (1976–86)**

Receptions (career): 586
- **Paul Lowe (1960–67)**
Rushing Yards (career): 4,963
- **Natrone Means (1993–95, 1998–99)**
Rushing Yards (season): 1,350 (1994)
- **Chuck Muncie (1980–84)**
Rushing TDs (career): 43
- **Kellen Winslow (1979–87)**
Receptions (game): 15 (Oct. 7, 1984)
Receiving TDs (game): 5 (Nov. 22, 1981)

Defense
- **Gill Byrd (1983–92)**
Interceptions (career): 42
- **Gary Johnson (1975–84)**
Sacks (season): 17.5 (1980)
- **Leslie O'Neal (1986–95)**
Sacks (game): 5 (Nov. 16, 1986)
Sacks (career): 105.5

LEAGUE HONORS
NFL MVP
- Dan Fouts (1982)

AFL Player of the Year
- Lance Alworth (1963)
- Paul Lowe (1965)

AFC Player of the Year
- Dan Fouts (1979, '82)
- Junior Seau (1992)

NFL Rookie of the Year
- Don Woods (1974)

Vital Stats

Stadium Address:
9449 Friars Rd.,
San Diego, Calif.
Phone: (619) 641-3100
Web: chargers.com
Box Office:
(619) 280-2121,
Mon.–Fri. 8–5
Media Coverage:
Radio: KFMB (760 AM)
TV: KFMB (Channel 8)
Training Facility:
University of California at
San Diego, La Jolla, Calif.

Pro Football Hall of Fame
- Lance Alworth (1978)
- Ron Mix (1979)
- Sid Gillman (1983)
- Dan Fouts (1993)
- Kellen Winslow (1995)
- Charlie Joiner (1996)

"Football is a team game — the satisfaction comes in winning."
— Hall-of-Famer Dan Fouts, the winningest QB in Charger history

Timeline

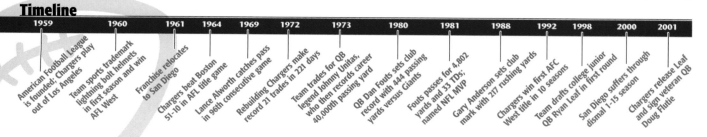

1959	1960	1961	1964	1969	1972	1973	1980	1981	1988	1992	1998	2000	2001

American Football League is founded; Chargers play out of Los Angeles

Team sports trademark lightning bolt helmets in first season and win AFL West

Franchise relocates to San Diego

Chargers beat Boston 51-10 in AFL title game

Lance Alworth catches pass in 96th consecutive game

Rebuilding Chargers make record 21 trades in 221 days

Team trades for QB legend Johnny Unitas, who then records career 40,000th passing yard

QB Dan Fouts sets club record with 444 passing yards versus Giants

Fouts passes for 4,802 yards and 33 TDs; named NFL MVP

Gary Anderson sets club mark with 217 rushing yards

Chargers win first AFC West title in 10 seasons

Team drafts college junior QB Ryan Leaf in first round

San Diego suffers through dismal 1-15 season

Chargers release Leaf and sign veteran QB Doug Flutie

QUALCOMM STADIUM: VENERABLE AND VERSATILE

SAN DIEGO STADIUM was built in 1967 as home to the expansion San Diego Chargers. Later renamed Jack Murphy Stadium in honor of the popular sportswriter who pushed for its construction, the "Q" is a multipurpose facility with a football capacity of more than 71,000. The biggest crowd in team history (68,274) came to watch a 1999 game versus the Packers. Despite its age, Qualcomm has excellent sight lines and up-to-date fan amenities. The stadium was host to Super Bowl XXXII and is slated to host the game again in 2003.

CONCESSIONS

Qualcomm Stadium provides fans with all the best in stadium food, including pretzels, hot dogs, burgers and pizza. Also available are fish tacos, a San Diego specialty.

GAME DAY TIPS

• **Gate hours:** Gates open 2.5 hours before kickoff.
• **Tailgating:** Tailgating is permitted in one's own parking stall in the inner ring. For larger parties, tailgate areas can be reserved at (619) 281-6316. Lots open four hours before a game.
• **Weather:** San Diego is warm in the summer and early fall, but rarely uncomfortably hot. Sunscreen and hats are a must on sunny days. Evenings can turn cool, so pack a light jacket. Winters are relatively mild in San Diego, with comfortable temperatures.
• **Prohibited items:** No alcohol or liquid containers of any kind can be brought into the stadium. Coolers are allowed provided they do not contain alcohol. Animals, except those trained to provide assistance to disabled visitors, are prohibited. Smoking is allowed in designated areas only.

Stadium Facts

Opened: Aug. 20, 1967
Cost: $27 million
Capacity: 71,000
Type: Outdoor
Surface: Grass
Home Sweet Home:
• Normally laid-back West Coasters can get pretty vocal when it comes to supporting their Chargers. The real diehards wear huge foam lightning bolts on their heads.

Seating Plan

- ☐ Club Level ....Prices vary
- ☐ Press Level $59
- ☐ Field, Plaza, Loge and View $43
- ☐ End Zone View $38
- ☐ Upper View $29
- ■ Lower Field (obstructed view) $24
- ■ Family - View 58 ....$24
- ATM Sections 14/15, 24/25, 27/28
- ♿ Throughout

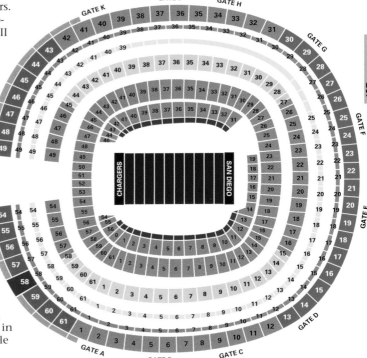

• **Ticket tips:** Single-game tickets are available for all games.
• **Lost and found:** (619) 641-3150.

Directions: *Take I-8 west, take exit I-15 north and follow to Friars Rd. exit. Right on Friars Rd. to Stadium exit. From I-15 south, exit Friars Rd. and turn right. Follow to Stadium exit. By Bus: The Chargers Express goes to and from the stadium from eight points with parking lots in town beginning two hours before games. Call (619) 238-0100 for information.*
Parking: *Lots surrounding the stadium can accommodate some 18,500 vehicles. More than 450 spaces are reserved for people with disabilities.*

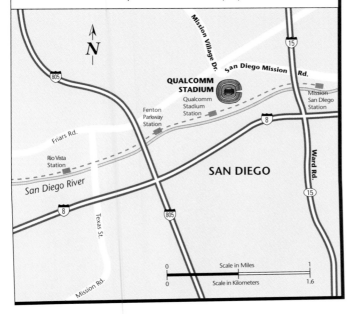

Nearby Hotels

▼▼▼ **Balboa Park Inn** *(Motel)*, 3402 Park Blvd. at Balboa Park (San Diego), (619) 298-0823, $89-$219
▼▼▼ **Comfort Suites-Hotel Circle** *(Suite Motel)*, 631 Camino Del Rio S. (San Diego), (619) 881-4000, $99-$169
▼▼▼ **Doubletree Hotel-San Diego Mission Valley** *(Hotel)*, 7450 Hazard Center Dr. (San Diego), (619) 297-5466, $129-$169
▼▼▼ **Radisson Hotel-San Diego** *(Hotel)*, 1433 Camino Del Rio S. (San Diego), (619) 260-0111, $209
▼▼▼ **San Diego Marriott Mission Valley** *(Hotel)*, 8757 Rio San Diego Dr. (San Diego), (619) 692-3800, $169-$189

Nearby Restaurants

▼▼▼▼ **Bertrand at Mister A's** *(California)*, 2550 Fifth Ave. in the Fifth Avenue Financial Center, top floor (San Diego), (619) 239-1377, $20-$40
▼▼ **City Delicatessen** *(American)*, 535 E. University Ave. (San Diego), (619) 295-2747, $4-$16
▼▼ **Islands Restaurant** *(Specialty)*, 2270 Hotel Circle in the Hanalei Hotel (San Diego), (619) 297-1101, $14-$25 (dinner only)
▼▼ **Monterey Whaling Company** *(Seafood)*, 901 Camino Del Rio S. in the Hilton San Diego Mission Valley (San Diego), (619) 543-9000, $9-$20
▼▼▼ **Prego** *(Italian)*, 1370 Frazee Rd. in the Hazard Center (San Diego), (619) 294-4700, $12-$25

SAN FRANCISCO 49ERS

SUCCESS WAS A LONG TIME COMING for the San Francisco 49ers. Through the team's first 24 seasons, including four in the old All-American Football Conference, the Niners never won a championship and only made it to the playoffs twice; this despite a host of great players, including future Hall-Of-Famers Y.A. Tittle, Leo "the Lion" Nomellini, Hugh "the King" McElhenny, Bob St. Clair and John Henry Johnson. The team's championship drought ended in 1970, when, led by QB John Brodie, the Niners went 10-3-1 and finally won the NFC West. The players must have liked the taste of success because the team won the division title again in '71 and '72. But Super Bowl champagne proved elusive as the 49ers were eliminated all three years by Dallas. That all changed in 1981. With young QB Joe Montana at the helm of Bill Walsh's complex offense and Jack "Hacksaw" Reynolds anchoring the defense, the 49ers took their division. Squaring off against the Cowboys yet again for the NFC championship, the 49ers looked beaten until Montana engineered one final drive and tossed a last-minute TD to Dwight Clark for the win. The team's 38-16 dismantling of Miami in Super Bowl XIX was almost anticlimactic. With one Super Bowl under their belt, the Niners never looked back, winning again in 1984, '88, '89 and '94 — an amazing five titles. Along the way the team has been blessed with incredible talent, producing seven NFL MVP awards from 1987 to '94 for work done by Montana, Steve Young, Roger Craig and the greatest receiver of all-time, Jerry Rice.

Vital Stats

Stadium Address:
3Com Park,
San Francisco, Calif.
Phone: (415) 656-4949
Web: sf49ers.com
Box Office:
(415) 656-4900,
Mon.–Fri. 9–5
Media Coverage:
Radio: KGO (810 AM)
TV: FOX (KTVU Channel 2)
Training Facility: Marie P. DeBartolo Sports Center, Santa Clara, Calif.

POSTSEASON

- **Super Bowl Championships** 5
(1981, '84, '88, '89, '94)
- **NFC Championships** 5
(1981, '84, '88, '89, '94)
- **NFC West Titles**..............18
(1970, '71, '72, '73, '81, '82, '83, '84, '86, '87, '88, '89, '90, '92, '93, '94, '95, '97)
- **Wild Card Berths**.............3
(1985, '96, '98)

RETIRED NUMBERS

- **John Brodie (12)**
- **Joe Montana (16)**
- **Joe Perry (34)**
- **Jimmy Johnson (37)**
- **Hugh McElhenny (39)**
- **Charlie Krueger (70)**
- **Leo Nomellini (73)**
- **Dwight Clark (87)**

Extra Point

- *QB Steve Young and WR Jerry Rice teamed up for 85 TD receptions to be the most prolific passing/catching duo in NFL history.*
- *Joe Montana retired with a 92.3 career quarterback rating — second only to teammate Steve Young. A clutch performer, Montana is the only player to win three Super Bowl MVPs.*

TEAM RECORDS
Offense

- **Roger Craig (1983–90)**
Carries (career): 1,686
Rushing Tds (career): 50 (tie)
1,000-Yard Seasons: 3
- **Jeff Garcia (1999–present)**
Comp. (season): 355 (2000)
Passing Yards (season): 4,278 (2000)
- **Garrison Hearst (1997–present)**
Rushing Yards (season); 1,570 (1998)
- **Joe Montana (1979–92)**
Comp. (career): 2,929
Passing Yards (career): 35,124
TD Passes (career): 244
300-Yard Games (career): 35
- **Joe Perry (1948–60, '63)**
Rushing Yards (career): 7,344
100-Yard Games (career): 18
- **Jerry Rice (1985–2000)**
Points (season): 138 (1987)
Points (career): 1,130
Receiving Yards (career): 19,248
Receiving Yards (season): 1,848 (1995)
Receptions (season): 122 (1995)
Receptions (career): 1,281
TDs (season): 23 (1987)
TDs (career): 187
1000-Yard Seasons: 12
- **Steve Young (1987–99)**
Comp. Pct. (career): 65.8
Comp. Pct. (season): 70.3 (1994)

QB Rating (career): 101.4
TD Passes (season): 36 (1998)

Defense

- **Fred Dean (1981–85)**
Sacks (game): 6 (Nov. 13, 1983)
- **Cedrick Hardman (1970–79)**
Sacks (season): 18 (1971)
Sacks (career): 112.5
- **Ronnie Lott (1981–90)**
Int. (season): 10 (1986)
Int. (career): 51

LEAGUE HONORS
NFL MVP

- **John Brodie (1970)**
- **Jerry Rice (1987, '90)**
- **Roger Craig (1988)**
- **Joe Montana (1989, '90)**
- **Steve Young (1992, '94)**

NFL Defensive MVP

- **Fred Dean (1981)**
- **Deion Sanders (1994)**
- **Dana Stubblefield (1997)**

NFL Coach of the Year

- **Bill Walsh (1981)**
- **George Seifert (1989, '94)**

Super Bowl MVP

- **Joe Montana**

"Who is this, the punter?"

— TE Dwight Clark, on first meeting QB Joe Montana, who would blossom into a three-time Super Bowl MVP and a Hall of Famer

Terrell Owens is one of the league's top young receivers.

(1981, '84, '89)
- **Jerry Rice (1988)**
- **Steve Young (1994)**

Pro Football Hall of Fame

- **Leo Nomellini (1969)**
- **Joe Perry (1969)**
- **Hugh McElhenny (1970)**
- **Y.A. Tittle (1971)**
- **John Henry Johnson (1987)**
- **Bob St-Clair (1990)**
- **Bill Walsh (1993)**
- **Jimmy Johnson (1994)**
- **Ronnie Lott (2000)**
- **Joe Montana (2000)**
- **Dave Wilcox (2000)**

Timeline

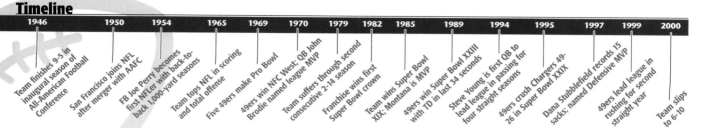

| 1946 | 1950 | 1954 | 1965 | 1969 | 1970 | 1979 | 1982 | 1985 | 1989 | 1994 | 1995 | 1997 | 1999 | 2000 |

- 1946 — Team finishes 9-5 in inaugural season of All-American Football Conference
- 1950 — San Francisco joins NFL after merger with AAFC
- 1954 — FB Joe Perry becomes first NFLer with back-to-back 1,000-yard seasons
- 1965 — Team tops NFL in scoring and total offense
- 1969 — Five 49ers make Pro Bowl
- 1970 — 49ers win NFC West; QB John Brodie named league MVP
- 1979 — Team suffers through second consecutive 2-14 season
- 1982 — Franchise wins first Super Bowl crown
- 1985 — Team wins Super Bowl XIX; Montana is MVP
- 1989 — 49ers win Super Bowl XXIII with TD in last 34 seconds
- 1994 — Steve Young is first QB to lead league in passing for four straight seasons
- 1995 — 49ers crush Chargers 49-26 in Super Bowl XXIX
- 1997 — Dana Stubblefield records 15 sacks; named Defensive MVP
- 1999 — 49ers lead league in rushing for second straight year
- 2000 — Team slips to 6-10

3COM PARK AT CANDLESTICK POINT: SAN FRANCISCO ICON

LIKE THE GOLDEN GATE BRIDGE, 3Com Park is a San Francisco landmark. Buffeted by relentless winds and shaken by the occasional earthquake, this venerable stadium has hosted everything from NFC championships and World Series, to the Beatles' last U.S. concert and Pope John Paul II. On top of its rich history, 3Com Park is known for its incredible lighting, with nine huge towers that literally turn night into day. When fans aren't watching replays on the huge video scoreboard, they can enjoy the view of the Bay.

CONCESSIONS

The concessions at 3Com include the traditional fare, as well as specialty items such as sausages, chili, clam chowder, garlic fries and barbecue. There are several vegetarian options, including garden burgers, burritos and three-cheese nachos.

Stadium Facts

Opened: *April 12, 1960*
Cost: *$24.6 million*
Capacity: *69,734*
Type: *Outdoor*
Surface: *Grass*
Home Sweet Home:
• *When it rains, the turf at 3Com Park can come up in large chunks, taking the feet from under players making sharp cuts. Swirling winds also wreak havoc on long passes and field goals.*

GAME DAY TIPS

• **Gate hours:** Gates open two hours prior to kickoff.
• **Tailgating:** Tailgating begins in the stadium lot four hours prior to kickoff.
• **Weather:** 3Com Park is notorious for its bad weather. Be prepared for cool, damp and very windy conditions, no matter how good the weather seems before going to the game.
• **Prohibited items:** Alcoholic beverages, cans, bottles, weapons, hard fruit, bullhorns, noisemakers, banners and signs are prohibited.
• **Ticket tips:** The 49ers have sold out every game they've played since 1981. They do put aside about 2,000 tickets for single-game sale. These tickets sell out extremely quickly, especially if they're for games against rival St. Louis Rams.

• **Lost and found:** (415) 656-4957 for lost items on game day or (650) 259-1985 Mon.–Fri.

Seating Plan

	$50		$50
	$50		$50
	$50	**ATM**	**Section 9 (blue)**
	$50	♿	**Sections 1, 4, 5, 9, 29, 41, 43 (yellow) ; 28, 30 (orange)**

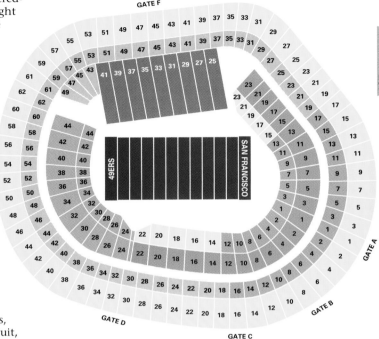

Directions: From north or south, take Hwy. 101 to 3Com Park exits. By Public Transportation: Streetcars, trains, ferries and buses are all available and limited parking makes these a good idea. Call stadium operations at (415) 656-4949 for help in planning the best route. *Parking:* Most of the stadium's 18,000 parking spots are reserved for season ticket holders; remaining spots are sold on first-come first-served basis. Overflow parking is accommodated by private lots in the area, including on Jamestown Ave. and Hunter's Point Expwy. Guests with disabilities can park in the stadium lot, where there is an ample number of reserved spots.

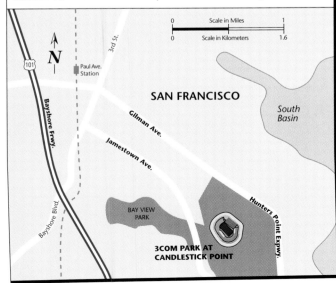

Nearby Hotels

▼▼▼ **Best Western Canterbury Hotel** *(Hotel)*, 750 Sutter St. (San Francisco), (415) 474-6464, $125-$375
▼▼▼ **Chancellor Hotel** *(Hotel)*, 433 Powell St. (San Francisco), (415) 362-2004, $140-$190
▼▼▼▼ **Hyatt Regency-San Francisco** *(Hotel)*, 5 Embarcadero Center (San Francisco), (415) 788-1234, $299-$324
▼▼▼▼▼ **The Ritz-Carlton, San Francisco** *(Hotel)*, 600 Stockton St. (San Francisco), (415) 296-7465, $480-$580
▼▼▼ **York Hotel** *(Hotel)*, 940 Sutter St. (San Francisco), (415) 885-6800, $129-$179

Nearby Restaurants

▼▼ **The Cliff House** *(American)*, 1909 Point Lobos at Ocean Beach (San Francisco), (415) 386-3330, $16-$25
▼▼ **Dante's** *(Seafood)*, on Pier 39 (San Francisco), (415) 421-5778, $17-$24
▼▼▼▼▼ **The Dining Room** *(Nouvelle French)*, 600 Stockton St. in The Ritz-Carlton, San Francisco (San Francisco), (415) 296-7465, $61-$87 (dinner only)
▼▼▼ **The Mandarin** *(Northern Chinese)*, 900 N. Point St. in the Woolen Mill Bldg., top floor (San Francisco), (415) 673-8812, $10-$20
▼▼ **Pompei's Grotto** *(Seafood)*, 340 Jefferson St. at Fisherman's Wharf (San Francisco), (415) 776-9265, $10-$20

SEATTLE SEAHAWKS

THE SEATTLE SEAHAWK'S first season in 1976 had all the hallmarks of an expansion team's inaugural year: a woeful record (2-12), a last-place finish and being outscored by opponents by 200 points. However, there were some bright spots, notably the emergence of two young stars: QB Jim Zorn and WR Steve Largent. For the next seven years, "Zorn to Largent" was frequently heard over PA systems around the league. In 1978 Zorn led the conference in completions while Largent was tops in receptions. Not surprisingly, the Seahawks enjoyed their first winning season that year and were one win away from a division title. QB Dave Krieg understudied for Zorn beginning in 1980 and finally took over in 1983. The lessons Krieg had learned on the sidelines proved invaluable as he led the team to the playoffs for the first time and tossed three TD passes in the Seahawks' 31-7 victory over Denver in the wild-card game. The 1980s was the team's best decade: The Seahawks made it to the postseason four times, while winning the AFC West in 1988. As well, the always-dependable Largent blossomed into the one of the game's great receivers. By the time he retired in 1989 Largent, originally considered too slow to play pro football, owned the record for most career receptions (819), receiving yards (13,089) and most TD receptions (100). The 1990s weren't as kind to Seattle, with the team losing 10 or more games in three successive seasons from 1991 to '93. But in '99 the Seahawks finished atop the AFC West and gave fans reason to hope that good things were in store for the team in the new millennium.

Vital Stats

Stadium Address:
3800 Montlake Blvd., Seattle, Wash.
Phone: (206) 543-2246
Web: seahawks.com
Box Office: (206) 515-4791, Mon.–Fri., 8–6 (Seahawks ticket office); Husky Stadium box office sells tickets only on game days 8–4:30
Media Coverage:
Radio: KIRO (710 AM)
TV: KOMO (Channel 4), KIRO (Channel 7), KCPQ (Channel 13)
Training Facility:
Seahawks Headquarters, Northwest College, Kirkland, Wash.

Extra Point

• Seahawks Head Coach Mike Holmgren is a proven winner. In seven seasons with the Packers, Holmgren amassed a 75-37 regular season record, made it to the playoffs six times and won Super Bowl XXXI. In his first year in Seattle in 1999, he led the team to its first playoffs since 1988.

POSTSEASON
• AFC West Titles 2
(1988, '99)
• AFC Wild Card Berths.....3
(1983, '84, '87)

RETIRED NUMBERS
• 12th Man
(Seattle Fans) (12)
• Steve Largent (80)

RING OF HONOR
• Steve Largent (1989)
• Jim Zorn (1991)
• Dave Brown (1992)
• Pete Gross (1992)
• Curt Warner (1994)
• Jacob Green (1995)

TEAM RECORDS
Offense
• Brian Blades (1988–98)
Receptions (season): 81 (1994)

• **Norm Johnson (1982–90)**
Field Goals (career): 159
Points (career): 810
• **Dave Krieg (1980–91)**
Comp (career): 2,096
Pass Att. (career): 3,576
Passing Yards (career): 26,132
TD Passes (season): 32 (1984)
TD Passes (career): 195
300-Yard Games (career): 11
• **Steve Largent (1976–89)**
Receiving Yards (game): 261 (Oct. 18, 1987)
Receiving Yards (season): 1,287
Receiving Yards (career): 13,089
Receptions (career): 819
TDs (career): 101
• **Warren Moon (1997–98)**
Comp. (season): 313 (1997)
Passing Yards (season): 3,678 (1997)
• **Todd Peterson (1995–98)**
Field Goals (season): 34 (1999)
Points (season): 134 (1999)
• **Curt Warner (1983–89)**
Carries (season): 335 (1983)
Carries (career): 1,649
Rushing TDs (career): 55
• **Chris Warren (1990–97)**

"I've seen the glory of this game."
— Steve Largent, during his 1995 induction into the Hall of Fame

Rushing Yards (season): 1,545 (1994)
Rushing Yards (career): 6,706
TDs (season): 16 (1995)
100-Yard Games (career): 24

Defense
• **Terry Beeson (1977–81)**
Tackles (season): 153 (1978)
• **Dave Brown (1976–86)**
Int. (career): 50
• **Kenny Easley (1984)**
Int. (season): 10 (1981) (tie)
• **Jacob Green (1981–91)**
Forced Fumbles (career): 28
Sacks (career): 116
• **John Harris (1978–85)**
Int. (season): 10 (tie) (1981)
• **Eugene Robinson (1985–95)**
Tackles (career): 984
• **Michael Sinclair (1991–present)**
Sacks (season): 16.5 (1998)

Special Teams
• **Bobby Joe Edmonds (1986–88)**
Punt Return Yards (career): 1,010
• **Steve Broussard (1995–98)**
Kickoff Return Yards (career): 4,060

LEAGUE HONORS
NFL Defensive Player of the Year
• Kenny Easley (1984)
• Cortez Kennedy (1992)

NFL Coach of the Year
• Jack Patera (1978)
• Chuck Knox (1984)

Pro Football Hall of Fame
• Steve Largent (1995)

Veteran RB Ricky Watters provides the Seahawks with a solid ground attack.

Timeline

1974	1975	1976	1978	1983	1984	1987	1988	1989	1992	1997	1988	1999	2000
Seattle is awarded NFL expansion franchise for 1976	Team is named Seahawks; 59,000 season tickets sold in first month of availability	Franchise gets first win in week six	QB Jim Zorn has most completions in AFC; team enjoys first winning season	Rookie Curt Warner is top AFC back; team makes first playoff appearance	Seahawks win franchise-record 12 games	WR Steve Largent becomes NFL's all-time reception leader	Seahawks win first AFC West crown	Largent retires with NFL-record 177 straight games with at least one catch	Seattle loses record 14 games	Forty-year-old QB Warren Moon passes for 25 TDs	Team has second consecutive .500 season	Seahawks win AFC West with 9-7 record	RB Ricky Watters has sixth straight 1,000-yard season

210

Husky Stadium:
That Old College Try

Husky Stadium was built in 1920 as the home for the University of Washington Huskies football team. Situated above Union Bay, the stadium is one of the nation's most picturesque. Fans in the north upper deck are treated to panoramic views of Mount Rainier, the Olympic Mountain Range and downtown Seattle. Fans should remember that Seattle can be cold and damp later in the season: Proper clothing is essential. The Seahawks' new stadium is under construction and will be completed for the 2002 season.

CONCESSIONS

Food at Husky Stadium is, as can be expected at a university installation, pretty basic. Besides the usual stadium food of hot dogs, hamburgers and soft drinks, fans can sample some specialty coffee and ice cream, along with clam chowder sold by a local seafood chain.

GAME DAY TIPS
- **Gate hours:** Gates open two hours prior to kickoff.
- **Tailgating:** Parking lot gates open three hours before kickoff.
- **Weather:** Although Seattle's fall weather is decent, it rains more often than anywhere else in the U.S., with occasional heavy fog. It's always best to be prepared for showers and chilly temperatures.
- **Prohibited items:** Alcohol, video cameras, horns, glass bottles, cans and thermos bottles in excess of two quarts are not permitted in the stadium. Picnic baskets and ice chests are also pro-

hibited. Smoking is allowed only in designated areas.
- **Ticket tips:** Single-game tickets for Seahawks games should be readily available, although games against the Oakland Raiders sell out quickly.
- **Lost and found:** (206) 543-2246.

Stadium Facts

Opened: Nov. 27, 1920
Cost: $600,000
Capacity: 68,589
Type: Outdoor
Surface: Field turf
Home Sweet Home:
- With nearly 70 percent of stadium seats located between the end zones, the noise can get pretty loud. Opposing QBs find it particularly distracting when they are calling audibles.

Seating Plan

■	$68	■	$22
■	$60	■	$15
■	$48	**ATM** Not available	
■	$38	♿ Lower level	
■	$28		

Directions: Take I-5 or I-405 to Hwy. 520 and exit at Montlake Blvd. (Hwy. 513). Follow signs to stadium. **By Bus:** Bus service is available to University of Washington campus and stadium. Call Metro Transit at (206) 553-3000 for information. **Parking:** About 3,500 parking spots are available around Husky Stadium, with another 2,500 elsewhere on university grounds. About 100 spaces are available for disabled visitors. Park-and-ride service is available at Union Station and Safeco Field.

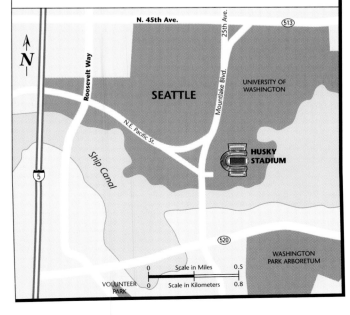

Nearby Hotels

▼▼▼ **Best Western University Tower** *(Hotel)*, 4507 Brooklyn Ave. NE (Seattle), (206) 634-2000, $99-$129
▼▼▼ **Ramada Inn Seattle at Northgate** *(Motel)*, 2140 N. Northgate Way (Seattle), (206) 365-0700, $87-$137
▼▼▼ **Silver Cloud Inn-University Village** *(Motel)*, 5036 25th Ave. NE (Seattle), (206) 526-5200, $110-$140
▼▼▼ **University Inn** *(Motor Inn)*, 4140 Roosevelt Way NE (Seattle), (206) 632-5055, $102-$144
▼▼▼▼ **The Westin Seattle** *(Hotel)*, 1900 5th Ave. (Seattle), (206) 728-1000, $139-$305

Nearby Restaurants

▼▼▼ **Chandlers Crabhouse & Fresh Fish Market** *(Seafood)*, 901 Fairview Ave. N. (Seattle), (206) 223-2722, $18-$28
▼▼ **Copper Sky Woodfire Grill & Bar** *(American)*, 550 NE Northgate Way (Seattle), (206) 363-9911, $11-$20
▼▼ **India House** *(Indian)*, 4737 Roosevelt Way NE (Seattle), (206) 632-5072, $9-$15
▼▼ **Mandarin Chef Restaurant** *(Chinese)*, 5022 University Way NE (Seattle), (206) 528-7596, $6-$9
▼▼ **Serafina** *(Italian)*, 2043 Eastlake Ave. E. (Seattle), (206) 323-0807, $10-$21

TAMPA BAY BUCCANEERS

EXPANSION TEAMS NEVER expect success to come quickly in the NFL, but no one warned the Tampa Bay Buccaneers exactly how rough it can be. Entering the league in 1976, the hapless Bucs stumbled and fumbled their way to a 0-14 record. By the time the final whistle mercifully ended their last game, Tampa Bay had been outscored 412-125 on the year and had suffered no fewer than five shutouts. The slide continued in 1977 as the team lost its first 12 matches and ran its winless streak to 26 games. However, the skid ended with a 33-14 win over the Saints, a game in which the Bucs set a NFL record by returning three interceptions for TDs. Success bred success and the team won five more times in 1978. But Tampa Bay really came into its own in 1979. Relying on sophomore QB Doug Williams, RB Ricky Bell and the stingiest defense in the NFL, the Bucs won the Central Division. The team had two more playoff appearances in 1981 and '82 before the lean years returned. From 1983 to '95 Tampa Bay never won more than seven games a season. The 1996 arrival of Tony Dungy as Head Coach buoyed the Bucs' floundering ship. Shoring up a punchless offense, the 1997 team relied on the one-two punch of backfield mates Warrick Dunn and Mike Alstott. The defense, led by Warren Sapp and Hardy Nickerson, allowed the fewest points in the NFC. Earning a wild-card berth, the team got to the NFC finals before losing to the Green Bay Packers. The Bucs made it back to the postseason in 1999 and again in 2000, building momentum for another run at the top.

Vital Stats

Stadium Address:
4201 N. Dale Mabry Hwy.,
Tampa, Fla.
Phone: (813) 870-2700
Web: buccaneers.com,
raymondjames.com/
stadium
Box Office:
(813) 879-2827,
Mon.–Fri., 8:30–5:30
Media Coverage:
Radio: WQYK (99.5 FM)
TV: WTOG (Channel 44)
Training Facility:
University of Tampa,
Tampa, Fla.

DT Warren Sapp is both a fearsome pass rusher and a smothering run-stopper.

POSTSEASON
• NFC Central Titles 4
(1979, '81, '99, 2000)
• NFC Wild Card Berths.....2
(1997, 2000)

Extra Point

• Buccaneer Cove, a huge pirate ship replica, is located in the north end zone. Whenever the Bucs score a TD, cannons blast confetti, mini-footballs and Buc merchandise into the stands.

TEAM HONORS
Retired
Numbers
• **Leroy Selmon (63)**

TEAM RECORDS
Offense
• **Mark Carrier (1987–92)**
Receptions (season): 86 (1989)
Receiving Yards (season): 1,422 (1989)
Receiving Yards (career): 5,018
100-Yard Games (season): 9 (1989)
• **Steve DeBerg (1984–87, 1992–93)**
Comp. (season): 308 (1984)
TD Passes (game): 5 (Sept. 13, 1987)
• **Trent Dilfer (1994–99)**
TD Passes (season): 21 (1997, '98)
• **Jimmie Giles (1978–86)**
TD Receptions (game): 4 (Oct. 20, 1985)
TD Receptions (career): 34
• **Martin Gramatica (1999–present)**
Field Goals (season): 28 (2000)
Points (season): 126 (2000)
• **Michael Husted (1993–98)**

Field Goals (career): 117
Longest Field Goal: 57 yards (Dec. 19, 1993)
Points (career): 502
• **Vinny Testaverde (1987–92)**
Pass Att. (career): 2,160
Comp. (game): 31 (Dec. 10, 1989)
Comp (career): 1,126
Passing Yards (career): 14,820
TD Passes (career): 77
• **James Wilder (1981–89)**
Combined Yardage (season): 2,229 (1984)
Receptions (career): 430
Rushing Yards (game): 219 (Nov. 6, 1983)
Rushing Yards (season): 1,544 (1984)
Rushing Yards (career): 5,957
Rushing TDs (season): 13 (1984)
Total TDs (career): 46
• **Doug Williams (1978–82)**
Passing Yards (game): 486 (Nov. 16, 1980)
Passing Yards (season): 3,563 (1981)

Defense
• **Cedric Brown (1976–84)**
Interceptions (season): 9 (1981)
Interceptions (career): 29
• **Hardy Nickerson (1993–99)**
Tackles (season): 214 (1993)
Tackles (career): 1,028

• **Lee Roy Selmon (1976–84)**
Sacks (season): 13 (1977)
Sacks (career): 78.5

Special Teams
• **Bobby Joe Edmonds (1995)**
Kick Return Yards (season): 1,147 (1995)
• **Karl Williams (1996–present)**
Punt Return Avg. (season): 21.1 (1996)
Punt Return Yards (season): 597 (1997)

LEAGUE HONORS
NFL Defensive Player of the Year
• Lee Roy Selmon (1979)
• Warren Sapp (1999)

NFL Rookie of the Year
• Santana Dotson (1992)
• Warrick Dunn (1997)

NFC Rookie of the Year
• Lawrence Dawsey (1991)

Pro Football Hall of Fame
• Lee Roy Selmon (1995)

"I'm in favor of it."
— Head Coach John MacKay,
when asked about his team's
execution after 0-14 1976 season

Timeline

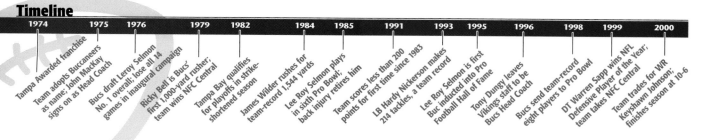

1974 — Tampa Awarded franchise
1975 — Team adopts Buccaneers as name; John MacKay signs on as Head Coach
1976 — Bucs draft Leroy Selmon No. 1 overall; lose all 14 games in inaugural campaign
1979 — Ricky Bell is Bucs' first 1,000-yard rusher; team wins NFC Central
1982 — Tampa Bay qualifies for playoffs in strike-shortened season
1984 — James Wilder rushes for team-record 1,544 yards
1985 — Lee Roy Selmon plays in sixth Pro Bowl; back injury retires him
1991 — Team scores less than 200 points for first time since 1983
1993 — LB Hardy Nickerson makes 214 tackles, a team record
1995 — Lee Roy Selmon is first Buc inducted into Pro Football Hall of Fame
1996 — Tony Dungy leaves Vikings staff to be Bucs Head Coach
1998 — Bucs send team-record eight players to Pro Bowl
1999 — DT Warren Sapp wins NFL Defensive Player of the Year; team takes NFC Central
2000 — Team trades for WR Keyshawn Johnson; finishes season at 10-6

RAYMOND JAMES STADIUM: COMFORT COMES FIRST

RAYMOND JAMES STADIUM IS BOTH an excellent football stadium and a great place to take the family. After being subjected to the hard benches in the old Tampa Stadium for 22 years, Bucs fans now watch games from the comfort of theater-style seats that come complete with cup holders. Two massive, high-definition videoboards (24 feet high by 92 feet long) at each end of the stadium show replays of the action at the stadium and even feature highlights from other NFL games.

CONCESSIONS

Fans at Raymond James Stadium have a variety of food choices to curb their hunger. In addition to the standard fare of pizza and hot dogs, the stadium's 600 food vendors offer lots of everything, from steaks and sausages to chicken wraps and vegetarian cuisine.

GAME DAY TIPS
- **Gate hours:** Gates open two hours prior to kickoff.
- **Tailgating:** The stadium boasts a grass parking lot, which opens three hours before kickoff.
- **Weather:** Tampa weather is semi-tropical, with comfortable fall temperatures. It's wise to tote along a windbreaker for evening games.
- **Prohibited items:** Cans, bottles and coolers, outside alcohol and food, umbrellas, strollers, and recording devices are prohibited. Smoking is allowed only in designated areas.
- **Ticket tips:** Seats for Bucs' games are always in short supply. Your best bet for buying tickets at the box office is to check on the availability of preseason games.
- **Lost and found:** (813) 673-4300.

Stadium Facts

Opened: Sept. 20, 1998
Cost: $168.5 million
Capacity: 65,647
Type: Open
Surface: Grass
Home Sweet Home:
- The Bucs' field ranked top overall in a survey of NFLers. Playing half their games on its impeccable grass surface means the Bucs are less prone to injuries from artificial turf.

Directions: From I-75 or I-4 west, take I-275 south. Exit 23-C (Himes Ave. N.) or 23-A (Dale Mabry Hwy.). By Bus: Several buses go to the stadium. For more information call Hillsborough Area Regional Transit (HART) at (813) 254-4278. **Parking:** There are about 10,000 spaces for cars in stadium lots and another 15,000 on surrounding streets such as Dale Mabry Hwy. and Dr. Martin Luther King Blvd. Wheelchair parking is available in lots A and C, while disabled parking is in lots 3 and 6.

Seating Plan

- ■ $60
- ■ $45
- ■ $45
- ▫ $34
- ■ $25
- ▪ .... N/A
- ATM **Sections 120, 144, 220, 245, 310, 335**
- ♿ **Throughout**

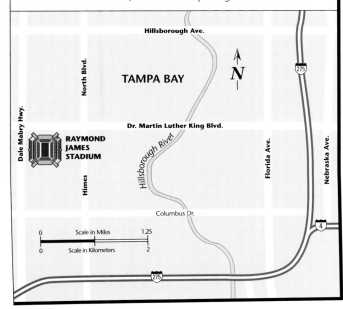

Nearby Hotels

▼▼▼ **Days Inn Airport Stadium** *(Motel)*, 2522 N. Dale Mabry Hwy. (Tampa), (813) 877-6181, $70-$105

▼▼▼ **Double Tree Hotel Tampa Airport-Westshore** *(Hotel)*, 4500 W. Cypress St. (Tampa), (813) 879-4800, $116-$134

▼▼▼ **Embassy Suites Hotel-Tampa/Airport/Westshore** *(Suite Hotel)*, 555 N. Westshore Blvd. (Tampa), (813) 875-1555, $129-$209

▼▼▼ **Holiday Inn Express Hotel & Suites Stadium/Airport** *(Motel)*, 4732 N. Dale Mabry Hwy. (Tampa), (813) 877-6061, $75-$95

▼▼▼▼ **Hyatt Regency Westshore** *(Hotel)*, 6200 Courtney Campbell Cswy. (Tampa), (813) 874-1234, $234-$259

Nearby Restaurants

▼▼▼▼ **Armani's** *(Northern Italian)*, 6200 Courtney Campbell Cswy. in the Hyatt Regency Westshore (Tampa), (813) 281-9165, $23-$35 (dinner only)

▼▼ **Crawdaddy's** *(American)*, 2500 Rocky Point Dr. (Tampa), (813) 281-0407, $16-$36 (dinner only)

▼▼ **Donatello** *(Northern Italian)*, 232 N. Dale Mabry Hwy. (Tampa), (813) 875-6660, $16-$29

▼▼ **Sam Seltzer's Steakhouse** *(Steak & Seafood)*, 4744 N. Dale Mabry Hwy. (Tampa), (813) 873-7267, $10-$19

▼▼▼ **Shula's Steakhouse** *(Steakhouse)*, 4860 W. Kennedy Blvd. in the Wyndham Westshore (Tampa), (813) 286-4366, $17-$33

TENNESSEE TITANS

RIGHT FROM THE START, the AFL Houston Oilers football team was built for excitement. Prior to the team's first season in 1960, owner Bud Adams signed Heisman Trophy running back Billy Cannon and lured QB George Blanda from the NFL. With Cannon bursting through opponents' lines and Blanda firing bombs, the Oilers exploded out of the blocks. When the dust settled three years later, Houston had won a pair of AFL crowns and had come within three points of taking a third. Apart from two playoff appearances in 1967 and '69 (both losses), Oilers fans didn't have much to cheer about until 1978. That year a massive rookie running back named Earl Campbell powered his way to a AFC-best 1,450 yards. One of the most intimidating backs in history, Campbell won MVP honors in his first three seasons and, not surprisingly, the Oilers made it to the playoffs all three years. The team's next run of greatness began in 1987, centering on a rifle-armed exile from the Canadian Football League. QB Warren Moon led to the Oilers postseason every year from 1987 to '93, but never to the Super Bowl. That momentous event would have to wait until 1999, when the team, now called the Titans and playing out of Nashville, lost Super Bowl XXXIV to the Rams by a score of 23-16. One of the most exciting championship games ever, Titans WR Kevin Dyson was tackled on the one-yard line as time expired. Led by superstars Eddie George, Steve McNair and Jevon "the Freak" Kearse, the Titans won the 2000 AFC Central crown and set themselves up as one of the NFL's elite teams.

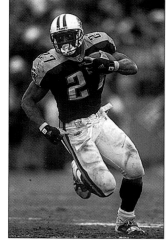

Eddie George provides the Titans with one of the NFL's most devastating running games.

> *"Somebody will always break your records. It's how you live that counts."*
>
> — *Earl Campbell, Hall-of-Fame running back*

POSTSEASON
- AFL Championships........2
(1960, '61)
- AFC Championships 1
(1998)
- AFC Central Titles 3
(1991, '93, 2000)
- AFC Wild Card Berths.....9
(1978, '79, '80, '87, '88, '89, '90, '92, '98)

RETIRED NUMBERS
- Earl Campbell (34)
- Jim Norton (43)
- Mike Munchak (63)
- Elvin Bethea (65)

Extra Point

• Trailing the Bills 16-15 with just seconds left in the 1999 AFC wild-card game, the Titans appeared to be finished. But Frank Wycheck took the ensuing kickoff and lateraled it to Kevin Dyson who was waiting near the sideline. Dyson sprinted 75 yards for the game-winning score in what is now referred to as "the Music City Miracle."

TEAM RECORDS
Offense
- **George Blanda (1960–66)**
TD Passes (game):
7 (Nov. 19, 1961)
TD Passes (season): 36 (1961)
- **Ernest Givins (1986–94)**
Receiving Yards (career):
7,935
Receptions (career): 542
- **Earl Campbell (1978–84)**
Rushing Yards (season):
1,934 (1980)
Rushing Yards (career): 8,574
Points (season): 136 (1998)
1,000-Yard Seasons: 5 (tie)
TDs (season): 19 (1979)
TDs (career): 73
- **Al Del Greco (1992–2000)**
Points (career): 1,060
Field Goals (season):
36 (1998)
Field Goals (career): 246
- **Eddie George (1996–present)**
Carries (season): 404
1,000-Yard Seasons: 5 (tie)
- **Charles Hennigan (1960–66)**
Receiving Yards (game):
272 (Oct. 13, 1961)
Receiving Yards (season):
1,746 (1961)
Receptions (season):

101 (1964)
TD Receptions (career): 51
- **Warren Moon (1984–93)**
Comp. (season): 404 (1991)
Comp. (career): 2,632
Passing Yards (game):
527 (Dec. 16, 1990)
Passing Yards (season):
4,690 (1991)
Passing Yards (career): 33,685
TD Passes (career): 196
300-Yard Games (career): 38
3,000-Yard Seasons: 6

Defense
- **Elvin Bethea (1968–83)**
Sacks (season): 16 (1973)
Sacks (career): 105
- **Freddie Glick (1961–66)**

Vital Stats

Stadium Address:
One Titans Wy.,
Nashville, Tenn.
Phone: (615) 565-4300
Web: titansonline.com
Box Office:
(615) 565-4200,
Mon.-Fri. 8:30-4:30
Media Coverage:
Radio: WGFX (104.5 FM)
TV: WKRN (Channel 2),
WTVF (Channel 5)
Training Facility:
Baptist Sports Park,
Nashville, Tenn.

Int. (season): 12 (tie) (1963)
- **Jim Norton (1960–68)**
Int. (career): 45
- **Mike Reinfeldt (1976–83)**
Int. (season): 12 (tie)

Special Teams
- **Billy "White Shoes" Johnson (1974–80)**
Punt Returns (career): 155
Punt Return Yards
(career): 2,040
- **Derrick Mason (1997–present)**
Punt Return Yards (season):
662 (2000)

LEAGUE HONORS
NFL MVP
- **Earl Campbell** (1978, '79, '80)

AFL MVP
- George Blanda (1961)

NFL Defensive Player of the Year
- Curley Culp (1975)

NFL Rookie of the Year
- Earl Campbell (1978)
- Eddie George (1996)

Pro Football Hall of Fame
- George Blanda (1981)
- Ken Houston (1986)
- Earl Campbell (1991)
- Charlie Joiner (1996)
- Mike Munchak (2001)

Timeline

1960	1961	1967	1973	1978	1980	1984	1991	1993	1994	1996	1998	1999	2000

- 1960: QB George Blanda leads team to AFL Championship
- 1961: Oilers repeat as AFL champs
- 1967: Team goes from last to first in one season
- 1973: Houston goes 1-13 for second consecutive year
- 1978: Rookie RB Earl Campbell leads AFC with 1,450 yards
- 1980: Campbell wins third straight MVP award; Oilers win wild-card spot
- 1984: QB Warren Moon wooed from Canadian Football League
- 1991: Moon completes NFL-record 404 passes
- 1993: Oilers make postseason for seventh straight season
- 1994: Moon leaves team; Oilers fall to 2-14
- 1996: Eddie George gains 1,368 yards; named NFL Rookie of the Year
- 1998: Franchise moves to Nashville
- 1999: Newly named Titans take wild-card spot with 13-3 record
- 2000: Heartbreaking loss in Super Bowl XXXIV; team rebounds in the following season with best record in NFL

ADELPHIA COLISEUM: NASHVILLE SKYLINE

SITUATED ON THE BANKS of the Cumberland River and over-looking downtown Nashville, Adelphia Coliseum is a beautiful venue in which to watch a football game. Adelphia has the state-of-the-art amenities expected by today's fans in an open-air stadium reminiscent of the game's golden years. While Adelphia's designers made sure they included the big-ticket items, such as two of the NFL's largest scoreboards, they also sweated out the details, such as seats that come with cup holders and pads of paper and pencils.

CONCESSIONS

Some 60 concession stands at Adelphia Coliseum offer fans the full range of stadium food, including burgers, hot dogs and popcorn. Franchise stands offer steaks, pizza and vegetarian food.

Stadium Facts

Opened: *Aug. 27, 1999*
Cost: *$292 million*
Capacity: *67,700*
Type: *Open*
Surface: *Grass*
Home Sweet Home:
• *In 1999 a national football magazine ranked Titans fans as the best in the NFL. Following one victory, Titans coach Jeff Fisher awarded the game ball to the team's faithful. The team went 9-0 in home games that year.*

GAME DAY TIPS

• **Gate hours:** Gates open two hours prior to kickoff.
• **Tailgating:** Parking lot gates open three hours before kickoff.
• **Weather:** Nashville is generally pleasantly mild, even during the early winter months. There are occasional light snowfalls, however, so check local forecasts and dress accordingly.
• **Prohibited items:** Coolers, bottles or cans, video cameras and umbrellas are prohibited. Hand-held still cameras are permitted. Smoking is allowed in designated areas.
• **Ticket tips:** Due to the team's popularity and recent success, the Titans have a limited number of single-game tickets available, usual-ly starting in July. They go quickly, however, particularly for games against AFC Central division rivals such as Jacksonville and Baltimore.
• **Lost and found:** (615) 565-4300.

Seating Plan

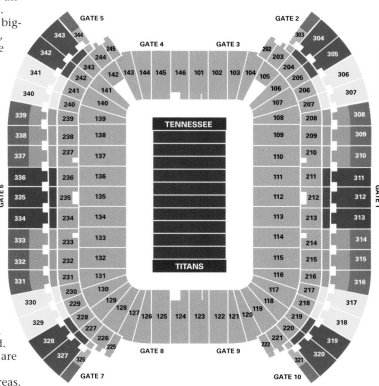

■	$40	▨	$18
■	$35	▨	$12
▨	$29	▨	Season tickets only
▨	$27	**ATM**	Gate 2, Gate 7
■	$25	♿	Throughout

Directions: *Exit I-65 at N. 1st St. or Interstate Dr. (from north) or Shelby St. (from south). Exit I-40 at Charlotte Ave., Church St. or Broadway. By Bus: Nashville Metro Transit Authority (MTA) shuttles operate from several locations around downtown Nashville. Call (615) 862-5950 for information.* **Parking:** *There are 7,500 parking spaces on-site, with 80 spots reserved for the disabled. More than 20,000 spots are also available near-by on S. 1st Ave., S. 5th Ave., Charlotte Ave., Commerce St. and Union St.*

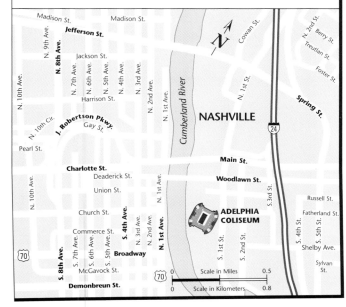

Nearby Hotels

▼▼ **Days Inn Downtown/Convention Center,** *(Motel)*, 711 Union St. (Nashville), (615) 242-4311, $79-$129
▼▼ **Ramada Inn Limited** *(Motel)*, 303 Interstate Dr. (Nashville), (615) 244-6690, $69-$129
▼▼▼ **Regal Maxwell House Nashville** *(Motor Inn)*, 2025 Metro Center Blvd. (Nashville), (615) 259-4343, $82
▼▼▼▼ **Renaissance Nashville Hotel** *(Hotel)*, 611 Commerce St. (Nashville), (615) 255-8400, $154-$215
▼▼▼▼ **Sheraton Nashville Downtown Hotel** *(Hotel)*, 623 Union St. (Nashville), (615) 259-2000, $95-$135

Nearby Restaurants

▼▼ **Big River Grille & Brewing Works** *(American)*, 111 Broadway St. (Nashville), (615) 251-4677, $7-$16
▼▼ **Demos' Steak & Spaghetti House** *(American)*, 300 Commerce St. (Nashville), (615) 256-4655, $13-$17
▼▼ **Market Street Brewery & Public House** *(American)*, 134 2nd Ave. N. (Nashville), (615) 259-9611, $7-$20
▼▼ **The Merchants** *(American)*, 401 Broadway St. (Nashville), (615) 254-1892, $15-$27
▼▼ **Stock Yard** *(Steakhouse)*, 901 2nd Ave. N. (Nashville), (615) 255-6464, $18-$35 (dinner only)

WASHINGTON REDSKINS

MIFFED BECAUSE THE BOSTON MEDIA had better coverage of a high-school field hockey game than his Boston Redskins' loss in the 1936 NFL championship, owner George Preston Marshall moved his team to Washington. The team subsequently won the 1937 crown, beginning a long-term love affair with the country's capital. But the team has had as many downs as it has had ups, including a 73-0 drubbing at the hands of the Chicago Bears in the 1940 title game. With his team facing the Bears again in the 1942 NFL championship, coach Ray Flaherty simply wrote "73-0" on the blackboard. A fired-up Sammy "Slingin'" Baugh threw for one TD and intercepted a Bears' pass in the end zone in Washington's 14-6 victory. Redskins faithful would have their patience tested after that — from 1949 to '68 the team had only two winning seasons. In 1971 Head Coach George Allen assembled a squad of battle-hardened veterans known as the "Over-the-Hill Gang." In the next six seasons, his team would make the playoffs five times. The 'Skins won their first Super Bowl in 1982, with game MVP John Riggins gobbling large chunks of real estate behind his massive offensive line, called "the Hogs." Washington won another championship in 1987, this time behind the strong arm of QB Doug Williams, who engineered a record 35 points in the second quarter. It was another quarterback, Mark Rypien, who next led the Redskins to the NFL summit in 1991, with 292 yards in the air and two TD strikes.

Vital Stats

Stadium Address:
FedEx Field, FedEx Way, Landover, Md.
Phone: (301) 276-6000
Web: redskins.com
Box Office: (301) 276-6050, Mon.–Fri. 9–5
Media Coverage:
Radio: WJFK (106.7 FM)
TV: WTTG (Channel 5), WJLA (Channel 7)
Training Facility:
Redskins Park, Ashburn, Va.

POSTSEASON
Super Bowl
Championships 3
(1982, '87, '91)
NFL Championships 2
(1937, '42)
NFC Championships..........5
(1972, '82, '83, '87, '91)
NFC East Titles....................7
(1972, '82, '83, '84, '87, '91, '99)
Wild Card Berths................7
(1971, '73, '74, '76, '86, '90, '92)

Stephen Davis led the Redskins with 11 touchdowns in 2000.

RETIRED NUMBERS
• Sammy Baugh (33)

TEAM RECORDS
Offense
• **Sammy Baugh (1937–52)**
QB Rating (season): 109.7 (1945)
TD Passes (career): 187
• **Stephen Davis (1996–present)**
Rushing Yards (season): 1,405 (1999)
• **Brad Johnson (1999–2000)**
Comp. (season): 316
Passing Yards (game): 471 (Dec. 26, 1999)
• **Sonny Jurgensen (1964–74)**
QB Rating (career): 85.0
TD Passes (season): 31 (1967)
• **Bobby Mitchell (1962–68)**
Receiving Yards (season): 1,436 (1963)
• **Art Monk (1980–93)**
Receiving Yards (career): 12,026
Receptions (season):

Extra Point

• In 1943, playing on offense, defense and special teams, Sammy Baugh completed a rare triple crown, leading the NFL in passing, punting and interceptions. Baugh was a charter member of the Hall of Fame.

106 (1984)
Receptions (career): 888
• **Mark Moseley (1974–86)**
Field Goals (season): 33 (1983)
Field Goals (career): 263
Points (Season): 161 (1983)
Points (career): 1,207
• **John Riggins (1976–79, 1981–85)**
Carries (career): 1,988
Rushing Yards (career): 7,472
TDs (season): 24 (1983)
• **Jay Schroeder (1984–87)**
Passing Yards (season): 4,109 (1986)
• **Charley Taylor (1964–77)**
TDs (career): 90
• **Joe Theismann (1974–85)**
Comp. (career): 2,044
Passing Yards (career): 25,206

Defense
• **Darrell Green (1983–present)**
Int. (career): 53
• **Dexter Manley (1981–89)**
Sacks (season): 18 (1986)
Sacks (career): 97.5
• **Dan Sandifer (1948–49)**
Int. (season): 13 (1948)

LEAGUE HONORS
NFL MVP
• Larry Brown (1972)
• Mark Moseley (1982)
• Joe Theismann (1982, '83)
• John Riggins (1983)

NFL Rookie of the Year
• Charley Taylor (1964)

Super Bowl MVP
• John Riggins (1982)
• Doug Williams (1987)
• Mark Rypien (1992)

Pro Football Hall of Fame
• Sammy Baugh (1963)
• Earl "Curly" Lambeau (1963)
• George Preston Marshall (1963)
• Otto Graham (1965)
• Bill Dudley (1966)
• Cliff Battles (1968)
• Wayne Millner (1968)
• Turk Edwards (1969)
• Vince Lombardi (1971)
• Ray Flaherty (1976)
• Deacon Jones (1980)
• Sam Huff (1982)
• Sonny Jurgensen (1982)
• Bobby Mitchell (1983)
• Charley Taylor (1984)
• Ken Houston (1986)
• Stan Jones (1991)
• John Riggins (1992)
• Joe Gibbs (1996)
• Paul Krause (1998)

"Ron may be President, but tonight I'm King."
— Redskin RB John Riggins, moments after being named MVP of Super Bowl XVII during the term of Ronald Reagan

Timeline

1932	1933	1937	1942	1955	1963	1971	1975	1983	1985	1988	1991	1999

Boston Braves football team goes 4-4 in first season

Braves change name to Redskins; play at Fenway Park

Team moves to Washington; wins first NFL Championship

Washington beats Bears for NFL championship, spoiling Chicago's bid for perfect season

Redskins score 21 points in 137 seconds against the Eagles

Bobby Mitchell sets team mark with 1,436 receiving yards

Team makes playoffs for first time in 25 years

QB Sonny Jurgensen retires after 18 NFL seasons

Skins beat Dolphins 27-17 in Super Bowl XVII

Joe Theismann suffers career-ending broken leg on Monday Night Football

QB Doug Williams leads team to 42-10 romp over Denver in Super Bowl XXII

Washington and Head Coach Joe Gibbs win third Super Bowl title

Redskins finish atop the NFC East

FedEx Field:
Getting Better All the Time

With a seating capacity of 85,000, FedEx Field is the largest outdoor stadium in the NFL. Good thing, too, as the Redskins have sold out every home game, regular season and playoffs, for the last 34 years. In 1999 new owner Daniel M. Snyder invested in detailed renovations. The improvements included replacing metal rails with glass rails to provide unobstructed views and upgrading the stadium sound system. Outside the stadium, the parking area was restructured to improve the flow of traffic.

CONCESSIONS

FedEx Field features a range of stadium food, including a number of fast food franchises. Visitors looking for something different should try the Memphis Barbecue and root beer from the Wild Goose Landing Microbrewery.

Vegetarian items are available.

GAME DAY TIPS

• **Gate hours:** Gates open three hours prior to kickoff.
• **Tailgating:** Parking lots open four hours before kickoff. Starting two hours prior to the game, field management will begin filling the lots from front to back. Arrive early if you want to meet people at a specific location.
• **Weather:** Early fall in Washington is comfortably warm. Late fall and early winter are usually snowy.
• **Prohibited items:** Bottles, jugs, coolers or other hard containers, alcohol, food, drinks, umbrellas, noise-making devices, and obscene or indecent clothing are

prohibited. Banners and video cameras are permitted. Smoking is allowed only in designated areas.
• **Ticket tips:** Redskins games have been sold out since 1966 so there are no single-

game tickets available at the box office. This is one of the largest stadiums in the NFL, so some of the intimacy may be lost in the higher seats.
• **Lost and found:** (301) 276-6000.

Stadium Facts

Opened: *Sept. 14, 1997*
Cost: *$250 million*
Capacity: *85,000*
Type: *Open*
Surface: *Grass*
Home Sweet Home:
• *While not as intimate as the old RFK Stadium, FedEx Field is still a noisy place when the fans get rocking. Skins fans are adept at drowning out opposing QB's snap counts.*

Directions: Take I-495/95 to exit 16 and turn west at Arena Dr. Or, take E. Capitol St., turn north onto Summerfield Blvd. and follow to stadium. By Bus: Washington Metro Area Transit Authority provides public transportation to FedEx Field. Shuttle buses leave for the stadium from the Addison Rd., Cheverly and Landover stations. Call WMATA at (202) 637-7000 for more information. **Parking:** Parking for approximately 6,000 cars is available nearby at U.S. Airways Arena and a shuttle from there runs to FedEx Field. Lots at FedEx Field are for permit holders only. Disabled parking for permit holders is available in lots E1 and H1.

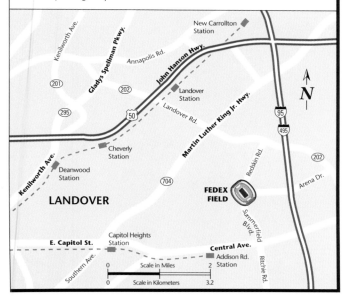

Seating Plan

▫	$75	■	N/A
▫	$65	**ATM**	**Sections 103, 116, 123, 124,**
■	$55		**131, 139, 303, 324, 330,**
■	$50		**334, 406, 422, 434, 449**
■	$40	♿	**Throughout**

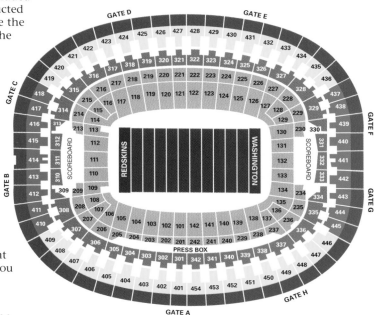

Nearby Hotels

▼▼ **Days Inn-Lanham** (*Motor Inn*), 9023 Annapolis Rd. (Lanham, Md.), (301) 459-6600, $70
▼▼ **Doubletree Club Hotel Washington DC-Largo** (*Motor Inn*), 9100 Basil Ct. (Largo, Md.), (301) 773-0700, $89-$129
▼▼▼ **Courtyard by Marriott-New Carrollton** (*Motor Inn*), 8330 Corporate Dr. (Landover, Md.), (301) 577-3373, $84-$148
▼▼▼ **The Greenbelt Marriott** (*Hotel*), 6400 Ivy Ln. (Greenbelt, Md.), (301) 441-3700, $89-$199
▼▼▼ **Holiday Inn Express Camp Springs** (*Motel*), 4783 Allentown Rd. (Camp Springs, Md.), (301) 420-2800, $99

Nearby Restaurants

▼▼ **94th Aero Squadron** (*American*), 5240 Paint Branch Pkwy. (College Park, Md.), (301) 699-9400, $13-$25
▼▼ **Royal Jade** (*Chinese*), 7701 Greenbelt Rd. (Greenbelt, Md.), (301) 441-8880, $7-$20
Sam's American Bar & Grill (*American*), 9421 West Largo Dr. in the Hampton Inn Washington/I-95 (Landover), (301) 808-0200
▼▼ **The Wayfarer Restaurant** (*Northern Italian*), 7401 Surratts Rd. in the Colony South Hotel & Conference Center (Clinton, Md.), (301) 856-3343, $12-$25

Hoc

KEY

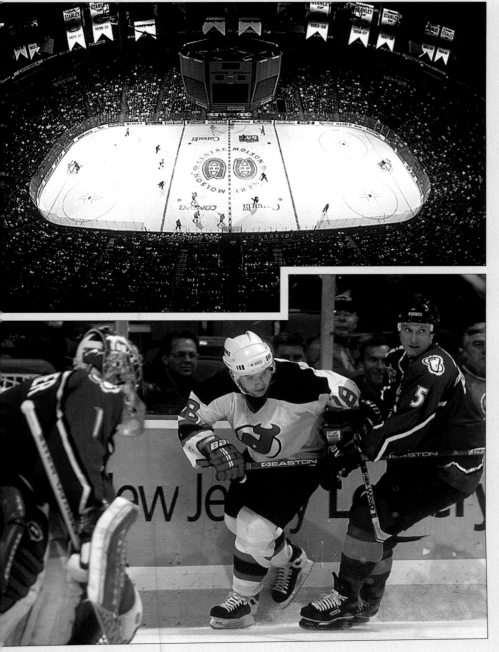

EASTERN CONFERENCE
Atlantic Division
New Jersey Devils
New York Islanders
New York Rangers
Philadelphia Flyers
Pittsburgh Penguins

Northeast Division
Boston Bruins
Buffalo Sabres
Montreal Canadiens
Ottawa Senators
Toronto Maple Leafs

Southeast Division
Atlanta Thrashers
Carolina Hurricanes
Florida Panthers
Tampa Bay Lightning
Washington Capitals

WESTERN CONFERENCE
Central Division
Chicago Blackhawks
Columbus Blue Jackets
Detroit Red Wings
Nashville Predators
St. Louis Blues

Northwest Division
Calgary Flames
Colorado Avalanche
Edmonton Oilers
Minnesota Wild
Vancouver Canucks

Pacific Division
Mighty Ducks of Anaheim
Dallas Stars
Los Angeles Kings
Phoenix Coyotes
San Jose Sharks

THE GAME

HOCKEY WAS BORN ON frozen ponds, lakes and rivers. And while the pro game is now played entirely in high-tech arenas, outdoor rinks can still be found everywhere there is snow, be they dotting the playgrounds of urban centers or on sections of iced-over lakes shoveled clear of snow by children before they begin to play. Wayne Gretzky himself, hockey's greatest player, began practicing the very moves he would one day use to tie NHL defenders in knots in his own backyard, flooded over and tended to by his father Walter. No matter how extravagant the light shows and pyrotechnics become in NHL arenas, no matter how loud the piped-in music or how jumbo the Jumbotron, hockey will always be a game of humble origins and proudly so.

For a game that relies so heavily on speed, many of hockey's most memorable images are forever frozen in time. There are the grainy black-and-white photographs of the game's earliest participants, helmetless men in wool sweaters and worn leather skates, made to look much smaller than today's players in large part due to their flimsy, almost nonexistent pads. This was hockey at the turn of the 20th century, a rough and tumble affair in which a participant needed to be deft on his skates and quick with his fists.

Georges Vezina looks characteristically unflappable in old photographs. A standout goalie for the Montreal Canadiens from 1910 to '25 and one of the best of all time, Vezina was known for his incredible cool under even the heaviest barrage of pucks. Diagnosed with tuberculosis prior to the 1925–26 season, Vezina didn't tell his teammates for fear that it would upset them. Instead he showed up to the Canadiens' dressing room in late March of '26 at his usual game-day time. When he found his equipment laid out for him as it always was before games, the stoic Vezina finally broke down and cried. Then, gathering his jersey under his arm, he left, never to return. A few days later, he was dead.

Eddie Shore, one of hockey's greatest defensemen, patrolled the blue line for the Boston Bruins throughout the '30s. Shots of Shore show a raw-boned man with angry eyes stopping opposing puck carriers dead in their tracks with ferocious body checks. While his notoriously short fuse led to numerous on-ice brawls, Shore was a blinding talent as well, the only defenseman in history to win four MVP awards.

THE ROCKET'S RED GLARE

When it came to fire in the eyes, none burned brighter than Maurice "Rocket" Richard. One of the most explosive players ever to lace up a pair of skates, the Rocket is best remembered as the first man to score 50 goals in a season — accomplishing this feat in the 50-game 1944–45 season. Normally a soft-spoken man, Richard was a whirling dervish on the ice, particularly when he swooped in on enemy goaltenders, black eyes ablaze. This was hockey of the 1940s and '50s, when players such as Richard, Gordie Howe and Bernie "Boom-Boom" Geoffrion were revolutionizing the game. Free-wheeling firebrand hockey was replacing the more traditional defensive game.

While hockey had started to open up and establish itself as the fastest game in the world, there was a group of courageous, if not a little crazy, players who were determined to keep games as low scoring as possible: the goalies. At the time, goaltending equipment was rudimentary at best and masks were unheard of. Crouched down low to face the blistering slap shots of the league's best snipers, men such as Terry Sawchuck, Turk Broda, Lorne "Gump" Worsley and Jacques Plante literally sacrificed their bodies — and faces — for the good of their team.

It was Plante who, after leaving a game to have the torn lip and nose used to block an Andy Bathgate shot stitched together, returned to the ice sporting a strange looking fiberglass mask that he usually wore in practice. A sign of hockey's blood-and-guts creed, many fans and members of the media criticized Plante when he began wearing the mask in games full-time.

Dominik Hasek's unorthodox style has made him one of the NHL's best goalies.

HIGH-FLYING THRILLS

While today's fans wouldn't see anything wrong with Plante's wanting to protect himself from a frozen puck winging in at 100 miles per hour, hockey has always put a premium on toughness. In the old days, the game's marquee players were often also the roughest. Looking to slow down Rocket Richard, the Rangers once called on the services of enforcer Bob "Killer" Dill. Richard and Dill dropped the gloves twice in their only meeting, with the Rocket, the biggest star of his era, knocking out Dill both times. In a 1956 playoff match against the Leafs, Detroit's Ted "Terrible" Lindsay displayed similar machismo by ignoring death threats to score the tying and winning goals. After the game-winning marker, a smiling Lindsay held his stick like a machine gun and rat-a-tat-tatted the booing Toronto fans.

But more than just a game of glorified roller derby, hockey at its best can be one of the most thrilling sports in the world. Darting through traffic and stick-handling their way around potential bone-rattling disaster, the game's skilled players are high-flying acrobats best exem-

Guy Lafleur of the Montreal Canadiens, one of the great stars of the 1970s, battles for a loose puck.

plified by the now-famous photo of Bobby Orr scoring the Cup-winning goal against St. Louis in 1970. Tripped while in mid-shot, Orr's flying body is parallel to the goal post, arms raised in victory, mouth open in childlike glee. Today it is players such as Mario Lemieux, Joe Sakic and Jaromir Jagr who pull the fans from their seats.

Of course, when it comes to debates about who is hockey's most skillful player, there can be only one answer: Wayne Gretzky. When "the Great One" finally retired in 1999, he held or shared some 61 NHL records. But he did more than break records; he obliterated them. The only player to score 200 points in a season, Gretzky did it an amazing four times. Whereas few players ever reach the 1,000-point plateau during their careers, Gretzky hung up his skates with 2,857 career points — more than 1,000 ahead of No. 2, Gordie Howe.

DREAMS OF THE CUP

As much as people remember the superstars, it is the great teams that are truly revered. The Ottawa Senators of the 1920s, Detroit in the early 1950s, the Leafs of the 1960s, the Canadiens of the 1970s, and the Islanders and Oilers of the 1980s — all powerful squads that managed to

Great Games in Great Venues

Montreal Forum: *What some people consider to be the greatest hockey game ever played was actually an exhibition game that ended in a 3-3 tie. On New Year's Eve 1975, in the midst of a short North American tour, the Soviet Union's powerful Central Red Army squad took on the high-flying Montreal Canadiens at Montreal's legendary Forum. The game featured up and down action and fierce goal-mouth scrambles. With the score tied late in the game, the Canadiens peppered the Red Army net, only to be denied by the acrobatics of goaltender Vladislav Tretiak. The crowd walked away stunned. Their heroes had been unable to dispatch the Soviets, but they had seen the game of hockey the way it was meant to be played.*

Chicago Stadium: *In nearly 50 years from the birth of the NHL in 1917, only three players had managed to score 50 goals in a single NHL season. One of them, Chicago's Bobby Hull, became the first ever to score more than 50. On March 12, 1966, the Blackhawks faithful in Chicago Stadium erupted as Hull notched his 51st goal of the season against New York Rangers netminder Cesare Maniago. Hull would finish the season with 54 goals.*

Detroit Olympia: *Hockeytown USA was the site of an act of incredible courage during the 1964 Stanley Cup finals. On April 23, despite breaking his ankle earlier in the game, Toronto defenseman Bobby Baun scored the winning goal in overtime of game six to give his Maple Leafs a 4-3 win over the hometown Red Wings. Two days later he played all of game seven with his leg taped and frozen by doctors. After Toronto clinched the deciding game to take the Stanley Cup, Baun was taken by ambulance to the hospital and his ankle was placed in a cast for the next six weeks.*

Maple Leaf Gardens, Toronto: *The fans of the 1970's Toronto Maple Leafs didn't have a great deal to cheer about, but on Feb. 7, 1976, they got to witness one of hockey's greatest individual feats. Maple Leafs captain Darryl Sittler set a record that still stands today, collecting 10 points (6 goals, 4 assists) in a 11-4 rout of the Boston Bruins. Bruins shellshocked goaltender Dave Reece never played another NHL game.*

Boston Garden: *In the 1938-39 Stanley Cup semifinals against the New York Rangers, Boston's Mel Hill earned himself the nickname to beat all others. Hill's overtime goals in game one in New York and two days later in game two back in Boston gave the Bruins a 2-0 lead in the series. After the Rangers rallied to send the series to a seventh and ultimate game back in the unfriendly confines of the Boston Garden, yet another overtime loss sent them packing and the Bruins were off to the finals against Toronto where they would capture their second Stanley Cup. The overtime hero in game seven? Mel "Sudden Death" Hill, of course.*

maintain their level of excellence over the years. In terms of sheer dominance, however, no team can touch the mighty Canadiens of the late 1950s, a squad that won an unprecedented five-straight Stanley Cups.

And ultimately, the Stanley Cup is what hockey really is all about. Almost right from the time children start teetering down the ice in their first tiny pair of skates, they think about hoisting the silver chalice over their head just like their heroes. Every pickup game becomes a Stanley Cup game seven, every goal the one that wins it and every homemade rink the place where, for a brief moment anyway, children's dreams come true.

KEY MOMENTS

The oldest of the major North American sports, hockey's origins are shrouded in mystery. Many historians believe it began in northern Europe. The following is a list of some the major developments that have helped shape the game we love today.

- **1820s Brits Take to the Ice**
Mad about field hockey, the residents of rural Bury Fen in England popularize a winter version of the sport played on ice. The game was called "bandy."
- **1870s Hockey Comes Across the Pond**
British soldiers stationed in Halifax, N. S., regale local residents with organized hockey matches. The game moves farther inland when students from Montreal's McGill University begin playing on a regular basis.
- **1892 Lord Stanley Donates Cup**
Lord Stanley of Preston, then the Governor-General of Canada, donates a silver bowl to be awarded to the best amateur hockey team in the country.
- **1904 Hockey Goes Pro**
The first pro hockey league is established in Michigan's upper peninsula region only to fold three years later.
- **1917 NHL is Born**
The National Hockey League is formed and is made up of five teams, the Montreal Canadiens, the Montreal Wanderers, the Ottawa Senators, the Toronto Arenas and the Quebec Bulldogs.
- **1922 Last Seven-on-Seven Game**
The last seven-on-seven pro game is won by the Toronto St. Patricks 6-0 over the Vancouver Millionaires. From then on, all games are played with five skaters a side.
- **1924 Canadiens Take Team's First Cup**
The Montreal Canadiens win their first NHL Stanley Cup. By century's end they will win a record 24 titles.
- **1930 Goalie Dons Mask**
After having his nose broken by a Howie Morenz shot, goalie Clint Benedict dons a makeshift mask. He discards it two games later because it impairs his visibility.
- **1937 Morenz Dies**
One of the NHL's first superstars, Howie Morenz, dies unexpectedly in the hospital after suffering a broken leg in a game. More than 10,000 fans paid their last respects as his body lay in state at the Montreal Forum.
- **1945 The Rocket Soars**
Maurice "Rocket" Richard is the first player in NHL history to score 50 goals in a season.
- **1946 Howe Plays First in Long String**
Rookie Gordie Howe plays first game in a career that will span a record 26 NHL seasons. When "Mr. Hockey" retires in 1980, he will have played in 1,767 NHL games.
- **1956 Hockey's First Great Dynasty**
Led by stars like "Rocket" Richard, Jacques Plante, Jean Beliveau and Doug Harvey, the Canadiens win first of five-straight Stanley Cups.
- **1959 Plante Makes Mask in Vogue**
All-Star goalie Jacques Plante develops mask after being badly cut on shot by Andy Bathgate. After going on a 10-game undefeated streak, Plante wears mask full-time.
- **1967 NHL Expands**
The era of the Original Six ends as the NHL welcomes six new teams to the league.
- **1969 Espo Cracks 100**
The Bruins' Phil Esposito is first NHL player to score 100 points in a single season.

Mario Lemieux's comeback in 2000–01, was instrumental in helping the Pittsburgh Penguins to the Eastern Conference Finals.

- **1970 Orr Revolutionizes Defenseman Position**
Bobby Orr stuns the hockey world by becoming first NHL defenseman to lead all scorers. The incomparable Orr would repeat this feat in the 1974–75 season.
- **1972 WHA Joins Pro Hockey Fray**
The 12-team World Hockey Association begins operations in direct competition with the NHL.
- **1975 Flyers Bully Their Way to Second Cup**
Philadelphia's infamous "Broad Street Bullies" steamroll their way to second straight Stanley Cup.
- **1979 Canadiens Dynasty, Part II**
Guy Lafleur, Larry Robinson and Ken Dryden lead Canadiens to fourth consecutive NHL championship.
- **1980 Gretzky Era Begins**
Nineteen-year-old Wayne Gretzky is youngest player to score 100 points in a season. Two years later Gretzky will set a new record by scoring 92 goals.
- **1983 Islanders Keep Rolling**
Led by sniper Mike Bossy and All-Star defenseman Denis Potvin, the New York Islanders take fourth straight Cup.
- **1986 The Great One Gets Even Greater**
Wayne Gretzky scores a record 215 points in the regular season and leads his Oilers to Stanley Cup.
- **1993 Mario Beats Cancer and Rest of NHL**
After missing a month to receive radiation treatment for cancer, Mario Lemieux returns to win NHL scoring title.
- **1998 Gretzky Alone at the Top**
Wayne Gretzky becomes first player to score 1,000 NHL goals (878 in regular season and 122 in playoffs).
- **2001 Colorado Takes Stanley Cup**
Goalie Patrick Roy leads the Avalanche to the franchise's second Stanley Cup title, defeating the New Jersey Devils.

Hockey Hall of Fame

HOCKEY'S ROOTS

Although hockey greats have been inducted into the Hockey Hall of Fame since 1945, there wasn't an actual building until 1961. That original structure proved to be too cramped for the ever-growing collection, so in 1993 a new complex expanded the Hall from 7,000 square feet to 52,000. Further expansion has seen the complex grow to more than 57,000 square feet and the extra room certainly has not gone to waste. The Hockey Hall of Fame is a wonderful place to visit, with a wide range of artifacts and exhibits that will please both young and old.

STORIES BEHIND THE GEAR

Of course, the centerpiece of the Hall is its collection of artifacts. More than just old bits of hockey gear, however, each piece of equipment speaks of hockey's formative years, be it the hand-held bells used by referees or a jersey of the defunct, but wonderfully named, California Golden Seals. And the items also tell the stories of the men who played the game. There are the simple leather skates worn by Maple Leafs defenseman Bill Barilko when he fired the Stanley Cup-winning goal past Montreal's Gerry McNeil in 1951. Barilko was killed in a light plane crash in the off-season, but his body, lost in the wilds of northern Ontario, wasn't recovered until 11 years later — the same year that the Leafs won their next Stanley Cup. Elsewhere fans can trace the development of the goalie mask, from Jacques Plante's earliest models right through to the streamlined, elaborately painted models of today.

One of the Hall's most popular stops is the Wayne Gretzky exhibit. With the help of Gretzky's father Walter, curators designed a display that covered "the Great One's" career, from the very first pair of flimsy skates he wore as a two-year-old right through to the full set of streamlined equipment he wore in his very last professional game. A hockey net on display looks like any other until fans realize that it was into this net that Gretzky fired his 802nd goal, the goal that moved him past his boyhood idol, Gordie Howe, as history's most prolific marksman. Other items include the key to the City of Edmonton and cereal boxes that bear Gretzky's likeness on the front.

The Grand Old Houses of Hockey display celebrates the NHL's most cherished venues — many of which have gone the way of the wrecking ball. Classic photos and historic artifacts transport fans to the great arenas, such as the Montreal Forum, the Boston Garden and the Detroit Olympia. Turnstiles, ticket booths, programs and ticket stubs are on display beside players' mementos such as the wool cap that Auriele Joliat sported as a dashing star of the Montreal Canadiens in the 1920s and the knee brace Bobby Orr was wearing when he scored his famous Cup-winning goal in 1970.

OLD AND THE NEW

One of the Hall's most unusual exhibits is a replica of the dressing room of hockey's most storied franchise, the Montreal Canadiens — re-created in exacting detail, down to the physiotherapy equipment and piles of dirty laundry. The Canadiens' famous red, white and blue jerseys hang in front of each locker and on the wall is a listing of each Montreal roster through the years.

Visitors can also relax and take in some of hockey's greatest moments at the Hall's beautiful theater. The high-resolution screen and surround sound help make fans feel like part of the action up on-screen. One recent film highlighted hockey's greatest dynasties, from the Ottawa Senators of 1919 to '27 to the Oilers juggernaut of the mid- to late '80s. A new film shows three players going through NHL training camp.

Interactive displays abound at the Hall. In one area, fans can don goalie equipment and get between the pipes to face a barrage of foam pucks fired at them at NHL speeds. Another game allows participants to test their scoring touch against an on-screen goalie using a real stick and pucks or, tables turned, control the goalie's movements as an animated attacker swoops in on them. In the Broadcast Zone, visitors can choose a classic hockey game of the past and settle in behind the microphone to try their hand at play-by-play.

Of course, the highlight of the Hall of Fame is the World Com Great Hall, where the life and career of each enshrinee is celebrated. Appropriately, the center of the room is dominated by showcases containing the NHL trophies, including the most coveted of them all, the world-famous Stanley Cup.

Vital Stats

Address:
BCE Place,
30 Yonge St.,
Toronto, Ont.
Phone: InfoLine (416) 360-7765, Switchboard (416) 360-7735
Web Site: hhof.com
Hours: Fall–spring Mon.–Fri. 10–5, Sat. 9:30–6, Sun. 10:30–5; summer Mon.–Sat. 9:30–6; closed Dec. 25, Jan. 1, Induction Day; special hours for March break, Christmas break
Admission: Adult $12; senior citizen $8; youth 4-18 $8; child under 4 free.
Directions: From Buffalo, take 427 south to QEW east (downtown Toronto). Continue east onto the Gardiner Expwy. Exit at Yonge St. and go north to Front St. From Detroit, cross at the Windsor Tunnel and take Hwy. 401 east. Take Hwy. 427 south to QEW and go east. Continue on the Gardiner Expwy. east. Go north on Yonge St. to Front St.

A display case in the popular Wayne Gretzky exhibit.

THE STARS

THE FOLLOWING IS A LIST OF THE NHL's most coveted records. Although hockey is often a game of intangibles, for sheer numbers alone you can see why Wayne Gretzky is considered by many to be the greatest player of all time. Active players are identified with an asterisk. For all career records, the nearest active players have been included so you can gauge how today's stars rank with the greats of eras past.

Service Records

Seasons (career):
1. Gordie Howe 26
2. Alex Delvecchio 24
   Tim Horton 24
4. Ray Bourque 22
   Mark Messier* 22

Games (career):
1. Gordie Howe 1,767
2. Larry Murphy* 1,615
3. Ray Bourque* 1,612

Scoring Records

Goals (career):
1. Wayne Gretzky 894

Possessing almost every NHL scoring record, Wayne Gretzky is aptly called "the Great One."

2. Gordie Howe 801
3. Marcel Dionne 731
6. Mark Messier* 651
7. Brett Hull* 649

Goals (season):
1. Wayne Gretzky
   92 (1981–82)
2. Wayne Gretzky,
   87 (1983–84)
3. Brett Hull*
   86 (1990–91)

Assists (career):
1. Wayne Gretzky 1,963
2. Ray Bourque 1,169
3. Ron Francis* 1,137

Assists (season):
1. Wayne Gretzky
   163 (1985–86)
2. Wayne Gretzky
   135 (1984–85)
3. Wayne Gretzky
   125 (1982–83)

Points (career):
1. Wayne Gretzky 2,857
2. Gordie Howe 1,850
3. Mark Messier* 1,781
5. Ron Francis* 1,624

Points (season):
1. Wayne Gretzky
   215 (1985–86)
2. Wayne Gretzky
   212 (1981–82)
3. Wayne Gretzky
   208 (1984–85)

Goaltending Records

Wins (career):
1. Patrick Roy* 484
2. Terry Sawchuk 447
3. Jacques Plante 435
7. Mike Vernon* 383

Wins (season):
1. Bernie Parent
   47 (1973–74)
2. Bernie Parent
   44 (1974–75)
   Terry Sawchuk
   44 (1951–52)
   Terry Sawchuk
   44 (1950–51)

Shutouts (career):
1. Terry Sawchuk 103
2. George Hainsworth 94
3. Glenn Hall 84
16. Ed Belfour* 57
17. Dominik Hasek* 56
18. Patrick Roy* 52

Shutouts (season):
1. George Hainsworth
   22 (1928–29)
2. Hal Winkler
   15 (1927–28)
   Alex Connell
   15 (1925–26)
   Alex Connell
   15 (1927–28)
   Tony Esposito
   15 (1969–70)

Goals Against Avg. (career):
1. Alex Connell 1.91
2. George Hainsworth
   1.93

3. Chuck Gardiner 2.02
7. Martin Brodeur* 2.21
9. Dominik Hasek* 2.24

Goals Against Avg. (season):
1. George Hainsworth
   0.92 (1928–29)
2. George Hainsworth
   1.06 (1927–28)
3. Alex Connell
   1.13 (1925–26)

Penalty Records

Penalty Minutes (career):
1. Dave "Tiger" Williams
   3,966
2. Dale Hunter 3,565
3. Marty McSorley 3,381
6. Bob Probert* 3,124

Penalty Minutes (season):
1. Dave Schultz
   472 (1974–75)
2. Paul Baxter
   409 (1981–82)
3. Mike Peluso
   408 (1991–92)

Team Records

Stanley Cup Championships:
1. Montreal Canadiens
   24
2. Toronto Maple Leafs
   13
3. Detroit Red Wings 9

Point Total (season):
1. Montreal Canadiens
   132 (1976–77)
2. Detroit Red Wings
   131 (1995–96)
3. Montreal Canadiens
   129 (1977–78)

Winning Pct. (season):
1. Boston Bruins
   .875 (1929–30)
2. Montreal Canadiens
   .830 (1943–44)
3. Montreal Canadiens
   .825 (1976–77)

Winning Streak:
1. Pittsburgh Penguins
   17 games (1992–93)
2. New York Islanders
   15 games (1981–82)
3. Boston Bruins
   14 games (1929–30)

Undefeated Streak:
1. Philadelphia Flyers
   35 games (1979–80)
2. Montreal Canadiens
   28 games (1977–78)
3. Philadelphia Flyers
   23 games (1975–76)
   Boston Bruins
   23 games (1940–41)

Leagues and Divisions

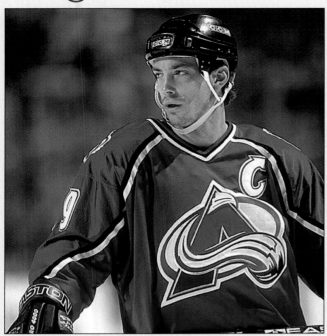

Joe Sakic is one of the NHL's brightest stars.

MYSTERIOUS BEGINNINGS

While the exact origin of hockey is murky, one thing is clear: The game did not originate in Canada. Many sports historians point to northern Europe as hockey's probable birthplace. There, where field hockey has long been a popular sport, many participants would play year-round, taking to the frozen ponds in the winter. In 17th-century Holland, people played a game called "kolven" and British poet William Cowper referred to boys playing a game "they call Hockey" as early as 1785.

Hockey made its way across the Atlantic in the late 19th century with British soldiers stationed on Canada's east coast. Organized hockey games began popping up in the 1870s and North America's first league was formed in Kingston, Ontario, in 1885.

LORD STANLEY'S CUP

In 1892 the Governor General of Canada, Lord Stanley of Preston, donated a silver chalice to be awarded each year to the country's top amateur hockey club. The trophy, now known as the Stanley Cup, is North America's oldest sporting prize, predating the National Hockey League by some 25 years.

The National Hockey League itself rose from the ashes of the old National Hockey Association and comprised five franchises, including the Montreal Canadiens and the Toronto Arenas (later the Maple Leafs). At the end of each season the top NHL team would square off against the champion from the Pacific Coast League to determine who would raise Lord Stanley's Cup. But the PCL folded prior to the 1926, making the Stanley Cup the sole possession of the NHL.

THE LEAGUE GROWS

The 1926–27 season also saw the league grow from seven to 10 franchises and divide itself into the Canadian and American Divisions. This arrangement would last through the 1937–38 season. Hard times and the clouds of war in Europe saw the league pared down to just seven teams in 1938–39. With the disappearance of the Brooklyn Americans following the 1941–42 season, the league was down to a half dozen teams.

The "Original Six" era of hockey, which included the Boston Bruins, Chicago Blackhawks, Detroit Red Wings, Montreal Canadiens, New York Rangers and Toronto Maple Leafs, ran until 1967 and is considered by many to be "the Golden Age of Hockey." Luminaries such as Gordie Howe, Rocket Richard, Ted Lindsay, Andy Bathgate, Jean Beliveau and Bobby Hull helped forge fierce rivalries that still burn today.

The league doubled in size prior to the 1967 season and the 12-team NHL was divided into two divisions. The most successful of the expansion teams has been the Philadelphia Flyers, winner of back-to-back Cups in 1973–74 and 1974–75.

THREAT FROM THE WHA

In 1972 the World Hockey Association played its first games. A direct competitor with the NHL, the WHA gained instant credibility when it lured megastar Bobby Hull from the NHL. Although the league would fold in 1979, it broke important new ground by actively seeking and signing European talent. Prior to the 1979–80 season, four WHA teams — Edmonton Oilers, New England Whalers, Quebec Nordiques and Winnipeg Jets — were admitted to the NHL. The league's most recent expansion saw the addition of teams in Columbus and Minnesota for the 2000–01 campaign.

NHL HARDWARE

In addition to the Stanley Cup, the league awards no fewer than 15 major trophies at season's end. The greatest single-season haul was achieved by Bobby Orr, who in 1969–70 walked off with four trophies: Hart, Ross, Norris and Smythe. Here is a list of the awards:

Art Ross Trophy: Player with the most total points.
Hart Trophy: Player judged most valuable to his team.
Lady Byng Trophy: Player who exhibits both high skill level and sportsmanship.
Vezina Trophy: League's top goaltender as voted by the general managers of each team.
William M. Jennings Trophy: Awarded to the goaltender(s) of the team that allows the fewest goals.
Calder Trophy: Rookie of the year.
James Norris Trophy: NHL's best defenseman.
Maurice "Rocket" Richard Trophy: Top goal scorer.
Bill Masterton Trophy: For perseverance and dedication to hockey.
Frank J. Selke Trophy: League's top defensive forward.
King Clancy Trophy: Leadership on and off the ice.
Lester Patrick Trophy: For outstanding service to hockey in the United States.
Lester B. Pearson Trophy: League's outstanding player as chosen by the NHL Players Association.
Jack Adams Trophy: NHL's best coach.
Conn Smythe Trophy: Playoff MVP.

MIGHTY DUCKS OF ANAHEIM

OWNED BY THE WALT DISNEY COMPANY and named after a successful Disney film, the Anaheim Mighty Ducks began their first season in 1993 with considerable fanfare. Roosting in a brand new arena and donning jerseys that sported a logo of a goalie mask shaped like a duck's beak, the team proved to be anything but traditional. For one thing, the Ducks didn't suffer from first-year malaise like so many other expansion teams. Applying coach Ron Wilson's system, the Ducks surprised everyone by remaining in the playoff hunt until late into the season. The team's 33 wins were the most ever by a first-year team and, most importantly, placed the Ducks ahead of that other southern California team, the Wayne Gretzky-led Los Angeles Kings. Although the next season was shortened by a strike, it marked the emergence of the franchise's greatest player, Paul Kariya. A fast skater with a sniper's eye, the rookie led the team in scoring. Midway through the 1995–96 season, the Ducks engineered a trade that brought Finnish scoring sensation Teemu Selanne to Anaheim. The prolific line mates spelled trouble for NHL goalies, with Selanne finishing second in the scoring race in 1996–97 and Kariya placing third. Qualifying for the playoffs, the high-flying Ducks beat Phoenix in the opening round before losing to the eventual Cup champion Red Wings. The Selanne/Kariya duo finished second and third in scoring again in 1998–99 and drove the team to the playoffs again. But with Selanne traded in 2001 it remains to be seen if Kariya and the rest of the Ducks will soar again.

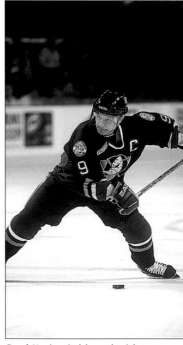

Paul Kariya is blessed with a quick and powerful shot.

POSTSEASON
• Playoff Appearances........2
(1996–97, 1998–99)

TEAM RECORDS
• **Bob Corkum (1993–96)**
Goals by a Center
(season): 23 (tie) (1993–94)
• **Todd Ewen (1993–96)**
Penalty Minutes (season): 285
• **Guy Hebert (1993–2000)**
Games by a Goalie
(career): 441
Goals Against Avg.

(season): 2.42
Minutes by a Goalie
(career): 25,206
Saves (season): 1,961
(1995–96)
Saves (career): 10,816
Shutouts (season): 6 (1998–99)
Shutouts (career): 27
Wins (season): 31 (1999–2000)
Wins (career): 173
• **Paul Kariya (1994–present)**
Assists (season): 62 (1998–99)
Assists (career): 288
Game-Winning Goals
(season): 10 (tie) (1996–97)
Games (career): 442
Goals by a Left Winger
(season): 50 (1995–96)
Goals by a Rookie (season):
18 (1994–95)
Goals (career): 243
Plus/Minus (season): +36
(1996–97)
Points by a Left Winger
(season): 108 (1995–96)
Points (career): 531
Power-Play Goals (career): 73
Shorthanded Goals
(career): 14
Shorthanded Points
(career): 19
Shots (season): 429 (1998–99)
Shots (career): 1,909
• **David Karpa (1994–98)**
Penalty Minutes (career): 788
• **Dimitri Mironov
(1996–98)**
Assists (game): 5
(Dec. 12, 1997)

> ### "In the back of my mind, Anaheim was the only one I wanted."
> — Nineteen-year-old Paul Kariya, after being drafted by the Ducks

• **Fredrik Olausson
(1995–96, 1998–2000)**
Assists by a Defenseman
(season): 40 (1998–99)
Goals by a Defenseman
(season): 16 (1998–99)
Points by a Defenseman
(season): 56 (1998–99)
• **Steve Rucchin
(1995–present)**
Assists by a Center (season):
48 (1996–97)
Goals by a Center (season):
23 (tie) (1998–99)
Points by a Center (season):
67 (1996–97)
• **Teemu Selanne
(1996–2001)**
Assists by a Right Winger
(season): 60 (1998–99)
Game-Winning Goals
(season): 10 (tie) (1997–98)
Game-Winning Goals
(career): 37 (tie)
Goals (season): 52 (1998–99)
Hat Tricks (career): 9
Points (season): 109 (1996–97)
Power-Play Goals (season):
25 (1998–99)

Slap Shot

• Paul Kariya really is the Ducks' franchise player, leading the team in career goals, assists and points. The team's first draft pick in 1993, he proved worthy of the high selection. His 464 points in the '90s is tops among expansion team players of the decade.
• Anaheim city politicians took a big gamble and had Arrowhead Pond built before the city was granted a NHL franchise. For a while it looked like the arena might go unused until Disney's Michael Eisner got involved.

Vital Stats

Stadium Address:
2695 E. Katella Ave.,
Anaheim, Calif.
Phone: (714) 704-2400
Web: mightyducks.com,
arrowheadpond.com
Box Office:
(714) 704-2500, Mon.–Fri.
10–6, Sat. 10–4, three
hours prior to Sun. events
Media Coverage:
Radio: XTRA (690 AM)
TV: KCAL (Channel 9),
Fox Sports Net 2
Training Facility:
Disney ICE,
Anaheim, Calif.

LEAGUE HONORS
Maurice Richard Trophy
• Teemu Selanne (1998–99)

Lady Byng Trophy
• Paul Kariya (1995–96,
1996–97)

Timeline

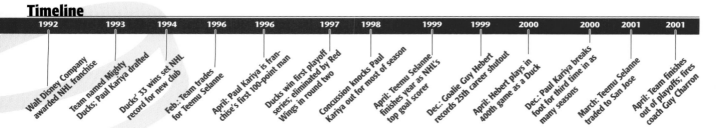

1992	1993	1994	1996	1996	1997	1998	1999	1999	2000	2000	2001	2001

Walt Disney Company awarded NHL franchise

Team named Mighty Ducks; Paul Kariya drafted

Ducks' 33 wins set NHL record for new club

Feb.: Team trades for Teemu Selanne

April: Paul Kariya is franchise's first 100-point man

Ducks win first playoff series; eliminated by Red Wings in round two

Concussion knocks Paul Kariya out for most of season

April: Teemu Selanne finishes year as NHL's top goal scorer

Dec.: Goalie Guy Hebert records 25th career shutout

April: Hebert plays in 400th game as a Duck

Dec.: Paul Kariya breaks foot for third time in as many seasons

March: Teemu Selanne traded to San Jose

April: Team finishes out of playoffs; fires coach Guy Charron

ARROWHEAD POND OF ANAHEIM: TOP FLIGHT ARENA

FANS WHO FLOCK to Arrowhead Pond to watch the Mighty Ducks are in for a first-rate sporting experience. To begin with, the Pond is a beautiful building, with a granite facade and sweeping green glass archways over the north and south entrances. Inside some 200,000 square feet of imported marble adorns the public concourses. In the bowl itself, excellent sight lines are enhanced by comfortable seating. This is especially true in the Plaza level, where fans sit very close to the action in luxurious padded seats.

CONCESSIONS

Arrowhead Pond offers fans an eating experience unlike any other. All the old arena favorites are here, of course, but there are also french fries with a variety of toppings, chicken tacos and sourdough bread bowls overflowing with clam chowder. Wash it down with a variety of imported and domestic beers.

GAME DAY TIPS
• **Gate hours:** Gates open one hour prior to opening faceoff.
• **Prohibited items:** Outside food or beverages, alcohol, coolers, video or audio recording equipment, professional cameras and laser pointers are strictly forbidden. Digital cameras are allowed. No signs are allowed and strollers are permitted only in the Suites. Smoking is not allowed inside the arena.
• **Ticket tips:** Anaheim tickets are usually available, but some games sell out well in advance. Games against the crosstown rival Kings are usually popular, as are Sunday Family Nights and the last game of the season. A good value is the first row of the Terrace. While high up, it's also close enough to see the game well. Avoid seats high in the corners and under the press box.
• **Lost and found:** (714) 704-2400.

Arena Facts

Opened: *June 17, 1993*
Cost: *$120 million*
Capacity: *17,174*
Home Sweet Home:
• *The Ducks attract boisterous crowds. Tradition dictates that a goal by the home team is celebrated by thousands of fans tooting their duck callers. Management encourages the practice by selling the callers at the arena.*

Seating Plan

PLAZA CONCOURSE	
■ Glass	$175
■ Rear Glass	$120
■ Main	$75
TERRACE CONCOURSE	
■ Lower	$44
■ Main	$32.50
■ Rear	$27

■ Rear Value	$15
CLUB CONCOURSE	
■ Club Seats	$75
■ Club/Plaza Suites	Call for prices
■ Disabled	Call for prices
ATM Sections 201, 401	
♿ Throughout	

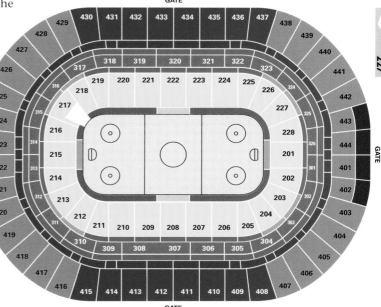

Directions

Directions: *Take Hwy. 57 to Ball Rd. or Katella Ave. exit. Go east and follow signs to arena. By Public Transportation: Orange County Transit Authority (OCTA) has bus service to Arrowhead Pond. Call (714) 636-7433 for more information. An Amtrak station is within walking distance. Call (800) USA-RAIL for information. Parking: There are 4,500 spaces available at the arena, of which 60 in lots 1 and 2 are reserved for disabled patrons. Extra parking is available on W. Katella Ave., The City Dr. and W. City Blvd.*

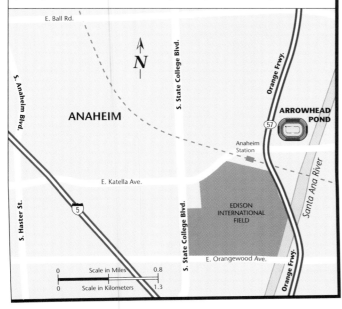

Nearby Hotels

▼▼▼ **Anaheim Towneplace Suites by Marriott** *(Motel)*, 1730 S. State College Blvd. (Anaheim), (714) 939-9700, $69-$99
▼▼▼ **Comfort Inn & Suites** *(Motel)*, 300 E. Katella Blvd. (Anaheim), (714) 772-8713, $89-$119
▼▼▼ **Hilton Suites Anaheim/Orange** *(Suite Hotel)*, 400 N. State College Blvd. (Orange), (714) 938-1111, $105-$210
▼▼▼ **Peacock Suite Resort** *(Suite Motel)*, 1745 S. Anaheim Blvd. (Anaheim), (714) 535-8255, $94-$130
▼▼▼ **Residence Inn by Marriott** *(Apartment)*, 1700 S. Clementine St. (Anaheim), (714) 533-3555, $199-$329

Nearby Restaurants

▼▼ **The Catch** *(Steak & Seafood)*, 1929 S. State College Blvd. (Anaheim), (714) 634-1829, $13-$25
▼▼▼ **Citrus City Grille** *(American)*, 122 N. Glassell St. (Orange), (714) 639-9600, $12-$24
▼▼ **King's Fish House** *(Seafood)*, 1521 W. Katella Ave. (Orange), (714) 771-6655, $10-$17
▼▼▼ **Mr. Stox Restaurant** *(American)*, 1105 E. Katella Ave. (Anaheim), (714) 634-2994, $16-$28
▼▼▼ **Rafaello Ristorante** *(Northern Italian)*, 1998 N. Tustin Ave. (Orange), (714) 283-8230, $11-$19

ATLANTA THRASHERS

THE GRANTING OF THE THRASHERS franchise to the city of Atlanta marked the return of NHL hockey to the Georgia capital. The previous franchise, the Flames, had been sold to new ownership in Calgary in 1980. The problems that brought about the sale of Atlanta's Flames — lack of a television contract and a financial crisis in the ownership — should not be issues this time around with Time Warner, Inc. as owner. And if there was any doubt about fan support for the team, it was quieted right from the start when a capacity crowd turned out to cheer for the Thrashers in its very first game. By the end of the season, the team had set an expansion record for attendance, attracting 705,389 fans to Philips Arena. What they saw on the ice was a lot of potential and little success, a common result for first-year franchises. The lineup was short on stars, but it did feature proven NHL netminder Damian Rhodes in goal and wily veteran captain Ray Ferraro up front. Ferraro, in fact, has had a rebirth in Atlanta. In the team's first season, his 19 goals matched his output from the previous two seasons combined. In 2000–01 he recorded 76 points, his best total in 1992. But Atlanta's hopes are not only pinned on their aging captain. Instead fans are looking to Patrik Stefan, the young Czech phenom the team chose first overall in the 1999 entry draft, to shine. Stefan showed flashes of brilliance in both his first two seasons, but the jury is still out on whether he can lift the franchise to its first playoff appearance any time soon. However, after 14 wins in year one and 23 in year two, the franchise definitely appears headed in the right direction.

Stadium Address:
1 Philips Dr.,
Atlanta, Ga.
Phone: (404) 878-3000
Web: atlantathrashers.com,
philipsarena.com
Box Office:
(404) 584-7825,
9:30–5 Mon.–Fri., weekend
events call for hours
Media Coverage:
Radio: WQXI (790 AM)
TV: WUPA (Channel 69),
Turner South
Practice Facility:
The IceForum, Duluth, Ga.

Team Records

• Donald Audette 1999–2001)
Goals (season): 32 (2000–01)
Plus/Minus (career): -1
Points by a Right Wing (season): 71 (2000–01)
Power-Play Goals (season): 13 (2000–01)
Shots (season): 187 (2000–01)
• Andrew Brunette (1999–present)
Game-Winning Goals (season): 4 (2000–2001)
Game-Winning Goals (career): 6
Points by a Left Wing (season): 59 (2000–01)

Shooting Pct. (season): 21.5 (1999–2000)
• Shean Donovan (1999–present)
Shorthanded Goals (season): 3 (2000–01)
Shorthanded Goals (career): 3
• Scott Fankhouser 1999–present)
Saves Pct. (season): .900 (2000–01)
• Ray Ferraro (1999–present)
Assists (season): 47 (2000–01)
Assists (career): 72
Games (career): 162
Goals (career): 48
Points (season): 76 (2000–01)
Points (career): 120
Power-Play Assists (season) 17 (2000–01)
Power-Play Goals (career): 21
Shots (career): 342
• Milan Hnilicka (2000–present)
Shutouts (season): 2 (2000–01)
Shutouts (career): 2
Wins (season): 12 (2000–01)
Wins (career): 12 (tie)
• Frantisek Kaberle (2000–present)

Plus/Minus (season): +11 (2000–01)
• Denny Lambert (1999–present)
Penalty Minutes (career): 434
• Gord Murphy (1999–present)
Blocked Shots (season): 132 (2000–01)
• Jeff Odgers (2000–present)
Games (season): 82 (2000–01)
Penalty Minutes (season): 226 (2000–01)
• Damian Rhodes (1999–present)
Minutes (season): 2,072 (2000–01)
Minutes (career): 3,633

Saves (season): 1,113 (2000–01)
Saves (career): 1,815
Shots Faced (season): 1,129 (2000–01)
Wins (career): 12
• Chris Tamer (1999–present)
Games (season): 82 (2000–01)
• Yannick Tremblay (1999–present)
Assists by a Defenseman (season): 21 (1999–2000)
Goals by a Defenseman (season): 10 (1999–2000)
Points by a Defenseman (season): 31 (1999–2000)
Points by a Defenseman (career): 43

Slap Shot

• The Thrasher name was inspired by Time Warner exec Ted Turner. He suggested the team be named for the Brown Thrasher, the official state bird of Georgia. The team describes the logo this way: "Our new 'look' is entertaining and fun; redefines sports logos; is truly surprising; communicates fierce determination and speed; and appeals to the entire community."

"No team has produced so much while being paid so little this season."

— Guy Curtright, sportswriter, on the 2000–01 Thrashers

Timeline

1997	1998	1999	2000	2001
NHL awards franchise to Atlanta	Thrashers unveil team logo	Team loses first regular season game to Devils	Team finishes first season with 14 wins	Veteran Ray Ferraro leads team with 76 points

Experienced veteran Ray Ferraro captains the Thrashers.

PHILIPS ARENA: CLOSE TO THE ACTION

PHILIPS ARENA HAS SEVERAL FEATURES that make it a special venue. For one, it is connected, practically and aesthetically, to the CNN Center and the city around it, blending seamlessly into the downtown Atlanta area. It also features a 400-foot interior street with numerous food, store and entertainment outlets. The seating also represents a bit of a breakthrough, with 60 percent of seats located on the lowest level. The seating rises or lowers depending on the event. The upper-level seats are closer to the action than in any other major venue.

CONCESSIONS

Most of the concession stands at Philips Arena are located along an indoor street running the length of the stadium. In addition to the standard fare, fans can feast on calzones, Buffalo wings, Texas chili and various grilled sandwiches.

Arena Facts

Opened: *Sept. 24, 1999*
Cost: *$213 million*
Capacity: *18,575*
Home Sweet Home:
• *The proximity of the fans to the ice at Philips Arena is a boon to the hometown Thrashers. The intense and very partisan atmosphere and the crowd noise can be both a distraction for visiting teams and a boost for the Thrashers.*

GAME DAY TIPS

• **Gate hours:** Gates open one hour prior to opening faceoff.
• **Prohibited items:** Glass bottles, aluminum cans, coolers, thermoses, outside food, and alcoholic beverages are prohibited. Banners and laser pointers are also forbidden. Smoking is allowed only in designated areas.
• **Ticket tips:** Thrashers tickets are quite popular. The team usually sells out against the Penguins, and it does well in games against Philadelphia and Detroit. The $10 seats are an especially good value here, as they are located closer to the ice than in other arenas. The team usually holds back some $10 tickets until two hours before game time, so it's worth trying to get some, even for potential sellouts.
• **Lost and found:** (404) 871-8960.

Seating Plan

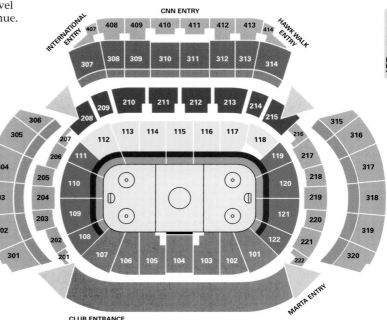

▨ Call for info	▨ $40
■ Call for info	▨ $36
░ $75	▨ $24
▩ $68	▨ $10
▩ $58	**ATM** Sections 208, 214
▩ $54	♿ Throughout
▨ $48	

Directions: *Exit I-75/85 south at Williams St. Turn right onto International Blvd. to arena. Exit I-75/85 north at International Blvd. and follow to arena. Exit I-20 at Windsor/Spring St. Follow to Marietta, turn left and follow signs to arena. By Public Transportation: A train station and several buses provide quick access to the arena. Call Metropolitan Atlanta Rapid Transit Authority (MARTA) at (404) 848-4800 for more information.* **Parking:** *There are 4,345 arena spaces (all deck lots have wheelchair-accessible spaces). More lots are on Jones Ave, Marietta St., Techwood Dr. and International Blvd.*

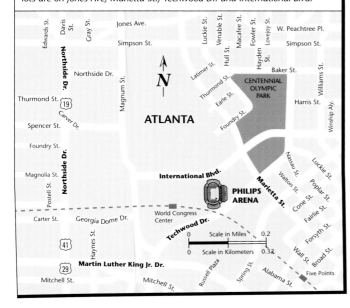

Nearby Hotels

▼▼▼ **Courtyard by Marriott-Downtown** *(Motor Inn)*, 175 Piedmont Ave. NE (Atlanta), (404) 659-2727, $89-$179
▼▼▼ **Fairfield Inn by Marriott-Downtown** *(Motel)*, 175 Piedmont Ave. NE (Atlanta), (404) 659-7777, $79-$139
▼▼▼ **Hampton Inn & Suites Atlanta Downtown** *(Motel)*, 161 Spring St. (Atlanta), (404) 589-1111, $79-$109
▼▼▼ **Omni Hotel at CNN Center** *(Hotel)*, 100 CNN Center (Atlanta), (404) 659-0000, $99-$224
▼▼ **Travelodge-Downtown** *(Motel)*, 311 Courtland St. NE (Atlanta), (404) 659-4545, $75-$135

Nearby Restaurants

▼▼▼ **The Atlanta Grill** *(Continental)*, 181 Peachtree St. NE in The Ritz-Carlton, Atlanta (Atlanta), (404) 659-0400, $16-$25
▼▼▼ **Hsu's Gourmet Chinese Restaurant** *(Chinese)*, 192 Peachtree Center Ave. (Atlanta), (404) 659-2788, $10-$20
▼▼▼▼ **Nikolai's Roof** *(Continental)*, 255 Courtland St. NE in the Hilton Atlanta & Towers (Atlanta), (404) 221-6362, $67-$116 (dinner only)
▼▼ **Pittypat's Porch** *(Regional American)*, 25 International Blvd. NW (Atlanta), (404) 525-8228, $19-$25 (dinner only)
[FYI] **The Varsity** *(American)*, 61 North Ave. NE (Atlanta), (404) 881-1706, $4-$10

BOSTON BRUINS

ONE OF THE OLDEST FRANCHISES in NHL history, the Boston Bruins is also one of the most storied. Finishing dead last in its inaugural 1924–25 season, the team battled its way to the NHL penthouse in 1928–29 with a sweep of the Rangers in the Stanley Cup finals. That squad was led by the "Dynamite Line" of Cooney Weiland, Dit Clapper and Dutch Gainor, hard-as-nails Eddie Shore on defense and Cecil "Tiny" Thompson between the pipes. But it wasn't until 1938–39 that the Bruins sipped champagne from the Stanley Cup again. This time the hero was Mel Hill, whose three over-time goals in the opening round of the playoffs earned him the nickname "Sudden Death." After another title in 1940–41, Boston had to endure a horrible drought, making it to the finals just five times in the next 28 seasons and coming away empty-handed each time. But the dry spell ended in dramatic fashion when defenseman Bobby Orr arrived on the scene in the 1960s. Unlike many of the lumbering defensemen of the time, Orr was a powerful skater and a brilliant stickhandler who had a knack for potting goals. In 1969–70 Orr became the first defenseman to lead the NHL in scoring, winning the league's MVP. Teamed up with another scoring machine, Phil Esposito, Orr spurred the Bruins to the Cup finals, winning it with his overtime goal in game four. Orr would repeat his heroics two years later, when he scored the Cup-winner in game six against the Rangers. Sadly, Orr's brilliant career was cut short by knee injuries and, not coincidentally, the Bruins have yet to win another Cup.

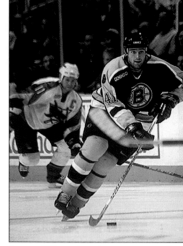

Jason Allison has become one of the NHL's regular scoring leaders.

POSTSEASON
- **Stanley Cup Championships** 5
(1928–29, 1938–39, 1940–41, 1969–70, 1971–72)
- **Wales Conference Championships** 2
(1987–88, 1989–90)
- **Eastern Division Championships** 3
(1970–71, 1971–72, 1973–74)
- **American Division Championships** 7
(1927–28, 1928–29, 1929–30, 1930–31, 1932–33, 1934–35, 1937–38)

HONORED NUMBERS
- Edward Shore (2)
- Lionel Hitchman (3)
- Bobby Orr (4)
- Aubrey Clapper (5)
- Phil Esposito (7)
- John Bucyk (9)
- Milt Schmidt (15)

TEAM RECORDS
- **Ray Bourque (1979–2000)**
Assists (career): 1,111
Games (career): 1,518
Points (career): 1,506
- **Johnny Bucyk (1957–78)**
Goals (career): 545
- **Phil Esposito (1967–76)**
Goals (season): 76 (1970–71)
Hat Tricks (career): 26
Points (season): 152 (1970–71)
50-Goal Seasons: 5
100-Point Seasons: 6 (tie)

"Forget about style, worry about results."

— Bobby Orr, who revolu-tionized the way defensemen play

- **Terry O'Reilly (1971–85)**
Penalty Minutes (career): 2,095
- **Bobby Orr (1966–76)**
Assists (season): 102 (1970–71)
Goals By Defenseman (season): 46 (1974–75)
100-Point Seasons: 6 (tie)
- **Cecil Thompson (1928–39)**
Shutouts: (career): 74
Wins (career): 252
- **Hal Winkler (1926–28)**
Goals Against Avg.

Slap Shot
- *The Hall of Fame has too many ex-Bruins to list here. In all, some 47 enshrinees have ties to the Bruins.*
- *Gerry Cheevers was one of the first goalies to deco-rate his mask. Whenever a puck hit him in the mask, he would paint a new scar on it to indicate what kind of damage would have been done to his face.*

(career): 1.56
Shutouts (season): 15 (1927–28)

LEAGUE HONORS
Hart Trophy
- Eddie Shore (1932–33, 1934–35, 1935–36, 1937–38)
- Bill Cowley (1940–41, 1942–43)
- Milt Schmidt (1950–51)
- Phil Esposito (1968–69, 1973–74)
- Bobby Orr (1969–70, 1970–71, 1971–72)

Art Ross Trophy
- Ralph Weiland (1929–30)
- Milt Schmidt (1939–40)
- Bill Cowley (1940–41)
- Herb Cain (1943–44)
- Phil Esposito (1968–69, 1970–71, 1971–72, 1972–73, 1973–74)
- Bobby Orr (1969–70, 1974–75)

James Norris Trophy
- Bobby Orr (1967–68, 1968–69, 1969–70, 1970–71, 1971–72, 1972–73, 1973–74, 1974–75)
- Ray Bourque (1986–87, 1987–88, 1989–90, 1990–91, 1993–94)

Vezina Trophy
- Cecil Thompson (1929–30, 1932–33, 1935–36, 1937–38)

Vital Stats

Stadium Address:
150 Causeway St., Boston, Mass.
Phone: (617) 624-1000
Web: bostonbruins.com, fleetcenter.com
Box Office: (617) 624-BEAR, Mon.–Sun. 11–7, off-season Mon.–Fri. 9–5
Media Coverage:
Radio: WBZ (1030 AM)
TV: UPN (Channel 38), NESN
Practice Facility:
Ristuccia Arena, Wilmington, Mass.

- Frank Brimsek (1938–39, 1941–42)
- Pete Peeters (1982–83)

Calder Trophy
- Frank Brimsek (1938–39)
- Jack Gelineau (1949–50)
- Larry Regan (1956–57)
- Bobby Orr (1966–67)
- Derek Sanderson (1967–68)
- Ray Bourque (1979–80)
- Sergei Samsonov (1997–98)

Conn Smythe Trophy
- Bobby Orr (1970, '72)

Timeline

1924	1927	1929	1933	1941	1951	1966	1970	1971	1980	1988	1994	1997	2000
Bruins play in first NHL season; team goes 6-24	Team enjoys first winning season	Boston beats Rangers in Stanley Cup finals	Eddie Shore is first defenseman to win league MVP award	Boston sweeps Detroit in Stanley Cup finals	Milt Schmidt named NHL's MVP	Bruins sign 18-year-old Bobby Orr	Orr wins first scoring title; Bruins win Cup	Phil Esposito sets NHL mark with 76 goals	Brad Park is only second defenseman to notch 500 career assists	Boston swept by Oilers in Cup finals	Cam Neely scores 50 goals in 44 games	Bruins tie team record with 47 losses	Ray Bourque records 1,500th career point; later traded to Colorado

230

FLEETCENTER:
NEW VENUE FOR HISTORIC TEAMS

OPENED IN 1995 TO REPLACE historic Boston Garden, the FleetCenter is home to two of pro sports' most storied franchises, the Bostons Celtics and the Bruins. Located behind the site of the now-demolished Garden, this multisport facility was built in just 27 months and provides fans with such luxuries as air conditioning, a multimillion dollar scoreboard and a pair of in-house restaurants. Although the FleetCenter lacks the history of the Boston Garden, its modern amenities make it an enjoyable place to cheer.

CONCESSIONS

The selection of food offered at the FleetCenter is truly dizzying. Aside from the traditional offerings, patrons can sample calzone, seasoned fries, lobster rolls and clam chowder. Vegetarians and the health-conscious will enjoy the fresh fruit, sandwiches and wraps, as well as a variety of salads. Beverages include frozen cocktails, microbrew and imported beers, wine and specialty coffees.

GAME DAY TIPS
• **Gate hours:** Gates open one hour prior to opening faceoff.
• **Prohibited items:** Food, beverages, cameras and recording devices are prohibited. Smoking is not allowed.
• **Ticket tips:** Getting tickets to see the Bruins play is not usually very hard, although Saturday night games and those against the Rangers tend to sell out quickly. The FleetCenter is known for having far better sight lines than the Boston Garden. Nevertheless, some fans complain that the less expensive seats are too far from the action.
• **Lost and found:** (617) 624-1331.

Arena Facts

Opened: *Sept. 30,1995*
Cost: *$160 million*
Capacity: *17,565*
Home Sweet Home:
• *Although the FleetCenter doesn't have the same history as the old Boston Garden, it still has many reminders of the franchise's great glory. Hanging from the rafters are five Stanley Cup banners and seven retired jersey numbers.*

Seating Plan

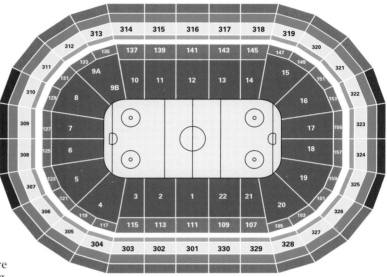

■	$143	■	$30
■	$80	■	$23
■	$60	**ATM**	**Sections 6, 7**
▫	$50	♿	**Sections 3, 14, 303, 314,**
■	$40		**318, 329**

Directions: *Exit I-93 at Storrow Dr. (exit 26) southbound and at Causeway St. (exit 25) northbound. By Subway: Take green or orange line to North Station. By Train: Take purple line to North Station. By Bus: Take Rte. 4 to North Station. Call MBTA at (617) 222-3200 for information.* **Parking:** *A garage under the stadium for 1,150 cars is accessible via Nashua St. The garage and the lot at nearby Tip O'Neil Federal Building have limited spots for people with disabilities. There are many private lots on Friend, Staniford and Portland Sts. and Lomansey Way.*

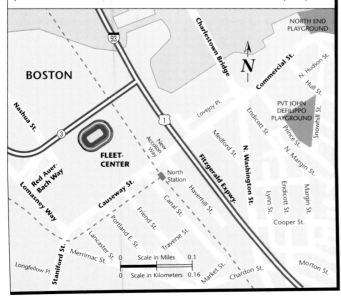

Nearby Hotels

▼▼▼▼ **Boston Harbor Hotel** *(Hotel)*, 70 Rowes Wharf (Boston), (617) 439-7000, $400-$2000
▼▼▼ **Boston Marriott Long Wharf Hotel** *(Hotel)*, 296 State St. (Boston), (617) 227-2867, $425-$600
▼▼▼ **Harborside Inn of Boston** *(Motor Inn)*, 185 State St. (Boston), (617) 723-7500, $145-$310
▼▼▼ **Holiday Inn Select-Boston Government Center** *(Hotel)*, 5 Blossom St. (Boston), (617) 742-7630, $149-$329
▼▼▼ **Millennium Bostonian Hotel** *(Hotel)*, Faneuil Hall Marketplace (Boston), (617) 523-3600, $305-$400

Nearby Restaurants

▼ **Durgin Park** *(Regional American)*, 340 Faneuil Hall Marketplace (Boston), (617) 227-2038, $6-$20
▼▼ **The Kinsale** *(Irish)*, 2 Center Plaza Government Center (Boston), (617) 742-5577, $9-$17
▼ **No Name Restaurant** *(Seafood)*, 17 Fish Pier (Boston), (617) 423-2705, $8-$15
▼▼▼ **Ristorante Davide** *(Northern Italian)*, 326 Commercial St. (Boston), (617) 227-5745, $18-$30
▼▼▼▼ **Rowes Wharf Restaurant** *(Regional American)*, 70 Rowes Wharf in the Boston Harbor Hotel (Boston), (617) 439-3995, $26-$35

BUFFALO SABRES

WHEN ALL IS SAID AND DONE, the two most important chapters in the Buffalo Sabres' story come down to breaks. A good break, in the form of a fortuitous coin toss, gave the nascent franchise the first pick in the 1970 draft. The expansion Sabres used their fortune wisely, selecting a standout center from Victoriaville, Quebec named Gilbert Perreault. Perreault, a dazzling stickhandler, won the Calder Trophy as rookie of the year. But the real magic was yet to come. When, the following season, Sabres coach Punch Imlach put two other young French Canadians, Richard Martin and Rene Robert, on the wings with Perreault, one of the NHL's most potent offensive lines was born. Known as the French Connection, the line led a formidable Sabres team all the way to the Stanley Cup Finals in 1975, where it lost to Philadelphia's Broad Street Bullies. The Sabres continued to put up strong regular season numbers throughout much of the 1970s and '80s, but postseason success was elusive. Even the hiring of legendary coach Scottie Bowman in 1979 could not bring the Sabres a Stanley Cup. Perreault retired in 1987, and it would take five years for the team's second franchise player to arrive, this time in the form of a slender Czech goalie named Dominik Hasek. Hasek, whose joints appeared to be made of rubber, revolutionized the goaltending position, flopping and rolling his way to five Vezina Trophies between 1994 and '99 and becoming the first goalie since Jacques Plante to take the Hart Trophy as league MVP. Hasek also backstopped the Sabres to the Stanley Cup Finals in 1999. There, the Sabres got the worst break of all — a missed foot-in-the-crease call that cost the team the Stanley Cup.

Miroslav Satan is a main cog in the Sabres offense.

POSTSEASON
• **Conference Championships**..................3
(1974–75, 1979–80, 1998–99)
• **Northeast Division Titles**......................1
(1996–97)
• **Adams Division Titles**.....3
(1974–75, 1979–80, 1980–81)

RETIRED NUMBERS
• Tim Horton (2)
• Rick Martin (7)
• Gilbert Perreault (11)
• Rene Robert (14)

TEAM RECORDS
• Dave Andreychuk (1982–93)

Slap Shot

• *Game four of the 1975 Stanley Cup finals is known as "the fog game." Held in Buffalo's Memorial Auditorium, the temperature was so warm that a fog covered the ice, making it almost impossible to see the puck. The game was stopped on a few occasions so that players could skate in circles to disperse the fog. The Sabres won the game 5-4 in overtime.*

Power-Play Goals (career): 153
• **Dominik Hasek (1992–2001)**
Goals Against Avg. (season): 1.87 (1998–99)
Shutouts (career): 55
Wins (career): 234
• **Pat LaFontaine (1991–97)**
Assists (season): 95 (1992–93)
Points (season): 148 (1992–93)
• **Rick Martin (1971–81)**
Hat Tricks (career): 21
40-Goal Seasons: 5
• **Alexander Mogilny (1989–95)**
Goals (season): 76 (1992–93)
• **Gilbert Perreault (1970–87)**
Assists (career): 814
Games (career): 1,191
Game-Winning Goals (career): 81
Goals (career): 512
Points (career): 1,326
30-Goal Seasons: 10
• **Craig Ramsay (1971–85)**
Consecutive Games: 776
Shorthanded Goals (career): 27
• **Rob Ray (1989–present)**
Penalty Minutes (career): 2,687

LEAGUE HONORS
Hart Trophy
• Dominik Hasek (1996–97, 1997–98)

Vezina Trophy
• Don Edwards (1979–80)
• Bob Sauve (1979–80)
• Tom Barrasso (1983–84)
• Dominik Hasek (1993–94, 1994–95, 1996–97, 1997–98, 1998–99, 2000–01)

Calder Trophy
• Gilbert Perreault (1970–71)
• Tom Barrasso (1983–84)

Lady Byng Trophy
• Gilbert Perreault (1972–73)

Frank J. Selke Trophy
• Craig Ramsay (1984–85)
• Michael Peca (1996–97)

Bill Masterton Trophy
• Don Luce (1974–75)
• Pat LaFontaine (1994–95)

Lester B. Pearson Award
• Dominik Hasek (1996–97, 1997–98)

William M. Jennings Trophy
• Tom Barrasso (1984–85)
• Bob Sauve (1984–85)
• Grant Fuhr (1993–94)
• Dominik Hasek (1993–94)

"Ruff has developed into one of the best coaches in this league."

— Bucky Gleason, sportswriter, on Sabres coach Lindy Ruff

Vital Stats

Stadium Address:
One Seymour H. Knox III Plaza, Buffalo, N.Y.
Phone: *(716) 855-4444*
Web: *sabres.com, hsbcarena.com*
Box Office:
(716) 855-4444 ext. 82, Mon.–Fri. 9–5
Media Coverage:
Radio: WNSA (107.7 FM) TV: Empire Sports Network
Practice Facility:
HSBC Arena, Buffalo, N.Y.

Jack Adams Award
• Ted Nolan (1996–97)

Hockey Hall of Fame
• Tim Horton (1977)
• Marcel Pronovost (1978)
• "Punch" Imlach (1984)
• Gilbert Perreault (1990)
• Scotty Bowman (1991)
• Seymour H. Knox III (1993)

Timeline

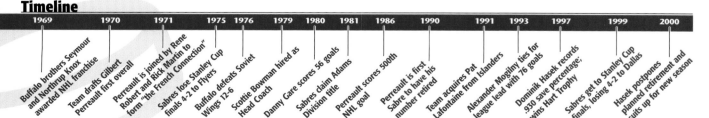

1969	1970	1971	1975	1976	1979	1980	1981	1986	1990	1991	1993	1997	1999	2000
Buffalo brothers Seymour and Northrup Knox awarded NHL franchise	Team drafts Gilbert Perreault first overall	Perreault is joined by Rene Robert and Rick Martin to form "the French Connection"	Sabres lose Stanley Cup finals 4-2 to Flyers	Buffalo defeats Soviet Wings 12-6	Scottie Bowman hired as Head Coach	Danny Gare scores 56 goals	Sabres claim Adams Division title	Perreault scores 500th NHL goal	Perreault is first Sabre to have his number retired	Team acquires Pat Lafontaine from Islanders	Alexander Mogilny ties for league lead with 76 goals	Dominik Hasek records .930 save percentage; wins Hart Trophy	Sabres get to Stanley Cup finals, losing 4-2 to Dallas	Hasek postpones planned retirement and suits up for new season

HSBC Arena: Sharp Digs for the Sabres

HSBC Arena was a radical change for the Buffalo Sabres and their fans. Ensconced in the cramped but intense confines of the Memorial Auditorium since the team's founding in 1970, both fans and players were thrilled when they saw HSBC. From its grand foyer, large food court, interactive displays and sports bar to the extensive team facilities, the new venue brings Buffalo in line with the most modern venues in the league. While perhaps lacking the charm of the Aud, HSBC more than compensates with modern comforts.

CONCESSIONS

Specialties served at HSBC Arena include roast beef on kimmelweck bread, fried bologna sandwiches with onions and peppers, and loganberry beverages. Also offered are Polish sausages, turkey burgers, tacos, barbecue, deli and salads.

Arena Facts

Opened: Sept. 21, 1996
Cost: $127.5 million
Capacity: 18,690
Home Sweet Home:
• *The Memorial Auditorium was famous for being small and exceptionally loud, giving the Sabres a distinct advantage at home. If the decibel level is any lower at HSBC, it's pretty hard to detect; this is still one very loud arena.*

GAME DAY TIPS

• **Gate hours:** Gates open two hours prior to opening faceoff.
• **Prohibited items:** Alcoholic beverages, laser pointers, helium balloons, weapons, illegal drugs, cameras, audio and video recorders, noisemakers, studded jewelry and fireworks are prohibited. Smoking is forbidden inside the arena, but patrons are allowed to exit in order to light up.
• **Ticket tips:** The Sabres' major rivals are the Maple Leafs and the Flyers. Expect sellouts when either of these teams come to town. In general, it's possible to get tickets for individual games, although seating choice will be limited. Fortunately, the sight lines at HSBC arena are good from anywhere.
• **Lost and found:** (716) 855-4454.

Seating Plan

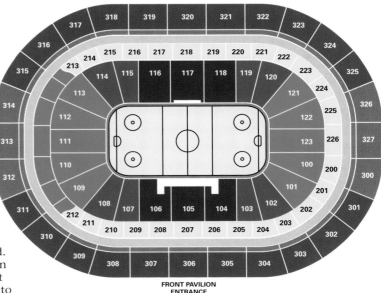

■	$100	■	$34
■	$79	■	$21
■	$59	■	$28
■	$51	**ATM**	**Sections 108/109, 115/116,**
░	$82		**300; Front Pavilion**
▓	**Suite Level** ... N/A	♿	**Throughout**

FRONT PAVILION ENTRANCE

Directions: *Exit I-190 south at exit 5 (Louisiana St.), turn left, then right onto Perry St. Exit I-190 north at exit 6 (Elm St.), turn right onto Seneca St., right onto Michigan St. By Subway: Take the train to the HSBC Arena stop. By Bus: Buses are available to and from the stadium. Call NFTA at (716) 855-7211 for information.* **Parking:** *The HSBC lot on Illinois St. holds 1,100 cars; 54 spots are reserved for people with disabilities. Off-site lots are on Scott, Perry, Exchange, Pearl and Main Sts.*

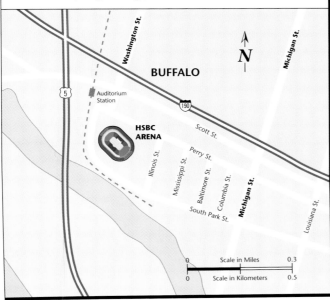

Nearby Hotels

▼▼▼ **Adam's Mark Hotel (*Hotel*)**, 120 Church St. (Buffalo), (716) 845-5100, $79-$129
▼▼ **Best Western Inn-On The Avenue (*Motel*)**, 510 Delaware Ave. (Buffalo), (716) 886-8333, $75-$149
▼▼▼ **Holiday Inn-Downtown (*Hotel*)**, 620 Delaware Ave. (Buffalo), (716) 886-2121, $99-$119
▼▼▼ **Hyatt Regency Buffalo (*Hotel*)**, Two Fountain Plaza (Buffalo), (716) 856-1234, $129-$154
▼▼▼ **Radisson Suite Hotel Buffalo (*Suite Hotel*)**, 601 Main St. (Buffalo), (716) 854-5500, $125-$179

Nearby Restaurants

▼ **Colter Bay Grill (*American*)**, 561 Delaware Ave. (Buffalo), (716) 882-1330, $6-$11
🄵🅈🄸 **E.B. Green's Steakhouse (*Steakhouse*)**, 2 Fountain Plaza in the Hyatt Regency (Buffalo), (716) 855-4870
▼▼▼ **Fiddle Heads Restaurant (*American*)**, 62 Allen St. (Buffalo), (716) 883-4166, $12-$22 (dinner only)
▼▼▼ **Hutch's (*American*)**, 1375 Delaware Ave. (Buffalo), (716) 885-0074, $12-$20 (dinner only)
▼▼ **Pettibone's Grille (*American*)**, 275 Washington St. (Buffalo), (716) 846-2100, $12-$20

CALGARY FLAMES

SOMETIMES A CHANGE OF SCENERY can make all the difference in the world. When the expansion Atlanta Flames first laced up their skates back in 1972, they surprised people by winning 25 games and proving they could compete with the rest of the league. The team was so competitive, in fact, that it fought its way into the playoffs six of its first eight years. Once in the postseason, however, the Flames seemed to flicker. In all six of those first playoff series the club was unceremoniously trounced, winning a grand total of two games out of 17 and getting swept four times. But the team's 1980 move to Calgary, Alta., seemed to be just the tonic to cure the round-one blues. That first season in Calgary saw Kent Nilsson set a club record with 131 points. The Flames shook the postseason monkey off their backs when they swept the Blackhawks in the opening round and, buoyed by their new-found success, they took out the Flyers in a game-seven thriller in the quarter-finals. The team would make the playoffs in each of the next seven seasons, but despite the presence of such stars as McDonald, Nilsson, Al MacInnis, Joe Nieuwendyk and goalie Mike Vernon, it could not win the coveted Cup. The arrival of veteran Doug Gilmore and rookie Theo Fleury for the 1988–89 season provided the missing pieces to Calgary's puzzle. Finishing with the best record in the NHL, the Flames beat Vancouver, Los Angeles and Chicago before defeating Montreal in the Stanley Cup finals. Although the Flames have made numerous postseason appearances since then, they have never again burned as bright.

Vital Stats

Stadium Address:
555 Saddledome Rise SE, Calgary, Alta.
Phone: *(403) 777-2177*
Web: *calgaryflames.com, pengrowthsaddledome.com*
Box Office: *(403) 777-4646, Mon.–Fri. 8:30–5*
Media Coverage:
Radio: 66CFR (660 AM)
TV: CTV SportsNet
Practice Facility:
Pengrowth Saddledome, Calgary, Alta.

Jerome Iginla is one of the Flames most dangerous snipers.

POSTSEASON
- Stanley Cup Championships 1 (1988–89)
- Campbell Conference Championships 2 (1985–86, 1988–89)
- Smythe Division Titles ...3 (1987–88, 1988–89, 1989–90)
- Pacific Division Titles.....2 (1993–94, 1994–95)

RETIRED NUMBERS
- Lanny MacDonald (9)

"Hockey is everything in Calgary."

— Joe Nieuwendyk, on the difference between playing in hockey-crazed Calgary for the first part of his career and then being traded to Dallas

TEAM RECORDS
- **Dan Bouchard (1972–81)** Shutouts (career): 20
- **Fred Brathwaite (1998–present)** Goals Against Avg. (season): 2.45 (1998–99)
- **Theo Fleury (1988–99)** Goals (career): 364 Hat Tricks (career): 13 (tie) Points (career): 830 Shorthanded Goals (game): 3 (March 9, 1991)

Slap Shot

- *The Flames have strong ties to the Montreal Canadiens. The team's first coach was Bernie "Boom Boom" Geoffrion, a Hall-of-Fame winger with the Habs in the 1950s and '60s. Doug Risebrough, a member of four Stanley Cup-winning Habs teams, served as a player, coach and GM of the Flames. Guy Lapointe, the Canadiens' Hall-of-Fame defenseman, was Calgary's assistant coach from 1990 to '99.*

- **Nick Fotiu (1985–87)** Penalty Minutes (period): 37 (March 8, 1987)
- **Tim Hunter (1981–92)** Penalty Minutes (season): 375 (1988–89) Penalty Minutes (career): 2,405
- **Al MacInnis (1981–94)** Assists (career): 609 Games (career): 803 Points by a Defenseman (season): 103 (1990–91)
- **Sergei Makarov (1989–93)** Points (game): 7 (Feb. 25, 1990)
- **Lanny McDonald (1981–89)** Goals (season): 66 (1982–83)
- **Joe Nieuwendyk (1986–95)** Goals (game): 5 (Jan. 11, 1989) Goals by a Rookie (season): 51 (1987–88) Points by a Rookie (season): 92 (1987–88) Power-Play Goals (season): 31 (1987–88)
- **Kent Nilsson (1979–85)** Assists (season): 82 (1980–81) Hat Tricks (career): 13 (tie) Shorthanded Goals (season): 9 (1984–85) Points (season): 133

(1980–81)
- **Neil Sheehy (1983–88, 1991–92)** Penalty Minutes (game): 41 (March 21, 1986)
- **Mike Vernon (1982–84, 1985–94, 2000–present)** Wins (season): 39 (1987–88) Wins (career): 260

LEAGUE HONORS
Calder Trophy
- Eric Vail (1974–75)
- Willi Plett (1976–77)
- Gary Suter (1985–86)
- Joe Nieuwendyk (1987–88)
- Sergei Makarov (1989–90)

Lady Byng Trophy
- Bob MacMillan (1978–79)
- Joe Mullen (1986–87, 1988–89)

Masterton Trophy
- Lanny MacDonald (1982–83)
- Gary Roberts (1995–96)

King Clancy Award
- Lanny MacDonald (1987–88)
- Joe Nieuwendyk (1994–95)

Conn Smythe Trophy
- Al MacInnis (1989)

Hockey Hall of Fame
- Glenn Hall (1975)
- Bob Johnson (1992)
- Lanny MacDonald (1992)
- Joe Mullen (2000)

Timeline

1972	1973	1974	1976	1980	1983	1984	1986	1989	1992	1995	1999	2000	2001
Atlanta Flames win first NHL game	Team notches 25 wins in inaugural campaign	Flames qualify for play-offs; lose in first round	Flames suffers first of five straight round-one eliminations	Flames relocate to Calgary	Lanny McDonald sets team record with 66 goals	Flames lose to Oilers in division finals	Canadiens beat Calgary in Cup finals	Team wins Stanley Cup; Lanny McDonald retires	Gary Roberts tallies 53 goals	Flames finish first in Pacific Division	Theo Fleury dealt to Avalanche	Phil Housley racks up 55 points – fourth best among NHL defensemen	Team struggles to 11th place finish in Western Conference

PENGROWTH SADDLEDOME: RIDING TALL IN THE SADDLE

WITH ITS UNIQUE SADDLE-SHAPED ROOF, the Pengrowth Saddledome is a perfect venue for Calgary, sometimes called "Canada's Cowtown." Inside a high-tech BOSE sound system affords the arena excellent acoustics. The Saddledome is also equipped with the latest in indoor pyrotechnic displays, including specially designed fireballs that are unleashed during player introductions and goal celebrations. Besides the Flames, the venue has hosted arena football, the 1988 Winter Olympics and, of course, numerous rodeos.

CONCESSIONS
The Saddledome offers all the traditional favorites, such as hot dogs, hamburgers, pizza and popcorn. Vegetarian food is available.

GAME DAY TIPS
• **Gate hours:** Gates open one hour prior to faceoff.

Arena Facts

Opened: Oct. 15, 1983
Cost: $176 million
Capacity: 17,139
Home Sweet Home:
• In order to make the Saddledome a premier concert venue, some 6,000 acoustic tiles were added to the concrete ceiling. Unfortunately, this tends to muffle crowd noise, taking away some of the Flames' home-ice advantage.

• **Prohibited items:** Food, beverages, cans, coolers and alcohol are prohibited. Banners and signs are allowed, as are non-mechanical noise-makers. Laser pointers, video cameras and flash cameras are not allowed. Smoking is allowed outside the west and east entrances.
• **Ticket tips:** Get your tickets well in advance. The Flames sold out 17 of their 41 home games in 1999–2000. Their arch rivals, the Oilers, as well as Colorado, Toronto and Montreal usually draw a crowd. The third level is high enough to make watching a game uncomfortable.
• **Lost and found:** (403) 777-4639.

Seating Plan

■ Air Canada Club	$114.95	■	$14.72
□	$114.95	**WC**	$45.93
▨ **Restaurant**	$82.01	**WC1**	$49.34
■	$84.11	**WC2**	$29.21
■	$73.83	**ATM** Sections 214, 228, Concourse, Lounge	
▦	$65.42	♿ End zone 100s, end zone 200s	
■	$42.06		
■	$32.24		
■	$23.83		

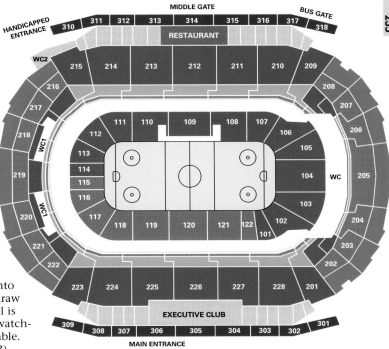

Directions: Take Memorial Dr. to 4th Ave. Turn right, follow to SE 1st St. Turn left, follow to 12 Ave., then to SE 5th St. and to arena. Or, take 9th Ave. to SE 1st St. Turn right, follow to 12th Ave. Turn left, follow to SE 5th St. Turn right, follow to arena. **By Public Transportation:** Several buses arrive in the vicinity. A light-rail transit station is nearby. Call Calgary Transit at (403) 974-4000 for information. **Parking:** About 750 spaces are available at Saddledome lots, with 15 reserved for the disabled. Extra parking is on SE MacLeod Trail, SW 11th Ave. and SW 12th Ave. and at Stampede Park.

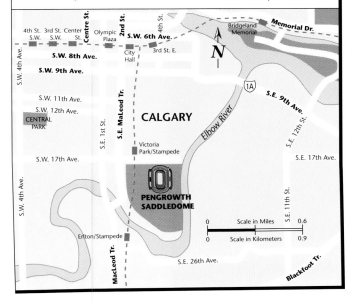

Nearby Hotels
▼▼▼ **Best Western Calgary Centre Inn** *(Motel)*, 3630 Macleod Tr. S. (Calgary), (403) 287-3900, $119-$189
▼▼▼ **Comfort Inn & Suites South** *(Motel)*, 4611 Macleod Tr. SW (Calgary), (403) 287-7070, $80-$179
▼▼▼▼ **The Fairmont Palliser** *(Classic Hotel)*, 133 9th Ave. SW (Calgary), (403) 262-1234, $169-$324
▼▼▼ **Holiday Inn Calgary Downtown** *(Hotel)*, 119 12th Ave. SW (Calgary), (403) 266-4611, $125-$135
▼▼▼▼ **Hyatt Regency Calgary** *(Hotel)*, 700 Centre St. S. (Calgary), (403) 717-1234, $145-$404

Nearby Restaurants
▼▼ **The Arden** *(Canadian)*, 1112 17th Ave. SW (Calgary), (403) 228-2821, $8-$13
▼▼ **La Brezza** *(Italian)*, 990 1st Ave. NE (Calgary), (403) 262-6230, $12-$22
▼▼▼▼ **La Chaumiere Restaurant** *(Continental)*, 139 17th Ave. SW (Calgary), (403) 228-5690, $19-$29
▼▼ **Thai Sa-On Restaurant** *(Thai)*, 351 10th Ave. SW (Calgary), (403) 264-3526, $6-$13
▼▼ **Whiskey Creek Steakhouse & Saloon** *(Canadian)*, 200 Barclay Parade SW (Calgary), (403) 262-9378, $10-$28

CAROLINA HURRICANES

THE PRESENT-DAY HURRICANES FRANCHISE is one of the most well-traveled clubs in professional hockey. Founded in 1971 as the WHA's New England Whalers, the team relocated from Springfield, Mass., to Hartford three years later to avoid competition for fans with the Bruins. The team joined the NHL in 1979 as the Hartford Whalers and played there for 17 seasons until the team's lackluster performances and poor crowds forced the team to seek refuge in Greensboro, N.C., in 1997. Renamed the Hurricanes, the team stayed there for two seasons before settling in its present home at the Entertainment and Sports Arena in Raleigh. Throughout their early years in the WHA, the Whalers enjoyed considerable success, thanks to a number of former NHL aces: Al Smith, Ted Green and Tom Williams. In 1973 the team won the Avco World Cup as the top team in the league. In the late 1970s the Whalers continued to raise eyebrows by icing a team that included such legendary veterans as Dave Keon, Bobby Hull and the great Gordie Howe, who all continued playing for the team when it began NHL play. In 1981 the team also drafted 18-year-old Ron Francis, who would become instrumental in the offensive lineup and who, after leaving the Whalers in 1991, would return to the franchise in '98 to lead the Hurricanes. Although the "Canes" have had a rough time during their first four seasons — making the playoffs only twice — they have a number of excellent players. With Ron Francis, Sami Kapanen and Rod Brind'Amour leading the charge and the amazing Arturs Irbe tending goal, the future holds much promise for this team.

Arturs Irbe is one of the team's great strengths.

POSTSEASON
• **Playoff Appearances** 10
(1979–80, 1985–86, 1986–87, 1987–88, 1988–89, 1989–90, 1990–91, 1991–92, 1998–99, 2000–01)

RETIRED NUMBERS
• **Gordie Howe (9)**

TEAM RECORDS
• **Sean Burke (1992–98)**
Games as a Goalie
(career): 281
• **Kevin Dineen**
(1984–91, 1995–99)
Penalty Minutes

Slap Shot

• *When the New England Whalers joined the NHL in 1979 — thus becoming the Hartford Whalers — Gordie Howe set an incredible longevity record with 26 seasons of NHL play and 32 seasons of pro hockey, spanning an unheard of five decades. His NHL records of 801 goals, 1049 assists and 1,850 points stood until the 1990s, when Wayne Gretzky began rewriting the career record book.*

(career): 1,441
Shorthanded Goals
(season): 4 (tie) (1984–85)
• **Ron Francis**
(1981–91, 1998–present)
Assists (game): 6
(March 5, 1987)
Assists (season): 69
(1989–90)
Assists (career): 688
Games (career): 956
Goals (game): 4
(Feb. 12, 1984)
Goals (career): 323
Points (career): 1,011
Power Play Goals
(career): 106
• **Arturs Irbe**
(1998–present)
Games as a Goalie
(season): 77 (2000–01)
Shutouts (season): 6
(2000–01)
Shutouts (career): 15
Wins (season):
37 (2000–01)
• **Trevor Kidd**
(1997–98)
Goals-Against Avg.
(season): 2.17 (1997–98)
Goals-Against Avg.
(career): 2.17
• **Mike Liut (1985–90)**
Wins (career): 115
• **Torrie Robertson**
(1983–88)
Penalty Minutes (season):
358 (1985–86)

"The door is open for us as long as we take care of business."
— *Hurricanes center Rod Brind'Amour*

• **Mike Rogers**
(1975–81)
Points (season): 105
(1980–81)
Goals by a Center
(season): 44 (1979–80)
Hat Tricks (season): 3 (tie)
(1980–81)
Shorthanded Goals
(season): 4 (tie)
(1980–81)
• **Geoff Sanderson**

Vital Stats

Stadium Address:
1400 Edwards Mill Rd.,
Raleigh, N.C.
Phone: (919) 861-2300
Web: caneshockey.com,
esa-today.com
Box Office:
(919) 861-2323,
Mon.–Fri. 9–5, event days
Sat. call for hours
Media Coverage:
Radio: WRBZ (850 AM)
TV: Fox Sports Net
Practice Facility:
IcePlex, Raleigh, N.C.

(1990–98)
Goals by a Left Wing
(season): 46 (1992–93)
Power Play Goals (season):
21 (1992–93)
Points by a Left Wing
(season): 89 (1982–83)
• **Blaine Stoughton**
(1978–84)
Game Winning Goals
(season): 9 (1979–80)
Goals (season):
56 (1979–80)
Hat Tricks (season): 3 (tie)
(1981–82)
Points by a Right Wing
(season): 100 (1979–80)
• **Dave Tippett**
(1984–90)
Shorthanded Goals
(career): 11

LEAGUE HONORS
Bill Masterton Trophy
• **Doug Jarvis**
(1986–87)

Hockey Hall of Fame
• **Gordie Howe (1972)**
• **Bobby Hull (1983)**
• **David Keon (1986)**

Timeline

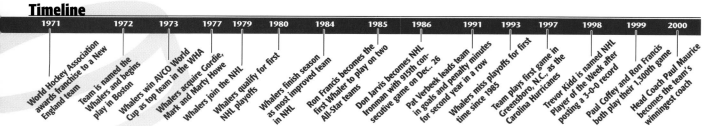

1971 — World Hockey Association awards franchise to a New England team

1972 — Team is named the Whalers and begins play in Boston

1973 — Whalers win AVCO World Cup as top team in the WHA

1977 — Whalers acquire Gordie, Mark and Marty Howe

1979 — Whalers join the NHL

1980 — Whalers qualify for first NHL playoffs

1984 — Whalers finish season as most improved team in NHL

1985 — Ron Francis becomes the first Whaler to play on two All-Star teams

1986 — Don Jarvis becomes NHL Ironman with 915th consecutive game on Dec. 26

1991 — Pat Verbeek leads team in goals and penalty minutes for second year in a row

1993 — Whalers miss playoffs for first time since 1985

1997 — Team plays first game in Greensboro, N.C., as the Carolina Hurricanes

1998 — Trevor Kidd is named NHL Player of the Week after posting a 3-0-0 record

1999 — Paul Coffey and Ron Francis both play their 1,300th game

2000 — Head Coach Paul Maurice becomes the team's winningest coach

ENTERTAINMENT AND SPORTS ARENA: RALEIGH'S GEM

THE 2000–01 SEASON MARKS the Hurricanes' second season at the E & S, the premier sports venue in the Southeast. Situated on a 140-acre plot of land next to the North Carolina State Fairgrounds and Carter-Finley Stadium, this new arena has become part of Raleigh's spectacular entertainment district. Inside the E & S was designed to optimize an intimate environment and proudly boasts a larger than usual lower deck to provide an abundance of close-to-the-action sight lines.

CONCESSIONS

With specialty stands for kids and a choice of domestic beers as well as wine, margaritas and coolers, the Entertainment and Sports Arena has something for everyone. Food choices include Tex/Mex, barbecue sandwiches, bratwurst and philly steak sandwiches.

Arena Facts

Opened: Oct. 29, 1999
Cost: $158 million
Capacity: 18,700
Home Sweet Home:
• With a greater number of seats concentrated at the home end of the arena (where the Hurricanes defend for two out of three periods), the E & S offers the home team more and louder crowd support than its competitors.

GAME DAY TIPS

• **Gate hours:** Gates open one hour prior to opening faceoff.
• **Prohibited items:** Video cameras, audio recorders, bottles, cans, coolers and alcoholic beverages are prohibited. Fireworks, sticks, laser pointers, aerosol cans, chains, studded bracelets, pets and noisemakers are also not permitted. Animals are prohibited, except for service animals. Smoking is not allowed, but patrons can exit near sections 107 and 116 in order to smoke.
• **Ticket tips:** Although some fans complain about narrow seats, the views at the arena are considered as excellent. Tickets to games are available, but sell more quickly on weekends and when the rival Washington Capitals are in town.
• **Lost and found:** (919) 861-2102.

Seating Plan

■ Club Ledge	$99	■ Lower Level-North	$40
▪ VIP Ledge and Front Row	$99	▪ The Mezzanine	$35
■ Club Level	$99	■ Balcony Premium	$22
■ Center Ice and Northern Club	$65	▨ Upper Goal Zone	$12
▨ Lower Level-South	$45	ᴬᵀᴹ Sections 111, 127, 334	
		♿ Throughout 100s, 200s	

Directions: From I-40, drive toward Raleigh to Wade Ave. (exit 289). Proceed to Edwards Mill Rd. exit. By Bus: Buses are available to and from the fair grounds, which are a short distance from the arena. Call TTA at (919) 549-9999 for information. **Parking:** There are 8,000 spots in the lots surrounding the arena. Fifty-eight spots are for patrons with disabilities; they are accessible via all three entrances. There is more parking at Carter Finley Stadium next to the arena.

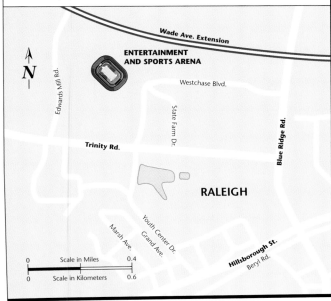

Nearby Hotels

▼▼ **Fairfield Inn** *(Motel)*, 1716 Walnut St. (Cary), (919) 481-4011, $54-$69

▼▼▼ **Hampton Inn & Suites** *(Motel)*, 111 Hampton Woods Ln. (Cary), (919) 233-1798, $89-$139

▼▼▼ **La Quinta Inn & Suites** *(Motel)*, 2211 Summit Park Ln. (Raleigh), (919) 785-0071, $79-$89

▼▼▼ **Raleigh Marriott Hotel-Crabtree Valley** *(Motor Inn)*, 4500 Marriott Dr. (Raleigh), (919) 781-7000, $139-$159

▼▼ **Red Roof Inn** *(Motel)*, 1800 Walnut St. (Cary), (919) 469-3400, $48-$73

Nearby Restaurants

▼▼ **42nd St. Oyster Bar & Seafood Grill** *(Seafood)*, 508 W. Jones St. (Raleigh), (919) 831-2811, $11-$18

▼▼ **Irregardless** *(American)*, 901 W. Morgan St. (Raleigh), (919) 833-8898, $12-$20

▼▼ **The Rathskeller** *(American)*, 2412 Hillsborough St. (Raleigh), (919) 821-5342, $12-$16

▼▼▼ **Simpson's Beef & Seafood** *(Steak & Seafood)*, 5625 Creedmoor Rd. in Creedmoor Crossings (Raleigh), (919) 783-8818, $14-$25

▼ **Wellspring Grocery** *(American)*, 3540 Wade Ave. in the Ridgewood Shopping Center (Raleigh), (919) 828-5805

CHICAGO BLACKHAWKS

ONE OF THE "ORIGINAL SIX" NHL FRANCHISES, the Chicago Blackhawks have certainly had their share of great players. From its very first season, when the legendary Dick Irvin led the Hawks with 18 goals, the team has featured some of the league's greatest offensive talents. In the 1930s it was scoring whiz Paul Thompson. He carried the team to its first title in 1934 and another in '38. The Hawks suffered a prolonged Stanley Cup dry spell through the 1940s and '50s, missing the playoffs 13 times and reaching the finals just once. Fans relied on future Hall-of-Famers the Bentley brothers, Max and Doug, Bill Mosienko and Roy Conacher to provide entertainment. In 1957 the Blackhawks acquired Bobby Hull, a powerful left winger who would shoot harder than any player before him. His blistering shot helped him become the first Hawk to score 50 goals in a season. Hull left the team in 1972 as the NHL all-time goals leader. Hull was complemented by a tough Czech-born centerman named Stan Mikita. Mikita would go from penalty-minutes leader to Lady Byng winner in one season and pick up two Hart trophies in his 22-year career. Together they brought Chicago its most recent Cup win in 1961. Tony Esposito's exceptional rookie season — he won the Calder and Vezina trophies — looked like a sure sign of more Cups to come, but two finals losses to the Canadiens in 1971 and '73 left the team empty. A trade that sent puck-control magician Denis Savard to Montreal for Chris Chelios in 1990 helped bring the squad to the finals once more in 1992, but the Hawks again fell short, losing four straight to the Penguins.

"When visiting clubs leave this place, I want them to know that they were involved in a war."

— *Blackhawks Head Coach Bryan Sutter*

Vital Stats

Stadium Address:
1901 W. Madison St., Chicago, Ill.
Phone: (312) 455-4500
Web:
chicagoblackhawks.com, united-center.com
Box Office:
(312) 559-1212, Mon.–Fri. 11–6, Sat. 11–4, game days until first intermission
Media Coverage:
Radio: WSCR (670 AM)
TV: Fox Sports Net
Practice Facility: The Edge, Bensenville, Ill.

POSTSEASON
• **Stanley Cup Championships** 3
(1933–34, 1937–38, 1960–61)

RETIRED NUMBERS
• Glenn Hall (1)
• Bobby Hull (9)
• Denis Savard (18)
• Stan Mikita (21)
• Tony Esposito (35)

TEAM RECORDS
• **Ed Belfour (1988–97)**
Games (season): 74 (1990–91)
Wins (season): 43 (1990–91)
• **Chris Chelios (1990–99)**
Penalty Minutes (career): 1,495
• **Tony Esposito (1969–84)**
Shutouts (season): 15

Slap Shot
• *Chicago goalie Glenn Hall owns a NHL record for endurance that will likely never be broken. Hall played 502 consecutive NHL games, all without a face mask. His durability earned him the nickname "Mr. Goalie."*
• *Of the "Original Six" NHL teams, Chicago has gone the longest since its last Stanley Cup — 40 years.*

(1969–70)
Shutouts (career): 74
Wins (career): 413
• **Bobby Hull (1957–72)**
Goals (season): 58 (1968–69)
Goals (career): 604
40-Goal Seasons: 8
• **Stan Mikita (1958–80)**
Assists (career): 926
Games (career): 1,394
Points (career): 1,467
• **Mike Peluso (1989–92)**
Penalty Minutes (season): 408 (1991–92)
• **Denis Savard (1980–90, 1995–97)**
Assists (season): 87 (twice)
Points (season): 131 (1987–88)

LEAGUE HONORS
Hart Trophy
• Max Bentley (1945–46)
• Al Rollins (1953–54)
• Bobby Hull (1964–65, 1965–66)
• Stan Mikita (1966–67, 1967–68)

Art Ross Trophy
• Doug Bentley (1942–43)
• Max Bentley (1945–46, 1946–47)
• Roy Conacher (1948–49)
• Bobby Hull (1959–60, 1961–62, 1965–66)
• Stan Mikita (1963–64, 1964–65, 1966–67, 1967–68)

Norris Trophy
• Pierre Pilote (1962–63, 1963–64, 1964–65)
• Doug Wilson (1981–82)
• Chris Chelios (1992–93, 1995–96)

Vezina Trophy
• Charles Gardiner (1931–32, 1933–34)
• Lorne Chabot (1934–35)
• Glenn Hall (1962–63, 1966–67)
• Denis de Jordy (1966–67)
• Tony Esposito (1969–70, 1971–72, 1973–74)
• Gary Smith (1971–72)
• Ed Belfour (1990–91, 1992–93)

Calder Trophy
• Mike Karakas (1935–36)
• Carl Dahlstrom (1937–38)
• Ed Litzenberger (1954–55)
• William Hay (1959–60)
• Tony Esposito (1969–70)
• Steve Larmer (1982–83)
• Ed Belfour (1990–91)

Lady Byng Trophy
• Elwin Romnes (1935–36)
• Max Bentley (1942–43)
• Clint Smith (1943–44)
• Bill Mosienko (1944–45)
• Ken Wharram (1963–64)
• Bobby Hull (1964–65)
• Stan Mikita (1966–67, 1967–68)

Tony Amonte gives the Hawks a deft scoring touch.

Jack Adams Award
• Orval Tessier (1982–83)

Timeline

1926	1930	1934	1941	1952	1961	1966	1971	1977	1982	1988	1992	1995	2000

Blackhawks win first game at Chicago Coliseum, 4-1 over Toronto Pats

Team has first winning season

Blackhawks win first Stanley Cup

Hawks goalie Sam Lopresti makes 80 saves against Boston, but Chicago loses 3-2

Bill Mosienko scores three goals in 21 seconds, a NHL record

Chicago wins Stanley Cup finals series in six games over Detroit

Bobby Hull becomes first Blackhawk to score 50 goals in a season

Montreal defeats Chicago in Stanley Cup finals

Stan Mikita scores 500th career goal

Denis Savard breaks Hull's single-season scoring mark with 131 points

Hawks sign Ed Belfour

Chicago loses finals to Pittsburgh

Hawks move into United Center

Team misses playoffs for third straight year

UNITED CENTER: OUT WITH THE OLD

OLD CHICAGO STADIUM WAS RENOWNED for its noise levels and its fervent fans. Like the Canadiens who moved from the Forum in Montreal, the Blackhawks franchise may have lost a bit of its home-ice edge when it moved into the new United Center in 1995. But the positives of the new facility certainly outweigh the negatives. Much improved player facilities, state-of-the-art fan amenities, good sight lines and an increased capacity all have made the United Center a welcome destination for the Blackhawks fans who flock there.

CONCESSIONS

The United Center has a number of must-try Chicago specialties, such as Italian beef sandwiches, thick-crust pizza, and foot-long hot dogs with unique toppings. The microbrewery serves a Blackhawks lager.

Arena Facts

Opened: Aug. 29, 1994
Cost: $175 million
Capacity: 20,500
Home Sweet Home:
• With almost 3,000 seats more than Chicago Stadium, the United Center allowed the Blackhawks to attract even larger crowds to their already boisterous home games. In 1995 the Hawks attracted an average of 20,415 fans per game, a NHL record.

Vegetarians have a choice of garden burgers, salads and fruit cups.

GAME DAY TIPS

• **Gate hours:** Gates open 90 minutes prior to opening faceoff.
• **Prohibited items:** Banners, food, beverages and video cameras are prohibited. Smoking is generally not allowed except in designated smoking areas outside the seating bowl.
• **Ticket tips:** The United Center has relatively good sight lines, but fans do complain that the great distance from the upper level to the ice surface makes it very difficult to see the action clearly. Fortunately, there

are usually plenty of lower seats to choose from. The only times you may have a problem are when the

Red Wings or the Blues are in town.
• **Lost and found:** (312) 455-4500.

Seating Plan

$250	$25
$75	$15
$60	**ATM** Sections 106, 116, 309
$50	♿ **Throughout**
$40	

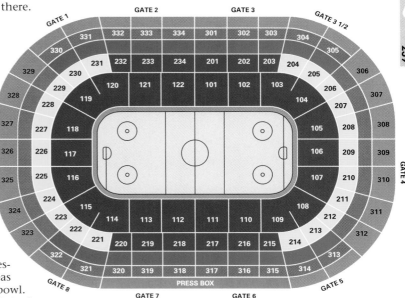

Directions: From I-90, take Madison exit and turn west on Madison St. From I-55 north, take Damen/Ashland exit, turn left and head north. From I-290 east, exit Damen St. and turn right on Madison St. By Train: Take Blue Line (Forest Park Train) to Medical Center stop. By Bus: Take No. 20 Madison or No. 19 Stadium Express. Call CTA at (312) 836-7000 for information. **Parking:** More than 6,000 parking spots are available at the center. Disabled parking is in lots G and H. Private lots are on W. Harrison, N. Paulina, W. Madison and W. Jackson Sts.

Nearby Hotels

▼▼ **Best Western Grant Park Hotel** *(Hotel)*, 1100 S. Michigan Ave. (Chicago), (312) 922-2900, $139-$335
▼▼▼ **Hyatt at University Village** *(Hotel)*, 625 S. Ashland Ave. (Chicago), (312) 491-1234, $190-$215
▼▼▼ **Hyatt on Printers Row** *(Hotel)*, 500 S. Dearborn St. (Chicago), (312) 986-1234, $205-$230
▼▼ **Quality Inn-Downtown** *(Hotel)*, 1 Mid City Plaza (Chicago), (312) 829-5000, $99-$169
▼▼▼ **W Chicago City Center** *(Classic Hotel)*, 172 W. Adams St. (Chicago), (312) 332-1200, $290-$464

Nearby Restaurants

▼▼ **Como Inn** *(Northern Italian)*, 546 Milwaukee Ave. (Chicago), (312) 421-5222, $12-$25
▼▼ **Harry Caray's Restaurant** *(Steakhouse)*, 33 W. Kinzie St. (Chicago), (312) 828-0966, $11-$33
▼▼▼ **Marche** *(French)*, 833 W. Randolph St. (Chicago), (312) 226-8399, $14-$34
▼▼▼▼ **OneSixtyBlue**, *(American)*, 160 N. Loomis St. (Chicago), (312) 850-0303, $19-$30
▼ **Wishbone** *(American)*, 1001 W. Washington Blvd. (Chicago), (312) 850-2663, $7-$14

COLORADO AVALANCHE

WHEN THE QUEBEC NORDIQUES jumped from the World Hockey Association to the NHL for the 1979–80 season, it immediately established one of pro sports' greatest rivalries. The upstart Nordiques shared the same province with one of the NHL's flagship teams, the venerable Montreal Canadiens, and the "Battle of Quebec" was waged with each meeting between the two teams. After a few tough years, the Nords began to climb up the rankings. This was due mostly to some shrewd draft picks in the 1970s and '80s. Among the future stars grabbed up were scoring sensation Michel Goulet, Dale Hunter and brothers Anton and Peter Stastny from Czechoslovakia. Quebec would win its division in 1985–86, only to be ambushed by the arch-nemesis Canadiens during the latter's march toward a record 23rd Stanley Cup. Although the Nords missed the playoffs from 1987–88 to 1991–92, a solid foundation was being laid with the drafting of such stalwarts as Joe Sakic, Mats Sundin, Adam Foote and Owen Nolan. In 1992 Peter Forsberg and five others were added to the team in a blockbuster trade with the Flyers for Eric Lindros. The team became a veritable force in 1995, when just months after moving to Colorado, it traded for superstar goalie Patrick Roy. With Roy slamming the door on opposition snipers, the newly named Avalanche defeated the heavily favored Detroit Red Wings to give the franchise its first-ever Stanley Cup in 1995–96. In 2000–01, the team again reached hockey's summit by defeating the defending champion New Jersey Devils in seven hard-fought games.

> ## "One goalie, one game against Russia for the championship of the world. I want Patrick."
> — *Hockey analyst, on goaltender Patrick Roy*

POSTSEASON
- **Stanley Cup Championships** 2
(1995–96, 2000–01)
- **Western Conference Championships** 2
(1995–96, 2000–01)
- **Northwest Division Titles** 3
(1998–99, 1999–2000, 2000–01)
- **Pacific Division Titles** 3
(1995–96, 1996–97, 1997–98)
- **Northeast Division Titles** 1
(1994–95)

- **Adams Division Titles**.....1
(1985–86)

TEAM RECORDS
- **Gord Donnelly (1983–88)**
Penalty Minutes (season): 301 (1987–88)
- **Steve Duchesne (1992–94)**
Points by a Defenseman (season): 82 (1992–93)
- **Michel Goulet (1979–90)**
Goals (season): 57 (1982–83)
Power Play Goals (season): 29 (1987–88)
Shorthanded Goals (season): 6 (tie) (1981–82)
- **Dale Hunter (1979–87)**
Penalty Minutes (career): 1,562
- **Sandis Ozolinsh (1995–2000)**
Goals by a Defenseman (season): 23 (1996–97)
- **Patrick Roy (1995–present)**
Games by a Goalie (season): 65 (1997–98)
Games by a Goalie (career): 352
Goals Against Avg. (season): 2.20 (2000–01)
Shutouts (season): 7 (1996–97)
Shutouts (career): 23
Ties (career): 44
Wins (season): 40 (2000–01)
Wins (career): 195
- **Joe Sakic (1988–present)**
Assists (career): 721
Game-Winning Goals (season): 12 (2000–01)
Games (career): 934
Points (career): 1,178
Goals (career): 457
Shorthanded Goals (career): 30
Shots (season): 332 (2000–01)
- **Anton Stastny (1979–89)**
Goals by a Rookie (season): 39 (tie) (1980–81)
- **Peter Stastny (1980–90)**
Assists (season): 93 (1981–82)
Goals by a Rookie (season): 39 (tie) (1980–81)
Points (season): 139 (1981–82)
100-Point Seasons (career): 7

LEAGUE HONORS
Hart Trophy
- Joe Sakic (2000–01)

Calder Trophy
- Peter Forsberg (1994–95)
- Peter Stastny (1980–81)
- Chris Drury (1998–99)

Lady Byng Trophy
- Joe Sakic (2000–01)

Jack Adams Award
- Marc Crawford (1994–95)

Conn Smythe Trophy
- Joe Sakic (1996)
- Patrick Roy (2001)

Hockey Hall of Fame
- Michel Goulet (1998)
- Peter Stastny (1998)

Vital Stats

Stadium Address:
1000 Chopper Pl., Denver, Colo.
Phone: (303) 405-8555
Web: pepsicenter.com, coloradoavalanche.com
Box Office:
(303) 405-1212, Mon.–Fri. 10–6, Sat. 10–3
Media Coverage:
Radio: KKFN (950 AM)
TV: KTVD (Channel 20), Fox Sports Net
Practice Facility:
Family Sports Center, Englewood, Colo.

Patrick Roy provides stellar netminding for the Avs.

Timeline

1972	1977	1979	1982	1984	1986	1987	1988	1992	1995	1996	1999	2000	2001
Quebec Nordiques play first WHA game	Team wins WHA crown	Nordiques join NHL	Peter Stastny sets team record with 139 points	Team enjoys first winning NHL season	Nordiques finish atop Adams Division	Team drafts Joe Sakic	Peter Stastny notches seventh 100-point season	Mats Sundin scores five times in game versus Hartford	Team moves to Colorado; name changed to Avalanche	Avs win Stanley Cup in first season in Colorado	Colorado wins fifth straight division title	Team trades for Raymond Bourque	Avs win Stanley Cup; Patrick Roy is playoff MVP

240

PEPSI CENTER: ALMOST PERFECT

SINCE THE PEPSI CENTER first opened its doors in 1999, reviews of the new venue have been mixed. With full training facilities, 95 luxury suites, decent sight lines and excellent sound, no one argues about the facility's technological standing — it's cutting edge all the way. Fans have complained, however, about the too-narrow seats and a lack of convenient bathroom facilities. Whatever is said about the Pepsi Center, it is an improvement over McNichols Arena, the Avalanche's previous venue.

CONCESSIONS

There are many options for those looking for something to eat at the Pepsi Center. Choices include hot dogs, hamburgers, cheese steak sandwiches, chicken wings, fish and chips, pizza and gyros. There are also several bars serving beer, wine and other beverages.

GAME DAY TIPS

• **Gate hours:** Gates open 90 minutes prior to opening faceoff.
• **Prohibited items:** Outside food and drinks, cans, bottles, coolers, thermoses, video cameras, and laser pointers are not allowed in the arena. Smoking is prohibited inside the arena, but guests are allowed to go outside to designated smoking areas.
• **Ticket tips:** The very new Pepsi Center is getting rave reviews for having excellent sight lines — even from "the nosebleed" sections. Patrons are very critical, however, of the narrow and uncomfortable seats in the upper deck. Anyone lucky enough to get tickets to see the Avalanche play shouldn't complain though — the team's home games sell out regularly and tickets are often difficult to come by.
• **Lost and found:** (720) 931-1581.

Arena Facts

Opened: Oct. 1, 1999
Cost: $160 million
Capacity: 18,007
Home Sweet Home:
• The Avs have enjoyed incredible fan support right from their very first game in 1995. In 2000–01 vocal Avs fans helped spur their team to a league-leading 28 wins at home. The team posted the best overall record in the NHL.

Seating Plan

- Rinkside (Row 1) $178
- Rinkside (Row 2-5) $123
- Prime Loge $101
- Corner Loge $87
- End Loge $79
- Lower Center Balcony ...$55
- Upper Center Balcony ...$50
- Lower Corner/
  End Balcony $39
- Corner Balcony,
  Mid-End Balcony $35
- Upper End Balcony $22
- ATM Sections 120, 144, 334, 366; box-office lobby
- Corners first level, throughout other levels

Directions: Exit I-25 north at Auraria Pkwy.; I-25 south at Speer Blvd. By Bus: Buses go close to the arena. Call (303) 299-6000 for information.
Parking: The center has 4,700 spots, with an additional 2,000 in a nearby lot. There are 100 wheelchair-accessible spots available immediately beside lot A. More parking is found on Wynkoop, Wazee, Blake, Market, 13th, 14th and 15th Sts.

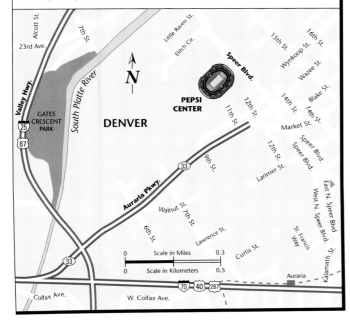

Nearby Hotels

▼▼▼▼ **Brown Palace Hotel** (*Classic Hotel*), 321 17th St. (Denver), (303) 297-3111, $234
▼▼ **Comfort Inn Downtown Denver** (*Hotel*), 401 17th St. (Denver), (303) 296-0400, $129
▼▼▼ **Denver Marriott Hotel City Center** (*Hotel*), 1701 California St. (Denver), (303) 297-1300, $189
▼▼▼ **Holiday Inn Denver Downtown** (*Hotel*), 1450 Glenarm Pl. (Denver), (303) 573-1450, $99-$139
▼▼▼▼ **Hotel Monaco** (*Hotel*), 1717 Champa St. (Denver), (303) 296-1717, $185-$240

Nearby Restaurants

▼▼▼ **McCormick's Fish House & Bar** (*Regional Seafood*), 1659 Wazee St. (Denver), (303) 825-1107, $8-$25
▼▼▼▼ **Palace Arms** (*Continental*), 321 17th St. in the Brown Palace Hotel (Denver), (303) 297-1311, $22-$38
▼▼▼ **Palm Restaurant** (*Steakhouse*), 1201 16th St. in the Westin Tabor Center Denver (Denver), (303) 825-2256, $14-$29
▼▼ **Rocky Mountain Diner** (*American*), 800 18th St. in the Ghost Building (Denver), (303) 293-8383, $9-$18
▼▼ **Rodizio Grill** (*Steakhouse*), 1801 Wynkoop St. (Denver), (303) 294-9277, $18

COLUMBUS BLUE JACKETS

PRIOR TO THE COLUMBUS BLUE JACKETS' first NHL season in 2000–01, team management was guarded about its expectations for the team. After all, expansion teams in every sport seemed destined for the cellar, often requiring years of tinkering before the right chemistry is found. The Columbus brain trust decided that if the team racked up 60 points by season's end, the campaign would be considered a success. Some experts, however, considered even that conservative goal to be ambitious. When the Columbus team took the ice on Oct. 7, 2000, for its first-ever game, it had all the hallmarks of an expansion team: lots of unproven rookies mixed with a selection of long-in-the-tooth veterans and nary a superstar in sight. The team started slowly, losing 19 of its first 27 games. But with veterans such as Lyle Odelein, Geoff Sanderson and Kevin Dineen keeping the younger players on an even keel, things started to click. There was a modest four-game winning streak in November, including a 3-2 win over the powerful Dallas Stars. Young David Vyborny emerged as an exciting prospect, scoring a variety of highlight-reel goals, including a rookie-record two on penalty shots. But it was longtime NHL netminder Ron Tugnutt who really anchored the team. Included among his expansion-record 22 wins were back-to-back 2-1 wins over St. Louis and Detroit, two of the league's premier teams. At season's end, the Blue Jackets found themselves ahead of the Islanders, Lightning, Thrashers, Panthers, Canadiens, Ducks and Wild and had 71 points in the bank. Mission accomplished and then some.

Veteran goalie Ron Tugnutt keeps the Jackets in the game.

TEAM RECORDS
- **Serge Aubin (2000–present)**
Games (season): 81 (2000–01) (tie)
- **Steve Heinze (2000–2001)**
Assists by a Right Winger (season): 20 (2000–01)

Slap Shot
- *The team is called the Blue Jackets in honor of the significant role the region played in the Civil War of 1861–65. Ohio contributed more of its population to the Union Army than any other state. A large number of the blue-jacketed uniforms worn by northern troops were manufactured in Columbus. The blue in the team's jersey is the same shade as was worn by the Union Army.*
- *The Blue Jackets' uniforms also pay tribute to the country's earliest history. The logo features an unfurled ribbon that forms the team's initials, CBJ. The 13 stars on the ribbon represent each of the original 13 U.S. colonies.*

Goals by a Right Winger (season): 22 (2000–01)
Points by a Right Winger (season): 42 (2000–01)
Power Play Goals (season): 14 (2000–01)
- **Jamie Heward (2000–present)**
Assists by a Defenseman (season): 16 (2000–01) (tie)
Goals by a Defenseman (season): 11 (2000–01)
Points by a Defenseman (season): 27 (2000–01)
Power Play Goals by a Defenseman (season): 9 (2000–01)
- **Espen Knutsen (2000–present)**
Assists (season): 42 (2000–01)
Points by a Center (season): 53 (2000–01)
Power Play Assists (season): 25 (2000–01)
Power Play Points (season): 27 (2000–01)
- **Robert Kron (2000–present)**
Shorthanded Goals (season): 1 (tie) (2000–01)
- **Lyle Odelein (2000–present)**
Games (season): 81 (2000–01) (tie)
- **Jamie Pushor (2000–present)**
Plus/Minus (season): +7 (2000–01)

Shorthanded Goals (season): 1 (tie) (2000–01)
- **Geoff Sanderson (2000–present)**
Assists by a Left Winger (season): 26 (2000–01)
Game-Winning Goals (season): 7
Goals (season): 30 (2000–01)
Points (season): 56 (2000–01)
Shots (season): 199
- **Ron Tugnutt (2000–present)**
Games by a Goalie (season): 53 (2000–01)
Goals Against Avg. (season): 2.44 (2000–01)
Losses (season): 25 (2000–01)
Minutes by a Goalie (season): 3,129 (2000–01)
Saves (season): 1,401 (2000–01)
Save Pct. (season): .917 (2000–01)
Shutouts (season): 4 (2000–01)
Starts by a Goalie (season): 53 (2000–01)
Ties (season): 5 (2000–01)
Wins (season): 22 (2000–01)
- **Tyler Wright (2000–present)**
Goals by a Center (season):

"Vote Tugnutt."
— Tongue-in-cheek Blue Jacket PR campaign, during U.S. presidential campaign that cashed in on the popularity of goalie Ron Tugnutt

Vital Stats

Stadium Address:
200 W. Nationwide Blvd., Columbus, Ohio
Phone: *(614) 246-2000*
Web: *columbusbluejackets.com, nationwidearena.com*
Box Office: *(614) 246-2000, Mon.–Fri. 10–6, Sat. 10–4, Sun. two hours prior to events*
Media Coverage: *Radio: WBNS (1460 AM), WWCD (101.1 FM) TV: Fox Sports Net*
Practice Facility: *CoreComm Ice Haus, Columbus, Ohio*

16 (2000–01)
Penalty Minutes (season): 140 (2000–01)

LEAGUE HONORS
NHL Player of the Week
- Marc Denis (Dec. 4–10, 2000)
- Ron Tugnutt (Mar. 12–18, 2001)

Timeline

1996	1997	1997	1998	1998	1999	1999	2000	2000	2000	2001	2001
Columbus applies for NHL franchise	June: NHL awards Columbus expansion team	Nov.: Team officials select Blue Jackets as team name	Feb.: Former Panthers coach Doug McLean named team's President and GM	July: Ground broken for new arena	Oct.: Blue Jackets unveil jerseys	Dec.: Team sells all executive suites and more than 10,000 season tickets	June: Rostislav Klesla is team's first-ever draft pick	July: Dave King is hired as Head Coach	Oct.: Blue Jackets lose home opener 5-3 to Blackhawks	Mar.: David Vyborny is first NHL rookie to score twice on penalty shots	April: Team ends first season with 28 wins

NATIONWIDE ARENA: RAISING THE BAR

WHEN THE NATIONWIDE ARENA opened on Sept. 9, 2000, it raised the bar for multipurpose venues. The building itself is beautiful, with a glass atrium, terrazzo floors and marble architectural details highlighted by a 135-foot-high light tower at the southeast corner of the arena. The open lobbies and concourses have been designed to give fans a great view of the ice the moment they set foot inside. Nationwide Arena is also the only NHL venue that has the team's practice facility, rink and all, attached to the main complex.

CONCESSIONS

In addition to traditional arena fare, hungry patrons can feast on quesadillas, tortilla wraps, lobster rolls, smokehouse pork sandwiches, grilled tuna steaks and chicken with caramelized onions, calzones, panini sandwiches and a variety of beers and liquors.

GAME DAY TIPS

• **Gate hours:** Gates open 90 minutes prior to opening faceoff.
• **Prohibited items:** Cans, bottles, coolers, food and alcohol are prohibited. Laser pointers, air horns, and noisemakers and projectiles of any kind are also prohibited. Video and flash cameras are not allowed. Smoking is allowed only in designated areas.
• **Ticket tips:** The Blue Jackets sold out 26 games in their first year of operations, including the last 15 of the season. This means that same-day tickets can often be very hard to come by. It's best to make your purchases ahead of time. Weekend games sell better, as do games against nearby teams such as the Red Wings and the Penguins.
• **Lost and found:** (614) 246-2000.

Arena Facts

Opened: *Sept. 9, 2000*
Cost: *$150 million*
Capacity: *18,500*
Home Sweet Home:
• *Not perceived as a hockey hotbed, Columbus has proven to be an enthusiastic hockey town. The Blue Jackets sold out 26 games in 2000–01. With their vocal fans behind them, the team notched 19 of its 28 wins at home.*

Directions: *Exit I-71 at Spring St. and go west, then north on N. Front St. Or, exit I-70/71 at N. Front St. and go north to parking entrance. By Bus: Several buses arrive at Nationwide Arena. Call Central Ohio Transit Authority (COTA) at (614) 228-1776 for information.* **Parking:** *More than 15,000 spaces are available in garages and lots within a 10-minute walk of the arena on Goodale Blvd., N. Front St. and N. 4th St. and at the Convention Center on N. High St. Most have parking for the disabled.*

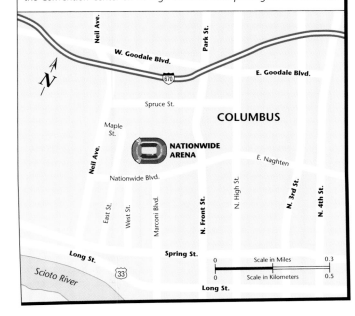

Seating Plan

▪ Glass Level	Sold Out
▪ Ticketmaster.com Lounge	Sold out
▫ Club Level 1	Sold out
▪ Club Level 2	Sold out
■ Lower Bowl A	$65
▪ Lower Bowl B	$55
▪ Lower Bowl C	$50
▪ Upper Bowl D	$43
▪ Upper Bowl E	$32
▪ Upper Bowl F	$22
▪ Upper Bowl G	$17
▪ Sky Terrace	$25
▫ Executive Suites	Call for Info
▫ Founders Suites	Call for Info
▪ Loge Box	Call for Info
▫ Club Terrace Table	Call for Info
▪ Party Tower	Call for Info
ATM Sections 110, 206, 213
♿ Throughout

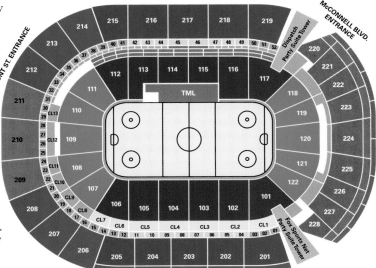

Nearby Hotels

▼▼▼ **Adam's Mark Columbus** *(Hotel)*, 50 N. Third St. (Columbus), (614) 228-5050, $89-$240
▼▼▼ **Courtyard by Marriott Downtown Columbus** *(Motel)*, 35 W. Spring St. (Columbus), (614) 228-3200, $139
▼▼▼ **Harrison House Bed & Breakfast** *(Historic Bed & Breakfast)*, 313 W. 5th Ave. (Columbus), (614) 421-2202, $109
▼▼▼ **The Lofts Hotel** *(Hotel)*, 55 E. Nationwide Blvd. (Columbus), (614) 461-2663, $219-$259
▼▼▼▼ **The Westin Great Southern Columbus** *(Classic Hotel)*, 310 S. High St. (Columbus), (614) 228-3800, $225-$235

Nearby Restaurants

▼▼ **The Columbus Brewing Company** *(American)*, 525 Short St. (Columbus), (614) 464-2739, $8-$18
▼▼▼ **Handke's Cuisine** *(American)*, 520 S. Front St. (Columbus), (614) 621-2500, $10-$26 (dinner only)
▼▼ **Schmidt's Restaurant and Sausage Haus** *(German)*, 240 E. Kossuth St. (Columbus), (614) 444-6808, $6-$12
▼▼▼ **R J Snapper's** *(Seafood)*, 700 N. High St. (Columbus), (614) 280-1070, $16-$23 (dinner only)
▼▼ **Tapatio Restaurant** *(Mexican)*, 491 N. Park St. (Columbus), (614) 221-1085, $9-$18

DALLAS STARS

THE STARS FRANCHISE BEGAN ITS LIFE in Minnesota when the NHL decided to expand the league to 12 teams in 1967. Based in Bloomington, the North Stars played 26 seasons in the Metropolitan Sports Center before moving to Dallas in 1993. The early years of the team were characterized by some often brilliant, but inconsistent hockey. In the early 1970s the North Stars came of age when coach Jack Gordon brought to his team such players as veteran Doug Mohns, defenseman Ted Harris and Lorne "Gump" Worsley, the tough, maskless goalie. Alongside the flamboyant Bill Goldsworthy, whose on-ice hustle endeared fans everywhere, these new players breathed life into the North Stars and helped the team rise in popularity and sell out games quickly. In the late 1970s a new team leader arrived in the shape of Bobby Smith, a remarkable young center who won the Calder Trophy in 1979 and helped the team take its first conference title in 1981. Throughout the 1980s the North Stars continued their uneven ways by winning a couple of division titles, but also falling into overwhelming slumps. During the team's ups and downs, it was players such as Neal Broten, Keith Acton, Dino Ciccarelli and Brian Bellows who led the Minnesota charge. By 1993 the North Stars were entangled in numerous financial and legal problems and it was decided the team would move to Dallas to become simply the Stars. Within a couple of years the Stars had reestablished themselves as a force, thanks to inspired players such as Guy Carbonneau, Joe Nieuwendyk, Ed Belfour, Sergei Zubov and Mike Modano. In the 1996–97 and 1997–98 seasons the Stars climbed to the top of the Central Division and in 1999 the team broke out to defeat the Sabres for the Stanley Cup. Since then the team has remained a threat, topping the Pacific Division in the last two seasons.

> *"I don't know if I'll ever get the privilege to coach a team like this again."*
> — *Stars coach Ken Hitchcock*

Vital Stats

Stadium Address:
2500 Victory Ave.,
Dallas, Texas
Phone: (214) 303-5535,
(214) 221-8326
Web: dallasstars.com,
americanairlinescenter.com
Box Office: (214) GO-
STARS, Mon.–Fri. 9–5,
Sat. 10–4, Sun. 12–4
Media Coverage:
Radio WBAP (820 AM)
TV: KDI (Channel 27),
Fox Sports Net
Practice Facility:
Stars Center,
Irving, Texas

POSTSEASON
• **Stanley Cup Championships** 1
(1998–99)
• **Western Conference Titles** 2
(1998–99, 1999–2000)
• **Prince of Wales Conference Titles**................2
(1980–81, 1990–91)
• **Pacific Division Titles** 3
(1998–99, 1999–2000, 2000–01)
• **Central Division Titles**....2
(1996–97, 1997–98)
• **Norris Division Titles** 2
(1981–82, 1983–84)

RETIRED NUMBERS
• Neal Broten (7)
• Bill Goldsworthy (8)
• Bill Masterton (19)

TEAM RECORDS
• **Brian Bellows (1982–92)**
Goals (season): 55 (tie)
(1989–90)
Points by a Left Wing
(season): 99 (1989–90)
Power-Play Goals (career): 134
• **Neal Broten (1980–95, 1996–97)**
Assists (season): 76 (1985–86)
Assists (career): 593
Games (career): 992
Shorthanded Goals (career): 24

• **Shane Churla (1988–96)**
Penalty Minutes
(career): 1,883
• **Dino Ciccarelli (1980–89)**
Goals (season): 55 (tie)
(1981–82)
Hat Tricks (career): 16
Points by a Right Wing
(season): 107 (1981–82)
Power-Play Goals
(season): 22 (1986–87)
• **Bill Goldsworthy (1967–77)**
Shots (season): 321 (1973–74)
• **Brett Hull (1998–present)**
Game-Winning Goals
(season): 11 (tie) (1998–99)
• **Basil McRae (1987–92)**

Slap Shot

• *The acclaimed NHL Masterton Trophy was inaugurated in 1968 after Bill Masterton, a strong North Stars player and legendary sportsman, died from a major head injury during a game. To this day the Masterton Trophy is one of the NHL's major awards, given each year for perseverance, sportsmanship and dedication to the game.*

The ever-dangerous sniper Mike Modano.

Penalty Minutes (season):
382 (1987–88)
• **Mike Modano (1988–present)**
Game-Winning Goals
(career): 62
Goals (career): 382
Goals by a Center
(season): 50 (1993–94)
Points (career): 900
• **Joe Nieuwendyk (1995–present)**
Game–Winning Goals
(season): 11 (tie) (1997–98)
• **Bobby Smith (1978–84, 1990–93)**
Points (season): 114 (1981–82)
Points (game): 7
(Nov. 11, 1981)
• **Tim Young (1975–83)**
Goals (game): 5 (Jan. 15, 1979)

LEAGUE HONORS
Calder Trophy
• Danny Grant (1968–69)
• Bobby Smith (1978–79)

Bill Masterton Trophy
• Al MacAdam (1979–80)

Lester Patrick Award
• Walter Bush (1972–73)
• John Mariucci (1976–77)
• Lou Nanne (1988–89)
• Neal Broten (1997–98)

Conn Smythe Trophy
• Joe Nieuwendyk (1999)

NHL Hall of Fame
• Gump Worsley (1980)
• John Mariucci (1985)
• Leo Boivin (1986)
• Bob Gainey (1992)
• Al Shaver (1993)

Timeline

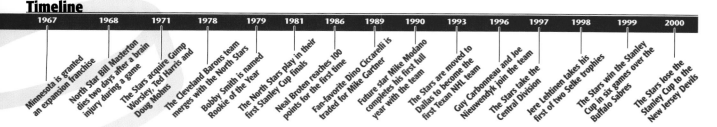

1967 — Minnesota is granted an expansion franchise

1968 — North Star Bill Masterton dies two days after a brain injury during a game

1971 — The Stars acquire Gump Worsley, Ted Harris and Doug Mohns

1978 — The Cleveland Barons team merges with the North Stars

1979 — Bobby Smith is named Rookie of the Year

1981 — The North Stars play in their first Stanley Cup finals

1986 — Neal Broten reaches 100 points for the first time

1989 — Fan-favorite Dino Ciccarelli is traded for Mike Gartner

1990 — Future star Mike Modano completes his first full year with the team

1993 — The Stars are moved to Dallas to become the first Texan NHL team

1996 — Guy Carbonneau and Joe Nieuwendyk join the team

1997 — The Stars take the Central Division

1998 — Jere Lehtinen takes his first of two Selke trophies

1999 — The Stars win the Stanley Cup in six games over the Buffalo Sabres

2000 — The Stars lose the Stanley Cup to the New Jersey Devils

AMERICAN AIRLINES CENTER: BEAUTY AND COMFORT

OPENED IN JULY 2001, the American Airlines Center is the new and improved home of the Stars. The arena's beautiful glass exterior offers spectacular views of downtown Dallas. Sweeping rotundas, terrazzo floors and coffered ceilings are just some of the venue's striking architectural details. The eight-sided scoreboard at the new arena is almost twice the size of the one at the old Reunion Arena and the state-of-the-art ice-making system promises that the rink will be one of the NHL's best.

CONCESSIONS

The American Airline Center offers hungry fans a wide variety of culinary treats, from down-home cooking to four-star food. Standard arena fare such as hot dogs, hamburgers and pizza are available, as well as a host of speciality items, including Southern-style barbecue.

Arena Facts

Opened: July 28, 2001
Cost: $325 million
Capacity: 18,500
• The Stars have a strong following, selling out every game since the beginning of the 1998–99 season. So, although the team has moved to a new arena, it will still benefit from the support of some of the most loyal and boisterous fans in the NHL.

GAME DAY TIPS

• **Gate hours:** Gates open 90 minutes prior to opening faceoff.
• **Prohibited items:** Food and drinks, pets (except for trained service animals and guide dogs), brooms, sticks, poles, video cameras, flash photography and other recording devices are prohibited. Patrons may be asked to refrain from using noisemakers if other fans complain. Smoking is permitted in designated areas outside the arena.
• **Ticket tips:** Retractable seating means that the arena can be reconfigured to offer optimum sight lines depending on the event. The new arena's seating bowl has been specially designed to put fans closer to the action; as a result, there are few bad seats. However,

Directions: From Hwy. 35 east, exit at Continental and follow east to N. Houston St. Turn left on N. Houston St. and follow to arena. By Public Transportation: Buses and light rail service the arena from Union Station. Call Dallas Area Rapid Transit (DART) at 214-979-1111 for information.
Parking: About 5,300 cars can be accommodated at the center; 165 spots are reserved for the physically disabled in lots F and S and the Platinum Parking Garage.

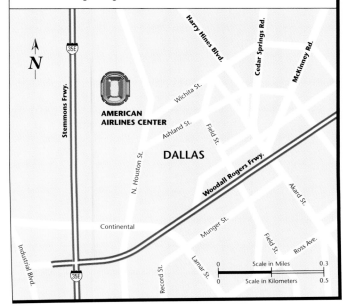

Seating Plan

- ■ Terrace .... **Call for info**
- ▨ Priority Terrace .... **Call for info**
- ■ Executive Terrace .... **Call for info**
- ▨ Platinum .... **Call for info**
- □ Executive .... **Call for info**
- ■ Celebrity .... **Call for info**
- ■ StarsClub Luxury .... **Call for info**
- ■ StarsClub Premium .... **Call for info**
- ATM Plaza Level, Terrace Level, Plaza Exterior
- ♿ Throughout

the Stars frequently sell out, so don't count on same-day tickets. Games against arch rivals such as Edmonton, San Jose and Colorado are most popular.
• **Lost and found:** (214) 222-3687.

Nearby Hotels

▼▼▼ **Amerisuites-West End (Suite Motel),** 1907 N. Lamar St. (Dallas), (214) 999-0500, $95-$130
▼▼▼ **Courtyard by Marriott-Market Center (Motor Inn),** 2150 Market Center Blvd. (Dallas), (214) 653-1166, $119-$129
▼▼▼ **Fairfield Inn Market Center (Motel),** 2110 Market Center Blvd. (Dallas), (214) 760-8800, $89-$124
▼▼▼ **Holiday Inn-Aristocrat Hotel (Historic Hotel),** 1933 Main St. (Dallas), (214) 741-7700, $189-$199
▼▼▼▼ **Hotel Adolphus (Historic Hotel),** 1321 Commerce St. (Dallas), (214) 742-8200, $355-$455

Nearby Restaurants

▼▼ **Baby Doe's Matchless Mine Restaurant (Steakhouse),** 3305 Harry Hines Blvd. (Dallas), (214) 871-7310, $17-$24
▼▼▼ **Bombay Cricket Club (Indian),** 2508 Maple Ave. (Dallas), (214) 871-1333, $12-$17
▼▼▼▼▼ **The French Room (Nouvelle French),** 1321 Commerce St. in the Hotel Adolphus (Dallas), (214) 742-8200, $52-$70 (dinner only)
▼▼▼ **Pomodoro (Italian),** 2520 Cedar Springs Rd. (Dallas), (214) 871-1924, $12-$26
▼▼ **Queen of Sheba (Ethiopian),** 3527 McKinney Ave. (Dallas), (214) 521-0491, $9-$12

DETROIT RED WINGS

IT IS ONLY FITTING THAT "HOCKEYTOWN, USA," should be home to the Red Wings, the most successful American franchise in NHL history. Only Montreal and Toronto have won more Stanley Cups. The Wings first came into prominence in the mid-1930s, when, led by Ebbie Goodfellow and Syd Howe, the team took back-to-back Stanley Cups. Although the Wings continued their winning ways into the '40s — including a third NHL title in 1943 — it wasn't until the 1950s that the team assembled the lineup that would become part of hockey lore. With a roster that included Ted Lindsay, Terry Sawchuck, Alex Delvecchio and the great Gordie Howe, Detroit was virtually unbeatable. From 1948 to 1955, the Wings racked up seven straight first-place seasons and won another four Stanley Cups that would secure them a place in posterity. For many fans, the rise of this stellar Detroit squad marks the advent of modern hockey; the Wings' teamwork and perseverance became the standard by which all teams were judged. For Howe, this incredible period marked the beginning of a brilliant career that would extend to 1980. After Wayne Gretzky, Howe remains the second-highest scorer in the game's history. Throughout the 1990s the Wings proved themselves to be one of the NHL's premier teams. Led by the talented likes of Sergei Fedorov, Brendan Shanahan and Steve Yzerman, the team won a pair Stanley Cups in the mid-1990s and to this day continues to be a major threat.

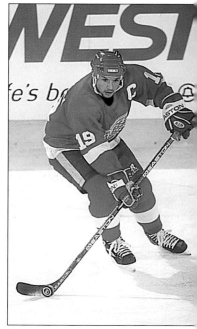

Steve Yzerman is a sure bet to make the Hall of Fame.

POSTSEASON
- Stanley Cup
Championships 9
(1935–36, 1936–37, 1942–43, 1949–50, 1951–52, 1953–54, 1954–55, 1996–97, 1997–98)

RETIRED NUMBERS
- Terry Sawchuck (1)
- Ted Lindsay (7)
- Gordie Howe (9)
- Alex Delvecchio (10)
- Sid Abel (12)

TEAM RECORDS
- Alex Delvecchio (1950–74)
Consecutive Games
(career): 548
- Sergei Fedorov
(1990–present)

Game-Winning Goals
(season): 11 (1995–96)
- **Gordie Howe (1946–71)**
Assists (career): 1,023
Games (career): 1,687
Goals (career): 786
Points (career): 1,809
Power-Play Goals
(career): 211
- **Syd Howe (1934–46)**
Goals (game): 6
(Feb. 3, 1944)
- **Terry Sawchuck (1949–55, 1957–64, 1968–69)**
Games by a Goaltender
(career): 734
Shutouts (career): 85
Shutouts (season):
12 (tie) (three times)
Wins (season): 44 (twice)
- **Steve Yzerman (1983–present)**
Assists (season): 90
(1988–89)
Goals (season): 65
(1988–89)
Points (season): 155
(1988–89)
Goals by a Rookie (season):
39 (1983–84)
Shots (season): 388
(1988–89)

LEAGUE HONORS
Art Ross Trophy
- Ted Lindsay (1949–50)
- Gordie Howe (1950–51, 1951–52, 1952–53, 1953–54, 1956–57, 1962–63)

Hart Trophy
- Ebbie Goodfellow
(1939–40)
- Sid Abel (1948–49)
- Gordie Howe (1951–52, 1952–53, 1956–57, 1957–58, 1959–60, 1962–63)
- Sergei Fedorov (1993–94)

James Norris Trophy
- Red Kelly (1953–54)
- Paul Coffey (1994–95)
- Nicklas Lidstrom
(2000–01)

Vezina Trophy
- Norm Smith (1936–37)
- John Mowers (1942–43)
- Terry Sawchuck (1951–52, 1952–53, 1954–55)

Calder Trophy
- Carl Voss (1932–33)
- Jim McFadden (1947–48)
- Terry Sawchuck
(1950–51)
- Glen Hall (1955–56)
- Roger Crozier (1964–65)

William M. Jennings Trophy
- Chris Osgood (1995–96)
- Mike Vernon (1995–96)

Jack Adams Award
- Bobby Kromm
(1977–78)
- Jacques Demers
(1986–87, 1987–88)
- Scotty Bowman
(1995–96)

Slap Shot

- *The Wings have one of the strangest rituals in pro sports — the octopus toss. Since 1952, when fishmongers Pete and Jerry Cusimano threw the first octopus, it has become customary for fans to toss one onto the ice during the playoffs. The creature's eight legs represented the number of wins it took to win the Stanley Cup back when only four teams made it to the postseason.*

Vital Stats

Stadium Address:
600 Civic Center Dr.,
Detroit, Mich.
Phone: (313) 396-7444
Web: detroitredwings.com,
olympiaentertainment.com
Box Office:
(313) 396-7575,
Mon.–Sat. 10–6, event days
Media Coverage:
Radio: WXYT (1270 AM)
TV: UPN (Channel 50),
Fox Sports Net
Practice Facility: Joe
Louis Arena, Detroit, Mich.

Conn Smythe Trophy
- Roger Crozier (1966)
- Mike Vernon (1997)
- Steve Yzerman (1998)

"If you've lost a game and learned nothing, then you've truly lost."
— *Red Wings legend Gordie Howe*

Timeline

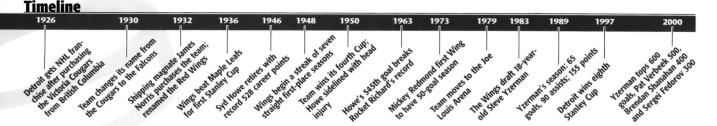

1926 — Detroit gets NHL franchise after purchasing the Victoria Cougars from British Columbia

1930 — Team changes its name from the Cougars to the Falcons

1932 — Shipping magnate James Norris purchases the team; renamed the Red Wings

1936 — Wings beat Maple Leafs for first Stanley Cup

1946 — Syd Howe retires with record 528 career points

1948 — Wings begin a streak of seven straight first-place seasons

1950 — Team wins fourth Cup; Howe sidelined with head injury

1963 — Howe's 545th goal breaks Rocket Richard's record

1973 — Mickey Redmond first Wing to have 50-goal season

1979 — Team moves to the Joe Louis Arena

1983 — The Wings draft 18-year-old Steve Yzerman

1989 — Yzerman's season: 65 goals, 90 assists, 155 points

1997 — Detroit wins eighth Stanley Cup

2000 — Yzerman tops 600 goals, Pat Verbeek 500, Brendan Shanahan 400 and Sergei Fedorov 300

JOE LOUIS ARENA:
IN THE HEART OF HOCKEYTOWN

KNOWN AS "THE JOE," Detroit's most famous arena has been home to the Wings since 1979. Located in the "Hockeytown" district, the Joe wasn't so popular when it first opened its doors; bleak and institutional, the arena was quickly nick-named "the Louis Warehouse" before it was re-vamped in 1982 by the Wings' new owners. Now the concourses are decorated with hockey murals and memorabilia, and the atmosphere is much more lively. The Joe also hosts many of Detroit's premier entertainment events and is the exclusive site for the Barnum and Bailey Circus troupe.

CONCESSIONS

From sausages and pizza to turkey sandwiches and gourmet ice cream, there is no shortage of choice when it comes to concessions at the Joe Louis Arena. Vegetarians will enjoy the pita stand

Arena Facts

Opened: *Dec. 12, 1979*
Cost: *$34 million*
Capacity: *19,983*
Home Sweet Home:
• *As one of the smallest venues in the NHL, the Joe Louis Arena has the advantage of almost always being filled to capacity. The boisterous fans imbue the Joe with pro-Wings energy that helps account for the team's high success rate at home.*

and salads. Beverage choices include specialty beers, wine and shakes.

GAME DAY TIPS

• **Gate hours:** Gates open one hour prior to opening faceoff.
• **Prohibited items:** Video cameras, flash photography, camera lenses bigger than 54mm, food, beverages, weapons, laser pointers, flag poles, air horns, umbrellas, bottles, cans and coolers are prohibited. Smoking is allowed only in the roped-off areas outside East and West gates.
• **Ticket tips:** The Red Wings are extremely popular, selling out on a regular basis. Rival teams include the

Seating Plan

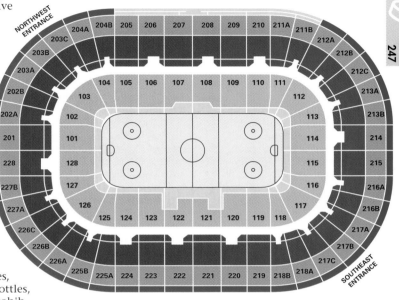

■ $20	■ $78
■ $41	**ATM** Sections 115, 128
■ $50	♿ Throughout
■ $70	

Rockies and the Blues. Those lucky enough to get tickets might enjoy the more raucous atmosphere in the upper level — despite the imperfect views.
• **Lost and found:** (313) 396-7460.

Directions: *From I-94, take Hwy. 10 south (John C. Lodge Frwy.) and exit at Jefferson Ave./Joe Louis Arena. From I-75, exit Rosa Parks Blvd. (Joe Louis Civic Center Parking) and turn right. By Bus: Buses and the People Mover are available to and from the stadium. Call the Detroit Department of Transportation at (313) 933-1300 for information.* **Parking:** *The arena lots hold 3,500 cars. Eighty disabled spots are in the garage on the lower level. There is more parking on W. Jefferson Ave., W. Congress St., Michigan Ave., Bagley St., W. Adams St. and E. Monroe St.*

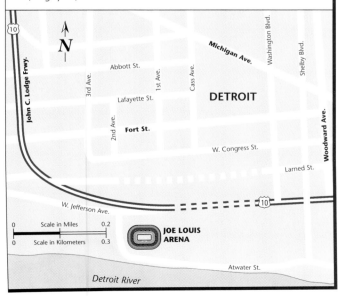

Nearby Hotels

▼▼▼▼ **The Atheneum Suite Hotel & Conference Center** *(Suite Hotel)*, 1000 Brush Ave. (Detroit), (313) 962-2323, $175-$700
▼▼ **Comfort Inn-Downtown Detroit** *(Motel)*, 1999 E. Jefferson Ave. (Detroit), (313) 567-8888, $79-$199
▼▼▼ **Courtyard by Marriott-Detroit Downtown** *(Motel)*, 333 E. Jefferson Ave. in the Millender Center (Detroit), (313) 222-7700, $139-$164
▼▼▼ **Crowne Plaza Pontchartrain** *(Hotel)*, 2 Washington Blvd., (313) 965-0200, $75-$139
▼▼ **Shorecrest Motor Inn** *(Motor Inn)*, 1316 E. Jefferson Ave. (Detroit), (313) 568-3000, $74-$104

Nearby Restaurants

▼ **America's Pizza Café** *(American)*, 2239 Woodward Ave. at the Fox Theater (Detroit), (313) 964-3122, $7-$13
▼▼ **Fishbones Rhythm Kitchen Café** *(Cajun)*, 400 Monroe St. in The Atheneum Suite Hotel & Conference Center (Detroit), (313) 965-4600, $5-$25
▼ **Lafayette Coney Island** *(American)*, 118 W. Lafayette St. (Detroit), (313) 964-8198, $2-$6
▼▼▼ **Opus One** *(American)*, 565 E. Larned St. (Detroit), (313) 961-7766, $20-$39
▼▼▼ **Whitney Restaurant** *(American)*, 4421 Woodward Ave. (Detroit), (313) 832-5700, $19-$35

EDMONTON OILERS

Goalie Tommy Salo.

IN THE NHL HISTORY BOOKS, the 1980s will be remembered as "the decade of the Oilers." Few teams have dominated the NHL the way the Oilers did during this golden period. After six moderately successful years in the WHA, the Oilers joined the NHL for the 1979–80 season and immediately began climbing the ranks. The architect of the Oilers' rise was Glen Sather, team President and General Manager, who became famous for his shrewd draft picks. Sather gambled by building the team around a slew of youngsters unproven at the NHL level, players such as Wayne Gretzky, Mark Messier and Paul Coffey. It was a gamble that had a huge payoff. In his first year of play, Gretzky tied Marcel Dionne for the most points in the league and by the end of the 1980–81 season he had set the league record of 164 points. The following season "the Great One" smashed Phil Esposito's NHL single-season goal record with a final tally of 92, a record that stands to this day. Following Gretzky's lead, the other Oilers rose to the occasion in 1982–83, with Messier and Glenn Anderson also topping the 100 point mark, but the team lost in the NHL finals. In 1984 Edmonton won its first Stanley Cup and repeated the feat in the next season as Gretzky set two more league records with 163 assists and a whopping 215 points. It wasn't until 1991 — three more Stanley Cups later — that a crack began to form in the Oiler dynasty. With the departure of Gretzky in 1988 and Messier, Anderson and goalie Grant Fuhr in 1991, the team seemed to lose its spark. Struggling for the next few years, the Oilers failed to make the playoffs from 1992–93 to 1995–96. However, led by Doug Weight and goalie Curtis Joseph, the team engineered a couple of good postseason runs in the late '90s, falling short twice in the semifinals. Over the past seasons, rising stars such as Weight, goalie Tommy Salo and left-winger Ryan Smyth have fans thinking of the glory years.

"I go to the rink happy and I leave it happy."

— Wayne Gretzky, former Oilers superstar

POSTSEASON
- **Stanley Cup Championships** 5
(1983–84, 1984–85, 1986–87, 1987–88, 1989–90)

RETIRED NUMBERS
- **Al Hamilton (3)**
- **Wayne Gretzky (99)**

TEAM RECORDS
- **Glenn Anderson (1981–91, 1995–96)**
Assists by a Right Winger (season): 67 (1981–82)
Game-Winning Goals (career): 73
Power-Play Goals (career): 126
- **Kelly Buchberger (1987–99)**
Penalty Minutes (career): 1,747
- **Paul Coffey (1981–87)**
Assists by a Defenseman (season): 90 (1985–86)
Goals by a Defenseman (season): 48 (1985–86)
Points by a Defenseman (season): 138 (1985–86)
- **Grant Fuhr (1982–91)**
Wins (career): 226
- **Wayne Gretzky (1980–88)**
Assists (game): 7 (Feb. 14, 1986)
Assists (season): 163 (1985–86)
Assists (career): 1086
Goals (game): 5 (Dec. 6, 1987)
Goals (season): 92 (1981–82)
Goals (career): 583
Points (season): 215 (1985–86)
Points (career): 1,669
Power-Play Goals (season): 20 (1983–84)
Shorthanded Goals (career): 55
Shots (season): 369 (1981–82)
- **Curtis Joseph (1996–98)**
Shutouts (season): 8 (1997–98)
Shutouts (career): 14
- **Jari Kurri (1981–90)**
Goals by a Right Winger (season): 71 (1984–85)
Points by a Right Winger (season): 135 (1984–85)
- **Kevin Lowe (1980–92, 1997–98)**
Games (career): 1,037
- **Mark Messier (1983–84)**
Assists by a Left Winger (season): 64 (1981–82)
Goals by a Left Winger (season): 50 (1981–82)
Points by a Left Winger (season): 106 (1982–83)
- **Steve Smith (1985–91)**
Penalty Minutes (season): 286 (1987–88)

LEAGUE HONORS
Hart Trophy
- **Wayne Gretzky (1980–81, 1981–82, 1982–83, 1983–84, 1984–85, 1985–86, 1986–87)**
- **Mark Messier (1989–90)**

Art Ross Trophy
- **Wayne Gretzky (1980–81, 1981–82, 1982–83, 1983–84, 1984–85, 1985–86, 1986–87)**

James Norris Trophy
- **Paul Coffey (1984–85, 1985–86)**

Vezina Trophy
- **Grant Fuhr (1987–88)**

Lady Byng Trophy
- **Wayne Gretzky (1979–80)**
- **Jari Kurri (1984–85)**

Slap Shot

- *In the spring of 1998 the future of the Oilers looked bleak. After a number of rough years, the Oilers dynasty was up for sale and the city was scrambling to find local investors to raise millions of dollars by a March 13 deadline. At the last possible moment, a group of 17 investors raised the money needed to keep the team in Edmonton and by 2000 the team was owned by 37 people.*

Vital Stats

Stadium Address:
7424 118th Ave., Edmonton, Alta.
Phone: (780) 471-7210
Web: edmontonoilers.com
Box Office:
(780) 414-GOAL
Mon.–Fri. 8:30–5, Sat. 9–5, game days at Skyreach
Media Coverage:
Radio: CHED (630 AM)
TV: A-Channel (CKEM Channel 51),
CTV Sports Net
Practice Facility: Skyreach Centre, Edmonton, Alta.

Lester B. Pearson
- Wayne Gretzky (1982–83, 1983–84, 1984–85, 1986–87)
- Mark Messier (1989–90)

Jack Adams Award
- Glen Sather (1985–86)

Conn Smythe Trophy
- Mark Messier (1984)
- Wayne Gretzky (1985, '88)
- Bill Ranford (1990)

Hockey Hall of Fame
- Glen Sather (1997)
- Wayne Gretzky (1999)

Timeline

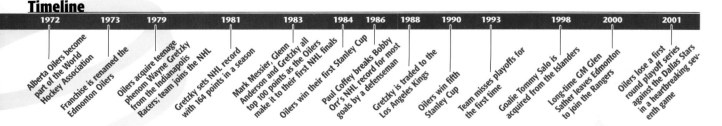

1972	1973	1979	1981	1983	1984	1986	1988	1990	1993	1998	2000	2001

- **1972** Alberta Oilers become part of the World Hockey Association
- **1973** Franchise is renamed the Edmonton Oilers
- **1979** Oilers acquire teenage phenom Wayne Gretzky from the Indianapolis Racers; team joins the NHL
- **1981** Gretzky sets NHL record with 164 points in a season
- **1983** Mark Messier, Glenn Anderson and Gretzky all top 100 points as the Oilers make it to their first NHL finals
- **1984** Oilers win their first Stanley Cup
- **1986** Paul Coffey breaks Bobby Orr's NHL record for most goals by a defenseman
- **1988** Gretzky is traded to the Los Angeles Kings
- **1990** Oilers win fifth Stanley Cup
- **1993** Team misses playoffs for the first time
- **1998** Goalie Tommy Salo is acquired from the Islanders
- **2000** Long-time GM Glen Sather leaves Edmonton to join the Rangers
- **2001** Oilers lose a first round playoff series against the Dallas Stars in a heartbreaking seventh game

SKYREACH CENTRE: RICH IN HOCKEY HISTORY

ORIGINALLY CALLED THE NORTHLANDS Coliseum, this plain looking arena belies the wealth of hockey history it has witnessed. By the mid-1980s, at the height of the Oiler's reign atop the NHL, the arena was one of the most famous in the world — on par with Yankee Stadium for the aura of excellence it exuded. These days the Skyreach has become a monument to the great teams of the past and, of course, Wayne Gretzky. "The Great One's" retired jersey is on display, a large bronze statue of him stands outside and a collection of Oilers memorabilia is housed inside.

CONCESSIONS

The choice of concessions offered at the Skyreach Centre includes pizza, beaver tails, hamburgers, German sausage, ice cream, gourmet pretzels and frozen yogurt. Vegetarians and the health-conscious can enjoy submarine sandwiches, salads, or veggies and dip.

GAME DAY TIPS

• **Gate hours:** Gates open 90 minutes prior to opening faceoff.
• **Prohibited items:** Bottles, cans, alcoholic beverages, video cameras and audio recording devices are prohibited. Smoking is not allowed in the arena, but patrons are allowed to exit through the north and south entrances in order to light up.
• **Ticket tips:** The Oilers have a large number of season ticket holders, which can make tickets a little hard to come by. Crowds will be larger if the arch rival Dallas Stars or any Canadian team is in town. The Skyreach Centre has good sight lines, which makes the less expensive tickets an especially good value.
• **Lost and found:** (780) 471-7316 or 471-7221.

Arena Facts

Opened: *Nov. 10, 1974*
Cost: *$17.3 million*
Capacity: *17,100*
Home Sweet Home:
• *Skyreach is famous for having the "fastest" ice in the NHL, perfect for teams with great skaters. The Oilers have always stacked their team with some of the fastest skaters in the league, who can use the Edmonton ice to its best advantage.*

Seating Plan

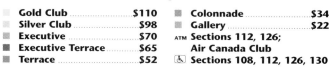

- Gold Club $110
- Silver Club $98
- Executive $70
- Executive Terrace $65
- Terrace $52
- Colonnade $34
- Gallery $22
- ATM Sections 112, 126; Air Canada Club
- ♿ Sections 108, 112, 126, 130

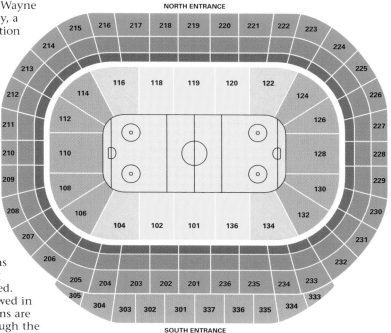

NORTH ENTRANCE

SOUTH ENTRANCE

Directions: *From Yellowhead Trail east or west, exit at Northlands Park. From Hwy. 2 north, take Whitemud Frwy. east and exit at 66th St./75th St. northbound. By Train: The LRT's Coliseum Station is just outside Skyreach Centre. By Bus: Several buses go to the arena. Call (780) 496-1611 for information.* **Parking:** *The on-site parking area at the arena is reserved for season ticket holders, but there are more than 2,700 spots available on the Northlands grounds. There are 40 on-site spots reserved for the disabled on a first-come first-served basis, with 50 more located on the grounds. There is also parking on 117th and 118th Aves.*

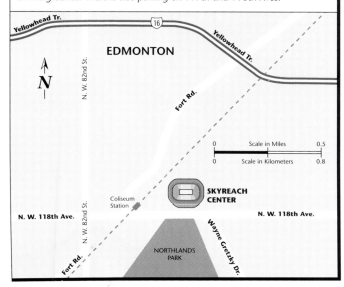

Nearby Hotels

▼▼ **Chateau Louis Hotel & Conference Centre** *(Motor Inn)*, 11727 Kingsway Ave. (Edmonton), (780) 452-7770, $89-$150
▼▼▼▼ **The Fairmont Hotel MacDonald** *(Classic Hotel)*, 10065 100th St. (Edmonton), (780) 424-5181, $179-$249
▼▼▼ **Glenora Bed & Breakfast Inn** *(Bed & Breakfast)*, 12327 102nd Ave. (Edmonton), (780) 488-6766
▼▼▼ **Ramada Hotel and Conference Centre** *(Motor Inn)*, 11834 Kingsway Ave. (Edmonton), (780) 454-5454, $139
▼▼▼ **Union Bank Inn** *(Historic Country Inn)*, 10053 Jasper Ave. (Edmonton), (780) 423-3600, $119-$179

Nearby Restaurants

▼▼▼ **Khazana** *(Indian)*, 10177 107th St. (Edmonton), (780) 702-0330, $10-$20
▼▼▼ **La Spiga** *(Italian)*, 10133 125th St. (Edmonton), (780) 482-3100, $15-$24
▼▼ **New Asian Village** *(Indian)*, 10143 Saskatchewan Dr. (Edmonton), (780) 433-3804, $10-$25
▼ **O'Byrne's Irish Pub** *(Irish)*, 10616 82nd Ave. (Edmonton), (780) 414-6766, $6-$15
▼▼ **Yiannis Taverna** *(Greek)*, 1044 82nd Ave. NW (Edmonton), (780) 433-6768, $13-$20

FLORIDA PANTHERS

ALTHOUGH MIAMI WAS GRANTED A PRO FRANCHISE with the upstart World Hockey Association in 1972, this team, the Screaming Eagles, never got off the ground. It wasn't until Blockbuster Chairman H. Wayne Huizenga launched his NHL project 20 years later that Miami finally had its own hockey team: the Florida Panthers. Under coach Roger Neilson, "the Cats" built an impressive roster that included Brian Skrudland, Scott Mellanby, Bill Lindsay and Tom Fitzgerald. The team also got a big break early when they acquired ex-Ranger John Vanbiesbrouck, one of the finest goaltenders in the game. The young squad racked up an impressive .494 winning percentage during the 1993–94 season — the best ever by a first-year team in any modern pro sport. The team continued to grow and mature during the course of the following season. In the 1994 entry draft, the Cats selected burly defenseman Ed Jovanovski and veteran Ray Sheppard and in 1995 the Panthers hired coach Doug MacLean to lead the team into its third season. The team responded well to these additions and suddenly began winning games. Early in the season the team got a boost when forward Scott Mellanby recorded his infamous "Rat Trick" by scoring two goals against Calgary and flinging one unfortunate rat across the Miami Arena dressing room to its death. The fans went wild with this story and for the rest of the season the Panthers were showered with support, as well as hundreds of plastic and rubber rats, after each goal. For the first time ever, the Panthers qualified for the playoffs. Expected to be eliminated quickly, the Cats surprised everyone as they systematically downed the Bruins, the Flyers and the Penguins to qualify for the Stanley Cup finals. Although they lost to the Colorado Avalanche after four hard-fought games, Florida won the honor of being one of the youngest teams to ever reach the finals. After this early magic, however, the team began to fall apart. For many fans, the loss of Fitzgerald, Sheppard and Vanbiesbrouck in 1998 signaled the end of Miami's popular underdog team. Since its Cinderella year, the Panthers have only seen postseason action on two occasions. With the acquisition of goal-scoring sensation Pavel Bure in 1999 and goalie Roberto Luongo in 2000, however, things may be looking up for the team in the future.

> *"I've never seen a guy who wants to score goals more than Pavel."*
>
> — *Ray Whitney, on Pavel Bure*

Vital Stats

Stadium Address:
One Panther Pkwy.,
Sunrise, Fla.
Phone: (954) 835-8000
Web: flpanthers.com,
national-ctr.com
Box Office:
(954) 835-TEAM,
Mon.–Fri.10–6, game days
Sat. 12–6
Media Coverage:
Radio: WQAM (560 AM)
TV: Fox Sports Net
Practice Facility:
Incredible Ice,
Coral Springs, Fla.

POSTSEASON
- **Eastern Conference Championships** 1
(1995–96)

TEAM RECORDS
- **Pavel Bure (1999–present)**
Game-Winning Goals
(season): 14 (1999–2000)
Game-Winning Goals
(career): 22

Slap Shot

- *Although the Panthers lost their 1996 Stanley Cup hopes to the Colorado Avalanche, their performance in the fourth and final game of the series is noteworthy. Deadlocked at 0-0 throughout the three periods, the game went into three sudden-death overtime periods before Uwe Kruppe, the powerful Avalanche defenseman, was able to fire a shot past John Vanbiesbrouck.*

Goals (game): 4 (tie)
(Feb. 10, 2001)
Goals (season): 59 (2000–01)
Points (season): 94
(1999–2000)
Shots on Goal (season): 384
(2000–01)
Power-Play Goals (season):
19 (tie) (2000–01)
- **Tom Fitzgerald (1993–98)**
Shorthanded Goals
(season): 6 (1995–96)
Shorthanded Goals
(career): 12
- **Victor Kozlov (1997–present)**
Assists (season): 53
(1999–2000)
- **Paul Laus (1993–present)**
Penalty Minutes (game): 30
(Mar. 16, 1995)
Penalty Minutes (season):
313 (1996–97)
Penalty Minutes
(career): 1,545
- **Roberto Luongo (2000–present)**
Shutouts (season): 5
(2000–01)
- **Scott Mellanby (1993–2000)**

Assists (game): 4 (tie)
(Nov. 26, 1997)
Games (career): 552
Goals (career): 157
Points (career): 354
Power-Play Goals (season):
19 (tie) (1995–96)
Power-Play Goals (career): 66
Shots (career): 1,296
- **Mark Parrish (1998–2000)**
Goals (game): 4
(tie) (Oct. 30,
1998)
- **Robert Svehla (1994–present)**
Assists
(career): 207
- **John Vanbiesbrouck (1993–98)**
Games by a
Goaltender
(career): 268
Wins (season):
27 (1996–97)
Wins
(career): 106
Shutouts
(career): 13
- **Ray Whitney (1997–2001)**

Assists (game): 4 (tie)
(Oct. 30, 2000)

LEAGUE HONORS
Maurice Richard Trophy
- Pavel Bure
(1999–2000, 2000–01)

Hockey Hall of Fame
- Bill Torrey (1995)

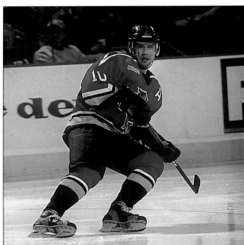

One of the league's best skaters is Pavel Bure.

Timeline

1992	1993	1994	1995	1995	1996	1996	1997	1998	1999	2000	2000

The NHL grants an expansion franchise to businessman H. Wayne Huizenga in Miami

Panthers win their home opener to a sellout crowd

John Vanbiesbrouck and Bob Kudelski named to NHL All-Star team

July: Doug MacLean named Head Coach of the Panthers

Oct.: Scott Mellanby kills a rat in the Panthers locker room, starting rubber rat craze among fans

April: The Panthers qualify for the playoffs for the first time

June: The Cats are swept by the Colorado Avalanche in the Stanley Cup finals

Vanbiesbrouck is 15th goalie to notch 300th win

Panthers begin play at the National Car Rental Center

The Cats acquire Pavel Bure from the Canucks

Jan.: Scott Mellanby scores his 500th NHL point

April: Panthers finish regular season with team record 43 wins

NATIONAL CAR RENTAL CENTER: THE CENTER OF IT ALL

IN 1995 SCOTT MELLANBY made news when he killed a rat in the old Miami Arena dressing room with a fierce slap shot. Although this incident instigated the Panthers' legendary tradition of tossing toy rats onto the ice, it also underlined the team's need for a new arena. This new arena arrived in the shape of the award-winning National Car Rental Center, billed as "the Center of it All." Renowned for its state-of-the-art facilities, unique design and innovative service for people with disabilities, this very new arena has become the standard for all hockey rinks.

CONCESSIONS

The food offered at the National Car Rental Center includes standard arena fare, such as hot dogs, burgers, nachos and popcorn, as well as more varied options such as Chinese stir-fry, gourmet pizza, Caesar salad and Cuban sandwiches — a Florida local specialty.

Arena Facts

Opened: Oct. 3, 1998
Cost: $185 million
Capacity: 19,250
Home Sweet Home:
• Designed with home-ice advantage in mind, the National Car Rental Center was built so that its steeper seating pitch would maximize noise levels of the hometown fans.

GAME DAY TIPS

• **Gate hours:** Gates open one hour prior to opening faceoff.
• **Prohibited items:** Food or beverages, coolers, cans, bottles, video cameras, audio recorders, weapons, horns or noisemakers, beachballs, frisbees and fireworks are prohibited. Animals are also prohibited, except those providing service to the disabled. Smoking is allowed outside in designated areas.
• **Ticket tips:** There is rarely any difficulty getting tickets to see the Panthers, although weekend games as well as games against the Penguins and the Red Wings draw bigger crowds. The Tampa Bay Lightning are an interstate rival and games against them often draw large crowds — many fans travel all the way from Tampa.
• **Lost and found:** (954) 835-8610.

Seating Plan

- ■ Emerald Club $95
- ■ Lower Bowl $67
- Club Level $75
- ■ Mezzanine $38
- ■ Sideline Balcony $30
- Goal Zone $25
- ■ Panther Pack Tickets $14
- ATM Sections 105, 131, 405
- ♿ Throughout

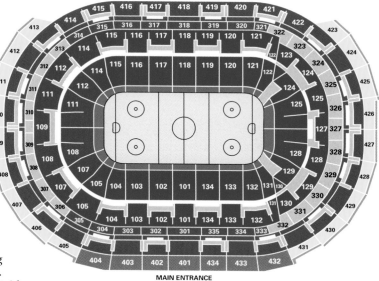

MAIN ENTRANCE

Directions: Exit Sawgrass Expwy. (Rte. 869) southbound at Oakland Park Blvd. and northbound at Pat Salerno Dr. After the toll plaza, proceed to Panther Pkwy. From I-595 west, take exit 1 (136th Ave.) and proceed north to the arena. By Bus: Buses are available to and from the arena. Call the Broward County Transit at (954) 357-8400 for more information. **Parking:** The lot at the National Car Rental Center can accommodate 7,500 cars and rarely fills up. There are 90 parking spaces for guests with disabilities on the northeast and southeast sides of the arena.

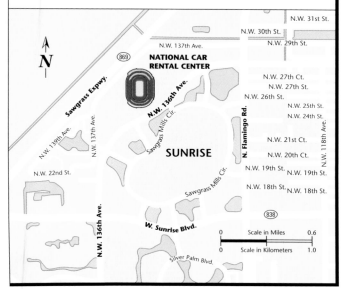

Nearby Hotels

▼▼▼ **AmeriSuites Plantation** (*Suite Motel*), 8530 W. Broward Blvd. (Plantation), (954) 370-2220, $79-$149
▼▼▼ **Baymont Inn & Suites-Sunrise Sawgrass** (*Motel*), 13651 NW 2nd St. (Sunrise), (954) 846-1200, $89-$114
▼▼▼ **La Quinta Inn & Suites** (*Motel*), 8101 Peters Rd. in the Crossroad Office Park (Plantation), (954) 476-6047, $89-$109
▼▼▼ **Sheraton Suites-Plantation** (*Suite Hotel*), 311 N. University Dr. at the Fashion Mall (Plantation), (954) 424-3300, $229-$349
▼▼▼ **Wyndham Resort & Spa, Ft. Lauderdale** (*Resort*), 250 Racquet Club Rd. (Weston), (954) 389-3300, $89-$270

Nearby Restaurants

▼▼ **Brasserie Max** (*American*), 321 N. University Dr. in the Fashion Mall (Plantation), (954) 424-8000, $8-$17
▼ **Davie Ale House** (*American*), 2080 University Dr. (Davie), (954) 236-0062, $6-$11
▼▼ **Emerald Coast** (*Chinese*), 4519 N. Pine Island Rd. (Sunrise), (954) 572-3822, $17
▼▼▼ **La Cucina Toscana** (*Italian*), 250 Racquet Club Rd. in the Wyndham Resort & Spa, Ft. Lauderdale (Weston), (954) 349-5712, $16-$25 (dinner only)
▼▼ **Legal Sea Foods** (*Seafood*), 2602 Sawgrass Mills Center (Sunrise), (954) 846-9011, $14-$30

LOS ANGELES KINGS

WHEN THE LATE JACK KENT COOKE brought hockey to Los Angeles in 1967, there were many who said he would fail. But the Canadian-born owner of the Los Angeles Lakers was passionate about the sport. He wanted his team to have a regal air, so he dubbed them "the Kings." Cooke also built a state-of-the-art palace, the Fabulous Forum. Cooke's original Kings featured a cast of colorful characters, many with nicknames coined by Cooke himself. Stars such as "Cowboy Bill" Flett and Eddie "the Jet" Joyal would entertain fans until bona fide stars such as Bob Pulford and Marcel Dionne arrived in the 1970s. Late in that decade, Dionne was joined by Charlie Simmer and Dave Taylor to form "the Triple Crown Line," one of the most potent scoring trios in league history. In 1988 the Kings brought true hockey royalty to town, acquiring perhaps the greatest player ever —Wayne Gretzky — from Edmonton. "The Great One" lived up to his billing, leading the Kings to their first Stanley Cup finals in 1993. Now ensconced in the ultramodern STAPLES Center, the Kings are relying on established stars Luc Robitaille and Adam Deadmarsh to lead the team to hockey's throne.

Longtime King Luc Robitaille continues to be a true sniper.

POSTSEASON
- **Campbell Conference Championships**..................1 (1992–93)
- **Smythe Division Titles**...1 (1990–91)
- **Playoff Appearances**.....22 (1967–68, 1968–69, 1973–74, 1974–75, 1975–76, 1976–77, 1977–78, 1978–79, 1979–80, 1980–81, 1981–82, 1984–85, 1986–87, 1987–88, 1988–89, 1989–90, 1990–91, 1991–92, 1992–93, 1997–98, 1999–2000, 2000–01)

RETIRED NUMBERS
- **Marcel Dionne (16)**
- **Dave Taylor (18)**
- **Rogie Vachon (30)**

TEAM RECORDS
- **Rob Blake (1989–2001)**
Assists by a Defenseman (career): 291
Goals by a Defenseman (career): 138
Points by a Defenseman (career): 429
- **Marcel Dionne (1975–87)**
Assists (career): 757
Consecutive Games: 324 (1978–82)
Game-Winning Goals (season): 9 (tie) (1980–81)
Goals (career): 550
Points (career): 1,307
30-goal seasons: 11 (tie)
100-point seasons: 7
- **Wayne Gretzky (1988–96)**
Assists (season): 122 (1990–91)
Playoff Points (career): 94
Points (season): 168 (1988–89)
- **Kelly Hrudey (1989–96)**
Playoff Wins (career): 26
- **Mario Lessard (1978–84)**
Wins (season): 35 (1980-81)
- **Marty McSorley (1988–96)**
Penalty Minutes (season): 399 (1992–93)
Penalty Minutes (career): 1,846
- **Bernie Nicholls (1981–90)**
Goals (season): 70 (1988–89)
Shorthanded Goals (season): 8 (1988–89)
Shots (season): 385 (1988–89)
- **Luc Robitaille (1986–94, 1997–present)**
Assists by a Left Winger (season): 63 (1991-92)
Goals by a Left Winger (season): 63 (1992–93)
Goals by a Rookie: 45 (1986–87)

Playoff Games (career): 94
Playoff Goals (career): 41
Points by a Left Winger (season): 125 (1992–93)
Power-Play Goals (season): 26 (1991–92)
Power-Play Goals (career): 195
30-Goal seasons: 11 (tie)
40-Goal Seasons: 9
- **Charlie Simmer (1977–85)**
Game-Winning Goals (season): 9 (tie) (1980–81)
- **Dave Taylor (1977–94)**
Games (career): 1,111
- **Rogie Vachon (1971–78)**
Games by a Goalie (career): 389
Games by a Goalie (season): 70 (1977–78)
Saves Pct. (season): .929 (1974–75)
Shutouts (season): 8 (1977–78)
Shutouts (career): 32
Goals Against Avg. (season): 2.24 (1974–75)
Wins (career): 171

LEAGUE HONORS
Art Ross Trophy
- **Marcel Dionne (1979–80)**
- **Wayne Gretzky (1989–90, 1990–91, 1993–94)**

Norris Trophy
- **Rob Blake (1997–98)**

Calder Trophy
- **Luc Robitaille (1986–87)**

Lady Byng Trophy
- **Marcel Dionne (1976–77)**
- **Butch Goring (1977–78)**
- **Wayne Gretzky (1990–91, 1991–92, 1993–94)**

Masterton Trophy
- **Butch Goring (1977–78)**
- **Bob Bourne (1987–88)**
- **Dave Taylor (1990–91)**

King Clancy Trophy
- **Dave Taylor (1990–91)**

Jack Adams Trophy
- **Bob Pulford (1974–75)**

Vital Stats

Stadium Address:
1111 S. Figueroa St.,
Los Angeles, Calif.
Phone: (213) 742-7100
Web: lakings.com,
staplescenter.com
Box Office: (213) 742-7340, Mon.–Sat. 10–7
Media Coverage:
Radio: KRLA (1110 AM)
TV: Fox Sports Net
Training Facility:
HealthSouth Training Center, El Segundo, Calif.

Slap Shot

- The STAPLES Center hosted the largest-ever hockey crowd in California: 18,478.
- Down 3-0 to Detroit in game four of their opening-round series in 2001, L.A. roared back from a 3-0 deficit with just seven minutes remaining to take the game and later the series.

"We turned some heads."
— Bryan Smolinski, on the Kings' improbable 2000–01 playoff run

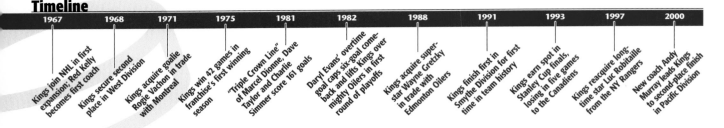

Timeline

1967	1968	1971	1975	1981	1982	1988	1991	1993	1997	2000
Kings join NHL in first expansion; Red Kelly becomes first coach	Kings secure second place in West Division	Kings acquire goalie Rogie Vachon in trade with Montreal	Kings win 42 games in franchise's first winning season	"Triple Crown Line" of Marcel Dionne, Dave Taylor and Charlie Simmer score 161 goals	Daryl Evans' overtime goal caps six-goal comeback and lifts Kings over mighty Oilers in first round of playoffs	Kings acquire superstar Wayne Gretzky in trade with Edmonton Oilers	Kings finish first in Smythe Division for first time in team history	Kings earn spot in Stanley Cup finals, losing in five games to the Canadiens	Kings reacquire longtime star Luc Robitaille from the NY Rangers	New coach Andy Murray leads Kings to second-place finish in Pacific Division

252

STAPLES CENTER
THE KINGS' CASTLE

OPENED IN 1999, the STAPLES Center has quickly established itself as one of the premier venues in all of sport. Home to both the Los Angeles Lakers and Clippers of the NBA as well as the Arena Football League's Los Angeles Avengers, the center is able to undergo complete changeovers to serve its various tenants in remarkably little time. It also hosts boxing events and concerts. The center features a wide array of fan conveniences, including 1,200 television monitors, two restaurants and about 6,000 parking spots.

CONCESSIONS

The center's 23 refreshment stands feature a wide variety of all the foods fans could expect, including hot dogs, pretzels, Chinese food, pizza, hamburgers, Mexican food and standard deli fare.

GAME DAY TIPS

• **Gate hours:** Gates open one hour prior to opening faceoff.

Arena Facts

Opened: Oct. 17, 1999
Cost: $400 million
Capacity: 18,118
Type: Indoor
Surface: Ice/Court floor
Home Sweet Home:
• Like so many people in Los Angeles, Kings fans love to be part of a show and are considered to be among the NHL's loudest.

• **Prohibited items:** Cameras with professional lenses, signs larger than 11 inches by 17 inches, food or beverages, strollers, skateboards, scooters and pets — except for service animals — are prohibited. Smoking is not permitted in the center; however, designated smoking terraces allow reentry to building.
• **Ticket tips:** Seats are typically available at every level for Kings games, but purchasing in advance is recommended, especially when popular opponents such as Dallas, Phoenix or the Mighty Ducks are in town. Entrance off Figueroa St. is least crowded during entry and exit times.
• **Lost and found:** (213) 742-7444.

Directions: Take I-405, I-105 or I-10 to I-110 north. Exit right onto Adams Blvd., then left onto Figueroa St., left onto 11th St. By Public Transportation: Many buses go to the arena. The Metro Blue Line and Red Line also pass nearby. Call the Metropolitan Transportation Authority (MTA) at 1-800-COMMUTE for information. **Parking:** Parking lots around the arena can accommodate about 6,000 cars; all are wheelchair-accessible. More parking is available on 8th, 9th, 11th and 12th Sts. and Olympic Blvd.

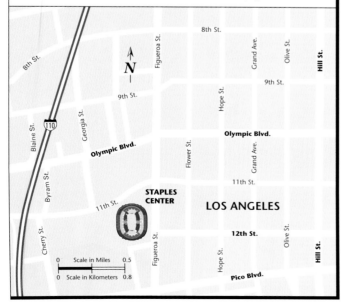

Seating Plan

□ .... N/A	■ .... N/A
▦ .... N/A	▨ **Premium Seating**
■ .... N/A	**ATM** Sections 109, 320;
▤ .... N/A	Star Plaza entry
■ .... N/A	♿ **Throughout**

11TH ST. ENTRY

FIGUEROA ST. ENTRY

STAR PLAZA ENTRY

Nearby Hotels

▼▼ **Best Western Dragon Gate Inn** *(Motor Inn)*, 818 N. Hill St. (Los Angeles), (213) 617-3077, $79-$189
▼▼▼▼ **Hyatt Regency Los Angeles** *(Hotel)*, 711 S. Hope St. (Los Angeles), (213) 683-1234, $210-$235
▼▼▼ **Los Angeles Downtown Marriott Hotel** *(Hotel)*, 333 S. Figueroa St. (Los Angeles), (213) 617-1133, $190-$149
▼▼▼ **The Millennium Biltmore Los Angeles** *(Classic Hotel)*, 506 S. Grand St. at 5th St. (Los Angeles), (213) 624-1011, $135-$155
▼▼▼ **Wyndham Checkers Hotel** *(Hotel)*, 535 S. Grand Ave. (Los Angeles), (213) 624-0000, $99-$199

Nearby Restaurants

▼▼▼ **A Thousand Cranes Restaurant** *(Japanese)*, 120 S. Los Angeles St. in the New Otani Hotel (Los Angeles), (213) 253-9255, $35-$90
▼▼▼ **Checkers Restaurant** *(Continental)*, 535 S. Grand Ave. in the Wyndham Checkers Hotel (Los Angeles), (213) 891-0519, $16-32 (dinner only)
▼▼ **Engine Company No. 28** *(American)*, 644 S. Figueroa St. (Los Angeles), (213) 624-6996, $10-$20
▼▼ **McCormick & Schmick's** *(Seafood)*, 633 W. 5th St. in the First Interstate World Center Bldg., 4th floor (Los Angeles), (213) 629-1929, $9-$20
▼▼▼ **The Tower** *(Continental)*, 1150 S. Olive St. in the Transamerica Center Bldg., 32nd floor (Los Angeles), (213) 746-1554, $35-$45

MINNESOTA WILD

FOLLOWING THE MINNESOTA WILD'S first NHL season in 2000–01, jokes surfaced about how the team might want to change its name. Playing in a system that stressed defense, the Wild's decidedly tame offense scored the fewest goals in the league. Minnesota's average of 2.04 goals per game pales in comparison to some of the NHL's most potent squads such as the Devils (3.5), the Avalanche (3.4) and the Senators (3.3). But this should hardly come as a surprise from a team coached by Jacques Lemaire. A Hall-of-Fame player for the Montreal Canadiens, Lemaire made his name as a coach in 1994–95, when he led the New Jersey Devils to the team's first Stanley Cup. With the Devils, Lemaire implemented his now-famous "neutral zone trap," in which opposing forwards are forced toward the boards when they have possession of the puck, effectively clogging up the middle of the ice and slowing down the most dangerous players. Stressing the fundamentals — and with 11 Stanley Cup rings to his credit Lemaire knows as much about the game's fundamentals as any man alive — the coach made no apologies for his team's conservative game plan. Knowledgeable Minnesotans appreciated the subtleties of the Wild's style of play, especially when it translated into an eight-game unbeaten streak in the middle of the season, including a 6-0 shellacking of the Dallas Stars. Although the team finished last in its division, it showed great potential with young stars such as Marian Gaborik and goaltender Manny Fernadez. With a solid first season under its belt, it won't be long before this team runs wild.

Manny Fernandez gives Wild fans high hopes for the future.

TEAM RECORDS
- **Jim Dowd (2000–present)**
Assists by a Center (season): 22 (2000–01)
- **Manny Fernandez (2000–present)**

Slap Shot

- *Although the team is new, the Wild's organization is full of proven winners. Vice President and General Manager Doug Riseborough won four Stanley Cups as a player with the Canadiens. He won a fifth in 1989 with the Flames as an assistant coach. Another ex-Hab, Head Coach Jacques Lemaire won 10 Cups in Montreal, eight as a player and two in front office. He won again in 1995 as Head Coach of the Devils. Assistant Coach Mario Tremblay sipped from four Cups as a Hab and Guy Lapointe, Coordinator of Amateur Scouting, was a member of six winning teams in Montreal. That's 26 Stanley Cup rings between them.*

Games by a Goalie (season): 42 (2000–01)
Goals Against Avg. (season): 2.24 (2000–01)
Minutes by a Goalie (season): 2,460 (2000–01)
Saves (season): 1,055
Save Pct. (season): .919 (2000–01)
Shutouts (season): 4 (2000–01)
Starts by a Goalie (season): 40 (2000–01)
Wins (season): 19 (2000–01)
- **Marian Gaborik (2000–present)**
Assists by a Left Winger (season): 18 (2000–01)
Goals (season): 18 (tie) (2000–01)
Goals by a Rookie: 18 (2000–01)
Points by a Left Winger (season): 36 (2000–01)
Power Play Goals (season): 6 (2000–01)
Shots (season): 179 (2000–01)
- **Darby Hendrikson (2000–present)**
Goals (season): 18 (tie) (2000–01)
- **Matt Johnson (2000–present)**
Penalty Minutes (season): 137 (2000–01)
- **Filip Kuba (2000–present)**
Game-Winning Goals (season): 4 (2000–01)
Power-Play Assists (season): 10 (2000–01)

Power-Play Goals by a Defenseman (season): 4 (tie) (2000–01)
Power-Play Points (season): 14 (2000–01)
- **Antti Laaksonen (2000–present)**
Games (season): 82 (2000–01)
- **Jamie McLennan (2000–present)**
Most Goals Against (season): 98 (2000–01)
Ties (season): 9 (2000–01)
Losses (season): 23 (2000–01)
- **Scott Pellerin (2000–01)**
Assists (season): 28 (2000–01)
Goals by a Right Winger (season): 11 (2000–01)
Plus/Minus (season): +6 (2000–01)
Points (season): 39 (2000–01)
- **Lubomir Sekeras (2000–present)**
Assists by a Defenseman (season): 23 (2000–01)
Goals by a Defenseman (season): 11 (2000–01)
Points by a Defenseman (season): 34 (2000–01)
Power-Play Goals by a

"I want players who follow systems and who put the team first."
— Coach Jacques Lemaire, on the type of players he wants on the Wild

Vital Stats

Stadium Address:
175 W. Kellogg Blvd., Saint Paul, Minn.
Phone: *(651) 265-4800*
Web: *wild.com, xcelenergycenter.com*
Box Office:
(651) 726-8240, Mon.–Fri. 10–6, events Sat.–Sun. call for hours
Media Coverage:
Radio: WCCO (830 AM) TV: KMSP (Channel 9), Fox Sports Net
Practice Facility:
Parade Ice Gardens, Minneapolis, Minn.

Defenseman (season): 4 (2000–01) (tie)
- **Wes Walz (2000–present)**
Games (season): 82 (tie) (2000–01)
Goals (season): 18 (tie) (2000–01)
Shorthanded Goals (season): 7 (2000–01)
Points by a Center (season): 30 (2000–01)

Timeline

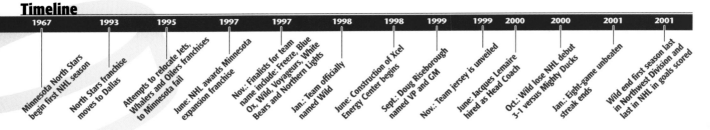

1967	1993	1995	1997	1997	1998	1998	1999	1999	2000	2000	2001	2001

Minnesota North Stars begin first NHL season

North Stars franchise moves to Dallas

Attempts to relocate Jets, Whalers and Oilers franchises to Minnesota fail

June: NHL awards Minnesota expansion franchise

Nov.: Finalists for team name include: Freeze, Blue Ox, Wild, Voyageurs, White Bears and Northern Lights

Jan.: Team officially named Wild

June: Construction of Xcel Energy Center begins

Sept.: Doug Riseborough named VP and GM

Nov.: Team jersey is unveiled

June: Jacques Lemaire hired as Head Coach

Oct.: Wild lose NHL debut 3-1 versus Mighty Ducks

Jan.: Eight-game unbeaten streak ends

Wild end first season last in Northwest Division and last in NHL in goals scored

XCEL ENERGY CENTER: FANS GO WILD

WITH ITS STUNNING GLASS EXTERIOR, the Xcel Energy Center is one of the NHL's most striking venues — and things only get better once fans go inside. Sight lines from all seats are excellent and, depending on the level, fans have access to a bistro, a cigar bar and small stages where live music and other acts take place. The Wild and the U.S. Hockey Hall of Fame also have added a number of displays on the premises so that hockey fans can trace the history of hockey in the Minnesota region.

CONCESSIONS

The concessions at Xcel Energy Center include a variety of foods to please all tastes. All the traditional arena favorites are here, including hamburgers, hot dogs and pizza, as well as garlic cheese bread, Italian sausage with marinara sauce, cheese curds, Buffalo wedges and kosher dogs. There are a variety of beers and liquors for refreshment.

GAME DAY TIPS
• **Gate hours:** Gates open 90 minutes prior to opening faceoff.
• **Prohibited items:** Food, beverages and cans, bottles or coolers are prohibited. Banners and signs are not permitted. Non-flash cameras are permitted, but video cameras are not. Laser pointer are strictly prohibited, as are weapons, beachballs, frisbees and projectiles of any kind. Smoking is permitted only in designated areas.
• **Ticket tips:** The Wild sold out every game in their inaugural season and things look similar for the coming year. There are about 2,000 single tickets available for each game, but they go quickly.
• **Lost and found:** (651) 265-4800.

Arena Facts

Opened: *Sept. 29, 2000*
Cost: *$130 million*
Capacity: *18,600*
Home Sweet Home:
• *Minnesota is the hockey capital of the U.S. As such, the Wild's fans are as knowledgeable as they are loud. Having sold out all 41 home games in the team's first season, the Wild may have the best fan support in the league.*

Seating Plan

■ Arena Club Level	**Call for info**
■ "On the Glass" Club	**Call for info**
■ Lower Level	**$64**
■ Lower Level	**$54**
■ Lower Level	**$44**
■ Upper Level	**$26**
■ Upper Level	**$10**
ATM Sections 114, 115, 302; Gate 1 near Box Office	
♿ Throughout	

Directions: *Exit I-35 east at Grand Ave. Turn right and follow to W. 7th St. Turn left and follow to arena. Exit I-35 east at Wacouta St. Follow to Kellogg Blvd., turn right and follow to arena.* **By Bus:** *Service is available to the center. Call Metro Transit at (612) 341-4287 for information. There are also free shuttles from points around the city.* **Parking:** *There are 25,000 spaces in lots on Kellogg Blvd. and 4th, 5th, 6th, Chestnut, Wabasha and Cedar streets; they have ample disabled parking.*

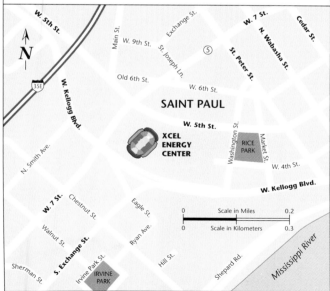

Nearby Hotels

▼▼▼ **Best Western Kelly Inn-State Capitol** *(Motor Inn)*, 161 St. Anthony Ave. (Saint Paul), (952) 227-8711, $89-$119
▼▼▼ **Embassy Suites Saint Paul** *(Suite Hotel)*, 175 E. 10th St. (Saint Paul), (952) 224-5400, $139-$259
FYI **Holiday Inn RiverCentre** *(Motel)*, 175 W. 7th St. (Saint Paul), (952) 225-1515, $109-$169
▼▼▼ **Radisson Riverfront Hotel Saint Paul** *(Hotel)*, 11 E. Kellogg Blvd. (Saint Paul), (952) 292-1900, $139-$189
▼▼▼▼ **The Saint Paul Hotel** *(Classic Hotel)*, 350 Market St. (Saint Paul), (952) 292-9292, $145

Nearby Restaurants

▼ **Elements Café** *(American)*, 120 W. Kellogg Blvd. in the Science Museum of Minnesota (Saint Paul), (952) 221-9444, $5-$9 (lunch only)
▼▼ **Leeann Chin Chinese Cuisine** *(Chinese)*, 214 E. 4th St. in Union Depot Place (Saint Paul), (952) 224-8814, $14
▼▼▼ **Pazzaluna** *(Italian)*, 360 St. Peter (Saint Paul), (952) 223-7000, $15-$40, (dinner only)
▼▼▼ **The St. Paul Grill** *(American)*, 350 Market St. in The Saint Paul Hotel (Saint Paul), (952) 224-7455, $10-$35
▼▼ **Sawatdee** *(Thai)*, 289 E. 5th St. (Saint Paul), (952) 222-5859, $6-$18

MONTREAL CANADIENS

WITH 24 STANLEY CUPS to the Montreal Canadiens' credit, the franchise is
® easily the most successful in hockey history. As might be expected, the team's
long and distinguished history is studded with names of the game's brightest
luminaries. Led by Aurele Joliat and Howie Morenz, the team electrified crowds in the 1920s
and '30s with their dashing style of play. The speed and skill of these "flying Frenchmen"
was to be the trademark of the team for generations to come. Perhaps none have flown higher than Maurice "Rocket" Richard, who in 1945 did the unthinkable and scored 50 goals in
50 games — the first man to do so. Richard was just one of the cornerstones on which the
first great Canadiens dynasty was built. In five straight seasons from 1955 to 1960, the
Canadiens won an unprecedented five Stanley Cups. Richard and his younger brother Henri,
"Boom-Boom" Geoffrion, Doug Harvey, Dickie Moore, Jacques Plante and the incomparable
Jean Beliveau were just some of the players from those teams to have been immortalized in
Hockey's Hall of Fame. This tradition of excellence was passed on to the players of the 1960s
and '70s, who in those 20 years won another 10 Cups. The second great Montreal dynasty, in
which the team won four straight titles to close out the '70s, was led by more Hall of Famers,
such as Guy Lafleur, Jacques Lemaire, Larry Robinson and Ken Dryden. Although the 1980s
and '90s reaped just two more championships — slim pickings by Canadiens' standards —
the team is hoping to bring glory back to this hockey hotbed soon into the new millennium.

"To you from failing hands we throw the torch; be yours to hold it high."

— Lines from poem "In Flanders Field," featured prominently in Montreal's dressing room

Vital Stats

Stadium Address:
1260 de la Gauchetière, Montreal, Que.
Phone: (514) 932-2582
Web: canadiens.com
centre-molson.com
Box Office:
(514) 989-2841,
Mon.–Fri. 12–6, event days
until 9, Sat.–Sun. during
hockey season 12–6
Media Coverage:
Radio: CJAD (800 AM)
TV: CBFT (Channel 2),
TQS (Channel 35)
Practice Facility:
Molson Centre,
Montreal, Que.

POSTSEASON
• **Stanley Cups**...................24
(1915–16, 1923–24, 1929–30,
1930–31, 1943–44, 1945–46,
1952–53, 1955–56, 1956–57,
1957–58, 1958–59, 1959–60,
1964–65, 1965–66, 1967–68,
1968–69, 1970–71, 1972–73,
1975–76, 1976–77, 1977–78,
1978–79, 1985–86, 1992–93)

RETIRED NUMBERS
• Jacques Plante (1)
• Doug Harvey (2)
• Jean Beliveau (4)
• Howie Morenz (7)
• Maurice Richard (9)
• Guy Lafleur (10)
• Henri Richard (16)

TEAM RECORDS
• **Ken Dryden**
(1970–73, 1974–79)
Wins (season): 42 (tie)
(1975–76)
• **Guy Lafleur** (1971–85)
Goals (season): 60 (tie)
(1977–78)
Points (season): 136

Slap Shot

• The team's power play
was so potent in the 1950s
that the rules had to be
changed to limit the team
with the man advantage to
just one goal per penalty.

Saku Koivu is Montreal's most dangerous scoring threat.

(1976–77)
Points (career): 1,246
• **Jacques Plante** (1952–63)
Wins (season): 42 (tie) (twice)
Wins (career): 311
• **Maurice Richard** (1942–60)
Goals (career): 544
• **Steve Shutt** (1972–85)
Goals (season): 60 (tie)
(1976–77)

LEAGUE HONORS
Hart Trophy
• Herb Gardiner (1926–27)
• Howie Morenz (1927–28,
1930–31, 1931–32)
• Aurele Joliat (1933–34)
• Babe Siebert (1936–37)

• Toe Blake (1938–39)
• Elmer Lach (1944–45)
• Maurice Richard (1946–47)
• Jean Beliveau
(1955–56, 1963–64)
• Bernie Geoffrion (1960–61)
• Jacques Plante (1961–62)
• Guy Lafleur
(1976–77, 1977–78)

Art Ross Trophy
• Joe Malone (1917–18)
• Newsy Lalonde
(1918–19, 1920–21)
• Howie Morenz
(1927–28, 1930–31)
• Toe Blake (1938–39)
• Elmer Lach
(1944–45, 1947–48)
• Bernie Geoffrion
(1954–55, 1960–61)
• Jean Beliveau (1955–56)
• Dickie Moore
(1957–58, 1958–59)
• Guy Lafleur (1975–76,
1976–77, 1977–78)

Vezina Trophy
• George Hainsworth
(1926–27, 1927–28, 1928–29)
• Bill Durnan (1943–44,
1944–45, 1945–46, 1946–47,
1948–49, 1949–50)
• Jacques Plante (1955–56,
1956–57, 1957–58, 1958–59,
1959–60, 1961–62)
• Charlie Hodge
(1963–64, 1965–66)
• Lorne Worsley

(1965–66, 1967–68)
• Rogatien Vachon (1967–68)
• Ken Dryden
(1972–73, 1975–76,
1976–77, 1977–78, 1978–79)
• Michel Larocque
(1976–77, 1977–78,
1978–79, 1980–81)
• Denis Herron (1980–81)
• Richard Sevigny (1980–81)
• Patrick Roy (1988–89,
1989–90, 1991–92)

Conn Smythe Trophy
• Jean Beliveau (1965)
• Serge Savard (1969)
• Ken Dryden (1971)
• Yvan Cournoyer (1973)
• Guy Lafleur (1977)
• Larry Robinson (1978)
• Bob Gainey (1979)
• Patrick Roy (1986, '93)

Timeline

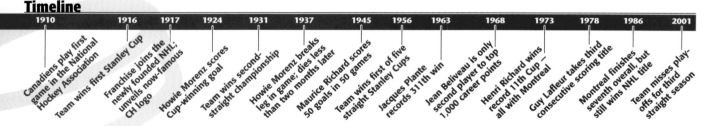

| 1910 | 1916 | 1917 | 1924 | 1931 | 1937 | 1945 | 1956 | 1963 | 1968 | 1973 | 1978 | 1986 | 2001 |

Canadiens play first game in the National Hockey Association

Team wins first Stanley Cup

Franchise joins the newly founded NHL; unveils now-famous CH logo

Howie Morenz scores Cup-winning goal

Team wins second-straight championship

Howie Morenz breaks leg in game; dies less than two months later

Maurice Richard scores 50 goals in 50 games

Team wins first of five straight Stanley Cups

Jacques Plante records 311th win

Jean Beliveau is only second player to top 1,000 career points

Henri Richard wins record 11th Cup — all with Montreal

Guy Lafleur takes third consecutive scoring title

Montreal finishes seventh overall, but still wins NHL title

Team misses play-offs for third straight season

MOLSON CENTRE: COMFORT IS KEY

IT ISN'T EASY REPLACING hockey's most venerable arenas, but that's exactly what the Canadiens did when the team moved from the old Montreal Forum to the Molson Centre in 1996. Many purists cried foul, claiming that leaving the storied building was to turn one's back on history. But what the Molson Centre lacks in tradition, it makes up for in comfort, with good sight lines and more comfortable seating for fans. Still, the Forum mystique has not be replaced. Since moving to the new arena, the Canadiens have struggled mightily.

CONCESSIONS

The Molson Centre offers fans a concession experience befitting North America's French metropolis. Fans can eat at 42 food stands serving all the arena standards, along with such local specialties as beavertails, Montreal-style smoked meat and, of course, poutine — french fries smothered with gravy and cheese curds.

GAME DAY TIPS
• **Gate hours:** Gates open 90 minutes prior to opening faceoff.
• **Prohibited items:** Food, beverages, bottles, cans and coolers, and professional and video cameras are prohibited. Banners and signs are also not permitted. Frisbees, pucks, weapons or projectiles of any sort are not allowed. Smoking is allowed only in designated areas.
• **Ticket tips:** Saturday night hockey is a tradition in Montreal, so tickets will be harder to come by for the weekend games. Games against Toronto are usually near-sellouts as Leafs fans arrive by the busloads. The Molson Centre is not steep, so the higher up seats tend to be far from the ice.
• **Lost and found:** (514) 989-2839.

Arena Facts

Opened: *Mar. 15, 1996*
Cost: *$230 million*
Capacity: *21,273*
Home Sweet Home:
• *When the team moved to the Molson Centre in 1996, it brought along its championship banners. Now, whenever visiting players look upward, they are reminded that they are playing against hockey's most successful team.*

257

Seating Plan

- ■ Prestige .... **Call for prices**
- ■ Red .... **Call for prices**
- ▢ Club .... **Call for prices**
- ☐ White .... **Call for prices**
- ▨ Gray .... **Call for prices**
- ■ Blue .... **Call for prices**
- ▨ Molson Zone .. **Call for prices**
- ATM **Sections 114, 313**
- ♿ **Sections 105, 107, 109, 117, 121**

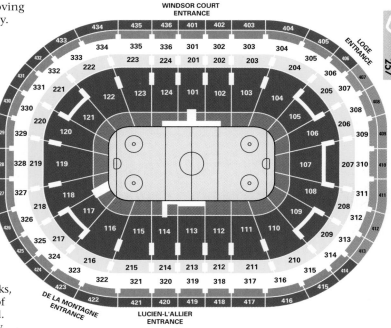

Directions: *From Hwy. 20/720 east, take de la Montagne/University exit. Turn left onto St. Antoine and follow to arena. From Hwy. 20/720 west, take University St. exit to Mansfield St. Go north on Mansfield, then left on de la Gauchetière and follow to arena. By Bus: Several bus routes service the district. Call (514) 288-6287 for information. By Subway: Take Line 2 (orange) to Bonaventure or Lucien L'Allier stations.* **Parking:** *Molson's lot has 550 spots; 10 for disabled. Additional parking is on Rue de la Montagne, Rue Saint-Antoine and de la Gauchetière.*

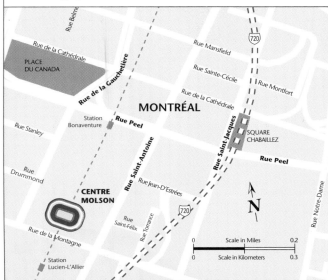

Nearby Hotels

▼▼▼ **Best Western Europa Downtown** *(Hotel)*, 1240 rue Drummond (Montreal), (514) 866-6492, $139-$189
▼▼▼ **Best Western Ville-Marie Hotel & Suites** *(Hotel)*, 3407 rue Peel (Montreal), (514) 288-4141, $99-$385
▼▼▼ **Hotel Le Cantlie Suites** *(Suite Hotel)*, 1110 rue Sherbrooke ouest (Montreal), (514) 842-2000, $115-$135
▼▼▼▼ **Hotel Omni Mont-Royal** *(Hotel)*, 1050 Sherbrooke ouest (Montreal), (514) 284-1110, $162-$224
▼▼▼▼ **Marriott Chateau Champlain** *(Hotel)*, 1 Place du Canada (Montreal), (514) 878-9000, $186-$241

Nearby Restaurants

▼▼ **Joe's Steak House** *(Steakhouse)*, 1430 rue Stanley (Montreal), (514) 842-4638, $7-$18
▼▼▼ **La Queue de Cheval Bar & Steakhouse** *(Steak & Seafood)*, 1221 boul Rene-Levesque ouest (Montreal), (514) 390-0090, $30-$40
▼▼▼▼ **Le Piment Rouge** *(Chinese)*, 1170 rue Peel (Montreal), (514) 866-7816, $19-$30
▼▼ **Mister Steer** *(American)*, 1198 Ste-Catherine ouest (Montreal), (514) 866-3233, $6-$15
▼▼ **Montreal Beer Museum** *(Continental)*, 2063 rue Stanley (Montreal), (514) 840-2020, $8-$15

NASHVILLE PREDATORS

ONE OF THE NEWEST TEAMS in the NHL, the Nashville Predators were admitted into the league in 1997, along with Atlanta, Minnesota and Columbus. Unlike the other NHL expansion teams, however, Nashville had already spent a number of years establishing its organization and hence became the first of these new teams to begin play. Although the Predators are still in their developmental phase and have yet to establish themselves as a major force on the ice, the team has quickly become one of the more successful in the league in terms of community support and fan loyalty. Many more established hockey clubs have been looking to Nashville to learn about generating this kind of local buzz. In terms of players, the Predators is one of the youngest squads in the league. Apart from team captain Tom Fitzgerald and Cliff Ronning, no other Nashville players have Stanley Cup experience and most of the team has only five seasons under their belt. In spite of this, the team has notched a number of winning streaks and some excellent performances. In its first two seasons, the Predators appeared to be in playoff contention up until the last part of the year, when inexperience showed and the team slumped badly. During the 2000–01 season, however, there were more signs that the squad was slowly approaching maturity. With Ronning, Patric Kjellberg, Scott Watson and goalie Mike Dunham all setting new team records and the young star David Legwand making news with his play, things can only be looking up for the Nashville Predators over the next few years.

Vital Stats

Stadium Address:
501 Broadway,
Nashville, Tenn.
Phone: (615) 770-2000
Web:
nashvillepredators.com,
gaylordentertainment
center.com
Box Office:
(615) 770-2040,
Mon.–Sat. 10–5:30
Media Coverage:
Radio: WWTN (99.7 FM)
TV: Fox Sports Net
Practice Facility:
Centennial Sportsplex,
Nashville, Tenn.

TEAM RECORDS

• **Patrick Cote (1999–2000)**
Penalty Minutes (season): 242 (1998–99)
Penalty Minutes (career): 312
• **Mike Dunham (1998–present)**
Goals Against Avg. (season): 2.28 (2000–01)
Saves (game): 52 (Oct. 21, 1998)
Saves Pct. (season): .923 (2000–01)
Shutouts (season): 4 (2000–01)
Shutouts (career): 5
Wins (season): 21 (2000–01)

Slap Shot

• Although Nashville has had its share of trouble racking up big NHL wins, the team has an unusually high percentage of players who excel on the world championship stage. Canadian Scott Watson, Finnish defensemen Kimmo Timonen and Karlis Skrastins, Czech Petr Sykora, Russian center Denis Arkhipov and American David Legwand have all made major contributions to their national teams in international competition.

"When teams come in here, they know what kind of energy we have . . . ."

— Tom Fitzgerald, Predators team captain

Wins (career): 56
• **Tom Fitzgerald (1998–present)**
Games Played (career): 244
• **Patric Kjellberg (1998–present)**
Assists by a Left Winger (season): 31 (2000–01)
Assists by a Left Winger (career): 74
Goals by a Left Winger (season): 23 (1999–2000)
Goals by a Left Winger (career): 48
Points by a Left Winger (season): 46 (1999–2000)
Points by a Left Winger (career): 122
• **Sergei Krivokrasov (1998–2000)**
Game-Winning Goals (season): 6 (1998–99)
Game-Winning Goals (career): 8
Goals by a Right Winger (season): 25 (1998–99)
Power-Play Goals (season): 10 (1998–99)
• **Cliff Ronning (1998–present)**
Assists (season): 43 (2000–01)
Assists (career): 114
Goals (season): 26

(1999–2000)
Goals (career): 63
Points (season): 62 (2000–01)
Points (career): 177
Power-Play Goals (career): 21
Shots (season): 248 (1999–2000)
Shots (career): 724
• **Kimmo Timonen (1998–present)**
Goals by a Defenseman (career): 24
• **Scott Walker (1998–present)**
Assists by a Right Winger (season): 29 (2000–01)
Assists by a Right Winger (career): 75
Goals by a Right Winger (season): 25 (2000–01)
Goals by a Right Winger (career): 47
Points by a Right Winger (season): 54 (2000–01)
Points by a Right Winger (career): 122

LEAGUE HONORS
All-Star Team
• Sergei Krivokrasov (1998–99)
• Kimmo Timonen (1999–2000)

Cliff Ronning gives Nashville grit up front.

Timeline

1996	1997	1997	1997	1998	1998	1998	1998	1999	1999	2000	2001
The new Nashville Arena opens its doors	June: Nashville is awarded a conditional franchise by the NHL	Aug.: Barry Trotz named as Nashville's first Head Coach	Nov.: Nashville fans select the name "Predators" for their new team	Mar.: Predators sell their first 12,000 season tickets	May: NHL officially accepts the Nashville franchise	July: Team names Tom Fitzgerald as its first team captain	Oct.: Predators win first-ever game against Carolina	April: Final game of the season features the NHL debut of David Legwand	Aug.: The Nashville Arena is renamed Gaylord Center	Legwand is among the league rookie scoring leaders with 28 points	Cliff Ronning breaks team records for points and assists

GAYLORD ENTERTAINMENT CENTER: EXPERIENCE THE EXCELLENCE

CONVENIENTLY LOCATED IN THE HEART of Music City, the Gaylord Center was designed as a tribute to Nashville's rich musical heritage. Facing the original site of the Grande Ole Opry, this arena is just minutes from the Country Music Hall of Fame and the historic Second Avenue District. The arena itself is an appropriately glitzy affair, loaded with high-tech scoreboards and sound equipment, amazing views, innovative acoustical engineering and the Tennessee Sports Hall of Fame. And for the gormandizing clientele, there's the popular Jack Daniels Old No. 7 Club, one of the best locally themed restaurants in NHL arenas.

CONCESSIONS

The Gaylord Entertainment Center has all the traditional food options, such as burgers, hot dogs, pizza and nachos, as well as deli wraps, quesadillas, chicken Caesar salad and wings.

Gourmet coffee and specialty beers are also available. The local specialty is the barbecue brisket sandwich.

GAME DAY TIPS

• **Gate hours:** Gates open 90 minutes prior to opening faceoff.
• **Prohibited items:** Food, beverages, bottles, cans, coolers, laser pointers, beachballs, frisbees, noisemakers, video cameras and large banners are all prohibited. There is no smoking in the arena, although smoking is permitted on the top level of the outside parking garage.
• **Ticket tips:** Getting tickets to see the Predators play is usually not too difficult, although they do sell more tickets on the weekends and when the Blues or the Red Wings are in town. Good sight lines mean the cheap seats won't disappoint you.
• **Lost and found:** (615) 770-2050.

Arena Facts

Opened: Dec. 18, 1996
Cost: $160 million
Capacity: 17,113
Home Sweet Home:
• *Games at the Gaylord Center are always a raucous affair, with fans simultaneously cheering the Predators and booing the competition. Predators fans also love to sing "Hockey Tonk," Nashville's theme song, to support their team.*

Seating Plan

☐ First Row	$95	■ Center Upper Level ... $27
▨ Second Row	$85	■ North Upper Level ... $16
■ Club Seats	$75	▨ Individual Game
■ Lower Level, Bottom	$65	Sales Only ... $10
■ Lower Level, Top	$55	ᴬᵀᴹ Sections 115/116, 309
■ North Club Seats	$44	♿ Throughout
■ South Upper Level	$33	

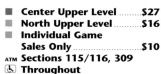

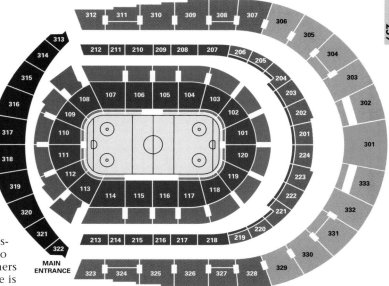

Directions: *Exit I-40 at Broadway westbound or eastbound. By Bus: Buses are available to and from the arena. Call Nashville MTA at (615) 862-5950 for information.* **Parking:** *The public is not allowed to park in the garage attached to the arena, but there are more than 10,000 spots within a 10-minute walk on Commerce St., Broadway, Demonbreun St., Church St. and McGavok St. Eight spots for the disabled are reserved in the on-site lot on first-come first-served basis.*

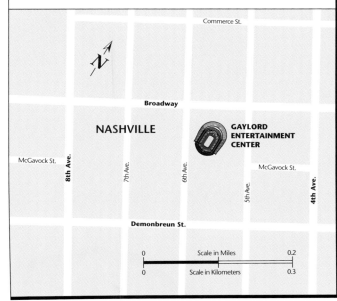

Nearby Hotels

▽▽ **Days Inn Downtown/Convention Center** *(Motel)*, 711 Union St. (Nashville), (615) 242-4311, $79-$129
▽▽ **Ramada Inn Limited** *(Motel)*, 303 Interstate Dr. (Nashville), (615) 244-6690, $69-$129
▽▽▽ **Regal Maxwell House Nashville** *(Motor Inn)*, 2025 Metro Center Blvd. (Nashville), (615) 259-4343, $82
▽▽▽▽ **Renaissance Nashville Hotel** *(Hotel)*, 611 Commerce St. (Nashville), (615) 255-8400, $154-$215
▽▽▽▽ **Sheraton Nashville Downtown Hotel** *(Hotel)*, 623 Union St. (Nashville), (615) 259-2000, $95-$135

Nearby Restaurants

▽▽ **Big River Grille & Brewing Works** *(American)*, 111 Broadway St. (Nashville), (615) 251-4677, $7-$16
▽▽ **Demos' Steak & Spaghetti House** *(American)*, 300 Commerce St. (Nashville), (615) 256-4655, $13-$17
▽▽ **Market Street Brewery & Public House** *(American)*, 134 2nd Ave. N. (Nashville), (615) 259-9611, $7-$20
▽▽▽ **The Merchants** *(American)*, 401 Broadway St. (Nashville), (615) 254-1892, $15-$27
▽▽ **Stock Yard** *(Steakhouse)*, 901 2nd Ave. N. (Nashville), (615) 255-6464, $18-$35 (dinner only)

NEW JERSEY DEVILS

THE NEW JERSEY DEVILS HAVE COME A LONG WAY. Largely the laughing stock of the NHL throughout the franchise's early history, the Devils have in five short years built a legacy of respect and dominance. The team entered the league as the Kansas City Scouts in 1974–75, the same year as the Washington Capitals. Both teams endured legendary struggles for legitimacy. The Scouts were short on talent. The team's only accomplishment was to outperform the Capitals by 20 points — scant praise since the Caps managed a paltry 21. A year later the Scouts were off to Colorado, where, now as the Rockies, the team continued to struggle, despite the coaching of Don Cherry for part of the six years the team was in Denver. The team relocated to New Jersey in 1982 with new owner Dr. John J. McMullen, but success was not quick to arrive. In fact, the Devils franchise languished in the division basement and was even called a "Mickey Mouse" franchise by Wayne Gretzky himself. That was until the 1987–88 season, when, with young talented forwards Kirk Muller, John MacLean and goalie Sean Burke, the Devils climbed to fourth place and earned the team's first playoff berth. The team acquired defenseman Scott Stevens in 1991 and, with a solid team defensive system created by coach Jacques Lemaire and executed perfectly by stars such as Claude Lemieux and Stephane Richer, the Devils took their first Stanley Cup in '95. Five years later, with new young stars Patrick Elias, Petr Sykora and Jason Arnott providing offensive punch, Stevens again captained the team to the top and a second Stanley Cup. And the Devils show no sign of slowing down. Once ridiculed, they are doing the laughing now.

> *"It sends a bit of a chill down our spines, hearing you scream."*
> — *Devils forward Randy McKay, to fans at Stanley Cup parade*

Vital Stats

Stadium Address:
50 Rte. 120,
E. Rutherford, N.J.
Phone: (201) 935-8500
Web: newjerseydevils.com,
meadowlands.com
Box Office:
(201) 935-3900,
Mon.–Fri. 9–6, Sat. 10–6,
Sun. 12–5
Media Coverage:
Radio: WABC (770 AM)
TV: MSGN,
Fox Sports Net
Practice Facility:
S. Mountain Arena,
West Orange, N.J.

POSTSEASON
- **Stanley Cup Championships** 2
(1994–95, 1999–2000)
- **Eastern Conference Championships** 3
(1994–95, 1999–2000, 2000–01)
- **Atlantic Division Titles**...4
(1996–97, 1997–98, 1998–99, 2000–01)
- **Patrick Division Titles** 1
(1987–88)

TEAM RECORDS
- **Martin Brodeur (1992–present)**
Goals-Against Avg. (season): 1.88 (1996–97)

Slap Shot

- *When a blizzard dropped 15 inches of snow on New Jersey on Jan. 22, 1986, the "334 Club" was born. That's how many fans made it to the game, a 7-5 Devils' victory over Calgary.*
- *The Devils' defense can be utterly frustrating for opponents. In the sixth game of the 2000 Conference Semi-Finals against Toronto, New Jersey allowed just six shots on goal, an NHL record.*

Shutouts (season): 10 (twice)
Shutouts (career): 51
Wins (season): 43 (twice)
Wins (career): 286
- **Doug Brown (1986–93)**
Shorthanded Goals (career): 11 (tie)
- **Ken Daneyko (1983–present)**
Games (career): 1,147
Penalty Minutes (career): 2,426
Seasons (career): 16
- **Patrik Elias (1995–present)**
Points (season): 96 (2000–01)
- **Tom Kurvers (1987–90)**
Assists (game): 5 (tie) (Feb. 13, 1989)
- **John MacLean (1983–98)**
Assists (career): 354
Game-Winning Goals (season): 11 (1989–90)
Game-Winning Goals (career): 55
Goals (career): 347
Hat Tricks (career): 6
Penalty Minutes (game): 42 (Dec. 11, 1990)
Points (career): 701
Power-Play Goals (season): 19 (1990–91)
Power-Play Goals (career): 92
Shots (season): 322 (1989–90)
- **John Madden (1999–present)**
Shorthanded Goals (season): 6 (1999–2000)

- **Kirk Muller (1984–91)**
Points (game): 6 (Oct. 29, 1986)
Power-Play Points (season): 37 (1987–88)
- **Krzysztof Oliwa (1996–2000)**
Penalty Minutes (season): 295 (1997–98)
- **Stephane Richer (1991–96)**
Shorthanded Goals (career): 11 (tie)
- **Scott Stevens (1991–present)**
Assists (season): 60 (1993-94)
Plus/Minus (season): +53 (1993-94)
Plus/Minus (career): +246
- **Pat Verbeek (1982–89)**
Goals (game): 4 (Feb. 28, 1988)
Goals (season): 46 (1987–88)

LEAGUE HONORS
Calder Trophy
- **Martin Brodeur (1993–94)**
- **Scott Gomez (1999–2000)**

Bill Masterton Trophy
- **Ken Daneyko (1999–2000)**

William M. Jennings Trophy
- **Martin Brodeur (1996–97, 1997–98)**
- **Mike Dunham (1996–97)**

Jack Adams Award
- Jacques Lemaire (1993–94)

Conn Smythe Trophy
- Claude Lemieux (1995)
- Scott Stevens (2000)

Martin Brodeur is one of the NHL's premiere netminders.

Timeline

1974	1976	1982	1984	1988	1992	1994	1995	1997	1998	1999	2000

- **1974** — Kansas City Scouts begin play in NHL
- **1976** — Scouts relocate to Colorado; change name to Rockies
- **1982** — Rockies sold to New Jersey group; team ties first game 3-3 with Penguins
- **1984** — Glenn Resch plays for Wales Conference All-Stars
- **1988** — Devils reach conference finals in first playoff year
- **1992** — Scott Stevens named Devils captain
- **1994** — Martin Brodeur wins Calder Trophy
- **1995** — Devils sweep Wings in Stanley Cup finals
- **1997** — Devils enjoy 15-game winning streak
- **1998** — Jacques Lemaire steps down as Head Coach
- **1999** — Ken Daneyko plays 1,000th game with franchise
- **2000** — Jason Arnott's goal in double OT of game six gives Devils second Stanley Cup

CONTINENTAL AIRLINES ARENA: DEVILISHLY GOOD

AS POORLY AS BASKETBALL'S New Jersey Nets have treated their supporters in recent years, the New Jersey Devils have been generous toward their fans, winning two Cups in the past five years. And attendance figures reflect it, as near capacity crowds are on hand for most games to fill the enormous Continental Airlines Arena. The space offers Devils fans great sight lines in a roomy environment. The Devils have announced plans for a new venue in the near future, so those interested should check out this arena while it's still in use.

CONCESSIONS

The food choices at the Continental Airlines Arena are quite varied, including the traditional hot dogs, nachos, hamburgers and fries as well as more exciting options, such as sausage, hand-carved meat sandwiches, and soup and chili in bread bowls. Vegetarians will enjoy a variety of salads, knishes and baked potatoes with assorted toppings.

GAME DAY TIPS
• **Gate hours:** Gates open one hour prior to opening faceoff.
• **Prohibited items:** Video cameras, weapons, air horns, megaphones, bottles, laser pointers, signs, banners and posters are prohibited. Smoking is prohibited inside the arena, but is allowed in designated areas outside Gate B and Gate D.
• **Ticket tips:** The Devils do not regularly sell out their games, but expect big crowds if they're playing their rivals, the New York Rangers. Most seats at the arena, even those in the upper level, offer a good view of the on-ice action.
• **Lost and found:** (201) 460-4341.

Arena Facts

Opened: July 2, 1981
Cost: $85 million
Capacity: 19,040
Home Sweet Home:
• The seating bowl at the Continental Airlines Arena slopes back from the ice surface more dramatically than most other venues. This creates strange sight lines for visiting goalies, who have been known to misplay easy shots.

Seating Plan

⬜ $85	⬛ $32
⬛ $85	⬛ $20
⬛ $65	**ATM** Section 101
⬛ $48	♿ End zone 100s

GATE C · GATE D · GATE B · GATE A

Directions: Take New Jersey Tpk. to exit 16W (Sports Complex) and follow signs to Sports Complex. By Bus: Buses are available from Port Authority in NYC. Call (212) 564-8484 for more information. **Parking:** The arena parking can hold 4,000 cars and there are 22,000 more spots available in the rest of the complex. Parking for people with disabilities is available in lots 21 and 23.

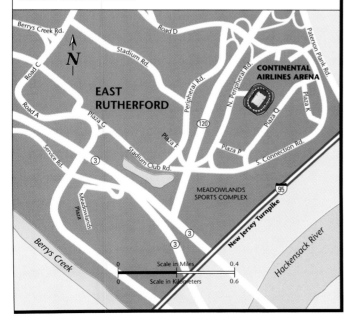

Nearby Hotels

▼▼▼ **Amerisuites** *(Motel)*, 41-01 Broadway (Fair Lawn), (201) 475-3888, $119-$199
▼▼▼ **Courtyard by Marriott** *(Motel)*, 455 Harmon Meadow Blvd. (Secaucus), (201) 617-8888, $180-$209
▼▼▼ **Fairfield Inn by Marriott** *(Motel)*, 850 SR 120 S. (East Rutherford), (201) 507-5222, $129
▼▼▼ **Hampton Inn** *(Motel)*, 250 Harmon Meadow Blvd. (Secaucus), (201) 867-4400, $135-$185
▼▼▼ **The Holiday Inn Harmon Meadow** *(Hotel)*, 300 Plaza Dr. (Secaucus), (201) 348-2000, $149-$209

Nearby Restaurants

▼▼ **Harold's New York Deli Restaurant** *(American)*, 10 Polito Ave. in the Quality Inn-Meadowlands (Lyndhurst), (201) 935-2600, $6-$20
▼▼ **La Dolce Vita** *(Italian)*, 316 Valley Brook Ave. (Lyndhurst), (201) 935-4260, $11-$25
▼▼ **Park & Orchard** *(American)*, 240 Hackensack St., (201) 939-9292 (East Rutherford), $13-$24
▼▼▼ **The River Palm Terrace** *(Steak & Seafood)*, 41-11 Broadway (Fair Lawn), (201) 703-3500, $19-$36
▼▼▼ **Sonoma Grill** *(American)*, 64 Hoboken Rd. (East Rutherford), (201) 507-8989, $17-$27

NEW YORK ISLANDERS

WHEN THE NEW YORK ISLANDERS first hit the ice in 1972–73, it looked like almost every expansion team that had come before it, finishing its first season deep in the cellar of the league standings. But in the off-season, Islanders GM Bill Torrey made two moves that laid the foundation for the club's future greatness. The first was hiring Al Arbour as Head Coach and the second was drafting a young defenseman named Denis Potvin. Another strong draft in 1974 reaped Clark Gillies, a prototype power forward who was as adept with his fists as he was at putting the puck in the net, and Bryan Trottier, a tenacious play-making center. Just two seasons removed from their last-place finish, the Islanders battled their way into the playoffs, where they staged upsets over the Rangers and Penguins before bowing out to the Flyers in a rugged semifinals. The final piece of the championship puzzle was put in place in 1978, when once again Torrey drafted brilliantly, selecting Mike Bossy. Bossy, as pure a sniper as the game has ever seen, was put on a line with Gillies and Trottier. The "Trio Grande" line was unstoppable, with Trottier leading the league in scoring and Bossy topping all goal scorers by potting 69. Squaring off against the mighty Philadelphia Flyers in the 1979–80 Stanley Cup, the underdog Islanders rose to the occasion and won their first championship on Bob Nystrom's overtime goal in game six. Having finally reached the summit, the team proved impossible to dislodge. The Isles won three more Cups in a row and established themselves as one of hockey's true dynasties.

Vital Stats

Stadium Address:
1255 Hempstead Tpk.,
Uniondale, N.Y.
Phone: (516) 794-9300
Web:
newyorkislanders.com,
nassaucoliseum.com
Box Office:
(800) 882-ISLES
Mon.–Sun. 9:30–4:45
Media Coverage:
Radio: WJWR (620 AM)
TV: Fox Sports Net
Practice Facility:
Iceworks, Syosset, N.Y.

POSTSEASON
• Stanley Cup
Championships...................4
(1979–80, 1980–81, 1981–82,
1982–83)
• Wales Conference
Championships...................3
(1981–82, 1982–83, 1983–84)

RETIRED NUMBERS
• Denis Potvin (5)
• Clark Gillies (9)
• Mike Bossy (22)
• Bob Nystrom (23)
• Bill Smith (31)
• Al Arbour (739)

TEAM RECORDS
• Mike Bossy (1977–88)
Goals by a Rookie (season):

Slap Shot

• With 573 goals in just 752 NHL games, Mike Bossy's goals-per-game average of .762 is second only to Mario Lemieux's.
• Likened to Bobby Orr when he was coming up through the Junior ranks, Denis Potvin proved to be the real deal. In 1986–87 Potvin passed Orr on his way to becoming the first defenseman to notch 1,000 career points.

53 (1977–78)
Goals (season): 69 (1978–79)
Goals (career): 573
Hat Tricks (season): 9
(1980–81)
Hat Tricks (career): 39
Points (season): 147 (1981–82)
• Denis Potvin (1973–88)
Points by a Defenseman
(season): 101 (1978–79)
• Felix Potvin (1998–2000)
Saves (game): 55 (tie)
(April 4, 1999)
• Glenn Resch (1974–81)
Longest Undefeated Streak:
23 games (1978–79)
Shutouts (season): 7
(1975–76)
Shutouts (career): 25
• Billy Smith (1972–89)
Saves (game): 55 (tie)
(Nov. 22, 1972)
Wins (season): 32 (1981–82)
Wins (career): 304
• Brian Trottier (1975–90)
Assists (season): 87 (1978–79)
Assists (career): 853
Points (game): 8
(Dec. 23, 1978)
Points (career): 1,353
• Nick Vukota (1988–96)
Penalty Minutes (game):
42 (Dec. 12, 1989)
Penalty Minutes
(career): 1,879

LEAGUE HONORS
Hart Trophy
• Bryan Trottier (1978–79)

Art Ross Trophy
• Bryan Trottier (1978–79)

James Norris Trophy
• Denis Potvin (1975–76,
1977–78, 1978–79)

Vezina Trophy
• Bill Smith (1981–82)

Calder Trophy
• Denis Potvin (1973–74)
• Bryan Trottier (1975–76)
• Mike Bossy (1977–78)
• Bryan Berard (1996–97)

Lady Byng Trophy
• Mike Bossy (1982–83,
1983–84, 1985–86)
• Pierre Turgeon (1992–93)

Bill Masterton Trophy
• Ed Westfall (1976–77)
• Mark Fitzpatrick
(1991–92)

King Clancy Trophy
• Bryan Trottier (1988–89)

William M. Jennings Trophy
• Roland Melanson
(1982–83)
• Bill Smith (1982–83)

Jack Adams Award
• Al Arbour (1978–79)

Conn Smythe Trophy
• Bryan Trottier (1980)

• Butch Goring (1980–81)
• Mike Bossy (1981–82)
• Bill Smith (1982–83)

Hockey Hall of Fame
• Mike Bossy (1991)
• Denis Potvin (1991)
• Bill Smith (1993)
• Bill Torrey (1995)
• Al Arbour (1996)
• Bryan Trottier (1997)

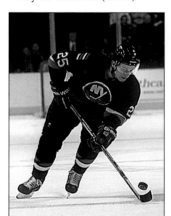

Mariusz Czerkawski provides much-needed scoring for the Islanders.

"We're the best that ever skated."
— Denis Potvin, following the Islanders' fourth-straight Stanley Cup

Timeline

1972	1973	1974	1975	1978	1980	1981	1983	1987	1988	1990	1994	2000	2001

Expansion Islanders lose home opener 3-2 to Atlanta Flames

Al Arbour named Head Coach; Denis Potvin drafted

Isles draft Clark Gillies and Bryan Trottier

Team loses in Cup semifinals

Mike Bossy is first rookie to score 50 goals

Isles win first Stanley Cup

Bossy is second player to pot 50 goals in 50 games; team wins second Cup

Islanders win fourth-straight championship

Pat LaFontaine scores in quadruple overtime to clinch Division semi-finals for Isles

Denis Potvin is first defense-man to score 300 goals

Bryan Trottier records 500th NHL goal

Al Arbour retires from second stint as coach

Isles draft goalie Rick DiPietro No. 1 overall

Team finishes with NHL's worst record

NASSAU VETERANS MEMORIAL COLISEUM: SCENE OF SOME GREAT MOMENTS

NASSAU COLISEUM OPENED in 1972, making it one of the NHL's older arenas. More than one spectator has likened the sound system to a transistor radio and there are a number of seats with obstructed views, especially in the upper sections. However, the arena has been spruced up of late, with a new paint job and recently added kids concessions. The venerable Coliseum has enjoyed its share of great moments and the four Stanley Cup banners hanging from the ceiling remind everyone of those heady times.

CONCESSIONS

The food at the Nassau Coliseum includes standard arena fare, such as burgers, chicken, pizza and popcorn, as well as Tex/Mex, foot-long hot dogs with special toppings and grilled meat sandwiches. Vegetarians will find salad and veggie burgers.

Arena Facts

Opened: *May 29, 1972*
Cost: *$32 million*
Capacity: *16,297*
Home Sweet Home:
• *New Yorkers are very vocal and can pump up their team. However, the Isles often lose this home-ice advantage when they play the crosstown Rangers and the Nassau Coliseum is filled with an equal mix of fans from both teams.*

GAME DAY TIPS

• **Gate hours:** Gates open one hour prior to opening faceoff.
• **Prohibited items:** Drugs, alcohol, weapons, glass containers and laser pointers are prohibited. Cameras and audio or video recording devices are not permitted in the arena. Signs and banners must be in good taste and cannot obstruct people's views. Smoking is not allowed anywhere in the arena.
• **Ticket tips:** Getting tickets for the Islanders' home games is usually extremely easy, unless their crosstown rival the Rangers is the opposing team. The Nassau Coliseum is fairly small, so spectators — even those seated in the upper decks — are quite close to the action. Watch out for obstructed views in the center of the upper deck.
• **Lost and found:** (516) 794-9303 ext. 132.

Seating Plan

■ **$71.50**		■ .... **N/A**	
▨ **$51.50**		▢ **Wheelchair Section**	
▦ **$39.50**		**ATM Main entrance lobby**	
▥ **$28.50**		♿ **Sections 202, 222**	
■ **$20.50**			

MAIN ENTRANCE

Directions: *From the Meadowbrook Pkwy. north or south, take exit M4 to Hempstead Tpk. west. Follow signs to Nassau Coliseum. By Train: Take the Long Island Railroad to Hempstead Station. Walk one block to the Hempstead Bus Terminal, where several buses go to the Coliseum. By Bus: Buses are available to and from the arena. Call (516) 766-6722 for information.* **Parking:** *The lot at the Nassau Coliseum can hold up to 6,869 cars and very rarely is full. There is ample parking for the disabled, located on the north and south sides of the building.*

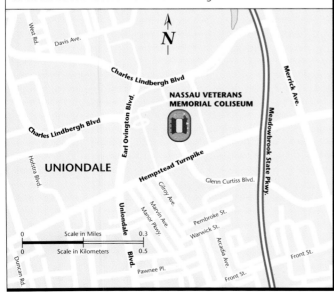

Nearby Hotels

▼▼ **Coliseum Motor Inn** *(Motel)*, 1650 Hempstead Tpke. (East Meadow), (516) 794-2100, $95-$110
ꀨ **Garden City Hotel** *(Hotel)*, 45 Seventh St. (Garden City), (516) 747-3000, $235-$350
▼▼ **Holiday Inn** *(Motor Inn)*, 101 James Doolittle Blvd. (Carle Place), (516) 997-5000, $219-$269
▼▼▼ **Long Island Marriott Hotel & Conference Center** *(Hotel)*, 101 James Doolittle Blvd. (Uniondale), (516) 794-3800, $219-$269
ꀨ **The Wingate Inn** *(Hotel)*, 821 Stewart Ave. (Garden City), (516) 705-9000

Nearby Restaurants

▼▼ **Arthur Ave** *(Italian)*, 2367 Hempstead Tpke. (East Meadow), (516) 520-9447, $6-$16
Benny's Ristorante *(Italian)*, 199 Post Ave. (Westbury), (516) 997-8111, $12-$20
Cheesecake Factory *(American)*, 1504 Old Country Rd. (Westbury), (516) 222-5500
▼▼▼ **La Cisterna Restaurant** *(Italian)*, 109 Mineola Blvd. (Mineola), (516) 248-2112, $18-$24
▼▼ **Riverbay Seafood Bar & Grill** *(Seafood)*, 700 Willis Ave. (Williston Park), (516) 742-9191, $12-$22

NEW YORK RANGERS

WITH NEW YORK BEING THE home of Broadway, it makes sense that the Rangers made a splashy entrance in their very first season in 1926–27. The team, assembled by hockey mastermind Conn Smythe and coached by the legendary Lester Patrick, stunned everyone by finishing first overall before bowing out in the playoffs. Led by a trio of future Hall of Famers, Frank Boucher, Bill Cook and Ivan "Ching" Johnson, the precocious Rangers took the Stanley Cup the following season, the only sophomore team ever to accomplish that feat. Hardly beginner's luck — the club won three Stanley Cups in its first 16 seasons, missing the playoffs just once. But World War II broke up the talented squad and in 1942–43, just two years after its championship, New York dropped to last place in the NHL. In the next 24 seasons, the Rangers would finish last or second-to-last an incredible 18 times, despite an influx of such future Hall of Famers as Andy Bathgate, Harry Howell and Gump Worsley. The drought ended in 1966–67, when the potent line of Rod Gilbert, Jean Ratelle and Vic Hadfield led the team to the first of nine straight playoff appearances. But still the Cup eluded the team's grasp. The 1993–94 Rangers squad was studded with talent, including Mike Richter in nets, Brian Leetch and Sergei Zubov on the blue line, and Adam Graves and Captain Mark Messier leading the charge up front. Finishing atop the league standings, the Rangers came from behind to win the Eastern Conference crown before copping the Stanley Cup on Messier's game-winner in game seven. Broadway was singing again.

Vital Stats

Stadium Address:
2 Pennsylvania Plaza, New York, N.Y.
Phone: (212) 465-6000
Web: newyorkrangers.com, thegarden.com
Box Office:
(212) 465-6741,
Mon.–Sat. 12–6,
event days 9–6
Media Coverage:
Radio: WFAN (66 AM),
WEVD (1050 AM)
TV: MSG
Practice Facility:
Playland Ice Casino, Rye, N.Y.

POSTSEASON
• Stanley Cup Championships 4
(1927–28, 1932–33, 1939–40, 1993–94)
• Eastern Conference Championships 1
(1993–94)
• American Division Titles 2
(1926–27, 1931–32)
• Patrick Division Titles 2
(1989–90, 1991–92)
• Atlantic Division Titles...1
(1993–94)

RETIRED NUMBERS
• Eddie Giacomin (1)
• Rod Gilbert (7)

TEAM RECORDS
• Eddie Giacomin (1965–76)
Shutouts (career): 49

Slap Shot

• In all, the Rangers have 39 players enshrined in the Hall of Fame. The most recent inductee was Wayne Gretzky in 1999.
• Gretzky retired from in 1999 after three seasons as a Ranger. In honor of his great career, every NHL team retired his No. 99.

"Chronologically, I'm 33. In hockey years, I'm 66."
— Rangers Captain Mark Messier, on the toll his style takes on his body

• **Rod Gilbert (1960–78)**
Goals (career): 406
Points (career): 1,021
• **Adam Graves (1991–present)**
Goals (season): 52 (1993–94)
• **Ron Greschner (1974–90)**
Penalty Minutes (career): 1,226
• **Harry Howell (1952–69)**
Games (career): 1,160
• **Brian Leetch (1987–present)**
Assists (season): 80 (1991–92)
Assists (career): 655
• **Jean Ratelle (1960–76)**
Points (season): 109 (1971–72)
30-Goal seasons: 6
• **Mike Richter (1989–present)**
Saves (game): 59 (Jan. 31, 1991)
Wins (season): 42 (1997–98)
Wins (career): 272
• **John Ross Roach (1928–32)**
Goals Against Avg. (season): 1.48 (1928–29)
Shutouts (season) 13 (1928–29)

LEAGUE HONORS
Hart Trophy
• Buddy O'Connor

(1947–48)
• Chuck Rayner (1949–50)
• Andy Bathgate (1958–59)
• Mark Messier (1991–92)

Art Ross Trophy
• Bill Cook (1926–27, 1932–33)
• Bryan Hextall (1941–42)

Norris Trophy
• Doug Harvey (1961–62)
• Harry Howell (1966–67)
• Brian Leetch (1991–92, 1996–97)

Vezina Trophy
• Dave Kerr (1939–40)
• Ed Giacomin (1970–71)
• Gilles Villemure (1970–71)
• John Vanbiesbrouck (1985–86)

Calder Trophy
• Kilby MacDonald (1939–40)
• Grant Warwick (1941–42)
• Edgar Laprade (1945–46)
• Pentti Lund (1948–49)
• Lorne Worsley (1952–53)
• Camille Henry (1953–54)

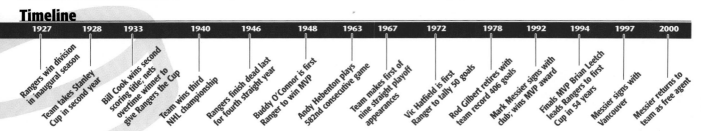

Defenseman Brian Leetch is a bona fide scoring threat.

• Steve Vickers (1972–73)
• Brian Leetch (1988–89)

Lady Byng Trophy
• Frank Boucher (1927–28, 1928–29, 1929–30, 1930–31, 1932–33, 1933–34, 1934–35)
• Clint Smith (1938–39)
• Buddy O'Connor (1947–48)
• Edgar Laprade (1949–50)
• Camille Henry (1957–58)
• Jean Ratelle (1971–72)
• Wayne Gretzky (1998–99)

Conn Smythe Trophy
• Brian Leetch (1994)

Timeline

| 1927 | 1928 | 1933 | 1940 | 1946 | 1948 | 1963 | 1967 | 1972 | 1978 | 1992 | 1994 | 1997 | 2000 |

- 1927: Rangers win division in inaugural season
- 1928: Team takes Stanley Cup in second year
- 1933: Bill Cook wins second scoring title; nets overtime winner to give Rangers the Cup
- 1940: Team wins third NHL championship
- 1946: Rangers finish dead last for fourth straight year
- 1948: Buddy O'Connor is first Ranger to win MVP
- 1963: Andy Hebenton plays 582nd consecutive game
- 1967: Team makes first of nine straight playoff appearances
- 1972: Vic Hatfield is first Ranger to tally 50 goals
- 1978: Rod Gilbert retires with team record 406 goals
- 1992: Mark Messier signs with club; wins MVP award
- 1994: Finals MVP Brian Leetch leads Rangers to first Cup in 54 years
- 1997: Messier signs with Vancouver
- 2000: Messier returns to team as free agent

MADISON SQUARE GARDEN: WORLD'S MOST FAMOUS ARENA

WITH TYPICAL NEW YORK BRAVADO, Madison Square Garden is billed as "the world's most famous arena." It certainly is one of the most storied, hosting everything from championship boxing, basketball, hockey and dog shows to singers ranging from Bing Crosby to Elvis Presley. The current structure is actually the fourth incarnation of MSG, with the first being built in 1874 by P.T. Barnum for his circus. Built in 1968, the current structure is as much a New York landmark as the Statue of Liberty and the Empire State Building.

CONCESSIONS

Madison Square Garden offers fans all the best in New York delicacies. There are hamburgers, hot dogs and pizza, as well as traditional snacks such as crackerjacks, popcorn and cotton candy. A selection of imported and local beers complements the food.

Arena Facts

Opened: Feb. 11, 1968
Cost: $43 million
Capacity: 18,200
Home Sweet Home:
• Maybe it's something in the water, but New York fans are among the loudest anywhere — regardless of the sport. Rangers faithful are as notorious for berating opposing players as they are for cheering the home team.

GAME DAY TIPS

• **Gate hours:** Gates open one hour prior to faceoff.
• **Prohibited items:** Food, beverages, alcohol and all kinds of containers are prohibited. Noisemakers and air horns are also forbidden, as are weapons and projectiles. Signs and banners are allowed as long as they do not obstruct views. Video and flash cameras are not allowed. Smoking is allowed only in designated areas.
• **Ticket tips:** The Rangers usually sell out all their games, often weeks or months in advance. Games against the crosstown rival

Seating Plan

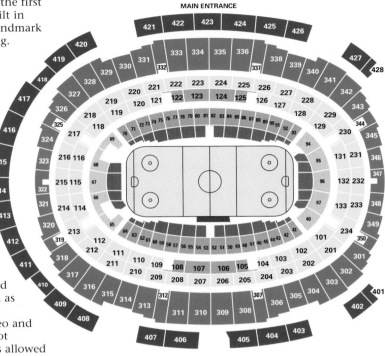

■ $700	■ $40
■ $150	■ $25
■ $130	**ATM** Box Office, 6th floor
■ $120	Tower A
■ $65	♿ Throughout

MAIN ENTRANCE

Islanders or Detroit are especially lively, as are weekend games. The view in the first few rows may be obstructed by fans walking in from the concourses.
• **Lost and found:** (212) 465-6299.

Directions: Located on 7th Ave. between 33rd St. and 31st St. By Bus: Several buses arrive at the arena. Call NYC Transit Authority at (718) 330-1234 for more information. By Subway: Lines 1, 2, 3 or 9 and A, C or E to 34th St./Penn Station. Or, lines B, D, F, N, Q, R or PATH to 34th St./Ave. of the Americas. **Parking:** Ten private parking lots and garages surround the arena, all of which have disabled parking. There is also some street parking on 7th, 8th, 9th and 10th Aves. and W. 35th St.

Nearby Hotels

▼▼▼ **The Avalon** *(Hotel)*, 16 E. 32nd St. (New York), (212) 299-7000, $175-$400
▼▼ **The Best Western Manhattan Hotel** *(Hotel)*, 17 W. 32nd St. (New York), (212) 736-1600, $109-$799
▼▼▼ **Courtyard by Marriott/Manhattan-Times Square South** *(Motel)*, 114 W. 40th St. (New York),(212) 391-0088, call for rates
▼▼▼ **Martinique on Broadway** *(Motor Inn)*, 49 W. 32nd St. (New York), (212) 736-3800, $199-$399
▼▼▼ **Southgate Tower Suite Hotel** *(Extended Stay Hotel)*, 371 7th Ave. (New York), (212) 563-1800, $229-$335

Nearby Restaurants

▼ **Carnegie Delicatessen & Restaurant** *(American)*, 854 7th Ave. (New York), (212) 757-2245, $10-$30
▼▼▼ **Chin Chin** *(Chinese)*, 216 E. 49th St. (New York), (212) 888-4555, $12-$21
▼▼▼▼ **Fifty-Seven Fifty-Seven Restaurant** *(American)*, 57 E. 57th St. in the Four Seasons Hotel (New York), (212) 758-5757, $28-$34
▼ **Mimi's Macaroni** *(Italian)*, 718 Amsterdam Ave. (New York), (212) 866-6311, $8-$15
Serendipity *(American)*, 225 E. 60th St. (New York), (212) 838-3531, $6-$20

OTTAWA SENATORS

ALTHOUGH THE MODERN-DAY SENATORS have only been in existence since 1992, organized hockey in Ottawa predates the NHL itself. The famed Ottawa Silver Seven, who boasted six future members of the Hall of Fame, won three straight Stanley Cups beginning in 1902–03. Changing its name to the Senators, the team won another championship in 1908–09 and was a charter member of the NHL when the new league began operations in 1917. In the Roaring '20s, no team roared louder than Ottawa as they skated to four more Cup victories. Among the players starring for the Sens during that era was Frank "King" Clancy, who in game two of the 1922–23 finals played every position, including goal while his team's netminder sat out a penalty. But the Senators' juggernaut came grinding to a halt when the team faltered in the early 1930s and was moved to St. Louis in 1934. Ottawa was without a NHL team for almost 60 years until the Senators reemerged for the 1992–93 season. Playing in the cramped Ottawa Civic Centre, the team struggled mightily, finishing dead last in the league for its first four campaigns. Ottawa turned the corner in 1996–97, however. With a strong cast of European talent that included Alexei Yashin, Daniel Alfredsson and Sergei Zholtok, the team finished third in its division and qualified for the postseason. The team has made the playoffs every year since then, but has shown a disheartening propensity for getting eliminated by less talented squads. In the meantime, Ottawa fans are waiting for the Senators to return to greatness.

Daniel Alfredsson is the leader of a talented Senators team.

POSTSEASON
- **Stanley Cup Championships** 8
(1902–03, 1903–04, 1904–05, 1908–09, 1919–20, 1920–21, 1922–23, 1926–27)
- **Northeast Division Titles** 2
(1998–99, 2000–01)
- **Canadian Division Titles** 1
(1926–27)

RETIRED NUMBERS
- Frank Finnigan (8)

TEAM RECORDS
- **Daniel Alfredsson (1995–present)**
Assists by a Right Winger (career): 216
Goals by a Right Winger (career): 113

Slap Shot

- *There are 33 former members of the old Ottawa Hockey Club, later called the Silver Seven and then the Senators, enshrined in the Hall of Fame.*
- *The Sens sold King Clancy to the Leafs for $35,000 in 1930 — a huge sum during the Great Depression.*

Points by a Right Winger (career): 339
- **Magnus Arvedson (1997–present)**
Shorthanded goals (season): 4 (1998–99)
Shorthanded Goals (career): 8
- **Marian Hossa (1999–present)**
Goals by a Right Winger (season): 32 (2000–01)
Points by a Right Winger (season): 75 (2000–01)
- **Patrick Lalime (1999–present)**
Shutouts (season): 7 (2000–01)
Wins (season): 36 (2000–01)
- **Shawn McEachern (1996–present)**
Assists by a Left Winger (career): 131
Goals by a Left Winger (season): 32 (2000–01)
Goals by a Left Winger (career): 127
Points by a Left Winger (season): 72 (2000–01)
Points by a Left Winger (career): 258
- **Mike Peluso (1992–93)**
Penalty Minutes (season): 318 (1992–93)
- **Damian Rhodes (1995–99)**
Saves (career): 4,156
- **Ron Tugnutt (1996–2000)**
Goals Against Avg. (season): 1.78 (1998–99)

Shutouts (career): 13
Wins (career): 72
- **Dennis Vial (1994–98)**
Penalty Minutes (career): 625
- **Alexei Yashin (1993–present)**
Assists (season): 50 (1998–99)
Assists (career): 273
Game-Winning Goals (season): 10 (2000–01)
Game-Winning Goals (career): 31
Goals (season): 44 (1998–99)
Goals (career): 218
Goals by a Rookie: 30 (1993–94)
Points (season): 94 (1998–99)
Points (career): 491
Points by a Rookie: 79 (1993–94)
Power-Play Goals (season): 19 (1998–99)
Power-Play Goals (career): 77
Shots (career): 1,671

LEAGUE HONORS
Hart Trophy
- Frank Nighbor (1923–24)

Ross Trophy
- Punch Broadbent (1921–22)
- Cy Denneny (1923–24)

"Fans have treated us unbelievably here."
— Sens' Jason York, on Ottawa's enthusiastic response to its NHL hockey team

Vital Stats

Stadium Address:
1000 Palladium Dr., Kanata, Ont.
Phone: (613) 599-0100
Web: ottawasenators.com, corelcentre.com
Box Office: (613) 599-0103, Mon.–Fri. 10–4; open Sat. 10–4 Sept.–Apr.
Media Coverage:
Radio: The Team (1200 AM), STAR (96 FM)
TV: CBC (Channel 4), CTV Sportsnet
Practice Facility:
Kanata Recreation Complex, Kanata, Ont.

Calder Trophy
- Daniel Alfredsson (1995–96)

Lady Byng Trophy
- Frank Nighbor (1924–25, 1925–26)

Adams Award
- Jacques Martin (1998–99)

Timeline

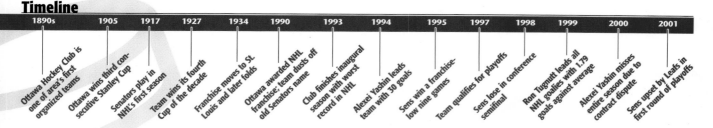

1890s — Ottawa Hockey Club is one of area's first organized teams
1905 — Ottawa wins third consecutive Stanley Cup
1917 — Senators play in NHL's first season
1927 — Team wins its fourth Cup of the decade
1934 — Franchise moves to St. Louis and later folds
1990 — Ottawa awarded NHL franchise; team dusts off old Senators name
1993 — Club finishes inaugural season with worst record in NHL
1994 — Alexei Yashin leads team with 30 goals
1995 — Sens win a franchise-low nine games
1997 — Team qualifies for playoffs
1998 — Sens lose in conference semifinal
1999 — Ron Tugnutt leads all NHL goalies with 1.79 goals against average
2000 — Alexei Yashin misses entire season due to contract dispute
2001 — Sens upset by Leafs in first round of playoffs

COREL CENTRE: PLUSH AND LIVELY

WHEN THEIR NEW ARENA opened in 1996, the Senators were able to leave the outdated Ottawa Civic Centre which had been home since 1992. The new venue, originally called the Palladium, has 18,500 plush seats, including 150 private suites and 2,500 club seats. With a smaller capacity than many arenas, the Corel Centre offers all fans, even those in the cheaper seats, a close-up view of the game. The arena is known for its family atmosphere and its in-house band that plays during breaks in the game.

CONCESSIONS

The main concourse at the Corel Centre has nine large concession stands and two mall-style food courts serving hamburgers, pizza, hot dogs and chicken wings, along with a traditional Canadian favorite, beavertails.

Arena Facts

Opened: Jan. 15, 1996
Cost: $170 million
Capacity: 18,500
Home Sweet Home:
• *Police officer Lyndon Slewidge sings both the American and Canadian anthems before each home game. The burly tenor is a local icon and his rousing performances always whip the fans into a frenzy before the puck is dropped.*

GAME DAY TIPS

• **Gate hours:** Gates usually open 90 minutes prior to opening faceoff.
• **Prohibited items:** Food, beverages, alcohol, containers and coolers of any kind are prohibited. Air horns and laser pointers are also forbidden. Still and digital cameras are permitted. Flash cameras are permitted only during the pregame warm-up. Video cameras are strictly forbidden. Banners, flags and signs are allowed if they do not obstruct any views. Smoking is allowed only in designated areas.
• **Ticket tips:** The Senators sold out 17 of 41 home games last season, sometimes weeks in advance. Games against Toronto,

Directions: *The Corel Centre is 15 minutes from downtown Ottawa. Take Hwy. 417 (Queensway) to Palladium Dr. exit and follow signs to the arena. By Bus: OC Transpo buses 401, 402, 403, 404 and 405 arrive at the Corel Centre. Call (613) 741-4390 for more information.* **Parking:** *There are 10,000 spaces at the Corel Centre. Parking for disabled guests is available on the south side of the arena (Gate 3), with 160 spaces in Lot 3. Valet parking is available at the VIP entrance (Gate 2).*

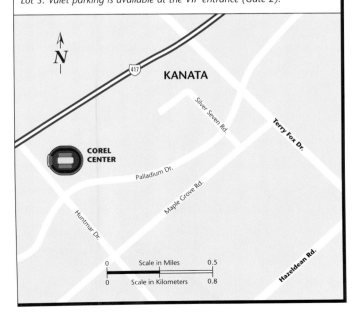

Seating Plan

- ■ Air Canada Club Seats ..$165
- ■ Reds $110
- ■ U1 ....$80
- ■ U2 ....$60
- ■ U3 ....$40
- ■ GM Power Seats $29
- ■ Coca-Cola Family Zone ...$21
- □ Penalty Box (includes dinner) $83
- ATM Gate 1
- ♿ Sections 101, 203, 219; top row 300s

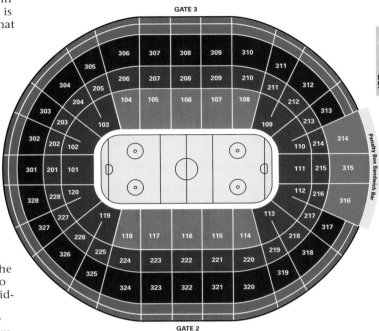

Montreal and Philadelphia do especially well, as do Saturday games. When it comes to picking seats, keep in mind that the luxury boxes cut off your view of the shot counter above row MM.
• **Lost and found:** (613) 599-0128.

Nearby Hotels

▼▼ **Best Western Barons Hotel** *(Motor Inn)*, 3700 Richmond Rd. (Nepean), (613) 828-2741, $129-$149
▼▼ **Comfort Inn** *(Motor Inn)*, 222 Hearst Way (Kanata), (613) 592-2200, $110-$120
▼▼▼ **The Days Inn Ottawa West** *(Motor Inn)*, 350 Moodie Dr. (Nepean), (613) 726-1717, $99
▼▼▼ **Holiday Inn Select** *(Motor Inn)*, 10 Lord Byng Way (Kanata), (613) 271-3057, $169-$230
▼▼ **Rideau Heights Motor Inn** *(Motel)*, 72 Rideau Heights Dr. (Nepean), (613) 226-4152, $71-$96

Nearby Restaurants

▼▼ **Canal Ritz** *(Italian)*, 375 Queen Elizabeth Dr. (Ottawa), (613) 238-8998, $8-$15
▼▼ **Friday's Roast Beef House** *(Steak & Seafood)*, 150 Elgin St. (Ottawa), (613) 237-5353, $15-$26
▼▼▼ **Le Jardin** *(French)*, 127 York St. (Ottawa), (613) 241-1424, $16-$30
▼▼▼ **Mamma Teresa Ristorante** *(Italian)*, 300 Somerset St. W. (Ottawa), (613) 236-3023, $10-$18
▼▼ **The Marble Works** *(Canadian)*, 14 Waller St. (Ottawa), (613) 241-6764, $16-$26

PHILADELPHIA FLYERS

FOR THOSE LOOKING FOR TELLTALE SIGNS OF SUCCESS, the Philadelphia Flyers' first season in the NHL provided decidedly mixed signals. Before the end of the season, the roof literally blew off the Spectrum where the team played its home games and the Flyers had to finish the year on the road. But the team did win the Western Division that year, showing the perseverance that would eventually take it to the top. Within three years, through successful trades and drafts, the team had added size to the lineup in the forms of enforcer Dave Schultz and defenseman Andre Dupont. It also picked up talented forwards in the persons of scrappy scorer Bobby Clarke, a junior star who was overlooked by many teams because he suffered from diabetes, Bill Barber and Rick MacLeish. Employing a brutally rough-and-ready style of hockey championed by coach Fred Shero, the Flyers enjoyed its first winning season in 1972–73 and earned the team the nickname "the Broad Street Bullies" in the process. The following season the Flyers defeated Boston to become the first expansion team to win a Stanley Cup. Goaltender Bernie Parent repeated as Conn Smythe winner the next year as the team won its second straight Cup. That success set the tone for the Flyers franchise. Through the 1980s, behind stars such as Brian Propp and power forward Tim Kerr, the team was a perennial contender. And after a tough stretch in the early 1990s Eric Lindros arrived to restore success to the franchise with another finals appearance in 1997. Unfortunately for Flyers' fans, no team since has shown the grit of the Broad Street Bullies — the grit required to win the franchise's third Stanley Cup.

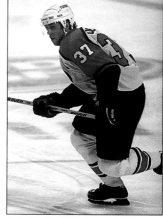

Eric Desjardins is a tower of strength on defense.

POSTSEASON
- Stanley Cup
Championships 2
(1973–74, 1974–75)
- Atlantic Division
Titles 3
(1994–95, 1995–96,
1999–2000)
- Patrick Division Titles 8
(1974–75, 1975–76, 1976–77,
1979–80, 1982–83, 1984–85,
1985–86, 1986–87)
- Western Division Titles ..2
(1967–68, 1973–74)

RETIRED NUMBERS
- Bernie Parent (1)
- Barry Ashbee (4)
- Bill Barber (7)
- Bobby Clarke (16)

Slap Shot
- *During the first period of a game at Vancouver on Feb. 8, 1972, Flyers goaltender Bruce Gamble suffered what was later diagnosed as a heart attack. Gamble finished the game, recording a 3-1 win.*
- *Flyer goalie Ron Hextall was the first NHL netminder to score a goal, notching a marker against Boston in December 1987.*

TEAM RECORDS
- **Bill Barber (1972–85)**
Goals (career): 420
- **Tom Bladon**
Points (game): 8
(Dec. 11, 1977)
- **Bobby Clarke (1969–84)**
Assists (season): 89 (twice)
Assists (career): 852
Points (career): 1,210
Games (career): 1,144
Seasons (career): 15
Shorthanded Goals
(career): 32
- **Ron Hextall**
(1986–92, 1994–99)
Wins (career): 240
- **Tim Kerr (1980–91)**
Power-Play Goals (season):
34 (1985–86)
Power-Play Goals (career): 145
- **Reggie Leach (1974–82)**
Goals (season): 61 (1975–76)
- **Eric Lindros**
(1992–2001)
Assists (game): 6
(Feb. 26, 1997)
- **Bernie Parent**
(1967–71, 1973–79)
Shutouts (season): 12 (twice)
Shutouts (career): 50
Wins (season): 47 (1973–74)
- **Brian Propp (1979–90)**
Game-Winning Goals
(season): 12 (1982–83)
- **Mark Recchi**
(1991–95, 1998–present)
Points (season): 123

(1992–93)
- **Dave Schultz (1971–76)**
Penalty Minutes (season):
472 (1974–75)
- **John Vanbiesbrouck**
(1998–2000)
Goals Against Avg.
(career): 2.19

LEAGUE HONORS
Hart Trophy
- Bobby Clarke (1972–73, 1974–75, 1975–76)
- Eric Lindros (1994–95)

Vezina Trophy
- Bernie Parent
(1973–74, 1974–75)
- Pelle Lindbergh (1984–85)
- Ron Hextall (1986–87)

Frank J. Selke Trophy
- Bobby Clarke (1982-83)
- Dave Poulin (1986–87)

Bill Masterton Trophy
- Bobby Clarke (1971–72)
- Tim Kerr (1988–89)

Jack Adams Award
- Fred Shero (1973–74)
- Pat Quinn (1979–80)
- Mike Keenan (1984–85)

Conn Smythe Trophy
- Bernie Parent (1974, '75)
- Reggie Leach (1976)
- Ron Hextall (1987)

Hockey Hall of Fame
- Bernie Parent (1984)
- Bobby Clarke (1987)
- Ed Snider(1988)
- Bill Barber (1990)
- Keith Allen (1992)
- Gene Hart (1997)

Vital Stats
Stadium Address:
*3601 S. Broad St.,
Philadelphia, Pa.*
Phone: *(215) 336-3600*
Web: *philadelphiaflyers.com,
comcast-spectacor.com*
Box Office:
*(215) 755-9700,
Mon.–Fri. 9–6*
Media Coverage:
*Radio: WIP (610 AM)
TV: UPN (Channel 57),
Comcast SportsNet*
Practice Facility:
*Flyers Skate Zone,
Voorheez, N.J.*

"If you love playing hockey, you love being a part of the team."

— *Flyers GM Bobby Clarke, on being a NHL player*

Timeline

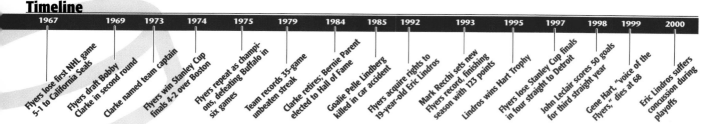

1967 — Flyers lose first NHL game 5-1 to California Seals
1969 — Flyers draft Bobby Clarke in second round
1973 — Clarke named team captain
1974 — Flyers win Stanley Cup finals 4-2 over Boston
1975 — Flyers repeat as champions, defeating Buffalo in six games
1979 — Team records 35-game unbeaten streak
1984 — Clarke retires; Bernie Parent elected to Hall of Fame
1985 — Goalie Pelle Lindberg killed in car accident
1992 — Flyers acquire rights to 19-year-old Eric Lindros
1993 — Mark Recchi sets new Flyers record, finishing season with 123 points
1995 — Lindros wins Hart Trophy
1997 — Flyers lose Stanley Cup finals in four straight to Detroit
1998 — John Leclair scores 50 goals for third straight year
1999 — Gene Hart, "voice of the Flyers," dies at 68
2000 — Eric Lindros suffers concussion during playoffs

268

FIRST UNION CENTER: SOMETHING FOR EVERYONE

FIRST UNION CENTER offers spectators everything they would expect in a new venue and a few things they wouldn't. Along with top-notch sight lines, seating and fan amenities, the stadium also features an in-arena microbrewery and cigar club. The venue also offers many interactive exhibits, including touch-screen video kiosks that allow fans to learn about the franchise and see some of its great moments. The first official event in the arena was a 5-3 win by the U.S. team in the 1996 Hockey World Cup.

CONCESSIONS

Given how popular they are in Philadelphia, it is no surprise that hoagies are a main attraction at the First Union Center. If the tuna, roast beef or cheese steak hoagies don't appeal, other options include hot dogs, gourmet pretzels, popcorn, pizza and microbrewery beer.

Arena Facts

Opened: Aug. 31, 1996
Cost: $210 million
Capacity: 19,519
Home Sweet Home:
• In the world of major-league baseball, Philadelphia fans are renowned as the most belligerent to opposing players. The city's hockey fans are no different, making First Union a difficult place for opposing teams to win.

GAME DAY TIPS

• **Gate hours:** Gates open 90 minutes prior to opening faceoff.
• **Prohibited items:** Video and audio recorders, laser pointers, noise-makers, brooms, weapons, sticks, bats, food, beverages, coolers, cans and bottles are all prohibited. Smoking is forbidden inside the stadium, but patrons are allowed to light up in a designated area outside the building.
• **Ticket tips:** The First Union Center is considered one of the best arenas in which to watch a game. The sight lines are excellent in all of the pricing areas, which is fortunate because Flyers tickets are not too easy to come by. Plan in advance to see the team in action, especially if division rivals such as New Jersey or Pittsburgh roll into town.
• **Lost and found:** (215) 389-9529.

Seating Plan

■ $150
■ ....Call for prices
■ $90
■ ....Call for prices
▓ $80

■ (First 11 rows) $50
■ (Last 4 rows) $37
ATM Sections 103, 219A
♿ Sections 112, 114, 121, 129, 202, 204A, 222

Directions: From I-95, exit at Broad St. First Union Center will be on your left. By Subway: Take the Broad St. line to the Pattison and Broad Sts. stop. By Bus: Various buses go to and from the arena. Call SEPTA at (215) 580-7800 for more information. **Parking:** There are 6,100 spots in the lot surrounding the center. Spots for patrons with disabilities are located in lots C and D. Overflow parking is accommodated by lots on S. Darien, S. 11th and S. Broad Sts.

Nearby Hotels

▼▼▼ **Courtyard by Marriott Airport** *(Motor Inn)*, 8900 Bartram Ave. (Philadelphia), (215) 365-2200, $159-$219
▼▼▼ **Hampton Inn-Philadelphia Airport** *(Motel)*, 8600 Bartram Ave. (Philadelphia), (215) 966-1300, $139-$169
▼▼▼ **Hilton Philadelphia Airport** *(Hotel)*, 4509 Island Ave. (Philadelphia), (215) 365-4150, $135-$195
▼▼▼ **Holiday Inn Philadelphia Stadium** *(Hotel)*, 900 Packer Ave. (Philadelphia), (215) 755-9500, $89-$149
▼▼▼ **Philadelphia Fairfield Inn** *(Motel)*, 8800 Bartram Ave. (Philadelphia), (215) 365-2254, $100

Nearby Restaurants

▼▼ **Bistro Romano** *(Italian)*, 120 Lombard St. (Philadelphia), (215) 925-8880, $10-$24
▼▼▼ **The Continental Restaurant & Martini Bar** *(Continental)*, 138 Market St. (Philadelphia), (215) 923-6069, $6-$19
▼▼ **Downey's Restaurant** *(American)*, 526 S. Front St. (Philadelphia), (215) 625-9500, $16-$20
▼ **Engine 46 Steak House** *(American)*, 10 Reed St. (Philadelphia), (215) 462-4646, $5-$19
▼▼▼ **The Plough and the Stars Irish Restaurant & Bar** *(Continental)*, 123 Chestnut St. (Philadelphia), (215) 733-0300, $14-$21

PHOENIX COYOTES

THE ROOTS OF PHOENIX'S HOCKEY FRANCHISE stretch some 1,300 miles to Winnipeg, Man., in western Canada. Originally called the Winnipeg Jets, the team was one of the original 12 clubs of the World Hockey Association. The WHA was a rival to the NHL, although the older league didn't take the new one very seriously at first. That all changed just months before the opening of the WHA's first season in 1972, when the Jets convinced one of the NHL's biggest stars, Bobby Hull, to jump ship and sign on with the team. With Hull, "the Golden Jet," blasting his trademark slap shots past shell-shocked goalies, the Jets went on to win three WHA crowns in seven years. With the WHA floundering in 1979, the Jets were admitted into the NHL, where after a couple of rough seasons the team rebounded with 10 playoff appearances in 12 years. But the club showed an alarming propensity for early exits from the postseason, winning only 17 of 52 games and advancing to the next round only twice. Undoubtedly the highlight of that period was the arrival of "the Finnish Flash," Teemu Selanne. In 1992 the slick speedster broke NHL rookie records by potting 76 goals and amassing 132 points. In 1996 the team moved from cold Canadian climes and set up shop in sunny Phoenix. The change of scenery did little to improve the newly named Coyotes' playoff woes, however. Despite the leadership of two of the game's most rugged and talented forwards, Keith Tkachuk and Jeremy Roenick, the Coyotes were eliminated in the first playoff round in five consecutive seasons.

"I can't wait for the White Out to hit Phoenix again."
— Former Coyote Keith Tkachuk, on the Phoenix fans' tradition of dressing all in white for home playoff games

Vital Stats

Stadium Address:
201 E. Jefferson St., Phoenix, Ariz.
Phone: (602) 379-2000
Web: phoenixcoyotes.com, americawestarena.com
Box Office: (602) 379-7800, Mon.–Fri. 10–5
Media Coverage:
Radio: KDUS (1060 AM), KDKB (93.3 FM)
TV: KASW (Channel 61), Fox Sports Net
Practice Facility:
ALLTEL Ice Den, Scottsdale, Ariz.

POSTSEASON
• **Playoff Appearances**......15
(1981–82, 1982–83, 1983–84, 1984–85, 1985–86, 1986–87, 1987–88, 1989–90, 1991–92, 1992–93, 1995–96, 1996–97, 1997–98, 1998–99, 1999–2000)
• **WHA Championships** 3
(1975–76, 1977–78, 1978–79)

RETIRED NUMBERS
• Bobby Hull (9)
• Thomas Steen (25)

TEAM RECORDS
• **Sean Burke (1999–present)**
Goals Against Avg. (career): 2.33

Slap Shot

• *From 1984 to '90, the Jets and the Oilers met five times in the playoffs. The Oilers, led at the time by Wayne Gretzky, won all five series and went on to win the Stanley Cup each year.*
• *In 1996–97, the Coyotes' first season in Phoenix, Keith Tkachuk gave fans plenty to cheer about. His 52 goals topped the league, making him the first U.S.-born player to be the NHL's premier sniper.*

• **Tie Domi (1992–95)**
Penalty Minutes (game): 49 (Feb. 9, 1995)
Penalty Minutes (season): 347 (1993–94)
• **Bob Essensa (1988–94, 1999–2000)**
Wins (season): 33 (tie) (1992–93)
Wins (career): 129
• **Brian Hayward (1982–86)**
Wins (season): 33 (tie) (1984–85)
• **Dale Hawerchuk (1981–90)**
Consecutive Games: 475 (Dec. 19, 1982–Dec. 10, 1988)
Goals (career): 379
Goals by a Center (season): 53 (1984–85)
Hat Tricks (career): 12
Points (career): 929
Power-Play Goals (career): 122
20-Goal Seasons: 9
30-Goal Seasons: 8
40-Goal Seasons:7
100-Point Seasons: 6
• **Phil Housley (1990–93)**
Assists (season): 79 (1992–93)
Goals by a Defenseman (season): 23 (twice)
• **Nikolai Khabibulin (1994–99)**
Shutouts (season): 8 (1998–99)
Shutouts (career): 21
20-Win Seasons: 4
30-Win Seasons: 3
• **Willy Lindstrom (1979–83)**

Goals (game): 5 (tie) (Mar. 2, 1982)
• **Paul MacLean (1981–88)**
Goals by a Right Wing (career): 248
• **Teemu Selanne (1992–96)**
Goals (season): 76 (1992–93)
Hat Tricks (season): 5 (1992–93)
Points (season): 132 (1992–93)
Power Play Goals (season): 24 (1992–93)
• **Doug Smail (1980–91)**
Shorthanded Goals (career): 25
• **Thomas Steen (1981–95)**

Phoenix fans pin their hopes on tough forward Jeremy Roenick.

Assists (career): 553
Games (career): 950
• **Keith Tkachuk (1991–2001)**
Goals by a Left Wing (season): 52 (1996–97)
Goals by a Left Wing (career): 323
Penalty Minutes (career): 1,508
50 Goal Seasons: 2
• **Alexei Zhamnov (1992–96)**
Goals (game): 5 (tie) (April 1, 1995)

LEAGUE HONORS
Calder Trophy
• Dale Hawerchuk (1981–82)
• Teemu Selanne (1992–93)

King Clancy Trophy
• Kris King (1995–96)

Adams Award
• Tom Watt (1981–82)
• Bob Murdoch (1989–90)

Timeline

1971 Winnipeg Jets are charter members of World Hockey Association

1975 Bobby Hull scores 50 goals in 50 games; goes on to pot a record 77 goals

1978 Team wins second of three WHA titles

1979 WHA folds; team joins NHL

1982 Jets eliminated in franchise's first NHL playoff series

1985 Team beats Flames in first playoff series win

1990 Jets drafts Keith Tkachuk and Alexei Zhamnov

1992 Teemu Selanne shatters NHL rookie records with 76 goals and 132 points

1994 Tie Domi leads team with 347 penalty minutes

1996 Team relocates to Phoenix; changes name to Coyotes

1997 Mike Gartner is only fifth player to reach 700-goals plateau

1999 Rick Tocchet notches 400th career goal

2000 Team makes playoffs for fifth straight season

2001 Wayne Gretzky becomes team's co-owner

AMERICA WEST ARENA: MODELED AFTER THE BEST

WHEN THE HOCKEY TEAM was relocated from Winnipeg to Phoenix in 1996, it moved right into one of the country's top sporting venues, the America West Arena. It is no accident that America West is an excellent place to take in a game. Prior to the arena's construction, management toured the world's top venues and incorporated the best of these designs into America West. Fans enjoy the downtown location and the concessions and design of this facility. Players like the on-site practice gym.

CONCESSIONS

Fans coming to America West Arena can expect all the old arena favorites: hamburgers, hot dogs, sausages, popcorn, corn on the cob and ice cream. Several local and national restaurant chains have franchises in the arena. Some regional beers are also available.

GAME DAY TIPS
• **Gate hours:** Gates open one hour prior to opening faceoff.
• **Prohibited items:** Bottles, cans, food or alcohol, video cameras, professional cameras, laser pointers and projectiles of any kind are prohibited. Signs and banners are permitted. Smoking is allowed only in designated outdoor areas.
• **Ticket tips:** Coyotes' tickets are fairly easy to come by. Games against Dallas, Detroit and some teams from the East do attract good crowds, although they rarely sell out. Keep in mind that since this was built as a basketball arena, the view of the north-end goal from some 4,000 seats is obstructed. In fact, the seats are situated directly above the goal.
• **Lost and found:** (602) 379-7776.

Arena Facts

Opened: *June 1, 1992*
Cost: *$90 million*
Capacity: *16,210*
Home Sweet Home:
• *Following a tradition that began when the franchise was in Winnipeg, Coyotes fans dress all in white for playoff games. The optical effect of 16,000 people dressed in white, combined with the loud cheers, helps fire up the team.*

Seating Plan

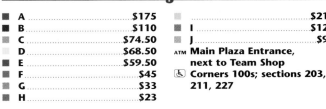

■ **A**	$175	▨		$21
■ **B**	$110	▨ **I**		$12
▨ **C**	$74.50	▨ **J**		$9
☐ **D**	$68.50			
■ **E**	$59.50			
■ **F**	$45			
▨ **G**	$33			
■ **H**	$23			

ATM **Main Plaza Entrance, next to Team Shop**
♿ **Corners 100s; sections 203, 211, 227**

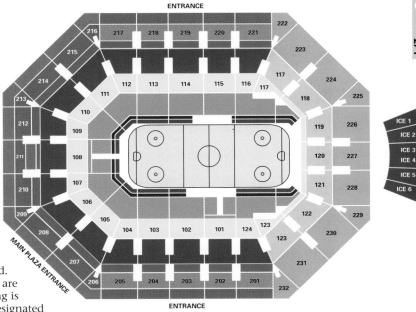

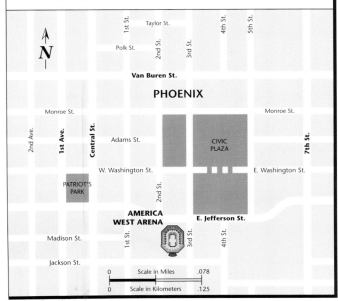

Directions: *Take I-10 to Washington St./Jefferson St. Follow Washington St. to 3rd St. and turn south to arena. By Bus: Several buses from downtown Phoenix arrive at the arena. Call ValleyMetro at (602) 253-5000 for information.* **Parking:** *The arena has a 900-space parking garage. Forty-five spaces are reserved for the disabled. There are more than 30,000 spots available in downtown Phoenix lots within a 15-minute walk on 1st, 2nd, 3rd, 4th, 5th and 7th Sts.*

Nearby Hotels

▼▼▼ **Best Western Executive Park Hotel** *(Hotel)*, 1100 N. Central Ave. (Phoenix), (602) 252-2100, $61-$91
▼▼▼ **Embassy Suites Hotel Airport West** *(Suite Hotel)*, 2333 E. Thomas Rd. (Phoenix), (602) 957-1910, $69-$139
▼▼▼ **Hilton Suites-Phoenix** *(Suite Hotel)*, 10 E. Thomas Rd. in Phoenix Plaza (Phoenix), (602) 222-1111, $59-$239
▼▼▼ **Hyatt Regency Phoenix** *(Hotel)*, 122 N. 2nd St. (Phoenix), (602) 252-1234, $224-$249
▼▼▼ **La Quinta Inn Thomas Rd** *(Motel)*, 2725 N. Black Canyon Hwy. (Phoenix), (602) 258-6271, $49-$99

Nearby Restaurants

▼▼▼ **Eddie Matney's** *(French)*, 2398 E. Camelback Rd. in Northern Trust Bank Tower (Phoenix), (602) 957-3214, $17-$25
▼▼ **Omaha Steakhouse** *(Southwest American)*, 2630 E. Camelback Rd. in Embassy Suites-Biltmore (Phoenix), (602) 955-3992, $11-$34
▼▼ **Rennicks** *(American)*, 2435 S. 47th St. (Phoenix), (480) 894-1600, $10-$19
▼▼ **Rose's** *(American)*, 1100 N. Central Ave. in Best Western Executive Park Hotel (Phoenix), (602) 252-2100, $9-$18
▼ **Stockyards Restaurant** *(American)*, 5001 E. Washington Ave. (Phoenix), (602) 273-7378, $14-$32

PITTSBURGH PENGUINS

EVEN BEFORE MARIO LEMIEUX became owner in 1999, the Pittsburgh Penguins has always been "Mario's team." There are players with greater numbers; Rocket Richard has more Cups, Gretzky has more points, Gordie Howe has more goals, but few have meant more to their team than "Super Mario." Before Lemieux burst onto the scene, Pittsburgh was a run-of-the-mill franchise. The team's first 17 years were marked by moderate successes, including a 1970 playoff sweep of Oakland. But while stars such as Jean Pronovost, Syl Apps and sniper Pierre Larouche kept things hopping at the Igloo, the team went bankrupt in 1975 and suffered a pair of last place finishes in 1982–83 and 1983–84. However, the franchise's fortunes changed forever in 1984 when it drafted an 18-year-old Mario Lemieux. Racking up 100 points as a rookie, the tall center won his first scoring title and MVP award in 1987–88. Plagued by back problems his whole career, Lemieux missed the first 50 games of the 1990–91 season following surgery, only to roar back and lead the Pens to their first Stanley Cup title. He bettered himself the following year, winning the scoring title, another Cup and a second playoff MVP award. In 1993 Lemieux underwent six weeks of radiation treatment to battle cancer and amazingly returned midway through the season to win the scoring title again. Retiring in 1997, Lemieux resurfaced in 1999 to buy the floundering franchise and save hockey in Pittsburgh. Remarkably, after more than three years out of hockey, Lemieux returned as a player in 2000–01 and led his Pens back to the playoffs.

Mario Lemieux returned to lead the Pens to the conference finals in 2001.

POSTSEASON
• Stanley Cup
Championships 2
(1990–91, 1991–92)

RETIRED NUMBERS
• Michel Briere (21)

TEAM RECORDS
• **Tom Barrasso (1988–2000)**
Goals Against Avg. (season): 2.07 (1997–98)
Saves (career): 12,064
Shutouts (season): 7 (1997–98)
Shutouts (career): 22
Wins (season): 43 (1992–93)
Wins (career): 226
• **Jaromir Jagr (1990–present)**

Slap Shot

• *From 1980–81 to 2000–01, only three players have won the NHL's Art Ross Trophy as the league's top scorer. Wayne Gretzky tops the list with 10 titles during that 21-year span. Mario Lemieux is next, with six crowns to his credit, followed by five-time winner Jaromir Jagr.*

• *Lemieux was a force the minute he stepped onto the ice. He scored his first NHL goal on his first shot on his first shift in his first game.*

Game-Winning Goals (season): 12 (1995–96)
Game-Winning Goals (career): 78
Shots (season): 403 (1995–96)
• **Mario Lemieux (1984–97, 2000–present)**
Assists (season): 114 (1988–89)
Assists (career): 922
Games (career): 788
Goals in a Period: 4 (Jan. 26, 1997)
Goals (season): 85 (1988–89)
Goals (career): 648
Points (season): 199 (1988–89)
Points (career): 1,570
Power-Play Assists (season): 58 (1987–88)
Power-Play Goals (season): 31 (1995–96)
Power Play Goals (career): 217
Power Play Points (season): 80 (1987–88)
Shorthanded Goals (season): 13 (1988–89)
Shorthanded Goals (career): 48

LEAGUE HONORS
Hart Trophy
• Mario Lemieux (1987–88, 1992–93, 1995–96)
• Jaromir Jagr (1998–99)

Art Ross Trophy
• Mario Lemieux (1987–88,

1988–89, 1991–92, 1992–93, 1995–96, 1996–97)
• Jaromir Jagr (1994–95, 1997–98, 1998–99, 1999–2000, 2000–01)

James Norris Trophy
• Randy Carlyle (1980–81)

Calder Trophy
• Mario Lemieux (1984–85)

Lady Byng Trophy
• Rick Kehoe (1980–81)
• Ron Francis (1994–95, 1997–98)

Frank J. Selke Trophy
• Ron Francis (1994–95)

Bill Masterton Trophy
• Lowell MacDonald (1972–73)
• Mario Lemieux (1992–93)

Lester B. Pearson Award
• Mario Lemieux (1985–86, 1987–88, 1992–93, 1995–96)
• Jaromir Jagr (1998–99, 1999–2000)

Conn Smythe Trophy
• Mario Lemieux (1991, '92)

"It's simple. Mario Lemieux saved hockey in Pittsburgh."
— *Player agent Tom Reich*

Vital Stats

Stadium Address:
66 Mario Lemieux Pl., Pittsburgh, Pa.
Phone: (412) 642-1800
Web:
pittsburghpenguins.com, mellonarena.com
Box Office:
(412) 642-PENS, Mon.–Fri. 10–5:30
Media Coverage:
Radio: 3-W-S (94.5 FM, 970 AM)
TV: WCWB (Channel 22), Fox Sports Net
Practice Facility:
Iceoplex of Southpointe, Canonsburg, Pa.

Hockey Hall of Fame
• Red Kelly (1969)
• Tim Horton (1977)
• Andy Bathgate (1978)
• Leo Boivin (1986)
• Scotty Bowman (1991)
• Bob Johnson (1992)
• Mario Lemieux (1997)
• Bryan Trottier (1997)
• Joe Mullen (2000)

Timeline

1967	1970	1972	1975	1978	1984	1988	1989	1990	1991	1997	1999	2000	2001
Pittsburgh part of six-team NHL expansion	Pens make first-ever playoff round	Team scores five goals in 2:07 versus St. Louis	Pierre Larouche leads rookie scorers	Ed DeBartolo buys club	Pens draft Mario Lemieux; Lemieux notches 100 points	Lemieux wins first scoring title; named MVP	Lemieux racks up 199 points	Team drafts Jaromir Jagr	Pens win first of two straight Stanley Cups	Pens lose captain as Lemieux retires	Lemieux becomes part owner of the team	Lemieux makes comeback as player	Pens lose conference finals to New Jersey

MELLON ARENA:
HOT TIMES AT THE IGLOO

THE OLDEST VENUE IN THE NHL, the Mellon Arena has hosted some of the NHL's greatest players, including Gordie Howe, Bobby Orr, Wayne Gretzky and, of course, the Penguins' very own dynamic duo, Jaromir Jagr and Mario Lemieux. Also known as the Igloo, the arena has undergone a series of renovations to keep pace with other, more modern venues. The arena was originally designed for the Civic Light Opera and, as such, is equipped with the largest retractable stainless steel roof in the world.

CONCESSIONS

As well as favorites such as burgers, nachos and pretzels, Mellon Arena offers gourmet fries with a variety of toppings, fresh-cut potato chips, hot roast beef sandwiches and a Pittsburgh specialty: foot-long hot dogs served with delicious coleslaw.

Arena Facts

Opened: Sept. 19, 1961
Cost: $22 million
Capacity: 16,958
Home Sweet Home:
• With Mario Lemieux as the NHL's biggest draw and no NBA team to compete against in the winter months, the Penguins always pull in large and boisterous crowds. The vocal fans give the team an added boost during games.

GAME DAY TIPS

• **Gate hours:** Gates open one hour prior to opening faceoff.
• **Prohibited items:** Food, beverages, cameras, and video and audio recorders are prohibited. Smoking is forbidden inside, but patrons may smoke outside via exits off the main concourse near sections B18 and B30.
• **Ticket tips:** The return of Mario Lemieux has made the Penguins a hot ticket in almost every city where they play — including their own. Weekend games, as well as matches against the Flyers, Rangers and Avalanche sell out especially quickly.
• **Lost and found:** (412) 842-1692.

Seating Plan

■ Igloo Seats	$125	
■ Club Seats	$80	
☐ A/B Level	$75	
▨ C Level	$65	
▨ D Level	$45	

■ E/F Balcony	$30	
■ Rear E Balcony	$20	
■ Suites	Call for info	
ATM Igloo; levels B, C		
♿ Sections EI-4, WI-1		

Directions

Directions: From I-579 south, exit at 6th Ave./Mellon Arena and turn left at light. From I-279 east, bear right through Fort Pitt Tunnel onto I-376 (toward Monroeville) and exit at Grant St. to 7th Ave. By Subway: Take the "T" to the Steel Plaza Station. By Bus: Buses are available to and from the arena. Call (412) 442-2000 for information. *Parking:* Five lots surround the arena. Wheelchair-accessible parking is available in the South and East lots. Other parking can be found on 4th, 6th, Oliver and Penn Aves.

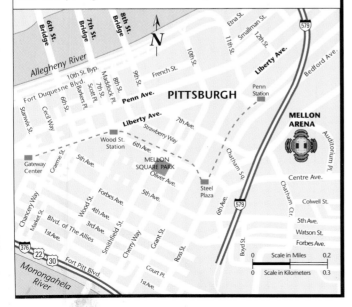

Nearby Hotels

▼▼▼ **Doubletree Hotel Pittsburgh** *(Hotel)*, 1000 Penn Ave. (Pittsburgh), (412) 281-3700, $99-$199
▼▼▼ **Hampton Inn** *(Motel)*, 4575 McKnight Rd. (Pittsburgh), (412) 939-3200, $84-$94
▼▼▼ **Hampton Inn-University Center** *(Motel)*, 3315 Hamlet St. (Pittsburgh), (412) 681-1000, $99-$109
▼▼▼ **Hilton Pittsburgh** *(Hotel)*, in the Gateway Center opposite Point State Park (Pittsburgh), (412) 391-4600, $84-$219
▼▼▼ **Sheraton Station Square Hotel** *(Hotel)*, 7 Station Square Dr. (Pittsburgh), (412) 261-2000, $139-$209

Nearby Restaurants

▼▼▼ **Grand Concourse Restaurant** *(Seafood)*, 1 Station Square in Pittsburgh and Lake Erie Railroad Terminal Bldg. (Pittsburgh), (412) 261-1717, $17-$25
▼▼ **Kiku's of Japan** *(Japanese)*, at Carson and Smithfield Sts. in the Shops at Station Square (Pittsburgh), (412) 765-3200, $15-$20
▼▼▼ **Pittsburgh Fishmarket Restaurant** *(Seafood)*, 1000 Penn Ave., in the Doubletree Hotel (Pittsburgh), (412) 227-3657, $12-$16
▼▼ **Khalil's II** *(Middle Eastern)*, 4757 Baum Blvd. (Pittsburgh), (412) 683-4757, $9-$16
▼▼▼▼ **Le Mont Restaurant** *(American)*, 1114 Grandview Ave. (Pittsburgh), (412) 431-3100, $22-$35 (dinner only)

St. Louis Blues

Vital Stats

Stadium Address:
1401 Clark Ave.,
St. Louis, Mo.
Phone: (314) 622-5400
Web: stlouisblues.com,
savviscenter.net
Box Office:
(314) 421-4400,
Mon.–Sun. 10–6, off-
season Mon.–Fri. 10–6
Media Coverage:
Radio: KTRS (550 AM)
TV: KPLR (Channel 11),
Fox Sports Net
Practice Facility:
U.S. Ice Complex,
Chesterfield, Mo.

THE ST. LOUIS BLUES HAVE NEVER HAD A SHORTAGE of stars in their lineup. In the early years veterans such as Dickie Moore, Doug Harvey and Hall-of-Fame goaltending duo Glenn Hall and Jacques Plante separated the Blues from the other expansion clubs and landed the franchise in three consecutive Stanley Cup finals. Fans in St. Louis didn't know how good they had it. The team dropped all three series and has not returned to the finals since, but the stars have kept coming. Ironman Garry Unger played 914 straight games, 662 with the Blues through the 1970s, and led the team in scoring for five seasons. Bernie Federko was a point-scoring machine during the 1980s, hitting the 100-point mark four times, while Mike Liut won more games during that decade than any other goaltender. The late '80s brought the dynamic duo of Adam Oates and Brett Hull, who shattered the franchise's single-season scoring marks, both topping the 100-point mark in 1989–90 and 1990–91. They were followed by young Brendan Shanahan, who potted 50 goals in 1993 and '94. But postseason success was limited to those first three seasons, where the competition was slim in the Western Division. When the team landed Wayne Gretzky in a trade late in the 1995–96 season, it looked like the team had assembled the horses to go all the way. That run was stopped by a double-overtime loss to Detroit in the conference semifinal and Gretzky was gone the following year. These days defense is the name of the game, with fans pinning their hopes on goalie Roman Turek, veteran defenseman Al MacInnis and rugged captain Chris Pronger.

"We might not be the best team in the league, but we're the most consistent."

— Former Blues defenseman Marc Bergevin

POSTSEASON
- **Western Division Titles...3**
(1967–68, 1968–69, 1969–70)
- **Smythe Division Titles....2**
(1976–77, 1980–81)
- **Norris Division Titles......2**
(1984–85, 1986–87)
- **Central Division Titles....1**
(1999–2000)

RETIRED NUMBERS
- Bob Gassoff (3)
- Barclay Plager (8)
- Brian Sutter (11)
- Bernie Federko (24)

Slap Shot
- *When Blues captain Chris Pronger won the Norris Trophy and the Hart Trophy in 1999–2000, he joined some elite company. He was the first to win both awards since Bobby Orr in 1972.*
- *The Blues have been a model of consistency in the NHL. The team has missed the playoffs just three times since joining the league for the 1967–68 season.*

TEAM RECORDS
- **Red Berenson
(1967–71, 1974–78)**
Goals (game): 6
(Nov. 7, 1968)
Points (game): 7 (tie)
(Nov. 7, 1968)
- **Bernie Federko (1976–89)**
Assists (career): 721
Games (career): 927
Points (game): 7 (tie)
(Nov. 7, 1968)
Points (career): 1,073
- **Glenn Hall (1967–71)**
Shutouts (career): 16
- **Brett Hull (1987–98)**
Game-Winning Goals
(season): 12 (1989–90)
Goals (season): 86 (1990–91)
Goals (career): 527
Hat Tricks (season): 8
(1991–92)
Points (season): 131 (1990–91)
Power-Play Goals (season):
29 (twice)
- **Mike Liut (1979–85)**
Minutes (career): 20,010
Wins (career): 151
- **Adam Oates (1989–92)**
Assists (season): 90 (1990–91)
- **Roman Turek
(1999–present)**
Goals-Against Average
(season): 1.95 (1999–2000)

Wins (season): 42
(1999–2000)
- **Garry Unger (1970–79)**
Consecutive Games: 662

LEAGUE HONORS
Hart Trophy
- Brett Hull (1990–91)
- Chris Pronger
(1999–2000)

James Norris Trophy
- Al MacInnis (1998–99)
- Chris Pronger
(1999–2000)

Vezina Trophy
- Jacques Plante (1968–69)
- Glen Hall (1968–69)

Lady Byng Trophy
- Phil Goyette (1969–70)

- Brett Hull (1989–90)
- Pavol Demitra
(1999–2000)

Bill Masterton Trophy
- Blake Dunlop (1980–81)
- Jamie McLennan
(1997–98)

Jack Adams Award
- Red Berenson (1980–81)
- Brian Sutter (1990–91)
- Joel Quenneville
(1999–2000)

Conn Smythe Trophy
- Glenn Hall (1968)

Hockey Hall of Fame
- Doug Harvey (1973)
- Dickie Moore (1974)
- Glenn Hall (1975)
- Jacques Plante (1978)
- Lynn Patrick (1980)
- Emile Francis (1982)
- Dan Kelly (1989)
- Scotty Bowman (1991)
- Al Arbour (1996)
- Peter Stastny (1998)
- Joe Mullen (2000)

Creative centerman Pierre Turgeon is one of the NHL's best passers.

Timeline

1967	Blues tie Minnesota in franchise's first game
1969	Jacques Plante records 1.96 GAA
1970	Blues lose third consecutive Stanley Cup finals
1975	Garry Unger leads team in scoring for fourth straight year
1978	Blues play penalty-free game with Montreal
1981	Wayne Babych becomes team's first 50-goal scorer with 54
1985	Goalie Mike Liut traded to Hartford
1987	Team signs Doug Gilmore; wins Norris Division
1991	Brett Hull wins Hart Trophy as league MVP
1994	Brendan Shanahan named to first All-Star team
1996	Team acquires Wayne Gretzky through trade with Kings
1999	Al MacInnis wins Norris Trophy
2000	Blues finish with best record in NHL

SAVVIS CENTER: THE ANSWER TO THE BLUES

FORMERLY THE KIEL CENTER, the Savvis Center is a great place to watch a hockey game. Like the St. Louis Arena where the Blues once played, the Savvis has wonderful sight lines. Unlike the old arena, however, Savvis also provides top-notch fan amenities — TV monitors, numerous rest rooms, scoreboards — and a selection of good food in the extensive food court and the three in-arena restaurants. The Savvis also features 1,700 club level seats, 91 suites and seven party rooms that can be rented on an event-by-event basis.

CONCESSIONS

St. Louis specialties at the Savvis Center include barbecue sandwiches, Southwest sausages and toasted ravioli. Other options include pizza, chicken wings, club sandwiches, snow cones, bratwurst and chili dogs. Specialty draft beers are also available.

Arena Facts

Opened: Oct. 8, 1994
Cost: $169.5 million
Capacity: 21,000
Home Sweet Home:
• Since the opening of the Savvis Center, the Blues have played in front of 126 sellout crowds. That kind of support was evident in the team's stunning 25-10-6 home record in 1999–2000.

GAME DAY TIPS

• **Gate hours:** Gates open one hour prior to opening faceoff.
• **Prohibited items:** Cans, bottles, coolers, outside food and beverages, helium balloons, laser pointers, sticks, pets (except for service animals for the disabled), weapons, and video cameras are all prohibited. Smoking is permitted only in designated areas inside the Savvis Center, but guests are also allowed to exit and reenter the arena through the West and 14th St. entrances in order to light up.
• **Ticket tips:** The Blues are a very popular team and frequently sell out their home games. Nonetheless, tickets are often available with a little bit of advanced planning. The Detroit Red Wings are the team's biggest rival, so tickets for games between the two teams are especially hard to come by.
• **Lost and found:** (314) 622-5431.

Seating Plan

- ■ **Club** $85
- ■ **Plaza** $80
- ■ **Plaza Ends** $70
- ■ **Plaza High End** (attack twice) $60
- ■ **Plaza High End** (attack once) $45
- ■ **Mezzanine Center** $42
- ■ **Mezzanine Ends** $30
- **Mezzanine High Center** .$23
- **Mezzanine High Ends** $15
- **ATM** **Sections 102/103, 302; Atrium near Box Office**
- ♿ **Throughout**

Nearby Hotels

▼▼▼ **Courtyard by Marriott Downtown (Motor Inn),** 2340 Market St. (St. Louis), (314) 241-9111, $109-$124
▼▼▼ **Drury Inn Union Station (Classic Motor Inn),** 201 S. 20th St. (St. Louis), (314) 231-3900, $109-$134
▼▼▼ **Hampton Inn Union Station (Hotel),** 2211 Market St. (St. Louis), (314) 241-3200, $99-$121
▼▼▼ **Holiday Inn Downtown Select (Hotel),** 811 N. 9th St. (St. Louis), (314) 421-4000, $89-$119
▼▼▼▼ **Hyatt Regency St. Louis at Union Station (Classic Hotel),** 1 St. Louis Union Station (St. Louis), (314) 231-1234, $185-$210

Nearby Restaurants

▼ **Broadway Oyster Bar (Cajun),** 736 S. Broadway (St. Louis), (314) 621-8811, $8-$14
▼ **St. Louis Brewery Tap Room (American),** 2100 Locust St. (St. Louis), (314) 241-2337, $5-$14
▼▼▼ **St. Louis Steakhouse (Steakhouse),** 101 S. 11th St. (St. Louis), (314) 241-1121, $19-$40 (dinner only)
▼▼▼ **Station Grill (American),** 1 St. Louis Union Station in the Hyatt Regency at Union Station (St. Louis), (314) 231-1234, $13-$26
▼▼▼ **Top of the Riverfront Restaurant (Regional American),** 200 S. 4th St. in the Regal Riverfront Hotel (St. Louis), (314) 241-3191, $16-$35 (dinner only)

Directions: Exit I-44 east at Jefferson Ave. Go to Chouteau Ave., then turn onto 18th St. and follow to Clark Ave.. Exit I-55 north at downtown Memorial Dr. Turn left at Market St., then left onto Tucker and go to Clark Ave. Exit I-64 west at 9th St., then turn left onto Clark Ave. By Public Transportation: MetroLink goes right to the arena; get off at Kiel Station. Buses are available to and from the center. Call (314) 231-2345 for more information. **Parking:** The on-site garage at the center is presold. There are about 6,500 spots available in the area surrounding the arena on Clark Ave., Chestnut St. and Pine St. Guests with disabilities can use reserved spots in the area lots or be dropped off at the 14th St. entrance.

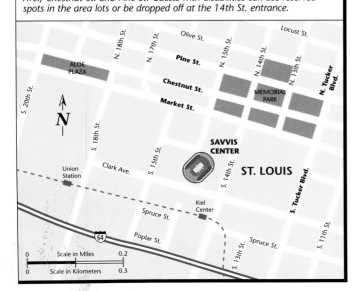

SAN JOSE SHARKS

THE SHARKS RECEIVED INCREDIBLE support when the team arrived in sunny California in 1991. To some that was a surprise. Fans in the Bay Area had not exactly come out in droves to support the Oakland/California Seals, a NHL franchise founded in 1967–68. The situation had forced the league to relocate the team to Cleveland following the 1975–76 season. The second time around would be different. With helmetless captain Doug Wilson anchoring the blue line and stellar young goalie Arturs Irbe in net, the expansion Sharks earned some respect, despite finishing in or near the NHL basement. By 1994, through successful NHL drafts and activity on the European market, the team had a mix of young stars such as Sandis Ozolinsh and Jeff Friesen and experienced veterans such as Russian standouts Sergei Makarov and Igor Larionov. The team's finesse-based play landed it in the playoffs in just its third season. Up against the number one seed Detroit Red Wings, the Sharks staged one of the greatest upsets in recent history, taking a dramatic game seven 3-2. The team then lost a heartbreaking seven-game tilt with the Maple Leafs that would have landed the team in the NHL semifinals. Fans were thrilled and doubters were converted. Since that year, the Sharks have continued to perform well. With Friesen and power forward Owen Nolan leading the charge, the Sharks have become a perennial playoff team and a threat to the top teams come playoff time. In fact, with the inspired play of young goalie Evgeni Nabokov, San Jose is now poised to become one of the NHL's marquee franchises.

276

Vital Stats

Stadium Address:
525 W. Santa Clara St.,
San Jose, Calif.
Phone: (408) 287-7070
Web: sj-sharks.com,
compaqcenteratsanjose.com
Box Office:
(408) 999-5757,
Mon.–Fri. 9:30–5:30,
during games Sat. 9:30–1
Media Coverage:
Radio: KFOX (98.5 FM)
TV: Fox Sports Net
Practice Facility:
Ice Center of San Jose,
San Jose, Calif.

POSTSEASON
• **Playoff Appearances**........6
(1995–94, 1994–95, 1997–98, 1998–99, 1999–2000, 2000–01)

TEAM RECORDS
• **Jamie Baker**
(1993–96, '98)
Shorthanded Goals
(game): 2 (Jan. 6, 1996)
• **Vincent Damphousse**
(1998–present)
Assists (game): 4
(Oct. 4, 1999)
• **Wade Flaherty (1991–97)**
Saves (period): 24
(Mar. 5, 1996)
• **Jeff Friesen (1994–2001)**
Assists (career): 201
Game-Winning Goals

(season): 7
(1997–98, 1999–2000)
Game-Winning Goals
(career): 25
Games (career): 512
Points (career): 350
Shorthanded Goals
(season): 6 (1997–98)
Shorthanded Goals
(career): 13
Shots (period): 6 (twice)
• **Rob Gaudreau (1992–95)**
Consecutive Games with
a Point: 12 (Dec. 3, 1992–
Dec. 29, 1992)
• **Jeff Hackett (1991–93)**
Saves (game): 57
(Dec. 26, 1992)
• **Bill Houlder (1997–99)**
Plus/Minus (career): +21
• **Arturs Irbe (1991–96)**
Consecutive Wins: 7
(Feb. 24, 1994–April 5, 1994)
Games (career): 183
Goals Allowed (career): 595
Wins (career): 57
• **Kelly Kisio (1991–93)**
Assists (season): 52 (1992–93)
• **Victor Kozlov (1994–97)**
Shots (game): 10
(Oct. 1, 1997)
• **Marty McSorley (1996–98)**
Penalty Minutes (game): 39
(Mar. 24, 1997)
• **Evgeni Nabokov**
(1999–present)
Goals Against Avg. (season):
2.18 (2000–01)
Shutouts (season): 6

(2000–01)
Wins (season): 32 (2000–01)
• **Bernie Nicholls (1996–98)**
Consecutive Games with
an Assist: 8 (twice)
• **Owen Nolan**
(1995–present)
Consecutive Games with
a Goal: 6 (Nov. 28, 1999–
Dec. 8, 1999)
Goals (game): 4
(Dec. 19, 1995)
Goals (season): 44
(1999–2000)
Goals (career): 161
Points (period): 4
(Dec. 19, 1995)
Points (game): 6
(Oct. 4, 1999)
Points (season): 84
(1999–2000)
Power-Play Goals (period): 3
(Dec. 19, 1995)
Power-Play Goals (season):
18 (1999–2000)
Power-Play Goals (career): 59
Shots (career): 1,259
• **Jeff Odgers (1991–96)**
Penalties (period): 6
(Jan. 26, 1993)
Penalty Minutes
(career): 1,001
• **Mike Ricci (1997–present)**
Consecutive Games: 223
(Nov. 22, 1997–April 9, 2000)
• **Steve Shields (1998–2000)**
Saves Pct. (season): .921
(1998–99)
Saves Pct. (career): .915

"This building is very special when it gets revved up."
— Sharks forward Tony Granato,
on the Compaq Center

Shutouts (career): 10
Shutout Streak: 141:46
(Oct. 10, 1999–Oct. 14, 1999)

LEAGUE HONORS
Calder Trophy
• Evgeni Nabokov
(2000–01)

Bill Masterton Trophy
• Tony Granato
(1996–97)

Slap Shot
• *The Sharks have featured some of the NHL's most durable veterans. Between 1996 and '99, four Sharks, Bernie Nicholls, Murray Craven, Bob Rouse and Vincent Damphousse, played their 1,000th game.*
• *Tony Granato was a deserving winner of the NHL 1997 award for perseverance. He'd undergone brain surgery in '96.*

Timeline

1990	1991	1993	1994	1995	1996	1997	1998	1999	2000
NHL grants Gordon and George Gund a franchise for the Bay Area	Sharks play first season at Cow Palace in San Francisco	Sharks move to the new San Jose Arena	Sharks record 58-point improvement, earn first playoff berth	Sharks rookie Jeff Friesen named to NHL All-Rookie team	Tony Granato makes successful return from brain surgery	Owen Nolan scores hat trick at first All-Star game held in San Jose	Goalie Mike Vernon posts 2.46 GAA; named team MVP	Shark forward Bernie Nicholls retires	Nolan sets team record with 84 points

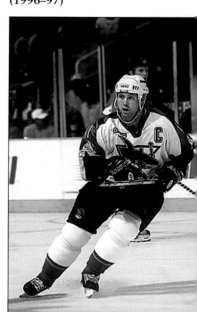

Owen Nolan is a potent combination of size, speed and strength.

COMPAQ CENTER AT SAN JOSE: ON THE CUTTING EDGE

BEING SITUATED IN SAN JOSE, the capital of Silicon Valley, it's no surprise that the Compaq Center represents the best in innovative technology. Plush seating, a state-of-the-art Sony Jumbotron scoreboard and the full range of modern fan and player amenities put this venue up with the most modern in the game. Outside, the stainless steel facade supports a stunning pyramid entryway. The rink has played an important role in the revitalization of downtown San Jose, drawing many fans to the area for Sharks games and other events.

CONCESSIONS

Although one could stick to the standard fare at the Compaq Center, there are lots of other interesting choices, such as specialty sausages, pasta, carved meat sandwiches and a barbecue stand. Vegetarians can have veggie burritos or submarines to satisfy their hunger.

GAME DAY TIPS
• **Gate hours:** Gates open 90 minutes prior to opening faceoff.
• **Prohibited items:** Bottles, cans, alcoholic beverages, video cameras and audio recording devices are prohibited. Smoking is not allowed anywhere in the building, but patrons are allowed to exit the arena through the north and south entrances in order to light up.
• **Ticket tips:** The popular Sharks sell out regularly, but a small number of tickets are put aside to be sold beginning at noon of every

evening home-game day. Rivals include any fellow California team, as well as the Dallas Stars and the St. Louis Blues. There are good

sight lines, but it is quite loud, thanks to the acoustics and the extremely vocal fans.
• **Lost and found:** (408) 999-5847.

Arena Facts

Opened: Sept. 7, 1993
Cost: $162.5 million
Capacity: 17,496
Home Sweet Home:
• *San Jose is one of the best-supported teams in the NHL, with near capacity or capacity crowds at virtually every game. The fans are loud and knowledgeable, having supported professional ice hockey in the area since the 1950s.*

Seating Plan

■ VIP Club Glass $102	■ Upper Rim (1st Row) $56
■ Sideline Club $89	■ Upper Reserved $34
■ End/Corner Club $79	☐ Upper Reserved $27
☐ Premium Glass $70	■ Upper Reserved $18
■ Premium Lower $61	**ATM** **Entrances**
■ Lower Reserved $54	♿ **Sections 102, 110, 112,**
■ Upper Reserved $39	**128, 213, 217**

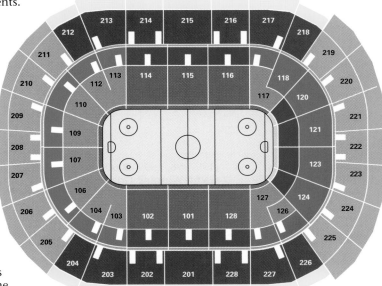

NORTH ENTRANCE

SOUTH ENTRANCE

Directions: Exit Guadalupe Pkwy. (Rte. 87) north at Santa Clara St. From I-280 south, exit at and turn left onto Bird Ave. **By Train:** The center is across the street from the Caltrain San Jose Diridon/Cahill St. Station. **By Bus:** The No.180 goes to downtown San Jose, where a free shuttle will take you to the center. Call (408) 321-2300 for information. **Parking:** The center lot can hold 1,600 cars; 35 spots are reserved for the disabled near the north entrance. Other parking can be found on Market, San Fernando, W. Santa Clara, 2nd and 3rd Sts. and S. Olmaden Blvd.

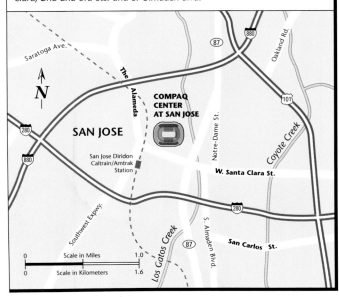

Nearby Hotels

▼▼▼ **Crowne Plaza San Jose** *(Hotel)*, 282 Almaden Blvd. (San Jose), (408) 998-0400, $79-$369

▼▼▼▼ **Fairmont Hotel** *(Hotel)*, 170 S. Market St. at Fairmont Plaza (San Jose), (408) 998-1900, $98-$406

▼▼▼▼ **Hotel de Anza** *(Hotel)*, 233 W. Santa Clara St. (San Jose), (408) 286-1000, $115-$344

▼▼▼ **Hyatt Sainte Claire-Downtown San Jose** *(Historic Hotel)*, 302 S. Market St. (San Jose), (408) 885-1234, $240-$315

▼▼▼ **San Jose Hilton & Towers** *(Hotel)*, 300 Almaden Blvd. (San Jose), (408) 287-2100, $129-$329

Nearby Restaurants

▼▼▼ **Emile's Restaurant** *(French)*, 545 S. 2nd St. (San Jose), (408) 289-1960, $25-$33 (dinner only)

▼▼ **Eulipia Restaurant & Bar** *(American)*, 374 S. 1st St. (San Jose), (408) 280-6161, $15-$30

▼▼▼ **Garden City Restaurant** *(American)*, 360 S. Saratoga Ave. (San Jose), (408) 244-4443, $9-$24

▼▼ **Lou's Village** *(Seafood)*, 1465 W. San Carlos St. (San Jose), (408) 293-4570, $15-$39

▼▼▼ **Madrone's** *(California)*, 2050 Gateway Pl. in the Doubletree Hotel (San Jose), (408) 453-4000, $15-$26

TAMPA BAY LIGHTNING

THE ARRIVAL OF THE NHL franchise in Tampa Bay really was like Lightning striking. The campaign for the franchise was launched by Hall-of-Famer Phil Esposito in March 1990 and by December the NHL had conditionally approved the bid. During training camp of that first season, Esposito shocked hockey people the world round by signing female goaltender Manon Rheaume to a tryout form. The following month she became the only female to play in one of the four major pro sports, stopping seven shots in 20 minutes in a preseason match against the Blues. When the Lightning took the ice for its first season, the team featured a cast of NHL castaways, including Brian Bradley who led the team with 86 points and defenseman Doug Crossman who provided a thrill in November when he recorded six points in a single game. The Lightning improved steadily over the next three seasons and by 1995–96 was challenging for a playoff spot. The emergence of team stars, including versatile defenseman Roman Hamrlik and goalie Daren Puppa, helped the team edge defending Stanley Cup champion New Jersey for the final East playoff spot. The Lightning lost, but the playoff appearance and the budding rivalry with the nearby Florida Panthers helped raise interest in the team. Unfortunately, that was the franchise's high point. There have been no playoff berths since, and injuries and continuing financial woes have left the team in a continual state of uncertainty. There are reasons for hope, however. Young Vincent Lecavalier has megastar potential and the signing of talented goalie Nikolai Khabibulin provides solidity in nets. Fans hope the two of them can brighten the Lightning's future.

Vincent Lecavalier has emerged as a top NHLer.

POSTSEASON
• Playoff Appearances........1
(1995–96)

TEAM RECORDS
• **Mikael Andersson (1992–99)**
Seasons: 7 (tie)
• **Brian Bradley (1992–98)**
Assists (season): 56 (1995–96)
Assists (career): 189
Consecutive Games with a Goal: 8 (Nov. 11, 1992–Nov. 24, 1992)
Consecutive Games with a Point: 13 (Nov. 1, 1992–Nov. 24, 1992)
Game-Winning Goals (season): 6 (tie) (1992–93)

Slap Shot

• *Fans in Tampa Bay have a lot of expectations for the 2001–02 season — new General Manager Rick Dudley has guaranteed a playoff spot for the franchise, which has been without one since 1995–96.*
• *Phil Esposito was fired as Lightning GM in 1998, but he's still a presence with the team, doing commentary for the team's TV broadcasts.*

Game-Winning Goals (career): 16
Goals (season): 42 (1992–93)
Goals (career): 111
Points (season): 86 (1992–93)
Points (career): 300
Power-Play Goals (season): 16 (1992–93)
Power-Play Goals (career): 37
Power-Play Points (career): 119
• **Marc Bureau (1992–95)**
Assists (game): 4 (tie) (Feb. 1, 1993)
• **Enrico Ciccone (1993–99)**
Penalty Minutes (season): 258 (1995–96)
• **Wendell Clark (1998–99)**
Hat Tricks (season): 3 (1998–99)
Hat Tricks (career): 3
• **Cory Cross (1993–99)**
Plus/Minus (game): +5
• **Doug Crossman (1992–93)**
Points (game): 6 (Nov. 7, 1992)
• **Chris Gratton (1993–2000)**
Penalty Minutes (career): 782
• **Roman Hamrlik (1992–98)**
Power-Play Points (season): 42 (1995–96)
Shots (season): 281 (1995–96)
• **Bill Houlder (1995–97, 1999–2000)**

"Goaltending is solid, the defense has enviable depth . . . that's the good news."
— Ira Kaufman, sportswriter, on the 2001 Lightning

Plus/Minus (season): +16
Plus/Minus (career): +14
• **Chris Kontos (1992–93)**
Goals (game): 4 (Oct. 7, 1992)
• **Daren Puppa (1993–2000)**
Goals Against Avg. (season): 2.46 (1995–96)
Goals Against Avg. (career): 2.68
Losses (season): 33 (tie) (1995–96)
Minutes (season): 3,653 (1995–96)
Shutouts (season): 5 (1995–96)
Shutouts (career): 12
Ties (season): 9 (1995–96)
Ties (career): 26
Wins (season): 29 (1995–96)
Wins (career): 77
• **Joe Reekie (1992–94)**
Assists (game): 4 (tie) (Oct. 7, 1992)
• **Mikael Renberg (1997–99)**
Goals (period): 3 (Mar. 21, 1998)
• **Darcy Tucker (1997–2000)**
Penalty Minutes (game): 49 (Dec. 27, 1999)
• **John Tucker (1992–96)**
Shots (game): 14 (Dec. 16, 1992)

Vital Stats

Stadium Address:
401 Channelside Dr., Tampa, Fla.
Phone: (813) 301-6500
Web:
tampabaylightning.com, icepalace.com
Box Office:
(813) 301-2500, Mon.–Fri. 9–6 or half an hour past end of event, Sat. 10–2 or half an hour past end of event
Media Coverage:
Radio: WDAE (620 AM)
TV: WTOG (Channel 44), Sunshine Network
Practice Facility:
Ice Sports Forum, Tampa, Fla.

• **Rob Zamuner (1992–99)**
Assists (period): 3 (Oct. 7, 1992)
Consecutive Games: 226
Games (career): 475
Points (rookie season): 43 (1992–93)
Seasons: 7 (tie)
Shorthanded Goals (season): 4 (1996–97)
Shorthanded Goals (career): 14

LEAGUE HONORS
Bill Masterton Trophy
• **John Cullen** (1998–99)

Timeline

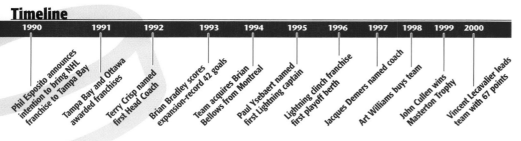

| 1990 | 1991 | 1992 | 1993 | 1994 | 1995 | 1996 | 1997 | 1998 | 1999 | 2000 |

Phil Esposito announces intention to bring NHL franchise to Tampa Bay

Tampa Bay and Ottawa awarded franchises

Terry Crisp named first Head Coach

Brian Bradley scores expansion-record 42 goals

Team acquires Brian Bellows from Montreal

Paul Ysebaert named first Lightning captain

Lightning clinch franchise first playoff berth

Jacques Demers named coach

Art Williams buys team

John Cullen wins Masterton Trophy

Vincent Lecavalier leads team with 67 points

ICE PALACE:
ONE HOT VENUE

DESIGNED SPECIFICALLY FOR HOCKEY, the Ice Palace is one of the best things about the pretty pitiful Lightning teams that have called it home since 1996. Along with 71 luxury suites, the venue features 3,000 Palace Club level seats, which come with many special services, including a reserved parking spot. There are no bad seats in the arena — all the sight lines are excellent and the amenities are both plentiful and well-placed. The Ice Palace is home to a large slate of other events and played host to the 1999 NHL All-Star game.

CONCESSIONS

Concession stands offer fans all the traditional arena favorites, including steak sandwiches and chicken wings. But for a change, you might want to try the "bloomin' onion" — a fried onion stuffed with spices, chili and garlic.

Arena Facts

Opened: Oct. 20, 1996
Cost: $160 million
Capacity: 19,758
Home Sweet Home:
• *Despite the team's poor showing, the Lightning has developed a loyal following. The volume in the arena can reach deafening levels as fans try their best to become like an extra player while they cheer for their perennial underdog team.*

GAME DAY TIPS

• **Gate hours:** Gates open 90 minutes prior to opening faceoff.
• **Prohibited items:** Food, beverages, alcohol and containers of any kind are prohibited. Non-professional, non-flash cameras are allowed, but video cameras are not. Tasteful banners and signs are allowed. Noisemaking devices and projectiles are forbidden. Smoking is permitted only in designated areas.
• **Ticket tips:** The Lightning only sold out six games last season, so tickets are generally available. Games are always

Seating Plan

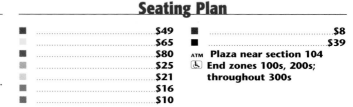

lively and near-capacity when the Panthers are in town, but Detroit, Toronto and Philadelphia also draw a crowd. While the upper level seats in the Palace are very high, the steep rise keeps the view decent.
• **Lost and found:** (813) 301-6502.

Directions: *From I-4 west, exit 1 south on 21st St. to Palm Ave., west to Nick Nuccio Pkwy., south on Channelside Dr. From I-275 north, exit 15 east on Gandy Blvd., east on Lee Roy Selmon to exit 4, east on W. Platt St./Channelside Dr.. From I-275 south, exit 26 south on Morgan St. By Bus: Several lines go to the arena. Call Hillsborough Area Regional Transit (HART) at (813) 254-4278.* **Parking:** *A 1,011-space garage is on site, with 40 spots reserved for the disabled. Another 10,000 spots are within walking distance on Ball, Morgan, Tampa and Whiting Sts., Channelside Dr., and JFK Blvd.*

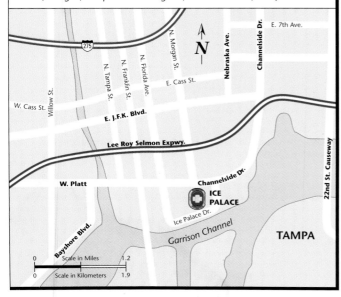

Nearby Hotels

▼▼▼ **Courtyard by Marriott-Downtown Tampa** *(Hotel)*, 102 E. Cass St. (Tampa), (813) 229-1100, $89-$149
▼▼▼ **Hilton Garden Inn/Tampa Ybor Historic District** *(Hotel)*, 1700 E. 9th Ave. (Tampa), (813) 769-9267, $99-$159
▼▼▼ **Holiday Inn City Centre** *(Hotel)*, 111 W. Fortune St. (Tampa), (813) 223-1351, $99-$153
▼▼▼ **Radisson Bay Harbor Hotel** *(Hotel)*, 7700 Courtney Campbell Cswy. (Tampa), (813) 281-8900, $112-$143
▼▼▼ **The Wyndham Harbour Island Hotel** *(Hotel)*, 725 S. Harbour Island Blvd. (Tampa), (813) 229-5000, $99-$139

Nearby Restaurants

▼▼ **The Cactus Club Southwestern Grill & Bar** *(Southwestern)*, 1601 Snow Ave. in Old Hyde Park (Tampa), (813) 251-4089, $7-$16
▼▼ **Cafe Creole** *(Cajun)*, 1330 9th Ave. (Tampa), (813) 247-6283, $12-$17
▼▼ **The Colonnade** *(Seafood)*, 3401 Bayshore Blvd. (Tampa), (813) 839-7558, $6-$21
▼▼ **Columbia Restaurant** *(Spanish)*, 2117 E. 7th Ave. (Tampa), (813) 248-4961, $14-$22
▼▼ **Mise En Place** *(American)*, 442 W. Kennedy Blvd. in Grand Central Place (Tampa), (813) 254-5373, $13-$23

TORONTO MAPLE LEAFS

IT'S BEEN MORE THAN 30 YEARS since the Maple Leafs have sipped from the Stanley Cup. The frustration and hopeful dedication of Toronto fans is legendary. But the franchise has not always treated its faithful this way. Between the team's debut in 1917 and its last Cup victory in 1967, the Leafs captured 13 titles and twice enjoyed minor dynasty status. In the 1940s the team won five Cups. The first, in 1942, featured a dramatic comeback from a 3-0 series deficit to Detroit. The Leafs took three straight titles starting in the spring of 1947. Before the following season, Leafs owner Conn Smythe traded several players to Chicago in order to obtain offensive star Max Bentley. Bentley did not disappoint, helping the Leafs retain the Cup for two more years. The team's 1950–51 championship is best remembered for Bill Barilko's overtime Cup-winning goal and his sudden death in a plane crash a few weeks later. The late 1950s brought a new crop of talent to Toronto, including long-time minor league goalie Johnny Bower, graceful center Dave Keon and scoring star Frank Mahovlich. Beginning in 1961–62, the team romped to three straight Cups once again. Perhaps the most dramatic moment came in the 1964 final, when Bobby Baun, playing on a cracked ankle, netted the winner in overtime. With the NHL's oldest roster, the Leafs won again in 1967. Since then, a host of stars from Darryl Sittler and Lanny MacDonald to Doug Gilmour and Wendell Clark have failed to recapture that glory. Today Leafs fans look to an aging team led by Curtis Joseph and Mats Sundin to bring the loyal fans what they want most: another Stanley Cup.

"The bricks and mortar you can get anywhere. It's the people I'll remember."
— *Dave "Tiger" Williams, on the closing of Maple Leaf Gardens*

Vital Stats

Stadium Address:
40 Bay St.,
Toronto, Ont.
Phone: (416) 815-5500
Web:
torontomapleleafs.com,
theaircanadacentre.com
Box Office:
(416) 872-5000,
Mon.–Thurs. 9:30–6, Fri.
9:30–8, Sat.–Sun. 9:30–5,
game day until one hour
after game starts
Media Coverage:
Radio: MOJO (640 AM)
TV: CFTO (Channel 9), TSN
Practice Facility:
Lakeshore Lions Arena,
Etobicoke, Ont.

POSTSEASON
• Stanley Cups 13
(1917–18, 1921–22, 1931–32, 1941–42, 1944–45, 1946–47, 1947–48, 1948–49, 1950–51, 1961–62, 1962–63, 1963–64, 1966–67)

RETIRED NUMBERS
• Bill Barilko (5)
• Irvine "Ace" Bailey (6)

HONORED NUMBERS
• Johnny Bower (1)
• Walter "Turk" Broda (1)
• Francis "King" Clancy (7)
• Tim Horton (7)
• Charlie Conacher (9)
• Ted Kennedy (9)
• Syl Apps (10)
• George Armstrong (10)

Slap Shot
• The Leafs franchise boasts an incredible 44 members of the Hockey Hall of Fame.
• Former Leaf Babe Pratt is the hockey equivalent to Shoeless Joe Jackson. A Hart Trophy winner in 1944, Pratt was expelled from hockey in 1945 for wagering on games. Though reinstated a year later, he ended his career in the minors.

TEAM RECORDS
• George Armstrong (1949–50, 1951–71)
Games (career): 1,187
• Walter "Turk" Broda (1936–43, 1945–52)
Shutouts (career): 62
Wins (career): 302
• Doug Gilmour (1991–97)
Assists (game): 6 (tie) (Feb. 13, 1993)
Assists (season): 95 (1992–93)
Points (season): 127 (1992–93)
• Curtis Joseph (1998–present)
Wins (season): 36 (1999–2000)
• Dave Keon (1960–75)
Shorthanded Goals (season): 8 (1970–71)
• Babe Pratt (1942–46)
Assists (game): 6 (tie) (Jan. 8, 1944)
• Dave Reid (1988–91)
Shorthanded Goals (season): 8 (tie) (1990–91)
• Borje Salming (1973–89)
Assists (career): 620
• Darryl Sittler (1970–82)
Goals (game): 6 (Feb. 7, 1976)
Goals (career): 389
• Rick Vaive (1979–87)
Goals (season): 54 (1981–82)
• Dave Williams

(1974–80)
Penalty Minutes (career): 1,670

LEAGUE HONORS
Hart Trophy
• Babe Pratt (1943–44)
• Ted Kennedy (1954–55)

Vezina Trophy
• Turk Broda (1940–41, 1947–48)
• Al Rollins (1950–51)
• Harry Lumley (1953–54)
• Johnny Bower (1960–61, 1964–65)
• Terry Sawchuk (1964–65)

Calder Trophy
• Syl Apps (1936–37)
• Gaye Stewart (1942–43)

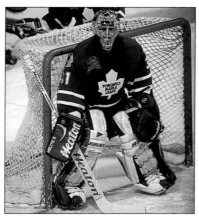
Curtis Joseph gives the Leafs some of the best goaltending in the NHL.

• Gus Bodnar (1943–44)
• Frank McCool (1944–45)
• Howie Meeker (1946–47)
• Frank Mahovlich (1957–58)
• Dave Keon (1960–61)
• Kent Douglas (1962–63)
• Brit Selby (1965–66)

Lady Byng Trophy
• Joe Primeau (1931–32)
• Gordie Drillon (1937–38)
• Syl Apps (1941–42)
• Sid Smith (1951–52, 1954–55)
• Red Kelly (1960–61)
• Dave Keon (1961–62, 1962–63)

Frank J. Selke Trophy
• Doug Gilmour (1992–93)

Conn Smythe Trophy
• Dave Keon (1967)

Timeline

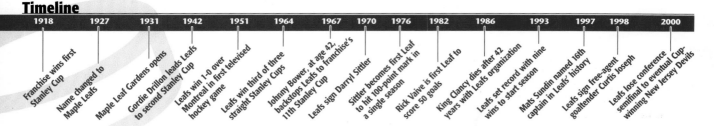

| 1918 | 1927 | 1931 | 1942 | 1951 | 1964 | 1967 | 1970 | 1976 | 1982 | 1986 | 1993 | 1997 | 1998 | 2000 |

- 1918: Franchise wins first Stanley Cup
- 1927: Name changed to Maple Leafs
- 1931: Maple Leaf Gardens opens
- 1931: Gordie Drillon leads Leafs to second Stanley Cup
- 1942: Leafs win 1-0 over Montreal in first televised hockey game
- 1951: Leafs win third of three straight Stanley Cups
- 1964: Johnny Bower, at age 42, backstops Leafs to franchise's 11th Stanley Cup
- 1967: Leafs sign Darryl Sittler
- 1970: Sittler becomes first Leaf to hit 100-point mark in a single season
- 1976: Rick Vaive is first Leaf to score 50 goals
- 1982: King Clancy dies after 42 years with Leafs organization
- 1986: Leafs set record with nine wins to start season
- 1993: Mats Sundin named 16th captain in Leafs' history
- 1997: Leafs sign free-agent goaltender Curtis Joseph
- 1998: Leafs lose conference semifinal to eventual Cup-winning New Jersey Devils

AIR CANADA CENTRE: DOWNTOWN GEM

OPENED IN 1999, the Air Canada Centre is widely acknowledged as one of the NHL's premier new venues. Set spectacularly in the heart of downtown Toronto, it features wide upholstered seats and excellent concessions, good news for the regular sellout crowds that take in the Leafs there. The top-flight sound system and television monitors make sure that you don't miss any action. The Air Canada Centre is also one of the few facilities in the NHL to be wholly owned by the team. The entire venture was privately funded.

CONCESSIONS
The Air Canada Centre offers food ranging from traditional hot dogs and hamburgers to sushi, chicken wings, pizza, submarines and deli. Vegetarians can choose from a variety of wraps, sandwiches and salads. There is also a pasta bar and an in-house brewery.

Arena Facts

Opened: *Feb. 20, 1999*
Cost: *$265 million*
Capacity: *18,819*
Home Sweet Home:
• *Leaf fans are without a doubt the most dedicated and supportive in all of hockey. Although the team has not won a Stanley Cup since 1967, the Leafs have sold out every home game they've played since the early 1940s.*

GAME DAY TIPS
• **Gate hours:** Gates open one hour prior to opening faceoff.
• **Prohibited items:** Bottles, cans, coolers, sticks, weapons, fireworks, skateboards, in-line skates, video cameras, audio recorders, helium balloons, and outside food and beverages are prohibited. Smoking is prohibited inside the arena, but patrons are allowed to exit at gates 4 and 5a in order to light up.
• **Ticket tips:** The Maple Leafs are a popular team. There are a large number of season ticket holders and games always sell out.

Seating Plan

▫ **Platinium Lounge**	$175	■	$70
■ **Platinium Lounge**	$165	■	$35
▫	$155	**ATM** Sections 105/106, 116/117, 323/324	
▫	$148		
■ **Air Canada Club Level**	Call for info	♿ Sections 105, 106, 309, 316, 317, 319	
■ **Club Level**	Call for info		

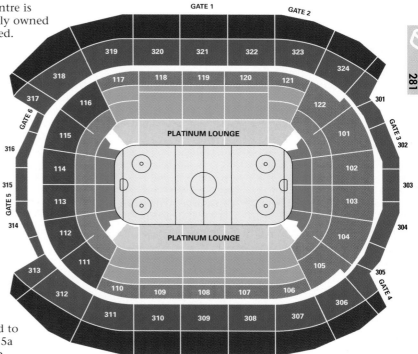

Tickets for Saturday night games go especially fast. Fortunately, the Air Canada Centre offers great views from all sections, even the "nosebleed" seats higher up.
• **Lost and found:** (416) 815-5982.

Directions: *Take Gardiner Expwy. to York St. exit, then continue one block north to arena. By Subway: Yonge-University-Spadina Line to Union Station. Call the Toronto Transit Commission at (416) 369-INFO for information. By Train: The GO Train to Union Station. Call (416) 869-3200 for schedules.* **Parking:** *Underground parking at the center is not public, but there are over 13,000 spaces available within walking distance on King St. W., York St., Lakeshore Blvd., and Queen's Quay St. Patrons with disabilities can call (416) 815-5743 to reserve a spot in the underground lot. A drop-off point is located on the west side of the arena.*

Nearby Hotels
▼▼▼▼ **Crowne Plaza Toronto Centre** *(Hotel)*, 225 Front St. W. (Toronto), (416) 597-1400, $189-$239
▼▼▼▼ **The Fairmont Royal York** *(Classic Hotel)*, 100 Front St. W. (Toronto), (416) 368-2511, $149-$249
▼▼▼ **Novotel Toronto Centre** *(Hotel)*, 45 The Esplanade (Toronto), (416) 367-8900, $225-$250
▼▼ **The Strathcona Hotel** *(Hotel)*, 60 York St. (Toronto), (416) 363-3321, $99-$149
▼▼▼▼ **The Westin Harbour Castle** *(Hotel)*, One Harbour Square (Toronto), (416) 869-1600, $149-$239

Nearby Restaurants
▼▼ **Hothouse Cafe Inc** *(American)*, 35 Church St. (Toronto), (416) 366-7800, $11-$13
▼▼ **Joe Badali's Ristorante Italiano** *(Italian)*, 156 Front St. W. (Toronto), (416) 977-3064, $9-$17
▼▼ **Shopsy's Delicatessen Restaurant** *(American)*, 33 Yonge St. (Toronto), (416) 365-3333, $8-$10
▼▼▼ **Tom Jones Steakhouse & Seafood** *(Steak & Seafood)*, 17 Leader Ln. (Toronto), (416) 366-6583, $21-$45
▼ **Wayne Gretzky's Restaurant** *(Canadian)*, 99 Blue Jays Way (Toronto), (416) 979-7825, $7-$26

VANCOUVER CANUCKS

A MONTH AFTER VANCOUVER was awarded its NHL franchise, the team lost a coin toss for first choice in the draft. Instead of franchise player Gilbert Perreault, the expansion Canucks ended up with defenseman Dale Tallon. Tallon was gone in a trade to Chicago after just two seasons. But one of the pickups in that trade, goaltender Gary Smith, led Vancouver to its first Smythe division title in 1974–75, the same year Perreault and the Sabres marched to the finals. The Canucks' first brush with big-time success came in the 1981–82 season. Led by first-year coach Roger Neilson and a lineup that included the graceful Thomas Gradin and hard-nosed captain Stan Smyl, Vancouver defeated Los Angeles and Chicago on the way to a Stanley Cup finals showdown with the Islanders. Losing the first two games in heartbreaking 6-5 decisions, the team was swept in four games. It would not be the Canucks' last close call. After picking up scoring sensation Pavel Bure in 1991, the Canucks suddenly found themselves with all the makings of a dominant team. Finishing second in the team's division during the regular season with solid scoring from Bure, Geoff Courtnall, and Cliff Ronning and unquestioned leadership from captain Trevor Linden, the Canucks toughed out an incredible first-round series with Calgary. The team trailed three games to one, won the final three games in overtime and rolled over Dallas and Toronto before falling in a dramatic seven-game tilt with the Rangers. Much has changed since that run. In fact, none of those players remain with the team. But the Canucks' youthful lineup has recently shown signs of mounting another charge to the Cup.

Vital Stats

Stadium Address:
800 Griffiths Way, Vancouver, B.C.
Phone: (604) 899-7889
Web: www.canucks.com, gmplace.com
Box Office: (604) 899-7676, Mon.–Sat. 9:30–6
Media Coverage:
Radio: CKNW (980 AM)
TV: VTV (Channel 9),
CTV SportsNet
Training Facility:
Larry Ashley Training Facility, GM Place, Vancouver, B.C.

"I had goose bumps."

— Canucks GM Brian Burke, on the two-minute ovation given to the team in GM Place during the final two minutes of a playoff loss

POSTSEASON
• **Western Conference Championships** 1
(1993–94)
• **Campbell Conference Championships** 1
(1981–82)
• **Smythe Division Titles** 3
(1974–75, 1991–92, 1992–93)

Slap Shot

• Based on the team's first 14 games at home, Canucks fans might have thought they'd inherited an established team, not an expansion one. Vancouver went 10-3-1 over that period, including a six-game winning streak.
• In 1979–80, gritty forward Stan Smyl led the Canucks in goals (31), assists (47), points (78) and penalty minutes (204). This still marks the last time any player has led his team in all four categories.

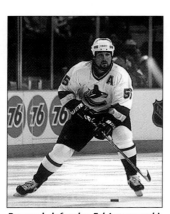

Rugged defender Ed Jovanovski.

• **Playoff Appearances**......17
(1974–75, 1975–76, 1978–79, 1979–80, 1980–81, 1981–82, 1982–83, 1983–84, 1985–86, 1988–89, 1990–91, 1991–92, 1992–93, 1993–94, 1994–95, 1995–96, 2000-01)

RETIRED NUMBERS
• **Stan Smyl (12)**

TEAM RECORDS
• **Rick Blight (1975–81)**
Power Play Goals (game): 3 (Oct. 6, 1976)
• **Andre Boudrias (1970–76)**

Assists (season): 62 (1974–75)
• **Donald Brashear (1996–present)**
Penalty Minutes (season): 372 (1997–98)
• **Pavel Bure (1991–98)**
Assists (period): 3 (Dec. 18, 1992)
Goals (period): 3 (tie) (Oct. 12, 1992)
Goals (game): 4 (tie) (Oct. 12, 1992)
Goals (season): 60 (1992–93, 1993–94)
Longest Goal-Scoring Streak: 8 games (1993–94)
Points (season): 110 (1992–93)
Points by a Rookie: 60 (tie) (1991–92)
Power Play Goals (season): 25 (1993–94)
Shorthanded Goals (game): 2 (tie) (Oct. 12, 1992)
Shorthanded Goals (career): 24
• **Trevor Linden (1988–98)**
Consecutive Games (career): 482
• **Kirk McLean (1987–98)**
Shutouts (career): 19
Wins (season): 38 (1991–92)
Wins (career): 205
• **Gino Odjick (1990–98)**
Penalty Minutes (game): 47 (Nov. 12, 1992)
Penalty Minutes (career): 2,127
• **Felix Potvin (1999–2001)**
Goals-Against Avg.

(career): 2.59
• **Cliff Ronning (1990–96)**
Points (period): 5 (April 15, 1993)
• **Patrick Sundstrom (1982–87)**
Assists (game): 6 (Feb. 29, 1984)
Points (game): 7 (Feb. 29, 1984)
• **Stan Smyl (1978–91)**
Assists (career): 411
Games (career): 896
Goals (career): 262
Seasons: 13
Shorthanded Goals (game): 2 (tie) (Jan. 25, 1985)
Points (career): 673
• **Tony Tanti (1982–90)**
Game-Winning Goals (career): 29
Goals (period): 3 (Jan. 7, 1989)
Goals (game): 4 (tie) (Jan. 13, 1988)
Hat Tricks (career): 10
Power-Play Goals (career): 102

LEAGUE HONORS
Calder Trophy
• **Pavel Bure (1991–92)**

King Clancy Award
• **Trevor Linden (1996–97)**

Jack Adams Award
• **Pat Quinn (1991–92)**

Timeline

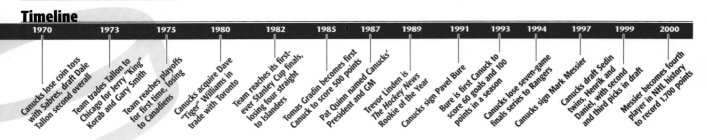

| 1970 | 1973 | 1975 | 1980 | 1982 | 1985 | 1987 | 1989 | 1991 | 1993 | 1994 | 1997 | 1999 | 2000 |

Canucks lose coin toss with Sabres, draft Dale Tallon second overall

Team trades Tallon to Chicago for Jerry "King" Korab and Gary Smith

Team reaches playoffs for first time, losing to Canadiens

Canucks acquire Dave "Tiger" Williams in trade with Toronto

Team reaches its first-ever Stanley Cup finals, losing four straight to Islanders

Tomas Gradin becomes first Canuck to score 500 points

Pat Quinn named Canucks' President and GM

Trevor Linden is The Hockey News Rookie of the Year

Canucks sign Pavel Bure

Bure is first Canuck to score 60 goals and 100 points in a season

Canucks lose seven-game finals series to Rangers

Canucks sign Mark Messier

Canucks draft Sedin twins, Henrik and Daniel, with second and third picks in draft

Messier becomes fourth player in NHL history to record 1,700 points

GENERAL MOTORS PLACE: WEST COAST GEM

LOCATED IN THE PICTURESQUE False Creek district of downtown Vancouver, GM Place has a definite West Coast ambience. From the quaint landscaped park around the arena to the incredible views of the mountains and ocean, the GM enjoys one of the most beautiful settings in pro sports. GM Place is also one of the busiest venues, hosting more than 200 events a year. It offers the latest in technology, from an eight-sided video scoreboard to a Bose sound system that provides acoustics among the best in North America.

CONCESSIONS

GM Place offers hungry patrons the usual concessions fare, including hamburgers, hot dogs, french fries, pizza and soft drinks. Thirsty fans can choose from specialty coffees and a selection of imported and local beers.

Arena Facts

Opened: *Sept. 21, 1995*
Cost: *$160 million*
Capacity: *18,422*
Home Sweet Home:
• *During a 1982 playoff game, coach Roger Neilson waved a white towel at the referees in mock surrender. Canucks fans followed suit and the team made it to the finals. Today, for important games, superstitious fans still wave towels.*

GAME DAY TIPS

• **Gate hours:** Gates open one hour prior to opening faceoff.
• **Prohibited items:** Signs, noisemakers, frisbees, beachballs, sticks, projectiles, cans, bottles and coolers are all prohibited. Fans may not bring in food or alcohol not purchased in the arena. Recording equipment of any sort is forbidden. Smoking is allowed only in designated areas.
• **Ticket tips:** With the Canucks' improved play, tickets have been harder to come by. There were 19 sellouts in the 1999–2000 season. The better teams in the conference, such as Detroit and Colorado, and historic favorites such as the Leafs and Canadiens usually draw the largest crowds, as do weekend games. Sight lines are excellent at GM Place and the seamless glass gives fans an unobstructed view of the action.
• **Lost and found:** (604) 899-7803.

Seating Plan

■ **Club Seats** $114.95
■ **Lower Bowl I** $92.99
■ **Lower Bowl II** $74
■ **Upper Bowl I** $65
■ **Brew House Grill** $65
□ **Upper Bowl II** $56.50
■ **Upper Bowl III** $47.75
□ **Wheelchair** $47.75
■ **Upper Bowl IV** $38
■ **Molson Canadian Zone** ... $31
■ **Upper Bowl V** $27.75
ATM **Sections 101, 114, 306, 318**
♿ **Sections 122, 312, 313, 318, 319**

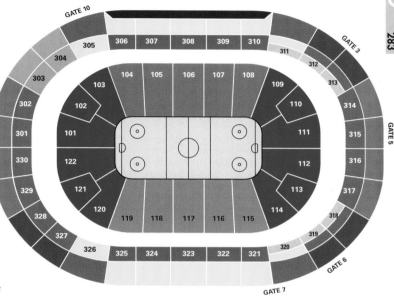

Directions: *From Hwy. 1 west, exit 1st Ave. and follow to Quebec St. Turn right, then left onto Expo Blvd. From Hwy. 99 north, exit Oak St. and follow to 49th Ave. Turn right, then right onto Cambie St. Follow to first exit onto Pacific Blvd. By Public Transportation: The SkyTrain and several buses go to GM Place. Call (604) 953-3333 for information.* **Parking:** *About 14,000 spaces are available under GM Place and nearby on Pender, Beatty, Smithe, Robson, Georgia, Nelson and Cambie Sts. Most lots have parking for the disabled. To reserve disabled parking underground, call (604) 899-7445.*

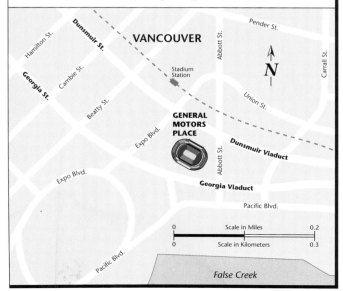

Nearby Hotels

▼▼▼ **Best Western Downtown Vancouver** (*Motor Inn*), 718 Drake St. (Vancouver), (604) 669-9888, $89-$229
▼▼▼▼ **Four Seasons Hotel Vancouver** (*Hotel*), 791 W. Georgia St. (Vancouver), (604) 689-9333, $290-$485
▼▼▼ **The Georgian Court Hotel** (*Hotel*), 773 Beatty St. (Vancouver), (604) 682-5555, $115-$260
▼▼▼ **Holiday Inn Hotel & Suites Vancouver Downtown** (*Hotel*), 1110 Howe St. (Vancouver), (604) 684-2151, $129-$319
▼▼▼▼ **The Westin Grand** (*Hotel*), 433 Robson St. (Vancouver), (604) 602-1999, $174-$279

Nearby Restaurants

▼▼▼▼ **Chartwell** (*Continental*), 791 W. Georgia St. in the Four Seasons Hotel Vancouver (Vancouver), (604) 689-9333, $19-$37
▼▼▼ **CinCin** (*Italian*), 1154 Robson St. (Vancouver), (604) 688-7338, $10-$22
▼▼▼ **Joe Fortes Seafood & Chop House** (*Seafood*), 777 Thurlow St. (Vancouver), (604) 669-1940, $12-$25
▼▼▼ **Villa De Lupo** (*Italian*), 869 Hamilton St. (Vancouver), (604) 688-7436, $18-$30 (dinner only)
▼▼▼ **The William Tell** (*Swiss*), 765 Beatty St. in The Georgian Court Hotel (Vancouver), (604) 688-3504, $18-$30

WASHINGTON CAPITALS

THE WASHINGTON CAPITALS WOULD like to forget its first eight years in the NHL. After nearly a decade of vying for the Stanley Cup, the team not only had no Cups, it also didn't even have a single winning season or a playoff appearance. Despite the heroic efforts of diminutive star Dennis Maruk, along with early stand-outs Mike Gartner and Guy Charron, the best the Caps could manage was 27 wins in 1979–80. By 1982 owner Abe Pollin had taken enough heat from the fans. He relieved General Manager Max McNab and replaced him with 33-year-old David Poile. Just a couple of weeks into the job, Poile orchestrated the deal that turned Washington's fortunes around. Poile dealt Ryan Walter and Rick Green to Montreal for defensemen Rod Langway and Brian Engblom and forwards Doug Jarvis and Craig Laughlin. Invigorated with winning spirit from the ex-Habs, the Caps recorded its first winning season and made its first playoff appearance, losing to the eventual Stanley Cup-winning New York Islanders. The Isles proved to be the Caps' nemesis come play-off time, knocking the team from the playoffs five times in the next 11 seasons. The Caps play-off learning curve was every bit as long and arduous as its regular season results. In its 14 consecutive playoff appearances, the team was a first-round casualty eight times and reached the third round just once, in 1989–90. But recent times have brought more success. With strong goaltending from Olaf Kolzig and scoring from longtime Cap sniper Peter Bondra, the team went to the finals in 1998, losing to Detroit. Tough defensively and capable on offense, the Caps may provide fans with a truly memorable moment yet.

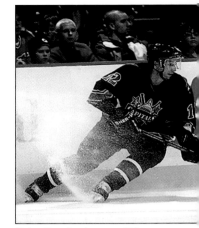

Peter Bondra is one of the NHL's elite players.

POSTSEASON
- **Eastern Conference Championships** 1 (1997–98)
- **Southeast Division Titles** 2 (1999–2000, 2000–01)
- **Patrick Division Titles** 1 (1988–89)
- **Playoff Appearances**......17 (1982–83, 1983–84, 1984–85, 1985–86, 1986–87, 1987–88, 1988–89, 1989–90, 1990–91, 1991–92, 1992–93, 1993–94, 1994–95, 1995–96, 1997–98, 1999–2000, 2000–01)

RETIRED NUMBERS
- Rod Langway (5)
- Yvon Labre (7)
- Dale Hunter (32)

Slap Shot
- *With its dreadful first sea-son, the Capitals set NHL records for fewest wins (minimum 70-game sea-son), most losses, most con-secutive losses (17) and most goals allowed (446).*
- *When Caps GM David Poile fired coach Bryan Murray midway in the 1989–90 season, he hired Murray's brother Terry.*

TEAM RECORDS
- **Peter Bondra (1990–present)** Game-Winning Goals (season): 13 (1997–98) Game-Winning Goals (career): 57 Goals (period): 4 (Feb. 5, 1994) Goals (game): 5 (Feb. 5, 1994) Hat Tricks (career): 14 Power-Play goals (season): 22 (2000–01) Power-Play Goals (career): 99 Shorthanded Goals (season): 6 (tie) (1994–95) Shorthanded Goals (career): 29
- **Jim Carey (1995–97)** Goals Against Avg. (season): 2.13 (1994–95) Goals Against Avg. (career): 2.37 Shutouts (season): 9 (1995–96)
- **Dino Ciccarelli (1988–92)** Points (game): 7 (Mar. 18, 1989)
- **Mike Gartner (1979–89)** Goals (career): 397 Points (career): 789 Shorthanded Goals (season): 6 (tie) (1986–87) Shots (season): 331 (1984–85)
- **Bengt Gustafsson (1979–89)** Goals (game): 5 (tie) (Jan. 8, 1984)
- **Alan Haworth (1982–87)**

Plus/Minus (season): +36 (1985–86)
- **Dale Hunter (1987–99)** Penalty Minutes (career): 2,003
- **Olaf Kolzig (1989, '92, 1994–present)** Save Pct. (season): .920 Shutouts (career): 21 Wins (season): 41 (1999–2000) Wins (career): 150
- **Rod Langway (1982–93)** Plus/Minus (career): +117
- **Dennis Maruk (1978–83)** Assists (season): 76 (1981–82) Goals (season): 60 (1981–82) Points (season): 136 (1981–82) Points (period): 5 (tie) (Mar. 5, 1982)
- **Alan May (1989–94)** Penalty Minutes (season): 339 (1989–90)
- **Kelly Miller (1986–99)** Games (career): 940
- **Adam Oates (1997–present)** Assists (period): 4 (tie) (Jan. 6, 1998)
- **Michal Pivonka (1986–99)** Assists (career): 418
- **Mike Ridley (1986–94)** Assists (game): 6 (Jan. 7, 1989)

"My plan is to try and win every season."
— Capitals GM George McPhee

Vital Stats
Stadium Address: 601 F St. NW, Washington, D.C.
Phone: (202) 628-3200
Web: washingtoncaps.com, mcicenter.com
Box Office: (202) 628-3200, Mon.–Sat. 10–5:30, event days
Media Coverage: Radio: WTEM (980 AM) TV: WBDC (Channel 50), Home Team Sports
Training Facility: Piney Orchard Ice Arena, Odenton, Md.

LEAGUE HONORS
Norris Trophy
- Rod Langway (1982–83, 1983–84)

Vezina Trophy
- Jim Carey (1995–96)
- Olaf Kolzig (1999–2000)

Adams Trophy
- Bryan Murray (1983–84)

Timeline
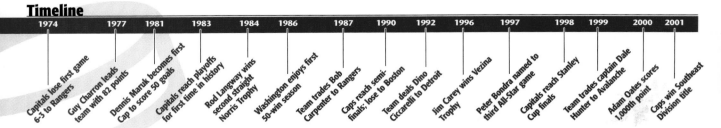

| 1974 | 1977 | 1981 | 1983 | 1984 | 1986 | 1987 | 1990 | 1992 | 1996 | 1997 | 1998 | 1999 | 2000 | 2001 |

- Capitals lose first game 6-3 to Rangers
- Guy Charron leads team with 82 points
- Dennis Maruk becomes first Cap to score 50 goals
- Capitals reach playoffs for first time in history
- Rod Langway wins second straight Norris Trophy
- Washington enjoys first 50-win season
- Team trades Bob Carpenter to Rangers
- Caps reach semi-finals; lose to Boston
- Team deals Dino Ciccarelli to Detroit
- Jim Carey wins Vezina Trophy
- Peter Bondra named to third All-Star game
- Capitals reach Stanley Cup finals
- Team trades captain Dale Hunter to Avalanche
- Adam Oates scores 1,000th point
- Caps win Southeast Division title

MCI CENTER:
A CAPITAL ARENA

THE WASHINGTON CAPITALS put the MCI Center on the world stage in record time, rolling to the Stanley Cup finals just six months after the arena's grand opening in 1997. The fans who flocked to the arena found a building with an exterior suited perfectly to its surroundings and a colorful interior that built excitement from the second they entered. The ultramodern facility includes restaurants and shops and is connected to a light rail station, which makes travel to the games easy and inexpensive.

CONCESSIONS

Fans have a full range of standard fare with a few extra treats. Visitors can try soft pretzels prepared in front of their eyes, food from a popular local Chinese restaurant and a wide range of tasty desserts. For vegetarians, one of the stands offers wraps.

Arena Facts

Opened: Dec. 2, 1997
Cost: $260 million
Capacity: 19,740
Home Sweet Home:
• After many years of tough times, Washington fans have been rewarded with a solid contender. As a result, Caps supporters are a loud bunch. It also helps the noise level that the upper level seats are closer to the ice than normal.

GAME DAY TIPS

• **Gate hours:** Gates open 90 minutes prior to opening faceoff.
• **Prohibited items:** Food, beverages, and alcohol are prohibited. Video cameras and flash cameras are not permitted. Banners and signs are allowed as long as no views are obstructed. Smoking is allowed only in designated areas.
• **Ticket tips:** The Washington Capitals sold out a quarter of their games last year, but tickets are still usually available on game day. Weekend games sell more quickly, as do games against nearby teams — Philadelphia, Pittsburgh and the Rangers among them. Seats in the upper level are closer to the ice than in many other stadiums.
• **Lost and found:** (202) 661-5678.

Seating Plan

☐	.....$170	■	.....$30
☐	.....$138	■	.....$18
■	.....$80	■	.....$10
■	.....$70		
☐	.....$65		
■	.....$48		

ATM Section 112, Discovery Store, F Street Lobby
♿ Throughout

(Arena seating diagram with sections: 7TH & G STREET ENTRANCE; sections 400–433, 100–121, 200–229, 400–431; GALLERY PLACE METRO ENTRANCE; F STREET ENTRANCE)

Directions: From I-66, exit Constitution Ave., left on 7th St. NW. From I-395 N, bear right and exit 12 St., right on Constitution Ave., left on 7th St. NW. From Rte. 50, exit New York Ave., left on 7th St. NW. By subway: Metrorail Red, Yellow or Green to Gallery Place/Chinatown station. Call Washington Metropolitan Area Transit Authority (WMATA) at (202) 637-7000 **Parking:** About 2,500 spots are available at the center garage, with 24 spaces for the disabled. Additional lots are on 5th, 6th, 7th, 8th, 9th, D, E and F Sts.

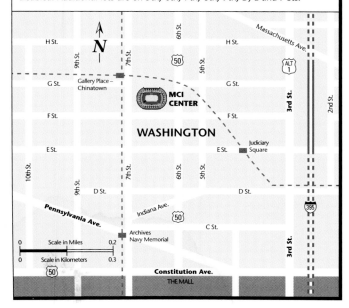

Nearby Hotels

▼▼▼ **Channel Inn Hotel** *(Motor Inn)*, 650 Water St. SW (Washington, D.C.), (202) 554-2400, $135-$150
▼▼▼ **Courtyard by Marriott-Convention Center** *(Hotel)*, 900 F St. NW (Washington, D.C.), (202) 638-4600, $79-$231
▼▼▼ **Grand Hyatt Washington at Washington Center** *(Hotel)*, 1000 H St. NW (Washington, D.C.), (202) 582-1234, $265-$290
▼▼▼ **Henley Park Hotel** *(Historic Hotel)*, 926 Massachusetts Ave. NW (Washington, D.C.), (202) 638-5200, $205-$265
▼▼ **Red Roof Inn Downtown** *(Motel)*, 500 H St. NW (Washington, D.C.), (202) 289-5959, $115-$175

Nearby Restaurants

▼▼▼ **701 Pennsylvania Avenue** *(Continental)*, 701 Pennsylvania Ave. NW (Washington, D.C.), (202) 393-0701, $15-$23
▼▼ **District Chophouse & Brewery** *(American)*, 509 7th St. NW (Washington, D.C.), (202) 347-3434, $19-$28
▼▼ **Hunan Chinatown** *(Chinese)*, 624 H St. NW (Washington, D.C.), (202) 783-5858, $10-$20
▼▼ **Les Halles** *(French)*, 1201 Pennsylvania Ave. NW (Washington, D.C.), (202) 347-6848, $14-$21
▼▼▼▼ **The Willard Room** *(American)*, 1401 Pennsylvania Ave. NW in The Willard Inter-Continental (Washington, D.C.), (202) 637-7440, $23-$29

TRIVIA

NOW THAT YOU'VE READ every single page in this book, you ought to have no trouble acing our trivia test. Go back to the opening photo spreads for each sport, study the pictures, and then test yourself and your friends to see if you're real pro sports fans.

Baseball pages 8–9

1	2	5
3	4	6

Photo 1: Braves outfielder Andruw Jones has won which fielding award three consecutive times from 1998 to 2000?

Gold Glove

Photo 2: Who is this player who broke baseball's color barrier and in which year did he do it?

Jackie Robinson in 1947

Photo 3: These fans are cheering in what legendary National League venue?

Wrigley Field

Photo 4: Which two teams are pictured here?

St. Louis Cardinals and Los Angeles Dodgers

Photo 5: Which team is this wacky fan rooting for?

Oakland Athletics

Photo 6: By wearing the number 5 on his sleeve, Yankees shortstop Derek Jeter is honoring which Yankee Hall of Famer?

Joe DiMaggio

Basketball pages 76–77

1	2	4
	3	5	6

Photo 1: Kareem Abdul-Jabbar is executing what patented shot in this picture?

Sky hook

When he began his career, Abdul-Jabbar went by what name?

Lew Alcindor

Photo 2: Which young Chicago Bulls star is this?

Ron Mercer

Photo 3: Julius Erving, pictured here, is known by what nickname?

Dr. J

Before joining the NBA, Erving playing in what rival league?

ABA

Photo 4: Jack Nicholson, seen in this photo, is a devoted fan of which NBA franchise?

Los Angeles Lakers

Photo 5: Which team eliminated Vince Carter and the Toronto Raptors from the 2001 NBA Playoffs?

Philadelphia 76ers

Photo 6: The Celtics won 16 NBA titles playing here, the team's former venue, which was famous for its parquet flooring. What was the venue called?

Boston Garden

Does the Celtics' current venue, the Fleet Center, have a parquet floor?

Yes

Football
pages 142–143

1 4
2 3 5 6

Photo 1: This pirate ship is located inside which NFL stadium?

Raymond James Stadium

Photo 2: This fan's bizarre headwear honors which Packers coach?

Vince Lombardi

That coach led the Packers to how many NFL titles?

Five

Packers fans are often referred to by what nickname?

Cheeseheads

Photo 3: This player is the NFL's all-time leader in receptions and receiving yards. Who is he?

Jerry Rice

How many Super Bowls has he won?

Three

Photo 4: Which two long-time NFL franchises are lining up here?

Green Bay Packers and Chicago Bears

Who is the Hall of Fame linebacker standing in the photo?

Ray Nitschke

Photo 5: This Vikings receiver was named Pro Bowl MVP in 1999 and 2000. Who is he?

Randy Moss

Photo 6: Emmit Smith shares the NFL record for consecutive seasons with 1,000-yards rushing. How many years in a row has he done this?

10

With whom does Smith share the record?

Barry Sanders

Hockey
pages 218–219

1 4
2 3 5

Photo 1: This Montreal Canadiens star was the first player in hockey history to score 50 goals in 50 games. Who is he?

Maurice "the Rocket" Richard

Photo 2: This legendary Boston Bruin was the first defenseman ever to win an NHL scoring title. Who is he?

Bobby Orr

Photo 3: The current captain of the Mighty Ducks of Anaheim, Paul Kariya has twice won the award as the NHL's most gentlemanly player. What is the award called?

The Lady Byng Trophy

Photo 4: Visitors to the Molson Centre in Montreal will see more Stanley Cup banners than they will in any other venue. How many cups has the Canadiens franchise won?

24

Photo 5: Which two NHL teams are squaring off in this picture?

Colorado Avalanche and New Jersey Devils

Both the Avalanche and the Devils franchises originated in other cities. Where did these franchises originate?

The Quebec Nordiques moved to Colorado and became the Avalanche following the 1994-95 NHL season. The Devils franchise has a longer history. The team began in 1974-75 as the Kansas City Scouts, moved to Colorado and competed as the Colorado Rockies between 1976-77 and 1981-82, and then relocated to New Jersey before the 1982-83 season.

Credits

PHOTO CREDITS

Front cover:
(upper left and upper right)
Michael Zito/
SportsChrome
*(lower left, center-both, spine
and back cover)*
Rob Tringali Jr./
SportsChrome

3 Rich Arden

8 *(upper left),* **8** *(lower left),*
9 *(lower),* **10, 12, 16, 18, 20,
22, 28, 30, 32, 38, 40, 42,
44, 46, 48, 50, 52, 54, 56,
58, 62, 64, 68, 70, 72, 74,
142** *(upper),* **143** *(lower right),*
**144, 148, 149, 151, 158,
170, 174, 180, 190, 192,
196, 202, 214, 216, 219**
(lower), **225, 264, 268, 284,
286** *(both),* **287** *(both)*
Rob Tringali Jr./
SportsChrome

8 *(upper right),* **11, 76**
(lower right), **218** *(upper)*
Bettmann/Corbis

8 *(lower right),* **34, 66, 77**
(upper left), **78, 128, 134, 142**
(lower right), **146, 168, 176,
204, 206, 208**
Michael Zito/
SportsChrome

9 *(upper),* **36, 80, 143** *(upper),*
**145, 198, 221, 222, 224,
230, 242, 258, 260, 270,
272, 276**
SportsChrome

13 National Baseball Hall
of Fame Library,
Cooperstown, N.Y.

14, 24, 26 Jonathan Kirn/
SportsChrome

15 Tony Tomsic/
SportsChrome

60 Steve Woltmann/
SportsChrome

76 *(left)* Brian Drake/
SportsChrome

76 *(upper right),* **77** *(lower
left),* **83, 84, 90, 92, 96,
102, 104, 106, 108, 110,
114, 116, 118, 120, 122,
124, 126, 130, 132, 136,
138, 140**
Brian Spurlock/
SportsChrome

77 *(right)* Brian Geddis/
Allsport

79 Jonathan Daniel/
Allsport

81 Layne Kennedy/
CORBIS

82 Manny Rubio/
SportsChrome

86 Nathaniel C. Butler/
Allsport

88, 94, 98, 112
Charles Small/
Brian Spurlock/
SportsChrome

100 Jed Jacobsohn/
Allsport

142 *(lower left),* **154, 166,
184, 210**
John Williamson/
SportsChrome

143 *(lower left),* **160, 162, 164,
172, 186, 194, 200, 212**
Vincent Manniello/
SportsChrome

147 Pro Football Hall
of Fame

150 Craig Rydlewski/
SportsChrome

156 Craig Melvin/
SportsChrome

178 AP/Wide World Photos

182, 188 Mark Friedman/
SportsChrome

218 *(lower left)*
Steven Goldstein/
SportsChrome

218 *(lower right),* **220, 226,
232, 238, 240, 250, 256,
262, 266, 278**
Gregg Forwerck/
SportsChrome

219 *(upper),* **223**
Robert Laberge/
Allsport

228 Nick Wass/
Allsport

234 Ian Tomlinson/
Allsport

236, 244, 246, 280
Layne Murdock/
SportsChrome

248, 282 Don Smith/
SportsChrome

252 Jason Wise/
SportsChrome

254 Rocky Widner/
SportsChrome

274 Elsa/Allsport

Great Grub Recipes (pages 152–153)

Bacon-Wrapped Tequila Lime Shrimp and *Mexican Corn on the Cob* courtesy of Shari and Kurt Butz, Great Grills and More,
 Green Bay, Wis.
Merrill's (Must-Try) Cheesy Roasted Wisconsin Potatoes and *Mad Dog's Grilled Wisconsin Potato Slices* courtesy of Mad Dog
 and Merrill, The Grilling Buddies
Twice-Dunked Yaki Hot Wings and *Drunken Grilled Brats* courtesy of the bbqzone (www.bbqgalore-online.com/tailgating)
Kansas City Style Pork Ribs courtesy of the Sonoran Grill, KNXV-TV, Phoenix, Ariz.

The editors would like to thank Major League Baseball, the National Basketball Association, the National Football League
and the National Hockey League, as well as the media relations departments for all the teams and stadiums.